ROBERT BROWNING'S POETRY

AUTHORITATIVE TEXTS
CRITICISM

A NORTON CRITICAL EDITION

ROBERT BROWNING'S POETRY

AUTHORITATIVE TEXTS
CRITICISM

Selected and Edited by

JAMES F. LOUCKS
THE OHIO STATE UNIVERSITY

W · W · NORTON & COMPANY
New York   London

ACKNOWLEDGMENTS

Harold Bloom: from *The Ringers in the Tower.* Copyright © 1971 by The University of Chicago. All rights reserved. Reprinted by permission of the author and The University of Chicago Press.

G. K. Chesterton: from *Robert Browning.* London: Macmillan, 1903. Reprinted by permission of Macmillan, London and Basingstoke.

Gerard Manley Hopkins: from *The Correspondence of Gerard Manley Hopkins and Richard Watson Dixon* edited by Claude Colleer Abbott, 1935. Reprinted by permission of Oxford University Press.

E. D. H. Johnson: "Robert Browning's Pluralistic Universe: A Reading of *The Ring and the Book,*" reprinted from *University of Toronto Quarterly* Vol. 31, (1961), by permission of the author and University of Toronto Press.

Roma A. King, Jr.: from *The Bow and the Lyre.* Ann Arbor: University of Michigan Press, 1957. Reprinted by permission of University of Michigan Press.

Robert Langbaum: from *The Poetry of Experience.* Copyright © 1957 by Robert Langbaum. Reprinted by permission of Random House, Inc., and Chatto & Windus Ltd.

J. Hillis Miller: from *The Disappearance of God: Five Nineteenth-Century Writers* by J. Hillis Miller. Cambridge, Mass.: The Belknap Press of Harvard University Press, Copyright © 1963 by the President and Fellows of Harvard College. Reprinted by permission of the author and publishers.

F. E. L. Priestley: "Blougram's Apologetics." Reprinted from *University of Toronto Quarterly,* Vol. 15 (Jan. 1946), by permission of the author and the University of Toronto Press.

William O. Raymond: from *The Infinite Moment and Other Essays in Robert Browning,* by William O. Raymond. Reprinted by permission of University of Toronto Press. © University of Toronto Press 1965.

George Santayana: from *Interpretations of Poetry and Religion.* Reprinted by permission of Constable Publishers.

W. David Shaw: from *The Dialectical Temper.* Copyright © 1969 by Cornell University. Used by permission of Cornell University Press.

Copyright © 1979 by W. W. Norton & Company, Inc.

Library of Congress Cataloging in Publication Data
Browning, Robert, 1812–1889.
   Robert Browning's poetry.
   (A Norton critical edition)
   Bibliography: p.
   Includes index.
   1. Browning, Robert, 1812–1889—Criticism and interpretation—Addresses, essays, lectures.   I. Loucks, James F.
PR4202.L59 1979   821'.8   79-10295
ISBN 0-393-04475-0
ISBN 0-393-09092-2 pbk.

Published simultaneously in Canada by Penguin Books Canada Ltd,
2801 John Street, Markham, Ontario L3R 1B4.

W. W. Norton & Company, Inc., 500 Fifth Avenue, New York, N.Y. 10110

3 4 5 6 7 8 9 0

Contents

Preface   ix

Browning: A Chronology   xi

List of Abbreviations   xiii

The Texts of the Poems

A Note on the Texts   xvi

The Experimental Phase (1833–45)
From *Pauline* (1833)   1
From *Paracelsus* (1835)   4
From *Sordello* (1840)   12
Pippa Passes (1841)   18
From *Dramatic Lyrics* (1842)   58
  My Last Duchess   58
  Count Gismond   59
  Soliloquy of the Spanish Cloister   62
  In a Gondola   64
  Cristina   70
  Johannes Agricola in Meditation   72
  Porphyria's Lover   74
  The Pied Piper of Hamelin   75
From *Dramatic Romances and Lyrics* (1845)   82
  "How They Brought the Good News
     from Ghent to Aix"   82
  Pictor Ignotus   84
  Home-Thoughts, from Abroad   86
  ["Here's to Nelson's Memory!"]   86
  Home-Thoughts, from the Sea   87
  The Bishop Orders His Tomb at St. Praxed's Church   87
  The Laboratory   91
  Meeting at Night; Parting at Morning   92
  Nationality in Drinks   93

The Major Phase (1855–69)
From *Men and Women* (1855)   94
  Love Among the Ruins   94
  A Lovers' Quarrel   96
  Evelyn Hope   100
  Up at a Villa—Down in the City   101
  A Woman's Last Word   104
  Fra Lippo Lippi   105
  A Toccata of Galuppi's   114
  By the Fire-Side   116

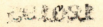

Any Wife to Any Husband 123
An Epistle . . . of Karshish, the Arab Physician 127
My Star 134
"Childe Roland to the Dark Tower Came" 134
Respectability 140
A Light Woman 140
The Statue and the Bust 142
How It Strikes a Contemporary 149
The Last Ride Together 151
Master Hugues of Saxe-Gotha 154
Bishop Blougram's Apology 158
Memorabilia 183
Andrea del Sarto 184
Saul [final version] 191
Women and Roses 200
Holy-Cross Day 201
The Guardian-Angel 205
Cleon 207
Popularity 215
Two in the Campagna 217
A Grammarian's Funeral 219
"Transcendentalism: A Poem in Twelve Books" 222
One Word More 224
From *Dramatis Personae* (1864) 229
  James Lee's Wife 229
  Dîs aliter Visum 239
  Abt Vogler 243
  Rabbi Ben Ezra 246
  Caliban upon Setebos 252
  Confessions 259
  Prospice 260
  Apparent Failure 261
  Epilogue 263
From *The Ring and the Book* (1868–69) 267
  Book V. Count Guido Franceschini 270
  Book VI. Giuseppe Caponsacchi 316
  Book X. The Pope 361

The Later Achievement (after 1870)
From *Fifine at the Fair* (1872) 409
  Prologue (Amphibian) 409
  Epilogue (The Householder) 411
From *Aristophanes' Apology* (1875) 412
  [Thamuris Marching] 412
From *Pacchiarotto and How He Worked in Distemper:
    With Other Poems* (1876) 415
  House 415
  Fears and Scruples 416
  Numpholeptos 418

From *Jocoseria* (1883)   421
  Adam, Lilith, and Eve   421
  Never the Time and the Place   422
From *Parleyings with Certain People of Importance*
    in Their Day (1887)   423
  With Christopher Smart   423
From *Asolando: Fancies and Facts* (1889)   430
  Prologue   430
  Bad Dreams, I–IV   431
  "Imperante Augusto Natus Est—"   436
  Development   440
  Epilogue   443

Prose
  From "Introductory Essay" to the *Letters*
    of Percy Bysshe Shelley (1852)   445

Criticism

Victorian Views
  John Forster · Evidences of a New Genius for
    Dramatic Poetry   455
  Thomas Carlyle · [Letter to Browning]   457
  George Eliot · [Review of *Men and Women*]   458
  William Morris · [Browning's Alleged Carelessness]   462
  John Ruskin · [Browning and the Italian
    Renaissance]   463
  Walter Bagehot · [Browning's Grotesque Art]   465
  Robert W. Buchanan · [*The Ring and the Book*]   469
  Alfred Austin · The Poetry of the Period:
    Mr. Browning   471
  Algernon Charles Swinburne · [Browning's Obscurity]   475
  Gerard Manley Hopkins · [Strictures on Browning]   479
  Oscar Wilde · [Browning as "Writer of Fiction"]   480
  Henry James · Browning in Westminster Abbey   482

Modern Essays in Criticism
  Revaluations   486
    George Santayana · The Poetry of Barbarism   486
    G. K. Chesterton · [Reply to Santayana]   493
    William O. Raymond · The Infinite Moment   496
    J. Hillis Miller · [Browning's Language]   509
  The Dramatic Monologue   514
    Robert Langbaum · The Dramatic Monologue:
      Sympathy versus Judgment   514
  Interpretations of Poems   536
    W. David Shaw · Browning's Duke as Theatrical
      Producer ["My Last Duchess"]   536
    Harold Bloom · Browning's "Childe Roland":
      All Things Deformed and Broken   544

viii · *Contents*

F. E. L. Priestley · Blougram's Apologetics   554

Roma A. King, Jr. · Eve and the Virgin:
"Andrea del Sarto"   563

E. D. H. Johnson · Robert Browning's Pluralistic
Universe: A Reading of *The Ring and the Book*   576

Selected Bibliography   596

Index of Titles   603

Preface

The aim of this edition is to offer as generous a selection of Browning's best poems as space allows. Inevitably (and regrettably), several fine long poems—"Christmas-Eve" and "Easter-Day," for example—have had to be omitted entirely, and other lengthy works, such as *Paracelsus, Sordello, The Ring and the Book,* and the *Parleyings,* are represented by excerpts. In general excerpting is done only when a poem's importance warrants its inclusion even in the aesthetically unsatisfactory form of a fragment, and when such fragments stand fairly well on their own, without the aid of heavy editorial apparatus. The result, I hope, is a convenient anthology presenting a balance of poetic forms and themes, demonstrating Browning's astonishing versatility as an artist and his fecundity as a thinker throughout a long, influential career.

A word about the annotation is perhaps in order. Browning has always been regarded as an unusually difficult, even obscure poet. Since much of the difficulty stems from the poet's habit of referring continually to little-known historical facts, forgotten persons, recondite fields of knowledge, and unread literature, I have devoted the bulk of my notes to providing information sufficient to enable one to read each selection without interruption. Critical interpretation, whether my own or that of others, has been avoided as tending to interfere with both the initial appreciation of a poem and its subsequent discussion in the classroom.

After each text I have cited the date of composition on the left, when known or strongly conjectured; the date of first printing in a periodical (prior to issuance in book form) is given on the right. For ready reference all line numberings in the excerpts correspond to those of the full text.

The Criticism section offers over a century of commentary on Browning's achievement. How a poet strikes his own contemporaries has a double value: such criticism allows us not only to chart the vicissitudes of the poet's reputation in his time, but also to estimate the moral and aesthetic values of his reading public. Hence I have given due place to representative Victorian assessments of Browning, selecting a jury of his peers—most of them creative writers or critics of the first rank—for the lasting validity of their insights. Their judgments range from the altogether negative (in Alfred Austin's sweeping condemnation) to the adulatory (in R. W. Buchanan's rhapsodizing upon *The Ring and the Book*), with most critics taking a judicious stance between these extremes.

Just as Henry James's magnificent tribute epitomizes the later Victorian acceptance (or veneration, indeed) of the poet-sage, so does George Santayana's censorious essay "The Poetry of Barbarism" (1900) indicate the extent of the reaction against Browning in the early decades of this century. In contrast, W. O. Raymond's "The Infinite Moment" (1950) represents a turning point in modern reappreciation for which groundwork was laid by scholars like William Clyde DeVane and Raymond himself in the 1930s and 1940s. The past twenty-five years have been marked by steadily increasing interest in Browning's life and work. Not only have three important biographies appeared, but such seminal books as Robert Langbaum's *The Poetry of Experience*, Roma King's *The Bow and the Lyre*, and J. Hillis Miller's *The Disappearance of God* have indicated fresh approaches to the poetry. The latter three critics are represented in this edition, together with W. David Shaw, Harold Bloom, F. E. L. Priestley, and E. D. H. Johnson. Only limitation of space prevented my offering the work of several other equally luminous critics; they are, however, named in the Selected Bibliography.

In preparing this edition I have accumulated many debts. Like all previous modern editors, I have relied heavily on DeVane's *A Browning Handbook*. A. K. Cook's full and accurate *A Commentary upon Browning's "The Ring and the Book"* has been indispensable. The notes in Charlotte Porter and Helen A. Clarke's "Florentine Edition" of Browning's poetry, as well as those in the Ohio University Press edition, have been informative and suggestive. The appearance in 1974 of William Irvine and Park Honan's masterly biography, *The Book, the Ring, and the Poet*, could not have been better timed; I have profited immensely from the authors' perceptive treatment of the poems as well as from their synthesis of several decades of Browning scholarship. I am grateful to Valparaiso University for its generous award of a University Research Professorship at a point when time was precious. And finally I should like to thank those individuals who have given help at various stages: Peter W. Phelps, John W. N. Francis, and Emily Garlin, of W. W. Norton & Company, for their encouragement and practical wisdom; Professors Richard D. Altick and Roma A. King, Jr., for their kind advice and assistance; and my wife Sandra for her forbearance and support. My mother contributed many an hour of proofreading; to her and to my father I affectionately dedicate this book.

JAMES F. LOUCKS

Browning: A Chronology

1812	Born May 7 at Camberwell (London suburb) to Robert and Sara Anna Wiedemann Browning.
ca. 1820–26	In boarding school near his home.
ca. 1824	Wrote a volume of Byronic verse called *Incondita,* which his parents tried unsuccessfully to have published. Browning later destroyed the volume, and only two of the poems have survived.
1826	Discovered Percy Bysshe Shelley's poetry. Read *Miscellaneous Poems, Queen Mab.*
1828	Enrolled in newly-founded University of London, but withdrew after only a few months.
1833	*Pauline,* anonymously published, went unsold and received scant notice.
1834	Journey to Russia in March and April.
1835	*Paracelsus* published at his father's expense.
1837	*Strafford,* a drama, was performed five nights. None of Browning's plays enjoyed commercial success, and he finally abandoned the stage.
1838	First Italian journey. Found material for *Sordello*.
1840	*Sordello* published. It was a critical failure, retarding the poet's reputation.
1841–46	Published *Pippa Passes,* first of eight pamphlets comprising *Bells and Pomegranates*. The others: (II) *King Victor and King Charles,* a drama, 1842; (III) *Dramatic Lyrics,* 1842; (IV) *The Return of the Druses,* a drama, 1843; (V) *A Blot in the 'Scutcheon,* a drama performed three nights, 1843; (VI) *Colombe's Birthday,* a drama, 1844; (VII) *Dramatic Romances and Lyrics,* 1845; (VIII) *Luria* and *A Soul's Tragedy,* both dramas, 1846.
1844	Second Italian journey.
1845	On January 10, wrote first letter to the poet Elizabeth Barrett, an invalid whose father was determined that his children should remain unmarried. On May 20, made first visit to Elizabeth at Wimpole Street.
1846	Married Elizabeth Barrett on September 12 without her father's knowledge. On September 19, they eloped to the Continent—their destination Pisa, Italy.

1847	Summer: Settled at Casa Guidi, in Florence.
1849	First collected edition of poems published. On March 9, a son, Robert Wiedemann Barrett, born. Shortly after, Browning's mother died.
1850	*Christmas-Eve and Easter-Day.*
1855	*Men and Women*, Browning's best single volume.
1855–56	Autumn-Winter: Visited London.
1860	Discovered the Old Yellow Book, source of *The Ring and the Book*, at a bookstall in Florence.
1861	June 29: Elizabeth Barrett Browning's death.
1862	Settled at 19 Warwick Crescent, London.
1863	Second collected edition of Browning's poems (called the "third").
1864	*Dramatis Personae*, a critical as well as a popular success. Browning lionized. That autumn, he began composing *The Ring and the Book*.
1866	Death of Browning's father.
1868–69	*The Ring and the Book* published; exceedingly well received. Browning's fame nearly equal to Tennyson's.
1871	*Balaustion's Adventure; Prince Hohenstiel-Schwangau.*
1872	*Fifine at the Fair.*
1873	*Red Cotton Night-Cap Country.*
1875	*Aristophanes' Apology; The Inn Album.*
1876	*Pacchiarotto and How He Worked in Distemper.*
1877	*The Agamemnon of Aeschylus.*
1878	*La Saisiaz* and *The Two Poets of Croisic.*
1879	*Dramatic Idyls.*
1880	*Dramatic Idyls: Second Series.*
1881	The Browning Society (London) founded.
1883	*Jocoseria.*
1884	*Ferishtah's Fancies.*
1887	*Parleyings with Certain People of Importance in Their Day.*
1888–89	*Poetical Works* in sixteen volumes, the last edition supervised by Browning.
1889	December 12: *Asolando* published; Browning died in Venice the same evening, at the house of his son. Burial December 31 in Westminster Abbey.

List of Abbreviations

The following list provides bibliographic data for books whose titles are abbreviated in the notes in order to save space. All quotations of Shakespeare are made with reference to *The Riverside Shakespeare*, ed. G. Blakemore Evans (Boston: Houghton Mifflin, 1974).

BRP	Irvine, William, and Park Honan. *The Book, The "The Ring and the Book," Oxford,* 1920. Reprint; *Browning.* New York: McGraw-Hill, 1974.
Cook	Cook, A. K. *A Commentary upon Browning's "The Ring and the Book."* Oxford, 1920 Reprint; Hamden, Conn.: Archon Books, 1966.
Curle	*Robert Browning and Julia Wedgwood: A Broken Friendship as Revealed by Their Letters.* Ed. Richard Curle. New York: Frederick A. Stokes, 1937.
Dearest Isa	*Dearest Isa: Robert Browning's Letters to Isabella Blagden.* Ed. Edward C. McAleer. Austin: University of Texas Press, 1951.
DeVane	DeVane, William Clyde. *A Browning Handbook.* 2nd ed. New York: Appleton-Century-Crofts, 1955.
G&M	Griffin, W. Hall, and H. C. Minchin. *The Life of Robert Browning.* 3rd ed. London: Methuen, 1938.
Grove	*Grove's Dictionary of Music and Musicians.* Ed. Eric Blom. 5th ed. 10 vols. New York: St. Martin's Press, 1954–61.
Hood	*Letters of Robert Browning Collected by Thomas J. Wise.* Ed. Thurman L. Hood. New Haven: Yale University Press, 1933.
Kintner	*The Letters of Robert Browning and Elizabeth Barrett Barrett 1845–1846.* Ed. Elvan Kintner. 2 vols. Cambridge, Mass.: The Belknap Press of Harvard University Press, 1969.
Learned Lady	*Learned Lady: Letters from Robert Browning to Mrs. Thomas FitzGerald, 1876–1889.* Ed. Edward C. McAleer. Cambridge, Mass.: Harvard University Press, 1966.
New Letters	*New Letters of Robert Browning.* Ed. William C. DeVane and K. L. Knickerbocker. London: John Murray, 1951.
OED	*Oxford English Dictionary.*
Orr, *Handbook*	Orr, Mrs. Sutherland (Alexandra Leighton). *A Handbook to the Works of Robert Browning.* 6th ed. London: G. Bell, 1892. Reprint; New York: Kraus Reprint Co., 1969.

Orr, *Life*   Orr, Mrs. Sutherland. *Life and Letters of Robert Browning*. Revised by Frederic G. Kenyon. Boston: Houghton Mifflin, 1908. Reprint; Westport, Conn.: Greenwood Press, 1973.

Portrait   Miller, Betty. *Robert Browning: A Portrait*. London: John Murray, 1952.

Turner   *Browning: Men and Women*. Ed. Paul Turner. London: Oxford University Press, 1972.

Vasari   Vasari, Giorgio. *Lives of the Most Eminent Painters, Sculptors, and Architects*. Trans. Mrs. Jonathan Foster. 2 vols. London, 1851.

The Texts of
The Poems

A Note on the Texts

The order of the poems is that of their initial publication in book form; the text followed, however, is the "Fourth and complete edition" of 1888–94 in seventeen volumes, all but the last having been supervised by Browning in the final months of his life. Alert and meticulous even in old age, Browning supplied the publisher, Smith, Elder, and Company, with a list of corrections—mostly in punctuation—that he wished to make in the first ten volumes of the 1889 reprint. Since not every correction was made (or made accurately) by the publisher, I have taken the course of emending the 1888–89 text in accordance with Browning's extant corrigenda, rather than relying on the 1889 reprint. Though the corrigenda sent to Smith, Elder have not been recovered, two presumably parallel sets of corrections in Browning's hand remain, differing in only a few particulars; these may be found in a list in the Brown University Library, and in the Dykes Campbell copy of the 1888–89 edition in the British Museum. I am indebted to Philip Kelley and William S. Peterson for their convenient tabulation of Browning's final revisions (*Browning Institute Studies*, 1 [1973], 109–17).

Browning's own corrections have been made silently. Below are listed my own verbal emendations; the edition followed, where relevant, is given in parentheses:

Cristina, 1. 63: "the next life" for "next life" (1849).
Bishop Blougram's Apology, 1. 608: "soil" for "soul" (1885).
Bishop Blougram's Apology, 1. 759: "other" for "others" (1855).
Saul, 1. 328: "off" for "oft" (1855).
The Ring and the Book, X.1141: "law's" for "laws."

The rare misspellings and obvious errors of punctuation in the 1888–89 edition have been silently corrected. Two peculiarities of Smith, Elder's house styling have been normalized: the inverted commas used to begin every line of continuous quoted material are suppressed; and the irregular practice of numbering half-lines of *The Ring and the Book* is not followed. The line numbering in that poem follows that of the "Florentine Edition."

The Experimental Phase
(1833-1845)

Pauline (1833)[1]

* * *

Sun-treader, life and light be thine for ever!
Thou art gone from us; years go by and spring
Gladdens and the young earth is beautiful,
Yet thy songs come not, other bards arise,
But none like thee: they stand, thy majesties,   155
Like mighty works which tell some spirit there
Hath sat regardless[2] of neglect and scorn,
Till, its long task completed, it hath risen
And left us, never to return, and all
Rush in to peer and praise when all in vain.   160
The air seems bright with thy past presence yet,
But thou art still for me as thou hast been
When I have stood with thee as on a throne
With all thy dim creations gathered round
Like mountains, and I felt of mould[3] like them,   165
And with them creatures of my own were mixed,
Like things half-lived, catching and giving life.
But thou art still for me who have adored
Tho' single panting but to hear thy name
Which I believed a spell to me alone,   170
Scarce deeming thou wast as a star to men!
As one should worship long a sacred spring
Scarce worth a moth's flitting, which long grasses cross,
And one small tree embowers droopingly—
Joying to see some wandering insect won   175
To live in its few rushes, or some locust
To pasture on its boughs, or some wild bird
Stoop for its freshness from the trackless air:
And then should find it but the fountain-head,
Long lost, of some great river washing towns   180
And towers, and seeing old woods which will live

1. Browning published *Pauline; A Fragment of a Confession* anonymously when he was twenty-one. Unsold and almost unnoticed by the reviewers, it was suppressed by the poet until 1868. Partly autobiographical, *Pauline* exhibits the strong early influence of Shelley, whose tribute is sung in these excerpts.
2. Heedless.
3. Earth.

1

But by its banks untrod of human foot,
Which, when the great sun sinks, lie quivering
In light as some thing lieth half of life
Before God's foot, waiting a wondrous change;   185
Then girt with rocks which seek to turn or stay
Its course in vain, for it does ever spread
Like a sea's arm as it goes rolling on,
Being the pulse of some great country—so
Wast thou to me, and art thou to the world!   190
And I, perchance, half feel a strange regret
That I am not what I have been to thee:
Like a girl one has silently loved long
In her first loneliness in some retreat,
When, late emerged, all gaze and glow to view   195
Her fresh eyes and soft hair and lips which bloom
Like a mountain berry: doubtless it is sweet
To see her thus adored, but there have been
Moments when all the world was in our praise,
Sweeter than any pride of after hours.   200
Yet, sun-treader, all hail! From my heart's heart
I bid thee hail! E'en in my wildest dreams,
I proudly feel I would have thrown to dust
The wreaths of fame which seemed o'erhanging me,
To see thee for a moment as thou art.   205

And if thou livest, if thou lovest, spirit!
Remember me who set this final seal
To wandering thought—that one so pure as thou
Could never die. Remember me who flung
All honour from my soul, yet paused and said   210
"There is one spark of love remaining yet,
For I have nought in common with him, shapes
Which followed him avoid me, and foul forms
Seek me, which ne'er could fasten on his mind;
And though I feel how low I am to him,   215
Yet I aim not even to catch a tone
Of harmonies he called profusely up;
So, one gleam still remains, although the last."
Remember me who praise thee e'en with tears,
For never more shall I walk calm with thee;   220
Thy sweet imaginings are as an air,
A melody some wondrous singer sings,
Which, though it haunt men oft in the still eve,
They dream not to essay; yet it no less
But more is honoured. I was thine in shame,[4]   225
And now when all thy proud renown is out,
I am a watcher whose eyes have grown dim
With looking for some star which breaks on him
Altered and worn and weak and full of tears.

* * *

4. I.e., I was your disciple when you were neglected.

My life has not been that of those whose heaven 360
Was lampless save where poesy shone out;
But as a clime where glittering mountain-tops
And glancing sea and forests steeped in light
Give back reflected the far-flashing sun;
For music (which is earnest[5] of a heaven, 365
Seeing we know emotions strange by it,
Not else to be revealed,) is like a voice,
A low voice calling fancy, as a friend,
To the green woods in the gay summer time:
And she fills all the way with dancing shapes 370
Which have made painters pale, and they go on
Till stars look at them and winds call to them
As they leave life's path for the twilight world
Where the dead gather. This was not at first,
For I scarce knew what I would do. I had 375
An impulse but no yearning—only sang.

And first I sang as I in dream have seen
Music wait on a lyrist for some thought,
Yet singing to herself until it came.
I turned to those old times and scenes where all 380
That's beautiful had birth for me, and made
Rude verses on them all; and then I paused—
I had done nothing, so I sought to know
What other minds achieved. No fear outbroke
As on the works of mighty bards I gazed, 385
In the first joy at finding my own thoughts
Recorded, my own fancies justified,
And their aspirings but my very own.
With them I first explored passion and mind,—
All to begin afresh! I rather sought 390
To rival what I wondered at than form
Creations of my own; if much was light
Lent by the others, much was yet my own.

I paused again: a change was coming—came:
I was no more a boy, the past was breaking 395
Before the future and like fever worked.
I thought on my new self, and all my powers
Burst out. I dreamed not of restraint, but gazed
On all things: schemes and systems went and came,
And I was proud (being vainest of the weak) 400
In wandering o'er thought's world to seek some one
To be my prize, as if you wandered o'er
The White Way[6] for a star.

              And my choice fell
Not so much on a system as a man—[7]
On one, whom praise of mine shall not offend, 405
Who was as calm as beauty, being such

5. Earnest: promise.
6. Milky Way.
         7. Shelley.

Unto mankind as thou to me, Pauline,—
Believing in them and devoting all
His soul's strength to their winning back to peace;
Who sent forth hopes and longings for their sake,   410
Clothed in all passion's melodies: such first
Caught me and set me, slave of a sweet task,
To disentangle, gather sense from song:
Since, song-inwoven, lurked there words which seemed
A key to a new world, the muttering   415
Of angels, something yet unguessed by man.
How my heart leapt as still I sought and found
Much there, I felt my own soul had conceived,
But there living and burning! Soon the orb
Of his conceptions dawned on me; its praise   420
Lives in the tongues of men, men's brows are high
When his name means a triumph and a pride,
So, my weak voice may well forbear to shame
What seemed decreed my fate: I threw myself
To meet it, I was vowed to liberty,   425
Men were to be as gods and earth as heaven,
And I—ah, what a life was mine to prove!
My whole soul rose to meet it. Now, Pauline,
I shall go mad, if I recall that time!

                    * * *

Sun-treader, I believe in God and truth   1020
And love; and as one just escaped from death
Would bind himself in bands of friends to feel
He lives indeed, so, I would lean on thee!
Thou must be ever with me, most in gloom
If such must come, but chiefly when I die,   1025
For I seem, dying, as one going in the dark
To fight a giant: but live thou for ever,
And be to all what thou hast been to me!
All in whom this wakes pleasant thoughts of me
Know my last state is happy, free from doubt   1030
Or touch of fear. Love me and wish me well.

1832

Paracelsus (1835)[1]

Part II

                    * * *

I hear a voice, perchance I heard[2]
Long ago, but all too low,

1. Browning's first acknowledged work, the ambitious dialogue-poem *Paracelsus* (1835) was a *succès d'estime*, setting the young poet before the London literary

So that scarce a care it stirred
If the voice were real or no:
I heard it in my youth when first   285
The waters of my life outburst:
But, now their stream ebbs faint, I hear
That voice, still low, but fatal-clear—
As if all poets, God ever meant
Should save the world, and therefore lent   290
Great gifts to, but who, proud, refused
To do his work, or lightly used
Those gifts, or failed through weak endeavour,
So, mourn cast off by him for ever,—
As if these leaned in airy ring   295
To take me; this the song they sing.

"Lost, lost! yet come,
With our wan troop make thy home.
Come, come! for we
Will not breathe, so much as breathe   300
Reproach to thee,
Knowing what thou sink'st beneath.
So sank we in those old years,
We who bid thee, come! thou last
Who, living yet, hast life o'erpast.   305
And altogether we, thy peers,
Will pardon crave for thee, the last
Whose trial is done, whose lot is cast
With those who watch but work no more,
Who gaze on life but live no more.   310
Yet we trusted thou shouldst speak
The message which our lips, too weak,
Refused to utter,—shouldst redeem
Our fault: such trust, and all a dream!
Yet we chose thee a birthplace   315
Where the richness ran to flowers:
Couldst not sing one song for grace?
Not make one blossom man's and ours?
Must one more recreant[3] to his race
Die with unexerted powers,   320
And join us, leaving as he found
The world, he was to loosen, bound?
Anguish! ever and for ever;
Still beginning, ending never.
Yet, lost and last one, come!   325

---

world. His essentially romantic vision led
him to portray Paracelsus (1493–1541),
Renaissance reformer of medicine and
pharmacology, as a Promethean hero
whose obsessive quest of universal
knowledge ultimately exhausts itself.
2. This lyric is sung by an Italian poet,
Aprile, whom Paracelsus encounters in
Constantinople. The two characters are
complementary: just as Paracelsus aspires to know all, Aprile "would love infinitely, and be loved" (II.420). The
poet is thought to be modeled after Shelley.
3. Unfaithful to duty or allegiance.

How couldst understand, alas,
What our pale ghosts strove to say,[4]
As their shades did glance and pass
Before thee night and day?
Thou wast blind as we were dumb: 330
Once more, therefore, come, O come!
How should we clothe, how arm the spirit
Shall next thy post of life inherit—
How guard him from thy speedy ruin?
Tell us of thy sad undoing   335
Here, where we sit, ever pursuing
Our weary task, ever renewing
Sharp sorrow, far from God who gave
Our powers, and man they could not save!"

* * *

Part IV

* * *

Heap cassia, sandal-buds and stripes[5]   190
    Of labdanum, and aloe-balls,
Smeared with dull nard an Indian wipes
    From out her hair: such balsam falls
    Down sea-side mountain pedestals,
From tree-tops where tired winds are fain,   195
Spent with the vast and howling main,
To treasure half their island-gain.

And strew faint sweetness from some old
    Egyptian's fine worm-eaten shroud
Which breaks to dust when once unrolled;   200
    Or shredded perfume, like a cloud
    From closet long to quiet vowed,
With mothed and dropping arras[6] hung,
Mouldering her lute and books among,
As when a queen, long dead, was young.   205

* * *

Over the sea our galleys went,[7]   450
With cleaving prows in order brave
To a speeding wind and a bounding wave,
    A gallant armament:
Each bark built out of a forest-tree
    Left leafy and rough as first it grew,   455

---

4. The "pale ghosts" recall the horde of the Indifferent in the Vestibule of Dante's hell (*Inferno*, III).
5. From IV.190–205. In the presence of his friend Festus, Paracelsus sings of his youthful fancies, represented in the first stanza by exotic spices.
6. Tapestry.
7. From IV.450–522. After singing this allegorical song to Festus, Paracelsus comments: " 'The sad rhyme of the men who proudly clung/To their first fault, and withered in their pride' " (526–27).

And nailed all over the gaping sides,
Within and without, with black bull-hides,
Seethed in fat and suppled in flame,
To bear the playful billows' game:
So, each good ship was rude to see,   460
Rude and bare to the outward view,
    But each upbore a stately tent
Where cedar pales[8] in scented row
Kept out the flakes of the dancing brine,
And an awning drooped the mast below,   465
In fold on fold of the purple fine,
That neither noontide nor starshine
Nor moonlight cold which maketh mad,
    Might pierce the regal tenement.[9]
When the sun dawned, oh, gay and glad   470
We set the sail and plied the oar;
But when the night-wind blew like breath,
For joy of one day's voyage more,
We sang together on the wide sea,
Like men at peace on a peaceful shore;   475
Each sail was loosed to the wind so free,
Each helm made sure by the twilight star,
And in a sleep as calm as death,
We, the voyagers from afar,
    Lay stretched along, each weary crew   480
In a circle round its wondrous tent
Whence gleamed soft light and curled rich scent,
    And with light and perfume, music too:
So the stars wheeled round, and the darkness past,
And at morn we started beside the mast,   485
And still each ship was sailing fast.

Now, one morn, land appeared—a speck
Dim trembling betwixt sea and sky:
"Avoid it," cried our pilot, "check
    The shout, restrain the eager eye!"   490
But the heaving sea was black behind
For many a night and many a day,
And land, though but a rock, drew nigh;
So, we broke the cedar pales away,
Let the purple awning flap in the wind,   495
    And a statue bright was on every deck!
We shouted, every man of us,
And steered right into the harbour thus,
With pomp and pæan[1] glorious.

A hundred shapes of lucid stone!   500
    All day we built its shrine for each,

---

8. Poles.
9. I.e., the "stately tent" of line 13.

1. Song of praise or triumph.

A shrine of rock for every one,
Nor paused till in the westering sun
   We sat together on the beach
To sing because our task was done.   505
When lo! what shouts and merry songs!
What laughter all the distance stirs!
A loaded raft with happy throngs
Of gentle islanders!
"Our isles are just at hand," they cried,   510
   "Like cloudlets faint in even sleeping;
Our temple-gates are opened wide,
   Our olive-groves thick shade are keeping
For these majestic forms"—they cried.
Oh, then we awoke with sudden start   515
From our deep dream, and knew, too late,
How bare the rock, how desolate,
Which had received our precious freight:
   Yet we called out—"Depart!
Our gifts, once given, must here abide.   520
   Our work is done; we have no heart
To mar our work,"—we cried.

* * *

Part V

* * *

Thus the Mayne glideth[2]
Where my Love abideth.
Sleep's no softer: it proceeds   420
On through lawns, on through meads,
On and on, whate'er befall,
Meandering and musical,
Though the niggard pasturage
Bears not on its shaven ledge   425
Aught but weeds and waving grasses
To view the river as it passes,
Save here and there a scanty patch
Of primroses too faint to catch
A weary bee.   430
           And scarce it pushes
Its gentle way through strangling rushes
Where the glossy kingfisher
Flutters when noon-heats are near,
Glad the shelving banks to shun,   435
Red and steaming in the sun,
Where the shrew-mouse with pale throat

2. From V.418–46. Festus sings to comfort the dying Paracelsus. Before joining the Rhine, the Mayne (Main) river flows through Würzburg, where Paracelsus had studied some thirty years before, and had known happiness with Festus and his wife Michal.

Burrows, and the speckled stoat;[3]
Where the quick sandpipers flit
In and out the marl[4] and grit   440
That seems to breed them, brown as they:
Nought disturbs its quiet way,
Save some lazy stork that springs,
Trailing it with legs and wings,
Whom the shy fox from the hill   445
Rouses, creep he ne'er so still.

* * *

I knew, I felt, (perception unexpressed,[5]
Uncomprehended by our narrow thought,
But somehow felt and known in every shift   640
And change in the spirit,—nay, in every pore
Of the body, even,)—what God is, what we are,
What life is—how God tastes an infinite joy
In infinite ways—one everlasting bliss,
From whom all being emanates, all power   645
Proceeds; in whom is life for evermore,
Yet whom existence in its lowest form
Includes; where dwells enjoyment there is he:
With still a flying point of bliss remote,
A happiness in store afar, a sphere   650
Of distant glory in full view; thus climbs
Pleasure its heights for ever and for ever.
The center-fire heaves underneath the earth,
And the earth changes like a human face;
The molten ore bursts up among the rocks,   655
Winds into the stone's heart, outbranches bright
In hidden mines, spots barren river-beds,
Crumbles into fine sand where sunbeams bask—
God joys therein. The wroth sea's waves are edged
With foam, white as the bitten lip of hate,   660
When, in the solitary waste, strange groups
Of young volcanos come up, cyclops-like,
Staring together with their eyes on flame—
God tastes a pleasure in their uncouth pride.
Then all is still; earth is a wintry clod: 665
But spring-wind, like a dancing psaltress, passes
Over its breast to waken it, rare verdure
Buds tenderly upon rough banks, between
The withered tree-roots and the cracks of frost,
Like a smile striving with a wrinkled face;   670
The grass grows bright, the boughs are swoln with blooms
Like chrysalids impatient for the air,

3. Ermine.
4. Silt.
5. From V.638–786. In this his dying speech, Paracelsus celebrates God's "scheme of being."
6. Dorbeetle, European dung beetle.

The shining dorrs[6] are busy, beetles run
Along the furrows, ants make their ado;
Above, birds fly in merry flocks, the lark   675
Soars up and up, shivering for very joy;
Afar the ocean sleeps; white fishing-gulls
Flit where the strand is purple with its tribe
Of nested limpets; savage creatures seek
Their loves in wood and plain—and God renews   680
His ancient rapture. Thus he dwells in all,
From life's minute beginnings, up at last
To man—the consummation of this scheme
Of being, the completion of this sphere
Of life: whose attributes had here and there   685
Been scattered o'er the visible world before,
Asking to be combined, dim fragments meant
To be united in some wondrous whole,
Imperfect qualities throughout creation,
Suggesting some one creature yet to make,   690
Some point where all those scattered rays should meet
Convergent in the faculties of man.
Power—neither put forth blindly, nor controlled
Calmly by perfect knowledge; to be used
At risk, inspired or checked by hope and fear: 695
Knowledge—not intuition, but the slow
Uncertain fruit of an enhancing toil,
Strengthened by love: love—not serenely pure,
But strong from weakness, like a chance-sown plant   700
Which, cast on stubborn soil, puts forth changed buds
And softer stains, unknown in happier climes;
Love which endures and doubts and is oppressed
And cherished, suffering much and much sustained,
And blind, oft-failing, yet believing love,
A half-enlightened, often-chequered trust:—   705
Hints and previsions of which faculties,
Are strewn confusedly everywhere about
The inferior natures, and all lead up higher,
All shape out dimly the superior race,
The heir of hopes too fair to turn out false,   710
And man appears at last. So far the seal
Is put on life; one stage of being complete,
One scheme wound up: and from the grand result
A supplementary reflux of light,
Illustrates all the inferior grades, explains   715
Each back step in the circle. Not alone
For their possessor dawn those qualities,
But the new glory mixes with the heaven
And earth; man, once descried, imprints for ever
His presence on all lifeless things: the winds   720
Are henceforth voices, wailing or a shout,

A querulous mutter or a quick gay laugh,
Never a senseless gust now man is born.
The herded pines commune and have deep thoughts,
A secret they assemble to discuss   725
When the sun drops behind their trunks which glare
Like grates of hell: the peerless cup afloat
Of the lake-lily is an urn, some nymph
Swims bearing high above her head: no bird
Whistles unseen, but through the gaps above   730
That let light in upon the gloomy woods,
A shape peeps from the breezy forest-top,
Arch with small puckered mouth and mocking eye.
The morn has enterprise, deep quiet droops
With evening, triumph takes the sunset hour,   735
Voluptuous transport ripens with the corn
Beneath a warm moon like a happy face:
—And this to fill us with regard for man.
With apprehension of his passing worth,
Desire to work his proper nature out,   740
And ascertain his rank and final place,
For these things tend still upward, progress is
The law of life, man is not Man as yet.
Nor shall I deem his object served, his end
Attained, his genuine strength put fairly forth,   745
While only here and there a star dispels
The darkness, here and there a towering mind
O'erlooks its prostrate fellows: when the host
Is out at once to the despair of night,
When all mankind alike is perfected,   750
Equal in full-blown powers—then, not till then,
I say, begins man's general infancy.
For wherefore make account of feverish starts
Of restless members of a dormant whole,
Impatient nerves which quiver while the body   755
Slumbers as in a grave? Oh long ago
The brow was twitched, the tremulous lids astir,
The peaceful mouth disturbed; half-uttered speech
Ruffled the lip, and then the teeth were set,
The breath drawn sharp, the strong right-hand
    clenched stronger,   760
As it would pluck a lion by the jaw;
The glorious creature laughed out even in sleep!
But when full roused, each giant-limb awake,
Each sinew strung, the great heart pulsing fast,
He shall start up and stand on his own earth,   765
Then shall his long triumphant march begin,
Thence shall his being date,—thus wholly roused,
What he achieves shall be set down to him.
When all the race is perfected alike

As man, that is; all tended to mankind,   770
And, man produced, all has its end thus far:
But in completed man begins anew
A tendency to God. Prognostics told
Man's near approach; so in man's self arise
August anticipations, symbols, types   775
Of a dim splendour ever on before
In that eternal circle life pursues.
For men begin to pass their nature's bound,
And find new hopes and cares which fast supplant
Their proper joys and griefs; they grow too great   780
For narrow creeds of right and wrong, which fade
Before the unmeasured thirst for good: while peace
Rises within them ever more and more.
Such men are even now upon the earth,
Serene amid the half-formed creatures round   785
Who should be saved by them and joined with them.

* * *

1834–35

Sordello (1840)

When after seven years of composition—and painstaking revision—the ambitious narrative poem *Sordello* was published in 1840, it was greeted with howls of protest or derision because of its obscurity of style and allusion. Despite generous praise from the great modern American poet Ezra Pound, *Sordello* remains among the most neglected of Browning's works, an irony since the poem provides a comprehensive view of the author's mind and art in his early phase. The historical setting of *Sordello* is the strife between two rival factions, the Guelphs and the Ghibellines, in northern Italy in the early thirteenth century. The protagonist is Sordello, a troubadour praised by Dante but otherwise obscure; Browning makes this figure his type of "Poet-as-Hero." Arthur Symons' characterization of the poem as a "psychological epic" is apt, for the focus is the developing conflict within Sordello between egoism and sympathy, art and society, contemplation and action—an internecine struggle that finally kills the hero. This passage, excerpted from Book II, lines 475–693, concerns Sordello's attitudes toward his art after he wins a song-contest in the Mantuan court by defeating his rival, Eglamor. Browning's own marginal glosses are helpful: "He has loved song's results, not song; so, must effect this [song] to obtain those [results]. He succeeds a little, but fails more; tries again, is no better satisfied, and declines from the ideal of song. What is the world's recognition worth? How poet no longer in unity with man, the whole visible Sordello goes wrong."

* * *
                    The evening star was high
When he reached Mantua, but his fame arrived
Before him: friends applauded, foes connived,
And Naddo[1] looked an angel, and the rest
Angels, and all these angels would be blest   480
Supremely by a song—the thrice-renowned
Goito-manufacture.[2] Then he found
(Casting about to satisfy the crowd)
That happy vehicle, so late allowed,
A sore annoyance; 't was the song's effect   485
He cared for, scarce the song itself: reflect!
In the past life, what might be singing's use?
Just to delight his Delians,[3] whose profuse
Praise, not the toilsome process which procured
That praise, enticed Apollo: dreams abjured,   490
No overleaping means for ends—take both
For granted or take neither! I am loth
To say the rhymes at last were Eglamor's;
But Naddo, chuckling, bade competitors
Go pine; "the master certes meant to waste   495
No effort, cautiously had probed the taste
He'd please anon: true bard, in short,—disturb
His title if they could; nor spur nor curb,
Fancy nor reason, wanting in him; whence
The staple of his verses, common sense: 500
He built on man's broad nature—gift of gifts,
That power to build! The world contented shifts
With counterfeits enough, a dreary sort
Of warriors, statesmen, ere it can extort
Its poet-soul—that's, after all, a freak   505
(The having eyes to see and tongue to speak)
With our herd's stupid sterling happiness
So plainly incompatible that—yes—
Yes—should a son of his improve the breed
And turn out poet, he were cursed indeed!"   510
"Well, there's Goito and its woods anon,
If the worst happen; best go stoutly on
Now!" thought Sordello.
                              Ay, and goes on yet!
You pother with your glossaries to get
A notion of the Troubadour's intent   515
In rondel, tenzon, virlai or sirvent[4]—

1. Naddo is "busiest of the tribe/Of genius-haunters" (*Sordello,* II.821–22).
2. Goito was Sordello's birthplace.
3. Natives of Delos, birthplace of Apollo, god of song.
4. Conventional French forms. *Rondel*: a lyric of fourteen lines on two rhymes, the first two lines becoming the refrain. *Tenzon*: a "contention" or imaginary verbal exchange upon some question of love or conduct. *Virlai*: or virelai, a complicated fixed form with refrains. *Sirvent*: Old Provençal poem in strophes, satiric or vituperative in tone, often about current events.

Much as you study arras[5] how to twirl
His angelot,[6] plaything of page and girl
Once; but you surely reach, at last,—or, no!
Never quite reach what struck the people so,   520
As from the welter of their time he drew
Its elements successively to view,
Followed all actions backward on their course,
And catching up, unmingled at the source,
Such a strength, such a weakness, added then   525
A touch or two, and turned them into men.
Virtue took form, nor vice refused a shape;
Here heaven opened, there was hell agape,
As Saint this simpered past in sanctity,
Sinner the other flared portentous by   530
A greedy people. Then why stop, surprised
At his success? The scheme was realized
Too suddenly in one respect: a crowd
Praising, eyes quick to see, and lips as loud
To speak, delicious homage to receive,   535
The woman's breath to feel upon his sleeve,
Who said, "But Anafest—why asks he less
Than Lucio, in your verses? how confess,
It seemed too much but yestereve!"—the youth,
Who bade him earnestly, "Avow the truth!   540
You love Bianca, surely, from your song;
I knew I was unworthy!"—soft or strong,
In poured such tributes ere he had arranged
Ethereal ways to take them, sorted, changed,
Digested. Courted thus at unawares,   545
In spite of his pretensions and his cares,
He caught himself shamefully hankering
After the obvious petty joys that spring
From true life, fain relinquish pedestal
And condescend with pleasures—one and all   550
To be renounced, no doubt; for, thus to chain
Himself to single joys and so refrain
From tasting their quintessence, frustrates, sure,
His prime design; each joy must he abjure
Even for love of it.   555
                He laughed: what sage
But perishes if from his magic page
He look because, at the first line, a proof
'T was heard salutes him from the cavern roof?
"On! Give yourself, excluding aught beside,
To the day's task; compel your slave provide   560
Its utmost at the soonest; turn the leaf
Thoroughly conned. These lays of yours, in brief—

---

5. Tapestries.   6. Flute-like instrument.

Cannot men bear, now, something better?—fly
A pitch beyond this unreal pageantry
Of essences? the period sure has ceased   565
For such: present us with ourselves, at least,
Not portions of ourselves, mere loves and hates
Made flesh: wait not!"
                 Awhile the poet waits
However. The first trial was enough:
He left imagining, to try the stuff   570
That held the imaged thing, and, let it writhe
Never so fiercely, scarce allowed a tithe
To reach the light—his Language. How he sought
The cause, conceived a cure, and slow re-wrought
That Language,—welding words into the crude   575
Mass from the new speech round him, till a rude
Armour was hammered out, in time to be
Approved beyond the Roman panoply
Melted to make it,—boots not. This obtained
With some ado, no obstacle remained   580
To using it; accordingly he took
An action with its actors, quite forsook
Himself to live in each, returned anon
With the result—a creature, and, by one
And one, proceeded leisurely to equip   585
Its limbs in harness of his workmanship.
"Accomplished! Listen, Mantuans!" Fond essay![7]
Piece after piece that armour broke away,
Because perceptions whole, like that he sought
To clothe, reject so pure a work of thought   590
As language: thought may take perception's place
But hardly co-exist in any case,
Being its mere presentment—of the whole
By parts, the simultaneous and the sole
By the successive and the many. Lacks   595
The crowd perception? painfully it tacks
Thought to thought, which Sordello, needing such,
Has rent perception into: it's to clutch
And reconstruct—his office to diffuse,
Destroy: as hard, then, to obtain a Muse[8]   600
As to become Apollo. "For the rest,
E'en if some wondrous vehicle expressed
The whole dream, what impertinence in me
So to express it, who myself can be
The dream! nor, on the other hand, are those   605
I sing to, over-likely to suppose
A higher than the highest I present

---

7. Foolish attempt.
8. To secure adequate expressive form.
                            The Muses were nine goddesses in Greek myth presiding over the arts.

Now, which they praise already: be content
Both parties, rather—they with the old verse,
And I with the old praise—far go, fare worse!"   610
A few adhering rivets loosed, upsprings
The angel, sparkles off his mail, which rings
Whirled from each delicatest limb it warps;
So might Apollo from the sudden corpse
Of Hyacinth[9] have cast his luckless quoits.   615
He set to celebrating the exploits
Of Montfort[1] o'er the Mountaineers.
                                Then came
The world's revenge: their pleasure, now his aim
Merely,—what was it? "Not to play the fool
So much as learn our lesson in your school!"   620
Replied the world. He found that, every time
He gained applause by any ballad-rhyme,
His auditory recognized no jot
As he intended, and, mistaking not
Him for his meanest hero, ne'er was dunce   625
Sufficient to believe him—all, at once.
His will . . . conceive it caring for his will!
—Mantuans, the main of them, admiring still
How a mere singer, ugly, stunted, weak,
Had Montfort at completely (so to speak)   630
His fingers' ends; while past the praise-tide swept
To Montfort, either's share distinctly kept:
The true meed for true merit!—his abates
Into a sort he most repudiates,
And on them angrily he turns. Who were   635
The Mantuans, after all, that he should care
About their recognition, ay or no?
In spite of the convention months ago,
(Why blink the truth?) was not he forced to help
This same ungrateful audience, every whelp   640
Of Naddo's litter, make them pass for peers
With the bright band of old Goito years,
As erst he toiled for flower or tree? Why, there
Sat Palma![2] Adelaide's funereal hair
Ennobled the next corner. Ay, he strewed   645
A fairy dust upon that multitude,
Although he feigned to take them by themselves;
His giants dignified those puny elves,
Sublimed their faint applause. In short, he found

9. Youth loved by both Apollo and Zephyrus. The latter out of jealousy blew a quoit thrown by Apollo so that it struck Hyacinthus, his partner in the game, instantly killing him.
1. Simon de Montfort, in the early thirteenth century, led a crusade to suppress the heretical Albigenses, whose strongholds were the mountainous regions of southern France and northern Italy.
2. Daughter of Eccelino by Agnes Este, and resident at Adelaide's court. Palma is loved by Sordello, who finds her beauty an inspiration.

Himself still footing a delusive round,   650
Remote as ever from the self-display
He meant to compass, hampered every way
By what he hoped assistance. Wherefore then
Continue, make believe to find in men
A use he found not?
                    Weeks, months, years went by; 655
And lo, Sordello vanished utterly,
Sundered in twain; each spectral part at strife
With each; one jarred against another life;
The Poet thwarting hopelessly the Man—
Who, fooled no longer, free in fancy ran   660
Here, there: let slip no opportunities
As pitiful, forsooth, beside the prize
To drop on him some no-time and acquit
His constant faith (the Poet-half's to wit—
That waiving any compromise between   665
No joy and all joy kept the hunger keen
Beyond most methods)—of incurring scoff
From the Man-portion—not to be put off
With self-reflectings by the Poet's scheme,
Though ne'er so bright. Who sauntered forth in dream,   670
Dressed any how, nor waited mystic frames,
Immeasurable gifts, astounding claims,
But just his sorry self?—who yet might be
Sorrier for aught he in reality
Achieved, so pinioned Man's the Poet-part,   675
Fondling, in turn of fancy, verse; the Art
Developing his soul a thousand ways—
Potent, by its assistance, to amaze
The multitude with majesties, convince
Each sort of nature that the nature's prince   680
Accosted it. Language, the makeshift, grew
Into a bravest of expedients, too;
Apollo, seemed it now, perverse had thrown
Quiver and bow away, the lyre alone
Sufficed. While, out of dream, his day's work went   685
To tune a crazy tenzon or sirvent—
So hampered him the Man-part, thrust to judge
Between the bard and the bard's audience, grudge
A minute's toil that missed its due reward!
But the complete Sordello, Man and Bard,   690
John's cloud-girt angel,[3] this foot on the land,
That on the sea, with, open in his hand,
A bitter-sweeting of a book—was gone.

* * *

3. Revelation 10:1–3. A mighty angel came down from heaven. "And he had in his hand a little book open: and he set his right foot upon the sea, and his left foot on the earth. . . ."

Pippa Passes (1841)[1]

Persons

PIPPA

OTTIMA

SEBALD

FOREIGN STUDENTS

GOTTLIEB

SCHRAMM

JULES

PHENE

AUSTRIAN POLICE

BLUPHOCKS

LUIGI and *his* MOTHER

POOR GIRLS

MONSIGNOR *and his* ATTENDANTS

Introduction

NEW YEAR'S DAY AT ASOLO IN THE TREVISAN[2]

SCENE.—*A large mean airy chamber. A girl,* PIPPA, *from the Silk-mills, springing out of bed.*

Day!
Faster and more fast,
O'er night's brim, day boils at last:
Boils, pure gold, o'er the cloud-cup's brim
Where spurting and suppressed it lay,   5
For not a froth-flake touched the rim
Of yonder gap in the solid gray
Of the eastern cloud, an hour away;
But forth one wavelet, then another, curled,
Till the whole sunrise, not to be suppressed,   10
Rose, reddened, and its seething breast
Flickered in bounds, grew gold, then overflowed the world.

Oh, Day, if I squander a wavelet of thee,
A mite of my twelve hours' treasure,
The least of thy gazes or glances,   15
(Be they grants thou art bound to or gifts above measure)
One of thy choices or one of thy chances,
(Be they tasks God imposed thee or freaks[3] at thy pleasure)
—My Day, if I squander such labour or leisure,
Then shame fall on Asolo, mischief on me!   20

Thy long blue solemn hours serenely flowing,
Whence earth, we feel, gets steady help and good—

1. *Pippa Passes* was published in 1841 as the first of a series of eight pamphlets with the general title *Bells and Pomegranates*. The poet's father bore the printing costs for the entire series. A product of Browning's first Italian visit in 1838, the play is set in Asolo, near Venice, where the poet was collecting materials for *Sordello* (1840).
2. Province of Treviso, north of Venice.
3. Capricious actions.

Thy fitful sunshine-minutes, coming, going,
As if earth turned from work in gamesome mood—
All shall be mine! But thou must treat me not   25
As prosperous ones are treated, those who live
At hand here, and enjoy the higher lot,
In readiness to take what thou wilt give,
And free to let alone what thou refusest;
For, Day, my holiday, if thou ill-usest   30
Me, who am only Pippa,—old-year's sorrow,
Cast off last night, will come again to-morrow:
Whereas, if thou prove gentle, I shall borrow
Sufficient strength of thee for new-year's sorrow.
All other men and women that this earth   35
Belongs to, who all days alike possess,
Make general plenty cure particular dearth,
Get more joy one way, if another, less:
Thou art my single day, God lends to leaven
What were all earth else, with a feel of heaven,—   40
Sole light that helps me through the year, thy sun's!
Try now! Take Asolo's Four Happiest Ones—
And let thy morning rain on that superb
Great haughty Ottima; can rain disturb
Her Sebald's homage? All the while thy rain   45
Beats fiercest on her shrub-house window-pane,
He will but press the closer, breathe more warm
Against her cheek; how should she mind the storm?
And, morning past, if mid-day shed a gloom
O'er Jules and Phene,—what care bride and groom   50
Save for their dear selves? 'T is their marriage-day;
And while they leave church and go home their way,
Hand clasping hand, within each breast would be
Sunbeams and pleasant weather spite of thee.
Then, for another trial, obscure thy eve   55
With mist,—will Luigi and his mother grieve—
The lady and her child, unmatched, forsooth,
She in her age, as Luigi in his youth,
For true content? The cheerful town, warm, close
And safe, the sooner that thou art morose,   60
Receives them. And yet once again, outbreak
In storm at night on Monsignor, they make
Such stir about,—whom they expect from Rome
To visit Asolo, his brothers' home,
And say here masses proper to release   65
A soul from pain,—what storm dares hurt his peace?
Calm would he pray, with his own thoughts to ward
Thy thunder off, nor want the angels' guard.
But Pippa—just one such mischance would spoil
Her day that lightens the next twelvemonth's toil   70
At wearisome silk-winding, coil on coil!

And here I let time slip for nought!
Aha, you foolhardy sunbeam, caught
With a single splash from my ewer!
You that would mock the best pursuer,   75
Was my basin over-deep?
One splash of water ruins you asleep,
And up, up, fleet your brilliant bits
Wheeling and counterwheeling,
Reeling, broken beyond healing: 80
Now grow together on the ceiling!
That will task your wits.
Whoever it was quenched fire first, hoped to see
Morsel after morsel flee
As merrily, as giddily . . .   85
Meantime, what lights my sunbeam on,
Where settles by degrees the radiant cripple?
Oh, is it surely blown, my martagon?[4]
New-blown and ruddy as St. Agnes'[5] nipple,
Plump as the flesh-bunch on some Turk bird's poll![6]   90
Be sure if corals, branching 'neath the ripple
Of ocean, bud there,—fairies watch unroll
Such turban-flowers; I say, such lamps disperse
Thick red flame through that dusk green universe!
I am queen of thee, floweret!   95
And each fleshy blossom
Preserve I not—(safer
Than leaves that embower it,
Or shells that embosom)
—From weevil and chafer?[7]   100
Laugh through my pane then; solicit the bee;
Gibe him, be sure; and, in midst of thy glee,
Love thy queen, worship me!

—Worship whom else? For am I not, this day,
Whate'er I please? What shall I please to-day?   105
My morn, noon, eve and night—how spend my day?
To-morrow I must be Pippa who winds silk,
The whole year round, to earn just bread and milk:
But, this one day, I have leave to go,
And play out my fancy's fullest games;   110
I may fancy all day—and it shall be so—
That I taste of the pleasures, am called by the names
Of the Happiest Four in our Asolo!
See! Up the hill-side yonder, through the morning,
Some one shall love me, as the world calls love: 115
I am no less than Ottima, take warning!
The gardens, and the great stone house above,

---

4. Kind of lily, also called Turk's cap.
5. Virgin martyr, killed at the age of twelve or thirteen.
6. Turkey's head.
7. Two species of beetle.

And other house for shrubs, all glass in front,
Are mine; where Sebald steals, as he is wont,
To court me, while old Luca yet reposes: 120
And therefore, till the shrub-house door uncloses,
I . . . what now?—give abundant cause for prate
About me—Ottima, I mean—of late,
Too bold, too confident she'll still face down
The spitefullest of talkers in our town.   125
How we talk in the little town below!
    But love, love, love—there's better love, I know!
This foolish love was only day's first offer;
I choose my next love to defy the scoffer:
For do not our Bride and Bridegroom sally   130
Out of Possagno church[8] at noon?
Their house looks over Orcana valley:
Why should not I be the bride as soon
As Ottima? For I saw, beside,
Arrive last night that little bride—   135
Saw, if you call it seeing her, one flash
Of the pale snow-pure cheek and black bright tresses,
Blacker than all except the black eyelash;
I wonder she contrives those lids no dresses!
—So strict was she, the veil   140
Should cover close her pale
Pure cheeks—a bride to look at and scarce touch,
Scarce touch, remember, Jules! For are not such
Used to be tended, flower-like, every feature,
As if one's breath would fray the lily of a creature?   145
A soft and easy life these ladies lead:
Whiteness in us were wonderful indeed.
Oh, save that brow its virgin dimness,
Keep that foot its lady primness,
Let those ankles never swerve   150
From their exquisite reserve,
Yet have to trip along the streets like me,
All but naked to the knee!
How will she ever grant her Jules a bliss
So startling as her real first infant kiss?   155
Oh, no—not envy, this!

—Not envy, sure!—for if you gave me
Leave to take or to refuse,
In earnest, do you think I'd choose
That sort of new love to enslave me?   160
Mine should have lapped me round from the beginning;
As little fear of losing it as winning:
Lovers grow cold, men learn to hate their wives,
And only parents' love can last our lives.

8. A church designed by the sculptor   Possagno, near Treviso.
Antonio Canova (1757–1822), born at

At eve the Son and Mother, gentle pair,   165
Commune inside our turret: what prevents
My being Luigi? While that mossy lair
Of lizards through the winter-time is stirred
With each to each imparting sweet intents
For this new-year, as brooding bird to bird—   170
(For I observe of late, the evening walk
Of Luigi and his mother, always ends
Inside our ruined turret, where they talk,
Calmer than lovers, yet more kind than friends)
—Let me be cared about, kept out of harm,   175
And schemed for, safe in love as with a charm;
Let me be Luigi! If I only knew
What was my mother's face—my father, too!
     Nay, if you come to that, best love of all
Is God's; then why not have God's love befall   180
Myself as, in the palace by the Dome,[9]
Monsignor?—who to-night will bless the home
Of his dead brother; and God bless in turn
That heart which beats, those eyes which mildly burn
With love for all men! I, to-night at least,   185
Would be that holy and beloved priest.

Now wait!—even I already seem to share
In God's love: what does New-year's hymn declare?
What other meaning do these verses bear?

> *All service ranks the same with God:*   190
> *Can work—God's puppets, best and worst,*
> *If now, as formerly he trod*
> *Paradise, his presence fills*
> *Our earth, each only as God wills*
> *Are we; there is no last nor first.*   195
>
> *Say not "a small event!" Why "small"?*
> *Costs it more pain that this, ye call*
> *A "great event," should come to pass,*
> *Than that? Untwine me from the mass*
> *Of deeds which make up life, one deed*   200
> *Power shall fall short in or exceed!*

And more of it, and more of it!—oh yes—
I will pass each, and see their happiness,
And envy none—being just as great, no doubt,
Useful to men, and dear to God, as they!   205
A pretty thing to care about
So mightily, this single holiday!
But let the sun shine! Wherefore repine?
—With thee to lead me, O Day of mine,
Down the grass path grey with dew,   210

9. Cathedral.

Under the pine-wood, blind with boughs,
Where the swallow never flew
Nor yet cicala[1] dared carouse—
No, dared carouse!

[*She enters the street.*]

Part I

MORNING

SCENE.—*Up the Hill-side, inside the Shrub-house.* LUCA'S *wife,*
OTTIMA, *and her paramour, the German* SEBALD.

SEBALD [*sings*].

> *Let the watching lids wink!*
> *Day's a-blaze with eyes, think!*
> *Deep into the night, drink!*

OTTIMA. Night? Such may be your Rhine-land nights perhaps;
But this blood-red beam through the shutter's chink   5
—We call such light, the morning: let us see!
Mind how you grope your way, though! How these tall
Naked geraniums straggle! Push the lattice
Behind that frame!—Nay, do I bid you!—Sebald,
It shakes the dust down on me! Why, of course   10
The slide-bolt catches. Well, are you content,
Or must I find you something else to spoil?
Kiss and be friends, my Sebald! Is 't full morning?
Oh, don't speak then!

SEBALD.   Ay, thus it used to be.
Ever your house was, I remember, shut   15
Till mid-day; I observed that, as I strolled
On mornings through the vale here; country girls
Were noisy, washing garments in the brook,
Hinds drove the slow white oxen up the hills:
But no, your house was mute, would ope no eye.   20
And wisely: you were plotting one thing there,
Nature, another outside. I looked up—
Rough white wood shutters, rusty iron bars,
Silent as death, blind in a flood of light.
Oh, I remember!—and the peasants laughed   25
And said, "The old man sleeps with the young wife."
This house was his, this chair, this window—his.

OTTIMA. Ah, the clear morning! I can see St. Mark's;[2]
That black streak is the belfry. Stop: Vicenza
Should lie . . . there's Padua, plain enough, that blue!   30
Look o'er my shoulder, follow my finger!

SEBALD.   Morning?

1. Cicada, locust.
2. Cathedral in Venice. Vicenza and Padua are to the south.

It seems to me a night with a sun added.
Where's dew, where's freshness? That bruised plant, I bruised
In getting through the lattice yestereve,
Droops as it did. See, here's my elbow's mark   35
I' the dust o' the sill.
OTTIMA.   Oh, shut the lattice, pray!
SEBALD. Let me lean out. I cannot scent blood here,
Foul as the morn may be.
                                There, shut the world out!
How do you feel now, Ottima? There, curse
The world and all outside! Let us throw off   40
This mask: how do you bear yourself? Let's out
With all of it.
OTTIMA.   Best never speak of it.
SEBALD. Best speak again and yet again of it,
Till words cease to be more than words. "His blood,"
For instance—let those two words mean "His blood"   45
And nothing more. Notice, I'll say them now,
"His blood."
OTTIMA.   Assuredly if I repented
The deed—
SEBALD.   Repent? Who should repent, or why?
What puts that in your head? Did I once say
That I repented?
OTTIMA.   No, I said the deed . . .   50
SEBALD. "The deed" and "the event"—just now it was
"Our passion's fruit"—the devil take such cant!
Say, once and always, Luca was a wittol,[3]
I am his cut-throat, you are . . .
OTTIMA.   Here's the wine;
I brought it when we left the house above,   55
And glasses too—wine of both sorts. Black? White then?
SEBALD. But am not I his cut-throat? What are you?
OTTIMA. There trudges on his business from the Duomo[4]
Benet the Capuchin,[5] with his brown hood
And bare feet; always in one place at church,   60
Close under the stone wall by the south entry.
I used to take him for a brown cold piece
Of the wall's self, as out of it he rose
To let me pass—at first, I say, I used:
Now, so has that dumb figure fastened on me,   65
I rather should account the plastered wall
A piece of him, so chilly does it strike.
This, Sebald?
SEBALD.   No, the white wine—the white wine!
Well, Ottima, I promised no new year
Should rise on us the ancient shameful way;   70

3. Man who knows his wife is unfaith-   5. Branch of the Franciscan order of
ful.   friars.
4. Cathedral.

Nor does it rise. Pour on! To your black eyes!
Do you remember last damned New Year's day?
OTTIMA. You brought those foreign prints. We looked at them
  Over the wine and fruit. I had to scheme
  To get him from the fire. Nothing but saying   75
  His own set wants the proof-mark,[6] roused him up
  To hunt them out.
SEBALD.   'Faith, he is not alive
  To fondle you before my face.
OTTIMA.   Do you
  Fondle me then! Who means to take your life
  For that, my Sebald?
SEBALD.   Hark you, Ottima!   80
  One thing to guard against. We'll not make much
  One of the other—that is, not make more
  Parade of warmth, childish officious coil,[7]
  Than yesterday: as if, sweet, I supposed
  Proof upon proof were needed now, now first,   85
  To show I love you—yes, still love you—love you
  In spite of Luca and what's come to him
  —Sure sign we had him ever in our thoughts,
  White sneering old reproachful face and all!
  We'll even quarrel, love, at times, as if   90
  We still could lose each other, were not tied
  By this: conceive you?
OTTIMA.   Love!
SEBALD.   Not tied so sure.
  Because though I was wrought upon, have struck
  His insolence back into him—am I
  So surely yours?—therefore forever yours?   95
OTTIMA. Love, to be wise, (one counsel pays another)
  Should we have—months ago, when first we loved,
  For instance that May morning we two stole
  Under the green ascent of sycamores—
  If we had come upon a thing like that   100
  Suddenly . . .
SEBALD.   "A thing"—there again—"a thing!"
OTTIMA. Then, Venus' body, had we come upon
  My husband Luca Gaddi's murdered corpse
  Within there, at his couch-foot, covered close—
  Would you have pored upon it? Why persist   105
  In poring now upon it? For 't is here
  As much as there in the deserted house:
  You cannot rid your eyes of it. For me,
  Now he is dead I hate him worse: I hate . . .
  Dare you stay here? I would go back and hold   110
  His two dead hands, and say, "I hate you worse,

6. Sign on a print showing it to be one of the first from the plate, and consequently valuable.
7. Fuss.

Luca, than . . ."

SEBALD.　　　　　Off, off—take your hands off mine,
'T is the hot evening—off! oh, morning is it?

OTTIMA. There's one thing must be done; you know what thing.
　　Come in and help to carry. We may sleep　　　　115
　　Anywhere in the whole wide house to-night.

SEBALD. What would come, think you, if we let him lie
　　Just as he is? Let him lie there until
　　The angels take him! He is turned by this
　　Off from his face beside,[8] as you will see.　　　120

OTTIMA. This dusty pane might serve for looking glass.
　　Three, four—four grey hairs! Is it so you said
　　A plait of hair should wave across my neck?
　　No—this way.

SEBALD.　　　　Ottima, I would give your neck,
　　Each splendid shoulder, both those breasts of yours,　　125
　　That this were undone! Killing! Kill the world,
　　So Luca lives again!—ay, lives to sputter
　　His fulsome dotage on you—yes, and feign
　　Surprise that I return at eve to sup,
　　When all the morning I was loitering here—　　130
　　Bid me despatch my business and begone.
　　I would . . .

OTTIMA.　　　See!

SEBALD.　　　　　No, I'll finish. Do you think
　　I fear to speak the bare truth once for all?
　　All we have talked of, is, at bottom, fine
　　To suffer; there's a recompense in guilt;　　135
　　One must be venturous and fortunate:
　　What is one young for, else? In age we'll sigh
　　O'er the wild reckless wicked days flown over;
　　Still, we have lived: the vice was in its place.
　　But to have eaten Luca's bread, have worn　　140
　　His clothes, have felt his money swell my purse—
　　Do lovers in romances sin that way?
　　Why, I was starving when I used to call
　　And teach you music, starving while you plucked me
　　These flowers to smell!

OTTIMA.　　　　My poor lost friend!

SEBALD.　　　　　　　　He gave me　　145
　　Life, nothing less: what if he did reproach
　　My perfidy, and threaten, and do more—
　　Had he no right? What was to wonder at?
　　He sat by us at table quietly:
　　Why must you lean across till our cheeks touched?　　150
　　Could he do less than make pretence to strike?
　　'T is not the crime's sake—I'd commit ten crimes

8. There is an old superstition that a　vengeance.
murdered man looks to the sky for

Greater, to have this crime wiped out, undone!
And you—O how feel you? Feel you for me?
OTTIMA. Well then, I love you better now than ever,   155
And best (look at me while I speak to you)—
Best for the crime; nor do I grieve, in truth,
This mask, this simulated ignorance,
This affectation of simplicity,
Falls off our crime; this naked crime of ours   160
May not now be looked over: look it down!
Great? let it be great; but the joys it brought,
Pay they or no its price? Come: they or it!
Speak not! The past, would you give up the past
Such as it is, pleasure and crime together?   165
Give up that noon I owned my love for you?
The garden's silence: even the single bee
Persisting in his toil, suddenly stopped,
And where he hid you only could surmise
By some campanula⁹ chalice set a-swing.   170
Who stammered—"Yes, I love you?"
SEBALD.   And I drew
Back; put far back your face with both my hands
Lest you should grow too full of me—your face
So seemed athirst for my whole soul and body!
OTTIMA. And when I ventured to receive you here,   175
Made you steal hither in the mornings—
SEBALD.   When
I used to look up 'neath the shrub-house here,
Till the red fire on its glazed windows spread
To a yellow haze?
OTTIMA.   Ah—my sign was, the sun
Inflamed the sere side of yon chestnut-tree   180
Nipped by the first frost.
SEBALD.   You would always laugh
At my wet boots: I had to stride thro' grass
Over my ankles.
OTTIMA.   Then our crowning night!
SEBALD. The July night?
OTTIMA.   The day of it too, Sebald!
When heaven's pillars seemed o'erbowed with heat,   185
Its black-blue canopy suffered descend
Close on us both, to weigh down each to each,
And smother up all life except our life.
So lay we till the storm came.
SEBALD.   How it came!
OTTIMA. Buried in woods we lay, you recollect;   190
Swift ran the searching tempest overhead;
And ever and anon some bright white shaft
Burned thro' the pine-tree roof, here burned and there,

9. Bell-flower.

As if God's messenger thro' the close wood screen
Plunged and replunged his weapon at a venture,   195
Feeling for guilty thee and me: then broke
The thunder like a whole sea overhead—
SEBALD. Yes!
OTTIMA. —While I stretched myself upon you, hands
To hands, my mouth to your hot mouth, and shook
All my locks loose, and covered you with them—   200
You, Sebald, the same you!
SEBALD.   Slower, Ottima!
OTTIMA. And as we lay—
SEBALD.   Less vehemently! Love me!
Forgive me! Take not words, mere words, to heart!
Your breath is worse than wine! Breathe slow, speak slow!
Do not lean on me!
OTTIMA.   Sebald, as we lay,   205
Rising and falling only with our pants,
Who said, "Let death come now! 'T is right to die!
Right to be punished! Nought completes such bliss
But woe!" Who said that?
SEBALD.   How did we ever rise?
Was 't that we slept? Why did it end?
OTTIMA.   I felt you   210
Taper into a point the ruffled ends
Of my loose locks 'twixt both your humid lips.
My hair is fallen now: knot it again!
SEBALD. I kiss you now, dear Ottima, now and now!
This way? Will you forgive me—be once more   215
My great queen?
OTTIMA.   Bind it thrice about my brow;
Crown me your queen, your spirit's arbitress,
Magnificent in sin. Say that!
SEBALD.   I crown you
My great white queen, my spirit's arbitress,
Magnificent . . .   220

[*From without is heard the voice of* PIPPA, *singing*—]

The year's at the spring
And day's at the morn;
Morning's at seven;
The hill-side's dew-pearled;
The lark's on the wing;   225
The snail's on the thorn:
God's in his heaven—
All's right with the world!

[PIPPA *passes.*]

SEBALD. God's in his heaven! Do you hear that? Who spoke?
You, you spoke!
OTTIMA.   Oh—that little ragged girl!   230
She must have rested on the step: we give them

But this one holiday the whole year round.
Did you ever see our silk-mills—their inside?
There are ten silk-mills now belong to you.
She stoops to pick my double heartsease[1]. . . Sh!   235
She does not hear: call you out louder!

SEBALD.   Leave me!
Go, get your clothes on—dress those shoulders!

OTTIMA.   Sebald?

SEBALD. Wipe off that paint! I hate you.

OTTIMA.   Miserable!

SEBALD. My God, and she is emptied of it now!
Outright now!—how miraculously gone   240
All of the grace—had she not strange grace once?
Why, the blank cheek hangs listless as it likes,
No purpose holds the features up together,
Only the cloven brow and puckered chin
Stay in their places: and the very hair,   245
That seemed to have a sort of life in it,
Drops, a dead web!

OTTIMA.   Speak to me—not of me!

SEBALD. —That round great full-orbed face, where not an angle
Broke the delicious indolence—all broken!

OTTIMA. To me—not of me! Ungrateful, perjured cheat!   250
A coward too: but ingrate's worse than all.
Beggar—my slave—a fawning, cringing lie!
Leave me! Betray me! I can see your drift!
A lie that walks and eats and drinks!

SEBALD.   My God!
Those morbid olive faultless shoulder-blades—   255
I should have known there was no blood beneath!

OTTIMA. You hate me then? You hate me then?

SEBALD.   To think
She would succeed in her absurd attempt,
And fascinate by sinning, show herself
Superior—guilt from its excess superior   260
To innocence! That little peasant's voice
Has righted all again. Though I be lost,
I know which is the better, never fear,
Of vice or virtue, purity or lust,
Nature or trick! I see what I have done,   265
Entirely now! Oh I am proud to feel
Such torments—let the world take credit thence—
I, having done my deed, pay too its price!
I hate, hate—curse you! God's in his heaven!

OTTIMA.   —Me!
Me! no, no, Sebald, not yourself—kill me!   270
Mine is the whole crime. Do but kill me—then
Yourself—then—presently—first hear me speak!

1. Kind of violet or pansy.

I always meant to kill myself—wait, you!
Lean on my breast—not as a breast; don't love me
The more because you lean on me, my own   275
Heart's Sebald! There, there, both deaths presently!
SEBALD. My brain is drowned now—quite drowned: all I feel
Is . . . is, at swift-recurring intervals,
A hurry-down within me, as of waters
Loosened to smother up some ghastly pit: 280
There they go—whirls from a black fiery sea!
OTTIMA. Not me—to him, O God, be merciful!

Talk by the way, while PIPPA *is passing from the hill-side to
Orcana.* FOREIGN STUDENTS *of painting and sculpture, from
Venice, assembled opposite the house of* JULES, *a young
French statuary, at Possagno.*

FIRST STUDENT. Attention! My own post is beneath this window,
but the pomegranate clump yonder will hide three or four of you
with a little squeezing, and Schramm and his pipe must lie flat in
the balcony. Four, five—who's a defaulter? We want everybody,
for Jules must not be suffered to hurt his bride when the jest's
found out.
SECOND STUDENT. All here! Only our poet's away—never having
much meant to be present, moonstrike him! The airs of that
follow, that Giovacchino! He was in violent love with himself,
and had a fair prospect of thriving in his suit, so unmolested was
it,—when suddenly a woman falls in love with him, too; and out
of pure jealously he takes himself off to Trieste,[2] immortal poem
and all: whereto is this prophetical epitaph appended already, as
Bluphocks assures me,—*"Here a mammoth-poem lies, Fouled to
death by butterflies."* His own fault, the simpleton! Instead of
cramp couplets, each like a knife in your entrails, he should write,
says Bluphocks, both classically and intelligibly.—*Æsculapius,*[3]
an Epic. Catalogue of the drugs: Hebe's[4] *plaister—One strip
Cools your lip. Phœbus'*[5] *emulsion—One bottle Clears your
throttle. Mercury's*[6] *bolus—One box Cures . . .*
THIRD STUDENT. Subside, my fine fellow! If the marriage was over
by ten o'clock, Jules will certainly be here in a minute with his
bride.
SECOND STUDENT. Good!—only, so should the poet's muse have
been universally acceptable, says Bluphocks, *et canibus nostris*[7]
. . . and Delia not better known to our literary dogs than the boy
Giovacchino!
FIRST STUDENT. To the point, now. Where's Gottlieb, the new-

2. City on the Adriatic across from Venice.
3. God of medicine. "Catalogue" refers to the epic convention of the catalogue or list of heroes.
4. Goddess of youth, cupbearer to the gods.
5. Apollo, god of song and of healing, father of Aesculapius.

6. Messenger of the gods. His emblem is the caduceus, symbol of medicine. Bolus: large pill. The rhyming word is "᾿ ox," i.e., syphilis.
7. "And to our dogs." Cf. Virgil, *Eclogues,* III.66–67: "But my flame Amyntas comes to me unbidden: insomuch that now our dogs know not Delia better" (Mackail translation).

comer? Oh,—listen, Gottlieb, to what has called down this piece of friendly vengeance on Jules, of which we now assemble to witness the winding-up. We are all agreed, all in a tale, observe, when Jules shall burst out on us in a fury by and by: I am spokesman—the verses that are to undeceive Jules bear my name of Lutwyche—but each professes himself alike insulted by this strutting stone-squarer, who came alone from Paris to Munich, and thence with a crowd of us to Venice and Possagno here, but proceeds in a day or two alone again—oh, alone indubitably!—to Rome and Florence. He, forsooth, take up his portion with these dissolute, brutalized, heartless bunglers!—so he was heard to call us all: now, is Schramm brutalized, I should like to know? Am I heartless?

GOTTLIEB. Why, somewhat heartless; for, suppose Jules a coxcomb as much as you choose, still, for this mere coxcombry, you will have brushed off—what do folks style it?—the bloom of his life. Is it too late to alter? These love-letters now, you call his—I can't laugh at them.

FOURTH STUDENT. Because you never read the sham letters of our inditing which drew forth these.

GOTTLIEB. His discovery of the truth will be frightful.

FOURTH STUDENT. That's the joke. But you should have joined us at the beginning: there's no doubt he loves the girl—loves a model he might hire by the hour!

GOTTLIEB. See here! "He has been accustomed," he writes, "to have Canova's women about him, in stone, and the world's women beside him, in flesh; these being as much below, as those above, his soul's aspiration: but now he is to have the reality." There you laugh again! I say, you wipe off the very dew of his youth.

FIRST STUDENT. Schramm! (Take the pipe out of his mouth, somebody!) Will Jules lose the bloom of his youth?

SCHRAMM. Nothing worth keeping is ever lost in this world: look at a blossom—it drops presently, having done its service and lasted its time; but fruits succeed, and where would be the blossom's place could it continue? As well affirm that your eye is no longer in your body, because its earliest favourite, whatever it may have first loved to look on, is dead and done with—as that any affection is lost to the soul when its first object, whatever happened first to satisfy it, is superseded in due course. Keep but ever looking, whether with the body's eye or the mind's, and you will soon find something to look on! Has the man done wondering at women?—there follow men, dead and alive, to wonder at. Has he done wondering at men?—there's God to wonder at: and the faculty of wonder may be, at the same time, old and tired enough with respect to its first object, and yet young and fresh sufficiently, so far as concerns its novel one. Thus . . .

FIRST STUDENT. Put Schramm's pipe into his mouth again! There, you see! Well, this Jules . . . a wretched fribble—oh, I watched his disportings at Possagno, the other day! Canova's gallery—you know: there he marches first resolvedly past great works by the dozen without vouchsafing an eye: all at once he stops full at the *Psiche-fanciulla*[8]—cannot pass that old acquaintance without a nod of encouragement—"In your new place, beauty? Then behave yourself as well here as at Munich—I see you!" Next he posts himself deliberately before the unfinished *Pietà*[9] for half an hour without moving, till up he starts of a sudden, and thrusts his very nose into—I say, into—the group; by which gesture you are informed that precisely the sole point he had not fully mastered in Canova's practice was a certain method of using the drill in the articulation of the knee-joint—and that, likewise, has he mastered at length! Good-bye, therefore, to poor Canova—whose gallery no longer needs detain his successor Jules, the predestinated novel thinker in marble!

FIFTH STUDENT. Tell him about the women: go on to the women!

FIRST STUDENT: Why, on that matter he could never be supercilious enough. How should we be other (he said) than the poor devils you see, with those debasing habits we cherish? He was not to wallow in that mire, at least: he would wait, and love only at the proper time, and meanwhile put up with the *Psiche-fanciulla*. Now, I happened to hear of a young Greek—real Greek girl at Malamocco;[1] a true Islander, do you see, with Alciphron's[2] "hair like sea-moss"—Schramm knows!—white and quiet as an apparition, and fourteen years old at farthest,—a daughter of Natalia, so she swears—that hag Natalia, who helps us to models at three *lire* an hour. We selected this girl for the heroine of our jest. So first, Jules received a scented letter—somebody had seen his Tydeus[3] at the Academy,[4] and my picture was nothing to it: a profound admirer bade him persevere—would make herself known to him ere long. (Paolina, my little friend of the *Fenice*,[5] transcribes divinely.) And in due time, the mysterious correspondent gave certain hints of her peculiar charms—the pale cheeks, the black hair—whatever, in short, had struck us in our Malamocco model: we retained her name, too—Phene, which is, by interpretation, sea-eagle. Now, think of Jules finding himself distinguished from the herd of us by such a creature! In his very first answer he proposed marrying his monitress: and fancy us over these letters, two, three times a day, to receive and despatch! I concocted the main of it: relations were in the way—secrecy must be observed—in fine, would he wed her on trust, and only speak to her when they were indissolubly united? St—st—Here they come!

SIXTH STUDENT. Both of them! Heaven's love, speak softly, speak within yourselves!

---

8. Canova's statue of Psyche with a butterfly.
9. Statue of Mary mourning over the body of Jesus.
1. Island near Venice.
2. Greek writer of the second century A.D. who authored fictitious letters admired for their style.
3. A hero of the Theban War.
4. Of Fine Arts, Venice.
5. The Phoenix, theatre in Venice.

FIFTH STUDENT. Look at the bridegroom! Half his hair in storm and half in calm,—patted down over the left temple,—like a frothy cup one blows on to cool it: and the same old blouse that he murders the marble in.

SECOND STUDENT. Not a rich vest like yours, Hannibal Scratchy![6] —rich, that your face may the better set it off.

SIXTH STUDENT. And the bride! Yes, sure enough, our Phene! Should you have known her in her clothes? How magnificently pale!

GOTTLIEB. She does not also take it for earnest, I hope?

FIRST STUDENT. Oh, Natalia's concern, that is! We settle with Natalia.

SIXTH STUDENT. She does not speak—has evidently let out no word. The only thing is, will she equally remember the rest of her lesson, and repeat correctly all those verses which are to break the secret to Jules?

GOTTLIEB. How he gazes on her! Pity—pity!

FIRST STUDENT. They go in: now, silence! You three,—not nearer the window, mind, than that pomegranate: just where the little girl, who a few minutes ago passed us singing, is seated!

Part II

NOON

SCENE.—*Over Orcana. The house of* JULES, *who crosses its threshold with* PHENE: *she is silent, on which* JULES *begins—*

Do not die, Phene! I am yours now, you
Are mine now; let fate reach me how she likes,
If you'll not die: so, never die! Sit here—
My work-room's single seat. I over-lean
This length of hair and lustrous front; they turn   5
Like an entire flower upward: eyes, lips, last
Your chin—no, last your throat turns: 't is their scent
Pulls down my face upon you. Nay, look ever
This one way till I change, grow you—I could
Change into you, beloved!
                                              You by me,   10
And I by you; this is your hand in mine,
And side by side we sit: all's true. Thank God!
I have spoken: speak you!
                                        O my life to come!
My Tydeus must be carved that's there in clay;
Yet how be carved, with you about the room?   15
Where must I place you? When I think that once
This room-full of rough block-work seemed my heaven

6. Play on the name of the Italian who began as a tailor.
painter Annibale Caracci (1540–1609),

Without you! Shall I ever work again,
Get fairly into my old ways again,
Bid each conception stand while, trait by trait, [20]
My hand transfers its lineaments to stone?
Will my mere fancies live near you, their truth—
The live truth, passing and repassing me,
Sitting beside me?
                    Now speak!
                              Only first,
See, all your letters! Was 't not well contrived? [25]
Their hiding-place is Psyche's robe; she keeps
Your letters next her skin: which drops out foremost?
Ah,—this that swam down like a first moonbeam
Into my world!
               Again those eyes complete
Their melancholy survey, sweet and slow, [30]
Of all my room holds; to return and rest
On me, with pity, yet some wonder too:
As if God bade some spirit plague a world,
And this were the one moment of surprise
And sorrow while she took her station, pausing [35]
O'er what she sees, finds good, and must destroy!
What gaze you at? Those? Books, I told you of;
Let your first word to me rejoice them, too:
This minion, a Coluthus,[7] writ in red
Bistre[8] and azure by Bessarion's scribe— [40]
Read this line . . . no, shame—Homer's be the Greek
First breathed me from the lips of my Greek girl!
This Odyssey in coarse black vivid type
With faded yellow blossoms 'twixt page and page,
To mark great places with due gratitude; [45]
"He said, and on Antinous[9] directed
A bitter shaft" . . . a flower blots out the rest!
Again upon your search? My statues, then!
—Ah, do not mind that—better that will look
When cast in bronze—an Almaign Kaiser,[1] that, [50]
Swart-green and gold, with truncheon based on hip.
This, rather, turn to! What, unrecognized?
I thought you would have seen that here you sit
As I imagined you,—Hippolyta,[2]
Naked upon her bright Numidian horse. [55]
Recall you this then? "Carve in bold relief"—
So you commanded—"carve, against I come,
A Greek, in Athens, as our fashion was,

---

7. Minion: darling. Coluthus: Greek poet of the sixth century A.D., one of whose poems was discovered by Cardinal Bessarion (line 40).
8. Dark brown.

9. One of Penelope's suitors, slain by Odysseus (*Odyssey*, XXII).
1. German ruler.
2. Queen of the Amazons.

Feasting, bay-filleted[3] and thunder-free,
Who rises 'neath the lifted myrtle-branch.   60
'Praise those who slew Hipparchus!'[4] cry the guests,
'While o'er thy head the singer's myrtle waves
As erst above our champion: stand up, all!' "
See, I have laboured to express your thought.
Quite round, a cluster of mere hands and arms,   65
(Thrust in all senses, all ways, from all sides,
Only consenting at the branch's end
They strain toward) serves for frame to a sole face,
The Praiser's, in the centre: who with eyes
Sightless, so bend they back to light inside   70
His brain where visionary forms throng up,
Sings, minding not that palpitating arch
Of hands and arms, nor the quick drip of wine
From the drenched leaves o'erhead, nor crowns cast off,
Violet and parsley crowns to trample on—   75
Sings, pausing as the patron-ghosts approve,
Devoutly their unconquerable hymn.
But you must say a "well" to that—say "well!"
Because you gaze—am I fantastic, sweet?
Gaze like my very life's-stuff, marble—marbly   80
Even to the silence! Why, before I found
The real flesh Phene, I inured myself
To see, throughout all nature, varied stuff
For better nature's birth by means of art:
With me, each substance tended to one form   85
Of beauty—to the human archetype.
On every side occurred suggestive germs
Of that—the tree, the flower—or take the fruit,—
Some rosy shape, continuing the peach,
Curved beewise o'er its bough; as rosy limbs,   90
Depending, nestled in the leaves; and just
From a cleft rose-peach the whole Dryad[5] sprang.
But of the stuffs one can be master of,
How I divined their capabilities!
From the soft-rinded smoothening facile chalk   95
That yields your outline to the air's embrace,
Half-softened by a halo's pearly gloom;
Down to the crisp imperious steel, so sure
To cut its one confided thought clean out
Of all the world. But marble!—'neath my tools   100
More pliable than jelly—as it were
Some clear primordial creature dug from depths
In the earth's heart, where itself breeds itself,
And whence all baser substance may be worked;

3. Crowned with bay leaves, supposed to protect the wearer against lightning.
4. Athenian tyrant whose murderers con- cealed their daggers in branches of myrtle at a festival.
5. Wood nymph.

Refine it off to air, you may,—condense it   105
Down to the diamond;—is not metal there,
When o'er the sudden speck my chisel trips?
—Not flesh, as flake off flake I scale, approach,
Lay bare those bluish veins of blood asleep?
Lurks flame in no strange windings where, surprised   110
By the swift implement sent home at once,
Flushes and glowings radiate and hover
About its track?
              Phene? what—why is this?
That whitening cheek, those still dilating eyes!
Ah, you will die—I knew that you would die!   115

PHENE *begins, on his having long remained silent.*
Now the end's coming; to be sure, it must
Have ended sometime! Tush, why need I speak
Their foolish speech? I cannot bring to mind
One half of it, beside; and do not care
For old Natalia now, nor any of them.   120
Oh, you—what are you?—if I do not try
To say the words Natalia made me learn,
To please your friends,—it is to keep myself
Where your voice lifted me, by letting that
Proceed: but can it? Even you, perhaps,   125
Cannot take up, now you have once let fall,
The music's life, and me along with that—
No, or you would! We'll stay then, as we are:
Above the world.
            You creature with the eyes!
If I could look for ever up to them,   130
As now you let me,—I believe, all sin,
All memory of wrong done, suffering borne,
Would drop down, low and lower, to the earth
Whence all that's low comes, and there touch and stay
—Never to overtake the rest of me,   135
All that, unspotted, reaches up to you,
Drawn by those eyes! What rises is myself,
Not me the shame and suffering; but they sink,
Are left, I rise above them. Keep me so,
Above the world!
           But you sink, for your eyes   140
Are altering—altered! Stay—"I love you, love" . . .
I could prevent it if I understood:
More of your words to me: was 't in the tone
Or the words, your power?
            Or stay—I will repeat
Their speech, if that contents you! Only change   145
No more, and I shall find it presently
Far back here, in the brain yourself filled up.
Natalia threatened me that harm should follow
Unless I spoke their lesson to the end,

But harm to me, I thought she meant, not you.   150
Your friends,—Natalia said they were your friends
And meant you well,—because, I doubted it,
Observing (what was very strange to see)
On every face, so different in all else,
The same smile girls like me are used to bear,   155
But never men, men cannot stoop so low;
Yet your friends, speaking of you, used that smile,
That hateful smirk of boundless self-conceit
Which seems to take possession of the world
And make of God a tame confederate,   160
Purveyor to their appetites . . . you know!
But still Natalia said they were your friends,
And they assented though they smiled the more,
And all came round me,—that thin Englishman
With light lank hair seemed leader of the rest;   165
He held a paper—"What we want," said he,
Ending some explanation to his friends—
"Is something slow, involved and mystical,
To hold Jules long in doubt, yet take his taste
And lure him on until, at innermost   170
Where he seeks sweetness' soul, he may find—this!
—As in the apple's core, the noisome fly:
For insects on the rind are seen at once,
And brushed aside as soon, but this is found
Only when on the lips or loathing tongue."   175
And so he read what I have got by heart:
I'll speak it,—"Do not die, love! I am yours."
No—is not that, or like that, part of words
Yourself began by speaking? Strange to lose
What cost such pains to learn! Is this more right?   180

> I am a painter who cannot paint;
> In my life, a devil rather than saint;
> In my brain, as poor a creature too:
> No end to all I cannot do!
> Yet do one thing at least I can—   185
> Love a man or hate a man
> Supremely: thus my lore began.
> Through the Valley of Love I went,
> In the lovingest spot to abide,
> And just on the verge where I pitched my tent,   190
> I found Hate dwelling beside.
> (Let the Bridegroom ask what the painter meant,
> Of his bride, of the peerless Bride!)
> And further, I traversed Hate's grove,
> In the hatefullest nook to dwell;   195
> But lo, where I flung myself prone, couched Love
> Where the shadow threefold fell.
> (The meaning—those black bride's-eyes above,
> Not a painter's lips should tell!)

"And here," said he, "Jules probably will ask,
'You have black eyes, Love,—you are, sure enough,
My peerless bride,—then do you tell indeed
What needs some explanation! What means this?' "
—And I am to go on, without a word—

So, I grew wise in Love and Hate,   205
From simple that I was of late.
Once, when I loved, I would enlace
Breast, eyelids, hands, feet, form and face
Of her I loved, in one embrace—
As if by mere love I could love immensely!   210
Once, when I hated, I would plunge
My sword, and wipe with the first lunge
My foe's whole life out like a sponge—
As if by mere hate I could hate intensely!
But now I am wiser, know better the fashion   215
How passion seeks aid from its opposite passion:
And if I see cause to love more, hate more
Than ever man loved, ever hated before—
And seek in the Valley of Love,
The nest, or the nook in Hate's Grove,   220
Where my soul may surely reach
The essence, nought less, of each,
The Hate of all Hates, the Love
Of all Loves, in the Valley or Grove,—
I find them the very warders   225
Each of the other's borders.
When I love most, Love is disguised
In Hate; and when Hate is surprised
In Love, then I hate most: ask
How Love smiles through Hate's iron casque,   230
Hate grins through Love's rose-braided mask,—
And how, having hated thee,
I sought long and painfully
To reach thy heart, nor prick
The skin but pierce to the quick—   235
Ask this, my Jules, and be answered straight
By thy bride—how the painter Lutwyche can hate!

JULES *interposes.*

Lutwyche! Who else? But all of them, no doubt,
Hated me: they at Venice—presently
Their turn, however! You I shall not meet: 240
If I dreamed, saying this would wake me.
                                                                    Keep
What's here, the gold—we cannot meet again,
Consider! and the money was but meant
For two years' travel, which is over now,
All chance or hope or care or need of it.   245
This—and what comes from selling these, my casts

And books and medals, except . . . let them go
Together, so the produce keeps you safe
Out of Natalia's clutches! If by chance
(For all's chance here) I should survive the gang   250
At Venice, root out all fifteen of them,
We might meet somewhere, since the world is wide.

        [*From without is heard the voice of* PIPPA, *singing*—]

    Give her but a least excuse to love me!
    When—where—
    How—can this arm establish her above me,   255
    If fortune fixed her as my lady there,
    There already, to eternally reprove me?
        ("Hist!"—said Kate the Queen;[6]
        But "Oh!"—cried the maiden, binding her tresses,
        " 'T is only a page that carols unseen,   260
        Crumbling your hounds their messes!")

    Is she wronged?—To the rescue of her honour,
    My heart!
    Is she poor?—What costs it to be styled a donor?
    Merely an earth to cleave, a sea to part.   265
    But that fortune should have thrust all this upon her!
        ("Nay, list!"—bade Kate the Queen;
        And still cried the maiden, binding her tresses,
        " 'T is only a page that carols unseen,
        Fitting your hawks their jesses!"[7])   270

        [PIPPA *passes.*]

JULES *resumes.*
    What name was that the little girl sang forth?
Kate? The Cornaro, doubtless, who renounced
The crown of Cyprus to be lady here
At Asolo, where still her memory stays,
And peasants sing how once a certain page   275
Pined for the grace of her so far above
His power of doing good to, "Kate the Queen—
She never could be wronged, be poor," he sighed,
"Need him to help her!"

                Yes, a bitter thing
To see our lady above all need of us;   280
Yet so we look ere we will love; not I,
But the world looks so. If whoever loves
Must be, in some sort, god or worshipper,
The blessing or the blest one, queen or page,
Why should we always choose the page's part?   285
Here is a woman with utter need of me,—
I find myself queen here, it seems!

                  How strange!

6. Caterina Cornaro (ca. 1454–1510), Venetian queen of Cyprus. In 1488 her abdication was forced by Venice, which gave her a castle at Asolo as residence.
7. In falconry, the strap on a hawk's leg for attaching a leash.

Look at the woman here with the new soul,
Like my own Psyche,—fresh upon her lips
Alit, the visionary butterfly,   290
Waiting my word to enter and make bright,
Or flutter off and leave all blank as first.
This body had no soul before, but slept
Or stirred, was beauteous or ungainly, free
From taint or foul with stain, as outward things   295
Fastened their image on its passiveness:
Now, it will wake, feel, live—or die again!
Shall to produce form out of unshaped stuff
Be Art—and further, to evoke a soul
From form be nothing? This new soul is mine!   300

Now, to kill Lutwyche, what would that do?—save
A wretched dauber, men will hoot to death
Without me, from their hooting. Oh, to hear
God's voice plain as I heard it first, before
They broke in with their laughter! I heard them   305
Henceforth, not God.
                    To Ancona[8]—Greece—some isle!
I wanted silence only; there is clay
Everywhere. One may do whate'er one likes
In Art: the only thing is, to make sure
That one does like it—which takes pains to know.   310
    Scatter all this, my Phene—this mad dream!
Who, what is Lutwyche, what Natalia's friends,
What the whole world except our love—my own,
Own Phene? But I told you, did I not,
Ere night we travel for your land—some isle   315
With the sea's silence on it? Stand aside—
I do but break these paltry models up
To begin Art afresh. Meet Lutwyche, I—
And save him from my statue meeting him?
Some unsuspected isle in the far seas!   320
Like a god going through his world, there stands
One mountain for a moment in the dusk,
Whole brotherhoods of cedars on its brow:
And you are ever by me while I gaze
—Are in my arms as now—as now—as now!   325
Some unsuspected isle in the far seas!
Some unsuspected isle in far-off seas!

Talk by the way, while PIPPA *is passing from Orcana to the
Turret. Two or three of the Austrian Police loitering with*
BLUPHOCKS, *an English vagabond, just in view of the Turret.*
BLUPHOCKS.[9] So, that is your Pippa, the little girl who passed us

---

8. A town on the Adriatic, south of
Venice.
9. "He maketh his sun to rise on the evil
and on the good, and sendeth rain on
the just and on the unjust" (Matthew
5:45). [*Browning's note.*]

singing? Well, your Bishop's Intendant's[1] money shall be honestly earned:—now, don't make me that sour face because I bring the Bishop's name into the business; we know he can have nothing to do with such horrors: we know that he is a saint and all that a bishop should be, who is a great man beside. *Oh were but every worm a maggot, Every fly a grig,[2] Every bough a Christmas faggot, Every tune a jig!* In fact, I have abjured all religions; but the last I inclined to, was the Armenian: for I have travelled, do you see, and at Koenigsberg,[3] Prussia Improper (so styled because there's a sort of bleak hungry sun there), you might remark over a venerable house-porch, a certain Chaldee[4] inscription; and brief as it is, a mere glance at it used absolutely to change the mood of every bearded passenger. In they turned one and all; the young and lightsome, with no irreverent pause, the aged and decrepit, with a sensible alacrity: 't was the Grand Rabbi's abode, in short. Struck with curiosity, I lost no time in learning Syriac—(these are vowels, you dogs,—follow my stick's end in the mud—*Celarent, Darii, Ferio!*[5]) and one morning presented myself, spelling-book in hand, a, b, c,—I picked it out letter by letter, and what was the purport of this miraculous posy? Some cherished legend of the past, you'll say—*"How Moses hocus-pocussed Egypt's land with fly and locust,"*—or, *"How to Jonah sounded harshish, Get thee up and go to Tarshish,"*[6]—or, *"How the angel meeting Balaam, Straight his ass returned a salaam."*[7] In no wise! *"Shackabrack—Boach—somebody or other—Isaach, Re-cei-ver, Pur-cha-ser and Ex-chan-ger of—Stolen Goods!"*[8] So, talk to me of the religion of a bishop! I have renounced all bishops save Bishop Beveridge[9]—mean to live so—and die—*As some Greek dog-sage, dead and merry, Hellward bound in Charon's wherry,[1] With food for both worlds, under and upper, Lupine-seed and Hecate's[2] supper, And never an obolus . . .* (Though thanks to you, or this Intendant through you, or this Bishop through his Intendant—I possess a burning pocketful of *zwanzigers*[3]) . . . *To pay the Stygian Ferry!*
FIRST POLICEMAN. There is the girl, then; go and deserve them the moment you have pointed out to us Signor Luigi and his mother. [*To the rest.*] I have been noticing a house yonder, this long while: not a shutter unclosed since morning!

SECOND POLICEMAN. Old Luca Gaddi's, that owns the silk-mills here: he dozes by the hour, wakes up, sighs deeply, says he should like to be Prince Metternich,[4] and then dozes again, after having bidden young Sebald, the foreigner, set his wife to playing draughts. Never molest such a household, they mean well.

BLUPHOCKS. Only, cannot you tell me something of this little Pippa, I must have to do with? One could make something of that name. Pippa—that is, short for Felippa—rhyming to *Panurge consults Hertrippa—Believest thou, King Agrippa?*[5] Something might be done with that name.

SECOND POLICEMAN. Put into rhyme that your head and a ripe musk-melon would not be dear at half a *zwanziger!* Leave this fooling, and look out; the afternoon's over or nearly so.

THIRD POLICEMAN. Where in this passport of Signor Luigi does our Principal instruct you to watch him so narrowly? There? What's there beside a simple signature? (That English fool's busy watching.)

SECOND POLICEMAN. Flourish all round—"Put all possible obstacles in his way;" oblong dot at the end—"Detain him till further advices reach you;" scratch at bottom—"Send him back on pretence of some informality in the above;" ink-spirt on right-hand side (which is the case here)—"Arrest him at once." Why and wherefore, I don't concern myself, but my instructions amount to this: if Signor Luigi leaves home to-night for Vienna—well and good, the passport deposed with us for our *visa* is really for his own use, they have misinformed the Office, and he means well; but let him stay over to-night—there has been the pretence we suspect, the accounts of his corresponding and holding intelligence with the Carbonari[6] are correct, we arrest him at once, to-morrow comes Venice, and presently Spielberg.[7] Bluphocks makes the signal, sure enough! That is he, entering the turret with his mother, no doubt.

Part III

EVENING

SCENE.—*Inside the Turret on the Hill above Asolo.* LUIGI *and his* MOTHER *entering.*

MOTHER. If there blew wind, you'd hear a long sigh, easing
    The utmost heaviness of music's heart.
LUIGI. Here in the archway?
MOTHER.   Oh no, no—in farther.

4. Austrian statesman (1773–1859), architect of his country's reactionary foreign policy.
5. "Panurge consults Hertrippa" about his marriage in Rabelais' *Gargantua and Pantagruel.* The question "King Agrippa, believest thou the prophets?" is put by St. Paul (Acts 26:27).
6. Secret society of patriots aiming to liberate Italy.
7. Austrian prison.

Where the echo is made, on the ridge.
LUIGI.   Here surely, then.
How plain the tap of my heel as I leaped up!   5
Hark—"Lucius Junius!"[8] The very ghost of a voice
Whose body is caught and kept by . . . what are those?
Mere withered wallflowers, waving overhead?
They seem an elvish group with thin bleached hair
That lean out of their topmost fortress—look   10
And listen, mountain men, to what we say,
Hand under chin of each grave earthy face.
Up and show faces all of you!—"All of you!"
That's the king dwarf with the scarlet comb; old Franz,[9]
Come down and meet your fate? Hark—"Meet your fate!"   15
MOTHER. Let him not meet it, my Luigi—do not
Go to his City! Putting crime aside,
Half of these ills of Italy are feigned:
Your Pellicos[1] and writers for effect,
Write for effect.
LUIGI.   Hush! Say A. writes, and B.   20
MOTHER. These A.s and B.s write for effect, I say.
Then, evil is in its nature loud, while good
Is silent; you hear each petty injury,
None of his virtues; he is old beside,
Quiet and kind, and densely stupid. Why   25
Do A. and B. not kill him themselves?
LUIGI.   They teach
Others to kill him—me—and, if I fail,
Others to succeed; now, if A. tried and failed,
I could not teach that: mine's the lesser task.
Mother, they visit night by night . . .
MOTHER.   —You, Luigi?   30
Ah, will you let me tell you what you are?
LUIGI. Why not? Oh, the one thing you fear to hint,
You may assure yourself I say and say
Ever to myself! At times—nay, even as now
We sit—I think my mind is touched, suspect   35
All is not sound: but is not knowing that,
What constitutes one sane or otherwise?
I know I am thus—so, all is right again.
I laugh at myself as through the town I walk,
And see men merry as if no Italy   40
Were suffering; then I ponder—"I am rich,
Young, healthy; why should this fact trouble me,
More than it troubles these?" But it does trouble.
No, trouble's a bad word: for as I walk

8. Lucius Junius Brutus, who drove the Tarquins from Rome and became one of the first two consuls of the republic (509 B.C.).
9. The Austrian emperor Francis I (ruled 1804–35).
1. Silvio Pellico, Italian dramatist, patriot, and Carbonarist, had been imprisoned in the Spielberg for ten years.

There's springing and melody and giddiness,   45
And old quaint turns and passages of my youth,
Dreams long forgotten, little in themselves,
Return to me—whatever may amuse me:
And earth seems in a truce with me, and heaven
Accords with me, all things suspend their strife,   50
The very cicala laughs "There goes he, and there!
Feast him, the time is short; he is on his way
For the world's sake: feast him this once, our friend!"
And in return for all this, I can trip
Cheerfully up the scaffold-steps. I go   55
This evening, mother!
MOTHER.   But mistrust yourself—
    Mistrust the judgment you pronounce on him!
LUIGI. Oh, there I feel—am sure that I am right!
MOTHER. Mistrust your judgment then, of the mere means
    To this wild enterprise. Say, you are right,—   60
    How should one in your state e'er bring to pass
    What would require a cool head, a cold heart,
    And a calm hand? You never will escape.
LUIGI. Escape? To even wish that, would spoil all.
    The dying is best part of it. Too much   65
    Have I enjoyed these fifteen years of mine,
    To leave myself excuse for longer life:
    Was not life pressed down, running o'er with joy,
    That I might finish with it ere my fellows
    Who, sparelier feasted, make a longer stay?   70
    I was put at the board-head, helped to all
    At first; I rise up happy and content.
    God must be glad one loves his world so much.
    I can give news of earth to all the dead
    Who ask me:—last year's sunsets, and great stars   75
    Which had a right to come first and see ebb
    The crimson wave that drifts the sun away—
    Those crescent moons with notched and burning rims
    That strengthened into sharp fire, and there stood,
    Impatient of the azure—and that day   80
    In March, a double rainbow stopped the storm—
    May's warm slow yellow moonlit summer nights—
    Gone are they, but I have them in my soul!
MOTHER. (He will not go!)
LUIGI.   You smile at me? 'T is true,—
    Voluptuousness, grotesqueness, ghastliness,   85
    Environ my devotedness as quaintly
    As round about some antique altar wreathe
    The rose festoons, goats' horns, and oxen's skulls.
MOTHER. See now: you reach the city, you must cross
    His threshold—how?
LUIGI.   Oh, that's if we conspired!   90

Then would come pains in plenty, as you guess—
But guess not how the qualities most fit
For such an office, qualities I have,
Would little stead me, otherwise employed,
Yet prove of rarest merit only here.   95
Every one knows for what his excellence
Will serve, but no one ever will consider
For what his worst defect might serve: and yet
Have you not seen me range our coppice yonder
In search of a distorted ash?—I find   100
The wry spoilt branch a natural perfect bow.
Fancy the thrice-sage, thrice-precautioned man
Arriving at the palace on my errand!
No, no! I have a handsome dress packed up—
White satin here, to set off my black hair;   105
In I shall march—for you may watch your life out
Behind thick walls, make friends there to betray you;
More than one man spoils everything. March straight—
Only, no clumsy knife to fumble for.
Take the great gate, and walk (not saunter) on   110
Thro' guards and guards——I have rehearsed it all
Inside the turret here a hundred times.
Don't ask the way of whom you meet, observe!
But where they cluster thickliest is the door
Of doors; they'll let you pass—they'll never blab   115
Each to the other, he knows not the favourite,
Whence he is bound and what's his business now.
Walk in—straight up to him; you have no knife:
Be prompt, how should he scream? Then, out with you!
Italy, Italy, my Italy!   120
You're free, you're free! Oh mother, I could dream
They got about me—Andrea from his exile,
Pier from his dungeon, Gaultier[2] from his grave!
MOTHER. Well, you shall go. Yet seems this patriotism
The easiest virtue for a selfish man   125
To acquire: he loves himself—and next, the world—
If he must love beyond,—but nought between:
As a short-sighted man sees nought midway
His body and the sun above. But you
Are my adored Luigi, ever obedient   130
To my least wish, and running o'er with love:
I could not call you cruel or unkind.
Once more, your ground for killing him!—then go!
LUIGI. Now do you try me, or make sport of me?
How first the Austrians got these provinces[3] . . .   135
(If that is all, I'll satisfy you soon)
—Never by conquest but by cunning, for

2. Other conspirators.
3. Northern Italian lands given to Austria by the Congress of Vienna (1815).

That treaty whereby . . .

MOTHER.   Well?

LUIGI.   (Sure, he's arrived,
The tell-tale cuckoo: spring's his confidant,
And he lets out her April purposes!)   140
Or . . . better go at once to modern time,
He has . . . they have . . . in fact, I understand
But can't restate the matter; that's my boast:
Others could reason it out to you, and prove
Things they have made me feel.

MOTHER.   Why go to-night?   145
Morn's for adventure. Jupiter is now
A morning star. I cannot hear you, Luigi!

LUIGI. "I am the bright and morning-star," saith God[4]—
And, "to such an one I give the morning-star."
The gift of the morning-star! Have I God's gift   150
Of the morning-star?

MOTHER.   Chiara will love to see
That Jupiter an evening-star next June.

LUIGI True, mother. Well for those who live through June!
Great noontides, thunder-storms, all glaring pomps
That triumph at the heels of June the god   155
Leading his revel through our leafy world.
Yes, Chiara will be here.

MOTHER.   In June: remember,
Yourself appointed that month for her coming.

LUIGI. Was that low noise the echo?

MOTHER.   The night-wind.
She must be grown—with her blue eyes upturned   160
As if life were one long and sweet surprise:
In June she comes.

LUIGI.   We were to see together
The Titian at Treviso.[5] There, again!

[*From without is heard the voice of* PIPPA, *singing*—]

A king lived long ago,
In the morning of the world,   165
When earth was nigher heaven than now:
And the king's locks curled,
Disparting o'er a forehead full
As the milk-white space 'twixt horn and horn
Of some sacrificial bull—   170
Only calm as a babe new-born:
For he was got to a sleepy mood,

4. Revelation 22:16: "I [Jesus] . . . am . . . the bright and morning star." Also Revelation 2:26–28: "And he that overcometh, and keepeth my works unto the end, to him will I give power over the nations: and he shall rule them with a rod of iron. . . . And I will give him the morning star."
5. Altarpiece, an *Annunciation* by the Venetian painter Titian (d. 1576) in the cathedral at Treviso.

So safe from all decrepitude,
Age with its bane, so sure gone by,
(The gods so loved him while he dreamed)   175
That, having lived thus long, there seemed
No need the king should ever die.

LUIGI. No need that sort of king should ever die!

Among the rocks his city was:
Before his palace, in the sun,   180
He sat to see his people pass,
And judge them every one
From its threshold of smooth stone.
They haled him many a valley-thief
Caught in the sheep-pens, robber-chief   185
Swarthy and shameless, beggar-cheat,
Spy-prowler, or rough pirate found
On the sea-sand left aground;
And sometimes clung about his feet,
With bleeding lip and burning cheek,   190
A woman, bitterest wrong to speak
Of one with sullen thickset brows:
And sometimes from the prison-house
The angry priests a pale wretch brought,
Who through some chink had pushed and pressed   195
On knees and elbows, belly and breast,
Worm-like into the temple,—caught
He was by the very god,
Who ever in the darkness strode
Backward and forward, keeping watch   200
O'er his brazen bowls, such rogues to catch!
These, all and every one,
The king judged, sitting in the sun.

LUIGI. That king should still judge sitting in the sun!

His councillors, on left and right,   205
Looked anxious up,—but no surprise
Disturbed the king's old smiling eyes
Where the very blue had turned to white.
'T is said, a Python[6] scared one day
The breathless city, till he came,   210
With forky tongue and eyes on flame,
Where the old king sat to judge alway;
But when he saw the sweepy hair
Girt with a crown of berries rare
Which the god will hardly give to wear   215
To the maiden who singeth, dancing bare
In the altar-smoke by the pine-torch lights,
At his wondrous forest rites,—

6. Enormous serpent that terrorized the folk until slain by Apollo.

> *Seeing this, he did not dare*
> *Approach that threshold in the sun,* 220
> *Assault the old king smiling there.*
> *Such grace had kings when the world begun!*
>
> [PIPPA *passes*.]

LUIGI. And such grace have they, now that the world ends!
  The Python at the city, on the throne,
  And brave men, God would crown for slaying him, 225
  Lurk in bye-corners lest they fall his prey.
  Are crowns yet to be won in this late time,
  Which weakness makes me hesitate to reach?
  'T is God's voice calls: how could I stay? Farewell!

> *Talk by the way, while* PIPPA *is passing from the Turret to the Bishop's Brother's House, close to the Duomo S. Maria.* POOR GIRLS *sitting on the steps.*

FIRST GIRL. There goes a swallow to Venice—the stout seafarer! 230
  Seeing those birds fly, makes one wish for wings.
  Let us all wish; you wish first!

SECOND GIRL.   I? This sunset
  To finish.

THIRD GIRL. That old—somebody I know,
  Greyer and older than my grandfather, 235
  To give me the same treat he gave last week—
  Feeding me on his knee with fig-peckers,[7]
  Lampreys and red Breganze-wine, and mumbling
  The while some folly about how well I fare,
  Let sit and eat my supper quietly: 240
  Since had he not himself been late this morning
  Detained at—never mind where,—had he not . . .
  "Eh, baggage, had I not!"—

SECOND GIRL.   How she can lie!

THIRD GIRL. Look there—by the nails!

SECOND GIRL.   What makes your fingers red?

THIRD GIRL. Dipping them into wine to write bad words with 245
  On the bright table: how he laughed!

FIRST GIRL.   My turn.
  Spring's come and summer's coming. I would wear
  A long loose gown, down to the feet and hands,
  With plaits here, close about the throat, all day;
  And all night lie, the cool long nights, in bed; 250
  And have new milk to drink, apples to eat,
  Deuzans and junetings, leather-coats[8] . . . ah, I should say,
  This is away in the fields—miles!

THIRD GIRL.   Say at once
  You'd be at home: she'd always be at home!
  Now comes the story of the farm among 255
  The cherry orchards, and how April snowed

7. Small birds, a delicacy, as are lamprey eels.   8. Varieties of apples.

White blossoms on her as she ran. Why, fool,
They've rubbed the chalk-mark out, how tall you were,
Twisted your starling's neck, broken his cage,
Made a dung-hill of your garden!
FIRST GIRL.   They, destroy   260
My garden since I left them? well—perhaps!
I would have done so: so I hope they have!
A fig-tree curled out of our cottage wall;
They called it mine, I have forgotten why,
It must have been there long ere I was born: 265
Cric—cric—I think I hear the wasps o'erhead
Pricking the papers strung to flutter there
And keep off birds in fruit-time—coarse long papers,
And the wasps eat them, prick them through and through.
THIRD GIRL. How her mouth twitches! Where was I?—before   270
She broke in with her wishes and long gowns
And wasps—would I be such a fool!—Oh, here!
This is my way: I answer every one
Who asks me why I make so much of him—
(If you say, "you love him"—straight "he'll not be gulled!")   275
"He that seduced me when I was a girl
Thus high—had eyes like yours, or hair like yours,
Brown, red, white,"—as the case may be: that pleases!
See how that beetle burnishes in the path!
There sparkles he along the dust: and, there—   280
Your journey to that maize-tuft spoiled at least!
FIRST GIRL. When I was young, they said if you killed one
Of those sunshiny beetles, that his friend
Up there, would shine no more that day nor next.
SECOND GIRL. When you were young? Nor are you young, that's
    true.   285
How your plump arms, that were, have dropped away!
Why, I can span them. Cecco beats you still?
No matter, so you keep your curious hair.
I wish they'd find a way to dye our hair
Your colour—any lighter tint, indeed,   290
Than black: the men say they are sick of black,
Black eyes, black hair!
FOURTH GIRL.   Sick of yours, like enough.
Do you pretend you ever tasted lampreys
And ortolans?[9] Giovita, of the palace,
Engaged (but there's no trusting him) to slice me   295
Polenta[1] with a knife that had cut up
An ortolan.
SECOND GIRL. Why, there! Is not that Pippa
We are to talk to, under the window,—quick,—
Where the lights are?

---

9. Another species of bird regarded as a   1. Pudding made of cornmeal.
delicacy.

FIRST GIRL.   That she? No, or she would sing.   300
  For the Intendant said . . .
THIRD GIRL.   Oh, you sing first!
  Then, if she listens and comes close . . . I'll tell you,—
  Sing that song the young English noble made,
  Who took you for the purest of the pure,
  And meant to leave the world for you—what fun!   305
SECOND GIRL [*sings*].

> You'll love me yet!—*and I can tarry*
>   *Your love's protracted growing:*
> *June reared that bunch of flowers you carry,*
>   *From seeds of April's sowing.*
>
> *I plant a heartful now: some seed*   310
>   *At least is sure to strike,*
> *And yield—what you'll not pluck indeed,*
>   *Not love, but, may be, like.*
>
> *You'll look at least on love's remains,*
>   *A grave's one violet:*   315
> *Your look?—that pays a thousand pains.*
>   *What's death? You'll love me yet!*

THIRD GIRL [*to* PIPPA *who approaches*]. Oh, you may come closer
—we shall not eat you! Why, you seem the very person that the
great rich handsome Englishman has fallen so violently in love
with. I'll tell you all about it.

Part IV

NIGHT

SCENE.—*Inside the Palace by the Duomo.* MONSIGNOR, *dismissing
his* ATTENDANTS.

MONSIGNOR. Thanks, friends, many thanks! I chiefly desire life now,
that I may recompense every one of you. Most I know something
of already. What, a repast prepared? *Benedicto benedicatur*[2] . . .
ugh, ugh! Where was I? Oh, as you were remarking, Ugo, the
weather is mild, very unlike winter-weather: but I am a Sicilian,
you know, and shiver in your Julys here. To be sure, when 't was
full summer at Messina,[3] as we priests used to cross in procession
the great square on Assumption Day,[4] you might see our thickest
yellow tapers twist suddenly in two, each like a falling star, or
sink down on themselves in a gore of wax. But go, my friends,
but go! [*To the* INTENDANT.] Not you, Ugo! [*The others leave
the apartment.*] I have long wanted to converse with you, Ugo.
INTENDANT. Uguccio—

2. A blessing.
3. Town in Sicily.

4. August 15. Feast celebrating the ascension of the Virgin Mary into heaven.

MONSIGNOR. . . . . 'guccio Stefani, man! of Ascoli, Fermo and Fossombruno;[5]—what I do need instructing about, are these accounts of your administration of my poor brother's affairs. Ugh! I shall never get through a third part of your accounts: take some of these dainties before we attempt it, however. Are you bashful to that degree? For me, a crust and water suffice.

INTENDANT. Do you choose this especial night to question me?

MONSIGNOR. This night, Ugo. You have managed my late brother's affairs since the death of our elder brother: fourteen years and a month, all but three days. On the Third of December, I find him . . .

INTENDANT. If you have so intimate an acquaintance with your brother's affairs, you will be tender of turning so far back: they will hardly bear looking into, so far back.

MONSIGNOR. Ay, ay, ugh, ugh,—nothing but disappointments here below! I remark a considerable payment made to yourself on this Third of December. Talk of disappointments! There was a young fellow here, Jules, a foreign sculptor I did my utmost to advance, that the Church might be a gainer by us both: he was going on hopefully enough, and of a sudden he notifies to me some marvellous change that has happened in his notions of Art. Here's his letter,—"He never had a clearly conceived Ideal within his brain till to-day. Yet since his hand could manage a chisel, he has practised expressing other men's Ideals; and, in the very perfection he has attained to, he foresees an ultimate failure: his unconscious hand will pursue its prescribed course of old years, and will reproduce with a fatal expertness the ancient types, let the novel one appear never so palpably to his spirit. There is but one method of escape: confiding the virgin type to as chaste a hand, he will turn painter instead of sculptor, and paint, not carve, its characteristics,"—strike out, I dare say, a school like Correggio:[6] how think you, Ugo?

INTENDANT. Is Correggio a painter?

MONSIGNOR. Foolish Jules! and yet, after all, why foolish? He may —probably will—fail egregiously; but if there should arise a new painter, will it not be in some such way, by a poet now, or a musician (spirits who have conceived and perfected an Ideal through some other channel), transferring it to this, and escaping our conventional roads by pure ignorance of them; eh, Ugo? If you have no appetite, talk at least, Ugo!

INTENDANT. Sir, I can submit no longer to this course of yours. First, you select the group of which I formed one,—next you thin it gradually,—always retaining me with your smile,—and so do you proceed till you have fairly got me alone with you between four stone walls. And now then? Let this farce, this chatter end now: what is it you want with me?

MONSIGNOR. Ugo!

5. Cities far to the south of Asolo, as are Forli and Cesena, mentioned later.
6. Antonio Allegri (ca. 1494–1534), Italian painter who took the name of his native town.

INTENDANT. From the instant you arrived, I felt your smile on me as you questioned me about this and the other article in those papers—why your brother should have given me this villa, that *podere*,[7]—and your nod at the end meant,—what?

MONSIGNOR. Possibly that I wished for no loud talk here. If once you set me coughing, Ugo!—

INTENDANT. I have your brother's hand and seal to all I possess: now ask me what for! what service I did him—ask me!

MONSIGNOR. I would better not: I should rip up old disgraces, let out my poor brother's weaknesses. By the way, Maffeo of Forli (which, I forgot to observe, is your true name), was the interdict ever taken off you, for robbing that church at Cesena?

INTENDANT. No, nor needs be: for when I murdered your brother's friend, Pasquale, for him . . .

MONSIGNOR. Ah, he employed you in that business, did he? Well, I must let you keep, as you say, this villa and that *podere*, for fear the world should find out my relations were of so indifferent a stamp? Maffeo, my family is the oldest in Messina, and century after century have my progenitors gone on polluting themselves with every wickedness under heaven: my own father . . . rest his soul!—I have, I know, a chapel to support that it may rest: my dear two dead brothers were,—what you know tolerably well; I, the youngest, might have rivalled them in vice, if not in wealth: but from my boyhood I came out from among them, and so am not partaker of their plagues. My glory springs from another source; or if from this, by contrast only,—for I, the bishop, am the brother of your employers, Ugo. I hope to repair some of their wrong, however; so far as my brother's ill-gotten treasure reverts to me, I can stop the consequences of his crime: and not one *soldo*[8] shall escape me. Maffeo, the sword we quiet men spurn away, you shrewd knaves pick up and commit murders with; what opportunities the virtuous forego, the villainous seize. Because, to pleasure myself apart from other considerations, my food would be millet-cake, my dress sackcloth, and my couch straw,—am I therefore to let you, the offscouring of the earth, seduce the poor and ignorant by appropriating a pomp these will be sure to think lessens the abominations so unaccountably and exclusively associated with it? Must I let villas and *poderi* go to you, a murderer and thief, that you may beget by means of them other murderers and thieves? No—if my cough would but allow me to speak!

INTENDANT. What am I to expect? You are going to punish me?

MONSIGNOR. —Must punish you, Maffeo. I cannot afford to cast away a chance. I have whole centuries of sin to redeem, and only a month or two of life to do it in. How should I dare to say . . .

INTENDANT. "Forgive us our trespasses"?

MONSIGNOR. My friend, it is because I avow myself a very worm, sinful beyond measure, that I reject a line of conduct you would applaud perhaps. Shall I proceed, as it were, a-pardoning?—I?—who have no symptom of reason to assume that aught less than my strenuousest efforts will keep myself out of mortal sin, much less keep others out. No: I do trespass, but will not double that by allowing you to trespass.

INTENDANT. And suppose the villas are not your brother's to give, nor yours to take? Oh, you are hasty enough just now!

MONSIGNOR. 1, 2—No. 3!—ay, can you read the substance of a letter, No. 3, I have received from Rome? It is precisely on the ground there mentioned, of the suspicion I have that a certain child of my late elder brother, who would have succeeded to his estates, was murdered in infancy by you, Maffeo, at the instigation of my late younger brother—that the Pontiff enjoins on me not merely the bringing that Maffeo to condign punishment, but the taking all pains, as guardian of the infant's heritage for the Church, to recover it parcel by parcel, howsoever, whensoever, and wheresoever. While you are now gnawing those fingers, the police are engaged in sealing up your papers, Maffeo, and the mere raising my voice brings my people from the next room to dispose of yourself. But I want you to confess quietly, and save me raising my voice. Why, man, do I not know the old story? The heir between the succeeding heir, and this heir's ruffianly instrument, and their complot's effect, and the life of fear and bribes and ominous smiling silence? Did you throttle or stab my brother's infant? Come now!

INTENDANT. So old a story, and tell it no better? When did such an instrument ever produce such an effect? Either the child smiles in his face; or, most likely, he is not fool enough to put himself in the employer's power so thoroughly: the child is always ready to produce—as you say—howsoever, wheresoever, and whensoever.

MONSIGNOR. Liar!

INTENDANT. Strike me? Ah, so might a father chastise! I shall sleep soundly to-night at least, though the gallows await me to-morrow; for what a life did I lead! Carlo of Cesena reminds me of his connivance, every time I pay his annuity; which happens commonly thrice a year. If I remonstrate, he will confess all to the good bishop—you!

MONSIGNOR. I see through the trick, caitiff! I would you spoke truth for once. All shall be sifted, however—seven times sifted.

INTENDANT. And how my absurd riches encumbered me! I dared not lay claim to above half my possessions. Let me but once unbosom myself, glorify Heaven, and die!

Sir, you are no brutal dastardly idiot like your brother I frightened to death: let us understand one another. Sir, I will make away with her for you—the girl—here close at hand; not the stupid obvious kind of killing; do not speak—know nothing of her nor of me! I see her every day—saw her this morning: of course there is to be no killing; but at Rome the courtesans perish off every three years, and I can entice her thither—have indeed begun operations already. There's a certain lusty blue-eyed

florid-complexioned English knave, I and the Police employ occasionally. You assent, I perceive—no, that's not it—assent I do
not say—but you will let me convert my present havings and
holdings into cash, and give me time to cross the Alps? 'T is but
a little black-eyed pretty singing Felippa, gay silk-winding girl. I
have kept her out of harm's way up to this present; for I always
intended to make your life a plague to you with her. 'T is as well
settled once and for ever. Some women I have procured will pass
Bluphocks, my handsome scoundrel, off for somebody; and once
Pippa entangled!—you conceive? Through her singing? Is it a
bargain?

[*From without is heard the voice of* PIPPA, *singing*—]

Overhead the tree-tops meet,
Flowers and grass spring 'neath one's feet;
There was nought above me, nought below,
My childhood had not learned to know:
For, what are the voices of birds
—Ay, and of beasts,—but words, our words,
Only so much more sweet?
The knowledge of that with my life begun.
But I had so near made out the sun,
And counted your stars, the seven and one,
Like the fingers of my hand:
Nay, I could all but understand
Wherefore through heaven the white moon ranges;
And just when out of her soft fifty changes
No unfamiliar face might overlook me—
Suddenly God took me.

[PIPPA *passes*.]

MONSIGNOR [*springing up*]. My people—one and all—all—
within there! Gag this villain—tie him hand and foot! He dares
. . . I know not half he dares—but remove him—quick! *Miserere
mei, Domine!*[9] Quick, I say!

SCENE.—PIPPA'S *chamber again. She enters it.*

The bee with his comb,
The mouse at her dray,[1]
The grub in his tomb,
Wile winter away;
But the fire-fly and hedge-shrew[2] and lob-worm, I pray,   5
How fare they?
Ha, ha, thanks for your counsel, my Zanze!
"Feast upon lampreys, quaff Breganze"—
The summer of life so easy to spend,
And care for to-morrow so soon put away!   10

9. "Lord, have mercy on me!"   2. Field mouse. Lob-worm: marine
1. Nest.   worm.

But winter hastens at summer's end,
And fire-fly, hedge-shrew, lob-worm, pray,
How fare they?
No bidding me then to . . . what did Zanze say?
"Pare your nails pearlwise, get your small feet shoes   15
More like" . . . (what said she?)—"and less like canoes!"
How pert that girl was!—would I be those pert
Impudent staring women! It had done me,
However, surely no such mighty hurt
To learn his name who passed that jest upon me: 20
No foreigner, that I can recollect,
Came, as she says, a month since, to inspect
Our silk-mills—none with blue eyes and thick rings
Of raw-silk-coloured hair, at all events.
Well, if old Luca keep his good intents,   25
We shall do better, see what next year brings.
I may buy shoes, my Zanze, not appear
More destitute than you perhaps next year!
Bluph . . . something! I had caught the uncouth name
But for Monsignor's people's sudden clatter   30
Above us—bound to spoil such idle chatter
As ours: it were indeed a serious matter
If silly talk like ours should put to shame
The pious man, the man devoid of blame,
The . . . ah but—ah but, all the same,   35
No mere mortal has a right
To carry that exalted air;
Best people are not angels quite:
While—not the worst of people's doings scare
The devil; so there's that proud look to spare!   40
    Which is mere counsel to myself, mind! for
I have just been the holy Monsignor:
And I was you too, Luigi's gentle mother,
And you too, Luigi!—how that Luigi started
Out of the turret—doubtlessly departed   45
On some good errand or another,
For he passed just now in a traveller's trim,
And the sullen company that prowled
About his path, I noticed, scowled
As if they had lost a prey in him.   50
And I was Jules the sculptor's bride,
And I was Ottima beside,
And now what am I?—tired of fooling.
Day for folly, night for schooling!
New year's day is over and spent,   55
Ill or well, I must be content.
    Even my lily's asleep, I vow:
Wake up—here's a friend I've plucked you:
Call this flower a heart's-ease now!
Something rare, let me instruct you,   60

Is this, with petals triply swollen,
Three times spotted, thrice the pollen;
While the leaves and parts that witness
Old proportions and their fitness,
Here remain unchanged, unmoved now; 65
Call this pampered thing improved now!
Suppose there's a king of the flowers
And a girl-show held in his bowers—
"Look ye, buds, this growth of ours,"
Says he, "Zanze from the Brenta,[3] 70
I have made her gorge polenta
Till both cheeks are near as bouncing
As her . . . name there's no pronouncing!
See this heightened colour too,
For she swilled Breganze wine 75
Till her nose turned deep carmine;
'T was but white when wild she grew.
And only by this Zanze's eyes
Of which we could not change the size,
The magnitude of all achieved 80
Otherwise, may be perceived."

Oh what a drear dark close to my poor day!
How could that red sun drop in that black cloud?
Ah Pippa, morning's rule is moved away,
Dispensed with, never more to be allowed! 85
Day's turn is over, now arrives the night's.
Oh lark, be day's apostle
To mavis, merle and throstle,[4]
Bid them their betters jostle
From day and its delights! 90
But at night, brother howlet,[5] over the woods,
Toll the world to thy chantry;
Sing to the bats' sleek sisterhoods
Full complines[6] with gallantry:
Then, owls and bats, 95
Cowls and twats,[7]
Monks and nuns, in a cloister's moods,
Adjourn to the oak-stump pantry!

[*After she has begun to undress herself.*]
Now, one thing I should like to really know:
How near I ever might approach all these 100
I only fancied being, this long day:
—Approach, I mean, so as to touch them, so
As to . . . in some way . . . move them—if you please,
Do good or evil to them some slight way.

3. River flowing to Venice.
4. Three species of birds.
5. Owl.
6. Seventh and last of the canonical hours.
7. Browning later said he thought the word referred to part of a nun's attire.

For instance, if I wind   105
Silk to-morrow, my silk may bind
                                    [*Sitting on the bedside.*]
And border Ottima's cloak's hem.
Ah me, and my important part with them,
This morning's hymn half promised when I rose!
True in some sense or other, I suppose.   110
                                    [*As she lies down.*]
God bless me! I can pray no more to-night.
No doubt, some way or other, hymns say right.

    All service ranks the same with God—
    With God, whose puppets, best and worst,
    Are we: there is no last nor first.   115
                                    [*She sleeps.*]

From *Dramatic Lyrics* (1842)

My Last Duchess[1]

FERRARA

That's my last Duchess painted on the wall,
Looking as if she were alive. I call
That piece a wonder, now: Frà Pandolf's[2] hands
Worked busily a day, and there she stands.
Will 't please you sit and look at her? I said   5
"Frà Pandolf" by design,[3] for never read
Strangers like you that pictured countenance,
The depth and passion of its earnest glance,
But to myself they turned (since none puts by
The curtain I have drawn for you, but I)   10
And seemed as they would ask me, if they durst,
How such a glance came there; so, not the first
Are you to turn and ask thus. Sir, 't was not
Her husband's presence only, called that spot
Of joy into the Duchess' cheek: perhaps   15
Frà Pandolf chanced to say "Her mantle laps
Over my lady's wrist too much,"[4] or "Paint
Must never hope to reproduce the faint
Half-flush that dies along her throat:" such stuff
Was courtesy, she thought, and cause enough   20
For calling up that spot of joy. She had
A heart—how shall I say?—too soon made glad,
Too easily impressed; she liked whate'er
She looked on, and her looks went everywhere.
Sir, 't was all one! My favour at her breast,   25
The dropping of the daylight in the West,
The bough of cherries some officious fool
Broke in the orchard for her, the white mule
She rode with round the terrace—all and each
Would draw from her alike the approving speech,   30
Or blush, at least. She thanked men,—good! but thanked
Somehow—I know not how—as if she ranked
My gift of a nine-hundred-years-old name[5]

1. First published with the contrasting poem, "Count Gismond" (below), under the caption "Italy and France." The duke closely resembles Alfonso II, fifth and last duke of Ferrara (1533–97), and last of the main branch of the powerful Este family, whose history Browning had studied while compiling material for his long Italian poem *Sordello* (1840). In 1558, Alfonso married Lucrezia, fourteen-year-old daughter of Cosimo I de' Medici, duke of Florence; in 1561 she died under mysterious circumstances.
2. Brother Pandolf, fictitious painter from a monastic order.
3. Purposely.
4. Her wrist is too beautiful to be hidden.
5. Lucrezia's family, the Medici, were comparative upstarts, the name being only a few generations old at the time.

With anybody's gift. Who'd stoop to blame
This sort of trifling? Even had you skill   35
In speech—(which I have not)—to make your will
Quite clear to such an one, and say, "Just this
Or that in you disgusts me; here you miss,
Or there exceed the mark"—and if she let
Herself be lessoned so, nor plainly set   40
Her wits to yours, forsooth, and made excuse,
—E'en then would be some stooping; and I choose
Never to stoop. Oh sir, she smiled, no doubt,
Whene'er I passed her; but who passed without
Much the same smile? This grew; I gave commands;[6]   45
Then all smiles stopped together. There she stands
As if alive. Will 't please you rise? We'll meet
The company below, then. I repeat,
The Count your master's known munificence
Is ample warrant that no just pretence[7]   50
Of mine for dowry will be disallowed;
Though his fair daughter's self, as I avowed
At starting, is my object. Nay, we'll go
Together down, sir. Notice Neptune,[8] though,
Taming a sea-horse,[9] thought a rarity,   55
Which Claus of Innsbruck[1] cast in bronze for me!

Count Gismond[1]

AIX IN PROVENCE

I

Christ God who savest man, save most
  Of men Count Gismond who saved me!
Count Gauthier, when he chose his post,
  Chose time and place and company
To suit it; when he struck at length   5
My honour, 't was with all his strength.

II

And doubtlessly ere he could draw
  All points to one, he must have schemed!
That miserable morning saw
  Few half so happy as I seemed,   10
While being dressed in queen's array
To give our tourney prize away.

6. The sense is ambiguous. Much later Browning said, "The commands were that she should be put to death," then added, "or he might have had her shut up in a convent."
7. Claim.
8. Old Italian deity identified with the Greek sea god Poseidon, creator of the horse.
9. Fabulous beast, half horse and half fish.

1. Imaginary sculptor. The mention of Innsbruck, seat of the Tyrolean Count, is calculated to flatter.
1. Originally the companion of "My Last Duchess" under the heading "Italy and France," this poem representing medieval France. Aix, capital of Provence in the Middle Ages, reached its zenith after the twelfth century under the patronage of the houses of Aragon and Anjou.

III

I thought they loved me, did me grace
    To please themselves; 't was all their deed;
God makes, or fair or foul, our face;   15
    If showing mine so caused to bleed
My cousins' hearts, they should have dropped
A word, and straight the play had stopped.

IV

They, too, so beauteous! Each a queen
    By virtue of her brow and breast;   20
Not needing to be crowned, I mean,
    As I do. E'en when I was dressed,
Had either of them spoke, instead
Of glancing sideways with still head!

V

But no: they let me laugh, and sing   25
    My birthday song quite through, adjust
The last rose in my garland, fling
    A last look on the mirror, trust
My arms to each an arm of theirs,
And so descend the castle-stairs—   30

VI

And come out on the morning-troop
    Of merry friends who kissed my cheek,
And called me queen, and made me stoop
    Under the canopy—(a streak
That pierced it, of the outside sun,   35
Powdered with gold its gloom's soft dun)—

VII

And they could let me take my state
    And foolish throne amid applause
Of all come there to celebrate
    My queen's-day—Oh I think the cause   40
Of much was, they forgot no crowd
Makes up for parents in their shroud!

VIII

However that be, all eyes were bent
    Upon me, when my cousins cast
Theirs down; 't was time I should present   45
    The victor's crown, but . . . there, 't will last
No long time . . . the old mist again
Blinds me as then it did. How vain!

IX

See! Gismond's at the gate, in talk
    With his two boys: I can proceed.   50
Well, at that moment, who should stalk
    Forth boldly—to my face, indeed—
But Gauthier, and he thundered "Stay!"
And all stayed. "Bring no crowns, I say!

X

"Bring torches! Wind the penance-sheet   55
  About her! Let her shun the chaste,
Or lay herself before their feet!
  Shall she whose body I embraced
A night long, queen it in the day?
For honour's sake no crowns, I say!"   60

XI

I? What I answered? As I live,
  I never fancied such a thing
As answer possible to give.
  What says the body when they spring
Some monstrous torture-engine's whole   65
Strength on it? No more says the soul.

XII

Till out strode Gismond; then I knew
  That I was saved. I never met
His face before, but, at first view,
  I felt quite sure that God had set   70
Himself to Satan; who would spend
A minute's mistrust on the end?

XIII

He strode to Gauthier, in his throat
  Gave him the lie, then struck his mouth
With one back-handed blow that wrote   75
  In blood men's verdict there. North, South,
East, West, I looked. The lie was dead.
And damned, and truth stood up instead.

XIV

This glads me most, that I enjoyed
  The heart of the joy, with my content   80
In watching Gismond unalloyed
  By any doubt of the event:
God took that on him—I was bid
Watch Gismond for my part: I did.

XV

Did I not watch him while he let   85
  His armourer just brace his greaves,[2]
Rivet his hauberk,[3] on the fret
  The while! His foot . . . my memory leaves
No least stamp out, nor how anon
He pulled his ringing gauntlets on.   90

XVI

And e'en before the trumpet's sound
  Was finished, prone lay the false knight,
Prone as his lie, upon the ground:
  Gismond flew at him, used no sleight
O' the sword, but open-breasted drove,   95
Cleaving till out the truth he clove.

2. Leg armor worn below the knee.   3. Protective tunic of chain mail.

XVII

Which done, he dragged him to my feet
    And said "Here die, but end thy breath
In full confession, lest thou fleet
    From my first, to God's second death!   100
Say, hast thou lied?" And, "I have lied
To God and her," he said, and died.

XVIII

Then Gismond, kneeling to me, asked
    —What safe my heart holds, though no word
Could I repeat now, if I tasked   105
    My powers for ever, to a third
Dear even as you are. Pass the rest
Until I sank upon his breast.

XIX

Over my head his arm he flung
    Against the world; and scarce I felt   110
His sword (that dripped by me and swung)
    A little shifted in its belt:
For he began to say the while
How South our home lay many a mile.

XX

So 'mid the shouting multitude   115
    We two walked forth to never more
Return. My cousins have pursued
    Their life, untroubled as before
I vexed them. Gauthier's dwelling-place
God lighten! May his soul find grace!   120

XXI

Our elder boy has got the clear
    Great brow; tho' when his brother's black
Full eye shows scorn, it . . . Gismond here?
    And have you brought my tercel[4] back?
       125I just was telling Adela
How many birds it struck since May.

Soliloquy of the Spanish Cloister[1]

I

Gr-r-r—there go, my heart's abhorrence!
    Water your damned flower-pots, do!
If hate killed men, Brother Lawrence,
    God's blood, would not mine kill you!
What? your myrtle-bush wants trimming?   5
    Oh, that rose has prior claims—
Needs its leaden vase filled brimming?

4. Male hawk. As William E. Harrold has observed, imagery from the sport of falconry attaches to the poem's characters throughout. In stanza I, for example, Gauthier "struck" the speaker's honor (*The Variance and the Unity,* [1973], p. 43).

1. Originally called "Cloister (Spanish)" and paired with "Camp (French)"; the poems were separated in 1849 and thereafter.

Hell dry you up with its flames!

II

At the meal we sit together:
    Salve tibi![2] I must hear
Wise talk of the kind of weather,
    Sort of season, time of year:
Not a plenteous cork-crop: scarcely
    Dare we hope oak-galls,[3] *I doubt:*
What's the Latin name for "parsley"?
    What's the Greek name for Swine's Snout?

III

Whew! We'll have our platter burnished,
    Laid with care on our own shelf!
With a fire-new spoon we're furnished,
    And a goblet for ourself,
Rinsed like something sacrificial
    Ere 't is fit to touch our chaps—
Marked with L. for our initial!
    (He-he! There his lily[4] snaps!)

IV

Saint, forsooth! While brown Dolores
    Squats outside the Convent bank
With Sanchicha, telling stories,
    Steeping tresses in the tank,
Blue-black, lustrous, thick like horsehairs,
    —Can't I see his dead eye glow,
Bright as 't were a Barbary corsair's?[5]
    (That is, if he'd let it show!)

V

When he finishes refection,
    Knife and fork he never lays
Cross-wise, to my recollection,
    As do I, in Jesu's praise.
I the Trinity illustrate,
    Drinking watered orange-pulp—
In three sips the Arian[6] frustrate;
    While he drains his at one gulp.

VI

Oh, those melons? If he's able
    We're to have a feast! so nice!
One goes to the Abbot's table,
    All of us get each a slice.
How go on your flowers? None double?
    Not one fruit-sort can you spy?
Strange!—And I, too, at such trouble,
    Keep them close-nipped on the sly!

2. "Hail to you" (Latin).
3. Swelling on oak leaf caused by fungi or parasites, yielding tannin used in tanning, dyeing, and the making of ink.
4. In Christian art, symbol of purity.
5. Pirate of the Barbary Coast of north-east Africa.
6. The Arians heretically rejected the orthodox doctrine of the Trinity, holding that the Son was created by and was subordinate to the Father.

VII

There's great text in Galatians,[7]
   Once you trip on it, entails   50
Twenty-nine distinct damnations,
   One sure, if another fails:
If I trip him just a-dying,
   Sure of heaven as sure can be,
Spin him round and send him flying   55
   Off to hell, a Manichee?[8]

VIII

Or, my scrofulous[9] French novel
   On grey paper with blunt type!
Simply glance at it, you grovel
   Hand and foot in Belial's[1] gripe: 60
If I double down its pages
   At the woeful[2] sixteenth print,
When he gathers his greengages,[3]
   Ope a sieve[4] and slip it in 't?

IX

Or, there's Satan!—one might venture   65
   Pledge one's soul to him, yet leave
Such a flaw in the indenture
   As he'd miss till, past retrieve,
Blasted lay that rose-acacia
   We're so proud of! *Hy, Zy, Hine* . . .[5]   70
'St, there's Vespers![6] *Plena gratiâ*
   Ave, Virgo![7] Gr-r-r—you swine!

In a Gondola[1]

He sings.

I send my heart up to thee, all my heart
   In this my singing.
For the stars help me, and the sea bears part;

---

7. Browning may have in mind Galatians 3:10: "For as many as are of the works of the law are under the curse: for it is written [Deuteronomy 28:15–44], Cursed is every one that continueth not in all things which are written in the book of the law to do them." The passage in Deuteronomy proceeds to list twenty-nine torments. Presumably the speaker hopes to prove Lawrence a heretic by requiring of him a deathbed interpretation of difficult Pauline doctrine such as that quoted.
8. Manichaeism was a popular dualistic heresy originating in third-century Persia, holding that Evil (Darkness) stands in eternal opposition to Good (Light). "Manichee" came to denote any dualistic philosophy considered heretical by the Roman Catholic church.
9. Morally corrupt, contaminated.
1. A prince of darkness. Cf. Milton's

Paradise Lost, I.490–92: "*Belial* came last, than whom a Spirit more lewd/Fell not from Heaven, or more gross to love/Vice for itself."
2. Bringing woe.
3. Small greenish plum.
4. Basket.
5. Probably a fragment of an incantation, presumably uttered to seal the pact with Satan.
6. Evening prayer, sixth canonical hour of the Breviary.
7. "Full of Grace, hail, Virgin!" Garbled Angelus prayer, which should begin *Ave Maria, gratiâ plena.*
1. The opening stanza of this lyrical drama was hastily written, at the urging of a friend, John Forster, to illustrate Daniel Maclise's painting *The Serenade*, exhibited in 1842.

The very night is clinging
Closer to Venice' streets to leave one space   5
   Above me, whence thy face
May light my joyous heart to thee its dwelling-place.

She speaks.

Say after me, and try to say
My very words, as if each word
Came from you of your own accord,   10
In your own voice, in your own way:
"This woman's heart and soul and brain
Are mine as much as this gold chain
She bids me wear; which" (say again)
"I choose to make by cherishing   15
A precious thing, or choose to fling
Over the boat-side, ring by ring."
And yet once more say . . . no word more!
Since words are only words. Give o'er!²

Unless you call me, all the same,   20
Familiarly by my pet name,
Which if the Three³ should hear you call,
And me reply to, would proclaim
At once our secret to them all.
Ask of me, too, command me, blame—   25
Do, break down the partition-wall
'Twixt us, the daylight world beholds
Curtained in dusk and splendid folds!
What's left but—all of me to take?
I am the Three's: prevent them, slake   30
Your thirst! 'T is said, the Arab sage,
In practising with gems, can loose
Their subtle spirit in his cruce⁴
And leave but ashes: so, sweet mage,
Leave them my ashes when thy use   35
Sucks out my soul, thy heritage!

He sings.

I

Past we glide, and past, and past!
   What's that poor Agnese doing
Where they make the shutters fast?
   Grey Zanobi's just a-wooing   40
To his couch the purchased bride:
   Past we glide!

---

2. Stop!
3. Later (lines 104–7) called Paul, Gian, and Himself (i.e., the woman's husband).
4. Crucible.

II

Past we glide, and past, and past!
   Why's the Pucci Palace flaring
Like a beacon to the blast?   45
   Guests by hundreds, not one caring
If the dear host's neck were wried:[5]
   Past we glide!

She sings.

I

The moth's kiss, first!
Kiss me as if you made believe   50
You were not sure, this eve,
How my face, your flower, had pursed
Its petals up; so, here and there
You brush it, till I grow aware
Who wants me, and wide ope I burst.   55

II

The bee's kiss, now!
Kiss me as if you entered gay
My heart at some noonday,
A bud that dares not disallow
The claim, so all is rendered up,   60
And passively its shattered cup
Over your head to sleep I bow.

He sings.

I

What are we two?
I am a Jew,
And carry thee, farther than friends can pursue,   65
To a feast of our tribe;
Where they need thee to bribe
The devil that blasts them unless he imbibe
Thy . . . Scatter the vision for ever! And now,
As of old, I am I, thou art thou!   70

II

Say again, what we are?
The sprite of a star,
I lure thee above where the destinies bar
My plumes their full play
Till a ruddier ray   75
Than my pale one announce there is withering away
Some . . Scatter the vision for ever! And now,
As of old, I am I, thou art thou!

5. Wrung.

He muses.

Oh, which were best, to roam or rest?
The land's lap or the water's breast?   80
To sleep on yellow millet-sheaves,
Or swim in lucid shallows just
Eluding water-lily leaves,
An inch from Death's black fingers, thrust
To lock you, whom release he must;   85
Which life were best on Summer eves?

He speaks, musing.

Lie back; could thought of mine improve you?
From this shoulder let there spring
A wing; from this, another wing;
Wings, not legs and feet, shall move you!   90
Snow-white must they spring, to blend
With your flesh, but I intend
They shall deepen to the end,
Broader, into burning gold,
Till both wings crescent-wise enfold   95
Your perfect self, from 'neath your feet
To o'er your head, where, lo, they meet
As if a million sword-blades hurled
Defiance from you to the world!

Rescue me thou, the only real!   100
And scare away this mad ideal
That came, nor motions to depart!
Thanks! Now, stay ever as thou art!

Still he muses.

I

What if the Three should catch at last
Thy serenader? While there's cast   105
Paul's cloak about my head, and fast
Gian pinions[6] me, Himself has past
His stylet[7] thro' my back; I reel;
And . . . is it thou I feel?

II

They trail me, these three godless knaves,   110
Past every church that saints and saves,
Nor stop till, where the cold sea raves
By Lido's[8] wet accursed graves,
They scoop mine, roll me to its brink,
And . . . on thy breast I sink!   115

6. Binds.
7. Stiletto, dagger.

8. Long narrow island containing the
Jewish cemetery, flooded at high tide.

She replies, musing.

Dip your arm o'er the boat-side, elbow-deep,
As I do: thus: were death so unlike sleep,
Caught this way? Death's to fear from flame or steel,
Or poison doubtless; but from water—feel!

Go find the bottom! Would you stay me? There!   120
Now pluck a great blade of that ribbon-grass
To plait in where the foolish jewel was,
I flung away: since you have praised my hair,
'T is proper to be choice in what I wear.

He speaks.

Row home? must we row home? Too surely   125
Know I where its front's demurely
Over the Giudecca[9] piled;
Window just with window mating,
Door on door exactly waiting,
All's the set face of a child: 130
But behind it, where's a trace
Of the staidness and reserve,
And formal lines without a curve,
In the same child's playing-face?
No two windows look one way   135
O'er the small sea-water thread
Below them. Ah, the autumn day
I, passing, saw you overhead!
First, out a cloud of curtain blew,
Then a sweet cry, and last came you—   140
To catch your lory[1] that must needs
Escape just then, of all times then,
To peck a tall plant's fleecy seeds,
And make me happiest of men.
I scarce could breathe to see you reach   145
So far back o'er the balcony
To catch him ere he climbed too high
Above you in the Smyrna peach
That quick the round smooth cord of gold,
This coiled hair on your head, unrolled,   150
Fell down you like a gorgeous snake
The Roman girls were wont, of old,
When Rome there was, for coolness' sake
To let lie curling o'er their bosoms.
Dear lory, may his beak retain   155
Ever its delicate rose stain
As if the wounded lotus-blossoms
Had marked their thief to know again!

Stay longer yet, for others' sake

9. Canal.   1. Parrot.

Than mine! What should your chamber do?   160
—With all its rarities that ache
In silence while day lasts, but wake
At night-time and their life renew,
Suspended just to pleasure you
Who brought against their will together   165
These objects, and, while day lasts, weave
Around them such a magic tether
That dumb they look: your harp, believe,
With all the sensitive tight strings
Which dare not speak, now to itself   170
Breathes slumberously, as if some elf
Went in and out the chords, his wings
Make murmur wheresoe'er they graze,
As an angel may, between the maze
Of midnight palace-pillars, on   175
And on, to sow God's plagues, have gone
Through guilty glorious Babylon.
And while such murmurs flow, the nymph
Bends o'er the harp-top from her shell
As the dry limpet[2] for the lymph   180
Come with a tune he knows so well.
And how your statues' hearts must swell!
And how your pictures must descend
To see each other, friend with friend!
Oh, could you take them by surprise,   185
You'd find Schidone's[3] eager Duke
Doing the quaintest courtesies
To that prim saint by Haste-thee-Luke![4]
And, deeper into her rock den,
Bold Castelfranco's[5] Magdalen   190
You'd find retreated from the ken[6]
Of that robed counsel-keeping Ser[7]—
As if the Tizian[8] thinks of her,
And is not, rather, gravely bent
On seeing for himself what toys   195
Are these, his progeny invent,
What litter now the board employs
Whereon he signed a document
That got him murdered! Each enjoys
Its night so well, you cannot break   200
The sport up, so, indeed must make
More stay with me, for others' sake.

2. Mollusk with tent-shaped shell, adhering to rocks of tidal areas. *Lymph*: water.

3. Bartolomeo Schedoni, or Schidone (ca. 1570–1615), Italian painter. The *Duke* and other art works described here are imaginary.

4. Or "Luca-fa-presto," nickname of Luca Giordano (1632–1705), prolific Neapolitan painter whose father, it is said, constantly admonished him to hurry.

5. Birthplace of the Italian painter Giorgione (ca. 1477–1510).

6. View.

7. Sir, gentleman.

8. A painting by Titian (d. 1576), most famous painter of the Venetian school.

She speaks.

I

To-morrow, if a harp-string, say,
Is used to tie the jasmine back
That overfloods my room with sweets,   205
Contrive your Zorzi somehow meets
My Zanze! If the ribbon's black,
The Three are watching: keep away!

II

Your gondola—let Zorzi wreathe
A mesh of water-weeds about   210
Its prow, as if he unaware
Had struck some quay or bridge-foot stair!
That I may throw a paper out
As you and he go underneath.

There's Zanze's vigilant taper; safe are we.   215
Only one minute more to-night with me?
Resume your past self of a month ago!
Be you the bashful gallant, I will be
The lady with the colder breast than snow.
Now bow you, as becomes, nor touch my hand   220
More than I touch yours when I step to land,
And say, "All thanks, Siora!"[9]—
                          Heart to heart
And lips to lips! Yet once more, ere we part,
Clasp me and make me thine, as mine thou art!
                   [*He is surprised, and stabbed.*[1]]
It was ordained to be so, sweet!—and best   225
Comes now, beneath thine eyes, upon thy breast.
Still kiss me! Care not for the cowards! Care
Only to put aside thy beauteous hair
My blood will hurt! The Three, I do not scorn
To death, because they never lived: but I   230
Have lived indeed, and so—(yet one more kiss)—can die!

Cristina[1]

I

She should never have looked at me
If she meant I should not love her!
There are plenty . . . men, you call such,

9. Signora, lady.
1. Browning later said the woman was not an accomplice.
1. Originally paired with "Rudel to the Lady of Tripoli" as Part II of "Queen-Worship." A notorious coquette, Maria Cristina I (1806–78), daughter of Francis I, king of the Two Sicilies, married Ferdinand VII, king of Spain, in 1829. Upon Ferdinand's death in 1833 she became regent with absolute power; but her secret marriage to an ex-sergeant (1833) antagonized many of her supporters, and the opposition of Spain's leading general prompted her resignation in 1840.

I suppose . . . she may discover
　All her soul to, if she pleases,　　　　　　　　5
　　And yet leave much as she found them:
But I'm not so, and she knew it
　When she fixed me, glancing round them.

II

What? To fix me thus meant nothing?
　But I can't tell (there's my weakness)　　10
What her look said!—no vile cant, sure,
　About "need to strew the bleakness
Of some lone shore with its pearl-seed,
　That the sea feels"—no "strange yearning
That such souls have, most to lavish　　　　15
　Where there's chance of least returning."

III

Oh, we're sunk enough here, God knows!
　But not quite so sunk that moments,
Sure tho' seldom, are denied us,
　When the spirit's true endowments　　　20
Stand out plainly from its false ones,
　And apprise it if pursuing
Or the right way or the wrong way,
　To its triumph or undoing.

IV

There are flashes struck from midnights,　　25
　There are fire-flames noondays kindle,
Whereby piled-up honours perish,
　Whereby swollen ambitions dwindle,
While just this or that poor impulse,
　Which for once had play unstifled,　　　30
Seems the sole work of a life-time
　That away the rest have trifled.

V

Doubt you if, in some such moment,
　As she fixed me, she felt clearly,
Ages past the soul existed,　　　　　　　35
　Here an age 't is resting merely,
And hence fleets again for ages,
　While the true end, sole and single,
It stops here for is, this love-way,
　With some other soul to mingle?　　　　40

VI

Else it loses what it lived for,
　And eternally must lose it;
Better ends may be in prospect,
　Deeper blisses (if you choose it),
But this life's end and this love-bliss　　45
　Have been lost here. Doubt you whether
This she felt as, looking at me,
　Mine and her souls rushed together?

VII

Oh, observe! Of course, next moment,
  The world's honours, in derision,   50
Trampled out the light for ever:
  Never fear but there's provision
Of the devil's to quench knowledge
  Lest we walk the earth in rapture!
—Making those who catch God's secret   55
  Just so much more prize their capture!

VIII

Such am I: the secret's mine now!
  She has lost me, I have gained her;
Her soul's mine: and thus, grown perfect,
  I shall pass my life's remainder.   60
Life will just hold out the proving
  Both our powers, alone and blended:
And then, come the next life quickly!
  This world's use will have been ended.

Johannes Agricola in Meditation[1]

There's heaven above, and night by night
  I look right through its gorgeous roof;
No suns and moons though e'er so bright
  Avail to stop me; splendour-proof[2]
I keep the broods of stars aloof: 5
For I intend to get to God,
  For 't is to God I speed so fast,
For in God's breast, my own abode,
  Those shoals of dazzling glory, passed,
I lay my spirit down at last.   10
I lie where I have always lain,
  God smiles as he has always smiled;
Ere suns and moons could wax and wane,
  Ere stars were thundergirt, or piled
The heavens, God thought on me his child;   15
Ordained a life for me, arrayed
  Its circumstances every one
To the minutest; ay, God said

1. First published with "Porphyria" ("Porphyria's Lover," below) in *The Monthly Repository* for January 1836 and signed "Z"; in *Dramatic Lyrics* (1842) the two poems are linked under the title "Madhouse Cells," but in the collections of 1863 and after, the poems are dissociated. The title figure, German Protestant reformer Johannes Agricola (born Schneider or Schnitter, 1494–1566), was the founder of Antinomianism, a heresy which held that while the unregenerate are still under the Mosaic Law, Christians are freed from it by grace, being under the Gospel alone. Moreover, good works are not efficacious; man is saved by faith alone, without regard to moral character. As C. R. Tracy has pointed out, part of Browning's intention may be to satirize the Calvinistic doctrines of election and reprobation (DeVane, pp. 124–25).

2. Perhaps an echo of Shelley's "The Cloud" (1820), line 65: "Sunbeam-proof, I hang like a roof."

This head this hand should rest upon
   Thus, ere he fashioned star or sun.   20
And having thus created me,
   Thus rooted me, he bade me grow,
Guiltless for ever, like a tree
   That buds and blooms, nor seeks to know
   The law by which it prospers so: 25
But sure that thought and word and deed
   All go to swell his love for me,
Me, made because that love had need
   Of something irreversibly
   Pledged solely its content to be.   30
Yes, yes, a tree which must ascend,
   No poison-gourd[3] foredoomed to stoop!
I have God's warrant, could I blend
   All hideous sins, as in a cup,
   To drink the mingled venoms up;   35
Secure my nature will convert
   The draught to blossoming gladness fast:
While sweet dews turn to the gourd's hurt,
   And bloat, and while they bloat it, blast,
   As from the first its lot was cast.   40
For as I lie, smiled on, full-fed
   By unexhausted power to bless,
I gaze below on hell's fierce bed,
   And those its waves of flame oppress,
   Swarming in ghastly wretchedness;   45
Whose life on earth aspired to be
   One altar-smoke, so pure!—to win
If not love like God's love for me,
   At least to keep his anger in;
   And all their striving turned to sin.   50
Priest, doctor, hermit, monk grown white
   With prayer, the broken-hearted nun,
The martyr, the wan acolyte,[4]
   The incense-swinging child,—undone
   Before God fashioned star or sun!   55
God, whom I praise; how could I praise,
   If such as I might understand,
Make out and reckon on his ways,
   And bargain for his love, and stand,
   Paying a price, at his right hand?[5]   60

ca. 1834   1836

3. Here a symbol for the damned; mentioned in 2 Kings 4:38–41.
4. Clergyman's assistant at services.
5. Symbol of election, exaltation, and power. Cf. Matthew 25:34: "Then shall the King say unto them on his right hand, Come, ye blessed of my Father, inherit the kingdom prepared for you from the foundation of the world. . . ."

Porphyria's Lover[1]

The rain set early in to-night,
    The sullen wind was soon awake,[2]
It tore the elm-tops down for spite,
    And did its worst to vex the lake:
    I listened with heart fit to break.   5
When glided in Porphyria; straight
    She shut the cold out and the storm,
And kneeled and made the cheerless grate
    Blaze up, and all the cottage warm;
    Which done, she rose, and from her form   10
Withdrew the dripping cloak and shawl,
    And laid her soiled gloves by, untied
Her hat and let the damp hair fall,
    And, last, she sat down by my side
    And called me. When no voice replied,   15
She put my arm about her waist,
    And made her smooth white shoulder bare,
And all her yellow hair displaced,
    And, stooping, made my cheek lie there,
    And spread, o'er all, her yellow hair,   20
Murmuring how she loved me—she
    Too weak, for all her heart's endeavour,
To set its struggling passion free
    From pride, and vainer ties dissever,
    And give herself to me for ever.   25
But passion sometimes would prevail,
    Nor could to-night's gay feast restrain
A sudden thought of one so pale
    For love of her, and all in vain:
    So, she was come through wind and rain.   30
Be sure I looked up at her eyes
    Happy and proud; at last I knew
Porphyria worshipped me; surprise
    Made my heart swell, and still it grew
    While I debated what to do.   35
That moment she was mine, mine, fair,
    Perfectly pure and good: I found
A thing to do, and all her hair
    In one long yellow string I wound
    Three times her little throat around,   40
And strangled her.   No pain felt she;

1. Thought to have been written in 1834 during a brief journey to St. Petersburg, Russia (*BRP*, p. 44). First published as "Porphyria" in *The Monthly Repository* for January 1836 with "Johannes Agricola." Browning was at this time experimenting with forms and styles that would best express his essentially dramatic impulse.

2. The projection of the speaker's mood onto nature anticipates Tennyson's *Maud* (1855), wherein the device—for which John Ruskin coined the pejorative term "pathetic fallacy"—is employed extensively.

I am quite sure she felt no pain.
As a shut bud that holds a bee,
   I warily oped her lids: again
   Laughed the blue eyes without a stain.   45
And I untightened next the tress
   About her neck; her cheek once more
Blushed bright beneath my burning kiss:
   I propped her head up as before,
   Only, this time my shoulder bore   50
Her head, which droops upon it still:
   The smiling rosy little head,
So glad it has its utmost will,
   That all it scorned at once is fled,
   And I, its love, am gained instead!   55
Porphyria's love: she guessed not how
   Her darling one wish would be heard.
And thus we sit together now,
   And all night long we have not stirred,
   And yet God has not said a word!   60

ca. 1834   1836

The Pied Piper of Hamelin;[1]

A *Child's Story*

(WRITTEN FOR, AND INSCRIBED TO, W. M. THE YOUNGER)

I

Hamelin Town's in Brunswick,
   By famous Hanover city;
The river Weser, deep and wide,
Washes its wall on the southern side;
A pleasanter spot you never spied;   5
   But, when begins my ditty,
Almost five hundred years ago,
To see the townsfolk suffer so
   From vermin, was a pity.

II

Rats!   10
They fought the dogs and killed the cats,
   And bit the babies in the cradles,
And ate the cheeses out of the vats,
   And licked the soup from the cooks' own ladles,
Split open the kegs of salted sprats,   15

1. Composed in May 1842 for Willie Macready, son of the famed actor William Charles Macready. The boy, sick at the time, was sent the poem to illustrate. In Hamelin (Hameln), a German town in the province of Hanover (not Brunswick), occurred a storied plague of rats in 1284. Browning's sources for the legend are Nathaniel Wanley's *Wonders of the Little World* (1678) and Richard Verstegen's *Restitution of Decayed Intelligence in Antiquities* (1605).

Made nests inside men's Sunday hats,
And even spoiled the women's chats
    By drowning their speaking
    With shrieking and squeaking
In fifty different sharps and flats.   20

III

At last the people in a body
    To the Town Hall came flocking:
"'T is clear," cried they, "our Mayor's a noddy;
    And as for our Corporation—shocking
To think we buy gowns lined with ermine   25
For dolts that can't or won't determine
What's best to rid us of our vermin!
You hope, because you're old and obese,
To find in the furry civic robe ease?
Rouse up, sirs! Give your brains a racking   30
To find the remedy we're lacking,
Or, sure as fate, we'll send you packing!"
At this the Mayor and Corporation
Quaked with a mighty consternation.

IV

An hour they sat in council,   35
    At length the Mayor broke silence:
"For a guilder[2] I'd my ermine gown sell,
    I wish I were a mile hence!
It's easy to bid one rack one's brain—
I'm sure my poor head aches again,   40
I've scratched it so, and all in vain.
Oh for a trap, a trap, a trap!"
Just as he said this, what should hap
At the chamber door but a gentle tap?
"Bless us," cried the Mayor, "what's that?"   45
(With the Corporation as he sat,
Looking little though wondrous fat;
Nor brighter was his eye, nor moister
Than a too-long-opened oyster,
Save when at noon his paunch grew mutinous   50
For a plate of turtle green and glutinous)
"Only a scraping of shoes on the mat?
Anything like the sound of a rat
Makes my heart go pit-a-pat!"

V

"Come in!"—the Mayor cried, looking bigger: 55
And in did come the strangest figure!
His queer long coat from heel to head
Was half of yellow and half of red,
And he himself was tall and thin,
With sharp blue eyes, each like a pin,   60

2. Or florin, standard gold currency of medieval Europe.

And light loose hair, yet swarthy skin,
No tuft on cheek nor beard on chin,
But lips where smiles went out and in;
There was no guessing his kith and kin:
And nobody could enough admire   65
The tall man and his quaint attire.
Quoth one: "It's as my great-grandsire,
Starting up at the Trump of Doom's tone,
Had walked this way from his painted tombstone!"

VI

He advanced to the council-table: 70
And, "Please your honours," said he, "I'm able,
By means of a secret charm, to draw
   All creatures living beneath the sun,
   That creep or swim or fly or run,
After me so as you never saw!   75
And I chiefly use my charm
On creatures that do people harm,
The mole and toad and newt and viper;
And people call me the Pied Piper."
(And here they noticed round his neck   80
   A scarf of red and yellow stripe,
To match with his coat of the self-same cheque;
   And at the scarf's end hung a pipe;
And his fingers, they noticed, were ever straying
As if impatient to be playing   85
Upon this pipe, as low it dangled
Over his vesture so old-fangled.)
"Yet," said he, "poor piper as I am,
In Tartary I freed the Cham,[3]
   Last June, from his huge swarms of gnats;   90
I eased in Asia the Nizam[4]
   Of a monstrous brood of vampyre-bats:
And as for what your brain bewilders,
   If I can rid your town of rats
Will you give me a thousand guilders?"   95
"One? fifty thousand!"—was the exclamation
Of the astonished Mayor and Corporation.

VII

Into the street the Piper stept,
   Smiling first a little smile,
As if he knew what magic slept   100
   In his quiet pipe the while;
Then, like a musical adept,
To blow the pipe his lips he wrinkled,
And green and blue his sharp eyes twinkled,
Like a candle-flame where salt is sprinkled;   105

---

3. Or khan, ruler of the Tartar empire   4. Ruler of Hyderabad, state in India.
in central Asia.

And ere three shrill notes the pipe uttered,
You heard as if an army muttered;
And the muttering grew to a grumbling;
And the grumbling grew to a mighty rumbling;
And out of the houses the rats came tumbling.   110
Great rats, small rats, lean rats, brawny rats,
Brown rats, black rats, grey rats, tawny rats,
Grave old plodders, gay young friskers,
　　Fathers, mothers, uncles, cousins,
Cocking tails and pricking whiskers,   115
　　Families by tens and dozens,
Brothers, sisters, husbands, wives—
Followed the Piper for their lives.
From street to street he piped advancing,
And step for step they followed dancing,   120
Until they came to the river Weser,
　　Wherein all plunged and perished!
—Save one who, stout as Julius Cæsar,[5]
Swam across and lived to carry
　　(As he, the manuscript he cherished)   125
To Rat-land home his commentary:
Which was, "At the first shrill notes of the pipe,
I heard a sound as of scraping tripe,[6]
And putting apples, wondrous ripe,
　　Into a cider-press's gripe: 130
And a moving away of pickle-tub-boards,
And a leaving ajar of conserve-cupboards,
And a drawing the corks of train-oil-flasks,[7]
And a breaking the hoops of butter-casks:
And it seemed as if a voice   135
　　(Sweeter far than by harp or by psaltery[8]
Is breathed) called out, 'Oh rats, rejoice!
　　The world is grown to one vast drysaltery![9]
So munch on, crunch on, take your nuncheon,[1]
Breakfast, supper, dinner, luncheon!'   140
And just as a bulky sugar-puncheon,[2]
All ready staved, like a great sun shone
Glorious scarce an inch before me,
Just as methought it said, 'Come, bore me!'
—I found the Weser rolling o'er me."   145

VIII

You should have heard the Hamelin people
Ringing the bells till they rocked the steeple.
"Go," cried the Mayor, "and get long poles,

---

5. Cæsar's ship was captured in 48 B.C. during the siege of Alexandria, and according to legend he swam to safety carrying aloft his *Commentaries on the Gallic War*.
6. Stomach tissue of ruminant (e.g., the ox), used as food.

7. Train-oil: whale oil.
8. Stringed instrument resembling the zither.
9. I.e., a place full of casks; warehouse.
1. Snack.
2. Cask of sugar.

Poke out the nests and block up the holes!
Consult with carpenters and builders, 150
And leave in our town not even a trace
Of the rats!"—when suddenly, up the face
Of the Piper perked in the market-place,
With a, "First, if you please, my thousand guilders!"

IX

A thousand guilders! The Mayor looked blue; 155
So did the Corporation too.
For council dinners made rare havoc
With Claret, Moselle, Vin-de-Grave, Hock;[3]
And half the money would replenish
Their cellar's biggest butt with Rhenish. 160
To pay this sum to a wandering fellow
With a gipsy coat of red and yellow!
"Beside," quoth the Mayor with a knowing wink,
"Our business was done at the river's brink;
We saw with our eyes the vermin sink, 165
And what's dead can't come to life, I think.
So, friend, we're not the folks to shrink
From the duty of giving you something for drink,
And a matter of money to put in your poke;
But as for the guilders, what we spoke 170
Of them, as you very well know, was in joke.
Beside, our losses have made us thrifty.
A thousand guilders! Come, take fifty!"

X

The Piper's face fell, and he cried
"No trifling! I can't wait, beside! 175
I've promised to visit by dinnertime
Bagdat,[4] and accept the prime
Of the Head-Cook's pottage, all he's rich in,
For having left, in the Caliph's[5] kitchen,
Of a nest of scorpions no survivor: 180
With him I proved no bargain-driver,
With you, don't think I'll bate a stiver![6]
And folks who put me in a passion
May find me pipe after another fashion."

XI

"How?" cried the Mayor, "d'ye think I brook 185
Being worse treated than a Cook?
Insulted by a lazy ribald
With idle pipe and vesture piebald?
You theaten us, fellow? Do your worst,
Blow your pipe there till you burst!" 190

XII

Once more he stept into the street

3. These and Rhenish are wines.
4. Baghdad, capital of Iraq.
5. The chief Mohammedan civil and
religious leader.
6. Lower my price by even a twentieth
of a guilder.

And to his lips again
Laid his long pipe of smooth straight cane;
And ere he blew three notes (such sweet
Soft notes as yet musician's cunning   195
   Never gave the enraptured air)
There was a rustling that seemed like a bustling
Of merry crowds justling at pitching and hustling,
Small feet were pattering, wooden shoes clattering,
Little hands clapping and little tongues chattering,   200
And, like fowls in a farm-yard when barley is scattering,
Out came the children running.
All the little boys and girls,
With rosy cheeks and flaxen curls,
And sparkling eyes and teeth like pearls,   205
Tripping and skipping, ran merrily after
The wonderful music with shouting and laughter.

XIII

The Mayor was dumb, and the Council stood
As if they were changed into blocks of wood.
Unable to move a step, or cry   210
To the children merrily skipping by,
—Could only follow with the eye
That joyous crowd at the Piper's back.
But how the Mayor was on the rack,
And the wretched Council's bosoms beat,   215
As the Piper turned from the High Street
To where the Weser rolled its waters
Right in the way of their sons and daughters!
However he turned from South to West,
And to Koppelberg Hill his steps addressed,   220
And after him the children pressed;
Great was the joy in every breast.
"He never can cross that mighty top!
He's forced to let the piping drop,
And we shall see our children stop!"   225
When, lo, as they reached the mountain-side,
A wondrous portal opened wide,
As if a cavern was suddenly hollowed;
And the Piper advanced and the children followed,
And when all were in to the very last,   230
The door in the mountain-side shut fast.
Did I say, all? No! One was lame,
   And could not dance the whole of the way;
And in after years, if you would blame
   His sadness, he was used to say,—   235
"It's dull in our town since my playmates left!
I can't forget that I'm bereft
Of all the pleasant sights they see,
Which the Piper also promised me.

For he led us, he said, to a joyous land,   240
Joining the town and just at hand,
Where waters gushed and fruit-trees grew
And flowers put forth a fairer hue,
And everything was strange and new;
The sparrows were brighter than peacocks here,   245
And their dogs outran our fallow deer,
And honey-bees had lost their stings,
And horses were born with eagles' wings:
And just as I became assured
My lame foot would be speedily cured,   250
The music stopped and I stood still,
And found myself outside the hill,
Left alone against my will,
To go now limping as before,
And never hear of that country more!"   255

XIV

Alas, alas for Hamelin!
   There came into many a burgher's pate
   A text[7] which says that heaven's gate
   Opes to the rich at as easy rate
As the needle's eye takes a camel in!   260
The mayor sent East, West, North and South,
To offer the Piper, by word of mouth,
   Wherever it was men's lot to find him,
Silver and gold to his heart's content,
If he'd only return the way he went,   265
   And bring the children behind him.
But when they saw 't was a lost endeavour,
And Piper and dancers were gone for ever,
They made a decree that lawyers never
   Should think their records dated duly   270
If, after the day of the month and year,
These words did not as well appear,
"And so long after what happened here
   On the Twenty-second of July,
Thirteen hundred and seventy-six:"   275
And the better in memory to fix
The place of the children's last retreat,
They called it, the Pied Piper's Street—
Where any one playing on pipe or tabor
Was sure for the future to lose his labour.   280
Nor suffered they hostelry or tavern
   To shock with mirth a street so solemn;
But opposite the place of the cavern
   They wrote the story on a column,
And on the great church-window painted   285
The same, to make the world acquainted

---

7. Matthew 19:24.

How their children were stolen away,
And there it stands to this very day.
And I must not omit to say
That in Transylvania there's a tribe   290
Of alien people who ascribe
The outlandish ways and dress
On which their neighbours lay such stress,
To their fathers and mothers having risen
Out of some subterraneous prison   295
Into which they were trepanned[8]
Long time ago in a mighty band
Out of Hamelin town in Brunswick land,
But how or why, they don't understand.

XV

So, Willy, let me and you be wipers   300
Of scores out with all men—especially pipers!
And, whether they pipe us free frόm rats or frόm mice,
If we've promised them aught, let us keep our promise!

1842

From *Dramatic Romances and Lyrics* (1845)

"How They Brought the Good News from Ghent to Aix"[1]

[16—.]

I

I sprang to the stirrup, and Joris, and he;
I galloped, Dirck galloped, we galloped all three;
"Good speed!" cried the watch, as the gate-bolts undrew;
"Speed!" echoed the wall to us galloping through;
Behind shut the postern,[2] the lights sank to rest,   5
And into the midnight we galloped abreast.

II

Not a word to each other; we kept the great pace
Neck by neck, stride by stride, never changing our place;
I turned in my saddle and made its girths tight,
Then shortened each stirrup, and set the pique[3] right,   10
Rebuckled the cheek-strap, chained slacker the bit,
Nor galloped less steadily Roland a whit.

---

8. Lured.
1. Browning later commented, ". . . there is *no* historical incident whatever commemorated by the Poem,— which I wrote at sea, off the African coast, with a merely general impression of the characteristic warfare and besieging which abound in the Annals of Flanders. This accounts for some difficulties in the time and space occupied by the ride in one night" (1883; Hood, pp. 215–16). Working without a map, Browning had described a somewhat devious route (about 120 miles) from Ghent, capital of East Flanders in Belgium, to Aix-la-Chapelle (Aachen) in West Germany.
2. Back door or gate in city wall.
3. The probable meaning is spur (cf. French *piquer*: "to spur").

III

'T was moonset at starting; but while we drew near
Lokeren, the cocks crew and twilight dawned clear;
At Boom, a great yellow star came out to see;   15
At Düffeld, 't was morning as plain as could be;
And from Mecheln church-steeple we heard the half-chime,
So, Joris broke silence with, "Yet there is time!"

IV

At Aershot, up leaped of a sudden the sun,
And against him the cattle stood black every one,   20
To stare thro' the mist at us galloping past,
And I saw my stout galloper Roland at last,
With resolute shoulders, each butting away
The haze, as some bluff river headland its spray:

V

And his low head and crest, just one sharp ear bent back   25
For my voice, and the other pricked out on his track;
And one eye's black intelligence,—ever that glance
O'er its white edge at me, his own master, askance!
And the thick heavy spume-flakes which aye and anon
His fierce lips shook upwards in galloping on.   30

VI

By Hasselt, Dirck groaned; and cried Joris, "Stay spur!
Your Roos galloped bravely, the fault's not in her,
We'll remember at Aix"—for one heard the quick wheeze
Of her chest, saw the stretched neck and staggering knees,
And sunk tail, and horrible heave of the flank,   35
As down on her haunches she shuddered and sank.

VII

So, we were left galloping, Joris and I,
Past Looz and past Tongres, no cloud in the sky;
The broad sun above laughed a pitiless laugh,
'Neath our feet broke the brittle bright stubble like chaff;   40
Till over by Dalhem a dome-spire⁴ sprang white,
And "Gallop," gasped Joris, "for Aix is in sight!"

VIII

"How they'll greet us!"—and all in a moment his roan
Rolled neck and croup⁵ over, lay dead as a stone;
And there was my Roland to bear the whole weight   45
Of the news which alone could save Aix from her fate,
With his nostrils like pits full of blood to the brim,
And with circles of red for his eye-sockets' rim.

IX

Then I cast loose my buffcoat,⁶ each holster let fall,
Shook off both my jack-boots,⁷ let go belt and all,   50
Stood up in the stirrup, leaned, patted his ear,

---

4. Dome of the Romanesque "Octagon," the Chapel begun by Charlemagne in 796 and (according to tradition) housing his remains.
5. Rump.

6. Close short-sleeved leather military coat worn for defense in the seventeenth century.
7. Heavy military boots extending above the knee.

Called my Roland his pet-name, my horse without peer;
Clapped my hands, laughed and sang, any noise, bad or good,
Till at length into Aix Roland galloped and stood.

X

And all I remember is—friends flocking round   55
As I sat with his head 'twixt my knees on the ground;
And no voice but was praising this Roland of mine,
As I poured down his throat our last measure of wine,
Which (the burgesses voted by common consent)
Was no more than his due who brought good news from Ghent.   60

ca. 1844

Pictor Ignotus[1]

FLORENCE, 15—

I could have painted pictures like that youth's
    Ye praise so. How my soul springs up! No bar
Stayed me—ah, thought which saddens while it soothes!
    —Never did fate forbid me, star by star,
To outburst on your night with all my gift   5
    Of fires from God: nor would my flesh have shrunk
From seconding my soul, with eyes uplift
    And wide to heaven, or, straight like thunder, sunk
To the centre, of an instant; or around
    Turned calmly and inquisitive, to scan   10
The licence and the limit, space and bound,
    Allowed to truth made visible in man.
And, like that youth ye praise so, all I saw,
    Over the canvas could my hand have flung,
Each face obedient to its passion's law,   15
    Each passion clear proclaimed without a tongue;
Whether Hope rose at once in all the blood,
    A-tiptoe for the blessing of embrace,
Or Rapture drooped the eyes, as when her brood
    Pull down the nesting dove's heart to its place;   20
Or Confidence[2] lit swift the forehead up,
    And locked the mouth fast, like a castle braved,[3]—
O human faces, hath it spilt, my cup?
    What did ye give me that I have not saved?
Nor will I say I have not dreamed (how well!)   25

1. First of Browning's monologues on painting, "Pictor Ignotus" foreshadows the theme of "Fra Lippo Lippi" and "Andrea del Sarto": the indissoluble relationship of art to the moral character of the artist. The Latin title means "painter unknown" (*ignotus* also means "ignoble"); the subtitle sets the poem in the High Renaissance, a period of unparalleled achievement in painting and sculpture, when Leonardo, Michelangelo, and Raphael made Florence the leading art center. (If we presume the living "youth" envied by the speaker at the opening of his monologue to be Raphael [1483–1520], the poem may be set about 1508, the end of Raphael's important Florentine Period.)
2. Being trusted, as with a secret.
3. Attacked.

Of going—I, in each new picture,—forth,
As, making new hearts beat and bosoms swell,
   To Pope or Kaiser,[4] East, West, South, or North,
Bound for the calmly-satisfied great State,
   Or glad aspiring little burgh, it went,   30
Flowers cast upon the car which bore the freight,
   Through old streets named afresh from the event,[5]
Till it reached home, where learnèd age should greet
   My face, and youth, the star not yet distinct
Above his hair, lie learning at my feet!—   35
   Oh, thus to live, I and my picture, linked
With love about, and praise, till life should end,
   And then not go to heaven, but linger here,
Here on my earth, earth's every man my friend,—
   The thought grew frightful, 't was so wildly dear!   40
But a voice changed it.[6] Glimpses of such sights
   Have scared me, like the revels through a door
Of some strange house of idols at its rites!
   This world seemed not the world it was before:
Mixed with my loving trusting ones, there trooped   45
   . . . Who summoned those cold faces that begun
To press on me and judge me? Though I stooped
   Shrinking, as from the soldiery a nun,
They drew me forth, and spite of me . . . enough!
   These buy and sell our pictures, take and give,   50
Count them for garniture and household-stuff,
   And where they live needs must our pictures live
And see their faces, listen to their prate,
   Partakers of their daily pettiness,
Discussed of,—"This I love, or this I hate,   55
   This likes[7] me more, and this affects me less!"
Wherefore I chose my portion. If at whiles
   My heart sinks, as monotonous I paint
These endless cloisters and eternal aisles
   With the same series, Virgin, Babe and Saint,   60
With the same cold calm beautiful regard,—
   At least no merchant traffics in my heart;
The sanctuary's gloom at least shall ward
   Vain tongues from where my pictures stand apart:
Only prayer breaks the silence of the shrine   65
   While, blackening in the daily candle-smoke,
They moulder on the damp wall's travertine,[8]

4. Emperor of the Holy Roman Empire. In the sixteenth century the best artists had immense prestige, attracting the patronage of rich princes and potentates ambitious for fame. Since the artist often dictated his own terms, he enjoyed unprecedented freedom.
5. Browning may have in mind Cimabue (ca. 1240–ca. 1302), whose colossal painting of the Madonna, according to Vasari, won such acclaim that the place where the painter worked was renamed Borgo Allegri, or "Joyful District." The completed painting was solemnly carried through the streets of Florence.
6. I.e., my own voice warned me against any thought of worldly success.
7. Pleases.
8. White limestone.

'Mid echoes the light footstep never woke.
So, die my pictures! surely, gently die!
O youth, men praise so,—holds their praise its worth?   70
Blown harshly, keeps the trump its golden cry?
Tastes sweet the water with such specks of earth?

1844?

Home-Thoughts, from Abroad[1]

I

Oh, to be in England
Now that April's there,
And whoever wakes in England
Sees, some morning, unaware,
That the lowest boughs and the brushwood sheaf   5
Round the elm-tree bole are in tiny leaf,
While the chaffinch sings on the orchard bough
In England—now!

II

And after April, when May follows,
And the whitethroat builds, and all the swallows!   10
Hark, where my blossomed pear-tree in the hedge
Leans to the field and scatters on the clover
Blossoms and dewdrops—at the bent spray's edge—
That's the wise thrush; he sings each song twice over,
Lest you should think he never could recapture   15
The first fine careless rapture!
And though the fields look rough with hoary dew
All will be gay when noontide wakes anew
The buttercups, the little children's dower
—Far brighter than this gaudy melon-flower!   20

ca. 1845

["Here's to Nelson's Memory!"][2]

Here's to Nelson's memory!
'T is the second time that I, at sea,
Right off Cape Trafalgar here,
Have drunk it deep in British Beer.
Nelson for ever—any time   5
And I his to command in prose or rhyme!
Give me of Nelson only a touch,

1. This title originally headed the three lyrics "Oh, to be in England," "Here's to Nelson's Memory!" and "Nobly Cape Saint Vincent."
2. This tribute to England's great naval hero was probably written while the poet was on board a ship bound for Italy in August 1844. The source of the Nelson anecdote, according to Browning, was the ship's captain (DeVane, p. 164). The poem was later placed in a group entitled "Nationality in Drinks" and called "Beer (Nelson)."

And I save it, be it little or much:
Here's one our Captain gives, and so
Down at the word, by George, shall it go!   10
He says that at Greenwich[3] they point the beholder
To Nelson's coat, "still with tar on the shoulder:
For he used to lean with one shoulder digging,
Jigging, as it were, and zig-zag-zigging
Up against the mizen-rigging!"[4]   15

1844

Home-Thoughts, from the Sea

Nobly, nobly Cape Saint Vincent[5] to the North-west died away;
Sunset ran, one glorious blood-red, reeking into Cadiz Bay;
Bluish 'mid the burning water, full in face Trafalgar lay;
In the dimmest North-east distance dawned Gibraltar grand and
  gray;
"Here and here did England help me: how can I help England?"
  —say,   5
Whoso turns as I, this evening, turn to God to praise and pray,
While Jove's planet[6] rises yonder, silent over Africa.

ca. 1844

The Bishop Orders His Tomb at Saint Praxed's Church[1]

ROME, 15—

Vanity, saith the preacher, vanity![2]
Draw round my bed: is Anselm keeping back?
Nephews—sons mine[3]. . . ah God, I know not! Well—
She, men would have to be your mother once,
Old Gandolf envied me, so fair she was!   5

3. Greenwich Hospital, then in possession of the coat worn by Nelson at the Battle of the Nile, August 1, 1798. He had lost his right arm as a result of his assault on Santa Cruz de Tenerife, July 24, 1797.
4. Stays supporting the mizzenmast, aft or next aft of the mainmast.
5. On the southwest tip of Portugal, where Nelson won a major naval battle on February 14, 1797. The other points named are on the Spanish coast. Nelson assisted in the bombardment of Cadiz (1800), and won the Battle of Trafalgar (October 21, 1805). Gibraltar was heroically defended in the siege of 1779 by its British governor, George Augustus Eliott (1717–90).
6. Jupiter.
1. First published in *Hood's Magazine*

for March 1845 as "The Tomb at St. Praxed's." Like his archrival Gandolf, the Bishop is fictitious; perhaps the closest analogue is the life of Cardinal Ippolito d'Este the Younger, who was vain, worldly, and notoriously stingy. The interior of the ornate little church of Santa Prassede, built in 822, had been restored just prior to the poet's first visit to Rome in 1844. It is named for a virgin saint, daughter of Pudens, a Roman senator of the second century. The splendid chapel, called "Garden of Paradise," is full of glittering mosaics. Opposite one entrance is the tomb of Cardinal Cetive (d. 1474); the carved effigy atop may have inspired the poem, though Browning's decorations are imaginary.
2. Ecclesiastes 1:2.
3. Illegitimate sons.

What's done is done, and she is dead beside,
Dead long ago, and I am Bishop since,
And as she died so must we die ourselves,
And thence ye may perceive the world's a dream.
Life, how and what is it? As here I lie   10
In this state-chamber, dying by degrees,
Hours and long hours in the dead night, I ask
"Do I live, am I dead?" Peace, peace seems all.
Saint Praxed's ever was the church for peace;
And so, about this tomb of mine. I fought   15
With tooth and nail to save my niche, ye know:
—Old Gandolf cozened[4] me, despite my care;
Shrewd was that snatch from out the corner South
He graced his carrion with, God curse the same!
Yet still my niche is not so cramped but thence   20
One sees the pulpit o' the epistle-side,[5]
And somewhat of the choir, those silent seats,
And up into the aery dome where live
The angels, and a sunbeam's sure to lurk:
And I shall fill my slab of basalt there,   25
And 'neath my tabernacle[6] take my rest,
With those nine columns round me, two and two,
The odd one at my feet where Anselm stands:
Peach-blossom marble all, the rare, the ripe
As fresh-poured red wine of a mighty pulse.[7]   30
—Old Gandolf with his paltry onion-stone,[8]
Put me where I may look at him! True peach,
Rosy and flawless: how I earned the prize![9]
Draw close: that conflagration of my church
—What then? So much was saved if aught were missed!   35
My sons, ye would not be my death? Go dig
The white-grape vineyard where the oil-press stood,
Drop water gently till the surface sink,
And if ye find . . . Ah God, I know not, I! . . .
Bedded in store of rotten fig-leaves soft,   40
And corded up in a tight olive-frail,[1]
Some lump, ah God, of *lapis lazuli*,[2]
Big as a Jew's head cut off at the nape,
Blue as a vein o'er the Madonna's breast . . .
Sons, all have I bequeathed you, villas, all,   45
That brave Frascati[3] villa with its bath,
So, let the blue lump poise between my knees,
Like God the Father's globe on both his hands

4. Defrauded.
5. Right side as one faces the altar, where the Epistle is read at Mass; liturgically inferior to the Gospel side.
6. Canopy.
7. Pulp of the grape.
8. Inferior marble that would flake off in layers.
9. Cf. Philippians 3:14: "I press toward the mark for the prize of the high calling of God in Christ Jesus."
1. Basket.
2. Semiprecious blue stone.
3. Fashionable resort town in the Alban Hills about fifteen miles southeast of Rome, where stand a number of elegant villas.

Ye worship in the Jesu Church[4] so gay,
For Gandolf shall not choose but see and burst!   50
Swift as a weaver's shuttle fleet our years:[5]
Man goeth to the grave, and where is he?[6]
Did I say basalt[7] for my slab, sons? Black—
'T was ever antique-black[8] I meant! How else
Shall ye contrast my frieze[9] to come beneath?   55
The bas-relief in bronze ye promised me,
Those Pans and Nymphs[1] ye wot of, and perchance
Some tripod, thyrsus,[2] with a vase or so,
The Saviour at his sermon on the mount,
Saint Praxed in a glory,[3] and one Pan   60
Ready to twitch the Nymph's last garment off,
And Moses with the tables . . . but I know
Ye mark me not! What do they whisper thee,
Child of my bowels, Anselm? Ah, ye hope
To revel down my villas while I gasp   65
Bricked o'er with beggar's mouldy travertine[4]
Which Gandolf from his tomb-top chuckles at!
Nay, boys, ye love me—all of jasper,[5] then!
'T is jasper ye stand pledged to, lest I grieve
My bath needs be left behind, alas!   70
One block, pure green as a pistachio-nut,
There's plenty jasper somewhere in the world—
And have I not Saint Praxed's ear to pray
Horses for ye, and brown Greek manuscripts,
And mistresses with great smooth marbly limbs?   75
—That's if ye carve my epitaph aright,
Choice Latin, picked phrase, Tully's[6] every word,
No gaudy ware like Gandolf's second line—
Tully, my masters? Ulpian[7] serves his need!
And then how I shall lie through centuries,   80
And hear the blessed mutter of the mass,
And see God made and eaten all day long,[8]
And feel the steady candle-flame, and taste
Good strong thick stupefying incense-smoke!
For as I lie here, hours of the dead night,   85

4. Il Gesù, ornate Jesuit church built between 1568 and 1584.
5. Cf. Job 7:6: "My days are swifter than a weaver's shuttle, and are spent without hope."
6. Cf. Job 21:13: "They spend their days in wealth, and in a moment go down to the grave."
7. Dark gray to black igneous rock.
8. Marble handsomer and more costly than basalt.
9. Sculptured band of stone.
1. Pan: Greek god of pastures and forests; nymphs: minor deities, beautiful woodland maidens.
2. Tripod: stool on which sat the oracles of Apollo at Delphi. Thyrsus: ornamented staff carried in processions by votaries of Dionysius (Bacchus), god of wine and fertility.
3. Halo.
4. Variety of limestone.
5. Semiprecious opaque quartz of several colors. The Bishop desires the translucent variety called green chalcedony, which has a waxlike luster.
6. Marcus Tullius Cicero (106–43 B.C.), orator and statesman, whose prose style was much admired in the Renaissance.
7. Domitius Ulpianus (d. 228), Roman jurist whose style reflects the loss of the Ciceronian classical purity.
8. Reference to the doctrine of transubstantiation, the mystical conversion of bread and wine into the body and blood of Christ during Mass.

Dying in state and by such slow degrees,
I fold my arms as if they clasped a crook,[9]
And stretch my feet forth straight as stone can point,
And let the bedclothes, for a mortcloth,[1] drop
Into great laps and folds of sculptor's-work: 90
And as yon tapers dwindle, and strange thoughts
Grow, with a certain humming in my ears,
About the life before I lived this life,
And this life too, popes, cardinals and priests,
Saint Praxed at his sermon on the mount,   95
Your tall pale mother with her talking eyes,
And new-found agate urns as fresh as day,
And marble's language, Latin pure, discreet,
—Aha, ELUCESCEBAT[2] quoth our friend?
No Tully, said I, Ulpian at the best!   100
Evil and brief hath been my pilgrimage.[3]
All *lapis*, all, sons! Else I give the Pope
My villas! Will ye ever eat my heart?
Ever your eyes were as a lizard's quick,
They glitter like your mother's for my soul,   105
Or ye would heighten my impoverished frieze,
Piece out its starved design, and fill my vase
With grapes, and add a vizor and a Term,[4]
And to the tripod ye would tie a lynx[5]
That in his struggle throws the thyrsus down,   110
To comfort me on my entablature[6]
Whereon I am to lie till I must ask
"Do I live, am I dead?" There, leave me, there!
For ye have stabbed me with ingratitude
To death—ye wish it—God, ye wish it! Stone—   115
Gritstone,[7] a-crumble! Clammy squares which sweat
As if the corpse they keep were oozing through—
And no more *lapis* to delight the world!
Well go! I bless ye. Fewer tapers there,
But in a row: and, going, turn your backs   120
—Ay, like departing altar-ministrants,
And leave me in my church, the church for peace,
That I may watch at leisure if he leers—
Old Gandolf, at me, from his onion-stone,
As still he envied me, so fair she was!   125

1844–45   1845

9. Shepherd's crook or crozier, symbolic of the Bishop's office.
1. Funeral pall.
2. "He was illustrious," in the decadent Latin of Ulpian's time; Cicero would have written *elucebat*. The Bishop had spitefully ordered bad Latin for Gandolf's tomb (line 100).
3. Genesis 47:9: "And Jacob said unto Pharaoh, The days of the years of my pilgrimage are an hundred and thirty years: few and evil have the days of the years of my life been. . . ."
4. Vizor: visor or mask of a helmet, a common decoration. Term: bust on a pedestal, of the sort erected to honor Terminus, Roman god of boundaries.
5. Dionysius was often represented with lynxes.
6. Here, a slab supported by columns.
7. Coarse sandstone.

The Laboratory[1]

ANCIEN RÉGIME

I

Now that I, tying thy glass mask[2] tightly,
May gaze thro' these faint smokes curling whitely,
As thou pliest thy trade in this devil's-smithy—
Which is the poison to poison her, prithee?

II

He is with her, and they know that I know   5
Where they are, what they do: they believe my tears flow
While they laugh, laugh at me, at me fled to the drear
Empty church, to pray God in, for them!—I am here.

III

Grind away, moisten and mash up thy paste,
Pound at thy powder,—I am not in haste!   10
Better sit thus, and observe thy strange things,
Than go where men wait me and dance at the King's.

IV

That in the mortar—you call it a gum?[3]
Ah, the brave tree whence such gold oozings come!
And yonder soft phial, the exquisite blue,[4]   15
Sure to taste sweetly,—is that poison too?

V

Had I but all of them, thee and thy treasures,
What a wild crowd of invisible pleasures!
To carry pure death in an earring, a casket,
A signet, a fan-mount, a filigree basket!   20

VI

Soon, at the King's, a mere lozenge to give,
And Pauline should have just thirty minutes to live!
But to light a pastile,[5] and Elise, with her head
And her breast and her arms and her hands, should drop dead!

VII

Quick—is it finished? The colour's too grim!   25
Why not soft like the phial's, enticing and dim?
Let it brighten her drink, let her turn it and stir,
And try it and taste, ere she fix[6] and prefer!

VIII

What a drop! She's not little, no minion[7] like me!

1. First published in *Hood's Magazine* for June 1844. The subtitle sets the poem in France before the Revolution of 1789. Browning probably had in mind the court of Louis XIV (1643–1715), shaken in the 1670s by a rash of poisonings.
2. Chemist's protective mask.
3. Probably gum arabic, exuded by the acacia tree, used in preparing emulsions and pills.
4. Perhaps blue vitriol (copper sulfate), a poisonous compound.
5. Tablet containing aromatic substances, burned to fumigate or deodorize the air.
6. Make up her mind.
7. Here in the rare sense of small and delicate (cf. French *mignon*, "darling").

That's why she ensnared him: this never will free   30
The soul from those masculine eyes,—say, "no!"
To that pulse's magnificent come-and-go.

IX

For only last night, as they whispered, I brought
My own eyes to bear on her so, that I thought
Could I keep them one half minute fixed, she would fall   35
Shrivelled; she fell not; yet this does it all!

X

Not that I bid you spare her the pain;
Let death be felt and the proof remain:
Brand, burn up, bite into its grace—
He is sure to remember her dying face!   40

XI

Is it done? Take my mask off! Nay, be not morose;
It kills her, and this prevents seeing it close:
The delicate droplet, my whole fortune's fee!
If it hurts her, beside, can it ever hurt me?

XII

Now, take all my jewels, gorge gold to your fill,   45
You may kiss me, old man, on my mouth if you will!
But brush this dust off me, lest horror it brings
Ere I know it—next moment I dance at the King's!

1844

Meeting at Night

I

The grey sea and the long black land;
And the yellow half-moon large and low;
And the startled little waves that leap
In fiery ringlets from their sleep,
As I gain the cove with pushing prow,   5
And quench its speed i' the slushy sand.

II

Then a mile of warm sea-scented beach;
Three fields to cross till a farm appears;
A tap at the pane, the quick sharp scratch
And blue spurt of a lighted match,   10
And a voice less loud, thro' its joys and fears,
Than the two hearts beating each to each!

Parting at Morning[1]

Round the cape of a sudden came the sea,
And the sun looked over the mountain's rim:

1. Answering a query in 1889, Browning said a man was the speaker in this and "Meeting at Night." This lyric "is *his* confession of how fleeting is the belief (implied in the first part) that such raptures are self-sufficient and enduring—as for the time they appear" (DeVane, p. 178).

And straight was a path of gold for him,[2]   15
And the need of a world of men for me.

Nationality in Drinks[1]

I

My heart sank with our claret-flask,
  Just now, beneath the heavy sedges[2]
That serve this pond's black face for mask;
  And still at yonder broken edges
O' the hole, where up the bubbles glisten,   5
After my heart I look and listen.

II

Our laughing little flask, compelled
  Thro' depth to depth more bleak and shady;
As when, both arms beside her held,
  Feet straightened out, some gay French lady   10
Is caught up from life's light and motion,
And dropped into death's silent ocean!

Up jumped Tokay on our table,
Like a pygmy castle-warder,
Dwarfish to see, but stout and able,   15
Arms and accoutrements all in order;[3]
And fierce he looked North, then, wheeling South,
Blew with his bugle a challenge to Drouth,
Cocked his flap-hat with the tosspot-feather,[4]
Twisted his thumb in his red moustache,   20
Jingled his huge brass spurs together,
Tightened his waist with its Buda[5] sash,
And then, with an impudence nought could abash,
Shrugged his hump-shoulder, to tell the beholder,
For twenty such knaves he should laugh but the bolder: 25
And so, with his sword-hilt gallantly jutting,
And dexter-hand[6] on his haunch abutting,
Went the little man, Sir Ausbruch,[7] strutting!

1844

2. The sun.
1. First appeared as "Claret and Tokay" in *Hood's Magazine* for June 1844. In 1863 "Here's to Nelson's Memory" was added as "Beer (Nelson)." Claret is a dry red French wine from Bordeaux, Tokay a sweet wine originally from Tokay in Hungary.
2. Tufted marsh plant.
3. Browning is evidently describing the figure on the label of the bottle.
4. Flap-hat: large-brimmed hat; tosspot: drunkard.
5. Old capital of Hungary, now part of Budapest.
6. Right hand.
7. As E. C. McAleer has shown, the term "Ausbruch" refers to the special hand-picking of the grapes for wines so identified.

The Major Phase
(1855-1869)

From *Men and Women* (1855)

Love Among the Ruins[1]

I

Where the quiet-coloured end of evening smiles,
    Miles and miles
On the solitary pastures where our sheep
    Half-asleep
Tinkle homeward thro' the twilight, stray or stop   5
    As they crop—
Was the site once of a city great and gay,
    (So they say)
Of our country's very capital, its prince
    Ages since   10
Held his court in, gathered councils, wielding far
    Peace or war.

II

Now,—the country does not even boast a tree,
    As you see,
To distinguish slopes of verdure, certain rills   15
    From the hills
Intersect and give a name to, (else they run
    Into one)
Where the domed and daring palace shot its spires
    Up like fires   20
O'er the hundred-gated circuit of a wall
    Bounding all,

1. Vexed at his laziness during 1851, Browning made a New Year's resolution to write a poem each day in 1852. The vow was kept for the first three days in January, when the poet composed "Love Among the Ruins," "Women and Roses," and "Childe Roland." The setting of "Love Among the Ruins" is unspecified, but since Browning's manuscript draft of the poem (now at Harvard) is entitled "Sicilian Pastoral," ancient Syracuse may have been the site originally in mind. Reports of recent excavations at Thebes, Babylon, and Nineveh—and the poet's reading of Shelley's "Ozymandias"—doubtless contributed to this vision of bygone opulence and power. The unusual versification may owe to the poet's "pet book" as a boy, Francis Quarles's *Emblems* (1635), one lyric of which has these echoic lines:

Boast not thy skill; the righteous man
    falls oft,
        Yet falls but soft:
There may be dirt to mire him, but no
    stones
        To crush his bones. . . .
        (II.xiv.13–16)

Made of marble, men might march on nor be pressed,
    Twelve abreast.

III

And such plenty and perfection, see, of grass   25
    Never was!
Such a carpet as, this summer-time, o'erspreads
    And embeds
Every vestige of the city, guessed alone,
    Stock[2] or stone—   30
Where a multitude of men breathed joy and woe
    Long ago;
Lust of glory pricked their hearts up, dread of shame
    Struck them tame;
And that glory and that shame alike, the gold   35
    Bought and sold.

IV

Now,—the single little turret that remains
    On the plains,
By the caper[3] overrooted, by the gourd
    Overscored,   40
While the patching houseleek's[4] head of blossom winks
    Through the chinks—
Marks the basement whence a tower in ancient time
    Sprang sublime,
And a burning ring, all round, the chariots traced   45
    As they raced,
And the monarch and his minions and his dames
    Viewed the games.

V

And I know, while thus the quiet-coloured eve
    Smiles to leave   50
To their folding, all our many-tinkling fleece
    In such peace,
And the slopes and rills in undistinguished grey
    Melt away—
That a girl with eager eyes and yellow hair   55
    Waits me there
In the turret whence the charioteers caught soul
    For the goal,
When the king looked, where she looks now, breathless, dumb
    Till I come.   60

VI

But he looked upon the city, every side,
    Far and wide,
All the mountains topped with temples, all the glades'
    Colonnades,

---

2. Stumps, lifeless things.
3. Low prickly Mediterranean shrub.

4. Pink-flowered European plant found on old walls and roofs.

All the causeys,⁵ bridges, aqueducts,—and then,   65
    All the men!
When I do come, she will speak not, she will stand,
    Either hand
On my shoulder, give her eyes the first embrace
    Of my face,   70
Ere we rush, ere we extinguish sight and speech
    Each on each.

VII

In one year they sent a million fighters forth
    South and North,
And they built their gods a brazen pillar high   75
    As the sky,
Yet reserved a thousand chariots in full force—
    Gold, of course.
Oh heart! oh blood that freezes, blood that burns!
    Earth's returns   80
For whole centuries of folly, noise and sin!
    Shut them in,
With their triumphs and their glories and the rest!
    Love is best.

1852

A Lovers' Quarrel¹

I

Oh, what a dawn of day!
How the March sun feels like May!
    All is blue again
    After last night's rain,
And the South dries the hawthorn-spray.   5
    Only, my Love's away!
I'd as lief that the blue were grey.

II

Runnels,² which rillets swell,
Must be dancing down the dell,
    With a foaming head   10
    On the beryl³ bed
Paven smooth as a hermit's cell;
    Each with a tale to tell,
Could my Love but attend⁴ as well.

III

Dearest, three months ago!   15
When we lived blocked-up with snow,—
    When the wind would edge

---

5. Causeways, raised roads.
1. The autobiographical element here is unmistakable. Browning and his wife differed strongly on the topics mentioned: Napoleon III and spiritualism.
2. Rivulets; rillets are small rivulets.
3. Hard mineral often used as a gem.
4. Heed.

In and in his wedge,
In, as far as the point could go—
  Not to our ingle,[5] though,
Where we loved each the other so!

IV
Laughs with so little cause!
We devised games out of straws.
  We would try and trace
  One another's face
In the ash, as an artist draws;
  Free on each other's flaws,
How we chattered like two church daws![6]

V
What's in the "Times"?—a scold
At the Emperor deep and cold;
  He has taken a bride
  To his gruesome side,
That's as fair as himself is bold:
  There they sit ermine-stoled,
And she powders her hair with gold.[7]

VI
Fancy the Pampas' sheen!
Miles and miles of gold and green
  Where the sunflowers blow
  In a solid glow,
And—to break now and then the screen—
  Black neck and eyeballs keen,
Up a wild horse leaps between![8]

VII
Try, will our table turn?
Lay your hands there light, and yearn
  Till the yearning slips
  Thro' the finger-tips
In a fire which a few discern,
  And a very few feel burn,
And the rest, they may live and learn![9]

VIII
Then we would up and pace,
For a change, about the place,
  Each with arm o'er neck:
  'T is our quarter-deck,[1]

5. Fireplace.
6. Jackdaws, resembling crows.
7. The opulent wedding of Napoleon III to Eugénie de Montijo, a Spanish countess, was reported in the [London] *Times* for January 31 and February 1, 1853.
8. In the *Times* for February 18, 1853, was a report of an attack on Buenos Aires by *gauchos*, cowboys of the *pampas*.
9. Spiritualism in its various forms—including rapping and table-turning—was at this time a craze in Florence. To Browning's dismay Elizabeth came to believe in it.
1. After part of ship's upper deck, reserved for officers. The lovers' snowbound cottage is compared to a storm-tossed ship.

We are seamen in woeful case.
　　Help in the ocean-space! 　　　　　　　　55
Or, if no help, we'll embrace.
　　　　　　IX
See, how she looks now, dressed
In a sledging-cap and vest!
　　'T is a huge fur cloak—
　　Like a reindeer's yoke 　　　　　　　60
Falls the lappet[2] along the breast:
　　Sleeves for her arms to rest,
Or to hang, as my Love likes best.
　　　　　　X
Teach me to flirt[3] a fan
As the Spanish ladies can, 　　　　　　65
　　Or I tint your lip
　　With a burnt stick's tip
And you turn into such a man!
　　Just the two spots that span
Half the bill of the young male swan. 　　70
　　　　　　XI
Dearest, three months ago
When the mesmerizer[4] Snow
　　With his hand's first sweep
　　Put the earth to sleep:
'T was a time when the heart could show 　　75
　　All—how was earth to know,
'Neath the mute hand's to-and-fro?
　　　　　　XII
Dearest, three months ago
When we loved each other so,
　　Lived and loved the same 　　　　　80
　　Till an evening came
When a shaft from the devil's bow
　　Pierced to our ingle-glow,
And the friends were friend and foe!
　　　　　　XIII
Not from the heart beneath— 　　　　　85
'T was a bubble born of breath,
　　Neither sneer nor vaunt,
　　Nor reproach nor taunt.
See a word, how it severeth!
　　Oh, power of life and death 　　　　90
In the tongue, as the Preacher saith![5]
　　　　　　XIV
Woman, and will you cast
For a word, quite off at last
　　Me, your own, your You,—
　　Since, as truth is true, 　　　　　95

2. Decorative flap or fold in a garment.
3. Flick or wave.
4. Mesmerism: precursor of hypnotism.
5. Ecclesiasticus 28:17: ". . . the stroke of a tongue will break bones."

I was You all the happy past—
   Me do you leave aghast
With the memories We amassed?
       XV
Love, if you knew the light
That your soul casts in my sight,   100
   How I look to you
   For the pure and true
And the beauteous and the right,—
   Bear with a moment's spite
When a mere mote threats the white!   105
       XVI
What of a hasty word?
Is the fleshy heart not stirred
   By a worm's pin-prick
   Where its roots are quick?
See the eye, by a fly's foot blurred—   110
   Ear, when a straw is heard
Scratch the brain's coat of curd![6]
      XVII
Foul be the world or fair
More or less, how can I care?
   'T is the world the same   115
   For my praise or blame,
And endurance is easy there.
   Wrong in the one thing rare—
Oh, it is hard to bear!
     XVIII
Here's the spring back or close,   120
When the almond-blossom blows:
   We shall have the word
   In a minor third[7]
There is none but the cuckoo knows:
   Heaps of the guelder-rose![8]   125
I must bear with it, I suppose.
      XIX
Could but November come,
Were the noisy birds struck dumb
   At the warning slash
   Of his driver's-lash—   130
I would laugh like the valiant Thumb[9]
   Facing the castle glum
And the giant's fee-faw-fum!
      XX
Then, were the world well stripped
Of the gear wherein equipped   135
   We can stand apart,

6. Whitish substance of the brain.
7. Interval between cuckoo's notes (here three semitones).
8. Shrub having clusters of white flowers and small red fruit.
9. Tom Thumb, from Henry Fielding's *Tom Thumb, a Tragedy* (1730).

Heart dispense with heart
In the sun, with the flowers unnipped,—
Oh, the world's hangings ripped,
We were both in a bare-walled crypt![1]   140

XXI

Each in the crypt would cry
"But one freezes here! and why?
When a heart, as chill,
At my own would thrill
Back to life, and its fires out-fly?   145
Heart, shall we live or die?
The rest, . . . settle by-and-by!"

XXII

So, she'd efface the score,
And forgive me as before.
It is twelve o'clock: 150
I shall hear her knock
In the worst of a storm's uproar,
I shall pull her through the door,
I shall have her for evermore![2]

ca. 1853

Evelyn Hope

I

Beautiful Evelyn Hope is dead!
Sit[1] and watch by her side an hour.
That is her book-shelf, this her bed;
She plucked that piece of geranium-flower,
Beginning to die too, in the glass;   5
Little has yet been changed, I think:
The shutters are shut, no light may pass
Save two long rays thro' the hinge's chink.

II

Sixteen years old when she died!
Perhaps she had scarcely heard my name;   10
It was not her time to love; beside,
Her life had many a hope and aim,
Duties enough and little cares,
And now was quiet, now astir,
Till God's hand beckoned unawares,—   15
And the sweet white brow is all of her.

III

Is it too late then, Evelyn Hope?
What, your soul was pure and true,
The good stars met in your horoscope,

---

1. This metaphor is found in the Brownings' love letters (cf. Kintner, I. 3–4, 5).
2. Cf. Browning's letter (Kintner, I. 262) alluding to this passage from Terence:

"*Amantium iræ amoris integratio est*" ("A lover's quarrel is a renewal of love"; *Andria*, III. ii. 23).
1. I shall sit.

Made you of spirit, fire and dew—   20
  And, just because I was thrice as old
 And our paths in the world diverged so wide,
Each was nought to each, must I be told?
  We were fellow mortals, nought beside?

IV

No, indeed! for God above   25
  Is great to grant, as mighty to make,
And creates the love to reward the love:
  I claim you still, for my own love's sake!
Delayed it may be for more lives yet,
  Through worlds I shall traverse, not a few: 30
Much is to learn, much to forget
  Ere the time be come for taking you.

V

But the time will come,—at last it will,
  When, Evelyn Hope, what meant (I shall say)
In the lower earth, in the years long still,   35
  That body and soul so pure and gay?
Why your hair was amber, I shall divine,
  And your mouth of your own geranium's red—
And what you would do with me, in fine,
  In the new life come in the old one's stead.   40

VI

I have lived (I shall say) so much since then,
  Given up myself so many times,
Gained me the gains of various men,
  Ransacked the ages, spoiled the climes;
Yet one thing, one, in my soul's full scope,   45
  Either I missed or itself missed me:
And I want and find you, Evelyn Hope!
  What is the issue? let us see!

VII

I loved you, Evelyn, all the while.
  My heart seemed full as it could hold?   50
There was place and to spare for the frank young smile,
  And the red young mouth, and the hair's young gold.
So, hush,—I will give you this leaf to keep:
  See, I shut it inside the sweet cold hand!
There, that is our secret: go to sleep!   55
  You will wake, and remember, and understand.

Up at a Villa—Down in the City[1]

(AS DISTINGUISHED BY AN ITALIAN PERSON OF QUALITY)

I

Had I but plenty of money, money enough and to spare,
The house for me, no doubt, were a house in the city-square;

---

1. The setting is probably the Tuscan   had taken a villa in the fall of 1850.
hills near Siena, where the Brownings

Ah, such a life, such a life, as one leads at the window there!

II

Something to see, by Bacchus,[2] something to hear, at least!
There, the whole day long, one's life is a perfect feast;   5
While up at a villa one lives, I maintain it, no more than a beast.

III

Well now, look at our villa! stuck like the horn of a bull
Just on a mountain-edge as bare as the creature's skull,
Save a mere shag of a bush with hardly a leaf to pull!
—I scratch my own, sometimes, to see if the hair's turned wool.   10

IV

But the city, oh the city—the square with the houses! Why?
They are stone-faced, white as a curd, there's something to take the
    eye!
Houses in four straight lines, not a single front awry;
You watch who crosses and gossips, who saunters, who hurries by;
Green blinds, as a matter of course, to draw when the sun gets
    high;   15
And the shops with fanciful signs which are painted properly.

V

What of a villa? Though winter be over in March by rights,
'T is May perhaps ere the snow shall have withered well off the
    heights:
You've the brown ploughed land before, where the oxen steam and
    wheeze,
And the hills over-smoked behind by the faint grey olive-trees.   20

VI

Is it better in May, I ask you? You've summer all at once;
In a day he leaps complete with a few strong April suns.
'Mid the sharp short emerald wheat, scarce risen three fingers well,
The wild tulip, at end of its tube, blows out its great red bell
Like a thin clear bubble of blood, for the children to pick and sell. 25

VII

Is it ever hot in the square? There's a fountain to spout and splash!
In the shade it sings and springs; in the shine such foam-bows flash
On the horses with curling fish-tails, that prance and paddle and
    pash[3]
Round the lady atop in her conch—fifty gazers do not abash.
Though all that she wears is some weeds round her waist in a sort
    of sash.   30

VIII

All the year long at the villa, nothing to see though you linger,
Except yon cypress that points like death's lean lifted forefinger.
Some think fireflies pretty, when they mix i' the corn and mingle,
Or thrid[4] the stinking hemp till the stalks of it seem a-tingle,
Late August or early September, the stunning cicala[5] is shrill,   35
And the bees keep their tiresome whine round the resinous firs on
  . the hill.

2. Common Italian oath: *per Bacco!*   4. Thread through.
3. Here, beat with hooves.   5. Locust.

Enough of the seasons,—I spare you the months of the fever and chill.

IX

Ere you open your eyes in the city, the blessed church-bells begin:
No sooner the bells leave off than the diligence[6] rattles in:
You get the pick of the news, and it costs you never a pin.   40
By-and-by there's the travelling doctor gives pills, lets blood, draws teeth;
Or the Pulcinello-trumpet[7] breaks up the market beneath.
At the post-office such a scene-picture—the new play, piping hot!
And a notice how, only this morning, three liberal thieves[8] were shot.
Above it, behold the Archbishop's most fatherly of rebukes,   45
And beneath, with his crown and his lion, some little new law of the Duke's![9]
Or a sonnet with flowery marge, to the Reverend Don So-and-so
Who is Dante, Boccaccio, Petrarca, Saint Jerome and Cicero,
"And moreover," (the sonnet goes rhyming,) "the skirts of Saint Paul has reached,
Having preached us those six Lent-lectures more unctuous than ever he preached."   50
Noon strikes,—here sweeps the procession! our Lady borne smiling and smart
With a pink gauze gown all spangles, and seven swords stuck in her heart![1]
Bang-whang-whang goes the drum, *tootle-te-tootle* the fife;[2]
No keeping one's haunches still: it's the greatest pleasure in life.

X

But bless you, it's dear—it's dear! fowls, wine, at double the rate.   55
They have clapped a new tax upon salt, and what oil pays passing the gate
It's a horror to think of. And so, the villa for me, not the city!
Beggars can scarcely be choosers: but still—ah, the pity, the pity!
Look, two and two go the priests, then the monks with cowls and sandals,
And the penitents dressed in white shirts, a-holding the yellow candles;   60
One, he carries a flag up straight, and another a cross with handles,
And the Duke's guard brings up the rear, for the better prevention of scandals:
Bang-whang-whang goes the drum, *tootle-te-tootle* the fife.[2]
Oh, a day in the city-square, there is no such pleasure in life!

ca. 1850

6. Public stagecoach.
7. Trumpet announcing a puppet show; the buffoon Pulcinello is the forerunner of Punch.
8. I.e., opponents of Austrian rule in Italy.
9. Upon his restoration in 1849 (with Austrian support), Leopold II, Grand Duke of Tuscany, dashed liberal hopes by enacting such repressive "little new law[s]" as the repeal in 1852 of the Tuscan constitution.
1. Symbol of St. Mary's seven sorrows.
2. Browning in 1864: "Do you see the 'Edinburg [*sic*] [*Review*]' that says all my poetry is summed up in 'Bang whang, whang, goes the Drum?' " (*Dearest Isa*, p. 196).

A Woman's Last Word[1]

I

Let's contend no more, Love,
   Strive nor weep:
All be as before, Love,
   —Only sleep!

II

What so wild as words are?   5
   I and thou
In debate, as birds are,
   Hawk on bough![2]

III

See the creature stalking
   While we speak!   10
Hush and hide the talking,
   Cheek on cheek!

IV

What so false as truth is,
   False to thee?[3]
Where the serpent's tooth is   15
   Shun the tree—

V

Where the apple reddens
   Never pry—
Lest we lose our Edens,
   Eve and I.   20

VI

Be a god and hold me
   With a charm!
Be a man and fold me
   With thine arm!

VII

Teach me, only teach, Love!   25
   As I ought
I will speak thy speech, Love,
   Think thy thought—

VIII

Meet, if thou require it,
   Both demands,   30
Laying flesh and spirit
   In thy hands.

1. One of Elizabeth Barrett's letters to Browning provides the best gloss on the dramatic situation of this lyric: "Oh, I understand perfectly, how as soon as ever a common man is sure of a woman's affections, he takes up the tone of right & might. . . . I have heard of the bitterest tears being shed by the victim as soon as ever, by one word of hers, she had placed herself in his power. Of such are 'Lovers' quarrels' for the most part. The growth of power on one side . . . & the struggle against it . . . on the other" (Kintner, II. 844).
2. As the hawk perches near the oblivious birds, so may love be threatened by discord.
3. Since it seems false.

IX

That shall be to-morrow
    Not to night:
I must bury sorrow   35
    Out of sight:

X

—Must a little weep, Love,
    (Foolish me!)
And so fall asleep, Love,
    Loved by thee.   40

Fra Lippo Lippi[1]

I am poor brother Lippo, by your leave!
You need not clap your torches to my face.
Zooks,[2] what's to blame? you think you see a monk!
What, 't is past midnight, and you go the rounds,
And here you catch me at an alley's end   5
Where sportive ladies leave their doors ajar?
The Carmine's my cloister: hunt it up,
Do,—harry out, if you must show your zeal,
Whatever rat, there, haps on his wrong hole,
And nip each softling of a wee white mouse,   10
Weke, weke, that's crept to keep him company!
Aha, you know your betters! Then, you'll take
Your hand away that's fiddling on my throat,
And please to know me likewise. Who am I?
Why, one, sir, who is lodging with a friend   15
Three streets off—he's a certain . . . how d'ye call?
Master—a . . . Cosimo of the Medici,[3]
I' the house that caps the corner. Boh! you were best!
Remember and tell me, the day you're hanged,
How you affected such a gullet's-gripe![4]   20

1. "Fra Lippo Lippi," Browning's most forceful statement upon the relation of art to life, is set in Florence near the middle of the fifteenth century. Browning's main source for the life of the painter-monk Fra Lippo Lippi (ca. 1406–69) is the sketch in Giorgio Vasari's *Lives of the Painters.* The accuracy of this account is questioned by modern scholars, and only the facts that seem well established are given here. Born in Florence, Lippi was orphaned at the age of two and was left in the hands of a poor aunt. In 1421 he was registered in the community of the Carmelite friars of S. Maria del Carmine in Florence, where he remained until 1432. His earliest known work, the *Reform of the Carmelite Rule* (ca. 1432), bore the influence of Masaccio, whom Lippi had watched at work in the Brancacci chapel of the Carmine (1426–27). After leaving the monastery he worked for a time in Padua, then returned to Florence, where he won the patronage of Cosimo de' Medici. In 1442 he was made rector of S. Quirico at Legnaia, but was dismissed for misconduct in 1455. While acting as chaplain of the convent of S. Margherita in Florence he eloped with a nun, Lucrezia Buti, who bore Filippino (ca. 1457–1504), himself a notable painter. From 1452–64 Lippi painted a series of monumental frescoes in the choir of the cathedral at Prato, near Florence; they are considered his greatest achievement. Though he painted exclusively religious subjects, his work is rich in human content.
2. "Gadzooks": a mild oath.
3. Cosimo the Elder (1389–1464), Florentine banker, virtual ruler of the city, and its leading art patron.
4. I.e., what prompted you to grip the throat of such a personage as me?

But you, sir, it concerns you that your knaves
Pick up a manner nor discredit you:
Zooks, are we pilchards,[5] that they sweep the streets
And count fair prize what comes into their net?
He's Judas to a tittle, that man is!   25
Just such a face! Why, sir, you make amends.
Lord, I'm not angry! Bid your hangdogs go
Drink out this quarter-florin[6] to the health
Of the munificent House that harbours me
(And many more beside, lads! more beside!)   30
And all's come square again. I'd like his face—
His, elbowing on his comrade in the door
With the pike and lantern,—for the slave that holds
John Baptist's[7] head a-dangle by the hair
With one hand ("Look you, now," as who should say)   35
And his weapon in the other, yet unwiped!
It's not your chance to have a bit of chalk,
A wood-coal or the like? or you should see!
Yes, I'm the painter, since you style me so.
What, brother Lippo's doings, up and down,   40
You know them and they take[8] you? like enough!
I saw the proper twinkle in your eye—
'Tell you, I liked your looks at very first.
Let's sit and set things straight now, hip to haunch.
Here's spring come, and the nights one makes up bands   45
To roam the town and sing out carnival,[9]
And I've been three weeks shut within my mew,[1]
A-painting for the great man, saints and saints
And saints again. I could not paint all night—
Ouf! I leaned out of window for fresh air.   50
There came a hurry of feet and little feet,
A sweep of lute-strings, laughs, and whiffs of song,—[2]
Flower o' the broom,
Take away love, and our earth is a tomb!
Flower o' the quince,   55
I let Lisa go, and what good in life since?
Flower o' the thyme—and so on. Round they went.
Scarce had they turned the corner when a titter
Like the skipping of rabbits by moonlight,—three slim shapes,
And a face that looked up . . zooks, sir, flesh and blood,   60
That's all I'm made of! Into shreds it went,
Curtain and counterpane and coverlet,
All the bed-furniture—a dozen knots,
There was a ladder! Down I let myself,

5. Sardines, small fish.
6. Florentine coin.
7. See note to line 196.
8. Please.
9. Festival of merrymaking before Lent.
1. Cage. According to Vasari, Lippi tol-
erated his confinement for only "a few
days," not three weeks.
2. The interspersed songs are imitations
of *stornelli*, three-line Italian folk songs
improvised on rhymes set by flower
names.

Hands and feet, scrambling somehow, and so dropped, 65
And after them. I came up with the fun
Hard by Saint Laurence,[3] hail fellow, well met,—
Flower o' the rose,
If I've been merry, what matter who knows?
And so as I was stealing back again 70
To get to bed and have a bit of sleep
Ere I rise up to-morrow and go work
On Jerome[4] knocking at his poor old breast
With his great round stone to subdue the flesh,
You snap me of the sudden. Ah, I see! 75
Though your eye twinkles still, you shake your head—
Mine's shaved[5]—a monk, you say—the sting's in that!
If Master Cosimo announced himself,
Mum's the word naturally; but a monk!
Come, what am I a beast for? tell us, now! 80
I was a baby when my mother died
And father died and left me in the street.
I starved there, God knows how, a year or two
On fig-skins, melon-parings, rinds and shucks,
Refuse and rubbish. One fine frosty day, 85
My stomach being empty as your hat,
The wind doubled me up and down I went.
Old Aunt Lapaccia trussed me with one hand,
(Its fellow was a stinger as I knew)
And so along the wall, over the bridge, 90
By the straight cut to the convent. Six words there,
While I stood munching my first bread that month:
"So, boy, you're minded," quoth the good fat father
Wiping his own mouth, 't was refection-time,—
"To quit this very miserable world? 95
Will you renounce" . . . "the mouthful of bread?" thought I;
By no means! Brief, they made a monk of me;
I did renounce the world, its pride and greed,
Palace, farm, villa, shop and banking-house,
Trash, such as these poor devils of Medici 100
Have given their hearts to—all at eight years old.
Well, sir, I found in time, you may be sure,
'T was not for nothing—the good bellyful,
The warm serge and the rope that goes all round,
And day-long blessed idleness beside! 105
"Let's see what the urchin's fit for"—that came next.
Not overmuch their way, I must confess.
Such a to-do! They tried me with their books:
Lord, they'd have taught me Latin in pure waste!

3. Church of San Lorenzo.
4. St. Jerome (ca. 347–ca. 420), zealous defender of monasticism and celibacy, and one of Lippi's more incongruous subjects. The *St. Jerome in Penitence* is highly praised by Vasari.
5. The crowns of monks' heads were shaved (tonsured) to betoken vows of chastity, poverty, and obedience.

Flower o' the clove,   110
All the Latin I construe is, "amo" I love!
But, mind you, when a boy starves in the streets
Eight years together, as my fortune was,
Watching folk's faces to know who will fling
The bit of half-stripped grape-bunch he desires,   115
And who will curse or kick him for his pains,—
Which gentleman processional and fine,[6]
Holding a candle to the Sacrament,
Will wink and let him lift a plate and catch
The droppings of the wax to sell again,   120
Or holla for the Eight[7] and have him whipped,—
How say I?—nay, which dog bites, which lets drop
His bone from the heap of offal in the street,—
Why, soul and sense of him grow sharp alike,
He learns the look of things, and none the less   125
For admonition from the hunger-pinch.
I had a store of such remarks, be sure,
Which, after I found leisure, turned to use.
I drew men's faces on my copy-books,
Scrawled them within the antiphonary's marge,[8]   130
Joined legs and arms to the long music-notes,
Found eyes and nose and chin for A's and B's,
And made a string of pictures of the world
Betwixt the ins and outs of verb and noun,
On the wall, the bench, the door. The monks looked black. 135
"Nay," quoth the Prior, "turn him out, d'ye say?
In no wise. Lose a crow and catch a lark.
What if at last we get our man of parts,
We Carmelites, like those Camaldolese[9]
And Preaching Friars,[1] to do our church up fine   140
And put the front on it that ought to be!"
And hereupon he bade me daub away.
Thank you! my head being crammed, the walls a blank,
Never was such prompt disemburdening.
First, every sort of monk, the black and white,[2]   145
I drew them, fat and lean: then, folk at church,
From good old gossips waiting to confess
Their cribs[3] of barrel-droppings, candle-ends,—
To the breathless fellow at the altar-foot,
Fresh from his murder, safe[4] and sitting there   150
With the little children round him in a row
Of admiration, half for his beard and half
For that white anger of his victim's son
Shaking a fist at him with one fierce arm,

Signing himself[5] with the other because of Christ   155
(Whose sad face on the cross sees only this
After the passion of a thousand years)
Till some poor girl, her apron o'er her head,
(Which the intense eyes looked through) came at eve
On tiptoe, said a word, dropped in a loaf,   160
Her pair of earrings and a bunch of flowers
(The brute took growling), prayed, and so was gone.
I painted all, then cried " 'T is ask and have;
Choose, for more's ready!"—laid the ladder flat,
And showed my covered bit of cloister-wall.   165
The monks closed in a circle and praised loud
Till checked, taught what to see and not to see,
Being simple bodies,—"That's the very man!
Look at the boy who stoops to pat the dog!
That woman's like the Prior's niece[6] who comes   170
To care about his asthma: it's the life!"
But there my triumph's straw-fire flared and funked;[7]
Their betters took their turn to see and say:
The Prior and the learned pulled a face
And stopped all that in no time. "How? what's here?   175
Quite from the mark of painting, bless us all!
Faces, arms, legs and bodies like the true
As much as pea and pea! it's devil's-game!
Your business is not to catch men with show,[8]
With homage to the perishable clay,   180
But lift them over it, ignore it all,
Make them forget there's such a thing as flesh.
Your business is to paint the souls of men—
Man's soul, and it's a fire, smoke . . . no, it's not . . .
It's vapour done up like a new-born babe—   185
(In that shape when you die it leaves your mouth)
It's . . . well, what matters talking, it's the soul!
Give us no more of body than shows soul!
Here's Giotto,[9] with his Saint a-praising God,
That sets us praising,—why not stop with him?   190
Why put all thoughts of praise out of our head
With wonder at lines, colours, and what not?
Paint the soul, never mind the legs and arms!
Rub all out, try at it a second time.
Oh, that white smallish female with the breasts,   195
She's just my niece . . . Herodias,[1] I would say,—

5. With sign of the Cross.
6. Probably euphemism for mistress.
7. Went out in smoke.
8. What follows is a delineation of the monastic ideal of painting—the mode of Fra Angelico and Lorenzo Monaco (see lines 235–36)—swiftly being supplanted by the natural style of Lippi and his contemporaries.
9. Giotto di Bondone (ca. 1267–1337), whose paintings of St. Francis are described in Vasari, was the most important medieval Italian artist.
1. Rather, Herodias' daughter Salome (the error is Vasari's as well as the Prior's). Her dancing so pleased Herod that he promised her whatever she wished; upon Herodias' instruction she demanded the head of John the Baptist (Matthew 14:3–12). Lippi soon corrects the Prior's self-betraying identification, calling the niece "patron-saint" (line 209).

Who went and danced and got men's heads cut off!
Have it all out!" Now, is this sense, I ask?
A fine way to paint soul, by painting body
So ill, the eye can't stop there, must go further   200
And can't fare worse! Thus, yellow does for white
When what you put for yellow's simply black,
And any sort of meaning looks intense
When all beside itself means and looks nought.
Why can't a painter lift each foot in turn,   205
Left foot and right foot, go a double step,
Make his flesh liker and his soul more like,
Both in their order? Take the prettiest face,
The Prior's niece . . . patron-saint—is it so pretty
You can't discover if it means hope, fear,   210
Sorrow or joy? won't beauty go with these?
Suppose I've made her eyes all right and blue,
Can't I take breath and try to add life's flash,
And then add soul and heighten them threefold?
Or say there's beauty with no soul at all—   215
(I never saw it—put the case the same—)
If you get simple beauty and nought else,
You get about the best thing God invents:
That's somewhat: and you'll find the soul you have missed,
Within yourself, when you return him thanks.   220
"Rub all out!" Well, well, there's my life, in short,
And so the thing has gone on ever since.
I'm grown a man no doubt, I've broken bounds:
You should not take a fellow eight years old
And make him swear to never kiss the girls.   225
I'm my own master, paint now as I please—
Having a friend, you see, in the Corner-house!
Lord, it's fast holding by the rings in front—
Those great rings serve more purposes than just
To plant a flag in, or tie up a horse!   230
And yet the old schooling sticks, the old grave eyes
Are peeping o'er my shoulder as I work,
The heads shake still—"It's art's decline, my son!
You're not of the true painters, great and old;
Brother Angelico's[2] the man, you'll find;   235
Brother Lorenzo[3] stands his single peer:
Fag on at flesh, you'll never make the third!"
Flower o' the pine,
You keep your mistr . . . manners, and I'll stick to mine!
I'm not the third, then: bless us, they must know!   240
Don't you think they're the likeliest to know,

2. The monastic name of Giovanni da
Fiesole (ca. 1400–1455), perhaps the
chief painter of the late medieval period,
whose style influenced Lippi's work of
the 1440s. It is said he was so devout he
painted while kneeling.
3. Lorenzo Monaco (ca. 1370–ca. 1425),
Camaldolese monk who exerted an important influence on Lippi's early work.

They with their Latin? So, I swallow my rage,
Clench my teeth, suck my lips in tight, and paint
To please them—sometimes do and sometimes don't;
For, doing most, there's pretty sure to come   245
A turn, some warm eve finds me at my saints—
A laugh, a cry, the business of the world—
(*Flower o' the peach,*
Death for us all, and his own life for each!)
And my whole soul revolves, the cup runs over,   250
The world and life's too big to pass for a dream,
And I do these wild things in sheer despite,
And play the fooleries you catch me at,
In pure rage! The old mill-horse, out at grass
After hard years, throws up his stiff heels so,   255
Although the miller does not preach to him
The only good of grass is to make chaff.[4]
What would men have? Do they like grass or no—
May they or mayn't they? all I want's the thing
Settled for ever one way. As it is,   260
You tell too many lies and hurt yourself:
You don't like what you only like too much,
You do like what, if given you at your word,
You find abundantly detestable.
For me, I think I speak as I was taught;   265
I always see the garden[5] and God there
A-making man's wife: and, my lesson learned,
The value and significance of flesh,
I can't unlearn ten minutes afterwards,

    You understand me: I'm a beast, I know.   270
But see, now—why, I see as certainly
As that the morning-star's about to shine,
What will hap some day. We've a youngster here
Comes to our convent, studies what I do,
Slouches and stares and lets no atom drop: 275
His name is Guidi[6]—he'll not mind the monks—
They call him Hulking Tom, he lets them talk—
He picks my practice up—he'll paint apace,
I hope so—though I never live so long,
I know what's sure to follow. You be judge!   280
You speak no Latin more than I, belike,
However, you're my man, you've seen the world
—The beauty and the wonder and the power,
The shapes of things, their colours, lights and shades,
Changes, surprises,—and God made it all!   285

---

4. Cf. 1 Peter 1:24 ("all flesh is as grass . . ."); and Matthew 3:12 ("[God] will burn up the chaff . . .").
5. Of Eden.
6. Tommaso Guidi (1401– ca. 1428), a pioneer of Italian Renaissance painting; known as Masaccio ("Sloppy Tom") because of his careless living habits. Following the annotation in his edition of Vasari, Browning erred in regarding Masaccio as Lippi's pupil, whereas the converse is true.

—For what? Do you feel thankful, ay or no,
For this fair town's face, yonder river's line,
The mountain round it and the sky above,
Much more the figures of man, woman, child,
These are the frame to? What's it all about?   290
To be passed over, despised? or dwelt upon,
Wondered at? oh, this last of course!—you say.
But why not do as well as say,—paint these
Just as they are, careless what comes of it?
God's works—paint any one, and count it crime   295
To let a truth slip. Don't object, "His works
Are here already; nature is complete:
Suppose you reproduce her—(which you can't)
There's no advantage! you must beat her, then."
For, don't you mark? we're made so that we love   300
First when we see them painted, things we have passed
Perpaps a hundred times nor cared to see;
And so they are better, painted—better to us,
Which is the same thing. Art was given for that;
God uses us to help each other so,   305
Lending our minds out. Have you noticed, now,
Your cullion's hanging face?[7] A bit of chalk,
And trust me but you should, though! How much more,
If I drew higher things with the same truth!
That were to take the Prior's pulpit-place,   310
Interpret God to all of you! Oh, oh,
It makes me mad to see what men shall do
And we in our graves! This world's no blot for us,
Nor blank; it means intensely, and means good:
To find its meaning is my meat and drink.   315
"Ay, but you don't so instigate to prayer!"
Strikes in the Prior: "when your meaning's plain
It does not say to folk—remember matins,[8]
Or, mind you fast next Friday!" Why, for this
What need of art at all? A skull and bones,   320
Two bits of stick nailed crosswise, or, what's best,
A bell to chime the hour with, does as well.
I painted a Saint Laurence[9] six months since
At Prato, splashed the fresco[1] in fine style:
"How looks my painting, now the scaffold's down?"   325
I ask a brother: "Hugely," he returns—
"Already not one phiz[2] of your three slaves
Who turn the Deacon off his toasted side,
But's scratched and prodded to our heart's content,
The pious people have so eased their own   330

7. Hangdog; deserving to be hanged.
Cullion: base fellow.
8. Morning services.
9. Martyred deacon of Pope Sixtus II,
who according to legend was broiled to
death on a gridiron (ca. 258); he is said
to have told his persecutors to turn him
over since he was done on one side.
1. Painting on fresh plaster.
2. Physiognomy, or face (slang).

With coming to say prayers there in a rage:
We get on fast to see the bricks beneath.
Expect another job this time next year,
For pity[3] and religion grow i' the crowd—
Your painting serves its purpose!" Hang the fools!   335

—That is—you'll not mistake an idle word
Spoke in a huff by a poor monk, God wot,
Tasting the air this spicy night which turns
The unaccustomed head like Chianti wine!
Oh, the church knows! don't misreport me, now!   340
It's natural a poor monk out of bounds
Should have his apt word to excuse himself:
And hearken how I plot to make amends.
I have bethought me: I shall paint a piece[4]
. . . There's for you![5] Give me six months, then go, see   345
Something in Sant' Ambrogio's! Bless the nuns!
They want a cast o' my office.[6] I shall paint
God in the midst, Madonna and her babe,
Ringed by a bowery flowery angel-brood,
Lilies and vestments and white faces, sweet   350
As puff on puff of grated orris-root[7]
When ladies crowd to Church at midsummer.
And then i' the front, of course a saint or two—
Saint John,[8] because he saves the Florentines,
Saint Ambrose,[9] who puts down in black and white   355
The convent's friends and gives them a long day,
And Job, I must have him there past mistake,
The man of Uz (and Us without the z,
Painters who need his patience).[1] Well, all these
Secured at their devotion, up shall come   360
Out of a corner when you least expect,
As one by a dark stair into a great light,
Music and talking, who but Lippo! I!—
Mazed, motionless and moonstruck—I'm the man!   365
Back I shrink—what is this I see and hear?
I, caught up with my monk's-things by mistake,
My old serge gown and rope that goes all round,
I, in this presence, this pure company!
Where's a hole, where's a corner for escape?
Then steps a sweet angelic slip of a thing   370
Forward, puts out a soft palm—"Not so fast!"
—Addresses the celestial presence, "nay—

---

3. Piety.
4. The promised altarpiece is the *Coronation of the Virgin,* commissioned in 1441 for the church of the Sant' Ambrogio nunnery in Florence.
5. There's a gift of sorts for you.
6. Sample of my work.
7. Root of the iris, used in perfumes and sachets.
8. The Baptist, patron saint of Florence.
9. Bishop of Milan, Ambrose (ca. 339–397) was one of the four great Church Fathers.
1. "Ye have heard of the patience of Job . . ." (James 5:11). Uz: Job's homeland (Job 1:1).

He made you and devised you, after all,
Though he's none of you! Could Saint John there draw—
His camel-hair[2] make up a painting-brush?   375
We come to brother Lippo for all that,
Iste perfecit opus!"[3] So, all smile—
I shuffle sideways with my blushing face
Under the cover of a hundred wings
Thrown like a spread of kirtles[4] when you're gay   380
And play hot cockles,[5] all the doors being shut,
Till, wholly unexpected, in there pops
The hothead husband! Thus I scuttle off
To some safe bench behind, not letting go
The palm of her, the little lily thing   385
That spoke the good word for me in the nick,
Like the Prior's niece . . . Saint Lucy,[6] I would say.
And so all's saved for me, and for the church
A pretty picture gained. Go, six months hence!
Your hand, sir, and good-bye: no lights, no lights!   390
The street's hushed, and I know my own way back,
Don't fear me! There's the grey beginning. Zooks!

1853?

A Toccata of Galuppi's[1]

I
Oh Galuppi, Baldassaro, this is very sad to find!
I can hardly misconceive you; it would prove me deaf and blind;
But although I take your meaning, 't is with such a heavy mind!

II
Here you come with your old music, and here's all the good it brings.
What, they lived once thus at Venice where the merchants were the kings,   5

2. "And John [the Baptist] was clothed with camel's hair . . ." (Mark 1:6).
3. Means either "this man executed the work" or "this man caused the work to be done." The words appear on a scroll in the lower right hand of the *Coronation* near the head of a kneeling figure Browning, following tradition, supposed to be Lippi. The figure is actually that of the convent's benefactor, the Canon Francesco Maringhi, who "caused the work to be done."
4. Gowns or skirts.
5. Game like blindman's buff; here, euphemism for sexual escapade.
6. Virgin martyr, killed ca. 304; she is patron of the eyes. In the *Coronation* St. Lucy appears in the right foreground.
1. As a boy Browning had the best professional instruction in music; his study of music theory (under John Relfe, musician to George III) is reflected in stan-
zas 7–9. Browning was competent at the piano and the organ, and in his repertoire were the toccatas of Baldassare Galuppi (1706–85), a prolific Venetian composer best known for his comic operas. "As for Galuppi," Browning wrote in 1887, "I had once in my possession two huge manuscript volumes almost exclusively made up of his 'Toccata-pieces' —apparently a slighter form of the Sonata to be 'touched' lightly off." No single work of Galuppi's, however, was the basis for the poem (*Grove's Dictionary*). A toccata (literally, "touch-piece") is a keyboard composition in free style with full chords and running passages. By Galuppi's time the Italian toccata had declined into a rapid type for exhibiting the performer's virtuosity (*Harvard Dictionary of Music,* 2nd ed.).
The poem's speaker is an imaginary Englishman, not Browning.

Where Saint Mark's[2] is, where the Doges used to wed the sea with
rings?[3]

III

Ay, because the sea's the street there; and 't is arched by . . . what
you call

. . . Shylock's bridge[4] with houses on it, where they kept the
carnival:

I was never out of England—it's as if I saw it all.

IV

Did young people take their pleasure when the sea was warm in
May?   10

Balls and masks begun at midnight, burning ever to mid-day,

When they made up fresh adventures for the morrow, do you say?

V

Was a lady such a lady, cheeks so round and lips so red,—

On her neck the small face buoyant, like a bell-flower on its bed,

O'er the breast's superb abundance where a man might base his
head?   15

VI

Well, and it was graceful of them—they'd break talk off and afford

—She, to bite her mask's black velvet—he, to finger on his sword,

While you sat and played Toccatas, stately at the clavichord?[5]

VII

What? Those lesser thirds so plaintive, sixths diminished,[6] sigh on
sigh,

Told them something? Those suspensions,[7] those solutions—"Must
we die?"   20

Those commiserating sevenths[8]—"Life might last! we can but try!"

VIII

"Were you happy?"—"Yes."—"And are you still as happy?"—
"Yes. And you?"

—"Then, more kisses!"—"Did *I* stop them, when a million seemed
so few?"

Hark, the dominant's[9] persistence till it must be answered to!

2. Ornate church named for the patron
saint of Venice and containing his relics.
Galuppi was named *maestro di cappella*
at St. Mark's in 1762.
3. To symbolize Venetian maritime
power, the doge or chief magistrate, in
an opulent annual ceremony, "wed" the
sea by casting a consecrated gold ring
into the waters of the Lido channel.
4. Bridge of the Rialto across the Grand
Canal, associated with Shylock because
it is mentioned by that character in
Shakespeare's *The Merchant of Venice*
(I.iii.107).
5. Precursor of the piano, its strings hit
by metal pins.
6. Lesser third: interval of three semitones, showing the key to be minor;
called "plaintive third" because supposed
to evoke moods of tenderness or grief.

Diminished sixth: interval of one semi-
tone less than a minor sixth; presumably
the musical equivalent of a "sigh."
7. Notes held over from one chord into
another, producing a momentary discord
and suspending the concord that the ear
expects; the resolution ("solution") is
the passage of a chord from dissonance
to consonance.
8. Perhaps diminished sevenths, producing mild discord.
9. Probably the "dominant seventh," so
called because the chord is built on the
fifth or "dominant" degree of the scale.
The natural resolution (or "answer") is
into the triad on C, which Galuppi
strikes an octave above the first presentation of the theme, giving the toccata's
close the effect of utter finality.

IX

So, an octave struck the answer. Oh, they praised you, I dare say!   25
"Brave[1] Galuppi! that was music! good alike at grave and gay!
I can always leave off talking when I hear a master play!"

X

Then they left you for their pleasure: till in due time, one by one,
Some with lives that came to nothing, some with deeds as well
    undone,
Death stepped tacitly and took them where they never see the
    sun.   30

XI

But when I sit down to reason, think to take my stand nor swerve,
While I triumph o'er a secret wrung from nature's close reserve,
In you come with your cold music till I creep thro' every nerve.

XII

Yes, you, like a ghostly cricket, creaking where a house was burned:
"Dust and ashes, dead and done with, Venice spent what Venice
    earned.   35
The soul, doubtless, is immortal—where a soul can be discerned.

XIII

"Yours for instance: you know physics, something of geology,
Mathematics are your pastime; souls shall rise in their degree;[2]
Butterflies may dread extinction,—you'll not die, it cannot be!

XIV

"As for Venice and her people, merely born to bloom and drop, 40
Here on earth they bore their fruitage, mirth and folly were the
    crop:
What of soul was left, I wonder, when the kissing had to stop?

XV

"Dust and ashes!" So you creak it, and I want the heart to scold.
Dear dead women, with such hair, too—what's become of all the
    gold
Used to hang and brush their bosoms? I feel chilly and grown
    old.   45

ca. 1853

By the Fire-Side[1]

I

How well I know what I mean to do
    When the long dark autumn-evenings come:
And where, my soul, is thy pleasant hue?
    With the music of all thy voices, dumb
In life's November too!   5

1. Excellent.
2. An old model of the world was that of the Great Chain of Being, with man in exalted "degree" just below the angels.
1. Though a dramatic monologue, this poem strongly reflects Browning's personal experience and attitudes, and was probably inspired by an 1853 excursion with his wife to a ruined chapel on a mountain path near Bagni di Lucca in Italy (DeVane, pp. 221–22).

II

I shall be found by the fire, suppose,
  O'er a great wise book as beseemeth age,
While the shutters flap as the cross-wind blows
  And I turn the page, and I turn the page,
Not verse now, only prose!   10

III

Till the young ones whisper, finger on lip,
  "There he is at it, deep in Greek:
Now then, or never, out we slip
  To cut from the hazels by the creek
A mainmast for our ship!"   15

IV

I shall be at it indeed, my friends:
  Greek puts already on either side
Such a branch-work forth as soon extends
  To a vista opening far and wide,
And I pass out where it ends.   20

V

The outside-frame, like your hazel-trees:
  But the inside-archway widens fast,[2]
And a rarer sort[3] succeeds to these,
  And we slope[4] to Italy at last
And youth, by green degrees.   25

VI

I follow wherever I am led,
  Knowing so well the leader's hand:
Oh woman-country, wooed not wed,
  Loved all the more by earth's male-lands,
Laid to their hearts instead!   30

VII

Look at the ruined chapel again
  Half-way up in the Alpine gorge!
Is that a tower, I point you plain,
  Or is it a mill, or an iron-forge
Breaks solitude in vain?   35

VIII

A turn, and we stand in the heart of things;
  The woods are round us, heaped and dim;
From slab to slab how it slips and springs,
  The thread of water single and slim,
Through the ravage some torrent brings![5]   40

IX

Does it feed the little lake below?
  That speck of white just on its marge

---

2. The first edition reads: "the inside-archway narrows fast."
3. Rarer than hazels; presumably the olives of Italy.
4. Go loiteringly (*OED*).
5. The Brownings had sought shelter in the chapel from a downpour.

Is Pella;[6] see, in the evening-glow,
    How sharp the silver spear-heads charge
When Alp meets heaven in snow!   45

X

On our other side is the straight-up rock;
    And a path is kept 'twixt the gorge and it
By boulder-stones where lichens mock
    The marks on a moth, and small ferns fit
Their teeth to the polished block.   50

XI

Oh the sense of the yellow mountain-flowers,
    And thorny balls, each three in one,
The chestnuts throw on our path in showers!
    For the drop of the woodland fruit's begun,
These early November hours,   55

XII

That crimson the creeper's leaf across
    Like a splash of blood, intense, abrupt,
O'er a shield else gold from rim to boss,[7]
    And lay it for show on the fairy-cupped
Elf-needled mat of moss,   60

XIII

By the rose-flesh mushrooms, undivulged
    Last evening—nay, in to-day's first dew
Yon sudden coral nipple bulged,
    Where a freaked[8] fawn-coloured flaky crew
Of toadstools peep indulged.   65

XIV

And yonder, at foot of the fronting ridge
    That takes the turn to a range beyond,
Is the chapel reached by the one-arched bridge
    Where the water is stopped in a stagnant pond
Danced over by the midge.[9]   70

XV

The chapel and bridge are of stone alike,
    Blackish-grey and mostly wet;
Cut hemp-stalks steep in the narrow dyke.[1]
    See here again, how the lichens fret
And the roots of the ivy strike!   75

XVI

Poor little place, where its one priest comes
    On a festa-day,[2] if he comes at all,
To the dozen folk from their scattered homes,
    Gathered within that precinct small
By the dozen ways one roams—   80

6. Village on the Lago d' Orta in Piedmont.
7. Raised ornament on shield.
8. Streaked with color.

9. Tiny fly.
1. Ditch.
2. Feast day, or religious holiday.

XVII

To drop from the charcoal-burners' huts,
    Or climbing from the hemp-dressers' low shed,
Leave the grange[3] where the woodman stores his nuts,
    Or the wattled cote[4] where the fowlers spread
Their gear on the rock's bare juts.   85

XVIII

It has some pretension too, this front,
    With its bit of fresco[5] half-moon-wise
Set over the porch, Art's early wont:
    'T is John in the Desert,[6] I surmise,
But has borne the weather's brunt—   90

XIX

Not from the fault of the builder, though,
For a pent-house[7] properly projects
Where three carved beams make a certain show,
    Dating—good thought of our architect's—
'Five, six, nine, he lets you know.   95

XX

And all day long a bird sings there,
    And a stray sheep drinks at the pond at times;
The place is silent and aware;
    It has had its scenes, its joys and crimes,
But that is its own affair.   100

XXI

My perfect wife, my Leonor,[8]
    Oh heart, my own, oh eyes, mine too,
Whom else could I dare look backward for,
    With whom beside should I dare pursue
The path grey heads abhor?   105

XXII

For it leads to a crag's sheer edge with them;
    Youth, flowery all the way, there stops—
Not they; age threatens and they contemn,
    Till they reach the gulf wherein youth drops,
One inch from life's safe hem!   110

XXIII

With me, youth led . . . I will speak now,
    Now longer watch you as you sit
Reading by fire-light, that great brow
    And the spirit-small hand propping it,
Mutely, my heart knows how—   115

XXIV

When, if I think but deep enough,
    You are wont to answer, prompt as rhyme;

3. Granary.
4. Light thatched shelter.
5. Painting made on fresh plaster.
6. John the Baptist in the wilderness.
7. Protective roof.
8. The faithful wife in Beethoven's opera *Fidelio*.

And you, too, find without rebuff
   Response your soul seeks many a time
Piercing its fine flesh-stuff.   120

XXV

My own, confirm me! If I tread
   This path back, is it not in pride
To think how little I dreamed it led
   To an age so blest that, by its side,
Youth seems the waste instead?   125

XXVI

My own, see where the years conduct!
   At first, 't was something our two souls
Should mix as mists do; each is sucked
   In each now: on, the new stream rolls,
Whatever rocks obstruct.   130

XXVII

Think, when our one soul understands
   The great Word which makes all things new,[9]
When earth breaks up and heaven expands,
   How will the change[1] strike me and you
In the house not made with hands?[2] 135

XXVIII

Oh I must feel your brain prompt mine,
   Your heart anticipate my heart,
You must be just before, in fine,
   See and make me see, for your part,
New depths of the divine!   140

XXIX

But who could have expected this
   When we two drew together first
Just for the obvious human bliss,
   To satisfy life's daily thirst
Within a thing men seldom miss?   145

XXX

Come back with me to the first of all,
   Let us lean and love it over again,
Let us now forget and now recall,
   Break the rosary in a pearly rain,
And gather what we let fall!   150

XXXI

What did I say?—that a small bird sings
   All day long, save when a brown pair
Of hawks from the wood float with wide wings
   Strained to a bell: 'gainst noon-day glare
You count the streaks and rings.   155

9. Revelation 21:5: "And he that sat upon the throne said, Behold, I make all things new."
1. Resurrection. See 1 Corinthians 15:51: "We shall not all sleep, but we shall all be changed."
2. 2 Corinthians 5:1: "We have a building of God, an house not made with hands, eternal in the heavens."

XXXII

But at afternoon or almost eve
   'T is better; then the silence grows
To that degree, you half believe
   It must get rid of what it knows,
Its bosom does so heave.   160

XXXIII

Hither we walked then, side by side,
   Arm in arm and cheek to cheek,
And still I questioned or replied,
   While my heart, convulsed to really speak,
Lay choking in its pride.   165

XXXIV

Silent the crumbling bridge we cross,
   And pity and praise the chapel sweet,
And care about the fresco's loss,
   And wish for our souls a like retreat,
And wonder at the moss.   170

XXXV

Stoop and kneel on the settle[3] under,
   Look through the window's grated square:
Nothing to see! For fear of plunder,
   The cross is down and the altar bare,
As if thieves don't fear thunder.   175

XXXVI

We stoop and look in through the grate,
   See the little porch and rustic door,
Read duly the dead builder's date;
   Then cross the bridge that we crossed before,
Take the path again—but wait!   180

XXXVII

Oh moment, one and infinite!
   The water slips o'er stock and stone;
The West is tender, hardly bright:
   How grey at once is the evening grown—
One star, its chrysolite![4]   185

XXXVIII

We two stood there with never a third,
   But each by each, as each knew well:
The sights we saw and the sounds we heard,
   The lights and the shades made up a spell
Till the trouble grew and stirred.   190

XXXIX

Oh, the little more, and how much it is!
   And the little less, and what worlds away!
How a sound shall quicken content to bliss,
   Or a breath suspend the blood's best play,
And life be a proof of this!   195

---

3. Bench.   4. Olive green stone, used as gem.

XL

Had she willed it, still had stood the screen
    So slight, so sure, 'twixt my love and her:
I could fix her face with a guard between,
    And find her soul as when friends confer,
Friends—lovers that might have been.   200

XLI

For my heart had a touch of the woodland-time,
    Wanting to sleep now over its best.
Shake the whole tree in the summer-prime,
    But bring to the last leaf no such test!
"Hold the last fast!" runs the rhyme.   205

XLII

For a chance to make your little much,
    To gain a lover and lose a friend,
Venture the tree and a myriad such,
    When nothing you mar but the year can mend:
But a last leaf—fear to touch!   210

XLIII

Yet should it unfasten itself and fall
    Eddying down till it find your face
At some slight wind—best chance of all!
    Be your heart henceforth its dwelling-place
You trembled to forestall!   215

XLIV

Worth how well, those dark grey eyes,
    That hair so dark and dear, how worth
That a man should strive and agonize,
    And taste a veriest hell on earth
For the hope of such a prize!   220

XLV

You might have turned and tried a man,
    Set him a space to weary and wear,
And prove which suited more your plan,
    His best of hope or his worst despair,
Yet end as he began.   225

XLVI

But you spared me this, like the heart you are,
    And filled my empty heart at a word.
If two lives join, there is oft a scar,
    They are one and one, with shadowy third;[5]
One near one is too far.   230

XLVII

A moment after, and hands unseen
    Were hanging the night around us fast;
But we knew that a bar was broken between
    Life and life: we were mixed at last
In spite of the mortal screen.   235

5. The Browning love letters several times mention a "third person," an imaginary outsider who objectively views their courtship (see Kintner, I.178,494–501).

XLVIII

The forests had done it; there they stood;
    We caught for a moment the powers at play:
They had mingled us so, for once and good,
    Their work was done—we might go or stay,
They relapsed to their ancient mood.   240

XLIX

How the world is made for each of us!
    How all we perceive and know in it
Tends to some moment's product thus,
    When a soul declares itself—to wit,
By its fruit,[6] the thing it does!   245

L

Be hate that fruit or love that fruit,
    It forwards the general deed of man,
And each of the Many helps to recruit
    The life of the race by a general plan;
Each living his own, to boot.   250

LI

I am named and known by that moment's feat;
    There took my station and degree;
So grew my own small life complete,
    As nature obtained her best of me—
One born to love you, sweet!   255

LII

And to watch you sink by the fire-side now
    Back again, as you mutely sit
Musing by fire-light, that great brow
    And the spirit-small hand propping it,
Yonder, my heart knows how!   260

LIII

So, earth has gained by one man the more,
    And the gain of earth must be heaven's gain too;
And the whole is well worth thinking o'er
    When autumn comes: which I mean to do
One day, as I said before.   265

1853?

Any Wife to Any Husband[1]

I

My love, this is the bitterest, that thou—
Who art all truth, and who dost love me now

6. See Matthew 7:16: "Ye shall know them by their fruits."
1. Though the immediate occasion for the poem may have been the involvement of the poet's father in a humiliating breach of promise suit, only three years after his wife's death, and his flight to Paris in 1852 to avoid payment of heavy damages (DeVane, p. 223), the poem proved oddly prophetic of Browning's own conduct after his wife's death. In September 1869 he proposed to a wealthy widow, Lady Louisa Ashburton, and was rejected owing to his frank declaration that it would be a marriage of convenience. He was never to forgive himself for what he construed as inconstancy to the memory of Elizabeth (*BRP*, chap. 24).

As thine eyes say, as thy voice breaks to say—
Shouldst love so truly, and couldst love me still
A whole long life through, had but love its will,   5
    Would death that leads me from thee brook delay.

II

I have but to be by thee, and thy hand
Will never let mine go, nor heart withstand
    The beating of my heart to reach its place.
When shall I look for thee and feel thee gone?   10
When cry for the old comfort and find none?
    Never, I know! Thy soul is in thy face.

III

Oh, I should fade—'t is willed so! Might I save,
Gladly I would, whatever beauty gave
    Joy to thy sense, for that was precious too.   15
It is not to be granted. But the soul
Whence the love comes, all ravage leaves that whole;
    Vainly the flesh fades; soul makes all things new.[2]

IV

It would not be because my eye grew dim
Thou couldst not find the love there, thanks to Him   20
    Who never is dishonoured in the spark
He gave us from his fire of fires, and bade
Remember whence it sprang, nor be afraid
    While that burns on, though all the rest grow dark.

V

So, how thou wouldst be perfect, white and clean   25
Outside as inside, soul and soul's demesne
    Alike, this body given to show it by!
Oh, three-parts through the worst of life's abyss,
What plaudits from the next world after this,
    Couldst thou repeat a stroke and gain the sky!   30

VI

And is it not the bitterer to think
That, disengage our hands and thou wilt sink
    Although thy love was love in very deed?
I know that nature! Pass a festive day,
Thou dost not throw its relic-flower away   35
    Nor bid its music's loitering echo speed.

VII

Thou let'st the stranger's glove lie where it fell;
If old things remain old things all is well,
    For thou art grateful as becomes man best:
And hadst thou only heard me play one tune,   40
Or viewed me from a window, not so soon
    With thee would such things fade as with the rest.

VIII

I seem to see! We meet and part; 't is brief;

2. Cf. 2 Corinthians 5:17: ". . . old   things are become new." (See line 38.)
things are passed away; behold, all

The book I opened keeps a folded leaf,
  The very chair I sat on, breaks the rank;   45
That is a portrait of me on the wall—
Three lines, my face comes at so slight a call:
  And for all this, one little hour to thank!

IX

But now, because the hour through years was fixed,
Because our inmost beings met and mixed,   50
  Because thou once hast loved me—wilt thou dare
Say to thy soul and Who may list beside,
"Therefore she is immortally my bride;
  Chance cannot change my love, nor time impair.

X

"So, what if in the dusk of life that's left,   55
I, a tired traveller of my sun bereft,
  Look from my path when, mimicking the same,
The fire-fly glimpses past me, come and gone?
—Where was it till the sunset? where anon
  It will be at the sunrise! What's to blame?"   60

XI

Is it so helpful to thee? Canst thou take
The mimic up, nor, for the true thing's sake,
  Put gently by such efforts at a beam?
Is the remainder of the way so long,
Thou need'st the little solace, thou the strong?   65
  Watch out thy watch, let weak ones doze and dream!

XII

—Ah, but the fresher faces! "Is it true,"
Thou'lt ask, "some eyes are beautiful and new?
  Some hair,—how can one choose but grasp such wealth?
And if a man would press his lips to lips   70
Fresh as the wilding hedge-rose-cup there slips
  The dew-drop out of, must it be by stealth?

XIII

"It cannot change the love still kept for Her,
More than if such a picture I prefer
  Passing a day with, to a room's bare side: 75
The painted form takes nothing she possessed,
Yet, while the Titian's Venus[3] lies at rest,
  A man looks. Once more, what is there to chide?"

XIV

So must I see, from where I sit and watch,
My own self sell myself, my hand attach   80
  Its warrant to the very thefts from me—
Thy singleness of soul that made me proud,
Thy purity of heart I loved aloud,
  Thy man's-truth I was bold to bid God see!

XV

Love so, then, if thou wilt! Give all thou canst   85

3. Probably the *Venus of Urbino*, in the Uffizi Gallery at Florence.

Away to the new faces—disentranced,
  (Say it and think it) obdurate no more:
Re-issue looks and words from the old mint,
Pass them afresh, no matter whose the print
  Image and superscription once they bore!   90
XVI
Re-coin thyself and give it them to spend,—
It all comes to the same thing at the end,
  Since mine thou wast, mine art and mine shalt be,
Faithful or faithless, sealing up the sum[4]
Or lavish of my treasure, thou must come   95
  Back to the heart's place here I keep for thee!
XVII
Only, why should it be with stain at all?
Why must I, 'twixt the leaves of coronal,
  Put any kiss of pardon on thy brow?
Why need the other women know so much,   100
And talk together, "Such the look and such
  The smile he used to love with, then as now!"
XVIII
Might I die last and show thee! Should I find
Such hardship in the few years left behind,
  If free to take and light my lamp, and go   105
Into thy tomb, and shut the door and sit,
Seeing thy face on those four sides of it
  The better that they are so blank, I know!
XIX
Why, time was what I wanted, to turn o'er
Within my mind each look, get more and more   110
  By heart each word, too much to learn at first;
And join thee all the fitter for the pause
'Neath the low doorway's lintel. That were cause
  For lingering, though thou calledst, if I durst!
XX
And yet thou art the nobler of us two: 115
What dare I dream of, that thou canst not do,
  Outstripping my ten small steps with one stride?
I'll say then, here's a trial and a task—
Is it to bear?—if easy, I'll not ask:
  Though love fail, I can trust on in thy pride.   120
XXI
Pride?—when those eyes forestall the life behind
The death I have to go through!—when I find,
  Now that I want thy help most, all of thee!
What did I fear? Thy love shall hold me fast
Until the little minute's sleep is past   125
  And I wake saved.—And yet it will not be!

---

4. Cf. Ezekiel 28:12: ". . . Thou sealest up the sum, full of wisdom, and perfect in beauty."

An Epistle[1]

CONTAINING THE

Strange Medical Experience of Karshish, the Arab Physician

Karshish, the picker-up of learning's crumbs,[2]
The not-incurious in God's handiwork
(This man's-flesh he hath admirably made,
Blown like a bubble, kneaded like a paste,
To coop up and keep down on earth a space   5
That puff of vapour from his mouth, man's soul)
—To Abib, all-sagacious in our art,
Breeder in me of what poor skill I boast,
Like me inquisitive how pricks and cracks
Befall the flesh through too much stress and strain,   10
Whereby the wily vapour fain would slip
Back and rejoin its source[3] before the term,—
And aptest in contrivance (under God)
To baffle it by deftly stopping such:—
The vagrant Scholar to his Sage at home   15
Sends greeting (health and knowledge, fame with peace)
Three samples of true snakestone[4]—rarer still,
One of the other sort, the melon-shaped,
(But fitter, pounded fine, for charms than drugs)
And writeth now the twenty-second time.   20

   My journeyings were brought to Jericho:
Thus I resume. Who studious in our art
Shall count a little labour unrepaid?
I have shed sweat enough, left flesh and bone
On many a flinty furlong of this land.   25
Also, the country-side is all on fire
With rumours of a marching hitherward:
Some say Vespasian[5] cometh, some, his son.
A black lynx snarled and pricked a tufted ear;
Lust of my blood inflamed his yellow balls: 30
I cried and threw my staff and he was gone.
Twice have the robbers stripped and beaten me,
And once a town declared me for a spy;
But at the end, I reach Jerusalem,

---

1. The title refers to an imaginary encounter between an itinerant Arab medical researcher and Lazarus in A.D. 66, long after the latter was raised from the dead by Jesus (John 11: 1–44). Since the conflict experienced by Karshish— that of positivism opposed by the will to believe—was shared by many of Browning's contemporaries, the poem has a modern resonance.
2. This epithet is evidently a translation of the writer's name, for "Karshish" derives from an Arabic word meaning "one who gathers." He and his teacher Abib are fictitious.
3. The world-soul.
4. Supposed to cure snake bites.
5. Roman emperor (from A.D. 69–79) who as Nero's general invaded Palestine in 67–68; his son Titus destroyed Jerusalem in 70.

Since this poor covert where I pass the night,   35
This Bethany, lies scarce the distance thence
A man with plague-sores at the third degree
Runs till he drops down dead. Thou laughest here!
'Sooth, it elates me, thus reposed and safe,
To void the stuffing of my travel-scrip[6]   40
And share with thee whatever Jewry yields.
A viscid choler[7] is observable
In tertians,[8] I was nearly bold to say;
And falling-sickness[9] hath a happier cure
Than our school wots of: there's a spider here   45
Weaves no web, watches on the ledge of tombs,
Sprinkled with mottles on an ash-grey back;
Take five and drop them . . . but who knows his mind,
The Syrian runagate I trust this to?
His service payeth me a sublimate[1]   50
Blown up his nose to help the ailing eye.
Best wait: I reach Jerusalem at morn,
There set in order my experiences,
Gather what most deserves, and give thee all—
Or I might add, Judæa's gum-tragacanth[2]   55
Scales off in purer flakes, shines clearer-grained,
Cracks 'twixt the pestle and the porphyry,[3]
In fine[4] exceeds our produce. Scalp-disease
Confounds me, crossing so with leprosy—
Thou hadst admired one sort I gained at Zoar[5]—   60
But zeal outruns discretion. Here I end.

    Yet stay: my Syrian blinketh gratefully,
Protesteth his devotion is my price—
Suppose I write what harms not, though he steal?
I half resolve to tell thee, yet I blush,   65
What set me off a-writing first of all.
An itch I had, a sting to write, a tang!
For, be it this town's barrenness—or else
The Man had something in the look of him—
His case has struck me far more than 't is worth.   70
So, pardon if—(lest presently I lose
In the great press of novelty at hand
The care and pains this somehow stole from me)
I bid thee take the thing while fresh in mind,
Almost in sight—for, wilt thou have the truth?   75
The very man is gone from me but now,
Whose ailment is the subject of discourse.
Thus then, and let thy better wit help all.
    'T is but a case of mania—subinduced

6. Pouch.
7. Gummy fluid.
8. Fevers recurring every third day.
9. Epilepsy.
1. Refined drug.

2. Soothing medicinal gum.
3. I.e., mortar.
4. In short.
5. Ancient town near Dead Sea on Jordanian border.

By epilepsy, at the turning-point   80
Of trance prolonged unduly some three days:
When, by the exhibition[6] of some drug
Or spell, exorcization, stroke of art
Unknown to me and which 't were well to know,
The evil thing out-breaking all at once   85
Left the man whole and sound of body indeed,—
But, flinging (so to speak) life's gates too wide,
Making a clear house of it too suddenly,
The first conceit[7] that entered might inscribe
Whatever it was minded on the wall   90
So plainly at that vantage, as it were,
(First come, first served) that nothing subsequent
Attaineth to erase those fancy-scrawls
The just-returned and new-established soul
Hath gotten now so thoroughly by heart   95
That henceforth she will read or these or none.
And first—the man's own firm conviction rests
That he was dead (in fact they buried him)
—That he was dead and then restored to life
By a Nazarene physician of his tribe: 100
—Sayeth, the same bade "Rise," and he did rise.
"Such cases are diurnal,"[8] thou wilt cry.
Not so this figment!—not, that such a fume,[9]
Instead of giving way to time and health,
Should eat itself into the life of life,   105
As saffron tingeth flesh, blood, bones and all!
For see, how he takes up the after-life.
The man—it is one Lazarus a Jew,
Sanguine, proportioned, fifty years of age,
The body's habit wholly laudable,   110
As much, indeed, beyond the common health
As he were made and put aside to show.
Think, could we penetrate by any drug
And bathe the wearied soul and worried flesh,
And bring it clear and fair, by three days' sleep!   115
Whence has the man the balm that brightens all?
This grown man eyes the world now like a child.
Some elders of his tribe, I should premise,
Led in their friend, obedient as a sheep,
To bear my inquisition. While they spoke,   120
Now sharply, now with sorrow,—told the case,—
He listened not except I spoke to him,
But folded his two hands and let them talk,
Watching the flies that buzzed: and yet no fool.
And that's a sample how his years must go.   125
Look, if a beggar, in fixed middle-life,

6. Application.   8. Everyday, commonplace.
7. Conception, notion.   9. Delusion.

Should find a treasure,—can he use the same
With straitened habits and with tastes starved small,
And take at once to his impoverished brain
The sudden element that changes things,   130
That sets the undreamed-of rapture at his hand
And puts the cheap old joy in the scorned dust?
Is he not such an one as moves to mirth—
Warily parsimonious, when no need,
Wasteful as drunkenness at undue times?   135
All prudent counsel as to what befits
The golden mean, is lost on such an one:
The man's fantastic will is the man's law.
So here—we call the treasure knowledge, say,
Increased beyond the fleshy faculty—   140
Heaven opened to a soul while yet on earth,
Earth forced on a soul's use while seeing heaven:
The man is witless of the size, the sum,
The value in proportion of all things,
Or whether it be little or be much.   145
Discourse to him of prodigious armaments
Assembled to besiege his city now,
And of the passing of a mule with gourds—
'T is one! Then take it on the other side,
Speak of some trifling fact,—he will gaze rapt   150
With stupor at its very littleness,
(Far as I see) as if in that indeed
He caught prodigious import, whole results;
And so will turn to us the bystanders
In ever the same stupor (note this point)   155
That we too see not with his opened eyes.
Wonder and doubt come wrongly into play,
Preposterously, at cross purposes.
Should his child sicken unto death,—why, look
For scarce abatement of his cheerfulness,   160
Or pretermission[1] of the daily craft!
While a word, gesture, glance from that same child
At play or in the school or laid asleep,
Will startle him to an agony of fear,
Exasperation, just as like. Demand   165
The reason why—" 't is but a word," object—
"A gesture"—he regards thee as our lord[2]
Who lived there in the pyramid alone,
Looked at us (dost thou mind?) when, being young,
We both would unadvisedly recite   170
Some charm's beginning, from that book of his,
Able to bid the sun throb wide and burst
All into stars, as suns grown old are wont.
Thou and the child have each a veil alike

1. Omission.   2. Teacher.

Thrown o'er your heads, from under which ye both   175
Stretch your blind hands and trifle with a match
Over a mine of Greek fire,[3] did ye know!
He holds on firmly to some thread of life—
(It is the life to lead perforcedly)
Which runs across some vast distracting orb   180
Of glory on either side that meagre thread,
Which, conscious of, he must not enter yet—
The spiritual life around the earthly life:
The law of that is known to him as this,
His heart and brain move there, his feet stay here.   185
So is the man perplext with impulses
Sudden to start off crosswise, not straight on,
Proclaiming what is right and wrong across,
And not along, this black thread through the blaze—
"It should be" baulked by "here it cannot be."   190
And oft the man's soul springs into his face
As if he saw again and heard again
His sage that bade him "Rise" and he did rise.
Something, a word, a tick o' the blood within
Admonishes: then back he sinks at once   195
To ashes, who was very fire before,
In sedulous recurrence to his trade
Whereby he earneth him the daily bread;
And studiously the humbler for that pride,
Professedly the faultier that he knows   200
God's secret, while he holds the thread of life.
Indeed the especial marking of the man
Is prone submission to the heavenly will—
Seeing it, what it is, and why it is.
'Sayeth, he will wait patient to the last   205
For that same death which must restore his being
To equilibrium, body loosening soul
Divorced even now by premature full growth:
He will live, nay, it pleaseth him to live
So long as God please, and just how God please.   210
He even seeketh not to please God more
(Which meaneth, otherwise) than as God please.
Hence, I perceive not he affects to preach
The doctrine of his sect whate'er it be,
Make proselytes as madmen thirst to do: 215
How can he give his neighbour the real ground,
His own conviction? Ardent as he is—
Call his great truth a lie, why, still the old
"Be it as God please" reassureth him.
I probed the sore as thy disciple should: 220
"How, beast," said I, "this stolid carelessness

---

3. Incendiary mixture used by the By-   vented much later than the time of the
zantine Greeks to burn enemy ships; in-   poem.

Sufficeth thee, when Rome is on her march
To stamp out like a little spark thy town,
Thy tribe, thy crazy tale and thee at once?"
He merely looked with his large eyes on me.   225
The man is apathetic, you deduce?
Contrariwise, he loves both old and young,
Able and weak, affects the very brutes
And birds—how say I? flowers of the field[4]—
As a wise workman recognizes tools   230
In a master's workshop, loving what they make.
Thus is the man as harmless as a lamb:
Only impatient, let him do his best,
At ignorance and carelessness and sin—
An indignation which is promptly curbed: 235
As when in certain travel I have feigned
To be an ignoramus in our art
According to some preconceived design,
And happened to hear the land's practitioners
Steeped in conceit sublimed[5] by ignorance,   240
Prattle fantastically on disease,
Its cause and cure—and I must hold my peace!

    Thou wilt object—Why have I not ere this
Sought out the sage himself, the Nazarene
Who wrought this cure, inquiring at the source,   245
Conferring with the frankness that befits?
Alas! it grieveth me, the learned leech[6]
Perished in a tumult[7] many years ago,
Accused,—our learning's fate,—of wizardry,
Rebellion, to the setting up a rule   250
And creed prodigious as described to me.
His death, which happened when the earthquake fell
(Prefiguring, as soon appeared, the loss
To occult learning in our lord the sage
Who lived there in the pyramid alone)   255
Was wrought by the mad people—that's their wont!
On vain recourse, as I conjecture it,
To his tried virtue, for miraculous help—
How could he stop the earthquake?[8] That's their way!
The other imputations must be lies: 260
But take one, though I loathe to give it thee,
In mere respect for any good man's fame.
(And after all, our patient Lazarus
Is stark mad; should we count on what he says?
Perhaps not: though in writing to a leech   265
'T is well to keep back nothing of a case.)

4. Matthew 6:28: "Consider the lilies of the field, how they grow; they toil not, neither do they spin. . . ."
5. Ironic reference to the chemical process of purification by distillation.
6. Physician.
7. Pilate delivered Jesus to the people after "a tumult was made." See Matthew 27:24.
8. The earthquake occurred at Jesus' death—not before, as Karshish presumes (Matthew 27:51).

This man so cured regards the curer, then,
As—God forgive me! who but God himself,
Creator and sustainer of the world,
That came and dwelt in flesh on it awhile! 270
—'Sayeth that such an one was born and lived,
Taught, healed the sick, broke bread at his own house,
Then died, with Lazarus by, for aught I know,
And yet was . . . what I said nor choose repeat,
And must have so avouched himself, in fact, 275
In hearing of this very Lazarus
Who saith—but why all this of what he saith?
Why write of trivial matters, things of price
Calling at every moment for remark?
I noticed on the margin of a pool 280
Blue-flowering borage,[9] the Aleppo sort,
Aboundeth, very nitrous. It is strange!

Thy pardon for this long and tedious case,
Which, now that I review it, needs must seem
Unduly dwelt on, prolixly set forth! 285
Nor I myself discern in what is writ
Good cause for the peculiar interest
And awe indeed this man has touched me with.
Perhaps the journey's end, the weariness
Had wrought upon me first. I met him thus: 290
I crossed a ridge of short sharp broken hills
Like an old lion's cheek teeth. Out there came
A moon made like a face with certain spots
Multiform, manifold and menacing:
Then a wind rose behind me. So we met 295
In this old sleepy town at unaware,
The man and I. I send thee what is writ.
Regard it as a chance, a matter risked
To this ambiguous Syrian—he may lose,
Or steal, or give it thee with equal good. 300
Jerusalem's repose shall make amends
For time this letter wastes, thy time and mine;
Till when, once more thy pardon and farewell!

The very God! think, Abib; dost thou think?
So, the All-Great, were the All-Loving too— 305
So, through the thunder comes a human voice
Saying, "O heart I made, a heart beats here!
Face, my hands fashioned, see it in myself!
Thou hast no power nor mayst conceive of mine,
But love I gave thee, with myself to love, 310
And thou must love me who have died for thee!"
The madman saith He said so: it is strange.

ca. 1854

9. Herb used as stimulant. Aleppo: Syrian town.

My Star[1]

All that I know
   Of a certain star
Is, it can throw
   (Like the angled spar)[2]
Now a dart of red,   5
   Now a dart of blue;[3]
Till my friends have said
   They would fain see, too,
My star that dartles[4] the red and the blue!
Then it stops like a bird; like a flower, hangs furled: 10
   They must solace themselves with the Saturn above it.
What matter to me if their star is a world?
   Mine has opened its soul to me; therefore I love it.

"Childe Roland to the Dark Tower Came"[1]

(See Edgar's song in "LEAR")

I

My first thought was, he lied in every word,
That hoary cripple, with malicious eye
Askance to watch the working of his lie
On mine, and mouth scarce able to afford

1. According to tradition the star is the poet's wife. When asked for his autograph, Browning customarily wrote out this lyric.
2. Iceland spar, transparent calcite which cleaves into rhomboid crystals, used for prisms.
3. The imagery of the poem probably derives from a letter of Elizabeth Barrett to Browning: "*Love*, I have learnt to believe in. I see the new light which Reichenbach shows pouring forth visibly from these chrystals [sic] tossed out. But when you say that the blue, I see, is red, and that the little chrystals are the fixed stars of the Heavens, how am I to think of you but that you are deluded . . . mistaken?" (April 21, 1846; Kintner, II.640). The chemist Karl von Reichenbach (1788–1869) claimed to have discovered a mesmeric influence emanating from certain crystals as light.
4. Shoots forth repeatedly.
1. In 1887, when asked whether he agreed with a certain allegorical analysis of this poem, Browning said, "Oh, no, not at all. Understand, I don't repudiate it, either. I only mean I was conscious of no allegorical intention in writing it. . . . Childe Roland came upon me as a kind of dream. I had to write it, then and there, and I finished it in the same day, I believe. But it was simply that I had to do it. I did not know then what

I meant beyond that, and I'm sure I don't know now. But I am very fond of it" (1887; DeVane, p. 229). When a churchman asked if the poem's meaning could be summed up in the phrase, "He that endureth to the end shall be saved," Browning replied, "Yes, just about that" (1888; DeVane, p. 231).

Scores of possible literary sources for "Childe Roland" have been suggested, despite Browning's repeated denial of any source other than the one cited in the subtitle, Edgar's song in *King Lear* (III.iv.182–84): "Childe Rowland to the dark tower came, / His word was still, 'Fie, foh, and fum, / I smell the blood of a British man.'" Edgar at this point in the play has taken the guise of a mad beggar, "Poor Tom," who describes his torment to King Lear: "Who gives any thing to poor Tom? whom the foul fiend hath led through fire and through flame, through [ford] and whirlpool, o'er bog and quagmire; . . . made him proud of heart, to ride on a bay trotting-horse over four-inch'd bridges, to course his own shadow for a traitor" (III.iv.51–58).

"Childe" is the title of a young warrior awaiting knighthood. Roland is a hero of the medieval French *Chanson de Roland* and of Ariosto's *Orlando Furioso* (1532).

Suppression of the glee, that pursed and scored 5
   Its edge, at one more victim gained thereby.

II

What else should he be set for, with his staff?
   What, save to waylay with his lies, ensnare
   All travelers who might find him posted there,
And ask the road? I guessed what skull-like laugh 10
Would break, what crutch 'gin write my epitaph
   For pastime in the dusty thoroughfare,

III

If at his counsel I should turn aside
   Into that ominous tract which, all agree,
   Hides the Dark Tower. Yet acquiescingly 15
I did turn as he pointed: neither pride
Nor hope rekindling at the end descried,
   So much as gladness that some end might be.

IV

For, what with my whole world-wide wandering,
   What with my search drawn out thro' years, my hope 20
   Dwindled into a ghost not fit to cope
With that obstreperous joy success would bring,—
I hardly tried now to rebuke the spring
   My heart made, finding failure in its scope.

V

As when a sick man very near to death[2] 25
   Seems dead indeed, and feels begin and end
   The tears and takes the farewell of each friend,
And hears one bid the other go, draw breath
Freelier outside, ("since all is o'er," he saith,
   "And the blow fallen no grieving can amend;") 30

VI

While some discuss if near the other graves
   Be room enough for this, and when a day
   Suits best for carrying the corpse away,
With care about the banners, scarves and staves:
And still the man hears all, and only craves 35
   He may not shame such tender love and stay.

VII

Thus, I had so long suffered in this quest,
   Heard failure prophesied so oft, been writ
   So many times among "The Band"—to wit,
The knights who to the Dark Tower's search addressed 40
Their steps—that just to fail as they, seemed best,
   And all the doubt was now—should I be fit?

VIII

So, quiet as despair, I turned from him,

2. Lines 25–30 echo John Donne's "A Valediction: Forbidding Mourning," lines 1–4: "As virtuous men pass mildly away,/ And whisper to their souls to go,/ Whilst some of their sad friends do say,/ 'The breath goes now,' and some say, 'No,' . . . ."

That hateful cripple, out of his highway
    Into the path he pointed. All the day   45
Had been a dreary one at best, and dim
Was settling to its close, yet shot one grim[3]
    Red leer to see the plain catch its estray.

IX

For mark! no sooner was I fairly found
    Pledged to the plain, after a pace or two,   50
    Than, pausing to throw backward a last view
O'er the safe road, 't was gone; grey plain all round:
Nothing but plain to the horizon's bound.
    I might go on; nought else remained to do.

X

So, on I went. I think I never saw   55
    Such starved ignoble nature; nothing throve:
    For flowers—as well expect a cedar grove!
But cockle, spurge,[4] according to their law
Might propagate their kind, with none to awe,[5]
    You'd think; a burr had been a treasure-trove.   60

XI

No! penury, inertness and grimace,
    In some strange sort, were the land's portion. "See
    Or shut your eyes," said Nature peevishly,
"It nothing skills:[6] I cannot help my case:
'T is the Last Judgment's fire must cure this place,   65
    Calcine[7] its clods and set my prisoners free."

XII

If there pushed any ragged thistle-stalk
    Above its mates, the head was chopped; the bents[8]
    Were jealous else. What made those holes and rents
In the dock's[9] harsh swarth leaves, bruised as to baulk   70
All hope of greenness? 't is a brute must walk
    Pashing their life out, with a brute's intents.

XIII

As for the grass, it grew as scant as hair
    In leprosy; thin dry blades pricked the mud
    Which underneath looked kneaded up with blood.   75
One stiff blind horse, his every bone a-stare,
Stood stupefied, however he came there:
    Thrust out past service from the devil's stud!

XIV

Alive? he might be dead for aught I know,
    With that red gaunt and colloped[1] neck a-strain,   80
    And shut eyes underneath the rusty mane;
Seldom went such grotesqueness with such woe;
I never saw a brute I hated so;
    He must be wicked to deserve such pain.

3. A stray domestic animal.
4. Weeds.
5. Nothing to check their growth.
6. It makes no difference.
7. Burn to a powder.

8. Coarse grasses.
9. Coarse weedy plant.
1. In folds or ridges. The horse was inspired by a figure in a tapestry of Browning's.

XV

I shut my eyes and turned them on my heart.   85
   As a man calls for wine before he fights,
    I asked one draught of earlier, happier sights,
Ere fitly I could hope to play my part.
Think first, fight afterwards—the soldier's art:
   One taste of the old time sets all to rights.   90

XVI

Not it! I fancied Cuthbert's reddening face
   Beneath its garniture of curly gold,
    Dear fellow, till I almost felt him fold
An arm in mine to fix me to the place,
That way he used. Alas, one night's disgrace!   95
   Out went my heart's new fire and left it cold.

XVII

Giles then, the soul of honour—there he stands
   Frank as ten years ago when knighted first.
    What honest man should dare (he said) he durst.[2]
Good—but the scene shifts—faugh! what hangman-hands   100
Pin to his breast a parchment? His own bands
   Read it. Poor traitor, spit upon and curst!

XVIII

Better this present than a past like that;
   Back therefore to my darkening path again!
    No sound, no sight as far as eye could strain.   105
Will the night send a howlet[3] or a bat?
I asked: when something on the dismal flat
   Came to arrest my thoughts and change their train.

XIX

A sudden little river crossed my path
   As unexpected as a serpent comes.   110
    No sluggish tide congenial to the glooms;
This, as it frothed by, might have been a bath
For the fiend's glowing hoof—to see the wrath
   Of its black eddy bespate[4] with flakes and spumes.

XX

So petty yet so spiteful! All along,   115
   Low scrubby alders kneeled down over it;
    Drenched willows flung them headlong in a fit
Of mute despair, a suicidal throng:
The river which had done them all the wrong,
   Whate'er that was, rolled by, deterred no whit.   120

XXI

Which, while I forded,—good saints, how I feared
   To set my foot upon a dead man's cheek,
    Each step, or fell the spear I thrust to seek
For hollows, tangled in his hair or beard!
—It may have been a water-rat I speared,   125

2. Cf. *Macbeth*, I.vii.46–47: "I dare do   3. Owl.
all that may become a man;/Who dares   4. Spattered.
do more is none."

But, ugh! it sounded like a baby's shriek.

XXII

Glad was I when I reached the other bank.
　　Now for a better country. Vain presage!
　　Who were the strugglers, what war did they wage,
Whose savage trample thus could pad the dank　　　　130
Soil to a plash?[5] Toads in a poisoned tank,
　　Or wild cats in a red-hot iron cage—

XIII

The fight must so have seemed in that fell cirque.[6]
　　What penned them there, with all the plain to choose?
　　No foot-print leading to that horrid mews,[7]　　　135
None out of it. Mad brewage set to work
Their brains, no doubt, like galley-slaves the Turk
　　Pits for his pastime, Christians against Jews.

XXIV

And more than that—a furlong on—why, there!
　　What bad use was that engine for, that wheel,　　　140
　　Or brake,[8] not wheel—that harrow fit to reel
Men's bodies out like silk? with all the air
Of Tophet's[9] tool, on earth left unaware,
　　Or brought to sharpen its rusty teeth of steel.

XXV

Then came a bit of stubbed ground, once a wood,　　　145
　　Next a marsh, it would seem, and now mere earth
　　Desperate and done with; (so a fool finds mirth,
Makes a thing and then mars it, till his mood
Changes and off he goes!) within a rood[1]—
　　Bog, clay and rubble, sand and stark black dearth.　　　150

XXVI

Now blotches rankling, coloured gay and grim,
　　Now patches where some leanness of the soil's
　　Broke into moss or substances like boils;
Then came some palsied oak, a cleft in him
Like a distorted mouth that splits its rim　　　155
　　Gaping at death, and dies while it recoils.

XXVII

And just as far as ever from the end!
　　Nought in the distance but the evening, nought
　　To point my footstep further! At the thought,
A great black bird, Apollyon's[2] bosom-friend,　　　160
Sailed past, nor beat his wide wing dragon-penned
　　That brushed my cap—perchance the guide I sought.

XXVIII

For, looking up, aware I somehow grew,
　　'Spite of the dusk, the plain had given place

5. Mire.
6. Terrible arena.
7. Cage or enclosure.
8. Toothed machine for processing flax.
9. Hell.
1. Quarter acre.

2. Or Abaddon, meaning "destroyer." In Revelation 9:11 he is "the angel of the bottomless pit." In *Pilgrim's Progress*, Part I, the "foul fiend" Apollyon has "wings like a dragon."

All round to mountains—with such name to grace 165
Mere ugly heights and heaps now stolen in view.
How thus they had surprised me,—solve it, you!
    How to get from them was no clearer case.

XXIX

Yet half I seemed to recognize some trick
    Of mischief happened to me, God knows when— 170
    In a bad dream perhaps. Here ended, then,
Progress this way. When, in the very nick
Of giving up, one time more, came a click
    As when a trap shuts—you're inside the den!

XXX

Burningly it came on me all at once, 175
    This was the place! those two hills on the right,
    Crouched like two bulls locked horn in horn in fight;
While to the left, a tall scalped mountain . . . Dunce,
Dotard, a-dozing at the very nonce,[3]
    After a life spent training for the sight! 180

XXXI

What in the midst lay but the Tower[4] itself?
    The round squat turret, blind as the fool's heart,
    Built of brown stone, without a counterpart
In the whole world. The tempest's mocking elf
Points to the shipman thus the unseen shelf[5] 185
    He strikes on, only when the timbers start.

XXXII

Not see? because of night perhaps?—why, day
    Came back again for that! before it left,
    The dying sunset kindled through a cleft:
The hills, like giants at a hunting, lay, 190
Chin upon hand, to see the game at bay,—
    "Now stab and end the creature—to the heft!"[6]

XXXIII

Not hear? when noise was everywhere! it tolled
    Increasing like a bell. Names in my ears
    Of all the lost adventurers my peers,— 195
How such a one was strong, and such was bold,
And such was fortunate, yet each of old
    Lost, lost! one moment knelled the woe of years.

XXXIV

There they stood, ranged along the hill-sides, met
    To view the last of me, a living frame 200
    For one more picture! in a sheet of flame
I saw them and I knew them all. And yet
Dauntless the slug-horn[7] to my lips I set,
    And blew. "*Childe Roland to the Dark Tower came.*"

1852

---

3. Crucial moment.
4. According to Browning this setting was based on "some recollection of a strange solitary little tower I have come upon more than once in Massa-Carrara, in the midst of low hills . . ." (*New Letters*, p. 173).
5. Sandbank or rock ledge.
6. Hilt.
7. *Slughorn* is an archaic form of *slogan*

Respectability[1]

I

Dear, had the world in its caprice
    Deigned to proclaim "I know you both,
    Have recognized your plighted troth,
Am sponsor for you: live in peace!"—
How many precious months and years   5
    Of youth had[2] passed, that speed so fast,
    Before we found it out at last,
The world, and what it fears?

II

How much of priceless life were spent
    With men that every virtue decks,   10
    And women models of their sex,
Society's true ornament,—
Ere we dared wander, nights like this,
    Thro' wind and rain, and watch the Seine,
    And feel the Boulevart[3] break again   15
To warmth and light and bliss?

III

I know! the world proscribes not love;
    Allows my finger to caress
    Your lips' contour and downiness,
Provided it supply a glove.   20
    The world's good word!—the Institute![4]
    Guizot receives Montalembert![5]
    Eh? Down the court three lampions[6] flare:
Put forward your best foot!

ca. 1852

A Light[1] Woman

I

So far as our story approaches the end,
    Which do you pity the most of us three?—
My friend, or the mistress of my friend
    With her wanton eyes, or me?

("battle cry"); Browning erroneously took it to be some sort of horn. The legendary Roland, badly outnumbered by the Saracens at Roncesvalles, thrice sounded his horn "Olivant" to communicate his plight to Charlemagne. The blasts were so loud the birds fell dead and the Saracens drew back in terror. After the battle Roland died.
1. The poem is set in Paris, 1852; the speaker is a man.
2. Would have.
3. Boulevard.
4. The lovers are approaching the august Institut de France, the agency governing France's learned societies, including (since 1795) the intellectually conservative Académie Française.
5. On February 5, 1852, the statesman François Guizot (1787–1874) was required by custom to deliver a speech welcoming his bitter opponent, the historian Charles Montalembert (1810–70) into the Académie Française upon the latter's election. Browning attended the ceremony.
6. Lamps.
1. The word suggests both frivolousness and sexual promiscuity.

II

My friend was already too good to lose,   5
    And seemed in the way of improvement yet,
When she crossed his path with her hunting-noose
    And over him drew her net.

III

When I saw him tangled in her toils,
    A shame, said I, if she adds just him   10
To her nine-and-ninety other spoils,
    The hundredth for a whim!

IV

And before my friend be wholly hers,
    How easy to prove to him, I said,
An eagle's the game her pride prefers,   15
    Though she snaps at a wren instead!

V

So, I gave her eyes my own eyes to take,
    My hand sought hers as in earnest need,
And round she turned for my noble sake,
    And gave me herself indeed.   20

VI

The eagle am I, with my fame in the world,
    The wren is he, with his maiden face.
—You look away and your lip is curled?
    Patience, a moment's space!

VII

For see, my friend goes shaking and white;   25
    He eyes me as the basilisk:[2]
I have turned, it appears, his day to night,
    Eclipsing his sun's disk.

VIII

And I did it, he thinks, as a very thief:
    "Though I love her—that, he comprehends—   30
One should master one's passions, (love, in chief)
    And be loyal to one's friends!"

IX

And she,—she lies in my hand as tame
    As a pear late basking over a wall;
Just a touch to try and off it came;   35
    'T is mine,—can I let it fall?

X

With no mind to eat it, that's the worst!
    Were it thrown in the road, would the case assist?
'T was quenching a dozen blue-flies' thirst
    When I gave its stalk a twist.   40

XI

And I,—what I seem to my friend, you see:
    What I soon shall seem to his love, you guess:

---

2. Fabulous reptile, supposed capable of killing its victims with a stare.

What I seem to myself, do you ask of me?
    No hero, I confess.

XII

'T is an awkward thing to play with souls,   45
    And matter enough to save one's own:
Yet think of my friend, and the burning coals
    He played with for bits of stone!

XIII

One likes to show the truth for the truth;
    That the woman was light is very true: 50
Bút suppose she says,—Never mind that youth!
    What wrong have I done to you?

XIV

Well, any how, here the story stays,
    So far at least as I understand;
And, Robert Browning, you writer of plays,[3]   55
    Here's a subject made to your hand!

The Statue and the Bust[1]

There's a palace in Florence, the world knows well,
And a statue watches it from the square,
And this story of both do our townsmen tell.

Ages ago, a lady there,
At the farthest window facing the East   5
Asked, "Who rides by with the royal air?"

The bridesmaids' prattle around her ceased;
She leaned forth, one on either hand;
They saw how the blush of the bride increased—

They felt by its beats her heart expand—   10
As one at each ear and both in a breath
Whispered, "The Great-Duke Ferdinand."

That self-same instant, underneath,
The Duke rode past in his idle way,
Empty and fine like a swordless sheath.   15

Gay he rode, with a friend as gay,
Till he threw his head back—"Who is she?"
—"A bride the Riccardi brings home to-day."

3. Wry reference to Browning's lack of success as a dramatist.
1. Here Browning retells an old Florentine legend, imaginatively adding a della Robbia bust of the lady to the "empty shrine" (line 189) faced by the equestrian statue of the Grand-Duke Ferdinand de' Medici (1549–1609), ruler of Florence 1587–1609. The statue, by Giovanni da Bologna (John of Douai, 1529–1608) stands in the Piazza della Annunziata. The palace of the first line, called the Riccardi-Manelli palace, was not actually acquired by the Riccardi (the family into which the lady married) until 1800.
    The rhyme scheme of the poem, though not the meter, is that of *terza rima*.

Hair in heaps lay heavily
Over a pale brow spirit-pure—   20
Carved like the heart of the coal-black tree,

Crisped like a war-steed's encolure[2]—
And vainly sought to dissemble[3] her eyes
Of the blackest black our eyes endure.

And lo, a blade for a knight's emprise   25
Filled the fine empty sheath of a man,—
The Duke grew straightway brave and wise.

He looked at her, as a lover can;
She looked at him, as one who awakes:
The past was a sleep, and her life began.   30

Now, love so ordered for both their sakes,
A feast was held that selfsame night
In the pile[4] which the mighty shadow makes.

(For Via Larga is three-parts light,
But the palace overshadows one,   35
Because of a crime which may God requite!

To Florence and God the wrong was done,
Through the first republic's murder there
By Cosimo and his cursed son.)[5]

The Duke (with the statue's face in the square)   40
Turned in the midst of his multitude
At the bright approach of the bridal pair.

Face to face the lovers stood
A single minute and no more,
While the bridgroom bent as a man subdued—   45

Bowed till his bonnet brushed the floor—
For the Duke on the lady a kiss conferred,
As the courtly custom was of yore.

In a minute can lovers exchange a word?
If a word did pass, which I do not think,   50
Only one out of the thousand heard.

That was the bridegroom. At day's brink
He and his bride were alone at last
In a bedchamber by a taper's blink.

Calmly he said that her lot was cast,   55

2. Curled like a war horse's mane.
3. Simulate.
4. The Medici (later Medici-Riccardi) palace in the Via Larga, now Via Cavour. Browning apparently did not know this palace was closed throughout Ferdinand's lifetime. (The editor wishes to thank Professor Allan Dooley for information on the palaces mentioned.)
5. Florence was a model republic until it came under the absolute rule of the Medici, beginning with Cosimo the Elder (1389–1464).

That the door she had passed was shut on her
Till the final catafalk[6] repassed.

The world meanwhile, its noise and stir,
Through a certain window facing the East,
She could watch like a convent's chronicler.   60

Since passing the door might lead to a feast,
And a feast might lead to so much beside,
He, of many evils, chose the least.

"Freely I choose too," said the bride—
"Your window and its world suffice,"   65
Replied the tongue, while the heart replied—

"If I spend the night with that devil twice,
May his window serve as my loop of hell
Whence a damned soul looks on paradise!

"I fly to the Duke who loves me well,   70
Sit by his side and laugh at sorrow
Ere I count another ave-bell.[7]

"'T is only the coat of a page to borrow,
And tie my hair in a horse-boy's trim,
And I save my soul—but not to-morrow"—   75

(She checked herself and her eye grew dim)
"My father tarries to bless my state:
I must keep it one day more for him.

"Is one day more so long to wait?
Moreover the Duke rides past, I know;   80
We shall see each other, sure as fate."

She turned on her side and slept. Just so!
So we resolve on a thing and sleep:
So did the lady, ages ago.

That night the Duke said, "Dear or cheap   85
As the cost of this cup of bliss may prove
To body or soul, I will drain it deep."

And on the morrow, bold with love,
He beckoned the bridegroom (close on call,
As his duty bade, by the Duke's alcove)   90

And smiled " 'T was a very funeral,
Your lady will think, this feast of ours,—
A shame to efface, whate'er befall!

"What if we break from the Arno[8] bowers,

---

6. Carriage on which a coffin rests during a state funeral.

7. Prayer bell rung morning and evening.
8. River flowing through Florence.

And try if Petraja,[9] cool and green,   95
Cure last night's fault with this morning's flowers?"

The bridegroom, not a thought to be seen
On his steady brow and quiet mouth,
Said, "Too much favour for me so mean!

"But, alas! my lady leaves[1] the South;   100
Each wind that comes from the Apennine[2]
Is a menace to her tender youth:

"Nor a way exists, the wise opine,
If she quits her palace twice this year,
To avert the flower of life's decline."   105

Quoth the Duke, "A sage and a kindly fear.
Moreover Petraja is cold this spring:
Be our feast to-night as usual here!"

And then to himself—"Which night shall bring
Thy bride to her lover's embraces, fool—   110
Or I am the fool, and thou art the king!

"Yet my passion must wait a night, nor cool—
For to-night the Envoy arrives from France[3]
Whose heart I unlock with thyself, my tool.

"I need thee still and might miss perchance.   115
To-day is not wholly lost, beside,
With its hope of my lady's countenance:

"For I ride—what should I do but ride?
And passing her palace, if I list,[4]
May glance at its window—well betide!"   120

So said, so done: nor the lady missed
One ray that broke from the ardent brow,
Nor a curl of the lips where the spirit kissed.

Be sure that each renewed the vow,
No morrow's sun should arise and set   125
And leave them then as it left them now.

But next day passed, and next day yet,
With still fresh cause to wait one day more
Ere each leaped over the parapet.

And still, as love's brief morning wore,   130
With a gentle start, half smile, half sigh,
They found love not as it seemed before.

9. Suburb of Florence on the southern slopes of Mount Morello.
1. Comes from.
2. Mountain range north of Florence.

3. Ferdinand wanted France as ally to offset Spanish influence in Italy.
4. Choose.

They thought it would work infallibly,
But not in despite of heaven and earth:
The rose would blow[5] when the storm passed by.   135

Meantime they could profit in winter's dearth
By store of fruits that supplant the rose:
The world and its ways have a certain worth:

And to press a point while these oppose
Were simple policy; better wait: 140
We lose no friends and we gain no foes.

Meantime, worse fates than a lover's fate,
Who daily may ride and pass and look
Where his lady watches behind the grate!

And she—she watched the square like a book   145
Holding one picture and only one,
Which daily to find she undertook:

When the picture was reached the book was done,
And she turned from the picture at night to scheme
Of tearing it out for herself next sun.   150

So weeks grew months, years; gleam by gleam
The glory dropped from their youth and love,
And both perceived they had dreamed a dream;

Which hovered as dreams do, still above:
But who can take a dream for a truth?   155
Oh, hide our eyes from the next remove!

One day as the lady saw her youth
Depart, and the silver thread that streaked
Her hair, and, worn by the serpent's tooth,

The brow so puckered, the chin so peaked,—   160
And wondered who the woman was,
Hollow-eyed and haggard-cheeked,

Fronting her silent in the glass—
"Summon here," she suddenly said,
"Before the rest of my old self pass,   165

"Him, the Carver, a hand to aid,
Who fashions the clay no love will change,
And fixes a beauty never to fade.

"Let Robbia's[6] craft so apt and strange
Arrest the remains of young and fair,   170
And rivet them while the seasons range.

"Make me a face on the window there,
Waiting as ever, mute the while,
My love to pass below in the square!

5. Burst into flower.
6. Luca della Robbia (1399–1482), head of a family workshop famed for its glazed terra cotta objects.

"And let me think that it may beguile   175
Dreary days which the dead must spend
Down in their darkness under the aisle,

"To say, 'What matters it at the end?
I did no more while my heart was warm
Than does that image, my pale-faced friend.'   180

"Where is the use of the lip's red charm,
The heaven of hair, the pride of the brow,
And the blood that blues the inside arm—

"Unless we turn, as the soul knows how,
The earthly gift to an end divine?   185
A lady of clay is as good, I trow."

But long ere Robbia's cornice, fine,
With flowers and fruits which leaves enlace,
Was set where now is the empty shrine—

(And, leaning out of a bright blue space,   190
As a ghost might lean from a chink of sky,
The passionate pale lady's face—

Eyeing ever, with earnest eye
And quick-turned neck at its breathless stretch,
Some one who ever is passing by—)   195

The Duke had sighed like the simplest wretch
In Florence, "Youth—my dream escapes!
Will its record stay?" And he bade them fetch

Some subtle moulder of brazen shapes—
"Can the soul, the will, die out of a man   200
Ere his body find the grave that gapes?

"John of Douay shall effect my plan,
Set me on horseback here aloft,
Alive, as the crafty sculptor can,

"In the very square I have crossed so oft: 205
That men may admire, when future suns
Shall touch the eyes to a purpose soft,

"While the mouth and the brow stay brave in bronze—
Admire and say, 'When he was alive
How he would take his pleasure once!'   210

"And it shall go hard but I contrive
To listen the while, and laugh in my tomb
At idleness which aspires to strive."

———————————

So! While these wait the trump of doom,
How do their spirits pass, I wonder,   215
Nights and days in the narrow room?

Still, I suppose, they sit and ponder
What a gift life was, ages ago,
Six steps out of the chapel yonder.

Only they see not God, I know,   220
Nor all that chivalry of his,
The soldier-saints who, row on row,

Burn upward each to his point of bliss—
Since, the end of life being manifest,
He had burned his way thro' the world to this.   225

I hear you reproach, "But delay was best,
For their end was a crime."—Oh, a crime will do
As well, I reply, to serve for a test,

As a virtue golden through and through,
Sufficient to vindicate itself   230
And prove its worth at a moment's view!

Must a game be played for the sake of pelf?[7]
Where a button goes, 't were an epigram
To offer the stamp of the very Guelph.[8]

The true has no value beyond the sham: 235
As well the counter as coin, I submit,
When your table's a hat, and your prize a dram.[9]

Stake your counter as boldly every whit,
Venture as warily, use the same skill,
Do your best, whether winning or losing it,   240

If you choose to play!—is my principle.
Let a man contend to the uttermost
For his life's set prize, be it what it will!

The counter our lovers staked was lost
As surely as if it were lawful coin: 245
And the sin I impute to each frustrate ghost

Is—the unlit lamp and the ungirt loin,[1]
Though the end in sight was a vice,[2] I say.
You of the virtue (we issue join)[3]
How strive you? *De te, fabula.*[4]   250

7. Money.
8. It would be a joke ("epigram") to play the game with silver coins ("stamp of the very Guelph") if any sort of counter would do. The Guelphs were a powerful faction in medieval Italy.
9. Drink.
1. Luke 12: 35–36: "Let your loins be girded about, and your lights burning; and ye yourselves like unto men that wait for their lord, when he will return from the wedding. . . ." The duke and the lady, Browning implies, are spiritually indifferent and thus unprepared to render their account before Christ.
2. "Crime" in first edition.
3. Take issue with, dispute.
4. *Quid rides? Mutato nomine de te / fabula narratur*: "Why do you laugh? Change the name, and the tale is about you" (Horace, *Satires*, I.i. 69–70).

How It Strikes a Contemporary[1]

I only knew one poet in my life:
And this, or something like it, was his way.

    You saw go up and down Valladolid,[2]
A man of mark, to know next time you saw.
His very serviceable suit of black   5
Was courtly once and conscientious still,
And many might have worn it, though none did:
The cloak, that somewhat shone and showed the threads,
Had purpose, and the ruff, significance.
He walked and tapped the pavement with his cane,   10
Scenting the world, looking it full in face,
An old dog, bald and blindish, at his heels.
They turned up, now, the alley by the church,
That leads nowhither; now, they breathed themselves
On the main promenade just at the wrong time: 15
You'd come upon his scrutinizing hat,
Making a peaked shade blacker than itself
Against the single window spared some house
Intact yet with its mouldered Moorish work,—
Or else surprise the ferrel[3] of his stick   20
Trying the mortar's temper 'tween the chinks
Of some new shop a-building, French and fine.
He stood and watched the cobbler at his trade,
The man who slices lemons into drink,
The coffee-roaster's brazier, and the boys   25
That volunteer to help him turn its winch.
He glanced o'er books on stalls with half an eye,
And fly-leaf ballads[4] on the vendor's string,
And broad-edge bold-print posters by the wall.
He took such cognizance of men and things,   30
If any beat a horse, you felt he saw;
If any cursed a woman, he took note;
Yet stared at nobody,—you stared at him,
And found, less to your pleasure than surprise,
He seemed to know you and expect as much.   35

1. May be a product of Browning's reflections on poetry and the poet while writing the *Essay on Shelley* (published 1852), particularly in defining the "subjective" poet; see the excerpt from the *Essay* in this edition. Cf. his letter of 1855 to John Ruskin: "A poet's affair is with God, to whom he is accountable, and of whom is his reward . . ." (W. G. Collingwood, *Life and Work of John Ruskin* [London, 1893] I: 234). After first publication in 1855, Browning removed the capitalization in all pronoun references to "our Lord the King"; evidently he wanted to make the allegory less obvious. Browning never visited Spain; the setting at Valladolid and other details may have been drawn from Lesage's *Gil Blas*, which the poet had read in 1835 (DeVane, pp. 236–37).
2. Town in north-central Spain, once the Castilian royal seat.
3. Ferrule, or metal tip.
4. Broadsides, popular verse printed on large folio sheets.

So, next time that a neighbour's tongue was loosed,
It marked the shameful and notorious fact,
We had among us, not so much a spy,
As a recording chief-inquisitor,
The town's true master if the town but knew![5]   40
We merely kept a governor for form,
While this man walked about and took account
Of all thought, said and acted, then went home,
And wrote it fully to our Lord the King
Who has an itch to know things, he knows why,   45
And reads them in his bedroom of a night.
Oh, you might smile! there wanted not a touch,
A tang of . . . well, it was not wholly ease
As back into your mind the man's look came.
Stricken in years a little,—such a brow   50
His eyes had to live under!—clear as flint
On either side the formidable nose
Curved, cut and coloured like an eagle's claw.
Had he to do with A.'s surprising fate?
When altogether old B. disappeared   55
And young C. got his mistress,—was't our friend,
His letter to the King, that did it all?
What paid the bloodless man for so much pains?
Our Lord the King has favourites manifold,
And shifts his ministry some once a month;   60
Our city gets new governors at whiles,—
But never word or sign, that I could hear,
Notified to this man about the streets
The King's approval of those letters conned
The last thing duly at the dead of night.   65
Did the man love his office? Frowned our Lord,
Exhorting when none heard—"Beseech me not!
Too far above my people,—beneath me!
I set the watch,—how should the people know?
Forget them, keep me all the more in mind!"   70
Was some such understanding 'twixt the two?

  I found no truth in one report at least—
That if you tracked him to his home, down lanes
Beyond the Jewry,[6] and as clean to pace,
You found he ate his supper in a room   75
Blazing with lights, four Titians[7] on the wall,
And twenty naked girls to change his plate!
Poor man, he lived another kind of life
In that new stuccoed third house by the bridge,
Fresh-painted, rather smart than otherwise!   80

5. Cf. the final sentence of Shelley's *A Defence of Poetry* (1840): "Poets are the unacknowledged legislators of the world."

6. Ghetto, or Jewish quarter.
7. Paintings by the Italian master Titian (d. 1576), famed for his glowing colors.

The whole street might o'erlook him as he sat,
Leg crossing leg, one foot on the dog's back,
Playing a decent cribbage with his maid
(Jacynth, you're sure her name was) o'er the cheese
And fruit, three red halves of starved winter-pears,   85
Or treat of radishes in April. Nine,
Ten, struck the church clock, straight to bed went he.

My father, like the man of sense he was,
Would point him out to me a dozen times;
"'St—'St," he'd whisper, "the Corregidor!"[8]   90
I had been used to think that personage
Was one with lacquered breeches, lustrous belt,
And feathers like a forest in his hat,
Who blew a trumpet and proclaimed the news,
Announced the bull-fights, gave each church its turn,   95
And memorized[9] the miracle in vogue!
He had a great observance from us boys;[1]
We were in error; that was not the man.

I'd like now, yet had haply been afraid,
To have just looked, when this man came to die,   100
And seen who lined the clean gay garret-sides
And stood about the neat low truckle-bed
With the heavenly manner of relieving guard.[2]
Here had been, mark, the general-in-chief,
Thro' a whole campaign of the world's life and death,   105
Doing the King's work all the dim day long,
In his old coat and up to knees in mud,
Smoked like a herring, dining on a crust,—
And, now the day was won, relieved at once!
No further show or need for that old coat,   110
You are sure, for one thing! Bless us, all the while
How sprucely we are dressed out, you and I!
A second, and the angels alter that.
Well, I could never write a verse,—could you?
Let's to the Prado[3] and make the most of time.   115

ca. 1852

The Last Ride Together

I

I said—Then, dearest, since 't is so,
Since now at length my fate I know,
Since nothing all my love avails,
Since all, my life seemed meant for, fails,
Since this was written and needs must be—   5

8. Chief magistrate.
9. Celebrated.
1. I.e., the boys paid him due reverence.
2. I.e., angels would come to relieve him of his duties.
3. The town's promenade.

My whole heart rises up to bless
Your name in pride and thankfulness!
Take back the hope you gave,—I claim
Only a memory of the same,
—And this beside, if you will not blame,   10
    Your leave for one more last ride with me.

II

My mistress bent[1] that brow of hers;
Those deep dark eyes where pride demurs
When pity would be softening through,
Fixed me a breathing-while or two   15
    With life or death in the balance: right!
The blood replenished me again;
My last thought was at least not vain:
I and my mistress, side by side
Shall be together, breathe and ride,   20
So, one day more am I deified.
    Who knows but the world may end to-night?

III

Hush! if you saw some western cloud
All billowy-bosomed, over-bowed
By many benedictions—sun's   25
And moon's and evening-star's at once—
    And so, you, looking and loving best,
Conscious grew, your passion drew
Cloud, sunset, moonrise, star-shine too,
Down on you, near and yet more near,   30
Till flesh must fade for heaven was here!—
Thus leant she and lingered—joy and fear!
    Thus lay she a moment on my breast.

IV

Then we began to ride. My soul
Smoothed itself out, a long-cramped scroll   35
Freshening and fluttering in the wind.
Past hopes already lay behind.
    What need to strive with a life awry?
Had I said that, had I done this,
So might I gain, so might I miss.   40
Might she have loved me? just as well
She might have hated, who can tell!
Where had I been now if the worst befell?
    And here we are riding, she and I.

V

Fail I alone, in words and deeds?   45
Why, all men strive and who succeeds?
We rode; it seemed my spirit flew,
Saw other regions, cities new,
    As the world rushed by on either side.
I thought,—All labour, yet no less   50

1. Inclined toward him.

Bear up beneath their unsuccess.
Look at the end of work, contrast
The petty done, the undone vast,
This present of theirs with the hopeful past!
    I hoped she would love me; here we ride.　　55

VI

What hand and brain went ever paired?
What heart alike conceived and dared?
What act proved all its thought had been?
What will but felt the fleshly screen?
    We ride and I see her bosom heave.　　60
There's many a crown for who can reach.
Ten lines, a statesman's life in each!
The flag stuck on a heap of bones,
A soldier's doing! what atones?
They scratch his name on the Abbey-stones.[2]　　65
    My riding is better, by their leave.

VII

What does it all mean, poet? Well,
Your brains beat into rhythm, you tell
What we felt only; you expressed
You hold things beautiful the best,　　70
    And pace them in rhyme so, side by side.
'T is something, nay 't is much: but then,
Have you yourself what's best for men?
Are you—poor, sick, old ere your time—
Nearer one whit your own sublime　　75
Than we who never have turned a rhyme?
    Sing, riding's a joy! For me, I ride.

VIII

And you, great sculptor—so, you gave
A score of years to Art, her slave,
And that's your Venus, whence we turn　　80
To yonder girl that fords the burn![3]
    You acquiesce, and shall I repine?
What, man of music, you grown grey
With notes and nothing else to say,
Is this your sole praise from a friend,　　85
"Greatly his opera's strains intend,
But in music we know how fashions end!"[4]
    I gave my youth; but we ride, in fine.[5]

IX

Who knows what's fit for us? Had fate
Proposed bliss here should sublimate[6]　　90

---

2. Honor him with burial in Westminster Abbey.
3. Wades across the creek.
4. Writing to Elizabeth Barrett, Browning cites a "startling axiom" of Claude Le Jeune: " 'In Music, the Beau Idéal changes every thirty years'—well, is not that *true*? The *Idea*, mind, changes,—the general standard . . .—next hundred years, who will be the Rossini?" (March 7, 1846; Kintner, I.523).
5. In short.
6. Elevate.

My being—had I signed the bond—
Still one must lead some life beyond,
   Have a bliss to die with, dim-descried.
This foot once planted on the goal,
This glory-garland round my soul,   95
Could I descry such? Try and test!
I sink back shuddering from the quest.
Earth being so good, would heaven seem best?
   Now, heaven and she are beyond this ride.

X

And yet—she has not spoke so long!   100
What if heaven be that, fair and strong
At life's best, with our eyes upturned
Whither life's flower is first discerned,
   We, fixed so, ever should so abide?
What if we still ride on, we two   105
With life for ever old yet new,
Changed not in kind but in degree,
The instant made eternity,—
And heaven just prove that I and she
   Ride, ride together, for ever ride?   110

Master Hugues of Saxe-Gotha

I

Hist, but a word, fair and soft!
   Forth and be judged, Master Hugues!
Answer the question I've put you so oft:
   What do you mean by your mountainous fugues?[1]
See, we're alone in the loft,—   5

II

I, the poor organist here,
   Hugues, the composer of note,
Dead though, and done with, this many a year:
   Let's have a colloquy, something to quote,
Make the world prick up its ear!   10

III

See, the church empties apace:
   Fast they extinguish the lights.
Hallo there, sacristan![2] Five minutes' grace!
   Here's a crank pedal wants setting to rights,
Baulks one of holding the base.[3]   15

1. The fugue is a complicated musical form in contrapuntal style based on a short melody, the subject or theme, which is stated at the beginning by one "voice" and then taken up by the other voices in close succession. The form was freed and perfected by J. S. Bach (1685–1750), born in the duchy of Saxe-Gotha in central Germany. Browning however said in 1887 that the imaginary Hugues was not the "glorious Bach" but "one of the dry-as-dust imitators who would elaborate some such subject as [a five-note phrase] for a dozen pages together" (H. E. Greene, *PMLA,* 62 [1947], 1098).
2. Church custodian.
3. Prevents my playing the bass properly.

IV

See, our huge house of the sounds,[4]
    Hushing its hundreds at once,
Bids the last loiterer back to his bounds!
    —O you may challenge them, not a response
Get the church-saints on their rounds!   20

V

(Saints go their rounds, who shall doubt?
    —March, with the moon to admire,
Up nave, down chancel, turn transept about,
    Supervise all betwixt pavement and spire,
Put rats and mice to the rout—   25

VI

Aloys and Jurien and Just—[5]
    Order things back to their place,
Have a sharp eye lest the candlesticks rust,
    Rub the church-plate, darn the sacrament-lace,
Clear the desk-velvet of dust.)   30

VII

Here's your book, younger folks shelve!
    Played I not off-hand and runningly,
Just now, your masterpiece, hard number twelve?
    Here's what should strike, could one handle it cunningly:
Help the axe, give it a helve![6]   35

VIII

Page after page as I played,
    Every bar's rest, where one wipes
Sweat from one's brow, I looked up and surveyed,
    O'er my three claviers,[7] yon forest of pipes
Whence you still peeped in the shade.   40

IX

Sure you were wishful to speak?
    You, with brow ruled like a score,
Yes, and eyes buried in pits on each cheek,
    Like two great breves,[8] as they wrote them of yore,
Each side that bar,[9] your straight beak!   45

X

Sure you said—"Good, the mere notes!
    Still, couldst thou take my intent,
Know what procured me our Company's votes—[1]
    A master were lauded and sciolists shent,[2]
Parted the sheep from the goats!"   50

4. The organ.
5. The "church-saints" of line 20.
6. Handle. I.e., if I could grasp your purpose, I could play your fugue better.
7. Here, keyboards or "manuals."
8. Old note value originally the shortest in use (Latin *brevis*, "short"), later the longest. Before 1450 it was written as a black square.
9. Vertical line marking a division in music.
1. I.e., why I was voted a "master" by the town's corporation ("Company") in a local competition.
2. Pretenders to knowledge disgraced.

XI

Well then, speak up, never flinch!
    Quick, ere my candle's a snuff[3]
—Burnt, do you see? to its uttermost inch—
    I believe in you, but that's not enough:
Give my conviction a clinch!   55

XII

First you deliver your phrase[4]
    —Nothing propound, that I see,
Fit in itself for much blame or much praise—
    Answered no less, where no answer needs be:
Off start the Two on their ways.   60

XIII

Straight must a Third interpose,
    Volunteer needlessly help;
In strikes a Fourth, a Fifth thrusts in his nose,
    So the cry's open, the kennel's a-yelp,
Argument's hot to the close.   65

XIV

One dissertates, he is candid;
    Two must discept,[5]—has distinguished;
Three helps the couple, if ever yet man did;
    Four protests; Five makes a dart at the thing wished:
Back to One, goes the case bandied.   70

XV

One says his say with a difference;
    More of expounding, explaining!
All now is wrangle, abuse, and vociferance;
    Now there's a truce, all's subdued, self-restraining:
Five, though, stands out all the stiffer hence.   75

XVI

One is incisive, corrosive;
    Two retorts, nettled, curt, crepitant;[6]
Three makes rejoinder, expansive, explosive;
    Four overbears them all, strident and strepitant:[7]
Five . . . O Danaides, O Sieve![8]   80

XVII

Now, they ply axes and crowbars;
    Now, they prick pins at a tissue
Fine as a skein of the casuist Escobar's[9]
    Worked on the bone of a lie. To what issue?
Where is our gain at the Two-bars?[1]   85

---

3. Charred wick.
4. Subject of fugue, "answered" by a second voice.
5. Disagree.
6. Crackling.
7. Boisterous.
8. The daughters of Danaüs king of Argos, forced to marry, killed their hus-bands. Condemned in Hades to keep filling perforated water-jars, they are emblematic of futile labor.
9. Escobar y Mendoza (1589–1669), theologian noted for subtle argumentation on moral issues.
1. Double vertical bar marking end of a section or whole piece of music.

XVIII

Est fuga, volvitur rota.[2]
    On we drift: where looms the dim port?
One, Two, Three, Four, Five, contribute their quota;
    Something is gained, if one caught but the import—
Show it us, Hugues of Saxe-Gotha!   90

XIX

What with affirming, denying,
    Holding, risposting, subjoining,[3]
All's like . . . it's like . . . for an instance I'm trying . . .
    There! See our roof, its gilt moulding and groining[4]
Under those spider-webs[5] lying!   95

XX

So your fugue broadens and thickens,
    Greatens and deepens and lengthens,
Till we exclaim—"But where's music, the dickens?
    Blot ye the gold, while your spider-web strengthens
—Blacked to the stoutest of tickens?"[6]   100

XXI

I for man's effort am zealous:
    Prove me such censure unfounded!
Seems it surprising a lover grows jealous—
    Hopes 't was for something, his organ-pipes sounded,
Tiring three boys at the bellows?   105

XXII

Is it your moral of Life?
    Such a web, simple and subtle,
Weave we on earth here in impotent strife,
    Backward and forward each throwing his shuttle,
Death ending all with a knife?   110

XXIII

Over our heads truth and nature—
    Still our life's zigzags and dodges,
Ins and outs, weaving a new legislature—
    God's gold just shining its last where that lodges,
Palled beneath man's usurpature.   115

XXIV

So we o'ershroud stars and roses,
    Cherub and trophy and garland;
Nothing grow something which quietly closes
    Heaven's earnest eye: not a glimpse of the far land
Gets through our comments and glozes.[7]   120

2. "There is a flight, the wheel turns." Cf. Ovid, *Metamorphoses*, IV. 461: *Volvitur Ixion et se sequiturque fugitique*: "There whirls Ixion on his wheel, both following himself and fleeing, all in one."
3. Retorting and adding.
4. Ribs covering the meeting of two intersecting vaults of a roof.
5. The spider's web as symbol of tiresome disputation may derive from Book I of Bacon's *Advancement of Learning* (1605), in which the medieval schoolmen are characterized as spiders who spin out "cobwebs of learning" without "substance and profit."
6. Ticking, material for bedding.
7. Glosses, interpretations.

XXV

Ah but traditions, inventions,
  (Say we and make up a visage)
So many men with such various intentions,
  Down the past ages, must know more than this age!
Leave we the web its dimensions!   125

XXVI

Who thinks Hugues wrote for the deaf,
  Proved a mere mountain in labour?[8]
Better submit; try again; what's the clef?
  'Faith, 't is no trifle for pipe and for tabor[9]—
Four flats, the minor in F.[1]   130

XXVII

Friend, your fugue taxes the finger:
  Learning it once, who would lose it?
Yet all the while a misgiving will linger,
  Truth's golden o'er us although we refuse it—
Nature, thro' cobwebs we string her.   135

XXVIII

Hugues! I advise *meâ poenâ*[2]
  (Counterpoint glares like a Gorgon)[3]
Bid One, Two, Three, Four, Five, clear the arena!
  Say the word, straight I unstop the full-organ,
Blare out the *mode Palestrina*.[4]   140

XXIX

While in the roof, if I'm right there,
  . . . Lo you, the wick in the socket!
Hallo, you sacristan, show us a light there!
  Down it dips, gone like a rocket.
What, you want, do you, to come unawares,   145
Sweeping the church up for first morning-prayers,
And find a poor devil has ended his cares
At the foot of your rotten-runged rat-riddled stairs?
  Do I carry the moon in my pocket?[5]

ca. 1853

Bishop Blougram's Apology

"Apology" in the title means a formal defense of one's beliefs or actions. Blougram is a fictitious Roman Catholic bishop speaking in the presence of a hostile agnostic journalist intent on exposing him as a hypocrite. The setting is London in the early 1850s.

8. "The mountains are in labor—they will give birth to a ridiculous mouse" (Horace, *Ars Poetica*, 139).
9. Small drum.
1. A difficult key.
2. At the risk of my punishment.
3. Female monster who could turn anyone looking at her to stone.
4. In the relatively severe, simple style of the school of Giovanni Pierluigi da Palestrina (ca. 1525–94), composer of religious music.
5. As R. D. Altick has shown, the line comes from Shakespeare's *Cymbeline* (III.i.42–44): "If Caesar can hide the sun from us with a blanket, or put the moon in his pocket, we will pay him tribute for light. . . ."

"Bishop Blougram's Apology" was designedly a poem for the times. In 1850 Pope Pius IX had created a furor in England by reestablishing there the Roman Catholic hierarchy, headed by the newly installed Archbishop of Westminster, Cardinal N.P.S. Wiseman (1802–65). The prime minister wrote a scathing open letter to the Bishop of Durham (November 4, 1850), declaring that "no foreign prince or potentate will be at liberty to fasten his fetters upon a nation which has so long and so nobly vindicated its right to freedom of opinion, civil, political, and religious." When "Blougram" appeared in 1855 it was obvious, especially to Catholics, that Browning had the worldly and sophisticated Wiseman in mind as the original of the Bishop; later the poet admitted as much. But he may also have drawn from the character of the brilliant controversialist John Henry Newman (1801–90), leader of the "Oxford Movement" until his conversion to Roman Catholicism in 1845. These Anglican conservatives voiced their opinions on a wide range of ecclesiastical issues in a pamphlet series, *Tracts for the Times* (1833–41)—hence their other name, "Tractarians." In the final number of the series, "Tract XC," Newman argued that the Thirty-Nine Articles of the Anglican church conflicted in no fundamental way with Roman Catholic doctrine. The episode of "Tract XC," according to C. F. Harrold, "gave a very unflattering impression of Newman's mind and for a long time the only conception of him in the mind of the English middle-class was that of a subtle-minded ecclesiastical hair-splitter and special pleader" (*J. H. Newman* [1945], p. 43). In the process of conversion, Newman had worked out a new, unorthodox, and rhetorically sophisticated form of apologetic. At the height of the "No-Popery" panic in England, he delivered two sets of apologetic lectures: *The Difficulties of Anglicans* (1850) and *The Present Position of Catholics in England* (1851). The intellectual side of this most conspicuous Catholic spokesman probably figured, however indirectly, in the composite portrait that is Browning's Blougram.

No more wine? then we'll push back chairs and talk.
A final glass for me, though: cool, i' faith!
We ought to have our Abbey[1] back, you see.
It's different, preaching in basilicas,[2]
And doing duty in some masterpiece   5
Like this of brother Pugin's, bless his heart!
I doubt if they're half baked, those chalk rosettes,
Ciphers and stucco-twiddlings everywhere;
It's just like breathing in a lime-kiln: eh?
These hot long ceremonies of our church   10
Cost us a little—oh, they pay the price,
You take me[3]—amply pay it! Now, we'll talk.

1. Westminster Abbey, taken from the Roman Catholic church at the English Reformation.
2. Ancient oblong churches with nave separated from side aisles by rows of columns. Blougram goes on to ridicule the Victorian "Gothic Revival," led by

English architect (and Catholic convert) A. W. N. Pugin (1812–52). Many of Pugin's churches suffered from being executed on a diminished scale, and from the introduction of shams like those named in lines 7–8.
3. Understand.

So, you despise me, Mr. Gigadibs.[4]
No deprecation,—nay, I beg you, sir!
Beside 't is our engagement: don't you know,   15
I promised, if you'd watch a dinner out,
We'd see truth dawn together?—truth that peeps
Over the glasses' edge when dinner's done,
And body gets its sop and holds its noise
And leaves soul free a little. Now's the time: 20
Truth's break of day! You do despise me then.
And if I say, "despise me,"—never fear!
I know you do not in a certain sense—
Not in my arm-chair, for example: here,
I well imagine you respect my place   25
(*Status, entourage,* worldly circumstance)
Quite to its value—very much indeed:
—Are up to the protesting eyes of you
In pride at being seated here for once—
You'll turn it to such capital account!   30
When somebody, through years and years to come,
Hints of the bishop,—names me—that's enough:
"Blougram? I knew him"—(into it you slide)
"Dined with him once, a Corpus Christi Day,[5]
All alone, we two; he's a clever man: 35
And after dinner,—why, the wine you know,—
Oh, there was wine, and good!—what with the wine . . .
'Faith, we began upon all sorts of talk!
He's no bad fellow, Blougram; he had seen
Something of mine he relished, some review: 40
He's quite above their[6] humbug in his heart,
Half-said as much, indeed—the thing's his trade.
I warrant, Blougram's sceptical at times:
How otherwise? I liked him, I confess!"
Che che,[7] my dear sir, as we say at Rome,   45
Don't you protest now! It's fair give and take;
You have had your turn and spoken your home-truths:
The hand's mine now, and here you follow suit.

    Thus much conceded, still the first fact stays—
You do despise me; your ideal of life   50
Is not the bishop's: you would not be I.
You would like better to be Goethe,[8] now,
Or Buonaparte, or, bless me, lower still,
Count D'Orsay,[9]—so you did what you preferred,

---

4. The name may come from British slang. *Gig*: "fool" and *dibs*: "money"; hence a fool who will do anything for money. A hack. (Turner, p. 340n.)
5. Feast honoring the Eucharist, or Lord's Supper.
6. Roman Catholics'.
7. "What, what?" (Italian exclamation of impatience or denial.)
8. Johann Wolfgang von Goethe (1749–1832), eminent German poet and man of letters.
9. Famous dandy, wit, and artist (1801–52), prominent in London society. He was an ardent Bonapartist.

Spoke as you thought, and, as you cannot help,   55
Believed or disbelieved, no matter what,
So long as on that point, whate'er it was,
You loosed your mind, were whole and sole yourself.
—That, my ideal never can include,
Upon that element of truth and worth   60
Never be based! for say they make me Pope—
(They can't[1]—suppose it for our argument!)
Why, there I'm at my tether's end, I've reached
My height, and not a height which pleases you:
An unbelieving Pope won't do, you say.   65
It's like those eerie stories nurses tell,
Of how some actor on a stage played Death,
With pasteboard crown, sham orb and tinselled dart,
And called himself the monarch of the world;
Then, going in the tire-room[2] afterward,   70
Because the play was done, to shift himself,
Got touched upon the sleeve familiarly,
The moment he had shut the closet door,
By Death himself. Thus God might touch a Pope
At unawares, ask what his baubles mean,   75
And whose part he presumed to play just now.
Best be yourself, imperial, plain and true!

So, drawing comfortable breath again,
You weigh and find, whatever more or less
I boast of my ideal realized   80
Is nothing in the balance when opposed
To your ideal, your grand simple life,
Of which you will not realize one jot.
I am much, you are nothing; you would be all,
I would be merely much: you beat me there.   85

No, friend, you do not beat me: hearken why!
The common problem, yours, mine, every one's,
Is—not to fancy what were fair in life
Provided it could be,—but, finding first
What may be, then find how to make it fair   90
Up to our means: a very different thing!
No abstract intellectual plan of life
Quite irrespective of life's plainest laws,
But one, a man, who is man and nothing more,
May lead within a world which (by your leave)   95
Is Rome or London, not Fool's-paradise.
Embellish Rome, idealize away,
Make paradise of London if you can,
You're welcome, nay, you're wise.
                       A simile!

---

1. Since the pontificate of Adrian VI of the Netherlands (1522–23), all popes had been Italian.
2. Dressing room.

We mortals cross the ocean of this world   100
Each in his average cabin of a life;
The best's not big, the worst yields elbow-room.
Now for our six months' voyage—how prepare?
You come on shipboard with a landsman's list
Of things he calls convenient: so they are!   105
An India screen is pretty furniture,
A piano-forte is a fine resource,
All Balzac's[3] novels occupy one shelf,
The new edition fifty volumes long;
And little Greek books, with the funny type   110
They get up well at Leipsic,[4] fill the next:
Go on! slabbed marble, what a bath it makes!
And Parma's pride, the Jerome,[5] let us add!
'T were pleasant could Correggio's fleeting glow
Hang full in face of one where'er one roams,   115
Since he more than the others brings with him
Italy's self,—the marvellous Modenese!—
Yet was not on your list before, perhaps.
—Alas, friend, here's the agent . . . is 't the name?
The captain, or whoever's master here—   120
You see him screw his face up; what's his cry
Ere you set foot on shipboard? "Six feet square!"
If you won't understand what six feet mean,
Compute and purchase stores accordingly—
And if, in pique because he overhauls[6]   125
Your Jerome, piano, bath, you come on board
Bare—why, you cut a figure at the first
While sympathetic landsmen see you off;
Not afterward, when long ere half seas over,[7]
You peep up from your utterly naked boards   130
Into some snug and well-appointed berth,
Like mine for instance (try the cooler jug—
Put back the other, but don't jog the ice!)[8]
And mortified you mutter "Well and good;
He sits enjoying his sea-furniture;   135
'T is stout and proper, and there's store of it:
Though I've the better notion, all agree,
Of fitting rooms up. Hang the carpenter,
Neat ship-shape fixings and contrivances—
I would have brought my Jerome, frame and all!"   140
And meantime you bring nothing: never mind—
You've proved your artist-nature: what you don't
You might bring, so despise me, as I say.

---

3. Honoré de Balzac (1799–1850), prolific French novelist. The new edition of
his complete works (fifty-five volumes)
began publication in 1856.
4. Teubner series of classical texts, published 1849 and after (Turner, 340n.).
5. The St. Jerome at Parma (called *Il*

Giorno or *Day*) is the work of Correggio, the name given Antonio Allegri
(1494–1534).
6. Hauls overboard.
7. Midway.
8. Ice was at that time a luxury in July,
when the interview takes place.

Now come, let's backward to the starting-place.
See my way: we're two college friends, suppose.   145
Prepare together for our voyage, then;
Each note and check the other in his work,—
Here's mine, a bishop's outfit; criticize!
What's wrong? why won't you be a bishop too?

Why first, you don't believe, you don't and can't,   150
(Not statedly, that is, and fixedly
And absolutely and exclusively)
In any revelation called divine.
No dogmas nail your faith; and what remains
But say so, like the honest man you are?   155
First, therefore, overhaul theology!
Nay, I too, not a fool, you please to think,
Must find believing every whit as hard:
And if I do not frankly say as much,
The ugly consequence is clear enough.   160

Now wait, my friend: well, I do not believe—
If you'll accept no faith that is not fixed,
Absolute and exclusive, as you say.
You're wrong—I mean to prove it in due time.
Meanwhile, I know where difficulties lie   165
I could not, cannot solve, nor ever shall,
So give up hope accordingly to solve—
(To you, and over the wine). Our dogmas then
With both of us, though in unlike degree,
Missing full credence—overboard with them!   170
I mean to meet you on your own premise:
Good, there go mine in company with yours!

And now what are we? unbelievers both,
Calm and complete, determinately fixed
To-day, to-morrow and for ever, pray?   175
You'll guarantee me that? Not so, I think!
In no wise! all we've gained is, that belief,
As unbelief before, shakes us by fits,
Confounds us like its predecessor. Where's
The gain? how can we guard our unbelief,   180
Make it bear fruit to us?—the problem here.
Just when we are safest, there's a sunset-touch,
A fancy from a flower-bell, some one's death,
A chorus-ending from Euripides,[9]—
And that's enough for fifty hopes and fears   185
As old and new at once as nature's self,
To rap and knock and enter in our soul,
Take hands and dance there, a fantastic ring,
Round the ancient idol, on his base again,—

9. **Fifth-century B.C. Greek dramatist, Browning's favorite.**

The grand Perhaps![1] We look on helplessly.   190
There the old misgivings, crooked questions are—
This good God,—what he could do, if he would,
Would, if he could—then must have done long since:
If so, when, where and how? some way must be,—
Once feel about, and soon or late you hit   195
Some sense, in which it might be, after all.
Why not, "The Way, the Truth, the Life?"[2]

                           —That way
Over the mountain, which who stands upon
Is apt to doubt if it be meant for a road;
While, if he views it from the waste itself,   200
Up goes the line there, plain from base to brow,
Not vague, mistakeable! what's a break or two
Seen from the unbroken desert either side?
And then (to bring in fresh philosophy)
What if the breaks themselves should prove at last   205
The most consummate of contrivances
To train a man's eye, teach him what is faith?
And so we stumble at truth's very test!
All we have gained then by our unbelief
Is a life of doubt diversifed by faith,   210
For one of faith diversifed by doubt:
We called the chess-board white,—we call it black.

    "Well," you rejoin, "the end's no worse, at least;
We've reason for both colours on the board:
Why not confess then, where I drop the faith   215
And you the doubt, that I'm as right as you?"

    Because, friend, in the next place, this being so,
And both things even,—faith and unbelief
Left to a man's choice,—we'll proceed a step,
Returning to our image, which I like.   220

    A man's choice, yes—but a cabin-passenger's—
The man made for the special life o' the world—
Do you forget him? I remember though!
Consult our ship's conditions and you find
One and but one choice suitable to all;   225
The choice, that you unluckily prefer,
Turning things topsy-turvy—they or it
Going to the ground.[3] Belief or unbelief
Bears upon life, determines its whole course,
Begins at its beginning. See the world   230
Such as it is,—you made it not, nor I;
I mean to take it as it is,—and you,

---

1. Deathbed saying ascribed to Rabelais: *Je vais quérir un grand Peut-Être* ("I go to seek a grand Perhaps").

2. John 14:6 (Christ's self-definition).

3. To defeat.

Not so you'll take it,—though you get nought else.
I know the special kind of life I like,
What suits the most my idiosyncrasy,   235
Brings out the best of me and bears me fruit
In power, peace, pleasantness and length of days.[4]
I find that positive belief does this
For me, and unbelief, no whit of this.
—For you, it does, however?—that, we'll try!   240
'T is clear, I cannot lead my life, at least,
Induce the world to let me peaceably,
Without declaring at the outset, "Friends,
I absolutely and peremptorily
Believe!"—I say, faith is my waking life: 245
One sleeps, indeed, and dreams at intervals,
We know, but waking's the main point with us
And my provision's for life's waking part.
Accordingly, I use heart, head and hand
All day, I build, scheme, study, and make friends;   250
And when night overtakes me, down I lie,
Sleep, dream a little, and get done with it,
The sooner the better, to begin afresh.
What's midnight doubt before the dayspring's faith?
You, the philosopher, that disbelieve,   255
That recognize the night, give dreams their weight—
To be consistent you should keep your bed,
Abstain from healthy acts that prove you man,
For fear you drowse perhaps at unawares!
And certainly at night you'll sleep and dream,   260
Live through the day and bustle as you please.
And so you live to sleep as I to wake,
To unbelieve as I to still believe?
Well, and the common sense o' the world calls you
Bed-ridden,—and its good things come to me.   265
Its estimation, which is half the fight,
That's the first-cabin[5] comfort I secure:
The next . . . but you perceive with half an eye!
Come, come, it's best believing, if we may;
You can't but own that!

                  Next, concede again,   270
If once we choose belief, on all accounts
We can't be too decisive in our faith,[6]
Conclusive and exclusive in its terms,
To suit the world which gives us the good things.
In every man's career are certain points   275
Whereon he dares not be indifferent;

4. Cf. Proverbs 3:16 [on wisdom]: "Length of days is in her right hand; and in her left hand riches and honour."
5. First class.

6. I.e., we dare not appear indecisive or indifferent. Cf. line 276. (The adverb "too" applies to "conclusive" and "exclusive" in the next line as well.)

The world detects him clearly, if he dare,
As baffled at the game, and losing life.
He may care little or he may care much
For riches, honour, pleasure, work, repose,   280
Since various theories of life and life's
Success are extant which might easily
Comport with either estimate of these;
And whoso chooses wealth or poverty,
Labour or quiet, is not judged a fool   285
Because his fellow would choose otherwise:
We let him choose upon his own account
So long as he's consistent with his choice.
But certain points, left wholly to himself,
When once a man has arbitrated on,   290
We say he must succeed there or go hang.
Thus, he should wed the woman he loves most
Or needs most, whatsoe'er the love or need—
For he can't wed twice.[7] Then, he must avouch,
Or follow, at the least, sufficiently,   295
The form of faith his conscience holds the best,
Whate'er the process of conviction was:
For nothing can compensate his mistake
On such a point, the man himself being judge:
He cannot wed twice, nor twice lose his soul.   300

    Well now, there's one great form of Christian faith
I happened to be born in—which to teach
Was given me as I grew up, on all hands,
As best and readiest means of living by;
The same on examination being proved   305
The most pronounced moreover, fixed, precise
And absolute form of faith in the whole world—
Accordingly, most potent of all forms
For working on the world. Observe, my friend!
Such as you know me, I am free to say,   310
I these hard latter days which hamper one,
Myself—by no immoderate exercise
Of intellect and learning, but the tact
To let external forces work for me,
—Bid the street's stones be bread and they are bread;[8]   315
Bid Peter's creed, or rather, Hildebrand's,[9]
Exalt me o'er my fellows in the world
And make my life an ease and joy and pride;
It does so,—which for me's a great point gained,
Who have a soul and body that exact   320

---

7. The Catholic church does not recognize divorce.
8. Ironic echo of Matthew 4:3–4. The devil tempts Jesus, saying, "If thou be the Son of God, command that these stones be made bread."

9. While the creed of Peter is the absolute authority of Christ (Acts 2:36), that of Hildebrand (Pope Gregory VII, 1073–85) was the ascendancy of the Pope over monarchs.

A comfortable care in many ways.
There's power in me and will to dominate
Which I must exercise, they hurt me else:
In many ways I need mankind's respect,
Obedience, and the love that's born of fear: 325
While at the same time, there's a taste I have,
A toy of soul, a titillating thing,
Refuses to digest these dainties crude.
The naked life is gross till clothed upon:
I must take what men offer, with a grace   330
As though I would not, could I help it, take!
An uniform I wear though over-rich—
Something imposed on me, no choice of mine;
No fancy-dress worn for pure fancy's sake
And despicable therefore! now folk kneel   335
And kiss my hand—of course the Church's hand.
Thus I am made, thus life is best for me,
And thus that it should be I have procured;
And thus it could not be another way,
I venture to imagine.

                  You'll reply,   340
So far my choice, no doubt, is a success;
But were I made of better elements,
With nobler instincts, purer tastes, like you,
I hardly would account the thing success
Though it did all for me I say.

                    But, friend,   345
We speak of what is; not of what might be,
And how 't were better if 't were otherwise.
I am the man you see here plain enough:
Grant I'm a beast, why, beasts must lead beasts' lives!
Suppose I own at once to tail and claws;   350
The tailless man exceeds me: but being tailed
I'll lash out lion fashion, and leave apes
To dock their stump[1] and dress their haunches up.
My business is not to remake myself,
But make the absolute best of what God made.   355
Or—our first simile—though you prove me doomed
To a viler berth still, to the steerage-hole,
The sheep-pen or the pig-stye, I should strive
To make what use of each were possible;
And as this cabin gets upholstery,   360
That hutch should rustle with sufficient straw.

    But, friend, I don't acknowledge quite so fast
I fail of all your manhood's lofty tastes
Enumerated so complacently,

---

1. Cut their tails short.

On the mere ground that you forsooth can find   365
In this particular life I choose to lead
No fit provision for them. Can you not?
Say you, my fault is I address myself
To grosser estimators than should judge?
And that's no way of holding up the soul,   370
Which, nobler, needs men's praise perhaps, yet knows
One wise man's verdict outweighs all the fools'—
Would like the two, but, forced to choose, takes that.
I pine among my million imbeciles
(You think) aware some dozen men of sense[2]   375
Eye me and know me, whether I believe
In the last winking Virgin,[3] as I vow,
And am a fool, or disbelieve in her
And am a knave,—approve in neither case,
Withhold their voices though I look their way: 380
Like Verdi[4] when, at his worst opera's end
(The thing they gave at Florence,—what's its name?)
While the mad houseful's plaudits near out-bang
His orchestra of salt-box, tongs and bones,[5]
He looks through all the roaring and the wreaths   385
Where sits Rossini[6] patient in his stall.

     Nay, friend, I meet you with an answer here—
That even your prime men who appraise their kind
Are men still, catch a wheel within a wheel,[7]
See more in a truth than the truth's simple self,   390
Confuse themselves. You see lads walk the street
Sixty the minute;[8] what's to note in that?
You see one lad o'erstride a chimney-stack;
Him you must watch—he's sure to fall, yet stands!
Our interest's on the dangerous edge of things.   395
The honest thief, the tender murderer,
The superstitious atheist, demirep[9]
That loves and saves her soul in new French books—
We watch while these in equilibrium keep
The giddy line midway: one step aside,   400
They're classed and done with. I, then, keep the line
Before your sages,—just the men to shrink
From the gross weights, coarse scales and labels broad

2. Cf. Pope's *Essay on Criticism*, line 391: "For fools admire, but men of sense approve."
3. In *Present Position of Catholics* Newman had affirmed his belief in two miracles: "the motion of the eyes of the pictures of the Madonna in the Roman States," and the "liquefaction of the blood of St. Januarius at Naples." (For the latter miracle see lines 726–30.)
4. Giuseppe Verdi (1813–1901), leading Italian operatic composer of the time. The "worst opera" may be the early work *Macbeth,* first performed in Florence in 1847.
5. Crude percussion instruments.
6. Gioacchino Rossini (1792–1868), Italian operatic composer, who could have seen *Macbeth* since he moved to Florence in 1847.
7. I.e., they see the complexity of existence. The symbol is from Ezekiel 1:16 and 10:10.
8. Very rapidly.
9. Contraction of "demi-reputation," applied to immoral women.

You offer their refinement. Fool or knave?
Why needs a bishop be a fool or knave   405
When there's a thousand diamond weights[1] between?
So, I enlist them. Your picked twelve,[2] you'll find,
Profess themselves indignant, scandalized
At thus being held unable to explain
How a superior man who disbelieves   410
May not believe as well: that's Schelling's[3] way!
It's through my coming in the tail of time,
Nicking the minute with a happy tact.
Had I been born three hundred years ago
They'd say, "What's strange? Blougram of course believes;"   415
And, seventy years since, "disbelieves of course."
But now, "He may believe; and yet, and yet
How can he?" All eyes turn with interest.
Whereas, step off the line on either side—
You, for example, clever to a fault,   420
The rough and ready man who write apace,
Read somewhat seldomer, think perhaps even less—
You disbelieve! Who wonders and who cares?
Lord So-and-so—his coat bedropped with wax,[4]
All Peter's chains about his waist,[5] his back   425
Brave with the needlework of Noodledom[6]—
Believes! Again, who wonders and who cares?
But I, the man of sense and learning too,
The able to think yet act, the this, the that,
I, to believe at this late time of day!   430
Enough; you see, I need not fear contempt.

    —Except it's yours! Admire me as these may,
You don't. But whom at least do you admire?
Present your own prefection, your ideal,
Your pattern man for a minute—oh, make haste,   435
Is it Napoleon you would have us grow?
Concede the means; allow his head and hand,
(A large concession, clever as you are)
Good! In our common primal element
Of unbelief (we can't believe, you know—   440
We're still at that admission, recollect!)
Where do you find—apart from, towering o'er
The secondary temporary aims
Which satisfy the gross taste you despise—
Where do you find his star?—his crazy trust   445
God knows through what or in what? it's alive

1. Units of troy weight, a system for measuring precious metal and jewels.
2. Jury.
3. F. W. J. von Schelling (1775–1854), German idealist philosopher, whose continual modification of his theological views gave rise to the charge of inconsistency.
4. From devotional candles.
5. Herod bound Peter in prison with two chains (Acts 12:6).
6. Vestment (probably a chasuble) splendidly embroidered by pious fools.

And shines and leads him, and that's all we want.
Have we aught in our sober night shall point
Such ends as his were, and direct the means
Of working out our purpose straight as his,   450
Nor bring a moment's trouble on success
With after-care to justify the same?
—Be a Napoleon, and yet disbelieve—
Why, the man's mad, friend, take his light away![7]
What's the vague good o' the world, for which you dare   455
With comfort to yourself blow millions up?
We neither of us see it! we do see
The blown-up millions—spatter of their brains
And writhing of their bowels and so forth,
In that bewildering entanglement   460
Of horrible eventualities
Past calculation to the end of time!
Can I mistake for some clear word of God
(Which were my ample warrant for it all)
His puff of hazy instinct, idle talk,   465
"The State, that's I,"[8] quack-nonsense about crowns,
And (when one beats the man to his last hold)
A vague idea of setting things to rights,
Policing people efficaciously,
More to their profit, most of all to his own;   470
The whole to end that dismallest of ends
By an Austrian marriage, cant to us the Church,[9]
And resurrection of the old *régime*?[1]
Would I, who hope to live a dozen years,
Fight Austerlitz[2] for reasons such and such?   475

No: for, concede me but the merest chance
Doubt may be wrong—there's judgment, life to come!
With just that chance, I dare not. Doubt proves right?
This present life is all?—you offer me
Its dozen noisy years, without a chance   480
That wedding an archduchess, wearing lace,
And getting called by divers new-coined names,
Will drive off ugly thoughts and let me dine,
Sleep, read and chat in quiet as I like!
Therefore I will not.

              Take another case;   485

7. An old treatment for madness.
8. *L'état, c'est moi.* Attributed to Louis XIV, not to Napoleon I.
9. Napoleon I, having divorced the Empress Joséphine because she had given him no heir, married Hapsburg Archduchess Marie Louise in 1810. By "cant" in the same line Blougram means Napoleon's hypocritical dealings with the church. The Concordat (1801) allowed free exercise of Catholic worship, but made it subject to the police power of the state. Later (1809) he annexed the papal states and imprisoned the Pope.
1. Napoleon's new relation by marriage to Europe's oldest reigning dynasty symbolized to many critics a betrayal of the Revolution.
2. Town northeast of Vienna, where in 1805 Napoleon defeated the combined Russian and Austrian armies.

Fit up the cabin yet another way.
What say you to the poets? shall we write
Hamlet, Othello—make the world our own,
Without a risk to run of either sort?
I can't!—to put the strongest reason first.   490
"But try," you urge, "the trying shall suffice;
The aim, if reached or not, makes great the life:
Try to be Shakespeare, leave the rest to fate!"
Spare my self-knowledge—there's no fooling me!
If I prefer remaining my poor self,   495
I say so not in self-dispraise but praise.
If I'm a Shakespeare, let the well alone;
Why should I try to be what now I am?
It I'm no Shakespeare, as too probable,—
His power and consciousness and self-delight   500
And all we want in common, shall I find—
Trying for ever? while on points of taste
Wherewith, to speak it humbly, he and I
Are dowered alike—I'll ask you, I or he,
Which in our two lives realizes most?   505
Much, he imagined—somewhat, I possess.
He had the imagination; stick to that!
Let him say, "In the face of my soul's works
Your world is worthless and I touch it not
Lest I should wrong them"—I'll withdraw my plea.   510
But does he say so? look upon his life!
Himself, who only can, gives judgment there.
He leaves his towers and gorgeous palaces[3]
To build the trimmest house in Stratford town;[4]
Saves money, spends it, owns the worth of things,   515
Giulio Romano's pictures, Dowland's[5] lute;
Enjoys a show, respects the puppets, too,
And none more, had he seen its entry once,
Than "Pandulph, of fair Milan cardinal."[6]
Why then should I who play that personage,   520
The very Pandulph Shakespeare's fancy made,
Be told that had the poet chanced to start
From where I stand now (some degree like mine
Being just the goal he ran his race to reach)
He would have run the whole race back, forsooth,   525
And left being Pandulph, to begin write plays?

3. Emblems of art and unreality in Shakespeare's last play, *The Tempest* (IV.i.152).
4. In 1597 Shakespeare acquired New Place, one of the largest houses in Stratford, where he retired about 1610.
5. Romano: Italian painter (ca. 1499–1546), mentioned in Shakespeare's *The Winter's Tale* (V.ii.97). John Dowland: English lutenist and songwriter (ca. 1563–ca. 1626), praised in a sonnet by Richard Barnfield that was reprinted in an unauthorized anthology, *The Passionate Pilgrim* (1599), attributed—on its title page—to Shakespeare.
6. As "holy legate of the Pope," Cardinal Pandulph curses and excommunicates King John (Shakespeare, *King John*, III.i.173ff.).

Ah, the earth's best can be but the earth's best!
Did Shakespeare live, he could but sit at home
And get himself in dreams the Vatican,
Greek busts, Venetian paintings, Roman walls,   530
And English books, none equal to his own,
Which I read, bound in gold (he never did).
—Terni's fall, Naples' bay and Gothard's top[7]—
Eh, friend? I could not fancy one of these;
But, as I pour this claret, there they are: 535
I've gained them—crossed St. Gothard last July
With ten mules to the carriage and a bed
Slung inside; is my hap the worse for that?
We want the same things, Shakespeare and myself,
And what I want, I have: he, gifted more,   540
Could fancy he too had them when he liked,
But not so thoroughly that, if fate allowed,
He would not have them also in my sense.
We play one[8] game; I send the ball aloft
No less adroitly that of fifty strokes   545
Scarce five go o'er the wall so wide and high
Which sends them back to me: I wish and get.
He struck balls higher and with better skill,
But at a poor fence level with his head,
And hit—his Stratford house, a coat of arms,[9]   550
Successful dealings in his grain and wool,[1]—
While I receive heaven's incense in my nose
And style myself the cousin of Queen Bess.[2]
Ask him, if this life's all, who wins the game?

Believe—and our whole argument breaks up.   555
Enthusiasm's the best thing, I repeat;
Only, we can't command it; fire and life
Are all, dead matter's nothing, we agree:
And be it a mad dream or God's very breath,
The fact's the same,—belief's fire, once in us,   560
Makes of all else mere stuff to show itself:
We penetrate our life with such a glow
As fire lends wood and iron—this turns steel,
That burns to ash—all's one, fire proves its power
For good or ill, since men call flare success.   565
But paint a fire, it will not therefore burn.
Light one in me, I'll find it food enough!
Why, to be Luther[3]—that's a life to lead,

7. Terni's fall: the famous waterfall, Cascate delle Marmore, in central Italy. Gothard's top: the St. Gotthard pass in the Alps, linking Switzerland and Italy. 8. The same. 9. In 1596 John Shakespeare, the poet's father, obtained a grant of arms; thereafter William signed himself as "gentleman."

1. Shakespeare had purchased farmland at Stratford. 2. Since bishops comprise the aristocracy of the Roman Catholic church, Blougram is in effect "cousin" to the English monarch, the constitutional head of the Anglican church. 3. Martin Luther (1483–1546), leader of the Reformation in Germany.

Incomparably better than my own.
He comes, reclaims God's earth for God, he says,   570
Sets up God's rule again by simple means,
Re-opens a shut book,[4] and all is done.
He flared out in the flaring of mankind;[5]
Such Luther's luck was: how shall such be mine?
If he succeeded, nothing's left to do: 575
And if he did not altogether—well,
Strauss[6] is the next advance. All Strauss should be
I might be also. But to what result?
He looks upon no future: Luther did.
What can I gain on the denying side?   580
Ice makes no conflagration. State the facts,
Read the text right, emancipate the world—
The emancipated world enjoys itself
With scarce a thank-you: Blougram told it first
It could not owe a farthing,—not to him   585
More than Saint Paul! 't would press its pay, you think?
Then add there's still that plaguy hundredth chance
Strauss may be wrong. And so a risk is run—
For what gain?[7] not for Luther's, who secured
A real heaven in his heart throughout his life,   590
Supposing death a little altered things.[8]

    "Ay, but since really you lack faith," you cry,
"You run the same risk really on all sides,
In cool indifference as bold unbelief.
As well be Strauss as swing 'twixt Paul and him.   595
It's not worth having, such imperfect faith,
No more available to do faith's work
Than unbelief like mine. Whole faith, or none!"

    Softly, my friend! I must dispute that point.
Once own the use of faith, I'll find you faith.   600
We're back on Christian ground. You call for faith:
I show you doubt, to prove that faith exists.[9]
The more of doubt, the stronger faith, I say,
If faith o'ercomes doubt. How I know it does?
By life and man's free will, God gave for that![1]   605
To mould life as we choose it, shows our choice:

4. Luther translated the New Testament into the vernacular (1522).
5. Showed his light in an age of enlightenment.
6. German scholar D. F. Strauss (1808–74), whose *Das Leben Jesu* was translated by George Eliot into English (1846). Most influential of the "higher" (i.e., historical and interpretive) biblical critics, Strauss concluded that the Gospels were myths rather than true historical accounts.
7. Cf. the "wager" passage in Pascal's *Pensées* (Brunschwig No. 233): belief is prudent, since one will gain eternal felicity if God exists, and will lose nothing if He does not.
8. Assuming Luther lost "heaven" at death, i.e., went to hell.
9. Cf. the *New Catholic Encyclopedia*: "Doubt and faith are mutually exclusive" (IV.1024).
1. Cf. the Thomistic doctrine that religious assent must be sufficiently free to be meritorious.

That's our one act, the previous work's his own.
You criticize the soil? it reared this tree—
This broad life and whatever fruit it bears!
What matter though I doubt at every pore, 610
Head-doubts, heart-doubts, doubts at my fingers' ends,
Doubts in the trivial work of every day,
Doubts at the very bases of my soul
In the grand moments when she probes herself—
If finally I have a life to show, 615
The thing I did, brought out in evidence
Against the thing done to me underground
By hell and all its brood, for aught I know?
I say, whence sprang this? shows it faith or doubt?
All's doubt in me; where's break of faith in this? 620
It is the idea, the feeling and the love,
God means mankind should strive for and show forth
Whatever be the process to that end,—
And not historic knowledge, logic sound,
And methaphysical acumen, sure! 625
"What think ye of Christ,"[2] friend? when all's done and said,
Like you this Christianity or not?
It may be false, but will you wish it true?
Has it your vote to be so if it can?
Trust you an instinct silenced long ago 630
That will break silence and enjoin you love
What mortified philosophy is hoarse,
And all in vain, with bidding you despise?
If you desire faith—then you've faith enough:
What else seeks God—nay, what else seek ourselves? 635
You form a notion of me, we'll suppose,
On hearsay; it's a favourable one:
"But still" (you add), "there was no such good man,
Because of contradiction in the facts.
One proves, for instance, he was born in Rome, 640
This Blougram; yet throughout the tales of him
I see he figures as an Englishman."
Well, the two things are reconcileable.
But would I rather you discovered that,
Subjoining—"Still what matter though they be? 645
Blougram concerns me nought, born here or there."

Pure faith indeed—you know not what you ask!
Naked belief in God the Omnipotent,
Omniscient, Omnipresent, sears too much
The sense of conscious creatures to be borne. 650
It were the seeing him, no flesh shall dare.
Some think, Creation's meant to show him forth:[3]

2. Jesus' question of the Pharisees in Matthew 22:42.
3. Blougram may have in mind the "natural theologians" of the eighteenth and early nineteenth centuries, who inferred from nature the providential design of a creative intelligence.

I say it's meant to hide him all it can,
And that's what all the blessed evil's for.[4]
Its use in Time is to environ us,   655
Our breath, our drop of dew, with shield enough
Against that sight till we can bear its stress.
Under a vertical sun, the exposed brain
And lidless eye and disemprisoned heart
Less certainly would wither up at once   660
Than mind, confronted with the truth of him.
But time and earth case-harden us to live;
The feeblest sense is trusted most; the child
Feels God a moment, ichors o'er the place,[5]
Plays on and grows to be a man like us.   665
With me, faith means perpetual unbelief
Kept quiet like the snake 'neath Michael's foot
Who stands calm just because he feels it writhe.[6]
Or, if that's too ambitious,—here's my box[7]—
I need the excitation of a pinch   670
Threatening the torpor of the inside-nose
Nigh on the imminent sneeze that never comes.
"Leave it in peace" advise the simple folk:
Make it aware of peace by itching-fits,
Say I—let doubt occasion still more faith!   675

   You'll say, once all believed, man, woman, child,
In that dear middle-age these noodles praise.[8]
How you'd exult if I could put you back
Six hundred years, blot out cosmogony,[9]
Geology, ethnology, what not,   680
(Greek endings, each the little passing-bell
That signifies some faith's about to die),[1]
And set you square with Genesis again,—
When such a traveller told you his last news,
He saw the ark a-top of Ararat[2]   685
But did not climb there since 't was getting dusk
And robber-bands infest the mountain's foot!
How should you feel, I ask, in such an age,
How act? As other people felt and did;
With soul more blank than this decanter's knob,   690

4. Blougram's optimistic conception of evil goes beyond the traditional view (as in Plotinus) that evil is the privation of goodness.
5. Ichor: a watery discharge that dries over a wound to protect it.
6. In religious art the archangel Michael is often depicted ready to slay the dragon (Satan) pinned beneath his foot.
7. Snuffbox.
8. At the time there was a wave of nostalgia for the Middle Ages. Blougram may have in mind Thomas Carlyle's *Past and Present* (1843), which in Book II praises the disciplined life of a medieval English monastery.
9. Scientific study of the creation of the universe. The authority of the Genesis account of the Creation in six days, and the concomitant belief that the earth's crust was about 6,000 years old, were severely shaken by the findings of geologists, who supported the theory that the processes of physical change took eons, not mere thousands of years.
1. Greek endings: the suffixes *gony* ("manner of coming into being") and *logy* ("science").
2. Mountain in Turkey, traditional resting place of Noah's ark (Genesis 8:4).

Believe—and yet lie, kill, rob, fornicate
Full in belief's face, like the beast you'd be!

No, when the fight begins within himself,
A man's worth something. God stoops o'er his head,
Satan looks up between his feet—both tug—   695
He's left, himself, i' the middle: the soul wakes
And grows. Prolong that battle through his life!
Never leave growing till the life to come!
Here, we've got callous to the Virgin's winks[3]
That used to puzzle people wholesomely: 700
Men have outgrown the shame of being fools.
What are the laws of nature, not to bend
If the Church bid them?—brother Newman asks.[4]
Up with the Immaculate Conception,[5] then—
On the rack with faith!—is my advice.   705
Will not that hurry us upon our knees,
Knocking our breasts, "It can't be—yet it shall!
Who am I, the worm, to argue with my Pope?
Low things confound the high things!" and so forth.
That's better than acquitting God with grace   710
As some folk do. He's tried—no case is proved,
Philosophy is lenient—he may go!

You'll say, the old system's not so obsolete
But men believe still: ay, but who and where?
King Bomba's lazzaroni[6] foster yet   715
The sacred flame, so Antonelli[7] writes;
But even of these, what ragamuffin-saint
Believes God watches him continually,
As he believes in fire that it will burn,
Or rain that it will drench him? Break fire's law,   720
Sin against rain, although the penalty
Be just a singe or soaking? "No," he smiles;
"Those laws are laws that can enforce themselves."

The sum of all is—yes, my doubt is great,
My faith's still greater, then my faith's enough.   725
I have read much, thought much, experienced much,
Yet would die rather than avow my fear
The Naples' liquefaction[8] may be false,

3. See note to line 377.
4. Newman maintained that the Divine Power occasionally circumvented the natural law to effect miracles.
5. In 1854 Pius IX promulgated the dogma that the soul of the Virgin Mary was from the moment of her conception preserved from original sin by divine grace. This doctrine is not to be confused with the Virgin Birth (Matthew 1:18–23).
6. Neapolitan beggars under the despotic rule of Ferdinand II, king of the Two Sicilies. He earned the nickname "Bomba" from his bombardment of the chief cities of Sicily to quell the 1848 revolt.
7. Powerful cardinal, secretary of state to Pius IX, 1852–70.
8. The dried blood of martyr St. Januarius, or St. Gennaro, patron saint of Naples (d. 305?) is said to liquefy twice a year while on public display in the Naples cathedral. Belief in such miracles is not required of Catholics, as the Bishop implies.

When set to happen by the palace-clock
According to the clouds or dinner-time.   730
I hear you recommend, I might at least
Eliminate, decrassify[9] my faith
Since I adopt it; keeping what I must
And leaving what I can—such points as this.
I won't—that is, I can't throw one away.   735
Supposing there's no truth in what I hold
About the need of trial to man's faith,
Still, when you bid me purify the same,
To such a process I discern no end.
Clearing off one excrescence to see two,   740
There's ever a next in size, now grown as big,
That meets the knife: I cut and cut again!
First cut the Liquefaction, what comes last
But Fichte's clever cut at God himself?[1]
Experimentalize on sacred things!   745
I trust nor hand nor eye nor heart nor brain
To stop betimes: they all get drunk alike.
The first step, I am master not to take.

    You'd find the cutting-process to your taste
As much as leaving growths of lies unpruned,   750
Nor see more danger in it,—you retort.
Your taste's worth mine; but my taste proves more wise
When we consider that the steadfast hold
On the extreme end of the chain of faith
Gives all the advantage, makes the difference   755
With the rough purblind mass we seek to rule:
We are their lords, or they are free of us,
Just as we tighten or relax our hold.
So, other matters equal, we'll revert
To the first problem—which, if solved my way   760
And thrown into the balance, turns the scale—
How we may lead a comfortable life,
How suit our luggage to the cabin's size.

    Of course you are remarking all this time
How narrowly and grossly I view life,   765
Respect the creature-comforts, care to rule
The masses, and regard complacently
"The cabin," in our old phrase. Well, I do.
I act for, talk for, live for this world now,
As this world prizes action, life and talk: 770
No prejudice to what next world may prove,
Whose new laws and requirements, my best pledge

9. Purify.
1. German idealist philosopher J. G.
Fichte (1762–1814), who as professor at
Jena delivered a paper "On the Basis of
Our Belief in a Divine Providence"
(1798), in which he asserted that the
"living and operative moral order is itself God. We need no other God, and
we cannot conceive any other."

To observe then, is that I observe these now,
Shall do hereafter what I do meanwhile.
Let us concede (gratuitously though)   775
Next life relieves the soul of body, yields
Pure spiritual enjoyment: well, my friend,
Why lose this life i' the meantime, since its use
May be to make the next life more intense?

   Do you know, I have often had a dream   780
(Work it up in your next month's article)
Of man's poor spirit in its progress, still
Losing true life for ever and a day
Through ever trying to be and ever being—
In the evolution of successive spheres—   785
Before its actual sphere and place of life,
Halfway into the next, which having reached,
It shoots with corresponding foolery
Halfway into the next still, on and off!
As when a traveller, bound from North to South,   790
Scouts[2] fur in Russia: what's its use in France?
In France spurns flannel: where's its need in Spain?
In Spain drops cloth, too cumbrous for Algiers!
Linen goes next, and last the skin itself,
A superfluity at Timbuctoo.   795
When, through his journey, was the fool at ease?
I'm at ease now, friend; worldly in this world,
I take and like its way of life; I think
My brothers, who administer the means,
Live better for my comfort—that's good too;   800
And God, if he pronounce upon such life,
Approves my service, which is better still.
If he keep silence,—why, for you or me
Or that brute beast pulled-up[3] in to-day's "Times,"
What odds is 't, save to ourselves, what life we lead? 805

   You meet me at this issue: you declare,—
All special-pleading done with—truth is truth,
And justifies itself by undreamed ways.
You don't fear but it's better, if we doubt,
To say so, act up to our truth perceived   810
However feebly. Do then,—act away!
'T is there I'm on the watch for you. How one acts
Is, both of us agree, our chief concern:
And how you'll act is what I fain would see
If, like the candid person you appear,   815
You dare to make the most of your life's scheme
As I of mine, live up to its full law
Since there's no higher law that counterchecks.

2. Rejects scornfully.   3. Arrested.

Put natural religion[4] to the test
You've just demolished the revealed with—quick,   820
Down to the root of all that checks your will,
All prohibition to lie, kill and thieve,
Or even to be an atheistic priest!
Suppose a pricking to incontinence—
Philosophers deduce you chastity   825
Or shame, from just the fact that at the first
Whoso embraced a woman in the field,
Threw club down and forewent his brains beside,
So, stood a ready victim in the reach
Of any brother savage, club in hand;   830
Hence saw the use of going out of sight
In wood or cave to prosecute his loves:
I read this in a French book t' other day.
Does law so analysed coerce you much?
Oh, men spin clouds of fuzz where matters end,   835
But you who reach where the first thread begins,
You'll soon cut that!—which means you can, but won't,
Through certain instincts, blind, unreasoned-out,
You dare not set aside, you can't tell why,
But there they are, and so you let them rule.   840
Then, friend, you seem as much a slave as I,
A liar, conscious coward and hypocrite,
Without the good the slave expects to get,
In case he has a master after all!
You own your instincts? why, what else do I,   845
Who want, am made for, and must have a God
Ere I can be aught, do aught?—no mere name
Want, but the true thing with what proves its truth,
To wit, a relation from that thing to me,
Touching from head to foot—which touch I feel,   850
And with it take the rest, this life of ours!
I live my life here; yours you dare not live.

    —Not as I state it, who (you please subjoin)
Disfigure such a life and call it names,
While, to your mind, remains another way   855
For simple men: knowledge and power have rights,
But ignorance and weakness have rights too.
There needs no crucial effort to find truth
If here or there or anywhere about:
We ought to turn each side, try hard and see,   860
And if we can't, be glad we've earned at least
The right, by one laborious proof the more,
To graze in peace earth's pleasant pasturage.
Men are not angels, neither are they brutes:

---

4. Natural religion laid stress on the operation of reason as a means of apprehending universal truth and attaining virtue, holding supernatural revelation to be unnecessary.

Something we may see, all we cannot see. 865
What need of lying? I say, I see all,
And swear to each detail the most minute
In what I think a Pan's[5] face—you, mere cloud:
I swear I hear him speak and see him wink,
For fear, if once I drop the emphasis, 870
Mankind may doubt there's any cloud at all.
You take the simple life—ready to see,
Willing to see (for no cloud's worth a face)—
And leaving quiet what no strength can move,
And which, who bids you move? who has the right? 875
I bid you; but you are God's sheep, not mine:
"Pastor est tui Dominus."[6] You find
In this the pleasant pasture of our life
Much you may eat without the least offence,
Much you don't eat because your maw[7] objects, 880
Much you would eat but that your fellow-flock
Open great eyes at you and even butt,
And thereupon you like your mates so well
You cannot please yourself, offending them;
Though when they seem exorbitantly sheep, 885
You weigh your pleasure with their butts and bleats
And strike the balance. Sometimes certain fears
Restrain you, real checks since you find them so;
Sometimes you please yourself and nothing checks:
And thus you graze through life with not one lie, 890
And like it best.

　　　　　But do you, in truth's name?
If so, you beat—which means you are not I—
Who needs must make earth mine and feed my fill
Not simply unbutted at, unbickered with,
But motioned to the velvet of the sward[8] 895
By those obsequious wethers'[9] very selves.
Look at me, sir; my age is double yours:
At yours, I knew beforehand, so enjoyed,
What now I should be—as, permit the word,
I pretty well imagine your whole range 900
And stretch of tether twenty years to come.
We both have minds and bodies much alike:
In truth's name, don't you want my bishopric,
My daily bread, my influence and my state?
You're young. I'm old; you must be old one day; 905
Will you find then, as I do hour by hour,
Women their lovers kneel to, who cut curls
From your fat lap-dog's ear to grace a brooch—
Dukes, who petition just to kiss your ring—

5. God of flocks and shepherds.
6. "The Lord is your shepherd" (paraphrase of Psalm 23:1).

7. Stomach.
8. Choicest part of the pasture.
9. Castrated male sheep.

With much beside you know or may conceive?   910
Suppose we die to-night: well, here am I,
Such were my gains, life bore this fruit to me,
While writing all the same my articles
On music, poetry, the fictile[1] vase
Found at Albano, chess, Anacreon's Greek.[2]   915
But you—the highest honour in your life,
The thing you'll crown yourself with, all your days,
Is—dining here and drinking this last glass
I pour you out in sign of amity
Before we part for ever. Of your power   920
And social influence, worldly worth in short,
Judge what's my estimation by the fact,
I do not condescend to enjoin, beseech,
Hint secrecy on one of all these words!
You're shrewd and know that should you publish one   926
The world would brand the lie—my enemies first,
Who'd sneer—"the bishop's an arch-hypocrite
And knave perhaps, but not so frank a fool."
Whereas I should not dare for both my ears
Breathe one such syllable, smile one such smile,   930
Before the chaplain who reflects myself—
My shade's so much more potent than your flesh.
What's your reward, self-abnegating friend?
Stood you confessed of those exceptional
And privileged great natures that dwarf mine—   935
A zealot with a mad ideal in reach,
A poet just about to print his ode,
A statesman with a scheme to stop this war,[3]
An artist whose religion is his art—
I should have nothing to object: such men   940
Carry the fire, all things grow warm to them,
Their drugget's[4] worth my purple, they beat me.
But you,—you're just as little those as I—
You, Gigadibs, who, thirty years of age,
Write statedly for Blackwood's Magazine,[5]   945
Believe you see two points in Hamlet's soul
Unseized by the Germans[6] yet—which view you'll print—
Meantime the best you have to show being still
That lively lightsome article we took
Almost for the true Dickens,—what's its name?   950

1. Of molded clay.
2. Albano Laziale: small town in central Italy, site of ancient Roman ruins. Anacreon: much imitated Greek lyric poet of the sixth century B.C., whose subjects were love and wine.
3. Crimean War (1854–56), in which Britain joined France to preserve the Ottoman Empire from Russian occupation.
4. Coarse woolen fabric, in contrast to the purple cloth symbolic of a bishop's office.
5. *Blackwood's Edinburgh Magazine*, a leading periodical founded 1817.
6. Noted for painstaking scholarship. The Bishop may have in mind Georg G. Gervinus, who wrote a four-volume study of Shakespeare (1849–52). (Turner, p. 346n.)

"The Slum and Cellar, or Whitechapel[7] life
Limned after dark!" it made me laugh, I know,
And pleased a month, and brought you in ten pounds.
—Success I recognize and compliment,
And therefore give you, if you choose, three words   955
(The card and pencil-scratch is quite enough)
Which whether here, in Dublin or New York,
Will get you, prompt as at my eyebrow's wink,
Such terms as never you aspired to get
In all our own[8] reviews and some not ours.   960
Go write your lively sketches! be the first
"Blougram, or The Eccentric Confidence"—
Or better simply say, "The Outward-bound."
Why, men as soon would throw it in my teeth
As copy and quote the infamy chalked broad   965
About me on the church-door opposite.
You will not wait for that experience though,
I fancy, howsoever you decide,
To discontinue—not detesting, not
Defaming, but at least—despising me!   970

———————————

Over his wine so smiled and talked his hour
Sylvester Blougram, styled *in partibus*
Episcopus, nec non[9]—(the deuce knows what
It's changed to by our novel hierarchy)
With Gigadibs the literary man,   975
Who played with spoons, explored his plate's design,
And ranged the olive-stones about its edge,
While the great bishop rolled him out a mind
Long crumpled, till creased consciousness lay smooth.

For Blougram, he believed, say, half he spoke.   980
The other portion, as he shaped it thus
For argumentatory purposes,
He felt his foe was foolish to dispute.
Some arbitrary accidental thoughts
That crossed his mind, amusing because new,   985
He chose to represent as fixtures there,
Invariable convictions (such they seemed
Beside his interlocutor's loose cards
Flung daily down, and not the same way twice)
While certain hell-deep instincts, man's weak tongue   990
Is never bold to utter in their truth
Because styled hell-deep ('t is an old mistake
To place hell at the bottom of the earth)

7. One of the most degraded London slum districts at the time.
8. Roman Catholic.
9. "In episcopal regions, and also . . ." The phrase refers to the change in Wise-man's title in 1850 from Bishop of Meli-potamus, *in partibus infidelium* ("in the regions of the faithless") to Archbishop of Westminster.

He ignored these,—not having in readiness
Their nomenclature and philosophy: 995
He said true things, but called them by wrong names.
"On the whole," he thought, "I justify myself
On every point where cavillers like this
Oppugn my life: he tries one kind of fence,[1]
I close, he's worsted, that's enough for him. 1000
He's on the ground: if ground should break away
I take my stand on, there's a firmer yet
Beneath it, both of us may sink and reach.
His ground was over mine and broke the first:[2]
So, let him sit with me this many a year!" 1005

He did not sit five minutes. Just a week
Sufficed his sudden healthy vehemence.
Something had struck him in the "Outward-bound"
Another way than Blougram's purpose was:
And having bought, not cabin-furniture 1010
But settler's-implements (enough for three)
And started for Australia—there, I hope,
By this time he has tested his first plough,
And studied his last chapter of St. John.[3]

Memorabilia[1]

I

Ah, did you once see Shelley plain,
    And did he stop and speak to you?
And did you speak to him again?
    How strange it seems and new!

II

But you were living before that, 5
    And also you are living after;
And the memory I started at—
    My starting moves your laughter.

III

I crossed a moor, with a name of its own
    And a certain use in the world no doubt, 10
Yet a hand's-breadth of it shines alone
    'Mid the blank miles round about:

1. *Oppugn*: assail. *Fence*: fencing tactic.
2. Gigadibs' ground, being abstract and idealistic, is loftier than the Bishop's pragmatic ground.
3. An ambiguous line which could mean (1) that Gigadibs may have ended his own critical study of "St. John" (i.e., the Gospels); or (2) that he may have reviewed the Gospels, particularly the final chapter of St. John (21). In that chapter Jesus, unrecognized by the disciples, makes himself known by telling them where to cast for a great haul of fish. Then he thrice tests Peter's love for him, each time commanding, "Feed my sheep." Perhaps Gigadibs' study of this passage amounts to an implicit "comment" on the inadequacy of Blougram's conception of his office as bishop, or Lord's shepherd.

1. Written as early as 1851, when Browning completed his *Essay on Shelley* (DeVane, p. 244). According to Browning the encounter took place in a London bookseller's shop.

IV

For there I picked up on the heather
And there I put inside my breast
A moulted feather, an eagle-feather!²   15
Well, I forget the rest.

ca. 1851

Andrea del Sarto

(CALLED "THE FAULTLESS PAINTER")

Contrasting markedly with the exuberant "Fra Lippo Lippi," this is Brown-
ing's classic study of moral and aesthetic failure. According to tradition,
Browning wrote the poem and sent it to his friend John Kenyon when he
was unable to comply with the latter's request for a copy of Andrea del
Sarto's self-portrait with his wife Lucrezia, which hung in the Pitti Palace,
Florence.

Browning's own portrait of the Florentine painter Andrea del Sarto
(1486–1531) is indebted to the somewhat biased account by Andrea's
pupil Giorgio Vasari in his *Lives of the Artists* (1550, 1568). After studying for some years with Piero di Cosimo, Andrea was employed by the
brotherhood of the Servites (1509–14). So excellent were his frescoes of
this period that he was called *Andrea senza errori* ("Andrew the unerring"); and in that medium—painting on fresh plaster—it was said that his
only rival was Raphael. Contented with his superior technical skill, he did
not aspire to be either an innovator or a leader in art. In 1516 he married a
handsome widow, Lucrezia del Fede, who served as model for several fine
Madonnas. Vasari describes her as overbearing, jealous, and faithless, exert-
ing a baneful influence over Andrea that cost him the respect of his associates and compromised his career. In 1518, at the invitation of Francis I,
Andrea went to the royal seat at Fontainebleau, near Paris, where for the
only time in his life he was adequately paid. But Lucrezia wrote Andrea
such bitter letters from Florence that he resolved to go there to settle his
affairs. He left Francis promising to return in a few months with statues
and pictures, for which the king had provided money. With it he purchased a house and "various pleasures," never returning to France. (Modern
scholars have doubted that such a misappropriation really occurred.)

In linking Andrea's artistic failure to flaws in character, Browning follows
Vasari, who found the master's work, though "entirely free of errors," wanting in "ardour and animation," owing to Andrea's "timidity of mind" and
utter lack of "elevation" (Vasari, III. 180).

But do not let us quarrel any more,
No, my Lucrezia; bear with me for once:
Sit down and all shall happen as you wish.
You turn your face, but does it bring your heart?

2. Memento of Shelley's brief earthly
life. Browning draws perhaps on the traditional association of the molted eagle
with renewed youth or resurrection.

I'll work then for your friend's friend, never fear, 5
Treat his own subject after his own way,
Fix his own time, accept too his own price,
And shut the money into this small hand
When next it takes mine. Will it? tenderly?
Oh, I'll content him,—but to-morrow, Love! 10
I often am much wearier than you think,
This evening more than usual, and it seems
As if—forgive now—should you let me sit
Here by the window with your hand in mine
And look a half-hour forth on Fiesole,[1] 15
Both of one mind, as married people use,
Quietly, quietly the evening through,
I might get up to-morrow to my work
Cheerful and fresh as ever. Let us try.
To-morrow, how you shall be glad for this! 20
Your soft hand is a woman of itself,
And mine the man's bared breast she curls inside.
Don't count the time lost, neither; you must serve
For each of the five pictures we require:
It saves a model. So! keep looking so— 25
My serpentining[2] beauty, rounds on rounds!
—How could you ever prick those perfect ears,
Even to put the pearl there! oh, so sweet—
My face, my moon, my everybody's moon,
Which everybody looks on and calls his, 30
And, I suppose, is looked on by in turn,
While she looks—no one's: very dear, no less.
You smile? why, there's my picture ready made,
There's what we painters call our harmony!
A common greyness silvers everything,— 35
All in a twilight, you and I alike
—You, at the point of your first pride in me
(That's gone you know),—but I, at every point;
My youth, my hope, my art, being all toned down
To yonder sober pleasant Fiesole. 40
There's the bell clinking from the chapel-top;
That length of convent-wall across the way
Holds the trees safer, huddled more inside;
The last monk leaves the garden; days decrease,
And autumn grows, autumn in everything. 45
Eh? the whole seems to fall into a shape
As if I saw alike my work and self
And all that I was born to be and do,
A twilight-piece. Love, we are in God's hand.
How strange now, looks the life he makes us lead; 50

1. Small town on a hill three miles from   2. Sinuous.
Florence.

So free we seem, so fettered fast we are!
I feel he laid the fetter: let it lie!
This chamber for example—turn your head—
All that's behind us! You don't understand
Nor care to understand about my art,   55
But you can hear at least when people speak:
And that cartoon,[3] the second from the door
—It is the thing, Love! so such things should be—
Behold Madonna!—I am bold to say.
I can do with my pencil what I know,   60
What I see, what at bottom of my heart
I wish for, if I ever wish so deep—
Do easily, too—when I say, perfectly,
I do not boast, perhaps: yourself are judge,
Who listened to the Legate's[4] talk last week,   65
And just as much they used to say in France.
At any rate 't is easy, all of it!
No sketches first, no studies, that's long past:
I do what many dream of, all their lives,
—Dream? strive to do, and agonize to do,   70
And fail in doing. I could count twenty such
On twice your fingers, and not leave this town,
Who strive—you don't know how the others strive
To paint a little thing like that you smeared
Carelessly passing with your robes afloat,—   75
Yet do much less, so much less, Someone says,
(I know his name, no matter)—so much less!
Well, less is more, Lucrezia: I am judged.
There burns a truer light of God in them,
In their vexed beating stuffed and stopped-up brain,   80
Heart, or whate'er else, than goes on to prompt
This low-pulsed forthright craftsman's hand of mine.
Their works drop groundward, but themselves, I know,
Reach many a time a heaven that's shut to me,
Enter and take their place there sure enough,   85
Though they come back and cannot tell the world.
My works are nearer heaven, but I sit here.
The sudden blood of these men! at a word—
Praise them, it boils, or blame them, it boils too.
I, painting from myself and to myself,   90
Know what I do, am unmoved by men's blame
Or their praise either. Somebody remarks
Morello's[5] outline there is wrongly traced,
His[6] hue mistaken; what of that? or else,
Rightly traced and well ordered; what of that?   95

3. Preparatory drawing for a picture.   ence.
4. Pope's envoy.   6. Its.
5. Mountain in Apennines north of Flor-

Speak as they please, what does the mountain care?
Ah, but a man's reach should exceed his grasp,[7]
Or what's a heaven for? All is silver-grey
Placid and perfect with my art: the worse!
I know both what I want and what might gain,   100
And yet how profitless to know, to sigh
"Had I been two, another and myself,
Our head would have o'erlooked the world!" No doubt.
Yonder's a work now, of that famous youth
The Urbinate[8] who died five years ago.   105
('T is copied, George Vasari sent it me.)
Well, I can fancy how he did it all,
Pouring his soul, with kings and popes to see,
Reaching, that heaven might so replenish him,
Above and through his art—for it gives way;   110
That arm is wrongly put—and there again—
A fault to pardon in the drawing's lines,
Its body, so to speak: its soul is right,
He means right—that, a child may understand.
Still, what an arm! and I could alter it: 115
But all the play, the insight and the stretch—
Out of me, out of me! And wherefore out?
Had you enjoined them on me, given me soul,
We might have risen to Rafael, I and you!
Nay, Love, you did give all I asked, I think—   120
More than I merit, yes, by many times.
But had you—oh, with the same perfect brow,
And perfect eyes, and more than perfect mouth,
And the low voice my soul hears, as a bird
The fowler's pipe, and follows to the snare—   125
Had you, with these the same, but brought a mind!
Some women do so. Had the mouth there urged
"God and the glory! never care for gain.
The present by the future, what is that?
Live for fame, side by side with Agnolo![9]   130
Rafael is waiting: up to God, all three!"
I might have done it for you. So it seems:
Perhaps not. All is as God over-rules.
Beside, incentives come from the soul's self;
The rest avail not. Why do I need you?   135

---

7. Browning's ideas on art, notably the glorification of the Imperfect, may partly derive from the great art critic John Ruskin. Cf. this passage from *The Stones of Venice* (1851–53): ". . . no good work whatever can be perfect, and *the demand for perfection is always a sign of a misunderstanding of the ends of art.* This for two reasons, both based on everlasting laws. The first, that no great man ever stops working till he has reached his point of failure; that is to say, his mind is always far in advance of his powers of execution. . . . The second reason is, that imperfection is . . . the sign of life in a mortal body, that is to say, of a state of progress and change" (II, chapter 6).
8. Raphael (Raffaello Sanzio, 1483–1520), born at Urbino.
9. Michelangelo (Michelagniolo Buonarroti, 1475–1564).

What wife had Rafael, or has Agnolo?[1]
In this world, who can do a thing, will not;
And who would do it, cannot, I perceive:
Yet the will's somewhat—somewhat, too, the power—
And thus we half-men struggle. At the end,   140
God, I conclude, compensates, punishes.
'T is safer for me, if the award be strict,
That I am something underrated here,
Poor this long while, despised, to speak the truth.
I dared not, do you know, leave home all day,   145
For fear of chancing on the Paris lords.[2]
The best is when they pass and look aside;
But they speak sometimes; I must bear it all.
Well may they speak! That Francis, that first time,
And that long festal year at Fontainebleau!   150
I surely then could sometimes leave the ground,
Put on the glory, Rafael's daily wear,
In that humane great monarch's golden look,—
One finger in his beard or twisted curl
Over his mouth's good mark that made the smile,   155
One arm about my shoulder, round my neck,
The jingle of his gold chain in my ear,
I painting proudly with his breath on me,
All his court round him, seeing with his eyes,
Such frank French eyes, and such a fire of souls   160
Profuse, my hand kept plying by those hearts,—
And, best of all, this, this, this face beyond,
This in the background, waiting on my work,
To crown the issue with a last reward!
A good time, was it not, my kingly days?   165
And had you not grown restless . . . but I know—
'T is done and past; 't was right, my instinct said;
Too live the life grew, golden and not grey,
And I'm the weak-eyed bat no sun should tempt
Out of the grange[3] whose four walls make his world.   170
How could it end in any other way?
You called me, and I came home to your heart.
The triumph was—to reach and stay there; since
I reached it ere the triumph, what is lost?
Let my hands frame your face in your hair's gold,   175
You beautiful Lucrezia that are mine!
"Rafael did this, Andrea painted that;
The Roman's[4] is the better when you pray,

1. Raphael finally married (with reluctance), but Michelangelo said, "I have a
wife too many already, namely this art,
which harries me incessantly, and my
works are my children . . ." (Vasari).

2. French nobles who have heard of Andrea's embezzlement.
3. Granary.
4. Raphael's. He went to Rome in 1508
to assist in decorating St. Peter's.

But still the other's Virgin was his wife—"
Men will excuse me. I am glad to judge   180
Both pictures in your presence; clearer grows
My better fortune, I resolve to think.
For, do you know, Lucrezia, as God lives,
Said one day Agnolo, his very self,
To Rafael . . . I have known it all these years . . .   185
(When the young man was flaming out his thoughts
Upon a palace-wall for Rome to see,
Too lifted up in heart because of it)
"Friend, there's a certain sorry little scrub[5]
Goes up and down our Florence, none cares how,   190
Who, were he set to plan and execute
As you are, pricked on by your popes and kings,
Would bring the sweat into that brow of yours!"
To Rafael's!—And indeed the arm is wrong.
I hardly dare . . . yet, only you to see,   195
Give the chalk here—quick, thus the line should go!
Ay, but the soul! he's Rafael! rub it out!
Still, all I care for, if he spoke the truth,
(What he? why, who but Michel Agnolo?
Do you forget already words like those?)   200
If really there was such a chance, so lost,—
Is, whether you're—not grateful—but more pleased.
Well, let me think so. And you smile indeed!
This hour has been an hour! Another smile?
If you would sit thus by me every night   205
I should work better, do you comprehend?
I mean that I should earn more, give you more.
See, it is settled dusk now; there's a star;
Morello's gone, the watch-lights show the wall,
The cue-owls speak the name we call them by.   210
Come from the window, love,—come in, at last,
Inside the melancholy little house
We built to be so gay with. God is just.
King Francis may forgive me: oft at nights
When I look up from painting, eyes tired out,   215
The walls become illumined, brick from brick
Distinct, instead of mortar, fierce bright gold,
That gold of his I did cement them with!
Let us but love each other. Must you go?
That Cousin[6] here again? he waits outside?   220
Must see you—you, and not with me? Those loans?
More gaming debts to pay? you smiled for that?
Well, let smiles buy me! have you more to spend?
While hand and eye and something of a heart

---

5. This anecdote is related by Vasari.   6. Renaissance euphemism for "lover."

Are left me, work's my ware, and what's it worth?   225
I'll pay my fancy. Only let me sit
The grey remainder of the evening out,
Idle, you call it, and muse perfectly
How I could paint, were I but back in France,
One picture, just one more—the Virgin's face,   230
Not yours this time! I want you at my side
To hear them—that is, Michel Agnolo—
Judge all I do and tell you of its worth.
Will you? To-morrow, satisfy your friend.
I take the subjects for his corridor,   235
Finish the portrait out of hand—there, there,
And throw him in another thing or two
If he demurs; the whole should prove enough
To pay for this same Cousin's freak. Beside,
What's better and what's all I care about,   240
Get you the thirteen scudi[7] for the ruff!
Love, does that please you? Ah, but what does he,
The Cousin! what does he to please you more?

 I am grown peaceful as old age to-night.
I regret little, I would change still less.   245
Since there my past life lies, why alter it?
The very wrong to Francis!—it is true
I took his coin, was tempted and complied,
And built this house and sinned, and all is said.
My father and my mother died of want.   250
Well, had I riches of my own? you see
How one gets rich! Let each one bear his lot.
They were born poor, lived poor, and poor they died:
And I have laboured somewhat in my time
And not been paid profusely. Some good son   255
Paint my two hundred pictures—let him try!
No doubt, there's something strikes a balance. Yes,
You loved me quite enough, it seems to-night.
This must suffice me here. What would one have?
In heaven, perhaps, new chances, one more chance—   260
Four great walls in the New Jerusalem,[8]
Meted on each side by the angel's reed,[9]
For Leonard,[1] Rafael, Agnolo and me
To cover—the three first without a wife,
While I have mine! So—still they overcome   265
Because there's still Lucrezia,—as I choose.

Again the Cousin's whistle! Go, my Love.

ca. 1853

---

7. Silver coin worth about one dollar.   9. Measured with an angel's rod.
8. Heaven; see Revelation 21:10–21.   1. Leonardo da Vinci (1452–1519).

Saul[1]

I

Said Abner,[2] "At last thou art come! Ere I tell, ere thou speak,
Kiss my cheek, wish me well!" Then I wished it, and did kiss his
    cheek.
And he, "Since the King, O my friend, for thy countenance sent,
Neither drunken nor eaten have we; nor until from his tent
Thou return with the joyful assurance the King liveth yet,   5
Shall our lip with the honey be bright, with the water be wet.
For out of the black mid-tent's silence, a space of three days,
Not a sound hath escaped to thy servants, of prayer nor of praise,
To betoken that Saul and the Spirit[3] have ended their strife,
And that, faint in his triumph, the monarch sinks back upon life.   10

II

"Yet now my heart leaps, O beloved! God's child with his dew
Only thy gracious gold hair, and those lilies still living and blue[4]
Just broken to twine round thy harp-strings, as if no wild heat
Were now raging to torture the desert!"

III

                         Then I, as was meet,
Knelt down to the God of my fathers, and rose on my feet,   15
And ran o'er the sand burnt to powder. The tent was unlooped;
I pulled up the spear that obstructed, and under I stooped;
Hands and knees on the slippery grass-patch, all withered and gone,
That extends to the second enclosure, I groped my way on
Till I felt where the foldskirts fly open. Then once more I prayed,   20
And opened the foldskirts and entered, and was not afraid
But spoke, "Here is David, thy servant!" And no voice replied.
At the first I saw nought but the blackness; but soon I descried
A something more black than the blackness—the vast, the upright
Main prop which sustains the pavilion: and slow into sight   25
Grew a figure against it, gigantic and blackest of all.
Then a sunbeam, that burst thro' the tent-roof, showed Saul.

IV

He stood as erect as that tent-prop, both arms stretched out wide
On the great cross-support in the centre, that goes to each side;

1. There are two versions of "Saul": the first, published in 1845 at the urging of Elizabeth Barrett, was admittedly a fragment; it comprised the first nine sections of the completed poem and concluded with the promissory words "End of Part the First." The final version (1855) incorporates the religious ideas Browning had evolved over the ten-year interim, notably the primacy of love and the centrality of the Incarnation. The ultimate source for "Saul" is the brief account of David's playing before Saul in 1 Samuel 16:14–23. But the impetus to treat the subject came from Browning's re-reading of Christopher Smart's visionary poem "A Song to David" (1763). For David's prophecy of Christ in stanza XVIII Browning's authority is the Pentecostal sermon of St. Peter: "Therefore [David] being a prophet, . . . spake of the resurrection of Christ . . ." (Acts 2:30–31).
2. Captain of Saul's army (1 Samuel 14:50).
3. "But the Spirit of the Lord departed from Saul, and an evil spirit from the Lord troubled him" (1 Samuel 16:14).
4. Blue water lily or lotus (according to Browning).

He relaxed not a muscle, but hung there as, caught in his pangs   30
And waiting his change, the king-serpent[5] all heavily hangs,
Far away from his kind, in the pine, till deliverance come
With the spring-time,—so agonized Saul, drear and stark, blind
    and dumb.

V

Then I turned my harp,—took off the lilies we twine round its
    chords
Lest they snap 'neath the stress of the noontide—those sunbeams
    like swords!   35
And I first played the tune all our sheep know, as, one after one,
So docile they come to the pen-door till folding be done.
They are white and untorn by the bushes, for lo, they have fed
Where the long grasses stifle the water within the stream's bed;
And now one after one seeks its lodging, as star follows star   40
Into eve and the blue far above us,—so blue and so far!

VI

—Then the tune, for which quails on the cornland will each leave
    his mate
To fly after the player; then, what makes the crickets elate
Till for boldness they fight one another: and then, what has weight
To set the quick jerboa[6] a-musing outside his sand house—   45
There are none such as he for a wonder, half bird and half mouse!
God made all the creatures and gave them our love and our fear,
To give sign, we and they are his children, one family here.

VII

Then I played the help-tune of our reapers, their wine-song, when
    hand
Grasps at hand, eye lights eye in good friendship, and great hearts
    expand   50
And grow one in the sense of this world's life.—And then, the last
    song
When the dead man is praised on his journey—"Bear, bear him
    along
With his few faults shut up like dead flowerets! Are balm-seeds not
    here
To console us? The land has none left such as he on the bier.
Oh, would we might keep thee, my brother!"—And then, the glad
    chaunt   55
Of the marriage,—first go the young maidens, next, she whom we
    vaunt
As the beauty, the pride of our dwelling.—And then, the great
    march[7]
Wherein man runs to man to assist him and buttress an arch[8]
Nought can break; who shall harm them, our friends?—Then, the
    chorus intoned
As the Levites[9] go up to the altar in glory enthroned.   60

5. Perhaps the boa constrictor, preparing to shed his skin.
6. Jumping rodent.
7. Battle song.
8. Semicircular battle formation.
9. Caste of priests.

But I stopped here: for here in the darkness Saul groaned.

VIII

And I paused, held my breath in such silence, and listened apart;
And the tent shook, for mighty Saul shuddered: and sparkles 'gan
    dart
From the jewels that woke in his turban, at once with a start,
All its lordly male-sapphires,[1] and rubies courageous at heart.   65
So the head: but the body still moved not, still hung there erect.
And I bent once again to my playing, pursued it unchecked,
As I sang,—

IX

        "Oh, our manhood's prime vigour! No spirit feels waste,
Not a muscle is stopped in its playing nor sinew unbraced.
Oh, the wild joys of living! the leaping from rock up to rock,   70
The strong rending of boughs from the fir-tree, the cool silver shock
Of the plunge in a pool's living water, the hunt of the bear,
And the sultriness showing the lion is couched in his lair.
And the meal, the rich dates yellowed over with gold dust divine,
And the locust-flesh steeped in the pitcher, the full draught   75
    of wine,
And the sleep in the dried river-channel where bulrushes tell
That the water was wont to go warbling so softly and well.
How good is man's life, the mere living! how fit to employ
All the heart and the soul and the senses for ever in joy!
Hast thou loved the white locks of thy father, whose sword thou
    didst guard   80
When he trusted thee forth with the armies, for glorious reward?
Didst thou see the thin hands of thy mother, held up as men sung
The low song of the nearly-departed, and hear her faint tongue
Joining in while it could to the witness, 'Let one more attest,
I have lived, seen God's hand thro' a lifetime, and all was
    for best?'   85
Then they sung thro' their tears in strong triumph, not much, but
    the rest.
And thy brothers, the help and the contest, the working whence
    grew
Such result as, from seething grape-bundles, the spirit strained true:
And the friends of thy boyhood—that boyhood of wonder and hope,
Present promise and wealth of the future beyond the eye's
    scope—   90
Till lo, thou are grown to a monarch; a people is thine;
And all gifts, which the world offers singly, on one head combine!
On one head, all the beauty and strength, love and rage (like the
    throe[2]
That, a-work in the rock, helps it labour and lets the gold go)
High ambition and deeds which surpass it, fame crowning them,—
    all   95
Brought to blaze on the head of one creature—King Saul!"

1. Blue gem-sapphire, "lordly" because   2. Earthquake, producing a fissure.
its color stood for royalty.

X

And lo, with the leap of my spirit,—heart, hand, harp and voice,
Each lifting Saul's name out of sorrow, each bidding rejoice
Saul's fame in the light it was made for—as when, dare I say,
The Lord's army, in rapture of service, strains through its array.   100
And upsoareth the cherubim-chariot[3]—"Saul!" cried I, and stopped,
And waited the thing that should follow. Then Saul, who hung propped
By the tent's cross-support in the centre, was struck by his name.
Have ye seen when Spring's arrowy summons goes right to the aim,
And some mountain, the last to withstand her, that held (he alone,   105
While the vale laughed in freedom and flowers) on a broad bust of stone
A year's snow bound about for a breastplate,—leaves grasp of the sheet?
Fold on fold all at once it crowds thunderously down to his feet,
And there fronts you, stark, black, but alive yet, your mountain of old,
With his rents, the successive bequeathings of ages untold—   110
Yea, each harm got in fighting your battles, each furrow and scar
Of his head thrust 'twixt you and the tempest—all hail, there they are!
—Now again to be softened with verdure, again hold the nest
Of the dove, tempt the goat and its young to the green on his crest
For their food in the ardours of summer. One long shudder thrilled   115
All the tent till the very air tingled, then sank and was stilled
At the King's self left standing before me, released and aware.
What was gone, what remained? All to traverse, 'twixt hope and despair;
Death was past, life not come: so he waited. Awhile his right hand
Held the brow, helped the eyes left too vacant forthwith to remand   120
To their place what new objects should enter: 't was Saul as before.
I looked up and dared gaze at those eyes, nor was hurt any more
Than by slow pallid sunsets in autumn, ye watch from the shore,
At their sad level gaze o'er the ocean—a sun's slow decline
Over hills which, resolved in stern silence, o'erlap and entwine   125
Base with base to knit strength more intensely: so, arm folded arm
O'er the chest whose slow heavings subsided.

XI

What spell or what charm,
(For, awhile there was trouble within me) what next should I urge
To sustain him where song had restored him?—Song filled to the verge
His cup with the wine of this life, pressing all that it yields   130
Of mere fruitage, the strength and the beauty: beyond, on what fields,

---

3. An image inspired by the vision of the cherubim and wheels in Ezekiel 10.

Glean a vintage more potent and perfect to brighten the eye
And bring blood to the lip, and commend them the cup they put
    by?
He saith, "It is good;" still he drinks not: he lets me praise life,
Gives assent, yet would die for his own part.

XII

                       The fancies grew rife   135
Which had come long ago on the pasture, when round me the sheep
Fed in silence—above, the one eagle wheeled slow as in sleep;
And I lay in my hollow and mused on the world that might lie
'Neath his ken, though I saw but the strip 'twixt the hill and the
    sky:
And I laughed—"Since my days are ordained to be passed with my
    flocks,   140
Let me people at least, with my fancies, the plains and the rocks,
Dream the life I am never to mix with, and image the show
Of mankind as they live in those fashions I hardly shall know!
Schemes of life, its best rules and right uses, the courage that gains,
And the prudence that keeps what men strive for." And now these
    old trains   145
Of vague thought came again; I grew surer; so, once more the string
Of my harp made response to my spirit, as thus—

XIII

                            "Yea, my King,"
I began—"thou dost well in rejecting mere comforts that spring
From the mere mortal life held in common by man and by brute:
In our flesh grows the branch of this life, in our soul it bears fruit. 150
Thou hast marked the slow rise of the tree,—how its stem trembled
    first
Till it passed the kid's lip, the stag's antler; then safely outburst
The fan-branches all round; and thou mindest when these too, in
    turn
Broke a-bloom and the palm-tree seemed perfect: yet more was to
    learn,
E'en the good that comes in with the palm-fruit. Our dates shall we
    slight,   155
When their juice brings a cure for all sorrow? or care for the plight
Of the palm's self whose slow growth produced them? Not so! stem
    and branch
Shall decay, nor be known in their place, while the palm-wine shall
    staunch
Every wound of man's spirit in winter. I pour thee such wine.
Leave the flesh to the fate it was fit for! the spirit be thine!   160
By the spirit, when age shall o'ercome thee, thou still shalt enjoy
More indeed, than at first when inconscious, the life of a boy.
Crush that life, and behold its wine running! Each deed thou hast
    done
Dies, revives, goes to work in the world; until e'en as the sun
Looking down on the earth, though clouds spoil him, though
    tempests efface,   165

Can find nothing his own deed produced not, must everywhere trace
The results of his past summer-prime,—so, each ray of thy will,
Every flash of thy passion and prowess, long over, shall thrill
Thy whole people, the countless, with ardour, till they too give forth
A like cheer to their sons, who in turn, fill the South and the
    North   170
With the radiance thy deed was the germ of. Carouse in the past!
But the license of age has its limit; thou diest at last:
As the lion when age dims his eyeball, the rose at her height,
So with man—so his power and his beauty for ever take flight.
No! Again a long draught of my soul-wine! Look forth o'er the
    years!   175
Thou hast done now with eyes for the actual; begin with the seer's!
Is Saul dead? In the depth of the vale make his tomb—bid arise
A grey mountain of marble heaped four-square, till, built to the
    skies,
Let it mark where the great First King slumbers: whose fame would
    ye know?
Up above see the rock's naked face, where the record shall go   180
In great characters cut by the scribe,—Such was Saul, so he did;
With the sages directing the work, by the populace chid,—
For not half, they'll affirm, is comprised there! Which fault to
    amend,
In the grove with his kind grows the cedar, whereon they shall spend
(See, in tablets 't is level before them) their praise, and record   185
With the gold of the graver, Saul's story,—the statesman's great
    word
Side by side with the poet's sweet comment. The river's a-wave
With smooth paper-reeds[4] grazing each other when prophet-winds
    rave:
So the pen gives unborn generations their due and their part
In thy being! Then, first of the mighty, thank God that thou
    art!"   190

XIV

And behold while I sang . . . but O Thou who didst grant me that
    day,
And before it not seldom hast granted thy help to essay,
Carry on and complete an adventure,—my shield and my sword
In that act where my soul was thy servant, thy word was my word,—
Still be with me, who then at the summit of human endeavour   195
And scaling the highest, man's thought could, gazed hopeless as
    ever
On the new stretch of heaven above me—till, mighty to save,
Just one lift of thy hand cleared that distance—God's throne from
    man's grave!
Let me tell out my tale to its ending—my voice to my heart
Which can scarce dare believe in what marvels last night I took
    part,   200

4. Papyrus.

As this morning I gather the fragments, alone with my sheep,
And still fear lest the terrible glory evanish like sleep!
For I wake in the grey dewy covert, while Hebron[5] upheaves
The dawn struggling with night on his shoulder, and Kidron[6] retrieves
Slow the damage of yesterday's sunshine.

XV

I say then,—my song [205]
While I sang thus, assuring the monarch, and ever more strong
Made a proffer of good to console him—he slowly resumed
His old motions and habitudes kingly. The right-hand replumed
His black locks to their wonted composure, adjusted the swathes
Of his turban, and see—the huge sweat that his countenance bathes, [210]
He wipes off with the robe; and he girds now his loins as of yore,
And feels slow for the armlets of price, with the clasp set before.
He is Saul, ye remember in glory,—ere error[7] had bent
The broad brow from the daily communion; and still, though much spent
Be the life and the bearing that front you, the same, God did choose, [215]
To receive what a man may waste, desecrate, never quite lose.
So sank he along by the tent-prop till, stayed by the pile
Of his armour and war-cloak and garments, he leaned there awhile,
And sat out my singing,—one arm round the tent-prop, to raise
His bent head, and the other hung slack—till I touched on the praise [220]
I foresaw from all men in all time, to the man patient there;
And thus ended, the harp falling forward. Then first I was 'ware
That he sat, as I say, with my head just above his vast knees
Which were thrust out on each side around me, like oak-roots which please
To encircle a lamb when it slumbers. I looked up to know [225]
If the best I could do had brought solace: he spoke not, but slow
Lifted up the hand slack at his side, till he laid it with care
Soft and grave, but in mild settled will, on my brow: thro' my hair
The large fingers were pushed, and he bent back my head, with kind power—
All my face back, intent to peruse it, as men do a flower. [230]
Thus held he me there with his great eyes that scrutinized mine—
And oh, all my heart how it loved him! but where was the sign?
I yearned—"Could I help thee, my father, inventing a bliss,
I would add, to that life of the past, both the future and this;
I would give thee new life altogether, as good, ages hence, [235]
As this moment,—had love but the warrant, love's heart to dispense!"

5. Mountain southwest of Jerusalem, and the city on it.
6. "The brook Cedron" (John 18:1), a ravine east of Jerusalem, is dry in summer.
7. Saul's "error" was disobedience of the Lord's command to destroy the Amalekites and all their goods; "the Lord repented that he had made Saul king over Israel" (1 Samuel 15).

XVI

Then the truth came upon me. No harp more—no song more![8]
  outbroke—

XVII

"I have gone the whole round of creation: I saw and I spoke:
I, a work of God's hand for that purpose, received in my brain
And pronounced on the rest of his handwork—returned
  him again   240
His creation's approval or censure: I spoke as I saw:
I report, as a man may of God's work—all's love, yet all's law.
Now I lay down the judgeship he lent me. Each faculty tasked
To perceive him, has gained an abyss, where a dewdrop was asked.
Have I knowledge? confounded it shrivels at Wisdom laid bare.   245
Have I forethought? how purblind, how blank, to[9] the Infinite Care!
Do I task any faculty highest, to image success?
I but open my eyes,—and perfection, no more and no less,
In the kind I imagined, full-fronts me, and God is seen God
In the star, in the stone, in the flesh, in the soul and the clod.   250
And thus looking within and around me, I ever renew
(With that stoop of the soul which in bending upraises it too)
The submission of man's nothing-perfect to God's all-complete,
As by each new obeisance in spirit, I climb to his feet.
Yet with all this abounding experience, this deity known,   255
I shall dare to discover some province, some gift of my own.
There's a faculty pleasant to exercise, hard to hoodwink,
I am fain to keep still in abeyance, (I laugh as I think)
Lest, insisting to claim and parade in it, wot ye, I worst
E'en the Giver in one gift.—Behold, I could love it if I durst!   260
But I sink the pretension as fearing a man may o'ertake
God's own speed in the one way of love: I abstain for love's sake.
—What, my soul? see thus far and no farther? when doors great
  and small,
Nine-and-ninety flew ope at our touch, should the hundredth appal?
In the least things have faith, yet distrust in the greatest of all? 265
Do I find love so full in my nature, God's ultimate gift,
That I doubt his own love can compete with it? Here, the parts
  shift?
Here, the creature surpass the Creator,—the end, what Began?
Would I fain in my impotent yearning do all for this man,
And dare doubt he alone shall not help him, who yet alone can?   270
Would it ever have entered my mind, the bare will, much less
  power,
To bestow on this Saul what I sang of, the marvellous dower
Of the life he was gifted and filled with? to make such a soul,
Such a body, and then such an earth for insphering the whole?
And doth it not enter my mind (as my warm tears attest)   275
These good things being given, to go on, and give one more, the
  best?

---

8. David implies that "song" (lyric po-
etry), while therapeutic, is not suitable for the higher function of prophecy.
9. Compared to.

Ay, to save and redeem and restore him, maintain at the height
This perfection,—succeed[1] with life's dayspring, death's minute of
    night?
Interpose at the difficult minute, snatch Saul the mistake,
Saul the failure, the ruin he seems now,—and bid him awake   280
From the dream, the probation, the prelude, to find himself set
Clear and safe in new light and new life,—a new harmony yet
To be run, and continued, and ended—who knows?—or endure!
The man taught enough, by life's dream, of the rest to make sure;
By the pain-throb, triumphantly winning intensified bliss,   285
And the next world's reward and repose, by the struggle in this.

XVIII

"I believe it! 'T is thou, God, that givest, 't is I who receive:
In the first is the last, in thy will is my power to believe.
All's one gift: thou canst grant it moreover, as prompt to my prayer
As I breathe out this breath, as I open these arms to the air.   290
From thy will, stream the worlds, life and nature, thy dread
       Sabaoth:[2]
I will?—the mere atoms despise me! Why am I not loth
To look that, even that in the face too?[3] Why is it I dare
Think but lightly of such impuissance? What stops my despair?
This;—'t is not what man Does which exalts him, but what man
       Would do!   295
See the King—I would help him but cannot, the wishes fall
       through.
Could I wrestle to raise him from sorrow, grow poor to enrich,
To fill up his life, starve my own out, I would—knowing which,
I know that my service is perfect. Oh, speak through me now!
Would I suffer for him that I love? So wouldst thou—so wilt
       thou!   300
So shall crown thee the topmost, ineffablest, uttermost crown—
And thy love fill infinitude wholly, nor leave up nor down
One spot for the creature to stand in! It is by no breath,
Turn of eye, wave of hand, that salvation joins issue with death!
As thy Love is discovered almighty, almighty be proved   305
Thy power, that exists with and for it, of being Beloved!
He who did most, shall bear most; the strongest shall stand the
       most weak.
'T is the weakness in strength, that I cry for! my flesh, that I seek
In the Godhead! I seek and I find it. O Saul, it shall be
A Face like my face that receives thee; a Man like to me,   310
Thou shalt love and be loved by, for ever: a Hand like this hand
Shall throw open the gates of new life to thee! See the Christ
       stand!"[4]

XIX

I know not too well how I found my way home in the night.

---

1. Follow.
2. Armies; hence, might.
3. In 1855 this line read: "and why am I loth / To look . . .?"

4. From his own intense love David is now able to infer the divine love that will necessarily culminate in God's Incarnation as Christ.

There were witnesses, cohorts[5] about me, to left and to right,
Angels, powers, the unuttered, unseen, the alive, the aware: 315
I repressed, I got through them as hardly, as strugglingly there,
As a runner beset by the populace famished for news—
Life or death. The whole earth was awakened, hell loosed with her
    crews;
And the stars of night beat with emotion, and tingled and shot
Out in fire the strong pain of pent knowledge: but I fainted not,   320
For the Hand still impelled me at once and supported, suppressed
All the tumult, and quenched it with quiet, and holy behest,
Till the rapture was shut in itself, and the earth sank to rest.
Anon at the dawn, all that trouble had withered from earth—
Not so much, but I saw it die out in the day's tender birth;   325
In the gathered intensity brought to the grey of the hills;
In the shuddering forests' held breath; in the sudden wind-thrills;
In the startled wild beasts that bore off, each with eye sidling still
Though averted with wonder and dread; in the birds stiff and chill
That rose heavily, as I approached them, made stupid with awe: 330
E'en the serpent that slid away silent,—he felt the new law.
The same stared in the white humid faces upturned by the flowers;
The same worked in the heart of the cedar and moved the vine-
    bowers:
And the little brooks witnessing murmured, persistent and low,
With their obstinate, all but hushed voices—"E'en so, it is so!"   335

ca. 1845–ca. 1853

Women and Roses[1]

I

I dream of a red-rose tree.
And which of its roses three
Is the dearest rose to me?

II

Round and round, like a dance of snow
In a dazzling drift, as its guardians, go   5
Floating the women faded for ages,
Sculptured in stone, on the poet's pages.
Then follow women fresh and gay,
Living and loving and loved to-day.
Last, in the rear, flee the multitude of maidens,   10
Beauties yet unborn. And all, to one cadence,
They circle their rose on my rose tree.

III

Dear rose, thy term is reached,
Thy leaf hangs loose and bleached:
Bees pass it unimpeached.[2]   15

IV

Stay then, stoop, since I cannot climb,
You, great shapes of the antique time!
How shall I fix you, fire you, freeze you,
Break my heart at your feet to please you?
Oh, to possess and be possessed! 20
Hearts that beat 'neath each pallid breast!
Once but of love, the poesy, the passion,
Drink but once and die!—In vain, the same fashion,
They circle their rose on my rose tree.

V

Dear rose, thy joy's undimmed, 25
Thy cup is ruby-rimmed,
Thy cup's heart nectar-brimmed.

VI

Deep, as drops from a statue's plinth[3]
The bee sucked in by the hyacinth,
So will I bury me while burning, 30
Quench like him at a plunge my yearning,
Eyes in your eyes, lips on your lips!
Fold me fast where the cincture[4] slips,
Prison all my soul in eternities of pleasure,
Girdle me for once! But no—the old measure, 35
They circle their rose on my rose tree.

VII

Dear rose without a thorn,
Thy bud's the babe unborn:
First streak of a new morn.

VIII

Wings, lend wings for the cold, the clear![5] 40
What is far conquers what is near.
Roses will bloom nor want beholders,
Sprung from the dust where our flesh moulders.
What shall arrive with the cycle's change?
A novel grace and a beauty strange. 45
I will make an Eve, be the artist that began her,
Shaped her to his mind!—Alas! in like manner
They circle their rose on my rose tree.

1852

Holy-Cross Day[1]

ON WHICH THE JEWS WERE FORCED TO ATTEND AN ANNUAL
CHRISTIAN SERMON IN ROME

["Now was come about Holy-Cross Day, and now must my lord preach his
first sermon to the Jews: as it was of old cared for in the merciful bowels[2]

---

3. Base.
4. Girdle.
5. Metaphor of the artist's imagination.

1. Holy-Cross Day (September 14), one
of the principal feasts of the Roman
Catholic church, originated in Jerusalem

of the Church, that, so to speak, a crumb at least from her conspicuous table here in Rome should be, though but once yearly, cast to the famishing dogs,[3] under-trampled and bespitten-upon beneath the feet of the guests. And a moving sight in truth, this, of so many of the besotted blind restif and ready-to-perish Hebrews! now maternally brought—nay (for He saith, 'Compel them to come in'[4]) haled, as it were, by the head and hair, and against their obstinate hearts, to partake of the heavenly grace. What awakening, what striving with tears, what working of a yeasty conscience! Nor was my lord wanting to himself on so apt an occasion; witness the abundance of conversions which did incontinently reward him: though not to my lord be altogether the glory."[5]—Diary by the Bishops' Secretary, 1600.]

What the Jews really said, on thus being driven to church, was rather to this effect:—

I

Fee, faw, fum! bubble and squeak![6]
Blessedest Thursday's[7] the fat of the week.
Rumble and tumble, sleek and rough,
Stinking and savoury, smug and gruff,
Take the church-road, for the bell's due chime   5
Gives us the summons—'t is sermon-time!

II

Boh, here's Barnabas! Job, that's you?
Up stumps Solomon—bustling too?
Shame, man! greedy beyond your years
To handsel the bishop's shaving-shears?[8]   10
Fair play's a jewel! Leave friends in the lurch?
Stand on a line ere you start for the church!

III

Higgledy piggledy, packed we lie,
Rats in a hamper, swine in a stye,
Wasps in a bottle, frogs in a sieve,   15
Worms in a carcase, fleas in a sleeve.
Hist! square shoulders, settle your thumbs[9]
And buzz for the bishop—here he comes.

to commemorate the dedication in 335 of the churches built by the Emperor Constantine on the sites of the Crucifixion and Holy Sepulcher. The practice of compelling Jews to attend conversionist sermons began in the papacy of Gregory XIII (1572–85) and continued into Browning's time; several times a year Jews were summoned to services in the church of St. Angelo in Pescheria, near the Roman ghetto. The diary entry preceding the poem is a fiction of Browning's.
2. Seat of pity or kindness.
3. In Matthew 15:25–27 the Canaanite woman begs Jesus to heal her daughter: "But he answered and said, It is not meet to take the children's bread, and to cast it to dogs. And she said, Truth, Lord: yet the dogs eat of the crumbs

which fall from their master's table."
4. Refers to the parable of the great supper from which the invited guests all excuse themselves. The angry master then sends his servants to "compel them [the poor, the handicapped] to come in" (Luke 14:23).
5. Paraphrase of Psalm 115:1: "Not unto us, O Lord, not unto us, but unto thy name give glory . . ."
6. Bubble and squeak: cold boiled potatoes and greens fried together.
7. Perhaps Holy Thursday, or Ascension Day. "Fat" because the three days preceding were appointed for fasting.
8. Handsel: to use for the first time. The shaving of a Jew was taken as a sign of conversion.
9. Get ready to bite your thumbs, an insulting gesture.

IV

Bow, wow, wow—a bone for the dog!
I liken his Grace to an acorned hog.[1]   20
What, a boy at his side, with the bloom of a lass,
To help and handle my lord's hour-glass!
Didst ever behold so lithe a chine?[2]
His cheek hath laps like a fresh-singed swine.

V

Aaron's asleep—shove hip to haunch,   25
Or somebody deal him a dig in the paunch!
Look at the purse with the tassel and knob,
And the gown with the angel and thingumbob!
What's he at, quotha?[3] reading his text!
Now you've his curtsey[4]—and what comes next.   30

VI

See to our converts—you doomed black dozen[5]—
No stealing away—nor cog nor cozen![6]
You five, that were thieves, deserve it fairly;
You seven, that were beggars, will live less sparely;
You took your turn and dipped in the hat,   35
Got fortune—and fortune gets you; mind that!

VII

Give your first groan—compunction's at work;
And soft! from a Jew you mount to a Turk.[7]
Lo, Micah,—the selfsame beard on chin
He was four times already converted in!   40
Here's a knife, clip quick—it's a sign of grace—
Or he ruins us all with his hanging-face.[8]

VIII

Whom now is the bishop a-leering at?
I know a point where his text falls pat.
I'll tell him to-morrow, a word just now   45
Went to my heart and made me vow
I meddle no more with the worst of trades[9]—
Let somebody else pay his serenades.

IX

Groan all together now, whee—hee—hee!
It's a-work, it's a-work, ah, woe is me!   50
It began, when a herd of us, picked and placed,
Were spurred through the Corso, stripped to the waist;[1]
Jew brutes, with sweat and blood well spent
To usher in worthily Christian Lent.

1. Hog fattened with acorns. The Jews reject pork as unclean.
2. Cut of meat including the backbone.
3. Quoth he (expression of contempt).
4. Genuflection.
5. Jews appointed by lot to act as though converted.
6. Neither cheat nor deceive.
7. I.e., you will rise to the status of mere barbarian in Christian eyes.
8. Hangdog look.
9. Usury, or money-lending, which the Jew will pretend to give up. Someone else will have to finance the hypocritical bishop's love-affairs (line 48).
1. Reference to the reported subsitution of Jews for horses in the annual race (*Corsa dei Berberi*) at Carnival time in Rome.

X

It grew, when the hangman entered our bounds,   55
Yelled, pricked us out to his church like hounds:
It got to a pitch, when the hand indeed
Which gutted my purse would throttle my creed:
And it overflows when, to even the odd,
Men I helped to their sins help me to their God.   60

XI

But now, while the scapegoats leave our flock,
And the rest sit silent and count the clock,
Since forced to muse the appointed time
On these precious facts and truths sublime,—
Let us fitly employ it, under our breath,   65
In saying Ben Ezra's Song of Death.[2]

XII

For Rabbi Ben Ezra, the night he died,
Called sons and sons' sons to his side,
And spoke, "This world has been harsh and strange;
Something is wrong: there needeth a change.   70
But what, or where? at the last or first?
In one point only we sinned, at worst.

XIII

"The Lord will have mercy on Jacob yet,
And again in his border see Israel set.
When Judah beholds Jerusalem,   75
The stranger-seed shall be joined to them:
To Jacob's House shall the Gentiles cleave.[3]
So the Prophet saith and his sons believe.

XIV

"Ay, the children of the chosen race
Shall carry and bring them to their place: 80
In the land of the Lord shall lead the same,
Bondsmen and handmaids. Who shall blame,
When the slaves enslave, the oppressed ones o'er
The oppressor triumph for evermore?

XV

"God spoke, and gave us the word to keep,   85
Bade never fold the hands nor sleep
'Mid a faithless world,—at watch and ward,
Till Christ at the end relieve our guard.
By His servant Moses the watch was set:
Though near upon cock-crow, we keep it yet.   90

XVI

"Thou! if thou wast He, who at mid-watch came,
By the starlight, naming a dubious name![4]
And if, too heavy with sleep—too rash

---

2. Abraham ibn Ezra (1092–1167), Jew-ish Bible commentator and scholar who taught in Rome after 1140. The "Song of Death" appears to be Browning's invention.
3. Lines 72–77 paraphrase Isaiah 14:1.

Browning adds a phrase from Jeremiah 3:18: "In those days the house of Judah shall walk with the house of Israel."
4. Jesus, whom the Jews do not regard as their Messiah.

With fear—O Thou, if that martyr-gash
Fell on Thee coming to take thine own,   95
And we gave the Cross, when we owed the Throne—

XVII

"Thou art the Judge. We are bruised thus.
But, the Judgment over, join sides with us!
Thine too is the cause! and not more thine
Than ours, is the work of these dogs and swine,   100
Whose life laughs through and spits at their creed!
Who maintain Thee in word, and defy Thee in deed!

XVIII

"We withstood Christ then? Be mindful how
At least we withstand Barabbas[5] now!
Was our outrage sore? But the worst we spared,   105
To have called these—Christians, had we dared!
Let defiance to them pay mistrust of Thee,
And Rome make amends for Calvary!

XIX

"By the torture, prolonged from age to age,
By the infamy, Israel's heritage,   110
By the Ghetto's[6] plague, by the garb's disgrace,
By the badge of shame, by the felon's place,
By the branding-tool, the bloody whip,
And the summons to Christian fellowship,—

XX

"We boast our proof that at least the Jew   115
Would wrest Christ's name from the Devil's crew.
Thy face took never so deep a shade
But we fought them in it, God our aid!
A trophy to bear, as we march, thy band,
South, East, and on to the Pleasant Land!"[7]   120

[*Pope Gregory XVI. abolished this bad business
of the Sermon.*—R. B.][8]

ca. 1854

The Guardian-Angel[1]

A PICTURE AT FANO

I

Dear and great Angel, wouldst thou only leave
That child, when thou hast done with him, for me!

5. According to the New Testament, at the demand of the Jews Pilate freed the murderer Barabbas and crucified Jesus.
6. Jewish quarter, formally established in 1555 in Rome by papal bull. The ghetto walls were not removed until 1870, at which time Roman Jews were accorded civil rights.
7. As Barbara Melchiori has shown, Browning adapts a passage from Jeremiah (3:17–19) in support of his final vision of unification of Christians and Jews. ". . . and all the nations shall be gathered unto it, to the name of the Lord, to Jerusalem. . . . and they [men of Judah and Israel] shall come together out of the land of the north to the land that I have given for an inheritance unto your fathers." The phrase "a pleasant land" occurs in verse 19.
8. The "bad business" ceased in 1846.
1. One of the very few poems Browning

Let me sit all the day here, that when eve
　　Shall find performed thy special ministry,
And time come for departure, thou, suspending 　　　5
Thy flight, mayst see another child for tending,
　　Another still, to quiet and retrieve.

II

Then I shall feel thee step one step, no more,
　　From where thou standest now, to where I gaze,
—And suddenly my head is covered o'er 　　　10
　　With those wings, white above the child who prays
Now on that tomb—and I shall feel thee guarding
Me, out of all the world; for me, discarding
　　Yon heaven thy home, that waits and opes its door.

III

I would not look up thither past thy head 　　　15
　　Because the door opes, like that child, I know,
For I should have thy gracious face instead,
　　Thou bird of God! And wilt thou bend me low
Like him, and lay, like his, my hands together,
And lift them up to pray, and gently tether 　　　20
　　Me, as thy lamb there, with thy garment's spread?

IV

If this was ever granted, I would rest
　　My head beneath thine, while thy healing hands
Close-covered both my eyes beside thy breast,
　　Pressing the brain, which too much thought expands, 　　　25
Back to its proper size again, and smoothing
Distortion down till every nerve had soothing,
　　And all lay quiet, happy and suppressed.

V

How soon all worldly wrong would be repaired!
　　I think how I should view the earth and skies 　　　30
And sea, when once again my brow was bared
　　After thy healing, with such different eyes.
O world, as God has made it! All is beauty:
And knowing this, is love, and love is duty.
　　What further may be sought for or declared? 　　　35

VI

Guercino drew this angel I saw teach
　　(Alfred,[2] dear friend!)—that little child to pray,
Holding the little hands up, each to each
　　Pressed gently,—with his own head turned away
Over the earth where so much lay before him 　　　40

---

wrote during the first three years of marriage, and one of his rare autobiographical utterances. Probably composed in Ancona, Italy, in late July 1848. At Fano, near Ancona on the Adriatic, the Brownings had been admiring *L'Angelo Custode,* by the Italian painter Giovanni Francesco Barbieri (1591–1666), called Guercino ("the squint-eyed").
2. Alfred Domett (1811–87), a confidant and fellow poet, whose emigration to New Zealand is the subject of Browning's "Waring" (1842).

Of work to do, though heaven was opening o'er him,
   And he was left at Fano by the beach.

VII

We were at Fano, and three times we went
   To sit and see him in his chapel there,
And drink his beauty to our soul's content   45
   —My angel[3] with me too: and since I care
For dear Guercino's fame (to which in power
And glory comes this picture for a dower,
   Fraught with a pathos so magnificent)—

VIII

And since he did not work thus earnestly   50
   At all times, and has else endured some wrong[4]—
I took one thought his picture struck from me,
   And spread it out, translating it to song.
My love is here. Where are you, dear old friend?
How rolls the Wairoa[5] at your world's far end?   55
   This is Ancona, yonder is the sea.

ca. 1848

Cleon[1]

"As certain also of your own poets have said" —

Cleon the poet (from the sprinkled isles,[2]
Lily on lily, that o'erlace the sea,
And laugh their pride when the light wave lisps "Greece")—
To Protus in his Tyranny:[3] much health!

   They give thy letter to me, even now: 5
I read and seem as if I heard thee speak.
The master of thy galley still unlades
Gift after gift; they block my court at last
And pile themselves along its portico
Royal with sunset,[4] like a thought of thee: 10
And one white she-slave from the group dispersed
Of black and white slaves (like the chequer-work
Pavement, at once my nation's work and gift,

3. Browning's wife.
4. Probably alludes to adverse criticism of Guercino's angels by the Brownings' friend, art critic Anna Jameson (*Sacred and Legendary Art* [1848] I: 82).
5. River in New Zealand.
1. This epistolary monologue is a formal and thematic companion to "An Epistle . . . of Karshish." The imaginary Cleon is a Greek of the late Hellenistic Age, and a contemporary of the Apostle Paul, whose European mission—including a period in Athens—commenced about A.D. 50. "Cleon" is regarded by some as Browning's reply to Matthew Arnold's

Empedocles on Etna (1852), in which the hero, a pagan philosopher in deep despair, takes his life after painful meditation upon the human condition. The epigraph to the present poem is from Acts 17: 28: "For in him [God] we live, and move, and have our being; as certain also of your own poets have said, For we are also his offspring."
2. The Sporades, scattered islands off the Greek coast near Crete.
3. *Tyranny* in Greek means absolute power, without necessarily implying oppression.
4. Crimson and purple were royal colors.

Now covered with this settle-down of doves),
One lyric[5] woman, in her crocus vest   15
Woven of sea-wools,[6] with her two white hands
Commends to me the strainer and the cup
Thy lip hath bettered ere it blesses mine.

Well-counselled, king, in thy munificence!
For so shall men remark, in such an act   20
Of love for him whose song gives life its joy,
Thy recognition of the use of life;
Nor call thy spirit barely adequate
To help on life in straight ways, broad enough
For vulgar souls, by ruling and the rest.   25
Thou, in the daily building of thy tower,[7]—
Whether in fierce and sudden spasms of toil,
Or through dim lulls of unapparent growth,
Or when the general work 'mid good acclaim
Climbed with the eye to cheer the architect,—   30
Didst ne'er engage in work for mere work's sake—
Hadst ever in thy heart the luring hope
Of some eventual rest a-top of it,
Whence, all the tumult of the building hushed,
Thou first of men mightst look out to the East: 35
The vulgar saw thy tower, thou sawest the sun.
For this, I promise on thy festival
To pour libation, looking o'er the sea,
Making this slave narrate thy fortunes, speak
Thy great words, and describe thy royal face—   40
Wishing thee wholly where Zeus lives the most,
Within the eventual element of calm.

Thy letter's first requirement[8] meets me here.
It is as thou hast heard: in one short life
I, Cleon, have effected all those things   45
Thou wonderingly dost enumerate.
That epos[9] on thy hundred plates of gold
Is mine,—and also mine the little chant,
So sure to rise from every fishing-bark
When, lights at prow, the seamen haul their net.   50
The image of the sun-god on the phare,[1]
Men turn from the sun's self to see, is mine;
The Pœcile,[2] o'er-storied its whole length,
As thou didst hear, with painting, is mine too.
I know the true proportions of a man   55
And woman also, not observed before;

5. Beautiful.
6. Wools dyed with sea-purple.
7. Protus' monument.
8. Inquiry. The first three inquiries are carefully answered; the fourth is dismissed in a postscript to the letter (337ff.).
9. Heroic poem, epic.
1. Lighthouse.
2. Portico at Athens decorated with battle scenes by great artists.

And I have written three books on the soul,
Proving absurd all written hitherto,
And putting us to ignorance again.
For music,—why, I have combined the moods,[3]   60
Inventing one. In brief, all arts are mine;
Thus much the people know and recognize,
Throughout our seventeen islands. Marvel not.
We of these latter days, with greater mind
Than our forerunners, since more composite,   65
Look not so great, beside their simple way,
To a judge who only sees one way at once,
One mind-point and no other at a time,—
Compares the small part of a man of us
With some whole man of the heroic age,   70
Great in his way—not ours, nor meant for ours.
And ours is greater, had we skill to know:
For, what we call this life of men on earth,
This sequence of the soul's achievements here
Being, as I find much reason to conceive,   75
Intended to be viewed eventually
As a great whole, not analyzed to parts,
But each part having reference to all,—
How shall a certain part, pronounced complete,
Endure effacement by another part?   80
Was the thing done?—then, what's to do again?
See, in the chequered pavement opposite,
Suppose the artist made a perfect rhomb,[4]
And next a lozenge,[5] then a trapezoid—
He did not overlay them, superimpose   85
The new upon the old and blot it out,
But laid them on a level in his work,
Making at last a picture; there it lies.
So, first the perfect separate forms were made,
The portions of mankind; and after, so,   90
Occurred the combination of the same.
For where had been a progress, otherwise?
Mankind, made up of all the single men,—
In such a synthesis the labour ends.
Now mark me! those divine men of old time   95
Have reached, thou sayest well, each at one point
The outside verge that rounds[6] our faculty;
And where they reached, who can do more than reach?
It takes but little water just to touch
At some one point the inside of a sphere,   100
And, as we turn the sphere, touch all the rest
In due succession: but the finer air

3. Or modes, ancient Greek musical scales differing in the arrangement of tones and semitones.
4. Equilateral parallelogram.
5. Diamond-shaped figure.
6. Limits.

Which not so palpably nor obviously,
Though no less universally, can touch
The whole circumference of that emptied sphere,   105
Fills it more fully than the water did;
Holds thrice the weight of water in itself
Resolved into a subtler element.
And yet the vulgar call the sphere first full
Up to the visible height—and after, void;   110
Not knowing air's more hidden properties.
And thus our soul, misknown,[7] cries out to Zeus
To vindicate his purpose in our life:
Why stay we on the earth unless to grow?
Long since, I imaged, wrote the fiction out,   115
That he or other god descended here
And, once for all, showed simultaneously
What, in its nature, never can be shown,
Piecemeal or in succession;—showed, I say,
The worth both absolute and relative   120
Of all his children from the birth of time,
His instruments for all appointed work.[8]
I now go on to image,—might we hear
The judgment which should give the due to each,
Show where the labour lay and where the ease,   125
And prove Zeus' self, the latent everywhere!
This is a dream:—but no dream, let us hope,
That years and days, the summers and the springs,
Follow each other with unwaning powers.
The grapes which dye thy wine are richer far,   130
Through culture, than the wild wealth of the rock;
The suave plum than the savage-tasted drupe;[9]
The pastured honey-bee drops choicer sweet;
The flowers turn double, and the leaves turn flowers;
That young and tender crescent-moon, thy slave,   135
Sleeping above her robe as buoyed by clouds,
Refines upon the women of my youth.
What, and the soul alone deteriorates?
I have not chanted verse like Homer, no—
Nor swept string like Terpander,[1] no—nor carved   140
And painted men like Phidias[2] and his friend:
I am not great as they are, point by point.
But I have entered into sympathy
With these four, running these into one soul,

---

7. Misunderstood.
8. In lines 115–27, Cleon's "fiction" of a divine revelation recalls the teaching of Auguste Comte (1798–1857), who proposed the worship of Humanity and the veneration of such benefactors of the human race as scientists, philosophers, painters, and poets.
9. Fruit with a pit; here, bitter wild plum.
1. Musician of Lesbos in the seventh century B.C., said to have devised the seven-stringed lyre.
2. Athenian sculptor and painter of the fifth century B.C. His "friend" is the statesman Pericles (ca. 495–429 B.C.), who employed Phidias to help decorate Athens.

Who, separate, ignored each other's art.   145
Say, it is nothing that I know them all?
The wild flower was the larger; I have dashed
Rose-blood upon its petals, pricked its cup's
Honey with wine,[3] and driven its seed to fruit,
And show a better flower if not so large: 150
I stand myself. Refer this to the gods
Whose gift alone it is! which, shall I dare
(All pride apart) upon the absurd pretext
That such a gift by chance lay in my hand,
Discourse of lightly or depreciate?   155
It might have fallen to another's hand: what then?
I pass too surely: let at least truth stay!

And next, of what thou followest on to ask.
This being with me as I declare, O king,
My works, in all these varicoloured kinds,   160
So done by me, accepted so by men—
Thou askest, if (my soul thus in men's hearts)
I must not be accounted to attain
The very crown and proper end of life?
Inquiring thence how, now life closeth up,   165
I face death with success in my right hand:
Whether I fear death less than dost thyself
The fortunate of men? "For" (writest thou)
"Thou leavest much behind, while I leave nought.
Thy life stays in the poems men shall sing,   170
The pictures men shall study; while my life,
Complete and whole now in its power and joy,
Dies altogether with my brain and arm,
Is lost indeed; since, what survives myself?
The brazen statue to o'erlook my grave,   175
Set on the promontory which I named.
And that—some supple courtier of my heir
Shall use its robed and sceptred arm, perhaps,
To fix the rope to, which best drags it down.
I go then: triumph thou, who dost not go!"   180

Nay, thou art worthy of hearing my whole mind.
Is this apparent, when thou turn'st to muse
Upon the scheme of earth and man in chief,
That admiration grows as knowledge grows?
That imperfection means perfection hid,   185
Reserved in part, to grace the after-time?
If, in the morning of philosophy,
Ere aught had been recorded, nay perceived,
Thou, with the light now in thee, couldst have looked
On all earth's tenantry, from worm to bird,   190
Ere man, her last, appeared upon the stage[4]—

3. Modified the sweetness with dry wine.   4. Cf. *Paracelsus*, V, 638–786.

Thou wouldst have seen them perfect, and deduced
The perfectness of others yet unseen.
Conceding which,—had Zeus then questioned thee
"Shall I go on a step, improve on this,   195
Do more for visible creatures than is done?"
Thou wouldst have answered, "Ay, by making each
Grow conscious in himself—by that alone.
All's perfect else: the shell sucks fast the rock,
The fish strikes through the sea, the snake both swims   200
And slides, forth range the beasts, the birds take flight,
Till life's mechanics can no further go—
And all this joy in natural life is put
Like fire from off thy finger into each,
So exquisitely perfect is the same.   205
But 't is pure fire, and they mere matter are;
It has them, not they it: and so I choose
For man, thy last premeditated work
(If I might add a glory to the scheme)
That a third thing should stand apart from both,   210
A quality arise within his soul,
Which, intro-active, made to supervise
And feel the force it has, may view itself,
And so be happy." Man might live at first
The animal life: but is there nothing more?   215
In due time, let him critically learn
How he lives; and, the more he gets to know
Of his own life's adaptabilities,
The more joy-giving will his life become.
Thus man, who hath this quality, is best.   220

But thou, king, hadst more reasonably said:
"Let progress end at once,—man make no step
Beyond the natural man, the better beast,
Using his senses, not the sense of sense."
In man there's failure, only since he left   225
The lower and inconscious forms of life.
We called it an advance, the rendering plain
Man's spirit might grow conscious of man's life,
And, by new lore so added to the old,
Take each step higher over the brute's head.   230
This grew the only life, the pleasure-house,
Watch-tower and treasure-fortress of the soul,[5]
Which whole surrounding flats of natural life
Seemed only fit to yield subsistence to;
A tower that crowns a country. But alas,   235
The soul now climbs it just to perish there!
For thence we have discovered ('t is no dream—
We know this, which we had not else perceived)

5. Cf. Tennyson's "Palace of Art" (1832): "I built my soul a lordly pleasure-house"
(line 1).

That there's a world of capability
For joy, spread round about us, meant for us,   240
Inviting us; and still the soul craves all,
And still the flesh replies, "Take no jot more
Than ere thou clombst the tower to look abroad!
Nay, so much less as that fatigue has brought
Deduction to it." We struggle, fain to enlarge   245
Our bounded physical recipiency,
Increase our power, supply fresh oil to life,
Repair the waste of age and sickness: no,
It skills not!⁶ life's inadequate to joy,
As the soul sees joy, tempting life to take.   250
They praise a fountain in my garden here
Wherein a Naiad⁷ sends the water-bow
Thin from her tube; she smiles to see it rise.
What if I told her, it is just a thread
From that great river which the hills shut up,   255
And mock her with my leave to take the same?
The artificer has given her one small tube
Past power to widen or exchange—what boots
To know she might spout oceans if she could?
She cannot lift beyond her first thin thread: 260
And so a man can use but a man's joy
While he sees God's. Is it for Zeus to boast,
"See, man, how happy I live, and despair—
That I may be still happier—for thy use!"
If this were so, we could not thank our lord,   265
As hearts beat on to doing; 't is not so—
Malice it is not. Is it carelessness?
Still, no. If care—where is the sign? I ask,
And get no answer, and agree in sum,
O king, with thy profound discouragement,   270
Who seest the wider but to sigh the more.
Most progress is most failure: thou sayest well.

   The last point now:—thou dost except a case—
Holding joy not impossible to one
With artist-gifts—to such a man as I   275
Who leave behind me living works indeed;⁸
For, such a poem, such a painting lives.
What? dost thou verily trip upon a word,
Confound the accurate view of what joy is
(Caught somewhat clearer by my eyes than thine)   280
With feeling joy? confound the knowing how
And showing how to live (my faculty)
With actually living?—Otherwise

6. Is of no use.
7. Water nymph.
8. A concept of immortality current in the Victorian age, notably among "unbe-lievers" like George Eliot and J. S. Mill, who denied personal immortality, and among the adherents of Comte.

Where is the artist's vantage o'er the king?
Because in my great epos I display   285
How divers men young, strong, fair, wise, can act—
Is this as though I acted? if I paint,
Carve the young Phœbus,[9] am I therefore young?
Methinks I'm older that I bowed myself
The many years of pain that taught me art!   290
Indeed, to know is something, and to prove
How all this beauty might be enjoyed, is more:
But, knowing nought, to enjoy is something too.
Yon rower, with the moulded muscles there,
Lowering the sail, is nearer it than I.   295
I can write love-odes: thy fair slave's an ode.
I get to sing of love, when grown too grey
For being beloved: she turns to that young man,
The muscles all a-ripple on his back.
I know the joy of kingship: well, thou art king!   300

    "But," sayest thou—(and I marvel, I repeat,
To find thee trip on such a mere word) "what
Thou writest, paintest, stays; that does not die:
Sappho[1] survives, because we sing her songs,
And Æschylus,[2] because we read his plays!"   305
Why, if they live still, let them come and take
Thy slave in my despite, drink from thy cup,
Speak in my place. Thou diest while I survive?
Say rather that my fate is deadlier still,
In this, that every day my sense of joy   310
Grows more acute, my soul (intensified
By power and insight) more enlarged, more keen;
While every day my hairs fall more and more,
My hand shakes, and the heavy years increase—
The horror quickening still from year to year,   315
The consummation coming past escape
When I shall know most, and yet least enjoy—
When all my works wherein I prove my worth,
Being present still to mock me in men's mouths,
Alive still, in the praise of such as thou,   320
I, I the feeling, thinking, acting man,
The man who loved his life so over-much,
Sleep in my urn. It is so horrible,
I dare at times imagine to my need
Some future state revealed to us by Zeus,   325
Unlimited in capability
For joy, as this is in desire for joy,
    —To seek which, the joy-hunger forces us:
That, stung by straitness of our life, made strait

9. The sun god Apollo, represented in
art as an ideally handsome youth.
1. Poet of Lesbos (born ca. 612 B.C.),

much admired in antiquity. Only a few
fragments of her work have survived.
2. Athenian tragic poet (525–456 B.C.).

On purpose to make prized the life at large— 330
Freed by the throbbing impulse we call death,
We burst there as the worm into the fly,
Who, while a worm still, wants his wings. But no!
Zeus has not yet revealed it; and alas,
He must have done so, were it possible! 335

Live long and happy, and in that thought die:
Glad for what was! Farewell. And for the rest,
I cannot tell thy messenger aright
Where to deliver what he bears of thine
To one called Paulus;[3] we have heard his fame 340
Indeed, if Christus be not one with him[4]—
I know not, nor am troubled much to know.
Thou canst not think a mere barbarian Jew
As Paulus proves to be, one circumcized,[5]
Hath access to a secret shut from us? 345
Thou wrongest our philosophy, O king,
In stooping to inquire of such an one,
As if his answer could impose at all!
He writeth, doth he? well, and he may write.
Oh, the Jew findeth scholars! certain slaves 350
Who touched on this same isle, preached him and Christ;
And (as I gathered from a bystander)
Their doctrine could be held by no sane man.

ca. 1854

Popularity[1]

I
Stand still, true poet that you are!
    I know you; let me try and draw you.
Some night you'll fail us: when afar
    You rise, remember one man saw you,
Knew you, and named a star! 5

II
My star, God's glow-worm! Why extend
    That loving hand of his which leads you,
Yet locks you safe from end to end
    Of this dark world, unless he needs you,
Just saves your light to spend? 10

III
His clenched hand shall unclose at last,
    I know, and let out all the beauty:

3. St. Paul.
4. I.e., the same person as Paul.
5. I.e., of the Jewish faith.
1. Browning's sympathy for the neglected literary genius of the poem may partly derive from his own frustrated quest for a wide audience. In 1855, the year this poem was published, Browning was entering middle age without having achieved true popularity in either drama or poetry after two decades of writing.

My poet holds the future fast,
    Accepts the coming ages' duty,
Their present for this past.   15
IV
That day, the earth's feast-master's brow
    Shall clear, to God the chalice raising;
"Others give best at first, but thou
    Forever set'st our table praising,
Keep'st the good wine till now!"[2]   20
V
Meantime, I'll draw you as you stand,
    With few or none to watch and wonder:
I'll say—a fisher, on the sand
    By Tyre the old,[3] with ocean-plunder,
A netful, brought to land.   25
VI
Who has not heard how Tyrian shells
    Enclosed the blue, that dye of dyes
Whereof one drop worked miracles,
    And coloured like Astarte's eyes[4]
Raw silk the merchant sells?   30
VII
And each bystander of them all
    Could criticize, and quote tradition
How depths of blue sublimed some pall[5]
    —To get which, pricked a king's ambition;
Worth sceptre, crown and ball.   35
VIII
Yet there's the dye, in that rough mesh,
    The sea has only just o'erwhispered!
Live whelks, each lip's beard dripping fresh,
    As if they still the water's lisp heard
Through foam the rock-weeds thresh.   40
IX
Enough to furnish Solomon
    Such hangings for his cedar-house,[6]
That, when gold-robed he took the throne
    In that abyss of blue, the Spouse
Might swear his presence shone   45
X
Most like the centre-spike of gold
    Which burns deep in the blue-bell's womb,
What time, with ardours manifold,

2. ". . . thou hast kept the good wine until now." Words of the "ruler of the feast" to the bridegroom after Jesus' miraculous conversion of the water into wine (John 2: 1–10).
3. Great city of ancient Phoenicia (now Lebanon), trade center famed for its purple dye, emblematic of royalty.
4. Semitic goddess representing the female principle.
5. Beautified a robe.
6. 1 Kings 7: Solomon's house and "porch of judgment," built of cedar; the blue wall hangings are not mentioned. The "Spouse" is Pharaoh's daughter, whom he wed and lavishly housed.

The bee goes singing to her groom,
Drunken and overbold.   50

XI

Mere conchs! not fit for warp or woof![7]
   Till cunning come to pound and squeeze
And clarify,—refine to proof[8]
   The liquor filtered by degrees,
While the world stands aloof.   55

XII

And there's the extract, flasked and fine,
   And priced and saleable at last!
And Hobbs, Nobbs, Stokes and Nokes[9] combine
   To paint the future from the past,
Put blue into their line.   60

XIII

Hobbs hints blue,—straight he turtle eats:
   Nobbs prints blue,—claret crowns his cup:
Nokes outdares Stokes in azure feats,—
   Both gorge. Who fished the murex[1] up?
What porridge[2] had John Keats?   65

Two in the Campagna[1]

I

I wonder do you feel to-day
   As I have felt since, hand in hand,
We sat down on the grass, to stray
   In spirit better through the land,
This morn of Rome and May?   5

II

For me, I touched a thought, I know,
   Has tantalized me many times,
(Like turns of thread the spiders throw
   Mocking across our path) for rhymes
To catch at and let go.   10

III

Help me to hold it! First it left
   The yellowing fennel, run to seed
There, branching from the brickwork's cleft,
   Some old tomb's ruin: yonder weed
Took up the floating weft,[2]   15

---

7. Unrefined, not ready for use in textiles.
8. To standard quality.
9. Imitators or plagiarists who batten on the "true poet's" pioneering efforts.
1. Genus of mollusc yielding purple dye, referred to in stanza VI.
2. Poor fare, symbolic of the poverty of John Keats (1795–1821) in his final years.

1. Inspired by a May 1854 outing with Elizabeth Barrett Browning in the Campagna di Roma, the plain surrounding Rome and site of the ruins of ancient Latium.
2. In weaving, threads crossing from side to side.

IV

Where one small orange cup amassed
    Five beetles,—blind and green they grope
Among the honey-meal: and last,
    Everywhere on the grassy slope
I traced it. Hold it fast!   20

V

The champaign with its endless fleece
    Of feathery grasses everywhere!
Silence and passion, joy and peace,
    An everlasting wash of air—
Rome's ghost since her decease.   25

VI

Such life here, through such lengths of hours,
    Such miracles performed in play,
Such primal naked forms of flowers,
    Such letting nature have her way
While heaven looks from its towers!   30

VII

How say you? Let us, O my dove,
    Let us be unashamed of soul,
As earth lies bare to heaven above!
    How is it under our control
To love or not to love?   35

VIII

I would that you were all to me,
    You that are just so much, no more.
Nor yours nor mine, nor slave nor free!
    Where does the fault lie? What the core
O' the wound, since wound must be?   40

IX

I would I could adopt your will,
    See with your eyes, and set my heart
Beating by yours, and drink my fill
    At your soul's springs,—your part my part
In life, for good and ill.   45

X

No. I yearn upward, touch you close,
    Then stand away. I kiss your cheek,
Catch your soul's warmth,—I pluck the rose[3]
    And love it more than tongue can speak—
Then the good minute goes.   50

XI

Already how am I so far
    Out of that minute? Must I go
Still like the thistle-ball, no bar,

---

3. Cf. Shakespeare's *Othello*, V.ii.13–15: "When I have pluck'd thy rose,/I cannot give it vital growth again,/It needs must wither." (This echo and the next are discussed by R. D. Altick [*PLL*, 3 (1967), 79].)

Onward, whenever light winds blow,
Fixed by no friendly star?[4]   55

XII

Just when I seemed about to learn!
Where is the thread now? Off again!
The old trick! Only I discern—
Infinite passion, and the pain
Of finite hearts that yearn.   60

1854

A Grammarian's Funeral,

SHORTLY AFTER THE REVIVAL OF LEARNING IN EUROPE[1]

Let us begin and carry up this corpse,
Singing together.
Leave we the common crofts, the vulgar thorpes[2]
Each in its tether[3]
Sleeping safe on the bosom of the plain,   5
Cared-for till cock-crow:
Look out if yonder be not day again
Rimming the rock-row!
That's the appropriate country; there, man's thought,
Rarer, intenser,   10
Self-gathered for an outbreak, as it is ought,
Chafes in the censer.[4]
Leave we the unlettered plain its herd and crop;
Seek we sepulture[5]
On a tall mountain, citied to the top,   15
Crowded with culture!
All the peaks soar, but one the rest excels;
Clouds overcome it;
No! yonder sparkle is the citadel's
Circling its summit.   20
Thither our path lies; wind we up the heights:
Wait ye the warning?[6]
Our low life was the level's and the night's;
He's for the morning.

4. **Cf.** Shakespeare's Sonnet 116: "[Love] is an ever fixed mark/That looks on tempests and is never shaken;/It is the star to every wand'ring bark. . . ."
1. The poem is set in fourteenth-century Italy, where the Renaissance began, marked by a humanistic revival of Greek and Latin learning. Scholars like Browning's anonymous Grammarian, who devoted their lives to the mastery of classical languages, were instrumental in the recovery of ancient texts. Though these specialists were in a sense the pioneers of the Renaissance, they inevitably became the butt of satire, as in Erasmus' *The Praise of Folly* (1510).

The Grammarian's eulogy is sung by a band of his former students, who are carrying the corpse to its burial place atop a mountain.
2. Fields and villages of the common folk.
3. Small radius.
4. Seethes in the incense burner.
5. Burial place.
6. Are you ready for the signal [to begin]?

Step to a tune, square chests, erect each head, [25]
    'Ware[7] the beholders!
This is our master, famous calm and dead,
    Borne on our shoulders.

Sleep, crop and herd! sleep, darkling thorpe and croft,
    Safe from the weather! [30]
He, whom we convoy to his grave aloft,
    Singing together,
He was a man born with thy face and throat,
    Lyric Apollo![8]
Long he lived nameless: how should spring take note [35]
    Winter would follow?
Till lo, the little touch, and youth was gone!
    Cramped and diminished,
Moaned he, "New measures, other feet anon!
    My dance is finished?" [40]
No, that's the world's way: (keep the mountain-side,
    Make for the city!)
He knew the signal, and stepped on with pride
    Over men's pity;
Left play for work, and grappled with the world [45]
    Bent on escaping:
"What's in the scroll," quoth he, "thou keepst furled?
    Show me their shaping,
Theirs who most studied man, the bard and sage,—
    Give!"—So, he gowned him,[9] [50]
Straight got by heart that book to its last page:
    Learned, we found him.
Yea, but we found him bald too, eyes like lead,
    Accents uncertain:
"Time to taste life," another would have said, [55]
    "Up with the curtain!"
This man said rather, "Actual life comes next?
    Patience a moment!
Grant I have mastered learning's crabbed text,
    Still there's the comment.[1] [60]
Let me know all! Prate not of the most or least,
    Painful or easy!
Even to the crumbs I'd fain eat up the feast,
    Ay, nor feel queasy."
Oh, such a life as he resolved to live, [65]
    When he had learned it,
When he had gathered all books had to give!
    Sooner, he spurned it.
Image the whole, then execute the parts—
    Fancy the fabric[2] [70]

7. Show your awareness of.
8. God of the sun, order, and song (the lyre), Apollo was represented as ideally handsome.
9. Became a scholar.
1. Textual commentary or annotation.
2. Structure.

Quite, ere you build, ere steel strike fire from quartz,
Ere mortar dab brick!

(Here's the town-gate reached: there's the market-place
Gaping before us.)
Yea, this in him was the peculiar grace   75
(Hearten our chorus!)
That before living he'd learn how to live—
No end to learning:
Earn the means first—God surely will contrive
Use for our earning.   80
Others mistrust and say, "But time escapes:
Live now or never!"
He said, "What's time? Leave Now for dogs and apes!
Man has Forever."
Back to his book then: deeper drooped his head: 85
Calculus[3] racked him:
Leaden before, his eyes grew dross[4] of lead:
Tussis[5] attacked him.
"Now, master, take a little rest!"—not he!
(Caution redoubled,   90
Step two abreast, the way winds narrowly!)
Not a whit troubled
Back to his studies, fresher than at first,
Fierce as a dragon
He (soul-hydroptic[6] with a sacred thirst)   95
Sucked at the flagon.
Oh, if we draw a circle premature,
Heedless of far gain,
Greedy for quick returns of profit, sure
Bad is our bargain!   100
Was it not great? did not he throw on God,
(He loves the burthen)—
God's task to make the heavenly period[7]
Perfect the earthen?
Did not he magnify the mind, show clear   105
Just what it all meant?
He would not discount life, as fools do here,
Paid by instalment.
He ventured neck or nothing—heaven's success
Found, or earth's failure: 110
"Wilt thou trust death or not?" He answered "Yes:
Hence with life's pale lure!"
That low man seeks a little thing to do,
Sees it and does it:
This high man, with a great thing to pursue,   115
Dies ere he knows it.

---

3. *Calculus:* "the stone." Perhaps gall-
stones or kidney stones.
4. Waste scum on surface of molten
metal.

5. Bronchial cough.
6. Unquenchably thirsty in his soul.
7. Sentence.

That low man goes on adding one to one
    His hundred's soon hit:
This high man, aiming at a million,
    Misses an unit.   120
That, has the world here—should he need the next,
    Let the world mind him!
This, throws himself on God, and unperplexed
    Seeking shall find him.
So, with the throttling hands of death at strife,   125
    Ground he at grammar;[8]
Still, thro' the rattle, parts of speech were rife:
    While he could stammer
He settled *Hoti's* business—let it be!—
    Properly based *Oun*—   130
Gave us the doctrine of the enclitic *De*,[9]
    Dead from the waist down.
Well, here's the platform, here's the proper place:
    Hail to your purlieus,[1]
All ye highfliers of the feathered race,   135
    Swallows and curlews!
Here's the top-peak; the multitude below
    Live, for they can, there:
This man decided not to Live but Know—
    Bury this man there?   140
Here—here's his place, where meteors shoot, clouds form,
    Lightnings are loosened,
Stars come and go! Let joy break with the storm,
    Peace let the dew send!
Lofty designs must close in like effects: 145
    Loftily lying,
Leave him—still loftier than the world suspects,
    Living and dying.

ca. 1854

"Transcendentalism: A Poem in Twelve Books"[1]

Stop playing, poet! May a brother speak?
'T is you speak, that's your error. Song's our art:
Whereas you please to speak these naked thoughts

---

8. Cf. Carlyle's denunciation of the "hidebound Pedants" of his own school days: "How can an inanimate, mechanical Gerund-Grinder . . . foster the growth of anything; much more of Mind . . .?" (*Sartor Resartus*, II.iii).
9. *Hoti, Oun, De*: Greek particles meaning respectively "that," "then," and "towards." The "enclitic *De*" is a suffix-forming particle which changes the accentual pattern in the word to which it is joined. In a letter to Tennyson, Browning said: "I wanted the grammarian 'dead from the waist down' . . . to spend his last breath on the biggest of the littlenesses; such an one is 'the enclitic δε' . . ." (July 1863).
1. Haunts.
1. This purports to be advice from a poet to one of his peers, the author of a long, arid philosophical poem entitled "Transcendentalism."

Instead of draping them in sights and sounds.[2]
—True thoughts, good thoughts, thoughts fit to treasure up!   5
But why such long prolusion[3] and display,
Such turning and adjustment of the harp,
And taking it upon your breast, at length,
Only to speak dry words across its strings?
Stark-naked thought is in request enough: 10
Speak prose and hollo it till Europe hears!
The six-foot Swiss tube, braced about with bark,
Which helps the hunter's voice from Alp to Alp—
Exchange our harp for that,—who hinders you?

But here's your fault; grown men want thought, you think;   15
Thought's what they mean by verse, and seek in verse:
Boys seek for images and melody,
Men must have reason—so, you aim at men.
Quite otherwise! Objects throng our youth, 't is true;
We see and hear and do not wonder much: 20
If you could tell us what they mean, indeed!
As German Boehme[4] never cared for plants
Until it happed, a-walking in the fields,
He noticed all at once that plants could speak,
Nay, turned with loosened tongue to talk with him.   25
That day the daisy had an eye indeed[5]—
Colloquized with the cowslip on such themes!
We find them extant yet in Jacob's prose.
But by the time youth slips a stage or two
While reading prose in that tough book he wrote   30
(Collating and emendating the same
And settling on the sense most to our mind),
We shut the clasps and find life's summer past.
Then, who helps more, pray, to repair our loss—
Another Boehme with a tougher book   35
And subtler meanings of what roses say,—
Or some stout Mage like him of Halberstadt,[6]
John, who made things Boehme wrote thoughts about?
He with a "look you!" vents a brace of rhymes,
And in there breaks the sudden rose herself,   40
Over us, under, round us every side,
Nay, in and out the tables and the chairs
And musty volumes, Boehme's book and all,—

---

2. In 1853 Browning wrote his friend Joseph Milsand: "I am writing—a first step toward popularity for me—lyrics with more music and painting than before, so as to get people to hear and see . . ." (G&M, p. 189).
3. Introduction.
4. Jacob Boehme or Behmen (1575–1624), shoemaker and mystic of Goerlitz, Germany, who spoke of "communion with the Herbs and Grass of the field," during which "in his inward Light he saw into their Essences, Use and Properties . . ." (*Works*, trans. William Law, 1764).
5. Daisy: "day's eye."
6. Johannes Teutonicus, canon of Halberstadt, Germany. A favorite childhood book of Browning's, Nathaniel Wanley's *Wonders of the Little World* (1678), contains an account of this medieval magician.

Buries us with a glory, young once more,
Pouring heaven into this shut house of life.   45

So come, the harp back to your heart again!
You are a poem, though your poem's naught.
The best of all you showed before, believe,
Was your own boy-face o'er the finer chords
Bent, following the cherub at the top   50
That points to God with his paired half-moon wings.

One Word More[1]

TO E. B. B.

I

There they are, my fifty men and women
Naming me the fifty poems finished!
Take them, Love, the book and me together:
Where the heart lies, let the brain lie also.

II

Rafael made a century of sonnets,[2]   5
Made and wrote them in a certain volume
Dinted with the silver-pointed pencil
Else he only used to draw Madonnas:
These, the world might view—but one, the volume.
Who that one, you ask? Your heart instructs you.   10
Did she live and love it all her life-time?
Did she drop, his lady of the sonnets,
Die, and let it drop beside her pillow
Where it lay in place of Rafael's glory,
Rafael's cheek so duteous and so loving—   15
Cheek, the world was wont to hail a painter's,
Rafael's cheek, her love had turned a poet's?

III

You and I would rather read that volume,
(Taken to his beating bosom by it)
Lean and list the bosom-beats of Rafael,   20
Would we not? than wonder at Madonnas—
Her, San Sisto names, and Her, Foligno,
Her, that visits Florence in a vision,
Her, that's left with lilies in the Louvre[3]—
Seen by us and all the world in circle.   25

1. This dedicatory epistle, appended to *Men and Women*, was written September 1855, after the rest of the manuscript had gone to the printer. As R. D. Altick has shown, the title derives from an 1845 letter of Elizabeth Barrett's: "Therefore we must leave this subject [of love]—& I must trust you to leave it without one word more . . ." (Kintner, I.179).
2. Vasari states that Raphael (1483–1520) was devoted to his mistress, and tradition holds that he addressed to the lady, Margherita (called "La Fornarina"), a hundred sonnets. Only three of Raphael's sonnets survive, with part of a fourth.
3. The four Madonnas are respectively: the *Sistine Madonna* (Dresden Gallery); the *Madonna di Foligno* (Vatican); the *Madonna del Granduca* (Pitti, Florence); and *La Belle Jardinière* (Louvre).

IV

You and I will never read that volume.
Guido Reni, like his own eye's apple
Guarded long the treasure-book and loved it.[4]
Guido Reni dying, all Bologna
Cried, and the world cried too, "Ours, the treasure!"   30
Suddenly, as rare things will, it vanished.

V

Dante once prepared to paint an angel:[5]
Whom to please? You whisper "Beatrice."
While he mused and traced it and retraced it,
(Peradventure with a pen corroded   35
Still by drops of that hot ink[6] he dipped for,
When, his left-hand i' the hair o' the wicked,
Back he held the brow and pricked its stigma,
Bit into the live man's flesh for parchment,
Loosed him, laughed to see the writing rankle,   40
Let the wretch go festering through Florence)—
Dante, who loved well because he hated,
Hated wickedness that hinders loving,
Dante standing, studying his angel,—
In there broke the folk of his Inferno.   45
Says he—"Certain people of importance"
(Such he gave his daily dreadful line to)
"Entered and would seize, forsooth, the poet."
Says the poet—"Then I stopped my painting."

VI

You and I would rather see that angel,   50
Painted by the tenderness of Dante,
Would we not?—than read a fresh Inferno.

VII

You and I will never see that picture.
While he mused on love and Beatrice,
While he softened o'er his outlined angel,   55
In they broke, those "people of importance:"
We and Bice[7] bear the loss for ever.

VIII

What of Rafael's sonnets, Dante's picture?
This: no artist lives and loves, that longs not
Once, and only once, and for one only,   60
(Ah, the prize!) to find his love a language
Fit and fair and simple and sufficient—

---

4. The manuscript of Raphael's sonnets is supposed to have passed into the hands of the Italian painter Guido Reni (1575–1642), after whose death it was lost.
5. Dante, in *Vita Nuova* (35), says that in 1291 as he began drawing a "resemblance of an angel"—his lady Beatrice Portinari—he was interrupted by the appearance of "certain people of importance." There is no evidence in *Vita Nuova* that they intended to "seize . . . the poet" (line 48).
6. Allusion to the *Inferno*, an anachronism since Dante began the *Divine Comedy* more than ten years after this incident.
7. Beatrice.

Using nature that's an art to others,
Not, this one time, art that's turned his nature.
Ay, of all the artists living, loving, 65
None but would forego his proper dowry,—
Does he paint? he fain would write a poem,—
Does he write? he fain would paint a picture,
Put to proof art alien to the artist's,
Once, and only once, and for one only, 70
So to be the man and leave the artist,
Gain the man's joy, miss the artist's sorrow.

IX

Wherefore? Heaven's gift[8] takes earth's abatement!
He who smites the rock and spreads the water,[9]
Bidding drink and live a crowd beneath him, 75
Even he, the minute makes immortal,
Proves, perchance, but mortal in the minute,
Desecrates, belike, the deed in doing.
While he smites, how can he but remember,
So he smote before, in such a peril, 80
When they stood and mocked—"Shall smiting help us?"
When they drank and sneered—"A stroke is easy!"
When they wiped their mouths and went their journey,
Throwing him for thanks—"But drought was pleasant."
Thus old memories mar the actual triumph; 85
Thus the doing savours of disrelish;
Thus achievement lacks a gracious somewhat;
O'er-importuned brows becloud the mandate,
Carelessness or consciousness—the gesture.[1]
For he bears an ancient wrong about him, 90
Sees and knows again those phalanxed faces,
Hears, yet one time more, the 'customed prelude—
"How shouldst thou, of all men, smite, and save us?"
Guesses what is like to prove the sequel—
"Egypt's flesh-pots—nay, the drought was better."[2] 95

X

Oh, the crowd must have emphatic warrant![3]
Theirs, the Sinai-forehead's cloven brilliance,[4]
Right-arm's rod-sweep,[5] tongue's imperial fiat.
Never dares the man put off the prophet.

XI

Did he love one face from out the thousands, 100

8. Divine inspiration.
9. Moses smote the rock for water (Exodus 17:1–7; Numbers 20:2–13).
1. Anxiety prevents clear perception of the poet's mandate to speak; imperfect execution mars the act of speech.
2. Exodus 16:2–3: Moses' ungrateful people long for the good things of the past and complain of their sufferings on the desert journey.
3. Adequate grounds for faith in their "prophets" (i.e., poets).
4. When he received the Commandments atop Mt. Sinai, Moses was allowed to witness indirectly God's glory from his place in a cloven rock; after he descended "the skin of Moses' face shone" (Exodus 33: 21–23; 34:35).
5. Aaron's rod (Exodus 7; Numbers 17).

(Were she Jethro's daughter,[6] white and wifely,
Were she but the Æthiopian bondslave,)
He would envy yon dumb patient camel,
Keeping a reserve of scanty water
Meant to save his own life in the desert;   105
Ready in the desert to deliver
(Kneeling down to let his breast be opened)
Hoard and life together for his mistress.

XII

I shall never, in the years remaining,
Paint you pictures, no, nor carve you statues,   110
Make you music that should all-express me;
So it seems: I stand on my attainment.
This of verse alone, one life allows me;
Verse and nothing else have I to give you.
Other heights in our lives, God willing: 115
All the gifts from all the heights, your own, Love!

XIII

Yet a semblance of resource avails us—
Shade so finely touched, love's sense must seize it.
Take these lines, look lovingly and nearly,
Lines I write the first time and the last time.   120
He who works in fresco, steals a hair-brush,
Curbs the liberal hand, subservient proudly,
Cramps his spirit, crowds its all in little,
Makes a strange art of an art familiar,
Fills his lady's missal-marge with flowerets.   125
He who blows thro' bronze, may breathe thro' silver,
Fitly serenade a slumbrous princess.
He who writes, may write for once as I do.

XIV

Love, you saw me gather men and women,
Live or dead or fashioned by my fancy,   130
Enter each and all, and use their service,
Speak from every mouth,—the speech, a poem.
Hardly shall I tell my joys and sorrows,
Hopes and fears, belief and disbelieving:
I am mine and yours—the rest be all men's,   135
Karshish, Cleon, Norbert and the fifty.
Let me speak this once in my true person,[7]
Not as Lippo, Roland or Andrea,
Though the fruit of speech be just this sentence:
Pray you, look on these my men and women,   140
Take and keep my fifty poems finished;
Where my heart lies, let my brain lie also!

6. Zipporah, Moses' wife (Exodus 2:21); he had also married an Ethiopian woman (Numbers 12:1).
7. Alludes to Browning's wife's having urged him to speak out directly, rather than through masks of "men and women"; cf. her letter of May 25, 1846 (Kintner, II.731–32).

Poor the speech;[8] be how I speak, for all things.

XV

Not but that you know me! Lo, the moon's self!
Here in London, yonder late in Florence,   145
Still we find her face, the thrice-transfigured.[9]
Curving on a sky imbrued with colour,
Drifted over Fiesole[1] by twilight,
Came she, our new crescent of a hair's-breadth.
Full she flared it, lamping Samminiato,[2]   150
Rounder 'twixt the cypresses and rounder,
Perfect till the nightingales applauded.
Now, a piece of her old self, impoverished,
Hard to greet, she traverses the houseroofs,
Hurries with unhandsome thrift of silver,   155
Goes dispiritedly, glad to finish.

XVI

What, there's nothing in the moon noteworthy?
Nay: for if the moon could love a mortal,
Use, to charm him (so to fit a fancy)
All her magic ('t is the old sweet mythos)[3]   160
She would turn a new side to her mortal,
Side unseen of herdsman, huntsman, steersman—
Blank to Zoroaster[4] on his terrace,
Blind to Galileo[5] on his turret,
Dumb to Homer,[6] dumb to Keats—him, even!   165
Think, the wonder of the moonstruck mortal—
When she turns round, comes again in heaven,
Opens out anew for worse or better!
Proves she like some portent of an iceberg
Swimming full upon the ship it founders,   170
Hungry with huge teeth of splintered crystals?
Proves she as the paved work of a sapphire
Seen by Moses when he climbed the mountain?
Moses, Aaron, Nadab and Abihu
Climbed and saw the very God, the Highest,   175
Stand upon the paved work of a sapphire.
Like the bodied heaven in his clearness
Shone the stone, the sapphire of that paved work,
When they ate and drank and saw God also![7]

8. Browning regarded his wife as a better poet than he.
9. The moon has passed through three phases—new or crescent, full, and waning—during the Brownings' journey from Florence to London.
1. Town three miles northeast of Florence.
2. San Miniato al Monte, church on a hill southeast of Florence.
3. The moon goddess Artemis (Diana) loved the mortal Endymion, visiting him in dreams. John Keats's *Endymion* (1818) is based on the myth; see line 165.
4. Persian prophet of the sixth century B.C. who founded a religion teaching the worship of Ormazd, or Ahura Mazda, a deity representing light and life.
5. Italian astronomer (1564–1642), who perfected the telescope. Just before going blind in 1637 he discovered the moon's oscillations in orbit.
6. Among the so-called Homeric Hymns is one to Artemis, identified with the moon.
7. Lines 174–79 closely paraphrase Exodus 24: 9–11.

XVII

What were seen? None knows, none ever shall know.   180
Only this is sure—the sight were other,
Not the moon's same side, born late in Florence,
Dying now impoverished here in London.
God be thanked, the meanest of his creatures
Boasts two soul-sides, one to face the world with,   185
Onc to show a woman when he loves her!

XVIII

This I say of me, but think of you, Love!
This to you—yourself my moon of poets!
Ah, but that's the world's side, there's the wonder,
Thus they see you, praise you, think they know you!   190
There, in turn I stand with them and praise you—
Out of my own self, I dare to phrase it.
But the best is when I glide from out them,
Cross a step or two of dubious twilight,
Come out on the other side, the novel   195
Silent silver lights and darks undreamed of,
Where I hush and bless myself with silence.

XIX

Oh, their Rafael of the dear Madonnas,
Oh, their Dante of the dread Inferno,
Wrote one song—and in my brain I sing it,   200
Drew one angel—borne, see, on my bosom!

R.B.

1855

From *Dramatis Personae* (1864)

James Lee's Wife[1]

I—JAMES LEE'S WIFE AT THE WINDOW[2]

I

Ah, Love, but a day
    And the world has changed!
The sun's away,
    And the bird estranged;
The wind has dropped,   5
    And the sky's deranged:
Summer has stopped.

1. The starting point for this lyric sequence was the early poem "Still ailing,
Wind?" published in *The Monthly Repository* for May 1836; the lyric is now
stanzas 1–6 of section VI.
    Of James Lee and wife, Browning said
he saw them as "people newly-married,
trying to realize a dream of being sufficient to each other, in a foreign land
(where you can try such an experiment)
and finding it break up,—the man being
tired first,—and tired precisely of the
love . . ." (Curle, p. 109).
2. The setting is Ste. Marie, near Pornic,
a lonely seaside hamlet. The poet had
rented the mayor's house for the summer
of 1862.

II

Look in my eyes!
  Wilt thou change too?
Should I fear surprise?
  Shall I find aught new
In the old and dear,
  In the good and true,
With the changing year?

III

Thou art a man,
  But I am thy love.
For the lake, its swan;
  For the dell, its dove;
And for thee—(oh, haste!)
  Me, to bend above,
Me, to hold embraced.

II—BY THE FIRESIDE

I

Is all our fire of shipwreck wood,
  Oak and pine?
Oh, for the ills half-understood,
  The dim dead woe
  Long ago
Befallen this bitter coast of France!
Well, poor sailors took their chance;
  I take mine.

II

A ruddy shaft our fire must shoot
  O'er the sea:
Do sailors eye the casement—mute,
  Drenched and stark,
  From their bark—
And envy, gnash their teeth for hate
O' the warm safe house and happy freight
  —Thee and me?

III

God help you, sailors, at your need!
  Spare the curse!
For some ships, safe in port indeed,
  Rot and rust,
  Run to dust,
All through worms i' the wood, which crept,
Gnawed our hearts out while we slept:
  That is worse.

IV

Who lived here before us two?
  Old-world pairs.

Did a woman ever—would I knew!—
    Watch the man
    With whom began   50
Love's voyage full-sail,—(now, gnash your teeth!)
When planks start, open hell beneath
    Unawares?

III—IN THE DOORWAY

I

The swallow has set her six young on the rail,
    And looks sea-ward: 55
The water's in stripes like a snake, olive-pale
    To the leeward,—
On the weather-side, black, spotted white with the wind.
"Good fortune departs, and disaster's behind,"—
Hark, the wind with its wants and its infinite wail!   60

II

Our fig-tree, that leaned for the saltness, has furled
    Her five fingers,
Each leaf like a hand opened wide to the world
    Where there lingers
No glint of the gold, Summer sent for her sake: 65
How the vines writhe in rows, each impaled on its stake!
My heart shrivels up and my spirit shrinks curled.

III

Yet here are we two; we have love, house enough,
    With the field there,
This house of four rooms, that field red and rough,   70
    Though it yield there,
For the rabbit that robs, scarce a blade or a bent;[3]
If a magpie alight now, it seems an event;
And they both will be gone at November's rebuff.

IV

But why must cold spread? but wherefore bring change   75
    To the spirit,
God meant should mate his with an infinite range,
    And inherit
His power to put life in the darkness and cold?
Oh, live and love worthily, bear and be bold!   80
Whom Summer made friends of, let Winter estrange!

IV—ALONG THE BEACH

I

I will be quiet and talk with you,
    And reason why you are wrong.
You wanted my love—is that much true?

---

3. Coarse beach grass.

And so I did love, so I do: 85
   What has come of it all along?
II
I took you—how could I otherwise?
   For a world to me, and more;
For all, love greatens and glorifies
Till God's a-glow, to the loving eyes,   90
   In what was mere earth before.
III
Yes, earth—yes, mere ignoble earth!
   Now do I mis-state, mistake?
Do I wrong your weakness and call it worth?
Expect all harvest, dread no dearth,   95
   Seal my sense up for your sake?
IV
Oh, Love, Love, no, Love! not so, indeed!
   You were just weak earth, I knew:
With much in you waste, with many a weed,
And plenty of passions run to seed,   100
   But a little good grain too.
V
And such as you were, I took you for mine:
   Did not you find me yours,
To watch the olive and wait the vine,
And wonder when rivers of oil and wine   105
   Would flow, as the Book assures?[4]
VI
Well, and if none of these good things came,
   What did the failure prove?
The man was my whole world, all the same,
With his flowers to praise or his weeds to blame,   110
   And, either or both, to love.
VII
Yet this turns now to a fault—there! there!
   That I do love, watch too long,
And wait too well, and weary and wear;
And 't is all an old story, and my despair   115
   Fit subject for some new song:
VIII
"How the light, light love, he has wings to fly
   At suspicion of a bond:
My wisdom has bidden your pleasure good-bye,
Which will turn up next in a laughing eye,   120
   And why should you look beyond?"

V—ON THE CLIFF

I

I leaned on the turf,
I looked at a rock

---

4. Conflation of Job 29:6 and 2 Chronicles 2:10.

Left dry by the surf;
For the turf, to call it grass were to mock: 125
Dead to the roots, so deep was done
The work of the summer sun.

II

And the rock lay flat
As an anvil's face:
No iron like that! 130
Baked dry; of a weed, of a shell, no trace:
Sunshine outside, but ice at the core,
Death's altar by the lone shore.

III

On the turf, sprang gay
With his films of blue, 135
No cricket, I'll say,
But a warhorse, barded and chanfroned[5] too,
The gift of a quixote-mage[6] to his knight,
Real fairy, with wings all right.

IV

On the rock, they scorch 140
Like a drop of fire
From a brandished torch,
Fall two red fans of a butterfly:
No turf, no rock: in their ugly stead,
See, wonderful blue and red! 145

V

Is it not so
With the minds of men?
The level and low,
The burnt and bare, in themselves; but then
With such a blue and red grace, not theirs,— 150
Love settling unawares!

VI—READING A BOOK, UNDER THE CLIFF

I

"Still ailing, Wind? Wilt be appeased or no?
   Which needs the other's office, thou or I?
Dost want to be disburthened of a woe,
   And can, in truth, my voice untie 155
Its links, and let it go?

II

"Art thou a dumb wronged thing that would be righted,
   Entrusting thus thy cause to me? Forbear!
No tongue can mend such pleadings; faith, requited
   With falsehood,—love, at last aware 160
Of scorn,—hopes, early blighted,—

5. Barded: equipped with horse armor.
Chanfron: chamfron, medieval armor for
a horse's head.
6. Self-deluded magician.

III

"We have them; but I know not any tone
    So fit as thine to falter forth a sorrow:
Dost think men would go mad without a moan,
    If they knew any way to borrow   165
A pathos like thy own?

IV

"Which sigh wouldst mock, of all the sighs? The one
    So long escaping from lips starved and blue,
That lasts while on her pallet-bed the nun
    Stretches her length; her foot comes through   170
The straw she shivers on;

V

"You had not thought she was so tall: and spent,
    Her shrunk lids open, her lean fingers shut
Close, close, their sharp and livid nails indent
    The clammy palm; then all is mute: 175
That way, the spirit went.

VI

"Or wouldst thou rather that I understand
    Thy will to help me?—like the dog I found
Once, pacing sad this solitary strand,
    Who would not take my food, poor hound,   180
But whined and licked my hand."

VII

All this, and more, comes from some young man's pride
    Of power to see,—in failure and mistake,
Relinquishment, disgrace, on every side,—
    Merely examples for his sake,   185
Helps to his path untried:

VIII

Instances he must—simply recognize?
    Oh, more than so!—must, with a learner's zeal,
Make doubly prominent, twice emphasize,
    By added touches that reveal   190
The god in babe's disguise.

IX

Oh, he knows what defeat means, and the rest!
    Himself the undefeated that shall be:
Failure, disgrace, he flings them you to test,—
    His triumph, in eternity   195
Too plainly manifest!

X

Whence, judge if he learn forthwith what the wind
    Means in its moaning—by the happy prompt
Instinctive way of youth, I mean; for kind
    Calm years, exacting their accompt   200
Of pain, mature the mind:

XI

And some midsummer morning, at the lull

Just about daybreak, as he looks across
A sparkling foreign country, wonderful
    To the sea's edge for gloom and gloss,   205
Next minute must annul,—

XII

Then, when the wind begins among the vines,
    So low, so low, what shall it say but this?
"Here is the change beginning, here the lines
    Circumscribe beauty, set to bliss   210
The limit time assigns."

XIII

Nothing can be as it has been before;
    Better, so call it, only not the same.
To draw one beauty into our hearts' core,
    And keep it changeless! such our claim;   215
So answered,—Never more!

XIV

Simple? Why this is the old woe o' the world;
    Tune, to whose rise and fall we live and die.
Rise with it, then! Rejoice that man is hurled
    From change to change unceasingly,   220
His soul's wings never furled!

XV

That's a new question; still replies the fact,
    Nothing endures: the wind moans, saying so;
We moan in acquiescence: there's life's pact,
    Perhaps probation—do *I* know?   225
God does: endure his act!

XVI

Only, for man, how bitter not to grave
    On his soul's hands' palms[7] one fair good wise thing
Just as he grasped it! For himself, death's wave;
    While time first washes—ah, the sting!—   230
O'er all he'd sink to save.

VII—AMONG THE ROCKS

I

Oh, good gigantic smile o' the brown old earth,
    This autumn morning! How he sets his bones
To bask i' the sun, and thrusts out knees and feet
For the ripple to run over in its mirth;   235
    Listening the while, where on the heap of stones
The white breast of the sea-lark twitters sweet.

II

That is the doctrine, simple, ancient, true;
    Such is life's trial, as old earth smiles and knows.

7. Cf. Isaiah 49:16: "Behold, I have graven thee upon the palms of my hands. . . ."

If you loved only what were worth your love, 240
Love were clear gain, and wholly well for you:
  Make the low nature better by your throes!
Give earth yourself, go up for gain above!

VIII—BESIDE THE DRAWING BOARD[8]

I

"As like as a Hand to another Hand!"
  Whoever said that foolish thing, 245
Could not have studied to understand
  The counsels of God in fashioning,
Out of the infinite love of his heart,
This Hand, whose beauty I praise, apart
From the world of wonder left to praise, 250
If I tried to learn the other ways
Of love in its skill, or love in its power.
  "As like as a Hand to another Hand":
  Who said that, never took his stand,
Found and followed, like me, an hour, 255
The beauty in this,—how free, how fine
To fear, almost,—of the limit-line!
As I looked at this, and learned and drew,
  Drew and learned, and looked again,
While fast the happy minutes flew, 260
  Its beauty mounted into my brain,
  And a fancy seized me; I was fain
To efface my work, begin anew,
Kiss what before I only drew;
Ay, laying the red chalk 'twixt my lips, 265
  With soul[9] to help if the mere lips failed,
  I kissed all right where the drawing ailed,
Kissed fast the grace that somehow slips
Still from one's soulless finger-tips.

II

'T is a clay cast, the perfect thing, 270
  From Hand live once, dead long ago:
Princess-like it wears the ring
  To fancy's eye, by which we know
That here at length a master found
  His match, a proud lone soul its mate, 275
As soaring genius sank to ground,
  And pencil could not emulate
The beauty in this,—how free, how fine

8. The estranged wife now ponders the idea of Beauty as she makes a chalk-drawing of a hand. Intuitively she grasps her situation: she has allowed her own idealism to divorce her from the living world.

9. Like "Imagination" for Coleridge, "soul" for Browning is both the perceptive and creative element in man, the *sine qua non* of great art. Cf. especially "Andrea del Sarto," lines 108ff.

To fear almost!—of the limit-line.
Long ago the god, like me   280
The worm, learned, each in our degree:
Looked and loved, learned and drew,
   Drew and learned and loved again,
While fast the happy minutes flew,
   Till beauty mounted into his brain   285
And on the finger which outvied
   His art he placed the ring that's there,
Still by fancy's eye descried,
   In token of a marriage rare:
   For him on earth, his art's despair,   290
For him in heaven, his soul's fit bride.

III

Little girl with the poor coarse hand
   I turned from to a cold clay cast—
I have my lesson, understand
   The worth of flesh and blood at last.   295
Nothing but beauty in a Hand?
   Because he could not change the hue,
   Mend the lines and make them true
To this which met his soul's demand,—
   Would Da Vinci[1] turn from you?   300
I hear him laugh my woes to scorn—
"The fool forsooth is all forlorn
Because the beauty, she thinks best,
Lived long ago or was never born,—
Because no beauty bears the test   305
In this rough peasant Hand! Confessed!
'Art is null and study void!'
   So sayest thou? So said not I,
   Who threw the faulty pencil by,
And years instead of hours employed,   310
Learning the veritable use
   Of flesh and bone and nerve beneath
   Lines and hue of the outer sheath,
If haply I might reproduce
   One motive of the powers profuse,   315
Flesh and bone and nerve that make
   The poorest coarsest human hand
   An object worthy to be scanned
A whole life long for their sole sake.
Shall earth and the cramped moment-space   320
Yield the heavenly crowning grace?
Now the parts and then the whole!
Who art thou, with stinted soul
   And stunted body, thus to cry

1. Browning has in mind a famous drawing, *Study of a Woman's Hands* *Folded over Her Breast* (ca. 1478) by Leonardo da Vinci.

'I love,—shall that be life's strait dole? 325
 I must live beloved or die!'
This peasant hand that spins the wool
 And bakes the bread, why lives it on,
 Poor and coarse with beauty gone,—
What use survives the beauty?" Fool! 330

Go, little girl with the poor coarse hand!
I have my lesson, shall understand.

IX—ON DECK[2]

I

There is nothing to remember in me,
 Nothing I ever said with a grace,
Nothing I did that you care to see, 335
 Nothing I was that deserves a place
In your mind, now I leave you, set you free.

II

Conceded! In turn, concede to me,
 Such things have been as a mutual flame.
Your soul's locked fast; but, love for a key, 340
 You might let it loose, till I grew the same
In your eyes, as in mine you stand: strange plea!

III

For then, then, what would it matter to me
 That I was the harsh ill-favoured one?
We both should be like as pea and pea; 345
 It was ever so since the world begun:
So, let me proceed with my reverie.

IV

How strange it were if you had all me,
 As I have all you in my heart and brain,
You, whose least word brought gloom or glee, 350
 Who never lifted the hand in vain—
Will hold mine yet, from over the sea!

V

Strange, if a face, when you thought of me,
 Rose like your own face present now,
With eyes as dear in their due degree, 355
 Much such a mouth, and as bright a brow,
Till you saw yourself, while you cried " 'T is She!"

VI

Well, you may, you must, set down to me
 Love that was life, like that was love;
A tenure of breath at your lips' decree, 360
 A passion to stand as your thoughts approve,
A rapture to fall where your foot might be.

---

2. The wife has left France and her hypercritical husband. She criticizes him in turn for his failure to reciprocate her love and forbearance.

VII

But did one touch for such love for me
   Come in a word or a look of yours,
Whose words and looks will, circling, flee   365
   Round me and round while life endures,—
Could I fancy "As I feel, thus feels he";

VIII

Why, fade you might to a thing like me,
   And your hair grow these coarse hanks of hair,
Your skin, this bark of a gnarled tree,—   370
   You might turn myself!—should I know or care
When I should be dead of joy, James Lee?

1862

Dîs aliter Visum;
or, Le Byron de nos Jours[1]

I

Stop, let me have the truth of that!
   Is that all true? I say, the day
Ten years ago when both of us
   Met on a morning, friends—as thus
We meet this evening, friends or what?—   5

II

Did you—because I took your arm
   And sillily smiled, "A mass of brass
That sea looks, blazing underneath!"
   While up the cliff-road edged with heath,
We took the turns nor came to harm—   10

III

Did you consider "Now makes twice
   That I have seen her, walked and talked
With this poor pretty thoughtful thing,
   Whose worth I weigh: she tries to sing;
Draws, hopes in time the eye grows nice;   15

IV

"Reads verse and thinks she understands;
   Loves all, at any rate, that's great,
Good, beautiful; but much as we
   Down at the bath-house love the sea,
Who breathe its salt and bruise its sands: 20

1. The title points up the poem's ironies. The first half, an allusion to *Aeneid*, II. 428, means "the gods saw it otherwise"; that is, the lovers deserved a better fate, but it was seemingly the gods' will that their love should be coldly dissected and destroyed by the man. The second half means "the modern Byron," referring to the very un-Byronic middle-aged poet of this monologue, who has finally carved out a respectable literary career.

The setting is a resort hotel in Pornic on the coast of Brittany, where the man has just given his version of their affair. Interrupting scornfully, the woman has the last word—the entire monologue.

V

"While . . . do but follow the fishing-gull
  That flaps and floats from wave to cave!
There's the sea-lover, fair my friend!
  What then? Be patient, mark and mend!
Had you the making of your scull?"   25

VI

And did you, when we faced the church
  With spire and sad slate roof, aloof
From human fellowship so far,
  Where a few graveyard crosses are,
And garlands for the swallows' perch,—   30

VII

Did you determine, as we stepped
  O'er the lone stone fence, "Let me get
Her for myself, and what's the earth
  With all its art, verse, music, worth—
Compared with love, found, gained, and kept?   35

VIII

"Schumann's[2] our music-maker now;
  Has his march-movement youth and mouth?
Ingres 's[3] the modern man that paints;
  Which will lean on me, of his saints?
Heine[4] for songs; for kisses, how?"   40

IX

And did you, when we entered, reached
  The votive frigate,[5] soft aloft
Riding on air this hundred years,
  Safe-smiling at old hopes and fears,—
Did you draw profit while she preached?   45

X

Resolving, "Fools we wise men grow!
  Yes, I could easily blurt out curt
Some question that might find reply
  As prompt in her stopped lips, dropped eye,
And rush of red to cheek and brow: 50

XI

"Thus were a match made, sure and fast,
  Mid the blue weed-flowers round the mound
Where, issuing, we shall stand and stay
  For one more look at baths and bay,
Sands, sea-gulls, and the old church last—   55

2. Robert Schumann (1810–56), German composer. Browning alludes to the stirring marches written after the Prussians confronted republican revolutionaries in Dresden, Schumann's home, in 1849.
3. Jean-Auguste-Dominique Ingres (1780–1867), much honored French painter. Though renowned for his nudes, he painted sacred subjects such as the *Martyrdom of St. Symphorian*, in the cathedral of Autun.
4. Heinrich Heine (1797–1856), German lyrical poet.
5. Thank offering in form of a model ship; hence pronoun "she" (line 45).

XII

"A match 'twixt me, bent, wigged and lamed,
  Famous, however, for verse and worse,
Sure of the Fortieth spare Arm-chair[6]
  When gout and glory seat me there,
So, one whose love-freaks pass unblamed,—   60

XIII

"And this young beauty, round and sound
  As a mountain-apple, youth and truth
With loves and doves, at all events
  With money in the Three per Cents,[7]
Whose choice of me would seem profound:—   65

XIV

"She might take me as I take her.
  Perfect the hour would pass, alas!
Climb high, love high, what matter? Still,
  Feet, feelings, must descend the hill:
An hour's perfection can't recur.   70

XV

"Then follows Paris and full time
  For both to reason: 'Thus with us!'
She'll sigh, 'Thus girls give body and soul
  At first word, think they gain the goal,
When 't is the starting-place they climb!   75

XVI

" 'My friend makes verse and gets renown;
  Have they all fifty years, his peers?
He knows the world, firm, quiet and gay;
  Boys will become as much one day:
They're fools; he cheats, with beard less brown.   80

XVII

" 'For boys say, *Love me or I die!*
  He did not say, *The truth is, youth
I want, who am old and know too much;*
  I'd catch youth: Lend me sight and touch!
Drop heart's blood where life's wheels grate dry!'   85

XVIII

"While I should make rejoinder"—(then
  It was, no doubt, you ceased that least
Light pressure of my arm in yours)
  " 'I can conceive of cheaper cures
For a yawning-fit o'er books and men.   90

XIX

" 'What? All I am, was, and might be,
  All, books taught, art brought, life's whole strife,
Painful results since precious, just

---

6. Allusion to the French Academy, to which the poet is sure of election upon the death of one of its forty members.

7. Her money is safely invested in Consols, British government bonds.

Were fitly exchanged, in wise disgust,
For two cheeks freshened by youth and sea?   95

XX

" 'All for a nosegay!—what came first;
    With fields on flower, untried each side;
I rally, need my books and men,
    And find a nosegay': drop it, then,
No match yet made for best or worst!"   100

XXI

That ended me. You judged the porch
    We left by, Norman;[8] took our look
At sea and sky; wondered so few
    Find out the place for air and view;
Remarked the sun began to scorch;   105

XXII

Descended, soon regained the baths,
    And then, good-bye! Years ten since then:
Ten years! We meet: you tell me, now,
    By a window-seat for that cliff-brow,
On carpet-stripes for those sand-paths.   110

XXIII

Now I may speak: you fool, for all
    Your lore! WHO made things plain in vain?
What was the sea for? What, the grey
    Sad church, that solitary day,
Crosses and graves and swallows' call?   115

XXIV

Was there nought better than to enjoy?
    No feat which, done, would make time break,
And let us pent-up creatures through
    Into eternity, our due?
No forcing earth teach heaven's employ?   120

XXV

No wise beginning, here and now,
    What cannot grow complete (earth's feat)
And heaven must finish, there and then?
    No tasting earth's true food for men,
Its sweet in sad, its sad in sweet?   125

XXVI

No grasping at love, gaining a share
    O' the sole spark for God's life at strife
With death, so, sure of range above
    The limits here? For us and love,
Failure; but, when God fails,[9] despair.   130

XXVII

This you call wisdom? Thus you add
    Good unto good again, in vain?

---

8. The church porch at Pornic, of Norman architecture.

9. When we fail God by denying love.

You loved, with body worn and weak;
  I loved, with faculties to seek:
Were both loves worthless since ill-clad?   135
XXVIII
Let the mere star-fish in his fault
  Crawl in a wash of weed, indeed,
Rose-jacynth to the finger-tips:
  He, whole in body and soul, outstrips
Man, found with either in default.   140
XXIX
But what's whole, can increase no more,
  Is dwarfed and dies, since here's its sphere.
The devil laughed at you in his sleeve!
  You knew not? That I well believe;
Or you had saved two souls: nay, four.   145
XXX
For Stephanie sprained last night her wrist,
  Ankle or something. "Pooh," cry you?
At any rate she danced, all say,
  Vilely; her vogue has had its day.
Here comes my husband from his whist.[1]   150

Abt Vogler[1]

(AFTER HE HAS BEEN EXTEMPORIZING UPON THE
MUSICAL INSTRUMENT OF HIS INVENTION)

I

Would that the structure[2] brave, the manifold music I build,
  Bidding my organ obey, calling its keys to their work,
Claiming each slave of the sound, at a touch, as when Solomon
    willed
  Armies of angels that soar, legions of demons that lurk,
Man, brute, reptile, fly,[3]—alien of end and of aim,   5

1. Card game with two sides of two partners. The name "whist" derives from the admonition to keep silence, and is thus appropriate to the dramatic action here.

1. Now all but forgotten, the German organist Georg Joseph Vogler (1749–1814)—called "Abt" or "Abbé" because he had taken holy orders—was an artist of importance in his day. One of his legendary feats was a competition with Beethoven at a party in 1803 to settle the question as to which of the two was the better extemporizer. In the opinion of at least one trained listener, Vogler won. According to *Grove's Dictionary of Music and Musicians,* "his extempore playing never failed to create an impression, and in the elevated fugal style he easily distanced all rivals." Vogler not only enjoyed a long and brilliant career as a concert organist, but was a noted music teacher, numbering among his pupils Meyerbeer, Gansbacher, and Weber. "The musical instrument of his invention" is the orchestrion, a portable organ nine feet square and six feet high, with nine hundred pipes and four manuals.

2. Friedrich von Schelling had called architecture "music in space, as it were a frozen music" (*Philosophy of Art,* trans. 1845).

3. According to Talmudic lore, Solomon received from heaven a great seal ring bearing the name of God. It gave him power to command supernatural forces, which helped him build the palace and temple at Jerusalem.

Adverse, each from the other heaven-high, hell-deep removed,—
Should rush into sight at once as he named the ineffable Name,[4]
And pile him a palace straight, to pleasure the princess he loved!

II

Would it might tarry like his, the beautiful building of mine,
This which my keys in a crowd pressed and importuned to raise!   10
Ah, one and all, how they helped, would dispart[5] now and now combine,
Zealous to hasten the work, heighten their master his praise!
And one would bury his brow with a blind plunge down to hell,
Burrow awhile and build, broad on the roots of things,
Then up again swim into sight, having based me my palace well,   15
Founded it, fearless of flame, flat on the nether springs.[6]

III

And another would mount and march, like the excellent minion[7] he was,
Ay, another and yet another, one crowd but with many a crest,
Raising my rampired[8] walls of gold as transparent as glass,
Eager to do and die, yield each his place to the rest: 20
For higher still and higher (as a runner tips with fire,
When a great illumination surprises a festal night—
Outlining round and round Rome's dome[9] from space to spire)
Up, the pinnacled glory reached, and the pride of my soul was in sight.

IV

In sight? Not half! for it seemed, it was certain, to match man's birth,   25
Nature in turn conceived, obeying an impulse as I;
And the emulous heaven yearned down, made effort to reach the earth,
As the earth had done her best, in my passion, to scale the sky:
Novel splendours burst forth, grew familiar and dwelt with mine,
Not a point nor peak but found and fixed its wandering star;   30
Meteor-moons, balls of blaze: and they did not pale nor pine,
For earth had attained to heaven, there was no more near nor far.

V

Nay more; for there wanted not who walked in the glare and glow,
Presences plain in the place; or, fresh from the Protoplast,[1]
Furnished for ages to come, when a kindlier wind should blow,   35
Lured now to begin and live, in a house to their liking at last;
Or else the wonderful Dead who have passed through the body and gone,
But were back once more to breathe in an old world worth their new:

4. Jehovah or Yahweh, a name so venerated by pious Jews that it was never pronounced; substitutes such as "Eloi" or "Ja" were used.
5. Separate.
6. The bed of hell.
7. Servant.
8. Having ramparts.
9. The poet had seen St. Peter's thus illuminated at Easter 1854.
1. Prototype.

What never had been, was now; what was, as it shall be anon;[2]
  And what is,—shall I say, matched both? for I was made perfect
    too.   40

VI

All through my keys that gave their sounds to a wish of my soul,
  All through my soul that praised as its wish flowed visibly forth,
All through music and me! For think, had I painted the whole,
  Why, there it had stood, to see, nor the process so wonder-worth:
Had I written the same, made verse—still, effect proceeds from
    cause,   45
  Ye know why the forms are fair, ye hear how the tale is told;
It is all triumphant art, but art in obedience to laws,
  Painter and poet are proud in the artist-list enrolled:—

VII

But here is the finger of God, a flash of the will that can,
  Existent behind all laws, that made them and, lo, they are!   50
And I know not if, save in this, such gift be allowed to man,
  That out of three sounds he frame, not a fourth sound, but a
    star.
Consider it well: each tone of our scale in itself is nought;
  It is everywhere in the world—loud, soft, and all is said:
Give it to me to use! I mix it with two in my thought: 55
  And, there! Ye have heard and seen: consider and bow the head!

VIII

Well, it is gone at last, the palace of music I reared;
  Gone! and the good tears start, the praises that come too slow;
For one is assured at first, one scarce can say that he feared,
  That he even gave it a thought, the gone thing was to go.   60
Never to be again![3] But many more of the kind
  As good, nay, better perchance: is this your comfort to me?
To me, who must be saved because I cling with my mind
  To the same, same self, same love, same God: ay, what was, shall
    be.

IX

Therefore to whom turn I but to thee, the ineffable Name?   65
  Builder and maker, thou, of houses not made with hands![4]
What, have fear of change from thee who art ever the same?
  Doubt that thy power can fill the heart that thy power expands?
There shall never be one lost good! What was, shall live as before;
  The evil is null, is nought, is silence implying sound;   70
What was good shall be good, with, for evil, so much good more;
  On the earth the broken arcs; in the heaven, a perfect round.

2. Inversion of the Gloria: "As it was in the beginning, is now, and ever shall be, world without end."
3. Cf. J. H. Newman: ". . . is it possible that that inexhaustible evolution and disposition of notes . . . should be a mere sound, which is gone and perishes? Can it be that those mysterious stirrings of heart, and keen emotions, . . . and awful impressions from we know not whence, should be wrought in us by what is unsubstantial, and comes and goes, and begins and ends in itself? It is not so; it cannot be" (*Theory of Developments in Religious Doctrine* [1843], sect. 39).
4. 2 Corinthians 5:1: "a building of God, an house not made with hands, eternal in the heavens."

X

All we have willed or hoped or dreamed of good shall exist;
  Not its semblance, but itself; no beauty, nor good, nor power
Whose voice has gone forth, but each survives for the melodist   75
  When eternity affirms the conception of an hour.
The high that proved too high, the heroic for earth too hard,
  The passion that left the ground to lose iself in the sky,
Are music sent up to God by the lover and the bard;
  Enough that he heard it once: we shall hear it by-and-by.   80

XI

And what is our failure here but a triumph's evidence
  For the fulness of the days? Have we withered or agonized?
Why else was the pause prolonged but that singing might issue
    thence?
  Why rushed the discords in but that harmony should be prized?[5]
Sorrow is hard to bear, and doubt is slow to clear,   85
  Each sufferer says his say, his scheme of the weal and woe:
But God has a few of us whom he whispers in the ear;
  The rest may reason and welcome: 't is we musicians know.[6]

XII

Well, it is earth with me; silence resumes her reign:
  I will be patient and proud, and soberly acquiesce.   90
Give me the keys. I feel for the common chord again,[7]
  Sliding by semitones, till I sink to the minor,—yes,
And I blunt it into a ninth, and I stand on alien ground,
  Surveying awhile the heights I rolled from into the deep;
Which, hark, I have dared and done, for my resting-place is found,   95
  The C Major of this life: so, now I will try to sleep.

Rabbi Ben Ezra[1]

I

Grow old along with me!
The best is yet to be,

5. The optimist Leibniz, in his *Théodicée* (1710), argues: "A little bitterness . . . often pleases more than sugar; shadows enhance colors; and even dissonance, in the right place, puts harmony into relief." Cf. Alexander Pope's *Essay on Man* (1733): "All discord, harmony not understood; / All partial evil, universal good" (I. 291–92).

6. Cf. Browning's "Parleying With Charles Avison": "There is no truer truth obtainable / By Man than comes of music" (138–39).

7. Symbolizing his transition from heaven to earth (musical ecstasy to silence), Vogler modulates stepwise ("by semitones") from the key in which he has been improvising: first he chooses a minor key (symbolic of "sorrow" or "woe" perhaps), then goes to the "alien" (i.e., middle) ground of a ninth —that is, to a discord requiring a resolu-

tion. This is produced by the modulation to C, an apt symbol both of repose and of the plane of ordinary life, since the key has no sharps or flats.

1. Browning first read the works of Abraham Ibn Ezra, or Abenezra (ca. 1090–1164) in the Vatican Library in 1853–54. Born in Toledo, Spain, the Jewish poet and scholar left his native country about 1140, traveling widely and gaining fame as a thinker, Hebrew philologist, and biblical exegete. His careful textual studies made him an important forerunner of modern biblical criticism. Philosophically he inclined toward both Neoplatonism and skepticism. Of his several hundred extant religious poems, many express a yearning for Zion. Browning purports to translate the rabbi's "Song of Death" in "Holy-Cross Day" (1855).

Part of Browning's intention, very

The last of life, for which the first was made:
      Our times are in His hand
      Who saith "A whole I planned, 5
Youth shows but half; trust God: see all nor be afraid!"

II

      Not that, amassing flowers,
      Youth sighed "Which rose make ours,
Which lily leave and then as best recall?"
      Not that, admiring stars, 10
      It yearned "Nor Jove, nor Mars;
Mine be some figured flame which blends, transcends them all!"

III

      Not for such hopes and fears
      Annulling youth's brief years,
Do I remonstrate: folly wide the mark! 15
      Rather I prize the doubt
      Low kinds exist without,
Finished and finite clods, untroubled by a spark.

IV

      Poor vaunt of life indeed,
      Were man but formed to feed 20
On joy, to solely seek and find and feast:
      Such feasting ended, then
      As sure an end to men;
Irks care the crop-full bird? Frets doubt the maw-crammed beast?[2]

V

      Rejoice we are allied 25
      To That which doth provide
And not partake, effect and not receive!
      A spark disturbs our clod;
      Nearer we hold of[3] God
Who gives, than of His tribes that take, I must believe. 30

VI

      Then, welcome each rebuff
      That turns earth's smoothness rough,
Each sting that bids nor sit nor stand but go!
      Be our joys three-parts pain!
      Strive, and hold cheap the strain; 35
Learn, nor account the pang; dare, never grudge the throe!

VII

      For thence,—a paradox
      Which comforts while it mocks,—
Shall life succeed in that it seems to fail:
      What I aspired to be, 40

---

probably, was to challenge the hedonism advocated in Edward FitzGerald's *The Rubáiyát of Omar Khayyám* (1859), the most popular poem of the Victorian age. The overwhelming optimism of "Rabbi Ben Ezra" elicited a reply, "Growing Old," from Matthew Arnold in 1867.
2. I.e., do care and doubt bother well-fed animals? This line is often cited as an instance of Browning's tendency toward roughness of diction and syntax.
3. Are related to.

And was not, comforts me:[4]
A brute I might have been, but would not sink i' the scale.[5]

VIII

What is he but a brute
Whose flesh has soul to suit,
Whose spirit works lest arms and legs want play?   45
To man, propose this test—
Thy body at its best,
How far can that project thy soul on its lone way?

IX

Yet gifts[6] should prove their use:
I own the Past profuse[7]   50
Of power each side, perfection every turn:
Eyes, ears took in their dole,
Brain treasured up the whole;
Should not the heart beat once "How good to live and learn?"

X

Not once beat "Praise be Thine!   55
I see the whole design,
I, who saw power, see now love perfect too:[8]
Perfect I call Thy plan:
Thanks that I was a man!
Maker, remake, complete,—I trust what Thou shalt do!"   60

XI

For pleasant in this flesh;
Our soul, in its rose-mesh[9]
Pulled ever to the earth, still yearns for rest;
Would we some prize might hold
To match those manifold   65
Possessions of the brute,—gain most, as we did best!

XII

Let us not always say
"Spite of this flesh to-day
I strove, made head, gained ground upon the whole!"
As the bird wings and sings,   70
Let us cry "All good things
Are ours, nor soul helps flesh more, now, than flesh helps soul!"[1]

XIII

Therefore I summon age
To grant youth's heritage,
Life struggle having so far reached its term: 75
Thence shall I pass, approved
A man, for aye removed
From the developed brute; a god though in the germ.

4. Cf. "Saul," line 295: ". . . 't is not what man Does which exalts him, but what man Would do!"
5. The scale or chain of being.
6. The endowments of youth; cf. line 74.
7. I.e., I admit the past is full.
8. For Browning, love completes God's tripartite nature, the other two elements being power and intelligence.
9. The net of flesh, with its veins and arteries.
1. Here Browning differs with Ibn Ezra, who taught that the soul and body were in conflict, and that the pursuit of wisdom was necessary to hold the passions in check.

XIV

And I shall thereupon
Take rest, ere I be gone   80
Once more on my adventure brave and new:
    Fearless and unperplexed,
    When I wage battle next,
What weapons to select, what armour to indue.[2]

XV

Youth ended, I shall try   85
My gain or loss thereby;
Leave the fire ashes, what survives is gold:
    And I shall weigh the same,
    Give life its praise or blame:
Young, all lay in dispute; I shall know, being old.   90

XVI

For note, when evening shuts,
A certain moment cuts
The deed off, calls the glory from the grey:
    A whisper from the west
    Shoots—"Add this to the rest,   95
Take it and try its worth: here dies another day."

XVII

So, still within this life,
Though lifted o'er its strife,
Let me discern, compare, pronounce at last,
    "This rage was right i' the main,   100
    That acquiescence vain:
The Future I may face now I have proved the Past."

XVIII

For more is not reserved
To man, with soul just nerved
To act to-morrow what he learns to-day: 105
    Here, work enough to watch
    The Master work, and catch
Hints of the proper craft, tricks of the tool's true play.

XIX

As it was better, youth
Should strive, through acts uncouth,   110
Toward making, than repose on aught found made:
    So, better, age, exempt
    From strife, should know, than tempt[3]
Further. Thou waitedest age: wait death nor be afraid!

XX

Enough now, if the Right   115
And Good and Infinite
Be named here, as thou callest thy hand thine own,
    With knowledge absolute,
    Subject to no dispute
From fools that crowded youth, nor let thee feel alone.   120

---

2. Put on.   3. Attempt.

XXI

Be there, for once and all,
Severed great minds from small,
Announced to each his station in the Past!
Was I,[4] the world arraigned,
Were they, my soul disdained,   125
Right? Let age speak the truth and give us peace at last!

XXII

Now, who shall arbitrate?
Ten men love what I hate,
Shun what I follow, slight what I receive;
Ten, who in ears and eyes   130
Match me: we all surmise,
They this thing, and I that: whom shall my soul believe?

XXIII

Not on the vulgar mass
Called "work," must sentence pass,[5]
Things done, that took the eye and had the price;   135
O'er which, from level stand,
The low world laid its hand,
Found straightway to its mind, could value in a trice:

XXIV

But all, the world's coarse thumb
And finger failed to plumb,   140
So passed in making up the main account;
All instincts immature,
All purposes unsure,
That weighed not as his work, yet swelled the man's amount:[6]

XXV

Thoughts hardly to be packed   145
Into a narrow act,
Fancies that broke through language and escaped;
All I could never be,
All, men ignored in me,
This, I was worth to God, whose wheel the pitcher shaped.   150

XXVI

Ay, note that Potter's wheel,[7]
That metaphor! and feel
Why time spins fast, why passive lies our clay,—

4. I [whom]. The next line has the same construction.
5. Browning may here be questioning the validity of the Victorian work ethic, which stressed productivity as a sign of individual worth.
6. The argument here is akin to the Evangelical belief that God judges a man's intentions, not his works. This principle underlies Browning's repeated glorification of the aspirant who fails in striving loftily.
7. Browning's metaphor of the potter's wheel appears to be a reply to the *Rubáiyát*, quatrains LIX–LXVI, first edition. Cf. Ecclesiastes 2 and The Wisdom of Solomon 2.

Thou, to whom fools propound,
When the wine makes its round,   155
"Since life fleets, all is change; the Past gone, seize to-day!"

XXVII

Fool! All that is, at all,
Lasts ever, past recall;
Earth changes, but thy soul and God stand sure:
What entered into thee,   160
That was, is, and shall be:
Time's wheel runs back or stops: Potter and clay endure.

XXVIII

He fixed thee mid this dance
Of plastic circumstance,
This Present, thou, forsooth, wouldst fain arrest: 165
Machinery just meant
To give thy soul its bent,
Try thee and turn thee forth, sufficiently impressed.

XXIX

What though the earlier grooves
Which ran the laughing loves   170
Around thy base,[8] no longer pause and press?
What though, about thy rim,
Scull-things in order grim
Grow out, in graver mood, obey the sterner stress?

XXX

Look not thou down but up!   175
To uses of a cup,
The festal board, lamp's flash and trumpet's peal,
The new wine's foaming flow,
The Master's lips a-glow!
Thou, heaven's consummate cup, what need'st thou with   180
   earth's wheel?

XXXI

But I need, now as then,
Thee, God, who mouldest men;
And since, not even while the whirl was worst,
Did I,—to the wheel of life
With shapes and colours rife,   185
Bound dizzily,—mistake my end, to slake Thy thirst:

XXXII

So, take and use Thy work:
Amend what flaws may lurk,
What strain o' the stuff, what warpings past the aim!
My times be in Thy hand!   190
Perfect the cup as planned!
Let age approve of youth, and death complete the same!

8. Of a cup being formed on the wheel; i.e., youth.

Caliban upon Setebos;
or, Natural Theology in the Island

"Caliban upon Setebos" has been the most widely admired poem of *Dramatis Personæ* (1864). Though evidently occasioned by the intellectual convulsion resulting from the publication in 1859 of Darwin's *The Origin of Species*—particularly the keen debate over the "missing link" between ape and man—"Caliban" has little to do with Darwinian theory. Rather, Browning's subject is man's inveterate tendency to create God in his own image. That the poem's intention is partly satirical is suggested by the subtitle, which alludes to one of the important forms of rational theology in the nineteenth century. *Natural Theology; or, Evidences of the Existence and Attributes of the Deity, collected from the Appearances of Nature* (1802) is the major work of an influential thinker, the latitudinarian Archdeacon William Paley (1743–1805). An elaboration of the eighteenth-century "argument from design," Paley's book professes that God's nature and purposes can be inferred empirically from natural phenomena. After drawing his famous "watchmaker-God" analogy, Paley adduces evidence of God's intelligence from the complexities of human anatomy, and His goodness from the "superaddition" of pleasure to other animal sensations. (Note that it is the prevalence of pain in his existence that forces Caliban to infer Setebos' essential cruelty.)

Several commentators have argued that another of Browning's satiric targets is orthodox Calvinism, which regarded man as depraved, and God as infinite and transcendent sovereign whose will and justice are inscrutable. The faithful, sincerely afraid of God, are impelled to repentance, which involves the denial of the flesh and the "old man" or Adam within. In accordance with God's ultimate purpose, men's souls are predestined to salvation or to condemnation and eternal death. Though Calvin insisted that man has free will, the doctrine of unconditional predestination implies that the individual exercise of free will is circumscribed by Providence. The mature Browning had largely rejected the Calvinistic elements of the Evangelical faith in which he was reared. After 1850 his stress fell heavily on the idea of a God of love.

From Calvin's thought Browning may have derived the germ of "Caliban upon Setebos." In his *Institutes* I.iii.1 ("The sense of the deity found in all men"), Calvin says, ". . . there is no nation so barbarous, no race so savage, as not to be firmly persuaded of the being of a God. Even those who in other respects appear to differ but little from brutes always retain some sense of religion. . . ." The original of Browning's brute is, of course, the spiteful humanoid of Shakespeare's *The Tempest*. Caliban, "abhorred slave" of the magician Prospero, is a "thing of darkness," "not honor'd with a human shape" (V.i.275; I.ii.283–4). Emblematizing the bestial in man (or in theological terms, unredeemed "natural man"), Shakespeare's Caliban, all appetite and fancy, is deficient in reason and therefore ineducable. While preserving Caliban's status—and his pungent speech—Browning significantly converts him from an object of loathing to a rational creature who elicits sympathy by his groping toward transcendence of his limited sphere.

The epigraph comes from Psalms 50:21: what God said to the wicked.

"Thou thoughtest that I was altogether such a one as thyself."

['Will[1] sprawl, now that the heat of day is best,
Flat on his belly in the pit's much mire,
With elbows wide, fists clenched to prop his chin.
And, while he kicks both feet in the cool slush,
And feels about his spine small eft-things[2] course,   5
Run in and out each arm, and make him laugh:
And while above his head a pompion-plant,[3]
Coating the cave-top as a brow its eye,
Creeps down to touch and tickle hair and beard,
And now a flower drops with a bee inside,   10
And now a fruit to snap at, catch and crunch,—
He looks out o'er yon sea which sunbeams cross
And recross till they weave a spider-web
(Meshes of fire, some great fish breaks at times)
And talks to his own self, howe'er he please,   15
Touching that other, whom his dam[4] called God.
Because to talk about Him, vexes—ha,
Could He but know! and time to vex is now,
When talk is safer than in winter-time.
Moreover Prosper and Miranda[5] sleep   20
In confidence he drudges at their task,
And it is good to cheat the pair, and gibe,
Letting the rank tongue blossom into speech.]

Setebos, Setebos, and Setebos!
'Thinketh, He dwelleth i' the cold o' the moon.   25

'Thinketh He made it, with the sun to match,
But not the stars; the stars came otherwise;
Only made clouds, winds, meteors, such as that:
Also this isle, what lives and grows thereon,
And snaky sea which rounds and ends the same.   30

'Thinketh, it came of being ill at ease:[6]
He hated that He cannot change His cold,
Nor cure its ache. 'Hath spied an icy fish
That longed to 'scape the rock-stream where she lived,
And thaw herself within the lukewarm brine   35
O' the lazy sea her stream thrusts far amid,
A crystal spike[7] 'twixt two warm walls of wave;
Only, she ever sickened, found repulse
At the other kind of water, not her life,
(Green-dense and dim-delicious, bred o' the sun)   40
Flounced back from bliss she was not born to breathe,
And in her old bounds buried her despair,
Hating and loving warmth alike: so He.

1. He (Caliban) will. Caliban usually refers to himself in the third person. The brackets indicate that Caliban is pondering silently or perhaps whispering.
2. Lizardlike creatures.
3. Pumpkin vine.
4. Sycorax, a witch, mother of Caliban and votary of Setebos, a Patagonian devil-god.

5. Prospero, protagonist of *The Tempest*, and his daughter.
6. By analogical reasoning Caliban projects his own misery onto his deity. Contrast Calvin's argument that because man is miserable and corrupt he must conclude that God alone exists in perfect felicity and goodness (*Institutes*, I.i.1).
7. Icy jet of water.

'Thinketh, He made thereat the sun, this isle,
Trees and the fowls here, beast and creeping thing.   45
Yon otter, sleek-wet, black, lithe as a leech;
Yon auk,[8] one fire-eye in a ball of foam,
That floats and feeds; a certain badger brown
He hath watched hunt with that slant white-wedge eye
By moonlight; and the pie[9] with the long tongue   50
That pricks deep into oakwarts[1] for a worm,
And says a plain word when she finds her prize,
But will not eat the ants; the ants themselves
That build a wall of seeds and settled stalks
About their hole—He made all these and more,   55
Made all we see, and us, in spite: how else?
He could not, Himself, make a second self
To be His mate; as well have made Himself:
He would not make what he mislikes or slights,
An eyesore to Him, or not worth His pains: 60
But did, in envy, listlessness or sport,[2]
Make what Himself would fain, in a manner, be—
Weaker in most points, stronger in a few,
Worthy, and yet mere playthings all the while,
Things He admires and mocks too,—that is it.   65
Because, so brave, so better though they be,
It nothing skills if He begin to plague.
Look now, I melt a gourd-fruit into mash,
Add honeycomb and pods, I have perceived,
Which bite like finches when they bill and kiss,—   70
Then, when froth rises bladdery, drink up all,
Quick, quick, till maggots scamper through my brain;[3]
Last, throw me on my back i' the seeded thyme,
And wanton, wishing I were born a bird.
Put case, unable to be what I wish,   75
I yet could make a live bird out of clay:
Would not I take clay, pinch my Caliban
Able to fly?—for, there, see, he hath wings,
And great comb like the hoopoe's[4] to admire,
And there, a sting to do his foes offence,   80
There, and I will that he begin to live,
Fly to yon rock-top, nip me off the horns
Of grigs[5] high up that make the merry din,
Saucy through their veined wings, and mind me not.
In which feat, if his leg snapped, brittle clay,   85
And he lay stupid-like,—why, I should laugh;
And if he, spying me, should fall to weep,

8. Diving seabird.
9. Magpie, bird related to the jay.
1. Growths on trunk of the oak.
2. Cf. Shakespeare's *King Lear*, IV.i.36–37: "As flies to wanton boys, are we to the gods; / They kill us for their sport."
3. In *The Tempest* Caliban worships Stephano because he "bears celestial liquor" (II.ii.117).
4. Colorful bird with large crest.
5. Crickets or grasshoppers.

Beseech me to be good, repair his wrong,
Bid his poor leg smart less or grow again,—
Well, as the chance were, this might take or else   90
Not take my fancy: I might hear his cry,
And give the mankin three sound legs for one,
Or pluck the other off, leave him like an egg,
And lessoned he was mine and merely clay.
Were this no pleasure, lying in the thyme,   95
Drinking the mash, with brain become alive,
Making and marring clay at will? So He.

'Thinketh, such shows nor right nor wrong in Him,
Nor kind, nor cruel: He is strong and Lord.
'Am strong myself compared to yonder crabs   100
That march now from the mountain to the sea;
'Let twenty pass, and stone the twenty-first,
Loving not, hating not, just choosing so.
'Say, the first straggler that boasts purple spots
Shall join the file, one pincer twisted off;   105
'Say, this bruised fellow shall receive a worm,
And two worms he whose nippers end in red;
As it likes me each time, I do: so He.[6]

Well, then, 'supposeth He is good i' the main,
Placable if His mind and ways were guessed,   110
But rougher than His handiwork, be sure!
Oh, He hath made things worthier than Himself,
And envieth that, so helped, such things do more
Than He who made them! What consoles but this?
That they, unless through Him, do nought at all,   115
And must submit: what other use in things?
'Hath cut a pipe of pithless elder-joint
That, blown through, gives exact the scream o' the jay
When from her wing you twitch[7] the feathers blue:
Sound this, and little birds that hate the jay   120
Flock within stone's throw, glad their foe is hurt:
Put case such pipe could prattle and boast forsooth
"I catch the birds, I am the crafty thing,
I make the cry my maker cannot make
With his great round mouth; he must blow through mine!" 125
Would not I smash it with my foot? So He.

But wherefore rough, why cold and ill at ease?
Aha, that is a question! Ask, for that,
What knows,—the something over Setebos[8]
That made Him, or He, may be, found and fought,   130
Worsted, drove off and did to nothing, perchance.

6. Browning in this passage appears to satirize the Calvinist doctrines of election, reprobation, and predestination, as these were popularly understood.
7. Pluck.

8. This superior force (called "Quiet" on line 137) is analogous to Aristotle's Unmoved Mover, the eternal and immaterial first cause, identified with the divine mind.

There may be something quiet o'er His head,
Out of His reach, that feels nor joy nor grief,
Since both derive from weakness in some way.
I joy because the quails come; would not joy   135
Could I bring quails here when I have a mind:
This Quiet, all it hath a mind to, doth.
'Esteemeth stars the outposts of its couch,
But never spends much thought nor care that way.
It may look up, work up,—the worse for those   140
It works on! 'Careth but for Setebos
The many-handed as a cuttle-fish,[9]
Who, making Himself feared through what He does,[1]
Looks up, first, and perceives he cannot soar
To what is quiet and hath happy life;   145
Next looks down here, and out of very spite
Makes this a bauble-world to ape yon real,[2]
These good things to match those as hips[3] do grapes.
'T is solace making baubles, ay, and sport.
Himself peeped late, eyed Prosper at his books   150
Careless and lofty, lord now of the isle:
Vexed, 'stitched a book of broad leaves, arrow-shaped,
Wrote thereon, he knows what, prodigious words;
Has peeled a wand and called it by a name;
Weareth at whiles for an enchanter's robe   155
The eyed skin of a supple oncelot;[4]
And hath an ounce[5] sleeker than youngling mole,
A four-legged serpent he makes cower and couch,
Now snarl, now hold its breath and mind his eye,
And saith she is Miranda and my wife: 160
'Keeps for his Ariel[6] a tall pouch-bill crane
He bids go wade for fish and straight disgorge;
Also a sea-beast, lumpish, which he snared,
Blinded the eyes of, and brought somewhat tame,
And split its toe-webs, and now pens the drudge   165
In a hole o' the rock and calls him Caliban;
A bitter heart that bides its time and bites.
'Plays thus at being Prosper in a way,
Taketh his mirth with make-believes: so He.

His dam held that the Quiet made all things   170
Which Setebos vexed only: 'holds not so.
Who made them weak, meant weakness He might vex.

9. Ten-armed mollusk.
1. Because Setebos shows intelligence and power but not love, Caliban responds appropriately with fear. Cf. "Cleon," in which the despairing speaker is unable to infer, from the human condition, a loving Zeus (lines 262ff.). For Browning, "love without a limit" demonstrates God's perfection (*The Ring and the Book*, X.1350ff.).

2. Cf. Plato's theory of Forms, developed in the *Phaedo*: there exists a transcendent world of ideal forms "imitated" in the material world.
3. Inedible fruit of the rose.
4. Ocelot, or spotted wild cat.
5. Snow leopard.
6. A spirit in Prospero's service (*Tempest*).

Had He meant other, while His hand was in,
Why not make horny eyes no thorn could prick,
Or plate my scalp with bone against the snow,   175
Or overscale my flesh 'neath joint and joint,
Like an orc's[7] armour? Ay,—so spoil His sport!
He is the One now: only He doth all.

'Saith, He may like, perchance, what profits Him.
Ay, himself loves what does him good; but why?   180
'Gets good no otherwise. This blinded beast
Loves whoso places flesh-meat on his nose,
But, had he eyes, would want no help, but hate
Or love, just as it liked him: He hath eyes.
Also it pleaseth Setebos to work,   185
Use all His hands, and exercise much craft,
By no means for the love of what is worked.
'Tasteth, himself, no finer good i' the world
When all goes right, in this safe summer-time,
And he wants little, hungers, aches not much,   190
Than trying what to do with wit and strength.
'Falls to make something: 'piled yon pile of turfs,
And squared and stuck there squares of soft white chalk,
And, with a fish-tooth, scratched a moon on each,
And set up endwise certain spikes of tree,   195
And crowned the whole with a sloth's skull a-top,
Found dead i' the woods, too hard for one to kill.
No use at all i' the work, for work's sole sake;
'Shall some day knock it down again: so He.

'Saith He is terrible: watch His feats in proof!   200
One hurricane will spoil six good months' hope.
He hath a spite against me, that I know,
Just as He favours Prosper, who knows why?
So it is, all the same, as well I find.
'Wove wattles[8] half the winter, fenced them firm   205
With stone and stake to stop she-tortoises
Crawling to lay their eggs here: well, one wave,
Feeling the foot of Him upon its neck,
Gaped as a snake does, lolled out its large tongue,
And licked the whole labour flat: so much for spite.   210
'Saw a ball[9] flame down late (yonder it lies)
Where, half an hour before, I slept i' the shade:
Often they scatter sparkles: there is force!
'Dug up a newt He may have envied once
And turned to stone, shut up inside a stone.   215
Please Him and hinder this?—What Prosper does?
Aha, if He would tell me how! Not He!
There is the sport: discover how or die!

7. Sea monster.   9. Meteorite.
8. Twigs.

All need not die, for of the things o' the isle
Some flee afar, some dive, some run up trees;   220
Those at His mercy,—why, they please Him most
When . . when . . well, never try the same way twice!
Repeat what act has pleased, He may grow wroth.
You must not know His ways, and play Him off,
Sure of the issue. 'Doth the like himself: 225
'Spareth a squirrel that[1] it nothing fears
But steals the nut from underneath my thumb,
And when I threat, bites stoutly in defence:
'Spareth an urchin[2] that contrariwise,
Curls up into a ball, pretending death   230
For fright at my approach: the two ways please.
But what would move my choler[3] more than this,
That either creature counted on its life
To-morrow and next day and all days to come,
Saying, forsooth, in the inmost of its heart,   235
"Because he did so yesterday with me,
And otherwise with such another brute,
So must he do henceforth and always."—Ay?
'Would teach the reasoning couple what "must" means!
'Doth as he likes, or wherefore Lord? So He.   240

'Conceiveth all things will continue thus,
And we shall have to live in fear of Him
So long as He lives, keeps His strength: no change,
If He have done His best, make no new world
To please Him more, so leave off watching this,—   245
If He surprise[4] not even the Quiet's self
Some strange day,—or, suppose, grow into it
As grubs grow butterflies: else, here are we,
And there is He, and nowhere help at all.

'Believeth with the life, the pain shall stop.   250
His dam held different, that after death
He both plagued enemies and feasted friends:
Idly![5] He does His worst in this our life,
Giving just respite lest we die through pain,
Saving last pain for worst,—with which, an end.   255
Meanwhile, the best way to escape His ire
Is, not to seem too happy.[6] 'Sees, himself,
Yonder two flies, with purple films and pink,
Bask on the pompion-bell above: kills both.
'Sees two black painful beetles roll their ball   260
On head and tail as if to save their lives:
Moves them the stick away they strive to clear.

1. In that, because.
2. Hedgehog.
3. Anger.
4. Attack.
5. I.e., Sycorax's belief in an afterlife is vain.
6. In lines 256–69 Browning seems to mock the sobriety of certain religious sects.

Even so, 'would have Him misconceive, suppose
This Caliban strives hard and ails no less,
And always, above all else, envies Him;   265
Wherefore he mainly dances on dark nights,
Moans in the sun, gets under holes to laugh,
And never speaks his mind save housed as now:
Outside, 'groans, curses. If He caught me here,
O'erheard this speech, and asked "What chucklest at?"   270
'Would, to appease Him, cut a finger off,[7]
Or of my three kid yearlings burn the best,
Or let the toothsome apples rot on tree,
Or push my tame beast for the orc to taste:
While myself lit a fire, and made a song   275
And sung it, "*What I hate, be consecrate*
To celebrate Thee and Thy state, no mate
For Thee; what see for envy in poor me?"
Hoping the while, since evils sometimes mend,
Warts rub away and sores are cured with slime,   280
That some strange day, will either the Quiet catch
And conquer Setebos, or likelier He
Decrepit may doze, doze, as good as die.

[What, what? A curtain o'er the world at once!
Crickets stop hissing; not a bird—or, yes,   285
There scuds His raven that has told Him all!
It was fool's play, this prattling! Ha! The wind
Shoulders the pillared dust, death's house o' the move,
And fast invading fires begin! White blaze—
A tree's head snaps—and there, there, there, there, there,   290
His thunder follows! Fool to gibe at Him!
Lo! 'Lieth flat and loveth Setebos!
'Maketh his teeth meet through his upper lip,
Will let those quails fly, will not eat this month
One little mess of whelks,[8] so he may 'scape!]   295

Confessions

I

What is he[1] buzzing in my ears?
  "Now that I come to die,
Do I view the world as a vale of tears?"
  Ah, reverend sir, not I!

II

What I viewed there once, what I view again   5
  Where the physic bottles stand
On the table's edge,—is a suburb lane,
  With a wall to my bedside hand.

7. Here and at the close Browning satirizes the concept of mortification or penance.

8. Shellfish.
1. The priest at hand.

III

That lane sloped, much as the bottles do,
   From a house you could descry   10
O'er the garden-wall: is the curtain blue
   Or green to a healthy eye?

IV

To mine, it serves for the old June weather
   Blue above lane and wall;
And that farthest bottle labelled "Ether"   15
   Is the house o'ertopping all.

V

At a terrace, somewhere near the stopper,
   There watched for me, one June,
A girl: I know, sir, it's improper,
   My poor mind's out of tune.   20

VI

Only, there was a way . . . you crept
   Close by the side, to dodge
Eyes in the house, two eyes except:
   They styled their house "The Lodge."

VII

What right had a lounger up their lane?   25
   But, by creeping very close,
With the good wall's help,—their eyes might strain
   And stretch themselves to Oes,

VIII

Yet never catch her and me together,
   As she left the attic, there,   30
By the rim of the bottle labelled "Ether,"
   And stole from stair to stair,

IX

And stood by the rose-wreathed gate. Alas,
   We loved, sir—used to meet:
How sad and bad and mad it was—   35
   But then, how it was sweet!

Prospice[1]

Fear death?—to feel the fog in my throat,
   The mist in my face,
When the snows begin, and the blasts denote
   I am nearing the place,
The power of the night, the press of the storm,   5
   The post of the foe;

1. The title means "look forward" or "be watchful." The poem first appeared in the *Atlantic Monthly* for June 1864 but was probably written shortly after Elizabeth Barrett Browning's death in 1861. At that time Browning wrote these words from Dante into his wife's Testament: "Thus I believe, thus I affirm, thus I am certain it is, that from this life I shall pass to another, there, where that lady lives of whom my soul was enamoured" (*Convivio*, II.9).

Where he stands, the Arch Fear in a visible form,
    Yet the strong man must go:
For the journey is done and the summit attained,
    And the barriers fall,   10
Though a battle's to fight ere the guerdon he gained,
    The reward of it all.
I was ever a fighter, so—one fight more,
    The best and the last!
I would hate that death bandaged my eyes, and forbore,   15
    And bade me creep past.
No! let me taste the whole of it, fare like my peers
    The heroes of old,
Bear the brunt, in a minute pay glad life's arrears
    Of pain, darkness and cold.   20
For sudden the worst turns the best to the brave,
    The black minute's at end,
And the elements' rage, the fiend-voices that rave,
    Shall dwindle, shall blend,
Shall change, shall become first a peace out of pain,   25
    Then a light, then thy breast,
O thou soul of my soul! I shall clasp thee again,
    And with God be the rest!

Apparent Failure[1]

"We shall soon lose a celebrated building."
                 Paris newspaper

I

No, for I'll save it! Seven years since,
    I passed through Paris, stopped a day
To see the baptism of your Prince;[2]
    Saw, made my bow, and went my way:
Walking the heat and headache off,   5
    I took the Seine-side, you surmise,
Thought of the Congress, Gortschakoff,[3]
    Cavour's appeal and Buol's replies,[4]
So sauntered till—what met my eyes?

II

Only the Doric[5] little Morgue!   10
    The dead-house where you show your drowned:

1. Written to help save the Paris Morgue from destruction. Since the events of stanza I occurred in 1856, the date of composition is 1863.
2. Louis Napoleon (1856–79), only son of Napoleon III and the Empress Eugénie. The Brownings witnessed the baptism in Paris in June 1856.
3. The Congress of Paris met from February 25 to April 16, 1856, to settle the Crimean War; the peace treaty was signed on March 30. Prince Aleksandr Gorchakov (1798–1883) was Russian foreign minister and a leading figure of the Congress.
4. Count Cavour (1810–61), prime minister of the Italian state of Piedmont, made an appeal on behalf of his state at the Congress. Count Buol-Schauenstein (1797–1865), as chief Austrian diplomat, responded to charges leveled by Cavour and others against Austria.
5. Simplest of classical Greek architectural styles.

Petrarch's Vaucluse makes proud the Sorgue,[6]
 Your Morgue has made the Seine renowned.
One pays one's debt in such a case;
 I plucked up heart and entered,—stalked,   15
Keeping a tolerable face
 Compared with some whose cheeks were chalked:
Let them! No Briton's to be baulked!

III

First came the silent gazers; next,
 A screen of glass, we're thankful for;   20
Last, the sight's self, the sermon's text,
 The three men who did most abhor
Their life in Paris yesterday,
 So killed themselves: and now, enthroned
Each on his copper couch, they lay   25
 Fronting me, waiting to be owned.
I thought, and think, their sin's atoned.

IV

Poor men, God made, and all for that!
 The reverence struck me; o'er each head
Religiously was hung its hat,   30
 Each coat dripped by the owner's bed,
Sacred from touch: each had his berth,
 His bounds, his proper place of rest,
Who last night tenanted on earth
 Some arch, where twelve such slept abreast,—   35
Unless the plain asphalte seemed best.

V

How did it happen, my poor boy?
 You wanted to be Buonaparte
And have the Tuileries[7] for toy,
 And could not, so it broke your heart?   40
You, old one by his side, I judge,
 Were, red as blood, a socialist,[8]
A leveller![9] Does the Empire grudge
 You've gained what no Republic missed?
Be quiet, and unclench your fist!   45

VI

And this—why, he was red in vain,
 Or black,—poor fellow that is blue!
What fancy was it turned your brain?
 Oh, women were the prize for you!
Money gets women, cards and dice   50
 Get money, and ill-luck gets just
The copper couch and one clear nice
 Cool squirt of water o'er your bust,
The right thing to extinguish lust!

6. River whose source is near the home of the Italian poet Petrarch (1304–74).
7. Royal palace adjacent to the Louvre, burned in 1871; now a public garden.
8. As today, red connoted radicalism or leftism in politics.
9. One advocating removal of social inequities.

VII

It's wiser being good than bad;   55
   It's safer being meek than fierce:
It's fitter being sane than mad.
   My own hope is, a sun will pierce
The thickest cloud earth ever stretched;
   That, after Last, returns the First,[1]   60
Though a wide compass round be fetched;
   That what began best, can't end worst,
Nor what God blessed once, prove accurst.

1863   1864

Epilogue[1]

FIRST SPEAKER, *as David*

I

On the first of the Feast of Feasts,
   The Dedication Day,[2]
When the Levites joined the Priests[3]
   At the Altar in robed array,
Give signal to sound and say,—   5

II

When the thousands, rear and van,
   Swarming with one accord
Became as a single man
   (Look, gesture, thought and word)
In praising and thanking the Lord,—   10

III

When the singers lift up their voice,
   And the trumpets made endeavour,
Sounding, "In God rejoice!"
   Saying, "In Him rejoice
Whose mercy endureth for ever!"—   15

IV

Then the Temple filled with a cloud,
   Even the House of the Lord;
Porch bent and pillar bowed:
   For the presence of the Lord,

1. Conflation of three biblical passages: Matthew 12:45, 19:30; Revelation 22:13.
1. The first two speakers represent contrasting strains of religious thought prevalent in England by mid-century: ritualism and rationalism, both of which are deplored by the third speaker, Browning in his own person. The first speaker, "David," gives the Roman Catholic–High Church Anglican position: the Temple is God's dwelling, and the institution is supported by its sacraments and hierarchies. The second speaker, "Renan," represents the skepticism and agnosticism attendant upon rational-historical criticism of Scripture. The third speaker argues that God continues to reveal Himself in the feeling and thought of the ordinary man. The poem marks the extent, by 1864, of Browning's departure from orthodox Christianity.
2. Dedication of Solomon's Temple at Jerusalem, when the Lord entered His house (1 Kings 8,9; and 2 Chronicles 5,6).
3. Levites: descendants of Levi, a sacred caste who aided the priests in ritualistic observations. Priests: descendants of Aaron; the superior clergy.

In the glory of His cloud,   20
    Had filled the House of the Lord.

SECOND SPEAKER, *as Renan*[4]

Gone now! All gone across the dark so far,
    Sharpening fast, shuddering ever, shutting still,
Dwindling into the distance, dies that star
    Which came, stood, opened once! We gazed our fill   25
With upturned faces on as real a Face[5]
    That, stooping from grave music and mild fire,
Took in our homage, made a visible place
    Through many a depth of glory, gyre on gyre,[6]
For the dim human tribute. Was this true?   30
    Could man indeed avail, mere praise of his,
To help by rapture God's own rapture too,
    Thrill with a heart's red tinge that pure pale bliss?
Why did it end? Who failed to beat the breast,
    And shriek, and throw the arms protesting wide,   35
When a first shadow showed the star addressed
    Itself to motion, and on either side
The rims contracted as the rays retired;
    The music, like a fountain's sickening pulse,
Subsided on itself; awhile transpired   40
    Some vestige of a Face no pangs convulse,
No prayers retard; then even this was gone,
    Lost in the night at last. We, lone and left
Silent through centuries, ever and anon
    Venture to probe again the vault bereft   45
Of all now save the lesser lights, a mist
    Of multitudinous points, yet suns, men say—
And this leaps ruby, this lurks amethyst,
    But where may hide what came and loved our clay?
How shall the sage detect in yon expanse   50
    The star which chose to stoop and stay for us?
Unroll the records! Hailed ye such advance
    Indeed, and did your hope evanish thus?
Watchers of twilight, is the worst averred?
    We shall not look up, know ourselves are seen,   55
Speak, and be sure that we again are heard,
    Acting or suffering, have the disk's serene[7]

4. Ernest Renan (1823–92), French scholar whose *Life of Jesus* Browning had read in 1863. Renan's purely historical interpretation of Christ's life denies any supernatural element or special revelation; his rationalistic conclusion that God had "disappeared" as a Personality informing the universe filled Renan with immense regret.
5. Of Christ.
6. Spiral. Browning may have found the word in Elizabeth Barrett Browning's *Aurora Leigh* (1856), IV.1167–68: ". . . graduating up in a spiral line / Of still expanding and ascending gyres. . . ."
7. A noun meaning "clear expanse of air," derived from Keats's "Chapman's Homer," 7–8: "Yet did I never breathe its pure serene / Till I heard Chapman speak out loud and bold."

Reflect our life, absorb an earthly flame,
    Nor doubt that, were mankind inert and numb,
Its core had never crimsoned all the same,   60
    Nor, missing ours, its music fallen dumb?
Oh, dread succession to a dizzy post,
    Sad sway of sceptre whose mere touch appals,
Ghastly dethronement, cursed by those the most
    On whose repugnant brow the crown next falls!   65

THIRD SPEAKER

I

Witless alike of will and way divine,
How heaven's high with earth's low should intertwine!
Friends, I have seen through your eyes: now use mine!

II

Take the least man of all mankind, as I;
Look at his head and heart, find how and why   70
He differs from his fellows utterly:

III

Then, like me, watch when nature by degrees
Grows alive round him, as in Arctic seas
(They said of old) the instinctive water flees

IV

Toward some elected point of central rock,[8]   75
As though, for its sake only, roamed the flock
Of waves about the waste: awhile they mock

V

With radiance caught for the occasion,—hues
Of blackest hell now, now such reds and blues
As only heaven could fitly interfuse,—   80

VI

The mimic monarch of the whirlpool, king
O' the current for a minute: then they wring
Up by the roots and oversweep the thing,

VII

And hasten off, to play again elsewhere
The same part, choose another peak as bare,   85
They find and flatter, feast and finish there.

VIII

When you see what I tell you,—nature dance
About each man of us, retire, advance,
As though the pageant's end were to enhance

IX

His worth, and—once the life, his product, gained—   90
Roll away elsewhere, keep the strife sustained,
And show thus real, a thing the North but feigned—

---

8. The description is that of the fabled maelstrom, or giant whirlpool.

X

When you acknowledge that one world could do
All the diverse work, old yet ever new,
Divide us, each from other, me from you,— 95

XI

Why, where's the need of Temple, when the walls
O' the world are that? What use of swells and falls
From Levites' choir, Priests' cries, and trumpet-calls?

XII

That one Face, far from vanish, rather grows,
Or decomposes but to recompose, 100
Become my universe that feels and knows.

From *The Ring and the Book* (1868-69)

The Ring and the Book, an epic-length poem in twelve books and Browning's acknowledged masterpiece, was published in four installments, 1868–69. It was a notable success despite its stupendous length: nearly 22,000 lines of blank verse. Browning's hold on fame was finally secured; he now rivaled his contemporary, Tennyson, and he was to enjoy two decades of lionization. The poem, which gave full scope to Browning's mind—compound as it was of earthiness and idealism, humor and high seriousness—is the product of his instinctive affinity to an obscure book and the lurid story it told. Maybe never has so ambitious a poem been based on so unpromising a subject as that of *The Ring and the Book*: an infamous triple murder that took place in Rome, 1698—once a *cause célèbre*, but a century and a half later merely a neglected chapter in the history of Roman jurisprudence. It was, as Carlyle is alleged to have said to Browning, "an old Bailey story that might have been told in ten lines, and only wants forgetting."

Browning chanced upon his source—always referred to as the Old Yellow Book—in a Florentine flea market on a June day in 1860. It was

> Small-quarto size, part print part manuscript;
> A book in shape but, really, pure crude fact
> Secreted from man's life when hearts beat hard,
> And brains, high-blooded, ticked two centuries since.
>
> (I.84–87)

This "pure crude fact" reposed in a bulky collection of documents—pleadings, affidavits, and letters—pertaining to a murder trial:

> "*Romana Homicidiorum*"—nay,
> Better translate—"A Roman murder-case:
> Position of the entire criminal cause
> Of Guido Franceschini, nobleman,
> With certain Four the cutthroats in his pay,
> Tried, all five, and found guilty and put to death
> By heading or hanging as befitted ranks,
> At Rome on February Twenty Two,
> Since our salvation Sixteen Ninety Eight:
> Wherein it is disputed if, and when,
> Husbands may kill adulterous wives, yet 'scape
> The customary forfeit."
>
> (I.118–29)

His curiosity piqued, Browning quickly purchased the book, pored over its contents delightedly—for he was a connoisseur of murder stories—and pieced together the following tale of greed, deception, passion, and cruelty:

In 1693 an impoverished, middle-aged nobleman of Arezzo named Guido Franceschini married the very young Francesca Pompilia, reared as the daughter of a bourgeois Roman couple, Pietro and Violante Comparini. Guido and wife went to Arezzo, followed soon by the Comparini, who had been led to believe they were allied to moneyed nobility. Finding only genteel poverty—and what they deemed poor treatment—they angrily returned to Rome, there bringing suit for the return of Pompilia's dowry. Their case was built on Violante's late revelation that Pompilia was not their daughter after all, but that of a Roman prostitute. The girl had been purchased in order that the Comparini could lay claim to an inheritance left them on the condition they produce an heir. Enraged at the suit, Guido entered a countersuit and (according to Pompilia's testimony) proceeded to make life torturous for his lowborn child-bride through constant harassment and petty cruelties. For his part, Guido declared that Pompilia was intractable and unfaithful. Pompilia, after several thwarted escape attempts, finally fled from Arezzo toward Rome on April 28–29, 1697, in the company of a young cleric, Giuseppe Caponsacchi. (Browning significantly altered the date to April 23, St. George's Day, to romanticize the event.) Giving chase, Guido caught them in an inn at Castelnuovo, near Rome, and had them arrested for flight and adultery. Tried and convicted at Rome, Caponsacchi was relegated to Civita Vecchia for three years; pending further inquiry, Pompilia was sent to a nunnery for penitent women. Because of pregnancy, however, she was soon bound over to the Comparini, in whose custody she gave birth to a son, Gaetano, on December 18, 1697. Apprised of the event, Guido went to Rome with four henchmen, and on January 2, 1698, after gaining entry into the Comparini house by pretending to be the bearer of a message from Caponsacchi, he murdered and mutilated the Comparini, leaving Pompilia for dead with twenty-two stab wounds. She lingered on four days, telling her story before dying. Quickly apprehended, Guido and the four were tried for murder before the tribunal of the Governor in Rome. At issue in the trial was whether a husband could kill his adulterous wife *honoris causâ*—for the sake of injured honor—with impunity. Behind this lay the still unresolved question of Pompilia's guilt or innocence. After the lawyers "wrangled, brangled, jangled" for a month, the court on February 18 found Guido guilty and sentenced him to be beheaded, his accomplices to be hanged. Pleading clerical privilege—he had held minor orders in the church—Guido unsuccessfully appealed to Pope Innocent XII to set aside the judgment. On February 22 Guido and his men were publicly executed.

Such was the raw "gold" of fact which, Browning tells us in Book I, would be combined with the "alloy" of the poetic imagination and then "wrought into a shapely ring," a work to be symbolically entitled *The Ring and the Book* and to contain Browning's mature reading of life. At first, however, Browning seems to have regarded the Old Yellow Book as material for a novel, not a poem; he tried—fortunately without success—to give the document away. His interest in the case grew, partly because of his penchant for history, and he sought further documents. In 1862 he obtained another pamphlet relating to the execution of Guido, now called the "Secondary Source." But not until 1864, owing to other commitments, did the actual composition begin; soon he was working at top speed, and by November 1865 he had three-fourths of the poem in hand. Thereafter he worked sporadically; three more years were needed to complete the task.

Though that gold of "pure crude fact" lay in rich profusion in the two sources, arriving at the whole truth as to the apportionment of guilt and innocence, praise and blame, was problematical in the extreme. Latent in the very argumentative nature of the material—the advocacy, the strong partisanship incident to such a trial—was an important theme: the elusive nature of truth itself. Is truth ascertainable in this sublunary world? To what extent is it relative to—and therefore vitiated by—individual human perspectives? The "plague of squint" seems universal; men accept for truth what they wish to believe. Judgment is at best impure, warped by private biases and prejudices; and language itself, in addition to possessing such inherent weaknesses as ambiguity, is notoriously liable to distortion or artful manipulation.

To embody his theme of the relation of truth to human perspective and belief, Browning daringly chose to tell his "Roman murder story" ten times over from as many distinct points of view. The risk of boredom through repetition was minimized by having each character emphasize, suppress, and distort various elements of the case according to his own interests and motives. These ten dramatic monologues are "framed"—introduced and concluded—by Browning himself in Books I and XII. Book I tells how the strange old volume took hold of the poet's imagination as he "mastered the contents, knew the whole truth/Gathered together, bound up in this book . . ." (I.115–16). His role as artist, he explains, is to "resuscitate" that body of inert historical matter by means of an inspiriting art. He goes on to impart much information on the case, and gives previews of each mono-loguist's performance. In the concluding book (XII) Browning gives glimpses of the trial's aftermath, then reaffirms his belief "That Art remains the one way possible/Of speaking truth, to mouths like mine at least" (XII.839–40). Books II through X are arranged in triads, the first composed of gossips called "Half-Rome," "The Other Half-Rome," and "Tertium Quid." Each speaker "swerves" from the truth because of private biases that are eventually betrayed. In the next triad, the three principals—Guido, Caponsacchi, and Pompilia—give their versions, Guido's being artful and self-serving, but those of the priest and his "Donna Angelicata" being as truthful as passionate, subjective involvement in the matter allows. The final triad begins with the ridiculous—two buffoonish lawyers interested solely in professional advancement—and concludes with the sublime: the magisterial judgment of the wise old Pope Innocent XII, who alone among the speakers possesses the insight and intuition necessary to approximate the whole truth. Though the poem could well have ended with that natural climax, Browning adds another monologue, in many ways the most remark-able of the ten: Guido speaks a second time, now as a desperate con-demned man who discovers belatedly both his real identity as a naturally amoral being and the full extent of his loathing for the vapid purity he sees in Pompilia—whom nonetheless he implores to save him from extinction at the end.

This colossal aggregation of dramatic monologues—each of major length —is a *tour de force,* one of the boldest literary experiments ever under-taken. It is one that could easily have failed, had it not been for Browning's deft, inventive treatment, his use, for example, of devices from the epic, the novel, and the drama. Instead of mere talk about the events, there is vivid portrayal, with gesture and dialogue. Browning's dramatic evocation of man-ners and morals in seventeenth-century Italy is Chaucerian in its cumulative power. Further, Browning imposes a remarkable unity on the work by paral-leling and contrasting both theme and character, and by weaving a dense, richly varied metaphorical pattern throughout. The final effect is not unlike that produced by the reading of Balzac or Dickens: the impression of a crowded, lively canvas depicting the *comédie humaine* in all its infinite variety.

The Ring and the Book

Book V

Count Guido Franceschini[1]

Thanks, Sir, but, should it please the reverend Court,
I feel I can stand somehow, half sit down
Without help, make shift to even speak, you see,[2]
Fortified by the sip of . . . why, 't is wine,
Velletri,[3]—and not vinegar and gall,[4]   5
So changed and good the times grow! Thanks, kind Sir!
Oh, but one sip's enough! I want my head
To save my neck, there's work awaits me still.
How cautious and considerate . . . aie, aie, aie,
Nor your fault, sweet Sir! Come, you take to heart   10
An ordinary matter. Law is law.
Noblemen were exempt, the vulgar thought,
From racking; but, since law thinks otherwise,
I have been put to the rack: all's over now,
And neither wrist—what men style, out of joint: 15
If any harm be, 't is the shoulder-blade,
The left one, that seems wrong i' the socket,—Sirs,
Much could not happen, I was quick to faint,
Being past my prime of life, and out of health.
In short, I thank you,—yes, and mean the word.   20
Needs must the Court be slow to understand
How this quite novel form of taking pain,
This getting tortured merely in the flesh,
Amounts to almost an agreeable change
In my case, me fastidious, plied too much   25
With opposite treatment, used (forgive the joke)
To the rasp-tooth toying with this brain of mine,
And, in and out my heart, the play o' the probe.

1. Book V presents the first of three "inside" accounts, that of Guido, who addresses the judges a few days after the murders. His defense is followed by the testimony of Caponsacchi (Book VI) and the dying confession of Pompilia (Book VII). Much of the interest of Guido's monologue lies in his resourceful use of rhetoric and special pleading.
2. Guido is to make the most of the fact that he still suffers after-effects of the torture. This means of extracting a confession was once standard for grave crimes in Roman court proceedings. On the use of judicial torture see A. K. Cook's *A Commentary upon Browning's "The Ring and the Book"* (New York: Oxford Univ. Press, 1920), App. VII.
3. Town near Rome, where a full-bodied wine is made.
4. Drink offered to Christ on the cross (Matthew 27:34).

Four years have I been operated on
I' the soul, do you see—its tense or tremulous part— 30
My self-respect, my care for a good name,
Pride in an old one, love of kindred—just
A mother, brothers, sisters, and the like,
That looked up to my face when days were dim,
And fancied they found light there—no one spot, 35
Foppishly sensitive, but has paid its pang.
That, and not this you now oblige me with,
That was the Vigil-torment,[5] if you please!
The poor old noble House that drew the rags
O' the Franceschini's once superb array 40
Close round her, hoped to slink unchallenged by,—
Pluck off these! Turn the drapery inside out
And teach the tittering town how scarlet[6] wears!
Show men the lucklessness, the improvidence
Of the easy-natured Count before this Count, 45
The father I have some slight feeling for,
Who let the world slide, nor foresaw that friends
Then proud to cap and kiss their patron's shoe,
Would, when the purse he left held spider-webs,
Properly push his child to wall one day! 50
Mimic the tetchy[7] humour, furtive glance,
And brow where half was furious, half fatigued,
O' the same son got to be of middle age,
Sour, saturnine,—your humble servant here,—
When things go cross and the young wife, he finds 55
Take to the window at a whistle's bid,
And yet demurs thereon, preposterous fool!—
Whereat the worthies judge he wants advice
And beg to civilly ask what's evil here,
Perhaps remonstrate on the habit they deem 60
He's given unduly to, of beating her:
. . . Oh, sure he beats her—why says John so else,
Who is cousin to George who is sib[8] to Tecla's self
Who cooks the meal and combs the lady's hair?
What! 'T is my wrist you merely dislocate 65
For the future when you mean me martyrdom?
—Let the old mother's economy alone,
How the brocade-strips saved o' the seamy side
O' the wedding-gown buy raiment for a year?
—How she can dress and dish up—lordly dish 70
Fit for a duke, lamb's head and purtenance[9]—
With her proud hands, feast household so a week?
No word o' the wine rejoicing God and man
The less when three-parts water? Then, I say,

---

5. The worse torture. The victim was tied to a bench, his legs elevated by a rod.
6. Rich cloth.
7. Touchy.
8. Kinsman.
9. Exodus 12:9. This is one of countless echoes from the Bible scattered through the poem.

A trifle of torture to the flesh, like yours,   75
While soul is spared such foretaste of hell-fire,
Is naught. But I curtail the catalogue
Through policy,—a rhetorician's trick,—
Because I would reserve some choicer points
O' the practice, more exactly parallel   80
(Having an eye to climax) with what gift,
Eventual grace the Court may have in store
I' the way of plague—what crown of punishments.
When I am hanged or headed, time enough
To prove the tenderness of only that,   85
Mere heading, hanging,—not their counterpart,
Not demonstration public and precise
That I, having married the mongrel of a drab,[1]
Am bound to grant that mongrel-brat, my wife,
Her mother's birthright-license as is just,—   90
Let her sleep undisturbed, i' the family style,
Her sleep out in the embraces of a priest,
Nor disallow their bastard[2] as my heir!
Your sole mistake,—dare I submit so much
To the reverend Court?—has been in all this pains   95
To make a stone roll down hill,—rack and wrench
And rend a man to pieces, all for what?
Why—make him ope mouth in his own defence,
Show cause for what he has done, the irregular deed,
(Since that he did it, scarce dispute can be)   100
And clear his fame a little, beside the luck
Of stopping even yet, if possible,
Discomfort to his flesh from noose or axe—
For that, out come the implements of law!
May it content my lords the gracious Court   105
To listen only half so patient-long
As I will in that sense profusely speak,
And—fie, they shall not call in screws to help!
I killed Pompilia Franceschini, Sirs;
Killed too the Comparini, husband, wife,   110
Who called themselves, by a notorious lie,[3]
Her father and her mother to ruin me.
There's the irregular deed: you want no more
Than right interpretation of the same,
And truth so far—am I to understand?   115
To that then, with convenient speed,—because
Now I consider,—yes, despite my boast,
There is an ailing in this omoplat[4]

---

1. Harlot. See headnote for Pompilia's background.
2. After his conviction, Guido acknowledges that he is really Gaetano's father (XI.1842ff.). Here, however, he must convince the judges that the murders were done to avenge his injured honor.

3. Pompilia's putative parents, the Comparini (Pietro and Violante) filed suit the year after the marriage to declare Pompilia illegitimate in the hope of recovering her dowry from Guido (who filed a countersuit).
4. Shoulder blade.

May clip my speech all too abruptly short,
Whatever the good-will in me. Now for truth!   120

I' the name of the indivisible Trinity!
Will my lords, in the plenitude of their light,
Weigh well that all this trouble has come on me
Through my persistent treading in the paths
Where I was trained to go,—wearing that yoke   125
My shoulder was predestined to receive,
Born to the hereditary stoop and crease?
Noble, I recognized my nobler still,
The Church, my suzerain; no mock-mistress, she;
The secular owned[5] the spiritual: mates of mine   130
Have thrown their careless hoofs up at her call
"Forsake the clover and come drag my wain!"
There they go cropping: I protruded nose
To halter, bent my back of docile beast,
And now am whealed,[6] one wide wound all of me,   135
For being found at the eleventh hour o' the day
Padding the mill-track, not neck-deep in grass:
—My one fault, I am stiffened by my work,
—My one reward, I help the Court to smile!

I am representative of a great line,   140
One of the first of the old families
In Arezzo, ancientest of Tuscan towns.
When my worst foe is fain to challenge this,
His worst exception runs—not first in rank
But second, noble in the next degree   145
Only; not malice' self maligns me more.
So, my lord opposite has composed, we know,
A marvel of a book, sustains the point
That Francis boasts the primacy 'mid saints;[7]
Yet not inaptly hath his argument   150
Obtained response from yon my other lord
In thesis published with the world's applause
—Rather 't is Dominic such post befits:
Why, at the worst, Francis stays Francis still,
Second in rank to Dominic it my be,   155
Still, very saintly, very like our Lord;
And I at least descend from Guido once
Homager to the Empire,[8] nought below—
Of which account as proof that, none o' the line
Having a single gift beyond brave blood,   160
Or able to do aught but give, give, give
In blood and brain, in house and land and cash,
Not get and garner as the vulgar may,

---

5. Admitted the claims of.
6. Flogged.
7. Guido alludes to the rivalry between two orders of friars, Franciscans and Dominicans.
8. Holder of a fief under the Emperor.

We became poor as Francis[9] or our Lord.
Be that as it likes you, Sirs,—whenever it chanced   165
Myself grew capable anyway of remark,[1]
(Which was soon—penury makes wit premature)
This struck me, I was poor who should be rich
Or pay that fault[2] to the world which trifles not
When lineage lacks the flag yet lifts the pole:[3]   170
On, therefore, I must move forthwith, transfer
My stranded self, born fish with gill and fin
Fit for the deep sea, now left flap bare-backed
In slush and sand, a show to crawlers vile
Reared of the low-tide and aright therein.   175
The enviable youth with the old name,
Wide chest, stout arms, sound brow and pricking veins,
A heartful of desire, man's natural load,
A brainful of belief, the noble's lot,—
All this life, cramped and gasping, high and dry   180
I' the wave's retreat,—the misery, good my lords,
Which made you merriment at Rome of late,[4]—
It made me reason, rather—muse, demand
—Why our bare dropping palace, in the street
Where such-an-one whose grandfather sold tripe   185
Was adding to his purchased pile a fourth
Tall tower, could hardly show a turret sound?
Why Countess Beatrice, whose son I am,
Cowered in the winter-time as she spun flax,
Blew on the earthen basket of live ash,   190
Instead of jaunting forth in coach and six
Like such-another widow who ne'er was wed?
I asked my fellows, how came this about?
"Why, Jack, the suttler's[5] child, perhaps the camp's,
Went to the wars, fought sturdily, took a town   195
And got rewarded as was natural.
She of the coach and six—excuse me there!
Why, don't you know the story of her friend?
A clown dressed vines on somebody's estate,
His boy recoiled from muck, liked Latin more,   200
Stuck to his pen and got to be a priest,
Till one day . . . don't you mind that telling tract
Against Molinos,[6] the old Cardinal wrote?

---

9. St. Francis (ca. 1182–1226), son of a wealthy merchant, devoted himself to a life of poverty.
1. Noticing.
2. Pay the penalty (of being poor).
3. When nobility fails to make proper display yet claims its rights.
4. Cf. Caponsacchi's castigation of the judges' "smirk" during his (and Pompilia's) trial for flight and adultery (VI.7–63).
5. Camp follower who peddled provisions to soldiers.
6. Spanish divine Miguel de Molinos (1627–96), who preached the concept of Quietism, the final stage of which entailed a rejection of all hindrances to direct union with God, including the church. Arrested by the Inquisition, Molinos was secretly tried, and his doctrines were condemned as heretical. He died in a prison at Rome in 1697. For the Pope's attitude to Molinism, see X.1863ff.

He penned and dropped it in the patron's desk
Who, deep in thought and absent much of mind,   205
Licensed the thing, allowed it for his own;
Quick came promotion,—*suum cuique*,[7] Count!
Oh, he can pay for coach and six, be sure!"
"—Well, let me go, do likewise:[8] war's the word—
That way the Franceschini worked at first,   210
I'll take my turn, try soldiership."—"What, you?
The eldest son and heir and prop o' the house,
So do you see your duty? Here's your post,
Hard by the hearth and altar. (Roam from roof,
This youngster, play the gipsy out of doors,   215
And who keeps kith and kin that fall on us?)
Stand fast, stick tight, conserve your gods at home!"
"—Well then, the quiet course, the contrary trade!
We had a cousin amongst us once was Pope,
And minor glories manifold. Try the Church,   220
The tonsure,[9] and,—since heresy's but half-slain
Even by the Cardinal's tract he thought he wrote,—
Have at Molinos!"—"Have at a fool's head!
You a priest? How were marriage possible?
There must be Franceschini till time ends—   225
That's your vocation. Make your brothers priests,
Paul shall be corporate,[1] and Girolamo step
Red-stockinged[2] in the presence when you choose,
But save one Franceschini for the age!
Be not the vine but dig and dung its root,[3]   230
Be not a priest but gird up priesthood's loins.
With one foot in Arezzo stride to Rome,
Spend yourself there and bring the purchase[4] back!
Go hence to Rome, be guided!"

                  So I was.

I turned alike from the hill-side zig-zag thread   235
Of way to the table-land a soldier takes,
Alike from the low-lying pasture-place
Where churchmen graze, recline and ruminate,
—Ventured to mount no platform like my lords
Who judge the world, bear brain I dare not brag—   240
But stationed me, might thus the expression serve,
As who should fetch and carry, come and go,
Meddle and make i' the cause my lords love most—
The public weal, which hangs to the law, which holds

7. "To each his own."
8. Luke 10:37.
9. I.e., the taking of holy orders. The tonsure is the monk's or priest's shaven crown.
1. Wear the cardinal's royal purple. Guido is represented as the first-born son; hence his responsibility to perpetu-ate the family name. The younger sons were free to seek preferment in the church.
2. In cardinal's stockings.
3. Luke 13:6–9. In effect, serve the church, but take no vows of celibacy.
4. Reward for service to the church.

By the Church, which happens to be through God himself. 245
Humbly I helped the Church till here I stand,—
Or would stand but for the omoplat, you see!
Bidden qualify for Rome, I, having a field,
Went, sold it, laid the sum at Peter's foot:[5]
Which means—I settled home-accounts with speed, 250
Set apart just a modicum should suffice
To hold the villa's head above the waves
Of weed inundating its oil and wine,
And prop roof, stanchion wall o' the palace so
As to keep breath i' the body, out of heart 255
Amid the advance of neighbouring loftiness—
(People like building where they used to beg)—
Till succoured one day,—shared the residue
Between my mother and brothers and sisters there,
Black-eyed babe Donna This and Donna That, 260
As near to starving as might decently be,
—Left myself journey-charges, change of suit,
A purse to put i' the pocket of the Groom
O' the Chamber of the patron, and a glove
With a ring to it for the digits of the niece 265
Sure to be helpful in his houshold,—then
Started for Rome, and led the life prescribed.
Close to the Church, thought clean of it, I assumed
Three or four orders of no consequence,[6]
—They cast out evil spirits and exorcise, 270
For example; bind a man to nothing more,
Give clerical savour to his layman's-salt,
Facilitate his claim to loaf and fish
Should miracle leave, beyond what feeds the flock,
Fragments to brim the basket of a friend[7]— 275
While, for the world's sake, I rode, danced and gamed,
Quitted me[8] like a courtier, measured mine
With whatsoever blade had fame in fence,
—Ready to let the basket go its round
Even though my turn was come to help myself, 280
Should Dives[9] count on me at dinner-time
As just the understander of a joke
And not immoderate in repartee.
Utrique sic paratus,[1] Sirs, I said,
"Here," (in the fortitude of years fifteen, 285
So good a pedagogue is penury)
"Here wait, do service,—serving and to serve!

5. That of the church. See Acts 4:36–37. (Barnabas, having sold his land, "brought the money, and laid it at the apostles' feet.")
6. What orders these were the records do not say. It is known that he served a Cardinal Nerli, and that his sojourn at Rome was unsuccessful.
7. Matthew 14:17–20.
8. Conducted myself.
9. The rich man of the parable (Luke 16:19–31).
1. "Thus prepared for either," i.e., for immediate or deferred advancement (Cook).

And, in due time, I nowise doubt at all,
The recognition of my service comes.
Next year I'm only sixteen. I can wait."   290

I waited thirty years, may it please the Court:
Saw meanwhile many a denizen o' the dung
Hop, skip, jump o'er my shoulder, make him wings
And fly aloft,—succeed, in the usual phrase.
Everyone soon or late comes round by Rome: 295
Stand still here, you'll see all in turn succeed.
Why, look you, so and so, the physician here,
My father's lacquey's son we sent to school,
Doctored and dosed this Eminence and that,
Salved the last Pope his certain obstinate sore,   300
Soon bought land as became him, names it now:
I grasp bell at his griffin-guarded gate,
Traverse the half-mile avenue,—a term,[2]
A cypress, and a statue, three and three,—
Deliver message from my Monsignor,   305
With varletry[3] at lounge i' the vestibule
I'm barred from who bear mud upon my shoe.
My father's chaplain's nephew, Chamberlain,[4]—
Nothing less, please you!—courteous all the same,
—He does not see me though I wait an hour   310
At his staircase-landing 'twixt the brace of busts,
A noseless Sylla, Marius[5] maimed to match,
My father gave him for a hexastich[6]
Made on my birthday,—but he sends me down,
To make amends, the relic I prize most—   315
The unburnt end o' the very candle, Sirs,
Purfled[7] with paint so prettily round and round,
He carried in such state last Peter's-day,—
In token I, his gentleman and squire,
Had held the bridle, walked his managed mule   320
Without a tittup[8] the procession through.
Nay, the official,—one you know, sweet lords!—
Who drew the warrant for my transfer late
To the New Prisons from Tordinona,[9]—he
Graciously had remembrance—"Francesc . . . ha?   325
His sire, now—how a thing shall come about!—
Paid me a dozen florins[1] above the fee,
For drawing deftly up a deed of sale
When troubles fell so thick on him, good heart,

2. Bust on a pillar, such as those honoring Terminus, god of boundaries.
3. Crowd of attendants or menials.
4. Highest ranking cardinal.
5. Lucius Sulla (138–78 B.C.) and Gaius Marius (157–86 B.C.), Roman generals who became bitter political rivals.
6. Epigram of six lines.
7. Here, decorated.
8. Prance.
9. The Carceri Nuove, or New Prisons, were built by Innocent X; the older papal prison was the Torre di Nona, a tower in the city walls (Cook).
1. Gold coins named for Florence.

And I was prompt and pushing! By all means!   330
At the New Prisons be it his son shall lie,—
Anything for an old friend!" and thereat
Signed name with triple flourish underneath.
These were my fellows, such their fortunes now,
While I—kept fasts and feasts innumerable,   335
Matins and vespers, functions to no end
I' the train of Monsignor and Eminence,
As gentleman-squire, and for my zeal's reward
Have rarely missed a place at the table-foot
Except when some Ambassador, or such like,   340
Brought his own people. Brief, one day I felt
The tick of time inside me, turning-point
And slight sense there was now enough of this:
That I was near my seventh climacteric,[2]
Hard upon, if not over, the middle life,   345
And, although fed by the east-wind,[3] fulsome-fine
With foretaste of the Land of Promise, still
My gorge gave symptom it might play me false;
Better not press it further,—be content
With living and dying only a nobleman,   350
Who merely had a father great and rich,
Who simply had one greater and richer yet,
And so on back and back till first and best
Began i' the night; I finish in the day.
"The mother must be getting old," I said;   355
"The sisters are well wedded away, our name
Can manage to pass a sister off, at need,
And do for dowry: both my brothers thrive—
Regular priests they are, nor, bat-like, 'bide
'Twixt flesh and fowl with neither privilege.   360
My spare revenue must keep me and mine.
I am tired: Arezzo's air is good to breathe;
Vittiano,—one limes[4] flocks of thrushes there;
A leathern coat costs little and lasts long:
Let me bid hope good-bye, content at home!"   365
Thus, one day, I disbosomed me and bowed.
Whereat began the little buzz and thrill
O' the gazers round me; each face brightened up:
As when at your Casino, deep in dawn,
A gamester says at last, "I play no more,   370
Forego gain, acquiesce in loss, withdraw
Anyhow:" and the watchers of his ways,
A trifle struck compunctious at the word,
Yet sensible of relief, breathe free once more,

2. I.e., nearly forty-nine years old, an exaggeration, since Browning has him married at forty-five. (The actual Guido, ten years younger, was executed at forty.)
3. Job 15:2: "Should a wise man . . . fill his belly with the east wind?"
4. Catches with birdlime, a sticky substance smeared on branches.

Break up the ring, venture polite advice—⁣   375
"How, Sir? So scant of heart and hope indeed?
Retire with neither cross nor pile⁵ from play?—
So incurious, so short-casting?⁶—give your chance
To a younger, stronger, bolder spirit belike,
Just when luck turns and the find throw sweeps all?"   380
Such was the chorus: and its goodwill meant—
"See that the loser leave door handsomely!
There's an ill look,—it's sinister, spoils sport,
When an old bruised and battered year-by-year
Fighter with fortune, not a penny in poke,   385
Reels down the steps of our establishment
And staggers on broad daylight and the world,
In shagrag beard and doleful doublet, drops
And breaks his heart on the outside: people prate
'Such is the profit of a trip upstairs!'   390
Contrive he sidle forth, baulked of⁷ the blow
Best dealt by way of moral, bidding down
No curse but blessings rather on our heads
For some poor prize he bears at tattered breast,
Some palpable sort of kind of good to set   395
Over and against the grievance: give him quick!"
Whereon protested Paul, "Go hang yourselves!
Leave him to me. Count Guido and brother of mine,
A word in your ear! Take courage, since faint heart
Ne'er won . . . aha, fair lady, don't men say?   400
There's a *sors*,⁸ there's a right Virgilian dip!
Do you see the happiness o' the hint? At worst,
If the Church want no more of you, the Court
No more, and the Camp as little, the ingrates,—come,
Count you are counted:⁹ still you've coat to back,   405
Not cloth of gold and tissue, as we hoped,
But cloth with sparks and spangles on its frieze¹
From Camp, Court, Church, enough to make a shine,
Entitle you to carry home a wife
With the proper dowry, let the worst betide!   410
Why, it was just a wife you meant to take!"

Now, Paul's advice was weighty: priests should know:²
And Paul apprised me, ere the week was out,
That Pietro and Violante, the easy pair,
The cits³ enough, with stomach to be more,   415
Had just the daughter and exact the sum
To truck⁴ for the quality of myself: "She's young,

---

5. Two sides of a coin (cf. "head nor tail"); hence penniless.
6. So apathetic, so cautious?
7. Spared from.
8. The *sors Virgiliana* was the Roman practice of opening Virgil at random in the hope of finding guidance.
9. You are a count who counts (Cook).

2. Guido alludes to the words of St. Paul, who after advising celibacy says, "But if they cannot contain, let them marry: for it is better to marry than to burn" (1 Corinthians 7:9).
3. Citizens, i.e., prosperous bourgeois.
1. Embroidered border.
4. Barter.

Pretty and rich: you're noble, classic, choice.
Is it to be a match?" "A match," said I.
Done! He proposed all, I accepted all,   420
And we performed all. So I said and did
Simply. As simply followed, not at first
But with the outbreak of misfortune, still
One comment on the saying and doing—"What?
No blush at the avowal you dared buy   425
A girl of age beseems your granddaughter,[5]
Like ox or ass? Are flesh and blood a ware?
Are heart and soul a chattel?"
                              Softly, Sirs!
Will the Court of its charity teach poor me
Anxious to learn, of any way i' the world,   430
Allowed by custom and convenience, save
This same which, taught from my youth up, I trod?
Take me along with you; where was the wrong step?
If what I gave in barter, style and state
And all that hangs to Franceschinihood,   435
Were worthless,—why, society goes to ground,
Its rules are idiot's-rambling. Honour of birth,—
If that thing has no value, cannot buy
Something with value of another sort,
You've no reward nor punishment to give   440
I' the giving or the taking honour; straight
Your social fabric, pinnacle to base,
Comes down a-clatter like a house of cards.
Get honour, and keep honour free from flaw,
Aim at still higher honour,—gabble o' the goose!   445
Go bid a second blockhead like myself
Spend fifty years in guarding bubbles of breath,
Soapsuds with air i' the belly, gilded brave,
Guarded and guided, all to break at touch
O' the first young girl's hand and first old fool's purse!   450
All my privation and endurance, all
Love, loyalty and labour dared and did,
Fiddle-de-dee!—why, doer and darer both,—
Count Guido Franceschini had hit the mark
Far better, spent his life with more effect,   455
As a dancer or a prizer,[6] trades that pay!
On the other hand, bid this buffoonery cease,
Admit that honour is a privilege,
The question follows, privilege worth what?
Why, worth the market-price,—now up, now down,   460
Just so with this as with all other ware:
Therefore essay the market, sell your name,
Style and condition to who buys them best!

---

5. Pompilia was thirteen when she mar-   6. Prize-fighter.
ried the forty-five-year-old Guido.

"Does my name purchase," had I dared inquire,
"Your niece, my lord?" there would have been rebuff   465
Though courtesy, your Lordship cannot else—
"Not altogether! Rank for rank may stand:
But I have wealth beside, you—poverty;
Your scale flies up there: bid a second bid
Rank too and wealth too!" Reasoned like yourself!   470
But was it to you I went with goods to sell?
This time 't was my scale quietly kissed the ground,
Mere rank against mere wealth—some youth beside,
Some beauty too, thrown into the bargain, just
As the buyer likes or lets alone. I thought   475
To deal o' the square: others find fault, it seems:
The thing is, those my offer most concerned,
Pietro, Violante, cried they fair or foul?
What did they make o' the terms? Preposterous terms?
Why then accede so promptly, close with such   480
Nor take a minute to chaffer? Bargain struck,
They straight grew bilious,[7] wished their money back,
Repented them, no doubt: why, so did I,
So did your Lordship, if town-talk be true,
Of paying a full farm's worth for that piece   485
By Pietro of Cortona[8]—probably
His scholar Ciro Ferri may have retouched—
You caring more for colour than design—
Getting a little tired of cupids too.
That's incident[9] to all the folk who buy!   490
I am charged, I know, with gilding fact by fraud;
I falsified and fabricated, wrote
Myself down roughly richer than I prove,[1]
Rendered a wrong revenue,—grant it all!
Mere grace, mere coquetry such fraud, I say: 495
A flourish round the figures of a sum
For fashion's sake, that deceives nobody.
The veritable back-bone, understood
Essence of this same bargain, blank and bare,
Being the exchange of quality for wealth,—   500
What may such fancy-flights be? Flecks of oil
Flirted by chapmen[2] where plain dealing grates.
I may have dripped a drop—"My name I sell;
Not but that I too boast my wealth"—as they,
"—We bring you riches; still our ancestor   505
Was hardly the rapscallion folk saw flogged,
But heir to we know who, were rights of force!"[3]
They knew and I knew where the backbone lurked
I' the writhings of the bargain, lords, believe!

7. Irate.
8. Baroque painter (1596–1669); Ferri (1634–89) was his chief pupil.
9. Likely to occur.

1. Guido had grossly (not mildly) exaggerated his income (Cook).
2. Sprinkled by merchants.
3. If justice were done.

I paid down all engaged for, to a doit,   510
Delivered them just that which, their life long,
They hungered in the hearts of them to gain—
Incorporation with nobility thus
In word and deed: for that they gave me wealth.
But when they came to try their gain, my gift,   515
Quit Rome and qualify for Arezzo, take
The tone o' the new sphere that absorbed the old,
Put away gossip Jack and goody Joan[4]
And go become familiar with the Great,
Greatness to touch and taste and handle now,[5]—   520
Why then,—they found that all was vanity,
Vexation, and what Solomon describes![6]
The old abundant city-fare was best,
The kindly warmth o' the commons, the glad clap
Of the equal on the shoulder, the frank grin   525
Of the underling at all so many spoons
Fire-new at neighbourly treat,—best, best and best
Beyond compare!—down to the loll itself
O' the pot-house[7] settle,—better such a bench
Than the stiff crucifixion by my dais   530
Under the piecemeal damask canopy
With the coroneted coat of arms a-top!
Poverty and privation for pride's sake,
All they engaged to easily brave and bear,—
With the fit upon them and their brains a-work,—   535
Proved unendurable to the sobered sots.
A banished prince, now, will exude a juice
And salamander-like[8] support the flame:
He dines on chestnuts, chucks the husks to help
The broil o' the brazier, pays the due baioc,[9]   540
Goes off light-hearted: his grimace begins
At the funny humours of the christening-feast
Of friend the money-lender,—then he's touched
By the flame and frizzles[1] at the babe to kiss!
Here was the converse trial, opposite mind: 545
Here did a petty nature split on rock
Of vulgar wants predestinate for such—
One dish at supper and weak wine to boot!
The prince had grinned and borne: the citizen[2] shrieked,
Summoned the neighbourhood to attest the wrong,   550
Made noisy protest he was murdered,—stoned
And burned and drowned and hanged,—then broke away,
He and his wife, to tell their Rome the rest.

---

4. Freely adapted from Ephesians 4:22–24.
5. Cf. Colossians 2:21.
6. In Ecclesiastes.
7. Tavern.
8. Like the salamander of myth, a lizard-like creature who could live in the midst of flame.
9. *Baiocco*, papal coin of small value.
1. Burns up; i.e., cannot endure.
2. Pietro (and Violante) Comparini, who left Arezzo for Rome after four months, bearing tales of poor treatment at Guido's house (see 762ff.).

And this you admire, you men o' the world, my lords?
This moves compassion, makes you doubt my faith? 555
Why, I appeal to . . . sun and moon? Not I!
Rather to Plautus, Terence, Boccaccio's Book,
My townsman, frank Ser Franco's merry Tales,[3]—
To all who strip a vizard[4] from a face,
A body from its padding, and a soul 560
From froth and ignorance it styles itself,—
If this be other than the daily hap
Of purblind[5] greed that dog-like still drops bone,
Grasps shadow, and then howls the case is hard!

So much for them so far: now for myself, 565
My profit or loss i' the matter: married am I:
Text whereon friendly censors burst to preach.
Ay, at Rome even, long ere I was left
To regulate her life for my young bride
Alone at Arezzo, friendliness outbroke 570
(Sifting my future to predict its fault)
"Purchase and sale being thus so plain a point,
How of a certain soul bound up, may-be,
I' the barter with the body and money-bags?
From the bride's soul what is it you expect?" 575
Why, loyalty and obedience,—wish and will
To settle and suit her fresh and plastic mind
To the novel, not disadvantageous mould!
Father and mother shall the woman leave,
Cleave to the husband, be it for weal or woe:[6] 580
There is the law: what sets this law aside
In my particular case? My friends submit
"Guide, guardian, benefactor,—fee, faw, fum,
The fact is you are forty-five years old,
Nor very comely even for that age: 585
Girls must have boys." Why, let girls say so then,
Nor call the boys and men, who say the same,
Brute this and beast the other as they do!
Come, cards on table! When you chaunt us next
Epithalamium[7] full to overflow 590
With praise and glory of white womanhood,
The chaste and pure—troll[8] no such lies o'er lip!
Put in their stead a crudity or two,
Such short and simple statement of the case
As youth chalks on our walls at spring of year! 595
No! I shall still think nobler of the sex,

3. **Guide** refers the judges to classics of comedy for analogues of the Comparini's greed. Plautus and Terence were Roman playwrights; "Boccaccio's Book" is the *Decameron* (1358), a collection of *novelle*; "Ser Franco" is Boccaccio's younger contemporary Franco Sacchetti, who also wrote *novelle*.
4. Mask.
5. Stupid.
6. Inversion of Genesis 2:24.
7. Wedding song.
8. Say glibly (Cook).

Believe a woman still may take a man
For the short period that his soul wears flesh,
And, for the soul's sake, understand the fault
Of armour frayed by fighting. Tush, it tempts   600
One's tongue too much! I'll say—the law's the law:
With a wife I look to find all wifeliness,
As when I buy, timber and twig, a tree—
I buy the song o' the nightingale inside.

Such was the pact: Pompilia from the first   605
Broke it, refused from the beginning day
Either in body or soul to cleave to mine,
And published it forthwith to all the world.
No rupture,—you must join ere you can break,—
Before we had cohabited a month   610
She found I was a devil and no man,—
Made common cause with those who found as much,
Her parents, Pietro and Violante,—moved
Heaven and earth to the rescue of all three.
In four months' time, the time o' the parents' stay,   615
Arezzo was a-ringing, bells in a blaze,
With the unimaginable story rife
I' the mouth of man, woman and child—to-wit
My misdemeanour. First the lighter side,
Ludicrous face of things,—how very poor   620
The Franceschini had become at last,
The meanness and the misery of each shift
To save a soldo,[9] stretch and make ends meet.
Next, the more hateful aspect,—how myself
With cruelty beyond Caligula's[1]   625
Had stripped and beaten, robbed and murdered them,
The good old couple, I decoyed, abused,
Plundered and then cast out, and happily so,
Since,— in due course the abominable comes,—
Woe worth[2] the poor young wife left lonely here!   630
Repugnant in my person as my mind,
I sought,—was ever heard of such revenge?
—To lure and bind her to so cursed a couch,
Such co-embrace with sulphur, snake and toad,
That she was fain to rush forth, call the stones   635
O' the common street to save her, not from hate
Of mine merely, but . . . must I burn my lips
With the blister of the lie? . . . the satyr-love
Of who but my own brother,[3] the young priest,
Too long enforced to lenten fare belike,   640
Now tempted by the morsel tossed him full

9. Small Tuscan coin.
1. Roman emperor who was exceedingly
cruel and probably mad (A.D. 12–41).
2. Woe be to.
3. Girolamo, who like Caponsacchi was

a canon of the Pieve church at Arezzo.
He was accused of making improper advances to Pompilia and of maltreating
the Comparini.

I' the trencher where lay bread and herbs at best.
Mark, this yourselves say!—this, none disallows,
Was charged to me by the universal voice
At the instigation of my four-months' wife!—   645
And then you ask "Such charges so preferred,
(Truly or falsely, here concerns us not)
Pricked you to punish now if not before?—
Did not the harshness double itself, the hate
Harden?" I answer "Have it your way and will!"   650
Say my resentment grew apace: what then?
Do you cry out on the marvel? When I find
That pure smooth egg which, laid within my nest,
Could not but hatch a comfort to us all,
Issues a cockatrice[4] for me and mine,   655
Do you stare to see me stamp on it? Swans are soft:
Is it not clear that she you call my wife,
That any wife of any husband, caught
Whetting a sting like this against his breast,—
Speckled with fragments of the fresh-broke shell,   660
Married a month and making outcry thus,—
Proves a plague-prodigy to God and man?
She married: what was it she married for,
Counted upon and meant to meet thereby?
"Love" suggests some one, "love, a little word   665
Whereof we have not heard one syllable."
So, the Pompilia, child, girl, wife, in one,
Wanted the beating pulse, the rolling eye,
The frantic gesture, the devotion due
From Thyrsis to Neæra![5] Guido's love—   670
Why not Provençal roses[6] in his shoe,
Plume to his cap, and trio of guitars
At casement, with a bravo[7] close beside?
Good things all these are, clearly claimable
When the fit price is paid the proper way.   675
Had it been some friend's wife, now, threw her fan
At my foot, with just this pretty scrap attached,
"Shame, death, damnation—fall these as they may,
So I find you, for a minute! Come this eve!"
—Why, at such sweet self-sacrifice,—who knows?   680
I might have fired up, found me at my post,
Ardent from head to heel, nor feared catch cough.
Nay, had some other friend's . . . say, daughter, tripped
Upstairs and tumbled flat and frank on me,
Bareheaded and barefooted, with loose hair   685
And garments all at large,—cried "Take me thus!
Duke So-and-So, the greatest man in Rome—

4. Mythical serpent hatched by a reptile from a cock's egg. Supposed to have the power of killing by its glance; hence, a treacherous person.
5. Stock names of lovers in pastoral poetry.
6. Ribbon rosettes (Cook).
7. Tough retainer.

To escape his hand and heart have I broke bounds,
Traversed the town and reached you!"—then, indeed,
The lady had not reached a man of ice!   690
I would have rummaged, ransacked at the word
Those old odd corners of an empty heart
For remnants of dim love the long disused,
And dusty crumblings of romance! But here,
We talk of just a marriage, if you please—   695
The every-day conditions and no more;
Where do these bind me to bestow one drop
Of blood shall dye my wife's true-love-knot[8] pink?
Pompilia was no pigeon, Venus' pet,
That shuffled from between her pressing paps   700
To sit on my rough shoulder,—but a hawk,
I bought at a hawk's price and carried home
To do hawk's service[9]—at the Rotunda,[1] say,
Where, six o' the callow nestlings in a row,
You pick and choose and pay the price for such.   705
I have paid my pound, await my penny's worth,
So, hoodwink,[2] starve and properly train my bird,
And, should she prove a haggard,[3]—twist her neck!
Did I not pay my name and style, my hope
And trust, my all? Through spending these amiss   710
I am here! 'T is scarce the gravity of the Court
Will blame me that I never piped a tune,
Treated my falcon-gentle[4] like my finch.
The obligation I incurred was just
To practise mastery, prove my mastership:—   715
Pompilia's duty was—submit herself,
Afford me pleasure, perhaps cure my bile.
Am I to teach my lords what marriage means,
What God ordains thereby and man fulfils
Who, docile to the dictate, treads the house?   720
My lords have chosen the happier part with Paul
And neither marry nor burn,[5]—yet priestliness
Can find a parallel to the marriage-bond
In its own blessed special ordinance
Whereof indeed was marriage made the type:[6]   725
The Church may show her insubordinate,
As marriage her refractory. How of the Monk
Who finds the claustral[7] regimen too sharp

---

8. Complicated double knot, symbol of love.
9. I.e., to obey its master.
1. The Piazza of the Pantheon, where birds are sold.
2. Blindfold. (The imagery is that of falconry.)
1 Here, an untrainable wild hawk. (Cf. *Othello*, III.iii.260–63 for a parallel metaphor.)

4. Goshawk, large brownish female hawk.
5. See note to V.412.
6. In Ephesians 5:22–25, St. Paul makes this analogy: husband is to wife as Christ is to church. "Therefore as the church is subject unto Christ, so let the wives be to their own husbands in every thing."
7. Monastic.

After the first month's essay? What's the mode
With the Deacon who supports indifferently[8]   730
The rod o' the Bishop when he tastes its smart
Full four weeks? Do you straightway slacken hold
Of the innocents, the all-unwary ones
Who, eager to profess,[9] mistook their mind?—
Remit a fast-day's rigour to the Monk   735
Who fancied Francis' manna meant roast quails,[1]—
Concede[2] the Deacon sweet society,
He never thought the Levite-rule[3] renounced,—
Or rather prescribe short chain and sharp scourge
Corrective of such peccant humours?[4] This—   740
I take to be the Church's mode, and mine.
If I was over-harsh,—the worse i' the wife
Who did not win[5] from harshness as she ought,
Wanted the patience and persuasion, lore
Of love, should cure me and console herself.   745
Put case that I mishandle, flurry and fright
My hawk through clumsiness in sportsmanship,
Twitch out five pens where plucking one would serve—
What, shall she bite and claw to mend the case?
And, if you find I pluck five more for that,   750
Shall you weep "How he roughs the turtle[6] there"?

Such was the starting; now of the further step.
In lieu of taking penance in good part,
The Monk, with hue and cry, summons a mob
To make a bonfire of the convent, say,—   755
And the Deacon's pretty piece of virtue (save
The ears o' the Court! I try to save my head)
Instructed by the ingenuous postulant,[7]
Taxes the Bishop with adultery, (mud
Needs must pair off with mud, and filth with filth)— 760
Such being my next experience. Who knows not—
The couple, father and mother of my wife,
Returned to Rome, published before my lords,
Put into print, made circulate far and wide
That they had cheated me who cheated them?   765
Pompilia, I supposed their daughter, drew
Breath first 'mid Rome's worst rankness, through the deed
Of a drab and a rogue, was by-blow bastard-babe
Of a nameless strumpet, passed off, palmed on me
As the daughter with the dowry. Daughter? Dirt   770
O' the kennel! Dowry? Dust o' the street! Nought more,
Nought less, nought else but—oh—ah—assuredly

---

8. Can hardly endure.
9. Take religious vows.
1. Numbers 11:31–33: quails fell like manna from the sky.
2. Do you allow . . . ?
3. Rules governing deacons.

4. Errant behavior.
5. Gain, improve.
6. Turtledove.
7. Candidate for admission into a religious order.

A Franceschini and my very wife!
Now take this charge as you will, for false or true,—
This charge, preferred before your very selves   775
Who judge me now,—I pray you, adjudge again,
Classing it with the cheats or with the lies,
By which category I suffer most!
But of their reckoning, theirs who dealt with me
In either fashion,—I reserve my word,   780
Justify that in its place; I am now to say,
Whichever point o' the charge might poison most,
Pompilia's duty was no doubtful one.
You put the protestation in her mouth
"Henceforward and forevermore, avaunt   785
Ye fiends, who drop disguise and glare revealed
In your own shape, no longer father mine
Nor mother mine! Too nakedly you hate
Me whom you looked as if you loved once,—me
Whom, whether true or false, your tale now damns,   790
Divulged thus to my public infamy,
Private perdition, absolute overthrow.
For, hate my husband to your hearts' content,
I, spoil and prey of you from first to last,
I who have done you the blind service, lured   795
The lion to your pitfall,—I, thus left
To answer for my ignorant bleating there,
I should have been remembered and withdrawn
From the first o' the natural fury, not flung loose
A proverb and a by-word men will mouth   800
At the cross-way, in the corner, up and down
Rome and Arezzo,—there, full in my face,
If my lord, missing them[8] and finding me,
Content himself with casting his reproach
To drop i' the street where such impostors die.   805
Ah, but—that husband, what the wonder were!—
If, far from casting thus away the rag
Smeared with the plague his hand had chanced upon,
Sewn to his pillow by Locusta's[9] wile,—
Far from abolishing, root, stem and branch,   810
The misgrowth of infectious mistletoe
Foisted into his stock for honest graft,[1]—
If he repudiate not, renounce nowise,
But, guarding, guiding me, maintain my cause
By making it his own, (what other way?)   815
—To keep my name for me, he call it his,
Claim it of who would take it by their lie,—
To save my wealth for me—or babe of mine
Their lie was framed to beggar at the birth—

8. The "impostors" of line 805; i.e., the
Comparini.
9. Female poisoner in the reigns of
Claudius and Nero.
1. Passed off as a viable graft onto the
Franceschini family tree.

He bid them loose grasp, give our gold again: 820
If he become no partner with the pair
Even in a game which, played adroitly, gives
Its winner life's great wonderful new chance,—
Of marrying, to-wit, a second time,—
Ah, if he did thus, what a friend were he! 825
Anger he might show,—who can stamp out flame
Yet spread no black o' the brand?—yet, rough albeit
In the act, as whose bare feet feel embers scorch,
What grace were his, what gratitude were mine!"
Such protestation should have been my wife's. 830
Looking for this, do I exact too much?
Why, here's the,—word for word, so much, no more,—
Avowal she made, her pure spontaneous speech
To my brother the Abate at first blush,
Ere the good impulse had begun to fade: 835
So did she make confession for the pair,
So pour forth praises in her own behalf.
"Ay, the false letter,"[2] interpose my lords—
"The simulated writing,—'t was a trick:
You traced the signs, she merely marked the same, 840
The product was not hers but yours." Alack,
I want no more impulsion to tell truth
From the other trick, the torture inside there!
I confess all—let it be understood—
And deny nothing! If I baffle you so, 845
Can so fence, in the plenitude of right,
That my poor lathen[3] dagger puts aside
Each pass o' the Bilboa,[4] beats you all the same,—
What matters inefficiency of blade?
Mine and not hers the letter,—conceded, lords! 850
Impute to me that practice!—take as proved
I taught my wife her duty, made her see
What it behoved her to see and say and do,
Feel in her heart and with her tongue declare,
And, whether sluggish or recalcitrant, 855
Forced her to take the right step, I myself
Was marching in marital rectitude!
Why who finds fault here, say the tale be true?
Would not my lords commend the priest whose zeal
Seized on the sick, morose or moribund, 860
By the palsy-smitten finger, made it cross
His brow correctly at the critical time?
—Or answered for the inarticulate babe
At baptism, in its stead declared the faith,
And saved what else would perish unprofessed? 865

2. Pompilia's letter of June 14, 1694, to Paolo (allegedly forged), in which she thanked him for having married her to Guido, and affirmed that life was peaceful since her parents' departure.
3. Latten, alloy resembling brass.
4. Sword made in Bilbao, Spanish town famed for its steel.

True, the incapable hand may rally yet,
Renounce the sign with renovated strength,—
The babe may grow up man and Molinist,—
And so Pompilia, set in the good path
And left to go alone there, soon might see   870
That too frank-forward, all too simple-straight
Her step was, and decline to tread the rough,
When here lay, tempting foot, the meadow-side,
And there the coppice rang with singing-birds!
Soon she discovered she was young and fair,   875
That many in Arezzo knew as much.[5]
Yes, this next cup of bitterness, my lords,
Had to begin go filling, drop by drop,
Its measure up of full disgust for me,
Filtered into by every noisome[6] drain—   880
Society's sink toward which all moisture runs.
Would not you prophesy—"She on whose brow is stamped
The note of the imputation that we know,—
Rightly or wrongly mothered with a whore,—
Such an one, to disprove the frightful charge,   885
What will she but exaggerate chastity,
Err in excess of wifehood, as it were,
Renounce even levities permitted youth,
Though not youth struck to age by a thunderbolt?
Cry 'wolf' i' the sheepfold, where's the sheep dares bleat,   890
Knowing the shepherd listens for a growl?"
So you expect. How did the devil decree?
Why, my lords, just the contrary of course!
It was in the house from the window, at the church
From the hassock,—where the theatre lent its lodge,[7]   895
Or staging for the public show left space,—
That still Pompilia needs must find herself
Launching her looks forth, letting looks reply
As arrows to a challenge; on all sides
Ever new contribution to her lap,   900
Till one day, what is it knocks at my clenched teeth
But the cup full, curse-collected all for me?
And I must needs drink, drink this gallant's praise,
That minion's prayer, the other fop's reproach,
And come at the dregs to—Caponsacchi! Sirs,   905
I,—chin-deep in a marsh of misery,
Struggling to extricate my name and fame
And fortune from the marsh would drown them all,
My face the sole unstrangled part of me,—
I must have this new gad-fly in that face,   910
Must free me from the attacking lover too!

5. In Guido's suit against Pompilia and Caponsacchi for flight and adultery (called the "Process of Flight," or *processus fugae*) it was alleged that Pompilia had many lovers in Arezzo. The allegation was quoted at the murder trial.
6. Filthy.
7. Loge or box.

Men say I battled ungracefully enough—
Was harsh, uncouth and ludicrous beyond
The proper part o' the husband: have it so!
Your lordships are considerate at least— 915
You order me to speak in my defence
Plainly, expect no quavering tuneful trills
As when you bid a singer solace you,—
Nor look that I shall give it, for a grace,
Stans pede in uno:[8]—you remember well 920
In the one case, 't is a plainsong too severe,[9]
This story of my wrongs,—and that I ache
And need a chair, in the other. Ask you me
Why, when I felt this trouble flap my face,
Already pricked with every shame could perch,— 925
When, with her parents, my wife plagued me too,—
Why I enforced not exhortation mild
To leave whore's-tricks and let my brows alone,
With mulct of comfits, promise of perfume?

"Far from that! No, you took the opposite course, 930
Breathed threatenings, rage and slaughter! What you will!
And the end has come, the doom is verily here,
Unhindered by the threatening. See fate's flare
Full on each face of the dead guilty three!
Look at them well, and now, lords, look at this! 935
Tell me: if on that day when I found first
That Caponsacchi thought the nearest way
To his church was some half-mile round by my door,
And that he so admired, shall I suppose,
The manner of the swallows' come-and-go 940
Between the props o' the window over-head—
That window happening to be my wife's,—
As to stand gazing by the hour on high,
Of May-eves, while she sat and let him smile,—
If I,—instead of threatening, talking big, 945
Showing hair-powder, a prodigious pinch,
For poison in a bottle,—making believe
At desperate doings with a bauble-sword,
And other bugaboo-and-baby-work,[1]—
Had, with the vulgarest household implement, 950
Calmly and quietly cut off, clean thro' bone
But one joint of one finger of my wife,
Saying "For listening to the serenade,
Here's your ring-finger shorter a full third:
Be certain I will slice away next joint, 955
Next time that anybody underneath
Seems somehow to be sauntering as he hoped

---

8. "Done standing on one foot"; i.e., an easy thing (Horace, *Satires*, I.iv.10).
9. Liturgical chant too austere in style.

1. In her actual deposition Pompilia alleged that Guido threatened to dispatch her by poisoning or stabbing.

A flower would eddy out of your hand to his
While you please fidget with the branch above
O' the rose-tree in the terrace!"—had I done so,   960
Why, there had followed a quick sharp scream, some pain,
Much calling for plaister, damage to the dress,
A somewhat sulky countenance next day,
Perhaps reproaches,—but reflections too!
I don't hear much of harm that Malchus did   965
After the incident of the ear, my lords!
Saint Peter took the efficacious way;
Malchus was sore but silenced for his life:[2]
He did not hang himself i' the Potter's Field
Like Judas, who was trusted with the bag   970
And treated to sops after he proved a thief.[3]
So, by this time, my true and obedient wife
Might have been telling beads with a gloved hand;
Awkward a little at pricking hearts and darts
On sampler possibly, but well otherwise: 975
Not where Rome shudders now to see her lie.
I give that for the course a wise man takes;
I took the other however, tried the fool's,
The lighter remedy, brandished rapier dread
With cork-ball at the tip, boxed Malchus' ear   980
Instead of severing the cartilage,
Called her a terrible nickname, and the like,
And there an end: and what was the end of that?
What was the good effect o' the gentle course?
Why, one night I went drowsily to bed,   985
Dropped asleep suddenly, not suddenly woke,
But did wake with rough rousing and loud cry,
To find noon in my face, a crowd in my room,
Fumes in my brain, fire in my throat, my wife
Gone God knows whither,—rifled vesture-chest,   990
And ransacked money-coffer. "What does it mean?"
The servants had been drugged too, stared and yawned
"It must be that our lady has eloped!"
—"Whither and with whom?"—"With whom but
        the Canon's self?
One recognizes Caponsacchi there!"—   995
(By this time the admiring neighbourhood
Joined chorus round me while I rubbed my eyes)
" 'T is months since their intelligence began,—
A comedy the town was privy to,—
He wrote and she wrote, she spoke, he replied,   1000
And going in and out your house last night
Was easy work for one . . . to be plain with you . . .
Accustomed to do both, at dusk and dawn

---

2. Guido suppresses the fact that Peter
was rebuked by Christ for this act (John

18:10–11).
3. John 13:26–30.

When you were absent,—at the villa, you know,
Where husbandry required the master-mind. 1005
Did not you know? Why, we all knew, you see!"
And presently, bit by bit, the full and true
Particulars of the tale were volunteered
With all the breathless zeal of friendship—"Thus
Matters were managed: at the seventh hour of night" . . . 1010
—"Later, at daybreak" . . . "Caponsacchi came" . . .
—"While you and all your household slept like death,
Drugged as your supper was with drowsy stuff" . . .
—"And your own cousin Guillichini[4] too—
Either or both entered your dwelling-place, 1015
Plundered it at their pleasure, made prize of all,
Including your wife . . ."—"Oh, your wife led the way,
Out of doors, on to the gate . . ."—"But gates are shut,
In a decent town, to darkness and such deeds:
They climbed the wall—your lady must be lithe— 1020
At the gap, the broken bit . . ."—"Torrione,[5] true!
To escape the questioning guard at the proper gate,
Clemente, where at the inn, hard by, 'the Horse,'
Just outside, a calash[6] in readiness
Took the two principals, all alone at last, 1025
To gate San Spirito, which o'erlooks the road,
Leads to Perugia, Rome and liberty."
Bit by bit thus made-up mosaic-wise,
Flat lay my fortune,—tesselated floor,
Imperishable tracery devils should foot 1030
And frolic it on, around my broken gods,
Over my desecrated hearth.

        So much
For the terrible effect of threatening, Sirs!
Well, this way I was shaken wide awake,
Doctored and drenched, somewhat unpoisoned so. 1035
Then, set on horseback and bid seek the lost,
I started alone, head of me, heart of me
Fire, and each limb as languid . . . ah, sweet lords,
Bethink you!—poison-torture, try persuade
The next refractory Molinist with that! . . . 1040
Floundered thro' day and night, another day
And yet another night, and so at last,
As Lucifer kept falling to find hell,
Tumbled into the court-yard of an inn[7]
At the end, and fell on whom I thought to find, 1045

4. A relative of Guido's accused, before the Arezzo court, of complicity in the elopement; Pompilia, in a letter to the Comparini, says he was to have accompanied her in the flight (Cook).
5. Bastion at northwest corner of Arezzo, adjacent to San Clemente gate. The evidence conflicted as to when and by what means Pompilia fled, and Browning in this passage seizes on that fact to underscore his theme of "our human testimony false."
6. Carriage.
7. At Castelnuovo, about fifteen miles north of Rome.

Even Caponsacchi,—what part once was priest,
Cast to the winds now with the cassock-rags.
In cape and sword a cavalier confessed,
There stood he chiding dilatory grooms,
Chafing that only horseflesh and no team   1050
Of eagles would supply the last relay,
Whirl him along the league, the one post more
Between the couple and Rome and liberty.
'T was dawn, the couple were rested in a sort,
And though the lady, tired,—the tenderer sex,—   1055
Still lingered in her chamber,—to adjust
The limp hair, look for any blush astray,—
She would descend in a twinkling,—"Have you out
The horses therefore!"
                         So did I find my wife.
Is the case complete? Do your eyes here see with mine?   1060
Even the parties dared deny no one
Point out of all these points
                              What follows next?
"Why, that then was the time," you interpose,
"Or then or never, while the fact was fresh,
To take the natural vengeance: there and thus   1065
They and you,—somebody had stuck a sword
Beside you while he pushed you on your horse,—
'Twas requisite to slay the couple, Count!"
Just so my friends say. "Kill!" they cry in a breath,
Who presently, when matters grow to a head   1070
And I do kill the offending ones indeed,—
When crime of theirs, only surmised before,
Is patent, proved indisputably now,—
When remedy for wrong,[8] untried at the time,
Which law professes shall not fail a friend,   1075
Is thrice tried[9] now, found threefold worse than null,—
When that might turn to transient shade, who knows?
Solidifies into a blot which breaks
Hell's black off in pale flakes for fear of mine,—
Then, when I claim and take revenge—"So rash?"   1080
They cry—"so little reverence for the law?"

Listen, my masters, and distinguish here!
At first, I called in law to act and help:
Seeing I did so, "Why, 't is clear," they cry,
"You shrank from gallant readiness and risk,   1085
Were coward: the thing's inexplicable else."
Sweet my lords, let the thing be! I fall flat,
Play the reed, not the oak, to breath of man.
Only inform my ignorance! Say I stand
Convicted of the having been afraid,   1090

8. Immediate revenge by manslaughter, excusable as a crime of passion.   9. In the three murders (with malice aforethought, hence inexcusable).

Proved a poltroon, no lion but a lamb,—
Does that deprive me of my right of lamb
And give my fleece and flesh to the first wolf?
Are eunuchs, women, children, shieldless quite
Against attack their own timidity tempts?   1095
Cowardice were misfortune and no crime!
—Take it that way, since I am fallen so low
I scarce dare brush the fly that blows my face,
And thank the man who simply spits not there,—
Unless the Court be generous, comprehend   1100
How one brought up at the very feet of law
As I, awaits the grave Gamaliel's[1] nod
Ere he clench fist at outrage,—much less, stab!
—How, ready enough to rise at the right time,
I still could recognise no time mature   1105
Unsanctioned by a move o' the judgment-seat,
So, mute in misery, eyed my masters here
Motionless till the authoritative word
Pronounced amercement.[2] There's the riddle solved:
This is just why I slew nor her nor him,   1110
But called in law, law's delegate in the place,
And bade arrest the guilty couple, Sirs!
We had some trouble to do so—you have heard
They braved me,—he with arrogance and scorn,
She, with a volubility of curse,   1115
A conversancy in the skill of tooth
And claw to make suspicion seem absurd,
Nay, and alacrity to put to proof
At my own throat my own sword, teach me so
To try conclusions better the next time,—   1120
Which did the proper service with the mob.
They never tried to put on mask at all:
To avowed lovers forcibly torn apart,
Upbraid the tyrant as in a playhouse scene,
Ay, and with proper clapping and applause   1125
From the audience that enjoys the bold and free.
I kept still, said to myself, "There's law!" Anon
We searched the chamber where they passed the night,
Found what confirmed the worst was feared before,
However needless confirmation now—   1130
The witches' circle intact, charms undisturbed
That raised the spirit and succubus,[3]—letters,[4] to-wit,

---

1. Teacher of the "law of the fathers" to St. Paul (Acts 22:3).
2. Penalty.
3. Female demon supposed to have sexual intercourse with a man while he sleeps.
4. The most damaging evidence against the pair. In her deposition of May 1697 (in the so-called "Process of Flight") Pompilia stated she could neither read nor write; Browning intuitively believed her, and persisted in regarding the love letters as Guido's forgery—despite evidence in the Old Yellow Book to the contrary. (See Cook, App. IV. B. Corrigan, in *Curious Annals* [Toronto, 1956], established, with reference to a document unknown to Browning, that Pompilia had four years of schooling.)

Love-laden, each the bag o' the bee that bore
Honey from lily and rose to Cupid's hive,—
Now, poetry in some rank blossom-burst,   1135
Now, prose,—"Come here, go there, wait such a while,
He's at the villa, now he's back again:
We are saved, we are lost, we are lovers all the same!"
All in order, all complete,—even to a clue
To the drowsiness that happed so opportune—   1140
No mystery, when I read "Of all things, find
What wine Sir Jealousy decided to drink—
Red wine? Because a sleeping-potion, dust
Dropped into white, discolours wine and shows."

—"Oh, but we did not write a single word!   1145
Somebody forged the letters in our name!—"
Both in a breath protested presently.
Aha, Sacchetti[5] again!—"Dame,"—quoth the Duke.
"What meaneth this epistle, counsel me,
I pick from out thy placket[6] and peruse,   1150
Wherein my page averreth thou art white
And warm and wonderful 'twixt pap and pap?"
"Sir," laughed the Lady, "'t is a counterfeit!
They page did never stroke but Dian's breast,
The pretty hound I nurture for thy sake: 1155
To lie were losel,[7]—by my fay, no more!"
And no more say I too, and spare the Court.

Ah, the Court! yes, I come to the Court's self;
Such the case, so complete in fact and proof,
I laid at the feet of law,—there sat my lords,   1160
Here sit they now, so may they ever sit
In easier attitude than suits my haunch!
In this same chamber did I bare my sores
O' the soul and not the body,—shun no shame,
Shrink from no probing of the ulcerous part,   1165
Since confident in Nature,—which is God,—
That she who, for wise ends, concocts a plague,
Curbs, at the right time, the plague's virulence too:
Law renovates even Lazarus,[8]—cures me!
Cæsar thou seekest? To Cæsar thou shalt go![9]   1170
Cæsar's at Rome: to Rome accordingly!

The case was soon decided: both weights, cast
I' the balance, vibrate, neither kicks the beam,
Here away, there away, this now and now that.
To every one o'my grievances law gave   1175
Redress, could purblind eye but see the point.

---

5. Guido here mimics the elegant style of Sacchetti's *Novelle*.
6. Skirt pocket.
7. No good.

8. Man raised from the dead by Jesus (John 11:1–46).
9. Acts 25:12; this is the answer to Paul's request to be judged by Caesar.

The wife stood a convicted runagate
From house and husband,—driven to such a course
By what she somehow took for cruelty,
Oppression and imperilment of life—   1180
Not that such things were, but that so they seemed:
Therefore, the end conceded lawful, (since
To save life there's no risk should stay our leap)
If follows that all means to the lawful end
Are lawful likewise,—poison, theft and flight.   1185
As for the priest's part, did he meddle or make,
Enough that he too thought life jeopardized;
Concede him then the colour charity
Casts on a doubtful course,—if blackish white
Or whitish black, will charity hesitate?   1190
What did he else but act the precept out,
Leave, like a provident shepherd, his safe flock
To follow the single lamb and strayaway?[1]
Best hope so and think so,—that the ticklish time
I' the carriage, the tempting privacy, the last   1195
Somewhat ambiguous accident at the inn,
—All may bear explanation: may? then, must!
The letters,—do they so incriminate?
But what if the whole prove a prank o' the pen,
Flight of the fancy, none of theirs at all,   1200
Bred of the vapours of my brain belike,
Or at worst mere exercise of scholar's-wit
In the courtly Caponsacchi: verse, convict?
Did not Catullus[2] write less seemly once?
Yet *doctus* and unblemished he abides.   1205
Wherefore so ready to infer the worst?
Still, I did righteously in bringing doubts
For the law to solve,—take the solution now!
"Seeing that the said associates, wife and priest,
Bear themselves not without some touch of blame   1210
—Else why the pother, scandal and outcry
Which trouble our peace and require chastisement?
We, for complicity in Pompilia's flight
And deviation, and carnal intercourse
With the same, do set aside and relegate   1215
The Canon Caponsacchi for three years
At Civita[3] in the neighbourhood of Rome:
And we consign Pompilia to the care
Of a certain Sisterhood of penitents[4]
I' the city's self, expert to deal with such."   1220

1. Matthew 18:12–13.
2. Greatest Roman lyricist (84?–54? B.C.), famed for his passionate love poems and scurrilous lampoons. On the strength of several longer works he was given the title of *doctus* ("learned").
3. Civita Vecchia, about thirty-five miles northwest of Rome.
4. In actuality the Scalette Convent, but all Browning's speakers mistakenly place her in the convent of the Convertites.

Word for word, there's your judgment! Read it, lords,
Re-utter your deliberate penalty
For the crime yourselves establish! Your award—
Who chop a man's right-hand off at the wrist
For tracing with forefinger words in wine   1225
O' the table of a drinking-booth that bear
Interpretation as they mocked the Church!
—Who brand a woman black between the breasts
For sinning by connection[5] with a Jew:
While for the Jew's self—pudency[6] be dumb!   1230
You mete out punishment such and such, yet so
Punish the adultery of wife and priest!
Take note of that, before the Molinists do,
And read me right the riddle, since right must be!
While I stood rapt away with wonderment,   1235
Voices broke in upon my mood and muse.
"Do you sleep?" began the friends at either ear,
"The case is settled,—you willed it should be so—
None of our counsel, always recollect!
With law's award, budge! Back into your place!   1240
Your betters shall arrange the rest for you.
We'll enter a new action, claim divorce:
Your marriage was a cheat themselves allow:
You erred i' the person,—might have married thus
Your sister or your daughter unaware.   1245
We'll gain you, that way, liberty at least,
Sure of so much by law's own showing. Up
And off with you and your unluckiness—
Leave us to bury the blunder, sweep things smooth!"
I was in humble frame of mind, be sure!   1250
I bowed, betook me to my place again.
Station by station I retraced the road,
Touched at this hostel, passed this post-house by,
Where, fresh-remembered yet, the fugitives
Had risen to the heroic stature: still—   1255
"That was the bench they sat on,—there's the board
They took the meal at,—yonder garden-ground
They leaned across the gate of,"—ever a word
O' the Helen and the Paris, with "Ha! you're he,
The . . . much-commiserated husband?"[7] Step   1260
By step, across the pelting, did I reach
Arezzo, underwent the archway's grin,
Traversed the length of sarcasm in the street,
Found myself in my horrible house once more,
And after a colloquy . . . no word assists!   1265
With the mother and the brothers, stiffened me
Straight out from head to foot as dead man does,

---

5. Sexual intercourse.   7. Helen's husband, Menelaus.
6. Modesty.

And, thus prepared for life as he for hell,
Marched to the public Square and met the world.
Apologize for the pincers, palliate screws?   1270
Ply me with such toy-trifles, I entreat!
Trust who has tried both sulphur and sops-in-wine![8]

I played the man as I best might, bade friends
Put non-essentials by and face the fact.
"What need to hang myself as you advise?   1275
The paramour is banished,—the ocean's width,
Or the suburb's length,—to Ultima Thule,[9] say,
Or Proxima Civitas,[1] what's the odds of name
And place? He's banished, and the fact's the thing.
Why should law banish innocence an inch?   1280
Here's guilt then, what else do I care to know?
The adulteress lies imprisoned,—whether in a well
With bricks above and a snake for company,
Or tied by a garter to a bed-post,—much
I mind what's little,—least's enough and to spare!   1285
The little fillip on the coward's cheek
Serves as though crab-tree cudgel broke his pate.
Law has pronounced there's punishment, less or more:
And I take note o' the fact and use it thus—
For the first flaw in the original bond,   1290
I claim release. My contract was to wed
The daughter of Pietro and Violante. Both
Protest they never had a child at all.
Then I have never made a contract: good!
Cancel me quick the thing pretended one.   1295
I shall be free.[2] What matter if hurried over
The harbour-boom[3] by a great favouring tide,
Or the last of a spent ripple that lifts and leaves?
The Abate is about it. Laugh who wins!
You shall not laugh me out of faith in law!   1300
I listen, through all your noise, to Rome!"
                                        Rome spoke.
In three months letters thence admonished me,
"Your plan for the divorce is all mistake.
It would hold, now, had you, taking thought to wed
Rachel of the blue eye and golden hair,   1305
Found swarth-skinned Leah cumber couch next day:[4]
But Rachel, blue-eyed golden-haired aright,
Proving to be only Laban's child, not Lot's,[5]

8. I.e., various mental torments.
9. Northernmost region of the habitable world to ancient geographers.
1. Nearby city; i.e., Civita Vecchia, to which Caponsacchi was "relegated."
2. According to the records, no divorce proceeding was initiated by the Franceschini, even though earlier (in 1694) such a suit had been contemplated (Cook).
3. Floating barrier across a harbor mouth.
4. I.e., a divorce is possible only on the ground of a mistake as to the identity of the spouse. Cf. V.1242–45. (Jacob, who loved Rachel, was tricked into marrying Leah instead; see Genesis 29:15–30.)
5. Lot, made drunk by his two daughters, conceived a son with each; he was unaware of his incestuous acts (Genesis 19:30–35).

Remains yours all the same for ever more.
No whit to the purpose is your plea: you err   1310
I' the person and the quality—nowise
In the individual,—that's the case in point!
You go to the ground,—are met by a cross-suit
For separation, of the Rachel here,
From bed and board,—she is the injured one,   1315
You did the wrong and have to answer it.
As for the circumstance of imprisonment
And colour it lends to this your new attack,
Never fear, that point is considered too!
The durance[6] is already at an end;   1320
The convent-quiet preyed upon her health,
She is transferred now to her parents' house
—No-parents, when that cheats and plunders you,
But parentage again confessed in full,
When such confession pricks and plagues you more—   1325
As now—for, this their house is not the house
In Via Vittoria wherein neighbours' watch
Might incommode the freedom of your wife,
But a certain villa smothered up in vines
At the town's edge by the gate i' the Pauline Way,   1330
Out of eye-reach, out of ear-shot, little and lone,
Whither a friend,—at Civita, we hope,
A good half-dozen-hours' ride off,—might, some eve,
Betake himself, and whence ride back, some morn,
Nobody the wiser: but be that as it may,   1335
Do not afflict your brains with trifles now.
You have still three suits to manage,[7] all and each
Ruinous truly should the event play false.
It is indeed the likelier so to do,
That brother Paul, your single prop and stay,   1340
After a vain attempt to bring the Pope
To set aside procedures, sit himself
And summarily use prerogative,
Afford us the infallible[8] finger's tact
To disentwine your tangle of affairs,   1345
Paul,—finding it moreover past his strength
To stem the irruption,[9] bear Rome's ridicule
Of . . . since friends must speak . . . to be round with you . . .
Of the old outwitted husband, wronged and wroth,
Pitted against a brace of juveniles—   1350

---

6. Forced confinement.
7. The three pending suits were: (1) Guido's countersuit (against the Comparini's claim of Pompilia's illegitimacy) to secure Pompilia's dowry; (2) Pompilia's suit for legal separation; and (3) Guido's suit against Pompilia for flight and adultery, brought at Arezzo. Paolo tried to have all three cases adjudicated simultaneously in a special session appointed by the pope, claiming that Guido, on the basis of having held holy orders, enjoyed ecclesiastical privilege. The pope, however, refused to intervene in the matter.
8. Allusion to the doctrine of papal infallibility; see note to X.150.
9. Invasion.

A brisk priest who is versed in Ovid's art[1]
More than his Summa,[2] and a gamesome wife
Able to act Corinna[3] without book,
Beside the waggish parents who played dupes
To dupe the duper—(and truly divers scenes   1355
Of the Arezzo palace, tickle rib
And tease eye till the tears come, so we laugh;
Nor wants the shock at the inn its comic force,
And then the letters and poetry—*merum sal!*)[4]
—Paul, finally, in such a state of things   1360
After a brief temptation to go jump
And join the fishes in the Tiber, drowns
Sorrow another and a wiser way:
House and goods, he has sold all off, is gone,
Leaves Rome,—whether for France or Spain, who knows? 1365
Or Britain almost divided from our orb.[5]
You have lost him anyhow."

          Now,—I see my lords
Shift in their seat,—would I could do the same!
They probably please expect my bile was moved
To purpose, nor much blame me: now, they judge,   1370
The fiery titillation urged my flesh
Break through the bonds. By your pardon, no, sweet Sirs!
I got such missives in the public place;
When I sought home,—with such news, mounted stair
And sat at last in the sombre gallery,   1375
('T was Autumn, the old mother in bed betimes,
Having to bear that cold, the finer frame
Of her daughter-in-law had found intolerable—
The brother, walking misery away
O' the mountain-side with dog and gun belike)   1380
As I supped, ate the coarse bread, drank the wine
Weak once, now acrid with the toad's-head-squeeze,[6]
My wife's bestowment,—I broke silence thus:
"Let me, a man, manfully meet the fact,
Confront the worst o' the truth, end, and have peace! 1385
I am irremediably beaten here,—
The gross illiterate vulgar couple,—bah!
Why, they have measured forces, mastered mine,
Made me their spoil and prey from first to last.
They have got my name,—'t is nailed now fast to theirs, 1390
The child or changeling is anyway my wife;
Point by point as they plan they execute,
They gain all, and I love all—even to the lure
That led to loss,—they have the wealth again

1. The *Art of Love* (*Ars Amatoria*).
2. The *Summa Theologica* of St. Thomas Aquinas, important in the development of Roman Catholic theology.
3. Ovid's mistress, celebrated in *Amores*.
4. "Very spicy" (Cook).
5. Phrase is borrowed from Virgil, *Eclogues*, I.67.
6. Toads were supposedly poisonous.

They hazarded awhile to hook me with,   1395
Have caught the fish and find the bait entire:
They even have their child or changeling back
To trade with, turn to account a second time.
The brother presumably might tell a tale
Or give a warning,—he, too, flies the field,[7]   1400
And with him vanish help and hope of help.
They have caught me in the cavern where I fell,
Covered my loudest cry for human aid
With this enormous paving-stone of shame.
Well, are we demigods or merely clay?   1405
Is success still attendant on desert?
Is this, we live on, heaven and the final state,
Or earth which means probation to the end?
Why claim escape from man's predestined lot
Of being beaten and baffled?—God's decree,   1410
In which I, bowing bruised head, acquiesce.
One of us Franceschini fell long since
I' the Holy Land, betrayed, tradition runs,
To Paynims[8] by the feigning of a girl
He rushed to free from ravisher, and found   1415
Lay safe enough with friends in ambuscade
Who flayed him while she clapped her hands and laughed:
Let me end, falling by a like device.
It will not be so hard. I am the last
O' my line which will not suffer any more.   1420
I have attained to my full fifty years,
(About the average of us all, 't is said,
Though it seems longer to the unlucky man)
—Lived through my share of life; let all end here,
Me and the house and grief and shame at once.   1425
Friends my informants,—I can bear your blow!"
And I believe 't was in no unmeet match
For the stoic's mood,[9] with something like a smile,
That, when morose December roused me next,
I took into my hand, broke seal to read   1430
The new epistle from Rome. "All to no use!
Whate'er the turn next injury take," smiled I,
"Here's one has chosen his part and knows his cue.
I am done with, dead now; strike away, good friends!
Are the three suits decided in a trice?   1435
Against me,—there's no question! How does it go?
Is the parentage of my wife demonstrated
Infamous to her wish? Parades she now
Loosed of the cincture that so irked the loin?
Is the last penny extracted from my purse   1440
To mulct me for demanding the first pound

---

7. Paolo had left Rome in 1697.   9. Insensibility to pain.
8. Infidels; a reference to the Crusades.

Was promised in return for value paid?
Has the priest, with nobody to court beside,
Courted the Muse in exile, hitched my hap
Into a rattling ballad-rhyme which, bawled   1445
At tavern-doors, wakes rapture everywhere,
And helps cheap wine down throat this Christmas time,
Beating the bagpipes? Any or all of these!
As well, good friends, you cursed my palace here
To its old cold stone face,—stuck your cap for crest   1450
Over the shield that's extant in the Square,—
Or spat on the statue's cheek, the impatient world
Sees cumber tomb-top in our family church:
Let him creep under covert as I shall do,
Half below-ground already indeed. Good-bye!   1455
My brothers are priests, and childless so; that's well—
And, thank God most for this, no child leave I—
None after me to bear till his heart break
The being a Franceschini and my son!"

"Nay," said the letter, "but you have just that!   1460
A babe, your veritable son and heir—
Lawful,—'t is only eight months since your wife
Left you,—so, son and heir, your babe was born
Last Wednesday in the villa,—you see the cause
For quitting Convent without beat of drum,   1465
Stealing a hurried march to this retreat
That's not so savage as the Sisterhood
To slips and stumbles: Pietro's heart is soft,
Violante leans to pity's side,—the pair
Ushered you into life a bouncing boy: 1470
And he's already hidden away and safe
From any claim on him you mean to make—
They need him for themselves,—don't fear, they know
The use o' the bantling,[1]—the nerve thus laid bare
To nip at, new and nice, with finger-nail!"   1475

Then I rose up like fire, and fire-like roared.
What, all is only beginning not ending now?
The worm which wormed its way from skin through flesh
To the bone and there lay biting, did its best,—
What, it goes on to scrape at the bone's self,   1480
Will wind to inmost marrow and madden me?
There's to be yet my representative,
Another of the name shall keep displayed
The flag with the ordure on it, brandish still
The broken sword has served to stir a jakes?[2]   1485
Who will he be, how will you call the man?
A Franceschini,—when who cut my purse,
Filched my name, hemmed me round, hustled me hard

1. Brat (and bastard).   2. Privy.

As rogues at a fair some fool they strip i' the midst,
When these count gains, vaunt pillage presently:— 1490
But a Caponsacchi, oh, be very sure!
When what demands its tribute of applause
Is the cunning and impudence o' the pair of cheats,
The lies and lust o' the mother, and the brave
Bold carriage of the priest, worthily crowned 1495
By a witness to his feat i' the following age,—
And how this three-fold cord could hook and fetch
And land leviathan that king of pride![3]
Or say, by some mad miracle of chance,
Is he indeed my flesh and blood, this babe?[4] 1500
Was it because fate forged a link at last
Betwixt my wife and me, and both alike
Found we had henceforth some one thing to love,
Was it when she could damn my soul indeed
She unlatched door, let all the devils o' the dark 1505
Dance in on me to cover her escape?
Why then, the surplusage of disgrace, the spilth
Over and above the measure of infamy,
Failing to take effect on my coarse flesh
Seasoned with scorn now, saturate with shame,— 1510
Is saved to instil on and corrode the brow,
The baby-softness of my first-born child—
The child I had died to see though in a dream,
The child I was bid strike out for, beat the wave
And baffle the tide of troubles where I swam, 1515
So I might touch shore, lay down life at last
At the feet so dim and distant and divine
Of the apparition, as 't were Mary's Babe
Had held, through night and storm, the torch aloft,—
Born now in very deed to bear this brand 1520
On forehead and curse me who could not save!
Rather be the town talk true, square's jest, street's jeer
True, my own inmost heart's confession true,
And he the priest's bastard and none of mine!
Ay, there was cause for flight, swift flight and sure! 1525
The husband gets unruly, breaks all bounds
When he encounters some familiar face,
Fashion of feature, brow and eyes and lips
Where he least looked to find them,—time to fly!
This bastard then, a nest for him is made, 1530
As the manner is of vermin, in my flesh:
Shall I let the filthy pest buzz, flap and sting,
Busy at my vitals and, nor hand nor foot
Lift, but let be, lie still and rot resigned?

3. Sea monster (Job 41); cf. the pope's treatment of leviathan (X.1096–1106).
4. Cf. XI.1842–97 for Guido's true attitude toward his son Gaetano; he concludes, "no use for son have I. . . ."

No, I appeal to God,—what says Himself,   1535
How lessons Nature when I look to learn?
Why, that I am alive, am still a man
With brain and heart and tongue and right-hand too—
Nay, even with friends, in such a cause as this,
To right me if I fail to take my right.   1540
No more of law; a voice beyond the law
Enters my heart, *Quis est pro Domino?*[5]

Myself, in my own Vittiano, told the tale
To my own serving-people summoned there:
Told the first half of it, scarce heard to end   1545
By judges who got done with judgment quick
And clamoured to go execute her 'hest—
Who cried "Not one of us that dig your soil
And dress your vineyard, prune your olive-trees,
But would have brained the man debauched our wife,   1550
And staked the wife whose lust allured the man,
And paunched[6] the Duke, had it been possible,
Who ruled the land yet barred us such revenge!"
I fixed on the first whose eyes caught mine, some four
Resolute youngsters with the heart still fresh,   1555
Filled my purse with the residue o' the coin
Uncaught-up by my wife whom haste made blind,
Donned the first rough and rural garb I found,
Took whatsoever weapon came to hand,
And out we flung and on we ran or reeled   1560
Romeward. I have no memory of our way,
Only that, when at intervals the cloud
Of horror about me opened to let in life,
I listened to some song in the ear, some snatch
Of a legend, relic of religion, stray   1565
Fragment of record very strong and old
Of the first conscience, the anterior right,
The God's-gift to mankind, impulse to quench
The antagonistic spark of hell and tread
Satan and all his malice into dust,   1570
Declare to the world the one law, right is right.
Then the cloud re-encompassed me, and so
I found myself, as on the wings of winds,
Arrived: I was at Rome on Christmas Eve.

Festive bells—everywhere the Feast o' the Babe,   1575
Joy upon earth, peace and good will to man!
I am baptized. I started and let drop
The dagger. "Where is it, His promised peace?"
Nine days o' the Birth-Feast did I pause and pray

---

5. "Who is on the Lord's side?" Having uttered this rallying cry, Moses, with "all the sons of Levi," killed 3,000 calf-idolaters (Exodus 32:26).
6. Stabbed in the belly.

To enter into no temptation more.   1580
I bore the hateful house, my brother's once,
Deserted,—let the ghost of social joy
Mock and make mouths at me from empty room
And idle door that missed the master's step,—
Bore the frank wonder of incredulous eyes,   1585
As my own people watched without a word,
Waited, from where they huddled round the hearth
Black like all else, that nod so slow to come.
I stopped my ears even to the inner call
Of the dread duty, only heard the song   1590
"Peace upon earth," saw nothing but the face
O' the Holy Infant and the halo there
Able to cover yet another face
Behind it, Satan's which I else should see.
But, day by day, joy waned and withered off: 1595
The Babe's face, premature with peak and pine,
Sank into wrinkled ruinous old age,
Suffering and death, then mist-like disappeared,
And showed only the Cross at end of all,
Left nothing more to interpose 'twixt me   1600
And the dread duty: for the angels' song,
"Peace upon earth," louder and louder pealed
"O Lord, how long, how long be unavenged?"[7]
On the ninth day, this grew too much for man.
I started up—"Some end must be!" At once,   1605
Silence: then, scratching like a death-watch-tick,[8]
Slowly within my brain was syllabled,
"One more concession, one decisive way
And but one, to determine thee the truth,—
This way, in fine, I whisper in thy ear: 1610
Now doubt, anon decide, thereupon act!"

"That is a way, thou whisperest in my ear!
I doubt, I will decide, then act," said I—
Then beckoned my companions: "Time is come!"

And so, all yet uncertain save the will   1615
To do right, and the daring aught save leave
Right undone, I did find myself at last
I' the dark before the villa with my friends,
And made the experiment, the final test,[9]
Ultimate chance that ever was to be   1620
For the wretchedness inside. I knocked, pronounced
The name, the predetermined touch for truth,
"What welcome for the wanderer? Open straight—"
To the friend, physician, friar upon his rounds,

7. Paraphrase of Revelation 6:10.
8. The sound of a death-watch beetle, supposed to foretell the death of an inmate of the house.
9. For a contrasting interpretation of this "test," see III.1590–1612.

Traveller belated, beggar lame and blind?   1625
No, but—"to Caponsachi!" And the door
Opened.
        And then,—why, even think, I think,
I' the minute that confirmed my worst of fears,
Surely,—I pray God that I think aright!—
Had but Pompilia's self, the tender thing   1630
Who once was good and pure, was once my lamb
And lay in my bosom, had the well-known shape
Fronted me in the door-way,—stood there faint
With the recent pang perhaps of giving birth
To what might, though by miracle, seem my child,—   1635
Nay more, I will say, had even the aged fool
Pietro, the dotard, in whom folly and age
Wrought, more than enmity or malevolence,
To practise and conspire against my peace,—
Had either of these but opened, I had paused.   1640
But it was she the hag, she that brought hell
For a dowry with her to her husband's house,
She the mock-mother, she that made the match
And married me to perdition, spring and source
O' the fire inside me that boiled up from heart   1645
To brain and hailed the Fury gave it birth,[1]—
Violante Comparini, she it was,
With the old grin amid the wrinkles yet,
Opened: as if in turning from the Cross,
With trust to keep the sight and save my soul,   1650
I had stumbled, first thing, on the serpent's head
Coiled with a leer at foot of it.
        There was the end!
Then was I rapt away by the impulse, one
Immeasurable everlasting wave of a need
To abolish that detested life. 'T was done: 1655
You know the rest and how the folds o' the thing,
Twisting for help, involved the other two
More or less serpent-like: how I was mad,
Blind, stamped on all, the earth-worms with the asp,
And ended so.
        You came on me that night,   1660
Your officers of justice,—caught the crime
In the first natural frenzy of remorse:
Twenty miles off, sound sleeping as a child
On a cloak i' the straw which promised shelter first,
With the bloody arms beside me,—was it not so?   1665
Wherefore not? Why, how else should I be found?
I was my own self, had my sense again,
My soul safe from the serpents. I could sleep:

1. Guido is attempting to diminish the force of the argument, urged repeatedly by the prosecution, that the murders were done in cold blood.

Indeed and, dear my lords, I shall sleep now,
Spite of my shoulder, in five minutes' space, 1670
When you dismiss me, having truth enough!
It is but a few days are passed, I find,
Since this adventure. Do you tell me, four?
Then the dead are scarce quiet where they lie,
Old Pietro, old Violante, side by side 1675
At the church Lorenzo,—oh, they know it well!
So do I. But my wife is still alive,
Has breath enough to tell her story yet,
Her way, which is not mine, no doubt at all.
And Caponsacchi, you have summoned him,— 1680
Was he so far to send for? Not at hand?
I thought some few o' the stabs were in his heart,
Or had not been so lavish: less had served.[2]
Well, he too tells his story,—florid prose
As smooth as mine is rough. You see, my lords, 1685
There will be a lying intoxication smoke
Born of the blood,—confusion probably,—
For lies breed lies—but all that rests with you!
The trial is no concern of mine; with me
The main of the care is over: I at least 1690
Recognize who took that huge burthen off,
Let me begin to live again. I did
God's bidding and man's duty, so, breathe free;
Look you to the rest! I heard Himself prescribe,
That great Physician, and dared lance the core 1695
Of the bad ulcer; and the rage abates,
I am myself and whole now: I prove cured
By the eyes that see, the ears that hear again,
The limbs that have relearned their youthful play,
The healthy taste of food and feel of clothes 1700
And taking to our common life once more,
All that now urges my defence from death.
The willingness to live, what means it else?
Before,—but let the very action speak!
Judge for yourselves, what life seemed worth to me 1705
Who, not by proxy but in person, pitched
Head-foremost into danger as a fool
That never cares if he can swim or no—
So he but find the bottom, braves the brook.
No man omits precaution, quite neglects 1710
Secrecy, safety, schemes not how retreat,
Having schemed he might advance. Did I so scheme?
Why, with a warrant which 't is ask and have,[3]
With horse thereby made mine without a word,

2. Pompilia sustained twenty-two stab wounds.
3. Guido had improvidently failed to obtain a pass through the city gates. The pope muses upon this "oversight" in X.810–41.

I had gained the frontier and slept safe that night.   1715
Then, my companions,—call them what you please,
Slave or stipendiary,⁴—what need of one
To me whose right-hand did its owner's work?
Hire an assassin yet expose yourself?
As well buy glove and then thrust naked hand   1720
I' the thorn-bush. No, the wise man stays at home,
Sends only agents out, with pay to earn:
At home, when they come back,—he straight discards
Or else disowns. Why use such tools at all
When a man's foes are of his house, like mine,   1725
Sit at his board, sleep in his bed? Why noise,
When there's the *acquetta* and the silent way?⁵
Clearly my life was valueless.

                    But now
Health is returned, and sanity of soul
Nowise indifferent to the body's harm.   1730
I find the instinct bids me save my life;
My wits, too, rally round me; I pick up
And use the arms that strewed the ground before,
Unnoticed or spurned aside: I take my stand,
Make my defence. God shall not lose a life   1735
May do Him further service, while I speak
And you hear, you my judges and last hope!
You are the law: 't is to the law I look.
I began life by hanging to the law,
To the law it is I hang till life shall end.   1740
My brother made appeal to the Pope, 't is true,
To say proceedings, judge my cause himself
Nor trouble law,—some fondness of conceit⁶
That rectitude, sagacity sufficed
The investigator in a case like mine,   1745
Dispensed with the machine of law. The Pope
Knew better, set aside my brother's plea
And put me back to law,—referred the cause
*Ad judices meos,*⁷—doubtlessly did well.
Here, then, I clutch my judges,—I claim law—   1750
Cry, by the higher law whereof your law
O' the land is humbly representative,—
Cry, on what point is it, where either accuse,
I fail to furnish you defence? I stand
Acquitted, actually or virtually,   1755
By every intermediate kind of court
That takes account of right or wrong in man,
Each unit in the series that begins
With God's throne, ends with the tribunal here.
God breathes, not speaks, his verdicts, felt not heard,   1760

4. Hireling.   6. Foolish conception.
5. I.e., poison.   7. "To my panel of jurors."

Passed on successively to each court I call
Man's conscience, custom, manners, all that make
More and more effort to promulgate, mark
God's verdict in determinable words,
Till last come human jurists—solidify   1765
Fluid result,—what's fixable lies forged,
Statute,—the residue escapes in fume,
Yet hangs aloft, a cloud, as palpable
To the finer sense as word the legist[8] welds.
Justinian's Pandects[9] only make precise   1770
What simply sparkled in men's eyes before,
Twitched in their brow or quivered on their lip,
Waited the speech they called but would not come.
These courts then, whose decree your own confirms,—
Take my whole life, not this last act alone,   1775
Look on it by the light reflected thence!
What has Society to charge me with?
Come, unreservedly,—favour none nor fear,—
I am Guido Franceschini, am I not?
You know the courses I was free to take?   1780
I took just that which let me serve the Church,
I gave it all my labour in body and soul
Till these broke down i' the service. "Specify?"
Well, my last patron was a Cardinal.
I left him unconvicted of a fault—   1785
Was even helped, by way of gratitude,
Into the new life that I left him for,[1]
This very misery of the marriage,—he
Made it, kind soul, so far as in him lay—
Signed the deed where you yet may see his name.   1790
He is gone to his reward,—dead, being my friend
Who could have helped here also,—that, of course!
So far, there's my acquittal, I suppose.
Then comes the marriage itself—no question, lords,
Of the entire validity of that!   1795
In the extremity of distress, 't is true,
For after-reasons, furnished abundantly,
I wished the thing invalid,[2] went to you
Only some months since, set you duly forth
My wrong and prayed your remedy, that a cheat   1800
Should not have force to cheat my whole life long.
"Annul a marriage? 'T is impossible!
Though ring about your neck be brass not gold,
Needs must it clasp, gangrene you all the same!"
Well, let me have the benefit, just so far,   1805

8. Lawyer.
9. Also known as the *Digest*, a compilation of juristic codes and decisions commissioned by Byzantine emperor Justinian the Great (483–565). The *Digest* was still the foundation of Roman law in 1698.
1. The patron, Cardinal Nerli, had rather dismissed Guido (Cook).
2. See note to line 1296

O' the fact announced,—my wife then is my wife,
I have allowance for a husband's right.
I am charged with passing right's due bound,—such acts
As I thought just, my wife called cruelty,
Complained of in due form,—convoked no court   1810
Of common gossipry, but took her wrongs—
And not once, but so long as patience served—
To the town's³ top, jurisdiction's pride of place,
To the Archbishop and Governor.
These heard her charge with my reply, and found   1815
That futile, this sufficient: they dismissed
The hysteric querulous rebel, and confirmed
Authority in its wholesome exercise,
They, with directest access to the facts.
"—Ay, for it was their friendship favoured you,   1820
Hereditary alliance against a breach
I' the social order: prejudice for the name
Of Franceschini!"—So I hear it said:
But not here. You, lords, never will you say
"Such is the nullity of grace and truth,   1825
Such the corruption of the faith, such lapse
Of law, such warrant have the Molinists
For daring reprehend us as they do,—
That we pronounce it just a common case,
Two dignitaries, each in his degree   1830
First, foremost, this the spiritual head, and that
The secular arm o' the body politic,
Should, for mere wrongs' love and injustice' sake,
Side with, aid and abet in cruelty
This broken beggarly noble,—bribed perhaps   1835
By his watered wine and mouldy crust of bread—
Rather than that sweet tremulous flower-like wife
Who kissed their hands and curled about their feet
Looking the irresistible loveliness
In tears that takes man captive, turns" . . . enough!   1840
Do you blast your predecessors? What forbids
Posterity to trebly blast yourselves
Who set the example and instruct their tongue?
You dreaded the crowd, succumbed to the popular cry,
Or else, would nowise seem defer thereto   1845
And yield to public clamour though i' the right!
You ridded your eye of my unseemliness,
The noble whose misfortune wearied you,—
Or, what's more probable, made common cause
With the cleric section, punished in myself   1850
Maladroit uncomplaisant laity,
Defective in behaviour to a priest
Who claimed the customary partnership

3. **Arezzo.**

I' the house and the wife. Lords, any lie will serve![4]
Look to it,—or allow me freed so far!   1855

Then I proceed a step, come with clean hands
Thus far, re-tell the tale told eight months since.
The wife, you allow so far, I have not wronged,
Has fled my roof, plundered me and decamped
In company with the priest her paramour: 1860
And I gave chase, came up with, caught the two
At the wayside inn where both had spent the night,
Found them in flagrant fault, and found as well,
By documents with name and plan and date,
The fault was furtive then that's flagrant now,   1865
Their intercourse a long established crime.
I did not take the license law's self gives
To slay both criminals o' the spot at the time,
But held my hand,—preferred play prodigy
Of patience which the world calls cowardice,   1870
Rather than seem anticipate the law
And cast discredit on its organs.—you.
So, to your bar I brought both criminals,
And made my statement: heard their counter-charge,
Nay,—their corroboration of my tale,   1875
Nowise disputing its allegements, not
I' the main, not more than nature's decency
Compels men to keep silence in this kind,—
Only contending that the deeds avowed
Would take another colour and bear excuse.   1880
You were to judge between us; so you did.
You disregard the excuse, you breathe away
The colour of innocence and leave guilt black,
"Guilty" is the decision of the court,
And that I stand in consequence untouched,   1885
One white integrity from head to heel.
Not guilty? Why then did you punish them?
True, punishment has been inadequate—
'T is not I only, not my friends that joke,
My foes that jeer, who echo "inadequate"—   1890
For, by a chance that comes to help for once,
The same case simultaneously was judged
At Arezzo, in the province of the Court
Where the crime had its beginning but not end.
They then, deciding on but half o' the crime,   1895
The effraction,[5] robbery,—features of the fault
I never cared to dwell upon at Rome,—
What was it they adjudged as penalty
To Pompilia,—the one criminal o' the pair
Amenable to their judgment, not the priest   1900

4. To sway the people against this court.   5. Forcible entry.

Who is Rome's?[6] Why, just imprisonment for life
I' the Stinche.[7] There was Tuscany's award[8]
To a wife that robs her husband: you at Rome—
Having to deal with adultery in a wife
And, in a priest, breach of the priestly vow[9]—   1905
Give gentle sequestration for a month
In a manageable Convent, then release,
You call imprisonment, in the very house
O' the very couple, which the aim and end
Of the culprits' crime was—just to reach and rest   1910
And there take solace and defy me: well,—
This difference 'twixt their penalty and yours
Is immaterial: make your penalty less—
Merely that she should henceforth wear black gloves
And white fan, she who wore the opposite—   1915
Why, all the same the fact o' the thing subsists.
Reconcile to your conscience as you may,
Be it on your own heads, you pronounced but half
O' the penalty for heinousness like hers
And his, that pays a fault at Carnival   1920
Of comfit-pelting past discretion's law,
Or accident to handkerchief in Lent
Which falls perversely as a lady kneels
Abruptly, and but half conceals her neck![1]
I acquiesce for my part: punished, though   1925
By a pin-point scratch, means guilty: guilty means
—What have I been but innocent hitherto?
Anyhow, here the offence, being punished, ends.

Ends?—for you deemed so, did you not, sweet lords?
That was throughout the veritable aim   1930
O' the sentence light or heavy,—to redress
Recognized wrong? You righted me, I think?
Well then,—what if I, at this last of all,
Demonstrate you, as my whole pleading proves,
No particle of wrong received thereby   1935
One atom of right?—that cure grew worse disease?
That in the process you call "justice done"
All along you have nipped away just inch
By inch the creeping climbing length of plague
Breaking my tree of life from root to branch,   1940
And left me, after all and every act
Of your interference,—lightened of what load?
At liberty wherein? Mere words and wind!
"Now I was saved, now I should feel no more

6. As an ecclesiastic, Caponsacchi was immune from prosecution in a civil court.
7. Prison at Florence.
8. Cf. the pope's assessment of "that strange shameful judgment" (X.830–40).
9. Though often called a priest, Caponsacchi was actually a subdeacon, a member of the lowest of the four major orders of clergy. He was bound by vows of celibacy, however.
1. Euphemism for bosom.

The hot breath, find a respite from fixed eye   1945
And vibrant tongue!" Why, scarce your back was turned,
There was the reptile, that feigned death at first,
Renewing its detested spire and spire
Around me, rising to such heights of hate
That, so far from mere purpose now to crush   1950
And coil itself on the remains of me,
Body and mind, and there flesh fang content,
Its aim is now to evoke life from death,
Make me anew, satisfy in my son
The hunger[2] I may feed but never sate,   1955
Tormented on to perpetuity,—
My son, whom, dead, I shall know, understand,
Feel, hear, see, never more escape the sight
In heaven that's turned to hell, or hell returned
(So rather say) to this same earth again,—   1960
Moulded into the image and made one,
Fashioned of soul as featured like in face,
First taught to laugh and lisp and stand and go
By that thief, poisoner and adulteress
I call Pompilia, he calls . . . sacred name,   1965
Be unpronounced, be unpolluted here!
And last led up to the glory and prize of hate
By his . . . foster-father, Caponsacchi's self,
The perjured priest, pink[3] of conspirators,
Tricksters and knaves, yet polished, superfine,   1970
Manhood to model adolescence by!
Lords, look on me, declare,—when, what I show,
Is nothing more nor less than what you deemed
And doled me out for justice,—what did you say?
For reparation, restitution and more,—   1975
Will you not thank, praise, bid me to your breasts
For having done the thing you thought to do,
And thoroughly trampled out sin's life at last?
I have heightened phrase to make your soft speech serve,
Doubled the blow you but essayed to strike,   1980
Carried into effect your mandate here
That else had fallen to ground: mere duty done,
Oversight of the master just supplied
By zeal i' the servant. I, being used to serve,
Have simply . . . what is it they charge me with?   1985
Blackened again, made legible once more
Your own decree, not permanently writ,
Rightly conceived but all too faintly traced.
It reads efficient, now, comminatory,[4]
A terror to the wicked, answers so   1990
The mood o' the magistrate, the mind of law.

2. For vengeance.   4. Effective . . . threatening.
3. The flower, or perfection.

Absolve, then, me, law's mere executant!
Protect your own defender,—save me, Sirs!
Give me my life, give me my liberty,
My good name and my civic rights again!   1995
It would be too fond, too complacent play
Into the hands o' the devil, should we lose
The game here, I for God: a soldier-bee
That yields his life, exenterate[5] with the stroke
O' the sting that saves the hive. I need that life.   2000
Oh. never fear! I'll find life plenty use
Though it should last five years more, aches and all!
For, first thing, there's the mother's age to help—
Let her come break her heart upon my breast,
Not on the blank stone of my nameless tomb!   2005
The fugitive brother[6] has to be bidden back
To the old routine, repugnant to the tread,
Of daily suit and service to the Church,—
Thro' gibe and jest, those stones that Shimei flung![7]
Ay, and the spirit-broken youth at home,[8]   2010
The awe-struck altar-ministrant, shall make
Amends for faith now palsied at the source,
Shall see truth yet triumphant, justice yet
A victor in the battle of this world!
Give me—for last, best gift—my son again,   2015
Whom law makes mine,—I take him at your word,
Mine be he, by miraculous mercy, lords!
Let me lift up his youth and innocence
To purify my palace, room by room
Purged of the memories, lend from his bright brow   2020
Light to the old proud paladin[9] my sire
Shrunk now for shame into the darkest shade
O' the tapestry, showed him once and shrouds him now!
Then may we,—strong from that rekindled smile,—
Go forward, face new times, the better day.   2025
And when, in times made better through your brave
Decision now,—might but Utopia be!—
Rome rife with honest women and strong men,
Manners reformed, old habits back once more,
Customs that recognize the standard worth,—   2030
The wholesome household rule in force again,
Husbands once more God's representative,
Wives like the typical Spouse[1] once more, and Priests
No longer men of Belial,[2] with no aim
At leading silly women captive, but   2035

5. Disemboweled.
6. Paolo.
7. 2 Samuel 16:5–13. The stones were cast at David and his servants.
8. Girolamo.
9. Paragon of chivalry.
1. See note to V.725.

2. I.e., worthless, licentious people. "Now the sons of Eli were sons of Belial; they knew not the Lord. . . . [Eli heard that his sons] lay with the women that assembled at the door of the tabernacle of the congregation" (1 Samuel 2:12, 22).

Of rising to such duties as yours now,—
Then will I set my son at my right-hand
And tell his father's story to this point,
Adding "The task seemed superhuman, still
I dared and did it, trusting God and law: 2040
And they approved of me: give praise to both!"
And if, for answer, he shall stoop to kiss
My hand, and peradventure start thereat,—
I engage to smile "That was an accident
I' the necessary process,—just a trip   2045
O' the torture-irons in their search for truth,—
Hardly misfortune, and no fault at all."

Book VI

Giuseppe Caponsacchi[1]

Answer you, Sirs? Do I understand aright?
Have patience! In this sudden smoke from hell,—
So things disguise themselves,—I cannot see
My own hand held thus broad before my face
And know it again. Answer you? Then that means   5
Tell over twice what I, the first time, told
Six months ago:[2] 't was here, I do believe,
Fronting you same three in this very room,
I stood and told you: yet now no one laughs,
Who then . . . nay, dear my lords, but laugh you did,   10
As good as laugh, what in a judge we style
Laughter—no levity, nothing indecorous, lords!
Only,—I think I apprehend the mood:
There was the blameless shrug, permissible smirk,
The pen's pretence at play with the pursed mouth,   15
The titter stifled in the hollow palm
Which rubbed the eyebrow and caressed the nose,
When I first told my tale: they meant, you know,
"The sly one, all this we are bound believe!
Well, he can say no other than what he says.   20
We have been young, too,—come, there's greater guilt!
Let him but decently disembroil himself,
Scramble from out the scrape nor move the mud,—
We solid ones may risk a finger-stretch!"
And now you sit as grave, stare as aghast   25
As if I were a phantom: not 't is—"Friend,
Collect yourself!"—no laughing matter more—

1. Giuseppe Maria Caponsacchi, church-man of Arezzo and rescuer of Pompilia, addresses the court on the day after Guido's testimony.
2. Caponsacchi and Pompilia were charged by Guido with unlawful flight and adultery in the summer of 1697, about eight months before the present trial.

"Counsel the Court in this extremity,
Tell us again!"—tell that, for telling which,
I got the jocular piece of punishment,   30
Was sent to lounge a little in the place
Whence now of a sudden here you summon me
To take the intelligence from just—your lips!
You, Judge Tommati, who then tittered most,—
That she I helped eight months since to escape   35
Her husband, was retaken by the same,
Three days ago, if I have seized your sense,—
(I being disallowed to interfere,
Meddle or make in a matter none of mine,
For you and law were guardians quite enough   40
O' the innocent, without a pert priest's help)—
And that he has butchered her accordingly,
As she foretold and as myself believed,—
And, so foretelling and believing so,
We were punished, both of us, the merry way: 45
Therefore, tell once again the tale! For what?
Pompilia is only dying while I speak!
Why does the mirth hang fire and miss the smile?
My masters, there's an old book, you should con
For strange adventures, applicable yet,   50
'T is stuffed with. Do you know that there was once
This thing: a multitude of worthy folk
Took recreation, watched a certain group
Of soldiery intent upon a game,—
How first they wrangled, but soon fell to play,   55
Threw dice,—the best diversion in the world.
A word in your ear,—they are now casting lots,
Ay, with the gesture quaint and cry uncouth,
For the coat of One[3] murdered an hour ago!
I am a priest,—talk of what I have learned.   60
Pompilia is bleeding out her life belike,
Gasping away the latest breath of all,
This minute, while I talk—not while you laugh?

Yet, being sobered now, what is it you ask
By way of explanation? There's the fact!   65
It seems to fill the universe with sight
And sound,—from the four corners of this earth
Tells itself over, to my sense at least.
But you may want to lower set i' the scale,—
Too vast, too close it clangs in the ear, perhaps;   70
You'd stand back just to comprehend it more.
Well then, let me, the hollow rock, condense
The voice o' the sea and wind, interpret you
The mystery of this murder. God above!

3. Jesus. The soldiers cast lots for his coat (John 19:23–24).

It is too paltry, such a transference   75
O' the storm's roar to the cranny of the stone!

This deed, you saw begin—why does its end
Surprise you? Why should the event enforce
The lesson, we ourselves learned, she and I,
From the first o' the fact, and taught you, all in vain?   80
This Guido from whose throat you took my grasp,
Was this man to be favoured, now, or feared,
Let do his will, or now his will restrained,
In the relation with Pompilia? Say!
Did any other man need interpose   85
—Oh, though first comer, though as strange at the work
As fribble⁴ must be, coxcomb, fool that's near
To knave as, say, a priest who fears the world—
Was he bound brave the peril, save the doomed,
Or go on, sing his snatch and pluck his flower,   90
Keep the straight path and let the victim die?
I held so; you decided otherwise,
Saw no such peril, therefore no such need
To stop song, loosen flower, and leave path. Law,
Law was aware and watching, would suffice,   95
Wanted no priest's intrusion, palpably
Pretence, too manifest a subterfuge!
Whereupon I, priest, coxcomb, fribble and fool,
Ensconced me in my corner, thus rebuked,
A kind of culprit, over-zealous hound   100
Kicked for his pains to kennel; I gave place
To you, and let the law reign paramount:
I left Pompilia to your watch and ward,
And now you point me—there and thus she lies!

Men, for the last time, what do you want with me?   105
Is it,—you acknowledge, as it were, a use,
A profit in employing me?—at length
I may conceivably help the august law?
I am free to break the blow, next hawk that swoops
On next dove, nor miss much of good repute?   110
Or what if this your summons, after all,
Be but the form of mere release, no more,
Which turns the key and lets the captive go?
I have paid enough in person at Civita,
Am free,—what more need I concern me with?   115
Thank you! I am rehabilitated then,
A very reputable priest. But she—
The glory of life, the beauty of the world,
The splendour of heaven, . . . well, Sirs, does no one move?
Do I speak ambiguously? The glory, I say,   120
And the beauty, I say, and splendour, still say I,

4. Frivolous person, trifler.

Who, priest and trained to live my whole life long
On beauty and splendour, solely at their source,
God,—have thus recognized my food in her,
You tell me, that's fast dying while we talk,   125
Pompilia! How does lenity to me,
Remit one death-bed pang to her? Come smile!
The proper wink at the hot-headed youth
Who lets his soul show, through transparent words,
The mundane love that's sin and scandal too!   130
You are all struck acquiescent now, it seems:
It seems the oldest, gravest signor here,
Even the redoubtable Tommati, sits
Chop-fallen,—understands how law might take
Service like mine, of brain and heart and hand,   135
In good part. Better late than never, law
You understand of a sudden, gospel too
Has a claim here, may possibly pronounce
Consistent with my priesthood, worthy Christ,
That I endeavoured to save Pompilia?

                          Then,   140
You were wrong, you see: that's well to see, though late:
That's all we may expect of man, this side
The grave: his good is—knowing he is bad:
Thus will it be with us when the books ope
And we stand at the bar on judgment-day.   145
Well then, I have a mind to speak, see cause
To relume the quenched flax[5] by this dreadful light,
Burn my soul out in showing you the truth.
I heard, last time I stood here to be judged,
What is priest's-duty,—labour to pluck tares   150
And weed the corn of Molinism;[6] let me
Make you hear, this time, how, in such a case,
Man, be he in the priesthood or at plough,
Mindful of Christ or marching step by step
With . . . what's his style, the other potentate[7]   155
Who bids have courage and keep honour safe,
Nor let minuter admonition tease?—
How he is bound, better or worse, to act.
Earth will not end through this misjudgment, no!
For you and the others like you sure to come,   160
Fresh work is sure to follow,—wickedness
That wants withstanding. Many a man of blood,
Many a man of guile will clamour yet,
Bid you redress his grievance,—as he clutched
The prey, forsooth a stranger stepped between,   165
And there's the good gripe in pure waste! My part

---

5. Isaiah 42:3: ". . . the smoking flax   6. I.e., heresy. See note to V.203.
shall he not quench: he shall bring forth   7. The civilized world.
judgment unto truth."

Is done; i' the doing it, I pass away
Out of the world. I want no more with earth.
Let me, in heaven's name, use the very snuff
O' the taper in one last spark shall show truth   170
For a moment, show Pompilia who was true!
Not for her sake, but yours: if she is dead,
Oh, Sirs, she can be loved by none of you
Most or least priestly! Saints, to do us good,
Must be in heaven, I seem to understand: 175
We never find them saints before, at least.
Be her first prayer then presently for you—
She has done the good to me . . .
                              What is all this?
There, I was born, have lived, shall die, a fool!
This is a foolish outset:—might with cause   180
Give colour[8] to the very lie o' the man,
The murderer,—make as if I loved his wife,
In the way he called love. He is the fool there!
Why, had there been in me the touch ot taint,
I had picked up so much of knaves'-policy   185
As hide it, keep one hand pressed on the place
Suspected of a spot would damn us both.
Or no, not her!—not even if any of you
Dares think that I, i' face the death, her death
That's in my eyes and ears and brain and heart,   190
Lie,—if he does, let him! I mean to say,
So he stop there, stay thought from smirching her
The snow-white soul that angels fear to take
Untenderly. But, all the same, I know
I too am taintless, and I bare my breast.   195
You can't think, men as you are, all of you,
But that, to hear thus suddenly such an end
Of such a wonderful white soul, that comes
Of a man and murderer calling the white black,
Must shake me, trouble and disadvantage. Sirs,   200
Only seventeen!

                    Why, good and wise you are!
You might at the beginning stop my mouth:
So, none would be to speak for her, that knew.
I talk impertinently, and you bear,
All the same. This it is to have to do   205
With honest hearts: they easily may err,
But in the main they wish well to the truth.
You are Christians; somehow, no one ever plucked
A rag, even, from the body of the Lord,
To wear and mock with, but despite himself,   210
He looked the greater and was the better. Yes,

8. Credibility.

I shall go on now. Does she need or not
I keep calm? Calm I'll keep as monk that croons
Transcribing battle, earthquake, famine, plague,
From parchment to his cloister's chronicle.   215
Not one word more from the point now!

                           I begin.
Yes, I am one of your body and a priest.
Also I am a younger son o' the House
Oldest now, greatest once, in my birth-town
Arezzo, I recognize no equal there—   220
(I want all arguments, all sorts of arms
That seem to serve,—use this for a reason, wait!)
Not therefore thrust into the Church, because
O' the piece of bread one gets there. We were first
Of Fiesole,[9] that rings still with the fame   225
Of Capo-in-Sacco our progenitor:
When Florence ruined Fiesole, our folk
Migrated to the victor-city, and there
Flourished,—our palace and our tower attest
In the Old Mercato,[1]—this was years ago,   230
Four hundred, full,—no, it wants fourteen just.
Our arms are those of Fiesole itself,
The shield quartered with white and red: a branch
Are the Salviati[2] of us, nothing more.
That were good help to the Church? But better still—   235
Not simply for the advantage of my birth
I' the way of the world, was I proposed for priest;
But because there's an illustration,[3] late
I' the day, that's loved and looked to as a saint
Still in Arezzo, he was bishop of,   240
Sixty years since: he spent to the last doit
His bishop's-revenue among the poor,
And used to tend the needy and the sick,
Barefoot, because of his humility.
He it was,—when the Granduke Ferdinand[4]   245
Swore he would raze our city, plough the place
And sow it with salt, because we Aretines
Had tied a rope about the neck, to hale
The statue of his father[5] from its base
For hate's sake,—he availed by prayers and tears   250
To pacify the Duke and save the town.
This was my father's father's brother. You see,
For his sake, how it was I had a right
To the self-same office, bishop in the egg,

9. Town near Florence.
1. Market in Florence. Cf. Dante, *Paradiso*, XVI.121–22: "Already Caponsacco had come down from Fiesole into the market-place" (Grandgent translation). "Capo-in-sacco" literally means "head-in-sack."
2. The Salviati were a leading Florentine family, one of whom was a cardinal.
3. Illustrious person.
4. Ferdinand II (1610–70).
5. Cosimo II (1590–1621).

So, grew i' the garb and prattled in the school,   255
Was made expect, from infancy almost,
The proper mood o' the priest; till time ran by
And brought the day when I must read the vows,
Declare the world renounced and undertake
To become priest and leave probation,—leap   260
Over the ledge into the other life,
Having gone trippingly hitherto up to the height
O'er the wan water. Just a vow to read!

I stopped short awe-struck. "How shall holiest flesh
Engage to keep such vow inviolate,   265
How much less mine? I know myself too weak,
Unworthy! Choose a worthier stronger man!"
And the very Bishop smiled and stopped my mouth
In its mid-protestation. "Incapable?
Qualmish of conscience? Thou ingenuous boy!   270
Clear up the clouds and cast they scruples far!
I satisfy thee there's an easier sense
Wherein to take such vow than suits the first
Rough rigid reading. Mark what makes all smooth,
Nay, has been even a solace to myself!   275
The Jews who needs must, in their synagogue,
Utter sometimes the holy name of God,
A thing their superstition boggles at,
Pronounce aloud the ineffable sacrosanct,—
How does their shrewdness help them? In this wise;   280
Another set of sounds they substitute,
Jumble so consonants and vowels—how
Should I know?—that there grows from out the old
Quite a new word that means the very same—
And o'er the hard place slide they with a smile.   285
Giuseppe Maria Caponsacchi mine,
Nobody wants you in these latter days
To prop the Church by breaking your back-bone,—
As the necessary way was once, we know,
When Diocletian[6] flourished and his like.   290
That building of the buttress-work was done
By martyrs and confessors: let it bide,
Add not a brick, but, where you see a chink,
Stick in a sprig of ivy or root a rose
Shall make amends and beautify the pile!   295
We profit as you were the painfullest
O' the martyrs, and you prove yourself a match
For the cruelest confessor ever was,
If you march boldly up and take your stand
Where their blood soaks, their bones yet strew the soil,   300
And cry 'Take notice, I the young and free

---

6. Roman emperor (245–313), persecutor of Christians.

And well-to-do i' the world, thus leave the world,
Cast in my lot thus with no gay young world
But the grand old Church: she tempts me of the two!'
Renounce the world? Nay, keep and give it us!   305
Let us have you, and boast of what you bring.
We want the pick o' the earth to practise with,
Not its offscouring, halt and deaf and blind
In soul and body. There's a rubble-stone
Unfit for the front o' the building, stuff to stow   310
In a gap behind and keep us weather-tight;
There's porphyry for the prominent place. Good lack!
Saint Paul has had enough and to spare, I trow,
Of ragged run-away Onesimus:[7]
He wants the right-hand with the signet-ring   315
Of King Agrippa,[8] now, to shake and use.
I have a heavy scholar cloistered up,
Close under lock and key, kept at his task
Of letting Fénelon[9] know the fool he is,
In a book I promise Christendom next Spring.   320
Why, if he covets so much meat, the clown,
As a lark's wing next Friday, or, any day,
Diversion beyond catching his own fleas,
He shall be properly swinged,[1] I promise him.
But you, who are so quite another paste[2]   325
Of a man,—do you obey me? Cultivate
Assiduous that superior gift you have
Of making madrigals—(who told me? Ah!)
Get done a Marinesque Adoniad[3] straight
With a pulse o' the blood a-pricking, here and there,   330
That I may tell the lady 'And he's ours!' "

So I became a priest: those terms changed all,
I was good enough for that, nor cheated so;
I could live thus and still hold head erect.
Now you see why I may have been before   335
A fribble and coxcomb, yet, as priest, break word
Nowise, to make you disbelieve me now.
I need that you should know my truth. Well, then,
According to prescription did I live,
—Conformed myself, both read the breviary   340
And wrote the rhymes, was punctual to my place
I' the Pieve,[4] and as diligent at my post
Where beauty and fashion rule. I throve apace,

7. Servant who became a disciple of St. Paul (Philemon 10 ff.).
8. Herod Agrippa II (271–100), king of Judea before whom St. Paul pleaded at Caesarea (Acts 26).
9. French writer (1651–1715), archbishop of Cambrai, whose mystical treatise *Maxims of the Saints* (1697) was condemned as unorthodox by Innocent XII in 1699.
1. Beaten.
2. Make, composition.
3. Poem in the florid style of the epic-length *Adone* (1622) of Giambattista Marino (or Marini, 1569–1625), about Venus and Adonis.
4. The Church of S. Maria della Pieve in Arezzo.

Sub-deacon, Canon, the authority
For delicate play at tarocs,[5] and arbiter   345
O' the magnitude of fan-mounts: all the while
Wanting no whit the advantage of a hint
Benignant to the promising pupil,—thus:
"Enough attention to the Countess now,
The young one; 't is her mother rules the roast,   350
We know where, and puts in a word: go pay
Devoir to-morrow morning after mass!
Break that rash promise to preach, Passion-week!
Has it escaped you the Archbishop grunts
And snuffles when one grieves to tell his Grace   355
No soul dares treat the subject of the day[6]
Since his own masterly handling it (ha, ha!)
Five years ago,—when somebody could help
And touch up an odd phrase in time of need,
(He, he!)—and somebody helps you, my son!   360
Therefore, don't prove so indispensable
At the Pieve, sit more loose i' the seat, nor grow
A fixture by attendance morn and eve!
Arezzo's just a haven midway Rome—
Rome's the eventual harbour,—make for port,   365
Crowd sail, crack cordage! And your cargo be
A polished presence, a genteel manner, wit
At will, and tact at every pore of you!
I sent our lump of learning, Brother Clout,
And Father Slouch, our piece of piety,   370
To see Rome and try suit the Cardinal.
Thither they clump-clumped, beads and book in hand,
And ever since 't is meat for man and maid
How both flopped down, prayed blessing on bent pate
Bald many an inch beyond the tonsure's need,   375
Never once dreaming, the two moony dolts,
There's nothing moves his Eminence so much
As—far from all this awe at sanctitude—
Heads that wag, eyes that twinkle, modified mirth
At the closet-lectures on the Latin tongue   380
A lady learns so much by, we know where.
Why, body o' Bacchus, you should crave his rule
For pauses in the elegiac couplet, chasms
Permissible only to Catullus![7] There!
Now go to duty: brisk, break Priscian's[8] head   385
By reading the day's office—there's no help.
You've Ovid[9] in your poke to plaster that;
Amen's at the end of all: then sup with me!"

<hr />

5. Card game.
6. The Molinist heresy.
7. Roman poet (87 B.C.–A.D. 54), whose elegant violation of metrical rules is endorsed by the Cardinal.

8. Break the rules for good classical Latin set down by Priscian, sixth-century grammarian.
9. Roman poet (43 B.C.–A.D. 17).

    Well, after three or four years of this life,
In prosecution of my calling, I   390
Found myself at the theatre one night
With a brother Canon, in a mood and mind
Proper enough for the place, amused or no:
When I saw enter, stand, and seat herself
A lady, young, tall, beautiful, strange and sad.   395
It was as when, in our cathedral once,
As I got yawningly through matin-song,
I saw *facchini*[1] bear a burden up,
Base it on the high-altar, break away
A board or two, and leave the thing inside   400
Lofty and lone: and lo, when next I looked,
There was the Rafael! I was still one stare,
When—"Nay, I'll make her give you back your gaze"—
Said Canon Conti; and at the word he tossed
A paper-twist of comfits to her lap,   405
And dodged and in a trice was at my back
Nodding from over my shoulder. Then she turned,
Looked our way, smiled the beautiful sad strange smile.
"Is not she fair? 'T is my new cousin," said he:
"The fellow lurking there i' the black o' the box   410
Is Guido, the old scapgrace: she's his wife,
Married three years since: how his Countship sulks!
He had brought little back from Rome beside,
After the bragging, bullying. A fair face,
And—they do say—a pocketful of gold   415
When he can worry both her parents dead.
I don't go much there, for the chamber's cold
And the coffee pale. I got a turn at first
Paying my duty: I observed they crouched
—The two old frightened family spectres—close   420
In a corner, each on each like mouse on mouse
I' the cat's cage: ever since, I stay at home.
Hallo, there's Guido, the black, mean and small,
Bends his brows on us—please to bend your own
On the shapely nether limbs of Light-skirts there   425
By way of a diversion! I was a fool
To fling the sweetmeats. Prudence, for God's love!
To-morrow I'll make my peace, e'en tell some fib,
Try if I can't find means to take you there."

That night and next day did the gaze endure,   430
Burnt to my brain, as sunbeam thro' shut eyes,
And not once changed the beautiful sad strange smile.
At vespers Conti leaned beside my seat
I' the choir,—part said, part sung—"*In ex-cel-sis*—
All's to no purpose; I have louted[2] low,   435

1. Porters.   2. Bowed.

But he saw you staring—*quia sub*—don't incline
To know you nearer: him we would not hold
For Hercules,—the man would lick your shoe
If you and certain efficacious friends
Managed him warily,—but there's the wife: 440
Spare her, because he beats her, as it is,
She's breaking her heart quite fast enough—*jam tu*—
So, be you rational and make amends
With little Light-skirts yonder—*in secula*
Secu-lo-o-o-o-rum. Ah, you rogue! Every one knows   445
What great dame she makes jealous: one against one,
Play, and win both!"
               Sirs, ere the week was out,
I saw and said to myself "Light-skirts hides teeth
Would make a dog sick,—the great dame shows spite
Should drive a cat mad: 't is but poor work this—   450
Counting one's fingers till the sonnet's crowned.
I doubt much if Marino really be
A better bard than Dante after all.
'T is more amusing to go pace at eve
I' the Duomo,[3]—watch the day's last gleam outside   455
Turn, as into a skirt of God's own robe,
Those lancet-windows' jewelled miracle,—
Than go eat the Archbishop's ortolans,[4]
Digest his jokes. Luckily Lent is near:
Who cares to look will find me in my stall   460
At the Pieve, constant to this faith at least—
Never to write a canzonet[5] any more."

So, next week, 't was my patron spoke abrupt,
In altered guise. "Young man, can it be ture
That after all your promise of sound fruit,   465
You have kept away from Countess young or old
And gone play truant in church all day long?
Are you turning Molinist?" I answered quick:
"Sir, what if I turned Christian? It might be.
The fact is, I am troubled in my mind,   470
Beset and pressed hard by some novel thoughts.
This your Arezzo is a limited world;
There's a strange Pope,—'t is said, a priest who thinks.
Rome is the port, you say: to Rome I go.
I will live alone, one does so in a crowd,   475
And look into my heart a little." "Lent
Ended,"—I told friends—"I shall go to Rome."

    One evening I was sitting in a muse
Over the opened "Summa,"[6] darkened round

---

3. Cathedral.
4. Small birds regarded as a table delicacy.

5. Light, graceful song.
6. The *Summa Theologica* of St. Thomas
Aquinas (ca. 1224–74).

By the mid-March twilight, thinking how my life   480
Had shaken under me,—broke short indeed
And showed the gap 'twixt what is, what should be,—
And into what abysm the soul may slip,
Leave aspiration here, achievement there,
Lacking omnipotence to connect extremes—   485
Thinking moreover . . . oh, thinking, if you like,
How utterly dissociated was I
A priest and celibate, from the sad strange wife
Of Guido,—just as an instance to the point,
Nought more,—how I had a whole store of strengths   490
Eating into my heart, which craved employ,
And she, perhaps, need of a finger's help,—
And yet there was no way in the wide world
To stretch out mine and so relieve myself,—
How when the page o' the Summa preached its best,   495
Her smile kept glowing out of it, as to mock
The silence we could break by no one word,—
There came a tap without the chamber-door,
And a whisper; when I bade who tapped speak out.
And, in obedience to my summons, last   500
In glided a masked muffled mystery,
Laid lightly a letter on the opened book,
Then stood with folded arms and foot demure,
Pointing as if to mark the minutes' flight.

I took the letter, read to the effect   505
That she, I lately flung the comfits to,
Had a warm heart to give me in exchange,
And gave it,—loved me and confessed it thus,
And bade me render thanks by word of mouth,
Going that night to such a side o' the house   510
Where the small terrace overhangs a street
Blind and deserted, not the street in front:
Her husband being away, the surly patch,[7]
At his villa of Vittiano

       "And you?"—I asked:
"What may you be?" "Count Guido's kind of maid—   515
Most of us have two functions in this house.
We all hate him, the lady suffers much,
'T is just we show compassion, furnish help,
Specially since her choice is fixed so well.
What answer may I bring to cheer the sweet   520
Pompilia?"

       Then I took a pen and wrote
"No more of this! That you are fair, I know:
But other thoughts now occupy my mind.

---

7. Fool.

I should not thus have played the insensible
Once on a time. What made you,—may one ask,—   525
Marry your hideous husband? 'T was a fault,
And now you taste the fruit of it. Farewell."

"There!" smiled I as she snatched it and was gone—
"There, let the jealous miscreant,—Guido's self,
Whose mean soul grins through this transparent trick,—   530
Be baulked so far, defrauded of his aim!
What fund of satisfaction to the knave,
Had I kicked this his messenger down stairs,
Trussed to the middle of her impudence,
And set his heart at ease so! No, indeed!   535
There's the reply which he shall turn and twist
At pleasure, snuff at till his brain grow drunk,
As the bear does when he finds a scented glove
That puzzles him,—a hand and yet no hand,
Of other perfume than his own foul paw!   540
Last month, I had doubtless chosen to play the dupe,
Accepted the mock-invitation, kept
The sham appointment, cudgel beneath cloak,
Prepared myself to pull the appointer's self
Out of the window from his hiding-place   545
Behind the gown of this part-messenger
Part-mistress who would personate the wife.
Such had seemed once a jest permissible:
Now I am not i' the mood."
                                    Back next morn brought
The messenger, a second letter in hand.   550
"You are cruel, Thyrsis, and Myrtilla[8] moans
Neglected but adores you, makes request
For mercy: why is it you dare not come?
Such virtue is scarce natural to your age.
You must love someone else; I hear you do,   555
The Baron's daughter or the Advocate's wife,
Or both,—all's one, would you make me the third—
I take the crumbs from table gratefully
Nor grudge who feasts there. 'Faith, I blush and blaze!
Yet if I break all bounds, there's reason sure.   560
Are you determinedly bent on Rome?
I am wretched here, a monster tortures me:
Carry me with you! Come and say you will!
Concert this very evening! Do not write!
I am ever at the window of my room   565
Over the terrace, at the *Ave.* Come!"

I questioned—lifting half the woman's mask
To let her smile loose. "So, you gave my line

8. Typical names of lovers in pastoral po-   adultery, and quoted in Browning's
etry, actually occurring in the love let-   source, the Old Yellow Book.
ters introduced at the trial for flight and

To the merry lady?" "She kissed off the wax,
And put what paper was not kissed away, 570
In her bosom to go burn: but merry, no!
She wept all night when evening brought no friend,
Alone, the unkind missive at her breast;
Thus Philomel,[9] the thorn at her breast too,
Sings" . . . "Writes this second letter?" "Even so! 575
Then she may peep at vespers forth?"—"What risk
Do we run o' the husband?"—"Ah,—no risk at all!
He is more stupid even than jealous. Ah—
That was the reason? Why, the man's away!
Beside, his bugbear is that friend of yours, 580
Fat little Canon Conti. He fears him,
How should he dream of you? I told you truth:
He goes to the villa at Vittiano—'t is
The time when Spring-sap rises in the vine—
Spends the night there. And then his wife's a child: 585
Does he think a child outwits him? A mere child:
Yet so full grown, a dish for any duke.
Don't quarrel longer with such cates,[1] but come!"

I wrote "In vain do you solicit me.
I am a priest: and you are wedded wife, 590
Whatever kind of brute your husband prove.
I have scruples, in short. Yet should you really show
Sign at the window . . . but nay, best be good!
My thoughts are elsewhere," "Take her that!"
                                          "Again
Let the incarnate meanness, cheat and spy, 595
Mean to the marrow of him, make his heart
His food, anticipate hell's worm once more!
Let him watch shivering at the window—ay,
And let this hybrid, this his light-of-love
And lackey-of-lies,—a sage economy,— 600
Paid with embracings for the rank brass coin,—
Let her report and make him chuckle o'er
The break-down of my resolution now,
And lour[2] at disappointment in good time!
—So tantalize and so enrage by turns, 605
Until the two fall each on the other like
Two famished spiders, as the coveted fly
That toys long, leaves their net and them at last!"
And so the missives followed thick and fast
For a month, say,—I still came at every turn 610
On the soft sly adder, endlong 'neath my tread.
I was met i' the street, made sign to in the church,
A slip was found i' the door-sill, scribbled word

---

9. Philomela, changed by the gods into a
nightingale to save her from death at the
hands of her tormentor, Tereus.

1. Dainty foods.
2. Frown.

'Twixt page and page o' the prayer-book in my place.
A crumpled thing dropped even before my feet,   615
Pushed through the blind, above the terrace-rail,
As I passed, by day, the very window once.
And ever from corners would be peering up
The messenger, with the self-same demand
"Obdurate still, no flesh but adamant?   620
Nothing to cure the wound, assuage the throe
O' the sweetest lamb that ever loved a bear?"
And ever my one answer in one tone—
"Go your ways, temptress! Let a priest read, pray,
Unplagued of vain talk, visions not for him!   625
In the end, you'll have your will and ruin me!"

One day, a variation: thus I read:
"You have gained little by timidity.
My husband has found out my love at length,
Sees cousin Conti was the stalking-horse,   630
And you the game he covered, poor fat soul!
My husband is a formidable foe,
Will stick at nothing to destroy you. Stand
Prepared, or better, run till you reach Rome!
I bade you visit me, when the last place   635
My tyrant would have turned suspicious at,
Or cared to seek you in, was . . . why say, where?
But now all's changed: beside, the season's past
At the villa,—wants the master's eye no more.
Anyhow, I beseech you, stay away   640
From the window! He might well be posted there."

I wrote—"You raise my courage, or call up
My curiosity, who am but man.
Tell him he owns the palace, not the street
Under—that's his and yours and mine alike.   645
If it should please me pad the path this eve,
Guido will have two troubles, first to get
Into a rage and then get out again.
Be cautious, though: at the *Ave!*"

                        You of the Court!
When I stood question here and reached this point   650
O' the narrative,—search notes and see and say
If someone did not interpose with smile
And sneer, "And prithee why so confident
That the husband must, of all needs, not the wife,
Fabricate thus,—what if the lady loved?   655
What if she wrote the letters?"

                          Learned Sir,
I told you there's a picture in our church.
Well, if a low-browed verger sidled up
Bringing me, like a blotch, on his prod's point,

A transfixed scorpion, let the reptile writhe,   660
And then said "See a thing that Rafael made—
This venom issued from Madonna's mouth!"
I should reply, "Rather, the soul of you
Has issued from your body, like from like,
By way of the ordure-corner!"
                            But no less,   665
I tired of the same long black teasing lie
Obtruded thus at every turn; the pest
Was far too near the picture, anyhow:
One does Madonna service, making clowns
Remove their dung-heap from the sacristy.   670
"I will to the window, as he tempts," said I:
"Yes, whom the easy love has failed allure,
This new bait of adventure tempts,—thinks he.
Though the imprisoned lady keeps afar,
There will they lie in ambush, heads alert,   675
Kith, kin, and Count mustered to bite my heel.
No mother nor brother viper of the brood
Shall scuttle off without the instructive bruise!"

So I went: crossed street and street: "The next street's turn,
I stand beneath the terrace, see, above,   680
The black of the ambush-window. Then, in place
Of hand's throw of soft prelude over lute,
And cough that clears way for the ditty last,"—
I began to laugh already—"he will have
'Out of the hole you hide in, on to the front,   685
Count Guido Franceschini, show yourself!
Hear what a man thinks of a thing like you,
And after, take this foulness in your face!' "

The words lay living on my lip, I made
The one-turn more—and there at the window stood,   690
Framed in its black square length, with lamp in hand,
Pompilia; the same great, grave, griefful air
As stands i' the dusk, on altar that I know,
Left alone with one moonbeam in her cell,
Our Lady of all the Sorrows. Ere I knelt—   695
Assured myself that she was flesh and blood—
She had looked one look and vanished.
                            I thought—"Just so:
It was herself, they have set her there to watch—
Stationed to see some wedding-band go by,
On fair pretence that she must bless the bride,   700
Or wait some funeral with friends wind past,
And crave peace for the corpse that claims its due.
She never dreams they used her for a snare,
And now withdraw the bait has served its turn.
Well done, the husband, who shall fare the worse!"   705

And on my lip again was—"Out with thee,
Guido!" When all at once she re-appeared;
But, this time, on the terrace overhead,
So close above me, she could almost touch
My head if she bent down; and she did bend,   710
While I stood still as stone, all eye, all ear.

She began—"You have sent me letters, Sir:
I have read none, I can neither read nor write;
But she you gave them to, a woman here,
One of the people in whose power I am,   715
Partly explained their sense, I think, to me
Obliged to listen while she inculcates
That you, a priest, can dare love me, a wife,
Desire to live or die as I shall bid,
(She makes me listen if I will or no)   720
Because you saw my face a single time.
It cannot be she says the thing you mean;
Such wickedness were deadly to us both:
But good true love would help me now so much—
I tell myself, you may mean good and true.   725
You offer me, I seem to understand,
Because I am in poverty and starve,
Much money, where one piece would save my life.
The silver cup upon the altar-cloth
Is neither yours to give nor mine to take;   730
But I might take one bit of bread therefrom,
Since I am starving, and return the rest,
Yet do no harm: this is my very case.
I am in that strait, I may not dare abstain
From so much of assistance as would bring   735
The guilt of theft on neither you nor me;
But no superfluous particle of aid.
I think, if you will let me state my case,
Even had you been so fancy-fevered here,
Not your sound self, you must grow healthy now—   740
Care only to bestow what I can take.
That it is only you in the wide world,
Knowing me nor in thought nor word nor deed,
Who, all unprompted save by your own heart,
Come proffering assistance now,—were strange   745
But that my whole life is so strange: as strange
It is, my husband whom I have not wronged
Should hate and harm me. For his own soul's sake,
Hinder the harm! But there is something more,
And that the strangest: it has got to be   750
Somehow for my sake too, and yet not mine,
—This is a riddle—for some kind of sake
Not any clearer to myself than you,
And yet as certain as that I draw breath,—

I would fain live, not die—oh, no, not die!   755
My case is, I was dwelling happily
At Rome with those dear Comparini, called
Father and mother to me; when at once
I found I had become Count Guido's wife:
Who then, not waiting for a moment, changed   760
Into a fury of fire, if once he was
Merely a man: his face threw fire at mine,
He laid a hand on me that burned all peace,
All joy, all hope, and last all fear away,
Dipping the bough of life, so pleasant once,   765
In fire which shrivelled leaf and bud alike,
Burning not only present life but past,
Which you might think was safe beyond his reach.
He reached it, though, since that beloved pair,
My father once, my mother all those years,   770
That loved me so, now say I dreamed a dream
And bid me wake, henceforth no child of theirs,
Never in all the time their child at all.
Do you understand? I cannot: yet so it is.
Just so I say of you that proffer help: 775
I cannot understand what prompts your soul,
I simply needs must see that it is so,
Only one strange and wonderful thing more.
They came here with me, those two dear ones, kept
All the old love up, till my husband, till   780
His people here so tortured them, they fled.
And now, is it because I grow in flesh
And spirit one with him their torturer,
That they, renouncing him, must cast off me?
If I were graced by God to have a child,   785
Could I one day deny God graced me so?
Then, since my husband hates me, I shall break
No law that reigns in this fell house of hate,
By using—letting have effect so much
Of hate as hides me from that whole of hate   790
Would take my life which I want and must have—
Just as I take from your excess of love
Enough to save my life with, all I need.
The Archbishop said to murder me were sin:
My leaving Guido were a kind of death   795
With no sin,—more death, he must answer for.
Hear now what death to him and life to you
I wish to pay and owe. Take me to Rome!
You go to Rome, the servant makes me hear.
Take me as you would take a dog, I think,   800
Masterless left for strangers to maltreat:
Take me home like that—leave me in the house
Where the father and the mother are; and soon
They'll come to know and call me by my name,

Their child once more, since child I am, for all   805
They now forget me, which is the worst o' the dream—
And the way to end dreams is to break them, stand,
Walk, go: then help me to stand, walk and go!
The Governor said the strong should help the weak:
You know how weak the strongest women are.   810
How could I find my way there by myself?
I cannot even call out, make them hear—
Just as in dreams: I have tried and proved the fact.
I have told this story and more to good great men,
The Archbishop and the Governor: they smiled.   815
'Stop your mouth, fair one!'—presently they frowned,
'Get you gone, disengage you from our feet!'
I went in my despair to an old priest,
Only a friar, no great man like these two,
But good, the Augustinian, people name   820
Romano,—he confessed me two months since:
He fears God, why then needs he fear the world?
And when he questioned how it came about
That I was found in danger of a sin—
Despair of any help from providence,—   825
'Since, though your husband outrage you,' said he,
'That is a case too common, the wives die
Or live, but do not sin so deep as this'—
Then I told—what I never will tell you—
How, worse than husband's hate, I had to bear   830
The love,—soliciting to shame called love,—
Of his brother,—the young idle priest i' the house[3]
With only the devil to meet there. 'This is grave—
Yes, we must interfere: I counsel,—write
To those who used to be your parents once,   835
Of dangers here, bid them convey you hence!'
'But,' said I, 'when I neither read nor write?'
Then he took pity and promised 'I will write.'
If he did so,—why, they are dumb or dead:
Either they give no credit to the tale,   840
Or else, wrapped wholly up in their own joy
Of such escape, they care not who cries, still
I' the clutches. Anyhow, no word arrives.
All such extravagance and dreadfulness
Seems incident to dreaming, cured one way,—   845
Wake me! The letter I received this morn,
Said—if the woman spoke you very sense—
'You would die for me:' I can believe it now:
For now the dream gets to involve yourself.
First of all, you seemed wicked and not good,   850
In writing me those letters: you came in
Like a thief upon me. I this morning said

3. The Canon Girolamo.

In my extremity, entreat the thief!
Try if he have in him no honest touch!
A thief might save me from a murderer.
'T was a thief said the last kind word to Christ:[4]   855
Christ took the kindness and forgave the theft:
And so did I prepare what I now say.
But now, that you stand and I see your face,
Though you have never uttered word yet,—well, I know, 860
Here too has been dream-work, delusion too,
And that at no time, you with the eyes here,
Ever intended to do wrong by me,
Nor wrote such letters therefore. It is false,
And you are true, have been true, will be true.   865
To Rome then,—when is it you take me there?
Each minute lost is mortal. When?—I ask."

I answered "It shall be when it can be.
I will go hence and do your pleasure, find
The sure and speedy means of travel, then   870
Come back and take you to your friends in Rome.
There wants a carriage, money and the rest,—
A day's work by to-morrow at this time.
How shall I see you and assure escape?"

She replied, "Pass, to-morrow at this hour.   875
If I am at the open window, well:
If I am absent, drop a handkerchief
And walk by! I shall see from where I watch,
And know that all is done. Return next eve,
And next, and so till we can meet and speak!"   880
"To-morrow at this hour I pass," said I.
She was withdrawn.
                Here is another point
I bid you pause at. When I told thus far,
Someone said, subtly, "Here at least was found
Your confidence in error,—you perceived   885
The spirit of the letters, in a sort,
Had been the lady's, if the body should be
Supplied by Guido: say, he forged them all!
Here was the unforged fact—she sent for you,
Spontaneously elected you to help,   890
—What men call, loved you: Guido read her mind,
Gave it expression to assure the world
The case was just as he foresaw: he wrote,
She spoke."
          Sirs, that first simile serves still,—
That falsehood of a scorpion hatched, I say,   895
Nowhere i' the world but in Madonna's mouth.
Go on! Suppose, that falsehood foiled, next eve

---

4. Luke 23:42: "Lord, remember me when thou comest into thy kingdom."

Pictured Madonna raised her painted hand,
Fixed the face Rafael bent above the Babe,
On my face as I flung me at her feet: 900
Such miracle vouchsafed and manifest,
Would that prove the first lying tale was true?
Pompilia spoke, and I at once received,
Accepted my own fact, my miracle
Self-authorized and self-explained,—she chose   905
To summon me and signify her choice.
Afterward,—oh! I gave a passing glance
To a certain ugly cloud-shape, goblin-shred
Of hell-smoke hurrying past the splendid moon
Out now to tolerate no darkness more,   910
And saw right through the thing that tried to pass
For truth and solid, not an empty lie:
"So, he not only forged the words for her
But words for me, made letters he called mine:
What I sent, he retained, gave these in place,   915
All by the mistress-messenger! As I
Recognized her, at potency of truth,
So she, by the crystalline soul, knew me,
Never mistook the signs. Enough of this—
Let the wraith go to nothingness again,   920
Here is the orb, have only thought for her!"

"Thought?" nay, Sirs, what shall follow was not thought:
I have thought sometimes, and thought long and hard.
I have stood before, gone round a serious thing,
Tasked my whole mind to touch and clasp it close,   925
As I stretch forth my arm to touch this bar.
God and man, and what duty I owe both,—
I dare to say I have confronted these
In thought: but no such faculty helped here.
I put forth no thought,—powerless, all that night   930
I paced the city: it was the first Spring.
By the invasion I lay passive to,
In rushed new things, the old were rapt away;[5]
Alike abolished—the imprisonment
Of the outside air, the inside weight o' the world   935
That pulled me down. Death meant, to spurn the ground,
Soar to the sky,—die well and you do that.
The very immolation made the bliss;
Death was the heart of life, and all the harm
My folly had crouched to avoid, now proved a veil   940
Hiding all gain my wisdom strove to grasp:
As if the intense centre of the flame
Should turn a heaven to that devoted fly
Which hitherto, sophist alike and sage,

5. 2 Corinthians 5:17: "[For the   behold, all things are become new."
Christian] old things   are   passed   away;

Saint Thomas[6] with his sober grey goose-quill, 945
And sinner Plato by Cephisian reed,[7]
Would fain, pretending just the insect's good,
Whisk off, drive back, consign to shade again.
Into another state, under new rule
I knew myself was passing swift and sure; 950
Whereof the initiatory pang approached,
Felicitous annoy, as bitter-sweet
As when the virgin-band, the victors chaste,
Feel at the end the earthly garments drop,
And rise with something of a rosy shame 955
Into immortal nakedness: so I
Lay, and let come the proper throe would thrill
Into the ecstasy and outthrob pain.

I' the grey of dawn it was I found myself
Facing the pillared front o' the Pieve—mine, 960
My church: it seemed to say for the first time
"But am not I the Bride, the mystic love
O' the Lamb,[8] who took thy plighted troth, my priest,
To fold thy warm heart on my heart of stone
And freeze thee nor unfasten any more? 965
This is a fleshly woman,—let the free
Bestow their life-blood, thou art pulseless now!"
See! Day by day I had risen and left this church
At the signal waved me by some foolish fan,
With half a curse and half a pitying smile 970
For the monk I stumbled over in my haste,
Prostrate and corpse-like at the altar-foot
Intent on his *corona*:[9] then the church
Was ready with her quip, if word conduced,
To quicken my pace nor stop for prating—"There! 975
Be thankful you are no such ninny, go
Rather to teach a black-eyed novice cards
Than gabble Latin and protrude that nose
Smoothed to a sheep's through no brains and much faith!"
That sort of incentive! Now the church changed tone— 980
Now, when I found out first that life and death
Are means to an end, that passion uses both,
Indisputably mistress of the man
Whose form of worship is self-sacrifice:
Now, from the stone lungs sighed the scrannel voice 985
"Leave that live passion, come be dead with me!"
As if, i' the fabled garden,[1] I had gone

6. St. Thomas Aquinas.
7. Plato is a "sinner" because a pagan. The reed (i.e., pen) is from the River Cephissus, flowing by Athens.
8. Revelation 21:9: ". . . I will shew thee the bride, the Lamb's wife."
9. Beads.

1. The Garden of the Hesperides, its golden apples guarded by a dragon, which Hercules killed to possess the fruit. The "seven-fold dragon," here the Church, is drawn from Revelation 12:3–9, where it is Satan, defeated by Michael and cast from heaven.

On great adventure, plucked in ignorance
Hedge-fruit, and feasted to satiety,
Laughing at such high fame for hips and haws,   990
And scorned the achievement: then come all at once
O' the prize o' the place, the thing of perfect gold,
The apple's self: and, scarce my eye on that,
Was 'ware as well o' the seven-fold dragon's watch.

Sirs, I obeyed. Obedience was too strange,—   995
This new thing that had been struck into me
By the look o' the lady,—to dare disobey
The first authoritative word. 'T was God's.
I had been lifted to the level of her,
Could take such sounds into my sense. I said   1000
"We two are cognisant o' the Master now;
She it is bids me bow the head: how true,
I am a priest! I see the function here;
I thought the other way self-sacrifice:
This is the true, seals up the perfect sum.   1005
I pay it, sit down, silently obey."

So, I went home. Dawn broke, noon broadened, I—
I sat stone-still, let time run over me.
The sun slanted into my room, had reached
The west. I opened book,—Aquinas blazed   1010
With one black name only on the white page.
I looked up, saw the sunset: vespers rang:
"She counts the minutes till I keep my word
And come say all is ready. I am a priest.
Duty to God is duty to her: I think   1015
God, who created her, will save her too
Some new way, by one miracle the more,
Without me. Then, prayer may avail perhaps."
I went to my own place i' the Pieve, read
The office: I was back at home again   1020
Sitting i' the dark. "Could she but know—but know
That, were there good in this distinct from God's,
Really good as it reached her, though procured
By a sin of mine,—I should sin: God forgives.
She knows it is no fear withholds me: fear?   1025
Of what? Suspense here is the terrible thing.
If she should, as she counts the minutes, come
On the fantastic notion that I fear
The world now, fear the Archbishop, fear perhaps
Count Guido, he who, having forged the lies,   1030
May wait the work, attend the effect,—I fear
The sword of Guido! Let God see to that—
Hating lies, let not her believe a lie!"

Again the morning found me. "I will work,
Tie down my foolish thoughts. Thank God so far!   1035

I have saved her from a scandal. stopped the tongues
Had broken else into a cackle and hiss
Around the noble name. Duty is still
Wisdom: I have been wise." So the day wore.

At evening—"But, achieving victory,   1040
I must not blink the priest's peculiar part,
Nor shrink to counsel, comfort: priest and friend—
How do we discontinue to be friends?
I will go minister, advise her seek
Help at the source,—above all, not despair: 1045
There may be other happier help at hand.
I hope it,—wherefore then neglect to say?"

There she stood—leaned there, for the second time,
Over the terrace, looked at me, then spoke:
"Why is it you have suffered me to stay   1050
Breaking my heart two days more than was need?
Why delay help, your own heart yearns to give?
You are again here, in the self-same mind,
I see here, steadfast in the face of you,—
You grudge to do no one thing that I ask.   1055
Why then is nothing done? You know my need.
Still, through God's pity on me, there is time
And one day more: shall I be saved or no?"
I answered—"Lady, waste no thought, no word
Even to forgive me! Care for what I care—   1060
Only! Now follow me as I were fate!
Leave this house in the dark to-morrow night,
Just before daybreak:—there's new moon this eve—
It sets, and then begins the solid black.
Descend, proceed to the Torrione, step   1065
Over the low dilapidated wall,
Take San Clemente, there's no other gate
Unguarded at the hour: some paces thence
An inn stands; cross to it; I shall be there."

She answered, "If I can but find the way.   1070
But I shall find it. Go now!"

                              I did go,
Took rapidly the route myself prescribed,
Stopped at Torrione,[2] climbed the ruined place,
Proved that the gate was practicable, reached
The inn, no eye, despite the dark, could miss,   1075
Knocked there and entered, made the host secure:
"With Caponsacchi it is ask and have;
I know my betters. Are you bound for Rome?
I get swift horse and trusty man," said he.

---

2. I.e., "keep" or fortification on the north wall of Arezzo; San Clemente Gate is
adjacent.

Then I retraced my steps, was found once more   1080
In my own house for the last time: there lay
The broad pale opened Summa. "Shut his book,
There's other showing! 'T was a Thomas[3] too
Obtained,—more favoured than his namesake here,—
A gift, tied faith fast, foiled the tug of doubt,—   1085
Our Lady's girdle; down he saw it drop
As she ascended into heaven, they say:
He kept that safe and bade all doubt adieu.
I too have seen a lady and hold a grace."

I know not how the night passed: morning broke;   1090
Presently came my servant. "Sir, this eve—
Do you forget?" I started. "How forget?
What is it you know?" "With due submission, Sir,
This being last Monday in the month but one
And a vigil, since to-morrow is Saint George,[4]   1095
And feast day, and moreover day for copes,[5]
And Canon Conti now away a month,
And Canon Crispi sour because, forsooth,
You let him sulk in stall and bear the brunt
Of the octave[6] . . . Well, Sir, 't is important!"

                                        "True!   1100

Hearken, I have to start for Rome this night.
No word, lest Crispi overboil and burst!
Provide me with a laic dress! Throw dust
I' the Canon's eye, stop his tongue's scandal so!
See there's a sword in case of accident."   1105
I knew the knave, the knave knew me.

                                        And thus
Through each familiar hindrance of the day
Did I make steadily for its hour and end,—
Felt time's old barrier-growth of right and fit
Give way through all its twines, and let me go.   1110
Use and wont recognized the excepted man,
Let speed the special service,—and I sped
Till, at the dead between midnight and morn,
There was I at the goal, before the gate,
With a tune in the ears, low leading up to loud,   1115
A light in the eyes, faint that would soon be flare,
Ever some spiritual witness new and new
In faster frequence, crowding solitude
To watch the way o' the warfare,—till, at last,
When the ecstatic minute must bring birth,   1120
Began a whiteness in the distance, waxed
Whiter and whiter, near grew and more near,

3. St. Thomas, who according to legend
was not witness to the Assumption of
the Virgin and was therefore skeptical
until she threw down her girdle to him to
end his doubt.

4. St. George's day, April 23.
5. Or mantles, worn by priests on feast
days.
6. The eight days after Easter.

Till it was she: there did Pompilia come:
The white I saw shine through her was her soul's,
Certainly, for the body was one black,   1125
Black from head down to foot. She did not speak,
Glided into the carriage,—so a cloud
Gathers the moon up. "By San Spirito,[7]
To Rome, as if the road burned underneath!
Reach Rome, then hold my head in pledge, I pay   1130
The run and the risk to heart's content!" Just that
I said,—then, in another tick of time,
Sprang, was beside her, she and I alone.

So it began, our flight thro' dusk to clear,
Through day and night and day again to night   1135
Once more, and to last dreadful dawn of all.
Sirs, how should I lie quiet in my grave
Unless you suffer me wring, drop by drop,
My brain dry, make a riddance of the drench
Of minutes with a memory in each,   1140
Recorded motion, breath or look of hers,
Which poured forth would present you one pure glass,
Mirror you plain,—as God's sea, glassed in gold,[8]
His saints,—the perfect soul Pompilia? Men,
You must know that a man gets drunk with truth   1145
Stagnant inside him! Oh, they've killed her, Sirs!
Can I be calm?

        Calmly! Each incident
Proves, I maintain, that action of the flight
For the true thing it was. The first faint scratch
O' the stone will test its nature, teach its worth   1150
To idiots who name Parian—coprolite.[9]
After all, I shall give no glare—at best
Only display you certain scattered lights
Lamping the rush and roll of the abyss:
Nothing but here and there a fire-point pricks   1155
Wavelet from wavelet: well!

           For the first hour
We both were silent in the night, I know:
Sometimes I did not see nor understand.
Blackness engulphed me,—partial stupor, say—
Then I would break way, breathe through the surprise,   1160
And be aware again, and see who sat
In the dark vest with the white face and hands.
I said to myself—"I have caught it, I conceive
The mind o' the mystery: 't is the way they wake
And wait, two martyrs somewhere in a tomb   1165
Each by each as their blessing was to die;

---

7. Southern gate of Arezzo.
8. Revelation 15:2: "And I saw as it were a sea of glass mingled with fire."

9. "Parian": fine marble; "coprolite": petrified reptile dung.

Some signal they are promised and expect,—
When to arise before the trumpet scares:
So, through the whole course of the world they wait
The last day, but so fearless and so safe!   1170
No otherwise, in safety and not fear,
I lie, because she lies too by my side."
You know this is not love, Sirs,—it is faith,
The feeling that there's God, he reigns and rules
Out of this low world: that is all; no harm!   1175
At times she drew a soft sigh—music seemed
Always to hover just above her lips,
Not settle,—break a silence music too.

In the determined morning, I first found
Her head erect, her face turned full to me,   1180
Her soul intent on mine through two wide eyes.
I answered them. "You are saved hitherto.
We have passed Perugia,—gone round by the wood,
Not through, I seem to think,—and opposite
I know Assisi; this is holy ground."[1]   1185
Then she resumed. "How long since we both left
Arezzo?" "Years—and certain hours beside."

It was at . . . ah, but I forget the names!
'T is a mere post-house and a hovel or two;
I left the carriage and got bread and wine   1190
And brought it her. "Does it detain to eat?"
"They stay perforce, change horses,—therefore eat!
We lose no minute: we arrive, be sure!"
This was—I know not where—there's a great hill
Close over, and the stream has lost its bridge,   1195
One fords it. She began—"I have heard say
Of some sick body that my mother knew,
'T was no good sign when in a limb diseased
All the pain suddenly departs,—as if
The guardian angel discontinued pain   1200
Because the hope of cure was gone at last:
The limb will not again exert itself,
It needs be pained no longer: so with me,
—My soul whence all the pain is past at once:
All pain must be to work some good in the end.   1205
True, this I feel now, this may be that good,
Pain was because of,—otherwise, I fear!"

She said,—a long while later in the day,
When I had let the silence be,—abrupt—
"Have you a mother?" "She died, I was born."   1210
"A sister then?" "No sister." "Who was it—
What woman were you used to serve this way,

---

1. "Holy" because it is the birthplace of St. Francis.

Be kind to, till I called you and you came?"
I did not like that word. Soon afterward—
"Tell me, are men unhappy, in some kind   1215
Of mere unhappiness at being men,
As women suffer, being womanish?
Have you, now, some unhappiness, I mean,
Born of what may be man's strength overmuch,
To match the undue susceptibility,   1220
The sense at every pore when hate is close?
It hurts us if a baby hides its face
Or child strikes at us punily, calls names
Or makes a mouth,—much more if stranger men
Laugh or frown,—just as that were much to bear! 1225
Yet rocks split,—and the blow-ball² does no more,
Quivers to feathery nothing at a touch;
And strength may have its drawback weakness 'scapes."

Once she asked "What is it that made you smile,
At the great gate with the eagles and the snakes, 1230
Where the company entered, 't is a long time since?"
"—Forgive—I think you would not understand:
Ah, but you ask me,—therefore, it was this.
That was a certain bishop's villa-gate,
I knew it by the eagles,—and at once   1235
Remembered this same bishop was just he
People of old were wont to bid me please
If I would catch preferment: so, I smiled
Because an impulse came to me, a whim—
What if I prayed the prelate leave to speak,   1240
Began upon him in his presence-hall
—'What, still at work so grey and obsolete?
Still rocheted and mitred³ more or less?
Don't you feel all that out of fashion now?
I find out when the day of things is done!' "   1245

At eve we heard the *angelus*:⁴ she turned—
"I told you I can neither read nor write.
My life stopped with the play-time; I will learn,
If I begin to live again: but you—
Who are a priest—wherefore do you not read   1250
The service at this hour? Read Gabriel's song,⁵
The lesson, and then read the little prayer
To Raphael,⁶ proper for us travellers!"
I did not like that, neither, but I read.

When we stopped at Foligno⁷ it was dark.   1255

2. Dandelion seed-head.
3. "Rochet": a bishop's surplice; "mitre": his hat.
4. Bell for prayer commemorating the Incarnation.
5. Perhaps the angel's salutation to the Virgin Mary: "Hail, thou that art highly favoured, the Lord is with thee: blessed art thou among women" (Luke 1:28).
6. The angel who traveled with Tobias (in the apocryphal Book of Tobit).
7. Town about ten miles south of Assisi.

The people of the post came out with lights:
The driver said, "This time to-morrow, may
Saints only help, relays continue good,
Nor robbers hinder, we arrive at Rome."
I urged, "Why tax your strength a second night?   1260
Trust me, alight here and take brief repose!
We are out of harm's reach, past pursuit: go sleep
If but an hour! I keep watch, guard the while
Here in the doorway." But her whole face changed,
The misery grew again about her mouth,   1265
The eyes burned up from faintness, like the fawn's
Tired to death in the thicket, when she feels
The probing spear o' the huntsman. "Oh, no stay!"
She cried, in the fawn's cry, "On to Rome, on, on—
Unless 't is you who fear,—which cannot be!"   1270

We did go on all night; but at its close
She was troubled, restless, moaned low, talked at whiles
To herself, her brow on quiver with the dream:
Once, wide awake, she menaced, at arms' length
Waved away something—"Never again with you!   1275
My soul is mine, my body is my soul's:
You and I are divided ever more
In soul and body: get you gone!" Then I—
"Why, in my whole life I have never prayed!
Oh, if the God, that only can, would help!   1280
Am I his priest with power to cast out fiends?
Let God arise and all his enemies
Be scattered!"[8] By morn, there was peace, no sigh
Out of the deep sleep.

         When she woke at last,
I answered the first look—"Scarce twelve hours more,   1285
Then, Rome! There probably was no pursuit,
There cannot now be peril: bear up brave!
Just some twelve hours to press through to the prize:
Then, no more of the terrible journey!" "Then,
No more o' the journey: if it might but last!   1290
Always, my life-long, thus to journey still!
It is the interruption that I dread,—
With no dread, ever to be here and thus!
Never to see a face nor hear a voice!
Yours is no voice; you speak when you are dumb;   1295
Nor face, I see it in the dark. I want
No face nor voice that change and grow unkind."
That I liked, that was the best thing she said.

In the broad day, I dared entreat, "Descend!"
I told a woman, at the garden-gate   1300

---

8. Psalm 68:1: "Let God arise, let his enemies be scattered."

By the post-house, white and pleasant in the sun,
"It is my sister,—talk with her apart!
She is married and unhappy, you perceive;
I take her home because her head is hurt;
Comfort her as you women understand!"   1305
So, there I left them by the garden-wall,
Paced the road, then bade put the horses to,
Came back, and there she sat: close to her knee,
A black-eyed child still held the bowl of milk,
Wondered to see know little she could drink,   1310
And in her arms the woman's infant lay.
She smiled at me "How much good this has done!
This is a whole night's rest and how much more!
I can proceed now, though I wish to stay.
How do you call that tree with the thick top   1315
That holds in all its leafy green and gold
The sun now like an immense egg of fire?"
(It was a million-leaved mimosa.) "Take
The babe away from me and let me go!"
And in the carriage "Still a day, my friend!   1320
And perhaps half a night, the woman fears.
I pray it finish since it cannot last:
There may be more misfortune at the close,
And where will you be? God suffice me then!"
And presently—for there was a roadside-shrine—   1325
"When I was taken first to my own church
Lorenzo in Lucina, being a girl,
And bid confess my faults, I interposed
'But teach me what fault to confess and know!'
So, the priest said—'You should bethink yourself: 1330
Each human being needs must have done wrong!'
Now, be you candid and no priest but friend—
Were I surprised and killed here on the spot,
A runaway from husband and his home,
Do you account it were in sin I died?   1335
My husband used to seem to harm me, not . . .
Not on pretence he punished sin of mine,
Nor for sin's sake and lust of cruelty,
But as I heard him bid a farming-man
At the villa take a lamb once to the wood   1340
And there ill-treat it, meaning that the wolf
Should hear its cries, and so come, quick be caught,
Enticed to the trap: he practised thus with me
That so, whatever were his gain thereby,
Others than I might become prey and spoil.   1345
Had it been only between our two selves,—
His pleasure and my pain,—why, pleasure him
By dying, nor such need to make a coil!⁹

9. Disturbance.

But this was worth an effort, that my pain
Should not become a snare, prove pain threefold   1350
To other people—strangers—or unborn—
How should I know? I sought release from that—
I think, or else from,—dare I say, some cause
Such as is put into a tree, which turns
Away from the north wind with what nest it holds,—   1355
The woman said that trees so turn: now, friend,
Tell me, because I cannot trust myself!
You are a man: what have I done amiss?"
You must conceive my answer,—I forget—
Taken up wholly with the thought, perhaps,   1360
This time she might have said,—might, did not say—
"You are a priest." She said, "my friend."
                              Day wore,
We passed the places, somehow the calm went,
Again the restless eyes began to rove
In new fear of the foe mine could not see.   1365
She wandered in her mind—addressed me once
"Gaetano!"—that is not my name: whose name?
I grew alarmed, my head seemed turning too.
I quickened pace with promise now, now threat:
Bade drive and drive, nor any stopping more.   1370
"Too deep i' the thick of the struggle, struggle through!
Then drench her in repose though death's self pour
The plenitude of quiet,—help us, God,
Whom the winds carry!"
                              Suddenly I saw
The old tower, and the little white-walled clump   1375
Of buildings and the cypress-tree or two,—
"Already Castelnuovo—Rome!" I cried,
"As good as Rome,—Rome is the next stage, think!
This is where travellers' hearts are wont to beat.
Say you are saved, sweet lady!" Up she woke.   1380
The sky was fierce with colour from the sun
Setting. She screamed out "No, I must not die!
Take me no farther, I should die: stay here!
I have more life to save than mine!"
                              She swooned.
We seemed safe: what was it foreboded so?   1385
Out of the coach into the inn I bore
The motionless and breathless pure and pale
Pompilia,—bore her through a pitying group
And laid her on a couch, still calm and cured
By deep sleep of all woes at once. The host   1390
Was urged "Let her stay an hour or two!
Leave her to us, all will be right by morn!"
Oh, my foreboding! But I could not choose.

I paced the passage, kept watch all night long.

I listened,—not one movement, not one sigh.   1395
"Fear not: she sleeps so sound!" they said: but I
Feared, all the same, kept fearing more and more,
Found myself throb with fear from head to foot,
Filled with a sense of such impending woe,
That, at first pause of night, pretence of gray,   1400
I made my mind up it was morn.—"Reach Rome,
Lest hell reach her! A dozen miles to make,
Another long breath, and we emerge!" I stood
I' the court-yard, roused the sleepy grooms. "Have out
Carriage and horse, give haste, take gold!" said I.   1405
While they made ready in the doubtful morn,—
'T was the last minute,—needs must I ascend
And break her sleep; I turned to go.
                               And there
Faced me Count Guido, there posed the mean man
As master,—took the field, encamped his rights,   1410
Challenged the world: there leered new triumph, there
Scowled the old malice in the visage bad
And black o' the scamp. Soon triumph suppled the tongue
A little, malice glued to his dry throat,
And he part howled, part hissed . . . oh, how he kept   1415
Well out o' the way, at arm's length and to spare!—
"My salutation to your priestship! What?
Matutinal,[1] busy with book so soon
Of an April day that's damp as tears that now
Deluge Arezzo at its darling's flight?   1420
'T is unfair, wrongs feminity at large,
To let a single dame monopolize
A heart the whole sex claims, should share alike:
Therefore I overtake you, Canon! Come!
The lady,—could you leave her side so soon?   1425
You have not yet experienced at her hands
My treatment, you lay down undrugged, I see!
Hence this alertness—hence no death-in-life
Like what held arms fast when she stole from mine.
To be sure, you took the solace and repose   1430
That first night at Foligno!—news abound
O' the road by this time,—men regaled me much,
As past them I came halting after you,
Vulcan pursuing Mars,[2] as poets sing,—
Still at the last here pant I, but arrive,   1435
Vulcan—and not without my Cyclops[3] too,
The Commissary and the unpoisoned arm
O' the Civil Force, should Mars turn mutineer.
Enough of fooling: capture the culprits, friend!

1. Early in the morning.
2. Vulcan, ugly and lame god of the forge, caught his unfaithful wife Venus and her lover Mars in a net, exposing them to the ridicule of the gods (*Odyssey*, VIII.266–366).
3. The Cyclops, one-eyed monsters, were Vulcan's servants.

Here is the lover in the smart disguise   1440
With the sword,—he is a priest, so mine lies still.
There upstairs hides my wife the runaway,
His leman:[4] the two plotted, poisoned first,
Plundered me after, and eloped thus far
Where now you find them. Do your duty quick!   1445
Arrest and hold him! That's done: now catch her!"
During this speech of that man,—well, I stood
Away, as he managed,—still, I stood as near
The throat of him,—with these two hands, my own,—
As now I stand near yours, Sir,—one quick spring,   1450
One great good satisfying gripe, and lo!
There had he laid abolished with his lie,
Creation purged o' the miscreate, man redeemed,
A spittle wiped off from the face of God!
I, in some measure, seek a poor excuse   1455
For what I left undone, in just this fact
That my first feeling at the speech I quote
Was—not of what a blasphemy was dared,
Not what a bag of venomed purulence
Was split and noisome,—but how splendidly   1460
Mirthful, how ludicrous a lie was launched!
Would Molière's[5] self wish more than hear such man
Call, claim such woman for his own, his wife,
Even though, in due amazement at the boast,
He had stammered, she moreover was divine?   1465
She to be his,—were hardly less absurd
Than that he took her name into his mouth,
Licked, and then let it go again, the beast,
Signed with his slaver. Oh, she poisoned him,
Plundered him, and the rest! Well, what I wished   1470
Was, that he would but go on, say once more
So to the world, and get his meed of men,
The fists's reply to the filth. And while I mused,
The minute, oh the misery, was gone!
On either idle hand of me there stood   1475
Really an officer, nor laughed i' the least:
Nay, rendered justice to his reason, laid
Logic to heart, as 't were submitted them
"Twice two makes four."
                          "And now, catch her!" he cried.
That sobered me. "Let myself lead the way—   1480
Ere you arrest me, who am somebody,
Being, as you hear, a priest and privileged,—
To the lady's chamber! I presume you—men
Expert, instructed how to find out truth,
Familiar with the guise of guilt. Detect   1485

4. Lover.
5. Leading French comic dramatist of the seventeenth century.

Guilt on her face when it meets mine, then judge
Between us and the mad dog howling there!"
Up we all went together, in they broke
O' the chamber late my chapel. There she lay,
Composed as when I laid her, that last eve,   1490
O' the couch, still breathless, motionless, sleep's self,
Wax-white, seraphic, saturate with the sun
O' the morning that now flooded from the front
And filled the window with a light like blood.
"Behold the poisoner, the adulteress,   1495
—And feigning sleep too! Seize, bind!" Guido hissed.

She started up, stood erect, face to face
With the husband: back he fell, was buttressed there
By the window all a flame with morning-red,
He the black figure, the opprobrious blur   1500
Against all peace and joy and light and life.
"Away from between me and hell!" she cried:
"Hell for me, no embracing any more!
I am God's, I love God, God—whose knees I clasp,
Whose utterly most just award I take,   1505
But bear no more love-making devils: hence!"
I may have made an effort to reach her side
From where I stood i' the door-way,—anyhow
I found the arms, I wanted, pinioned fast,
Was powerless in the clutch to left and right   1510
O' the rabble pouring in, rascality
Enlisted, rampant on the side of hearth
Home and the husband,—pay in prospect too!
They heaped themselves upon me. "Ha!—and him
Also you outrage? Him, too, my sole friend,   1515
Guardian and saviour? That I baulk you of,
Since—see how God can help at last and worst!"
She sprang at the sword the hung beside him, seized,
Drew, brandished it, the sunrise burned for joy
O' the blade, "Die," cried she, "devil, in God's name!"   1520
Ah, but they all closed round her, twelve to one
—The unmanly men, no woman-mother made,
Spawned somehow! Dead-white and disarmed she lay.
No matter for the sword, her word sufficed
To spike the coward through and through: he shook,   1525
Could only spit between the teeth—"You see?
You hear? Bear witness, then! Write down . . but no—
Carry these criminals to the prison-house,
For first thing! I begin my search meanwhile
After the stolen effects, gold, jewels, plate,   1530
Money and clothes, they robbed me of and fled,
With no few amorous pieces, verse and prose,
I have much reason to expect to find."

When I saw that—no more than the first mad speech,

Made out the speaker made and a laughing-stock, 1535
So neither did this next device explode
One listener's indignation,—that a scribe
Did sit down, set himself to write indeed,
While sundry knaves began to peer and pry
In corner and hole,—that Guido, wiping brow 1540
And getting him a countenance, was fast
Losing his fear, beginning to strut free
O' the stage of his exploit, snuff here, sniff there,—
Then I took truth in, guessed sufficiently
The service for the moment. "What I say, 1545
Slight at your peril! We are aliens here,
My adversary and I, called noble both;
I am the nobler, and a name men know.
I could refer our cause to our Court
In our own country, but prefer appeal 1550
To the nearer jurisdiction. Being a priest,
Though in a secular garb,—for reasons good
I shall adduce in due time to my peers,—
I demand that the Church I serve, decide
Between us, right the slandered lady there. 1555
A Tuscan noble, I might claim the Duke:
A priest, I rather choose the Church,—bid Rome
Cover the wronged with her inviolate shield."

There was no refusing this: they bore me off,
They bore her off, the separate calls o' the same 1560
Ignoble prison, and, separate, thence to Rome.
Pompilia's face, then and thus, looked on me
The last time in this life: not one sight since,
Never another sight to be! And yet
I thought I had saved her. I appealed to Rome: 1565
It seems I simply sent her to her death.
You tell me she is dying now, or dead:
I cannot bring myself to quite believe
This is a place you torture people in:
What if this your intelligence were just 1570
A subtlety, an honest wile to work
On a man at unawares? 'T were worthy you.
No, Sirs, I cannot have the lady dead!
That erect form, flashing brow, fulgurant eye,
That voice immortal (oh, that voice of hers!) 1575
That vision in the blood-red day-break—that
Leap to life of the pale electric sword
Angels go armed with,—that was not the last
O' the lady! Come, I see through it, you find—
Know the manœuvre! Also herself said 1580
I saved her: do you dare say she spoke false?
Let me see for myself if it be so!
Though she were dying, a Priest might be of use,

The more when he's a friend too,—she called me
Far beyond "friend." Come, let me see her—indeed   1585
It is my duty, being a priest: I hope
I stand confessed, established, proved a priest?
My punishment had motive that, a priest
I, in a laic garb, a mundane mode,
Did what were harmlessly done otherwise.   1590
I never touched her with my finger-tip
Except to carry her to the couch, that eve,
Against my heart, beneath my head, bowed low,
As we priests carry the paten:[6] that is why
—To get leave and go see her for your grace—   1595
I have told you this whole story over again.
Do I deserve grace? For I might lock lips,
Laugh at your jurisdiction: what have you
To do with me in the matter? I suppose
You hardly think I donned a bravo's dress   1600
To have a hand in the new crime; on the old,
Judgment's delivered, penalty imposed,
I was chained fast at Civita hand and foot—
She had only you to trust to, you and Rome,
Rome and the Church, and no pert meddling priest   1605
Two days ago, when Guido, with the right,
Hacked her to pieces. One might well be wroth;
I have been patient, done my best to help:
I come from Civita and punishment
As friend of the Court—and for pure friendship's sake 1610
Have told my tale to the end,—nay, not the end—
For, wait—I'll end—not leave you that excuse!

When we were parted,—shall I go on there?
I was presently brought to Rome—yes, here I stood
Opposite yonder very crucifix—   1615
And there sat you and you, Sirs, quite the same.
I heard charge, and bore question, and told tale
Noted down in the book there,—turn and see
If, by one jot or tittle, I vary now!
I' the colour the tale takes, there's change perhaps; 1620
'T is natural, since the sky is different,
Eclipse in the air now; still, the outlined stays.
I showed you how it came to be my part
To save the lady. Then your clerk produced
Papers, a pack of stupid and impure   1625
Banalities called letters about love—
Love, indeed,—I could teach who styled them so,
Better, I think, though priest and loveless both!
"—How was it that a wife, young, innocent,
And stranger to your person, wrote this page?"—   1630

6. Plate used for carrying the bread of the Eucharist.

"—She wrote it when the Holy Father wrote
The bestiality that posts thro' Rome,
Put in his mouth by Pasquin."[7] "Nor perhaps
Did you return these answers, verse and prose,
Signed, sealed and sent the lady? There's your hand!"   1635
"—This precious piece of verse, I really judge,
Is meant to copy my own character,[8]
A clumsy mimic; and this other prose,
Not so much even; both rank forgery:
Verse, quotha? Bembo's[9] verse! When Saint John wrote   1640
The tract *'De Tribus,'*[1] I wrote this to match."
"—How came it, then, the documents were found
At the inn on your departure?"—"I opine,
Because there were no documents to find
In my presence,—you must hide before you find.   1645
Who forged them hardly practised in my view;
Who found them waited till I turned my back."
"—And what of the clandestine visits paid,
Nocturnal passage in and out the house
With its lord absent? 'T is alleged you climbed . . ."   1650
"—Flew on a broomstick to the man i' the moon!
Who witnessed or will testify this trash?"
"—The trusty servant, Margherita's self,
Even she who brought you letters, you confess,
And, you confess, took letters in reply: 1655
Forget not we have knowledge of the facts!"
"—Sirs, who have knowledge of the facts, defray
The expenditure of wit I waste in vain,
Trying to find out just one fact of all!
She who brought letters from who could not write,   1660
And took back letters to who could not read,—
Who was that messenger, of your charity?"
"—Well, so far favours you the circumstance
That this same messenger . . . how shall we say? . . .
Sub imputatione meretricis   1665
Laborat,[2]—which makes accusation null:
We waive this woman's: nought makes void the next.
Borsi, called Venerino, he who drove,
O' the first night when you fled away, at length
Deposes to your kissings in the coach,   1670
—Frequent, frenetic . . ." "When deposed he so?"
"After some weeks of sharp imprisonment . . ."
"—Granted by friend the Governor, I engage—"
"—For his participation in your flight!

7. Pasquino, fifteenth-century Roman tailor and writer of epigrams. On a statue in Rome named for him were posted lampoons and witticisms (*pasquinades*) on current events.
8. Handwriting.
9. Pietro Bembo (1470–1547), Italian cardinal and scholar whose verses were admired for their classical purity.
1. *De Tribus Impostoribus* ("Of Three Impostors"), a medieval tract criticizing Moses, Christ, and Mohammed.
2. "Was reputed to be a prostitute."

At length his obduracy melting made   1675
The avowal mentioned . ." "Was dismissed forthwith
To liberty, poor knave, for recompense.
Sirs, give what credit to the lie you can!
For me, no word in my defence I speak,
And God shall argue for the lady!"
                         So   1680
Did I stand question, and make answer, still
With the same result of smiling disbelief,
Polite impossibility of faith
In such affected virtue in a priest;
But a showing fair play, an indulgence, even,   1685
To one no worse than others after all—
Who had not brought disgrace to the order, played
Discreetly, ruffled gown nor ripped the cloth
In a bungling game at romps: I have told you, Sirs—
If I pretended simply to be pure   1690
Honest and Christian in the case,—absurd!
As well go boast myself above the needs
O' the human nature, careless how meat smells,
Wine tastes,—a saint above the smack! But once
Abate my crest, own flaws i' the flesh, agree   1695
To go with the herd, be hog no more nor less,
Why, hogs in common herd have common rights:
I must not be unduly borne upon,
Who just romanced a little, sowed wild oats,
But 'scaped without a scandal, flagrant fault.   1700
My name helped to a mirthful circumstance:
"Joseph" would do well to amend his plea:
Undoubtedly—some toying with the wife,
But as for ruffian violence and rape,
Potiphar pressed too much on the other side![3]   1705
The intrigue, the elopement, the disguise,—well charged!
The letters and verse looked hardly like the truth.
Your apprehension was—of guilt enough
To be compatible with innocence,
So, punished best a little and not too much.   1710
Had I struck Guido Franceschini's face,
You had counselled me withdraw for my own sake,
Baulk him of bravo-hiring. Friends came round,
Congratulated, "Nobody mistakes!
The pettiness o' the forfeiture defines   1715
The peccadillo: Guido gets his share:
His wife is free of husband and hook-nose,
The mouldy viands and the mother-in-law.
To Civita with you and amuse the time,

3. In Egypt, Joseph serves Potiphar, whose wife's sexual advances he rejects. She accuses Joseph of trying to seduce her, and Potiphar casts him in prison (Genesis 39).

Travesty us 'De Raptu Helenæ!'[4]   1720
A funny figure must the husband cut
When the wife makes him skip,—too ticklish, eh?
Do it in Latin, not the Vulgar, then!
Scazons[5]—we'll copy and send his Eminence.
Mind—one iambus in the final foot!   1725
He'll rectify it, be your friend for life!"
Oh, Sirs, depend on me for much new light
Thrown on the justice and religion here
By this proceeding, much fresh food for thought!

And I was just set down to study these   1730
In relegation, two short days ago,
Admiring how you read the rules, when, clap,
A thunder comes into my solitude—
I am caught up in a whirlwind and cast here,
Told of a sudden, in this room where so late   1735
You dealt out law adroitly, that those scales,
I meekly bowed to, took my allotment from,
Guido has snatched at, broken in your hands,
Metes to himself the murder of his wife,
Full measure, pressed down, running over now!   1740
Can I assist to an explanation?—Yes,
I rise in your esteem, sagacious Sirs,
Stand up a renderer of reasons, not
The officious priest would personate Saint George[6]
For a mock Princess in undragoned days.   1745
What, the blood startles you? What, after all
The priest who needs must carry sword on thigh
May find imperative use for it? Then, there was
A Princess, was a dragon belching flame,
And should have been a Saint George also? Then,   1750
There might be worse schemes than to break the bonds
At Arezzo, lead her by the little hand,
Till she reached Rome, and let her try to live?
But you were law and gospel,—would one please
Stand back, allow your faculty elbow-room?   1755
You blind guides who must needs lead eyes that see![7]
Fools, alike ignorant of man and God!
What was there here should have perplexed your wit
For a wink of the owl-eyes of you? How miss, then,
What's now forced on you by this flare of fact—   1760
As if Saint Peter failed to recognize
Nero as no apostle, John or James,
Till someone burned a martyr, made a torch

4. "The Rape of Helen," late Greek poem in imitation of Homer.
5. Lines in a "limping" iambic meter ending in a spondee or trochee instead of the normal iamb.
6. Legendary soldier-saint and patron of England, said to have fought a dragon in order to rescue a king's daughter, who was about to be sacrificed. Departing from strict historical truth, Browning has Caponsacchi rescue Pompilia on the saint's day, April 23.
7. Matthew 23:24: "Ye blind guides. . . ."

O' the blood and fat to show his features by!
Could you fail read this cartulary[8] aright   1765
On head and front of Franceschini there,
Large-lettered like hell's masterpiece of print,—
That he, from the beginning pricked at heart
By some lust, letch[9] of hate against his wife,
Plotted to plague her into overt sin   1770
And shame, would slay Pompilia body and soul,
And save his mean self—miserably caught
I' the quagmire of his own tricks, cheats and lies?
—That himself wrote those papers,—from himself
To himself,—which, i' the name of me and her,   1775
His mistress-messenger gave her and me,
Touching us with such pustules of the soul
That she and I might take the taint, be shown
To the world and shuddered over, speckled so?
—That the agent put her sense into my words,   1780
Made substitution of the thing she hoped,
For the thing she had and held, its opposite,
While the husband in the background bit his lips
At each fresh failure of his precious plot?
—That when at the last we did rush each on each,   1785
By no chance but because God willed it so—
The spark of truth was struck from out our souls—
Made all of me, descried in the first glance,
Seem fair and honest and permissible love
O' the good and true—as the first glance told me   1790
There was no duty patent in the world
Like daring try be good and true myself,
Leaving the shows of things to the Lord of Show
And Prince o' the Power of the Air.[1] Our very flight,
Even to its most ambiguous circumstance,   1795
Irrefragably proved how futile, false . . .
Why, men—men and not boys—boys and not babes—
Babes and not beasts—beasts and not stocks and stones!—
Had the liar's lie been true one pin-point speck,
Were I the accepted suitor, free o' the place,   1800
Disposer of the time, to come at a call
And go at a wink as who should say me nay,—
What need of flight, what were the gain the therefrom
But just damnation, failure or success?
Damnation pure and simple to her the wife   1805
And me the priest—who bartered private bliss
For public reprobation, the safe shade
For the sunshine which men see to pelt me by:
What other advantage,—we who led the days
And nights alone i' the house,—was flight to find?   1810
In our whole journey did we stop an hour,
Diverge a foot from straight road till we reached

8. Register.
9. Passion.

1. Satan. The latter phrase is found in
Ephesians 2:2.

Or would have reached—but for that fate of ours—
The father and mother, in the eye of Rome,
The eye of yourselves we made aware of us   1815
At the first fall of misfortune? And indeed
You did so far give sanction to our flight,
Confirm its purpose, as lend helping hand,
Deliver up Pompilia not to him
She fled, but those the flight was ventured for.   1820
Why then could you, who stopped short, not go on
One poor step more, and justify the means,
Having allowed the end?—not see and say
"Here's the exceptional conduct that should claim
To be exceptionally judged on rules   1825
Which, understood, make no exception here"—
Why play instead into the devil's hands
By dealing so ambiguously as gave
Guido the power to intervene like me,
Prove one exception more? I saved his wife   1830
Against law: against law he slays her now:
Deal with him!

     I have done with being judged.
I stand here guiltless in thought, word and deed,
To the point that I apprise you,—in contempt
For all misapprehending ignorance   1835
O' the human heart, much more the mind of Christ,—
That I assuredly did bow, was blessed
By the revelation of Pompilia. There!
Such is the final fact I fling you, Sirs,
To mouth and mumble and misinterpret: there!   1840
"The priest's in love," have it the vulgar way!
Unpriest me, rend the rags o' the vestment, do—
Degrade deep, disenfranchise all you dare—
Remove me from the midst, no longer priest
And fit companion for the like of you—   1845
Your gay Abati with the well-turned leg
And rose i' the hat-rim, Canons, cross at neck
And silk mask in the pocket of the gown,
Brisk Bishops with the world's musk still unbrushed
From the rochet; I'll no more of these good things: 1850
There's a crack somewhere, something that's unsound
I' the rattle!
    For Pompilia—be advised,
Build churches, go pray! You will find me there,
I know, if you come,— and you will come, I know.
Why, there's a Judge weeping! Did not I say   1855
You were good and true at bottom? You see the truth—
I am glad I helped you: she helped me just so.
But for Count Guido,—you must counsel there!
I bow my head, bend to the very dust,
Break myself up in shame of faultiness.   1860

I had him one whole moment, as I said—
As I remember, as will never out
O' the thoughts of me,—I had him in arm's reach
There,—as you stand, Sir, now you cease to sit,—
I could have killed him ere he killed his wife,   1865
And did not: he went off alive and well
And then effected this last feat—through me!
Me—not through you—dismiss that fear! 'T was you
Hindered me staying here to save her,—not
From leaving you and going back to him   1870
And doing service in Arezzo. Come,
Instruct me in procedure! I conceive—
In all due self-abasement might I speak—
How you will deal with Guido: oh, not death!
Death, if it let her life be: otherwise   1875
Not death,—your lights will teach you clearer! I
Certainly have an instinct of my own
I' the matter: bear with me and weigh its worth!
Let us go away—leave Guido all alone
Back on the world again that knows him now!   1880
I think he will be found (indulge so far!)
Not to die so much as slide out of life,
Pushed by the general horror and common hate
Low, lower,—left o' the very ledge of things,
I seem to see him catch convulsively   1885
One by one at all honest forms of life,
At reason, order, decency and use—
To cramp[2] him and get foothold by at least;
And still they disengage them from his clutch.
"What, you are he, then, had Pompilia once   1890
And so forwent her? Take not up with us!"
And thus I see him slowly and surely edged
Off all the table-land whence life upsprings
Aspiring to be immortality,
As the snake, hatched on hill-top by mischance,   1895
Despite his wriggling, slips, slides, slidders down
Hill-side, lies low and prostrate on the smooth
Level of the outer place, lapsed in the vale:
So I lose Guido in the loneliness,
Silence and dusk, till at the doleful end,   1900
At the horizontal line, creation's verge,
From what just is to absolute nothingness—
Whom is it, straining onward still, he meets?
What other man deep further in the fate,
Who, turning at the prize of a footfall   1905
To flatter him and promise fellowship,
Discovers in the act a frightful face—
Judas, made monstrous by much solitude!
The two are at one now! Let them love their love

2. Give him a secure hold.

That bites and claws like hate, or hate their hate   1910
That mops and mows[3] and makes as it were love!
There, let them each tear each in devil's-fun,
Or fondle this the other while malice aches—
Both teach, both learn detestability!
Kiss him the kiss, Iscariot! Pay that back,   1915
That smatch[4] o' the slaver blistering on your lip,
By the better trick, the insult he spared Christ—
Lure him the lure o' the letters, Aretine!
Lick him o'er slimy-smooth with jelly-filth
O' the verse-and-prose pollution in love's guise!   1920
The cockatrice is with the basilisk![5]
There let them grapple, denizens o' the dark,
Foes or friends, but indissolubly bound,
In their one spot out of the ken of God
Or care of man, for ever and ever more!   1925

Why, Sirs, what's this? Why, this is sorry and strange!
Futility, divagation:[6] this from me
Bound to be rational, justify an act
Of sober man!—whereas, being moved so much,
I give you cause to doubt the lady's mind: 1930
A pretty sarcasm for the world! I fear
You do her wit injustice,—all through me!
Like my fate all through,—ineffective help!
A poor rash advocate I prove myself.
You might be angry with good cause: but sure   1935
At the advocate,—only at the undue zeal
That spoils the force of his own plea, I think?
My part was just to tell you how things stand,
State facts and not be flustered at their fume.
But then 't is a priest speaks: as for love,—no!   1940
If you let buzz a vulgar fly like that
About your brains, as if I loved, forsooth,
Indeed, Sirs, you do wrong! We had no thought
Of such infatuation, she and I:
There are many points that prove it: do be just!   1945
I told you,—at one little roadside-place
I spent a good half-hour, paced to and fro
The garden; just to leave her free awhile,
I plucked a handful of Spring herb and bloom:
I might have sat beside her on the bench   1950
Where the children were: I wish the thing had been,
Indeed: the event could not be worse, you know:
One more half-hour of her saved! She's dead now, Sirs!
While I was running on at such a rate,
Friends should have plucked me by the sleeve: I went   1955
Too much o' the trivial outside of her face

3. Grimaces.   glance was supposed to be fatal.
4. Smack, taste.   6. Digression.
5. Both are legendary reptiles whose

And the purity that shone there—plain to me,
Not to you, what more natural? Nor am I
Infatuated,—oh, I saw, be sure!
Her brow had not the right line, leaned too much,   1960
Painters would say; they like the straight-up Greek:
This seemed bent somewhat with an invisible crown
Of martyr and saint, not such as art approves.
And how the dark orbs dwelt deep underneath,
Looked out of such a sad sweet heaven on me!   1965
The lips, compressed a little, came forward too,
Careful for a whole world of sin and pain.
That was the face, her husband makes his plea,
He sought just to disfigure,—no offence
Beyond that! Sirs, let us be rational!   1970
He needs must vindicate his honour,—ay,
Yet shirks, the coward, in a clown's disguise,
Away from the scene, endeavours to escape.
Now, had he done so, slain and left no trace
O' the slayer,—what were vindicated, pray?   1975
You had found his wife disfigured or a corpse,
For what and by whom? It is too palpable!
Then, here's another point involving law:
I use this argument to show you meant
No calumny against us by that title   1980
O' the sentence,—liars try to twist it so:
What penalty it bore, I had to pay
Till further proof should follow of innocence—
Probationis ob defectum,[7]—proof?
How could you get proof without trying us?   1985
You went through the preliminary form,
Stopped there, contrived this sentence to amuse
The adversary. If the title ran
For more than fault imputed and not proved,
That was a simple penman's error, else   1990
A slip i' the phrase,—as when we say of you
"Charged with injustice"—which may either be
Or not be,—'t is a name that sticks meanwhile.
Another relevant matter: fool that I am!
Not what I wish true, yet a point friends urge: 1995
It is not true,—yet, since friends think it helps,—
She only tried me when some others failed—
Began with Conti, whom I told you of,
And Guillichini, Guido's kinsfolk both,
And when abandoned by them, not before,   2000
Turned to me. That's conclusive why she turned.
Much good they got by the happy cowardice!
Conti is dead, poisoned a month ago:
Does that much strike you as a sin? Not much,
After the present murder,—one mark more   2005

7. "For lack of proof," with reference to adultery.

On the Moor's skin,—what is black by blacker still?
Conti had come here and told truth. And so
With Guillichini; he's condemned of course
To the galleys, as a friend in this affair,
Tried and condemned for no one thing i' the world,   2010
A fortnight since by who but the Governor?—
The just judge, who refused Pompilia help
At first blush, being her husband's friend, you know.
There are two tales to suit the separate courts,
Arezzo and Rome: he tells you here, we fled   2015
Alone, unhelped,—lays stress on the main fault,
The spiritual sin, Rome looks to: but elsewhere
He likes best we should break in, steal, bear off,
Be fit to brand and pillory and flog—
That's the charge goes to the heart of the Governor: 2020
If these unpriest me, you and I may yet
Converse, Vincenzo Marzi-Medici![8]
Oh, Sirs, there are worse men than you, I say!
More easily duped, I mean; this stupid lie,
Its liar never dared propound in Rome,   2025
He gets Arezzo to receive,—nay more,
Gets Florence and the Duke to authorize!
This is their Rota's[9] sentence, their Granduke
Signs and seals! Rome for me henceforward—Rome,
Where better men are,—most of all, that man   2030
The Augustinian of the Hospital,[1]
Who writes the letter,—he confessed, he says,
Many a dying person, never one
So sweet and true and pure and beautiful.
A good man! Will you make him Pope one day?   2035
Not that he is not good too, this we have—
But old,—else he would have his word to speak,
His truth to teach the world: I thirst for truth,
But shall not drink it till I reach the source.

Sirs, I am quiet again. You see, we are   2040
So very pitiable, she and I,
Who had conceivably been otherwise.
Forget distemperature and idle heat!
Apart from truth's sake, what's to move so much?
Pompilia will be presently with God;   2045
I am, on earth, as good as out of it,
A relegated priest; when exile ends,
I mean to do my duty and live long.
She and I are mere strangers now: but priests
Should study passion; how else cure mankind,   2050
Who come for help in passionate extremes?
I do but play with an imagined life
Of who, unfettered by a vow, unblessed

8. Governor of Arezzo.
9. Tuscan ecclesiastical court subject to
papal review.
1. Pompilia's confessor, Fra Celestino.

By the higher call,—since you will have it so,—
Leads it companioned by the woman there.   2055
To live, and see her learn, and learn by her,
Out of the low obscure and petty world—
Or only see one purpose and one will
Evolve themselves i' the world, change wrong to right:
To have to do with nothing but the true,   2060
The good, the eternal—and these, not alone
In the main current of the general life,
But small experiences of every day,
Concerns of the particular hearth and home:
To learn not only by a comet's rush   2065
But a rose's birth,—not by the grandeur, God—
But the comfort, Christ. All this, how far away!
Mere delectation, meet for a minute's dream!—
Just as a drudging student trims his lamp,
Opens his Plutarch,[2] puts him in the place   2070
Of Roman, Grecian; draws the patched gown close,
Dreams, "Thus should I fight, save or rule the world!"—
Then smilingly, contentedly, awakes
To the old solitary nothingness.
So I, from such communion, pass content . . .   2075

O great, just, good God! Miserable me!

Book X

The Pope[1]

Like to Ahasuerus, that shrewd prince,[2]
I will begin,—as is, these seven years now,

2. Roman historian whose *Parallel Lives*
compares great Romans with their Greek
counterparts.
1. Antonio Pignatelli (1615–1700), a
Neapolitan, was elected pope in 1691 to
succeed Alexander VIII. He took the
name of Innocent XII as a sign that he
wished to emulate the papacy of Innocent XI, a vigorous reformer. Pignatelli
had been vice-legate of Urbino, governor
of Perugia, and nuncio to Tuscany, to
Poland, and to Austria; he had been created cardinal and archbishop of Naples
by Innocent XI. Pignatelli as Innocent
XII put an end to nepotism and the sale
of offices. He was benevolent, charitable,
and frugal, and called the poor his relations; the Roman nobles, on the other
hand, he severely punished for all viola-
tions of the law.
  The soliloquy of Browning's pope is
set on February 21, 1698, the day before
Guido and his accomplices are to be executed. Pleading ecclesiastical privilege
—he had taken minor orders in the
church—Guido has appealed his case to
the pope. Morally certain of Guido's

culpability, Innocent refuses to intervene,
and the civil court's death sentence is
forthwith carried out. The pope is represented as an aged man aware that his
own death cannot be far off, and anxious therefore that this possibly final act
of judgment be right in the eyes of God.
Meditating somberly on the Franceschini
case, he finds in it the deepest human
concerns: truth and falsehood, good and
evil, faith and doubt. His speculations
on these issues amount to an anatomy of
the world as it stands at the close of the
seventeenth century. Inevitably arises the
question of the future of Western culture
—with particular reference to religious
faith—in the coming Age of Reason. The
pope voices Browning's own creed,
rather than that of orthodox Roman Catholicism; but he is no mere mouthpiece
for the poet, who has created in the
pope a fully realized dramatic character,
one of the great philosophic heroes in
literature.
2. Persian king who, one sleepless night,
read of an abortive plot against him
(Esther 6:1–3).

My daily wont,—and read a History[3]
(Written by one whose deft right hand was dust
To the last digit, ages ere my birth)   5
Of all my predecessors, Popes of Rome:
For though mine ancient early dropped the pen,
Yet others picked it up and wrote it dry,
Since of the making books there is no end.[4]
And so I have the Papacy complete   10
From Peter first to Alexander last;
Can question each and take instruction so.
Have I to dare?—I ask, how dared this Pope?
To suffer?—Suchanone, how suffered he?
Being about to judge, as now, I seek   15
How judged once, well or ill, some other Pope;
Study some signal judgment that subsists
To blaze on, or else blot, the page which seals
The sum up of what gain or loss to God
Came of His one more Vicar in the world.   20
So, do I find example, rule of life;
So, square and set in order the next page,
Shall be stretched smooth o'er my own funeral cyst.[5]

Eight hundred years exact before the year
I was made Pope, men made Formosus[6] Pope,   25
Say Sigebert[7] and other chroniclers.
Ere I confirm or quash the Trial here
Of Guido Franceschini and his friends,
Read,—How there was a ghastly Trial once
Of a dead man by a live man, and both, Popes: 30
Thus—in the antique penman's very phrase.

"Then Stephen, Pope and seventh of the name,[8]
Cried out, in synod as he sat in state,
While choler quivered on his brow and beard,
'Come into court, Formosus, thou lost wretch,   35
That claimedst to be late Pope as even I!'

"And at the word the great door of the church
Flew wide, and in they brought Formosus' self,
The body of him, dead, even as embalmed
And buried duly in the Vatican   40
Eight months before, exhumed thus for the nonce.

3. No single *History* has been identified.
4. Ecclesiastes 12:12.
5. Coffin.
6. Pope from 891–896, he sided with Arnulf, king of Germany, against the princes of Spoleto, and in 895 crowned Arnulf emperor. After his death the validity of his acts was contested, and Stephen VI, treating him as a usurper, disinterred his body in 897. Theodore II restored it to Christian burial, and John

IX declared Formosus' pontificate valid. The violence described by Innocent in lines 32–149 was typical of the period.
7. Medieval chronicler Sigebert of Gembloux (ca. 1030–1112).
8. Actually the sixth, pope from 896–897. The other papacies named are: Romanus (897), Theodore II (897), John IX (898–900), and Sergius III (904–911) (lines 105–41).

They set it, that dead body of a Pope,
Clothed in pontific vesture now again,
Upright on Peter's chair as if alive.

"And Stephen, springing up, cried furiously   45
'Bishop of Porto, wherefore didst presume
To leave that see and take this Roman see,
Exchange the lesser for the greater see,
—A thing against the canons of the Church?'

"Then one—(a Deacon who, observing forms,   50
Was placed by Stephen to repel the charge,
Be advocate and mouthpiece of the corpse)—
Spoke as he dared, set stammeringly forth
With white lips and dry tongue,—as but a youth,
For frightful was the corpse-face to behold,—   55
How nowise lacked there precedent for this.

"But when, for his last precedent of all,
Emboldened by the Spirit, out he blurts
'And, Holy Father, didst not thou thyself
Vacate the lesser for the greater see,   60
Half a year since change Arago for Rome?'
'—Ye have the sin's defence now, Synod mine!'
Shrieks Stephen in a beastly froth of rage:
'Judge now betwixt him dead and me alive!
Hath he intruded, or do I pretend?   65
Judge, judge!'—breaks wavelike one whole foam of wrath.

"Whereupon they, being friends and followers,
Said 'Ay, thou art Christ's Vicar, and not he!
Away with what is frightful to behold!
This act was uncanonic and a fault.'   70

"Then, swallowed up in rage, Stephen exclaimed
'So, guilty! So, remains I punish guilt!
He is unpoped, and all he did I damn:
The Bishop, that ordained him, I degrade:
Depose to laics those he raised to priests: 75
What they have wrought is mischief nor shall stand,
It is confusion, let it vex no more!
Since I revoke, annul and abrogate
All his decrees in all kinds: they are void!
In token whereof and warning to the world,   80
Strip me yon miscreant of those robes usurped,
And clothe him with vile serge befitting such!
Then hale the carrion to the market-place:
Let the town-hangman chop from his right hand
Those same three fingers which he blessed withal; 85
Next cut the head off once was crowned forsooth:
And last go fling them, fingers, head and trunk,
To Tiber that my Christian fish may sup!'

—Either because of ΙΧΟΥΣ which means Fish[9]
And very aptly symbolizes Christ,   90
Or else because the Pope is Fisherman,[1]
And seals with Fisher's-signet.
                                   "Anyway,
So said, so done: himself, to see it done,
Followed the corpse they trailed from street to street
Till into Tiber[2] wave they threw the thing.   95
The people, crowded on the banks to see,
Were loud or mute, wept or laughed, cursed or jeered,
According as the deed addressed their sense;
A scandal verily: and out spake a Jew
'Wot ye your Christ had vexed our Herod thus?'   100

"Now when, Formosus being dead a year,
His judge Pope Stephen tasted death in turn,
Made captive by the mob and strangled straight,
Romanus, his successor for a month,
Did make protest Formosus was with God,   105
Holy, just, true in thought and word and deed.
Next Theodore, who reigned but twenty days,
Therein convoked a synod, whose decree
Did reinstate, repope the late unpoped,
And do away with Stephen as accursed.   110
So that when presently certain fisher-folk
(As if the queasy river could not hold
Its swallowed Jonas, but discharged the meal)
Produced the timely product of their nets,
The mutilated man, Formosus,—saved   115
From putrefaction by the embalmer's spice,
Or, as some said, by sanctity of flesh,—
'Why, lay the body again,' bade Theodore,
'Among his predecessors, in the church
And burial-place of Peter!' which was done.   120
'And,' addeth Luitprand,[3] 'many of repute,
Pious and still alive, avouch to me
That, as they bore the body up the aisle,
The saints in imaged row bowed each his head
For welcome to a brother-saint come back.'   125
As for Romanus and this Theodore,
These two Popes, through the brief reign granted each,
Could but initiate what John came to close
And give the final stamp to: he it was
Ninth of the name, (I follow the best guides)   130
Who,—in full synod at Ravenna held

9. Initial letters of the phrase "Jesus Christ, son of God, Savior," which comprise the Greek word for "fish," an early symbol of Christianity.
1. Christ said to Peter and Andrew: "Follow me, and I will make you fishers of men" (Matthew 4:19). The pope's signet ring represents St. Peter fishing from a boat.
2. River flowing through Rome.
3. Or Liudprand (ca. 922–972), Italian historian and bishop of Cremona.

With Bishops seventy-four, and present too
Eude[4] King of France with his Archbishopry,—
Did condemn Stephen, anathematize[5]
The disinterment, and make all blots blank,   135
'For,' argueth here Auxilius[6] in a place
De Ordinationibus, 'precedents
Had been, no lack, before Formosus long,
Of Bishops so transferred from see to see,—
Marinus,[7] for example:' read the tract.   140

"But, after John, came Sergius,[8] reaffirmed
The right of Stephen, cursed Formosus, nay
Cast out, some say, his corpse a second time.
And here,—because the matter went to ground,
Fretted by new griefs, other cares of the age,—   145
Here is the last pronouncing of the Church,
Her sentence that subsists unto this day.
Yet constantly opinion hath prevailed
I' the Church, Formosus was a holy man."

Which of the judgments was infallible?[9]   150
Which of my predecessors spoke for God?
And what availed Formosus that this cursed,
That blessed, and then this other cursed again?
"Fear ye not whose power can kill the body
And not the soul," saith Christ, "but rather those   155
Can cast both soul and body into hell!"[1]

John judged thus in Eight Hundred Ninety Eight,
Exact eight hundred years ago to-day
When, sitting in his stead, Vice-gerent here,
I must give judgment on my own behoof.   160
So worked the predecessor: now, my turn!

In God's name! Once more on this earth of God's,
While twilight lasts and time wherein to work,
I take His staff with my uncertain hand,
And stay my six and fourscore years, my due   165
Labour and sorrow, on His judgment-seat,
And forthwith think, speak, act, in place of Him—
The Pope for Christ. Once more appeal is made
From man's assize[2] to mine: I sit and see
Another poor weak trembling human wretch   170
Pushed by his fellows, who pretend the right,

4. Eudes (or Odo, d. 898), king of the
Franks.
5. Condemn.
6. Frankish priest of the tenth century,
who defended the papacy of Formosus.
7. Marinus I (or Martin II), pope from
882–884. He restored Formosus, then in
exile, to his see as cardinal-bishop of
Porto.

8. Between the two were Benedict IV
(900–903) and Leo V (903).
9. Allusion to the controversial issue, in
the 1860s, of papal infallibility, which
was made an article of faith by the Vatican Council of 1870.
1. Matthew 10:28.
2. Superior civil court.

Up to the gulf which, where I gaze, begins
From this world to the next,—gives way and way,
Just on the edge over the awful dark:
With nothing to arrest him but my feet.   175
He catches at me with convulsive face,
Cries "Leave to live the natural minute more!"
While hollowly the avengers echo "Leave?
None! So has he exceeded man's due share
In man's fit license, wrung by Adam's fall,   180
To sin and yet not surely die,[3]—that we,
All of us sinful, all with need of grace,
All chary of our life,—the minute more
Or minute less of grace which saves a soul,—
Bound to make common cause with who craves time,   185
—We yet protest against the exorbitance
Of sin in this one sinner, and demand
That his poor sole remaining piece of time
Be plucked from out his clutch: put him to death!
Punish him now! As for the weal or woe   190
Hereafter, God grant mercy! Man be just,
Nor let the felon boast he went scot-free!"
And I am bound, the solitary judge,
To weigh the worth, decide upon the plea,
And either hold a hand out, or withdraw   195
A foot and let the wretch drift to the fall.
Ay, and while thus I dally, dare perchance
Put fancies for a comfort 'twixt this calm
And yonder passion that I have to bear,—
As if reprieve were possible for both   200
Prisoner and Pope,—how easy were reprieve!
A touch o' the hand-bell here, a hasty word
To those who wait, and wonder they wait long,
I' the passage there, and I should gain the life!—
Yea, though I flatter me with fancy thus,   205
I know it is but nature's craven-trick.
The case is over, judgment at an end,
And all things done now and irrevocable:
A mere dead man is Franceschini here,
Even as Formosus centuries ago.   210
I have worn through this sombre wintry day,
With winter in my soul beyond the world's,
Over these dismalest of documents
Which drew night down on me ere eve befell,—
Pleadings and counter-pleadings, figure of fact   215
Beside fact's self, these summaries to-wit,—
How certain three were slain by certain five:
I read here why it was, and how it went,

3. Genesis 3:4: "And the serpent said unto the woman, Ye shall not surely die."

And how the chief o' the five preferred excuse,
And how law rather chose defence should lie,— 220
What argument he urged by wary word
When free to play off wile, start subterfuge,
And what the unguarded groan told, torture's feat
When law grew brutal, outbroke, overbore
And glutted hunger on the truth, at last,— 225
No matter for the flesh and blood between.
All 's a clear rede[4] and no more riddle now.
Truth, nowhere, lies yet everywhere in these—
Not absolutely in a portion, yet
Evolvible from the whole: evolved at last 230
Painfully, held tenaciously by me.
Therefore there is not any doubt to clear
When I shall write the brief word presently
And chink the hand-bell, which I pause to do.
Irresolute? Not I, more than the mound 235
With the pine-trees on it yonder! Some surmise,
Perchance, that since man's wit is fallible,
Mine may fail here? Suppose it so,—what then?
Say,—Guido, I count guilty, there's no babe
So guiltless, for I misconceive the man! 240
What's in the chance should move me from my mind?
If, as I walk in a rough country-side,
Peasants of mine cry "Thou art he can help,
Lord of the land and counted wise to boot:
Look at our brother, strangling in his foam, 245
He fell so where we find him,—prove thy worth!"
I may presume, pronounce, "A frenzy-fit,
A falling-sickness or a fever-stroke!
Breathe a vein, copiously let blood at once!"
So perishes the patient, and anon 250
I hear my peasants—"All was error, lord!
Our story, thy prescription: for there crawled
In due time from our hapless brother's breast
The serpent which had stung him: bleeding slew
Whom a prompt cordial had restored to health." 255
What other should I say than "God so willed:
Mankind is ignorant, a man am I:
Call ignorance my sorrow, not my sin!"
So and not otherwise, in after-time,
If some acuter wit, fresh probing, sound 260
This multifarious mass of words and deeds
Deeper, and reach through guilt to innocence,
I shall face Guido's ghost nor blench a jot.
"God who set me to judge thee, meted out
So much of judging faculty, no more: 265
Ask Him if I was slack in use thereof!"

4. Account.

I hold a heavier fault imputable
Inasmuch as I changed a chaplain once,
For no cause,—no, if I must bare my heart,—
Save that he snuffled somewhat saying mass.   270
For I am ware it is the seed of act,
God holds appraising in His hollow palm,
Not act grown great thence on the world below,
Leafage and branchage, vulgar eyes admire.
Therefore I stand on my integrity,   275
Nor fear at all: and if I hesitate,
It is because I need to breathe awhile,
Rest, as the human right allows, review
Intent the little seeds of act, my tree,—
The thought, which, clothed in deed, I give the world   280
At chink of bell and push of arrased door.

O pale departure, dim disgrace of day!
Winter's in wane, his vengeful worst art thou,
To dash the boldness of advancing March!
Thy chill persistent rain has purged our streets   285
Of gossipry; pert tongue and idle ear
By this, consort 'neath archway, portico.
But wheresoe'er Rome gathers in the grey,
Two names now snap and flash from mouth to mouth—
(Sparks, flint and steel strike) Guido and the Pope.   290
By this same hour to-morrow eve—aha,
How do they call him?—the sagacious Swede[5]
Who finds by figures how the chances prove,
Why one comes rather than another thing,
As, say, such dots turn up by throw of dice,   295
Or, if we dip in Virgil[6] here and there
And prick for such a verse, when such shall point.
Take this Swede, tell him, hiding name and rank,
Two men are in our city this dull eve;
One doomed to death,—but hundreds in such plight   300
Slip aside, clean escape by leave of law
Which leans to mercy in this latter time;
Moreover in the plenitude of life
Is he, with strength of limb and brain adroit,
Presumably of service here: beside,   305
The man is noble, backed by nobler friends:
Nay, they so wish him well, the city's self
Makes common cause with who—house-magistrate,
Patron of hearth and home, domestic lord—
But ruled his own, let aliens cavil. Die?   310
He'll bribe a gaoler or break prison first!

5. Still unidentified. It is possible Browning had in mind Swedish mathematician, scientist, and (late in life) mystic, Emanuel Swedenborg (1688–1772), whom Elizabeth Barrett Browning deeply admired. Swedenborg would have been only a boy in 1698, however.
6. See note to V.401.

Nay, a sedition may be helpful, give
Hint to the mob to batter wall, burn gate,
And bid the favourite malefactor march.
Calculate now these chances of escape!   315
"It is not probable, but well may be."
Again, there is another man, weighed now
By twice eight years beyond the seven-times-ten,
Appointed overweight to break our branch.
And this man's loaded branch lifts, more than snow,   320
All the world's cark and care, though a bird's nest
Were a superfluous burthen: notably
Hath he been pressed, as if his age were youth,
From to-day's dawn till now that day departs,
Trying one question with true sweat of soul   325
"Shall the said doomed man fitlier die or live?"
When a straw swallowed in his posset,⁷ stool
Stumbled on where his path lies, any puff
That's incident to such a smoking flax,⁸
Hurries the natural end and quenches him!   330
Now calculate, thou sage, the chances here,
Say, which shall die the sooner, this or that?
"That, possibly, this in all likelihood."
I thought so: yet thou tripp'st, my foreign friend!
No, it will be quite otherwise,—to-day   335
Is Guido's last: my term is yet to run.

But say the Swede were right, and I forthwith
Acknowledge a prompt summons and lie dead:
Why, then I stand already in God's face
And hear "Since by its fruit a tree is judged,⁹   340
Show me thy fruit, the latest act of thine!
For in the last is summed the first and all,—
What thy life last put heart and soul into,
There shall I taste thy product." I must plead
This condemnation of a man to-day.   345

Not so! Expect nor question nor reply
At what we figure as God's judgment-bar!
None of this vile way by the barren words
Which, more than any deed, characterize
Man as made subject to a curse: no speech—   350
That still bursts o'er some lie which lurks inside,
As the split skin across the coppery snake,
And most denotes man! since, in all beside,
In hate or lust or guile or unbelief,
Out of some core of truth the excrescence comes,   355
And, in the last resort, the man may urge

7. Hot drink.
8. Isaiah 42:3: ". . . the smoking flax
shall he [Christ] not quench: he shall
bring forth judgment unto truth."
9. Matthew 12:33: ". . . the tree is
known by his fruit."

"So was I made, a weak thing that gave way
To truth, to impulse only strong since true,
And hated, lusted, used guile, forwent faith."
But when man walks the garden of this world   360
For his own solace, and, unchecked by law,
Speaks or keeps silence as himself sees fit,
Without the least incumbency to lie,
—Why, can he tell you what a rose is like,
Or how the birds fly, and not slip to false   365
Though truth serve better? Man must tell his mate
Of you, me and himself, knowing he lies,
Knowing his fellow knows the same,—will think
"He lies, it is the method of a man!"
And yet will speak for answer "It is truth"   370
To him who shall rejoin "Again a lie!"
Therefore these filthy rags of speech, this coil
Of statement, comment, query and response,
Tatters all too contaminate for use,
Have no renewing: He, the Truth, is, too,   375
The Word.[1] We men, in our degree, may know
There, simply, instantaneously, as here
After long time and amid many lies,
Whatever we dare think we know indeed
—That I am I, as He is He,—what else?   380
But be man's method for man's life at least!
Wherefore, Antonio Pignatelli, thou
My ancient self, who wast no Pope so long
But studiedst God and man, the many years
I' the school, i' the cloister, in the diocese   385
Domestic, legate-rule in foreign lands,[2]—
Thou other force in those old busy days
Than this grey ultimate decrepitude,—
Yet sensible of fires that more and more
Visit a soul, in passage to the sky,   390
Left nakeder than when flesh-robe was new—
Thou, not Pope but the mere old man o' the world,
Supposed inquisitive and dispassionate,
Wilt thou, the one whose speech I somewhat trust,
Question the after-me, this self now Pope,   395
Hear his procedure, criticize his work?
Wise in its generation is the world.[3]

This is why Guido is found reprobate.
I see him furnished forth for his career,
On starting for the life-chance in our world,   400
With nearly all we count sufficient help:.
Body and mind in balance, a sound frame,

---

1. John 14:6 and 1:14.
2. Innocent had been bishop in Italy and had represented the pope in Poland and Germany.
3. Luke 16:8.

A solid intellect: the wit to seek,
Wisdom to choose, and courage wherewithal
To deal in whatsoever circumstance   405
Should minister to man, make life succeed.
Oh, and much drawback! what were earth without?
Is this our ultimate stage, or starting-place
To try man's foot, if it will creep or climb,
'Mid obstacles in seeming, points that prove   410
Advantage for who vaults from low to high
And makes the stumbling-block a stepping-stone?
So, Guido, born with appetite, lacks food:
Is poor, who yet could deftly play-off[4] wealth:
Straitened, whose limbs are restless till at large.   415
He, as he eyes each outlet of the cirque[5]
And narrow penfold for probation, pines
After the good things just outside its grate,
With less monition, fainter conscience-twitch,
Rarer instinctive qualm at the first feel   420
Of greed unseemly, prompting grasp undue,
Than nature furnishes her main mankind,—
Making it harder to do wrong than right
The first time, careful lest the common ear
Break measure, miss the outstep of life's march.   425
Wherein I see a trial fair and fit
For one else too unfairly fenced about,
Set above sin, beyond his fellows here:
Guarded from the arch-tempter all must fight,
By a great birth, traditionary name,   430
Diligent culture, choice companionship,
Above all, conversancy with the faith
Which puts forth for its base of doctrine just
"Man is born nowise to content himself,
But please God."[6] He accepted such a rule,   435
Recognized man's obedience; and the Church,
Which simply is such rule's embodiment,
He clave to, he held on by,—nay, indeed,
Near pushed inside of, deep as layman durst,
Professed so much of priesthood as might sue   440
For priest's-exemption where the layman sinned,—
Got his arm frocked which, bare, the law would bruise.
Hence, at this moment, what's his last resource,
His extreme stay and utmost stretch of hope
But that,—convicted of such crime as law   445
Wipes not away save with a worldling's blood,—
Guido, the three-parts consecrate, may 'scape?
Nay, the portentous[7] brothers of the man
Are veritably priests, protected each

4. Feign.
5. Arena.
6. Romans 15:1 and 1 Thessalonians 4:1.
7. Sinister.

May do his murder in the Church's pale,   450
Abate Paul, Canon Girolamo!
This is the man proves irreligiousest
Of all mankind, religion's parasite!
This may forsooth plead dinned ear, jaded sense,
The vice o' the watcher who bides near the bell,   455
Sleeps sound because the clock is vigilant,
And cares not whether it be shade or shine,
Doling out day and night to all men else!
Why was the choice o' the man to niche himself
Perversely 'neath the tower where Time's own tongue   460
Thus undertakes to sermonize the world?
Why, but because the solemn is safe too,
The belfry proves a fortress of a sort,
Has other uses than to teach the hour:
Turns sunscreen, paravent and ombrifuge[8]   465
To whoso seeks a shelter in its pale,
—Ay, and attractive to unwary folk
Who gaze at storied portal, statued spire,
And go home with full head but empty purse,
Nor dare suspect the sacristan[9] the thief!   470
Shall Judas,—hard upon the donor's heel,
To filch the fragments of the basket,—plead
He was too near the preacher's mouth, nor sat
Attent with fifties in a company?
No,—closer to promulgated decree,   475
Clearer the censure of default. Proceed!

I find him bound, then, to begin life well;
Fortified by propitious circumstance,
Great birth, good breeding, with the Church for guide,
How lives he? Cased thus in a coat of proof,   480
Mailed like a man-at-arms, though all the while
A puny starveling,—does the breast pant big,
The limb swell to the limit, emptiness
Strive to become solidity indeed?
Rather, he shrinks up like the ambiguous fish,   485
Detaches flesh from shell and outside show,
And steals by moonlight (I have seen the thing)
In and out, now to prey and now to skulk.
Armour he boasts when a wave breaks on beach,
Or bird stoops for the prize: with peril nigh,—   490
The man of rank, the much-befriended-man,
The man almost affiliate to the Church,
Such is to deal with, let the world beware!
Does the world recognize, pass prudently?
Do tides abate and sea-fowl hunt i' the deep?   495
Already is the slug from out its mew,

8. Refuge from wind and rain; i.e., from   9. Custodian of church's sacred vessels.
the world's buffeting.

Ignobly faring with all loose and free,
Sand-fly and slush-worm at their garbage-feast,
A naked blotch no better than they all:
Guido has dropped nobility, slipped the Church,   500
Plays trickster if not cut-purse, body and soul
Prostrate among the filthy feeders—faugh!
And when Law takes him by surprise at last,
Catches the foul thing on its carrion-prey,
Behold, he points to shell left high and dry,   505
Pleads "But the case out yonder is myself!"
Nay, it is thou, Law prongs amid thy peers,
Congenial vermin; that was none of thee,
Thine outside,—give it to the soldier-crab![1]

For I find this black mark impinge the man,   510
That he believes in just the vile of life.
Low instinct, base pretension, are these truth?
Then, that aforesaid armour, probity
He figures in,[2] is falsehood scale on scale;
Honour and faith,—a lie and a disguise,   515
Probably for all livers in this world,
Certainly for himself! All say good words
To who will hear, all do thereby bad deeds
To who must undergo; so thrive mankind!
See this habitual creed exemplified   520
Most in the last deliberate act; as last,
So, very sum and substance of the soul
Of him that planned and leaves one perfect piece,
The sin brought under jurisdiction now,
Even the marriage of the man: this act   525
I sever from his life as sample, show
For Guido's self, intend to test him by,
As, from a cup filled fairly at the fount,
By the components we decide enough
Or to let flow as late, or staunch the source.   530

He purposes this marriage, I remark,
On no one motive that should prompt thereto—
Farthest, by consequence, from ends alleged
Appropriate to the action; so they were:
The best, he knew and feigned, the worst he took   535
Not one permissible impulse moves the man,
From the mere liking of the eye and ear,
To the true longing of the heart that loves,
No trace of these: but all to instigate,
Is what sinks man past level of the brute   540
Whose appetite if brutish is a truth.
All is the lust for money: to get gold,—

---

1. Hermit crab, which lives in empty
shells.
2. Cf. Ephesians 6:13–14: "the whole armour of God . . . the breastplate of
righteousness."

Why, lie, rob, if it must be, murder! Make
Body and soul wring gold out, lured within
The clutch of hate by love, the trap's pretence!   545
What good else get from bodies and from souls?
This got, there were some life to lead thereby,
—What, where or how, appreciate those who tell
How the toad lives: it lives,—enough for me!
To get this good,—with but a groan or so,   550
Then, silence of the victims,—were the feat.
He foresaw, made a picture in his mind,—
Of father and mother stunned and echoless
To the blow, as they lie staring at fate's jaws
Their folly danced into, till the woe fell;   555
Edged in a month by strenuous cruelty
From even the poor nook whence they watched the wolf
Feast on their heart, the lamb-like child his prey;
Plundered to the last remnant of their wealth,
(What daily pittance pleased the plunderer dole)   560
Hunted forth to go hide head, starve and die,
And leave the pale awe-stricken wife, past hope
Of help i' the world now, mute and motionless,
His slave, his chattel, to first use, then destroy.
All this, he bent mind how to bring about,   565
Put plain in act and life, as painted plain,
So have success, reach crown of earthly good,
In this particular enterprise of man,
By marriage—undertaken in God's face
With all these lies so opposite God's truth,   570
For end so other than man's end.

                            Thus schemes
Guido, and thus would carry out his scheme:
But when an obstacle first blocks the path,
When he finds none may boast monopoly
Of lies and tricks i' the tricking lying world,—   575
That sorry timid natures, even this sort
O' the Comparini, want nor trick nor lie
Proper to the kind,—that as the gor-crow[3] treats
The bramble-finch so treats the finch the moth,
And the great Guido is minutely matched   580
By this same couple,—whether true or false
The revelation of Pompilia's birth,
Which in a moment brings his scheme to nought,—
Then, he is piqued, advances yet a stage,
Leaves the low region to the finch and fly,   585
Soars to the zenith whence the fiercer fowl
May dare the inimitable swoop. I see.
He draws now on the curious[4] crime, the fine

---

3. Carrion crow.   4. Singular, cunning.

Felicity and flower of wickedness;
Determines, by the utmost exercise   590
Of violence, made safe and sure by craft,
To satiate malice, pluck one last arch-pang
From the parents, else would triumph out of reach,
By punishing their child, within reach yet,
Who, by thought, word or deed, could nowise wrong 595
I' the matter that now moves him. So plans he,
Always subordinating (note the point!)
Revenge, the manlier sin, to interest
The meaner,—would pluck pang forth, but unclench
No gripe in the act, let fall no money-piece.   600
Hence a plan for so plaguing, body and soul,
His wife, so putting, day by day, hour by hour,
The untried torture to the untouched place,
As must precipitate an end foreseen,
Goad her into some plain revolt, most like   605
Plunge upon patent suicidal shame,
Death to herself, damnation by rebound
To those whose hearts he, holding hers, holds still:
Such plan as, in its bad completeness, shall
Ruin the three together and alike,   610
Yet leave himself in luck and liberty,
No claim renounced, no right a forfeiture,
His person unendangered, his good fame
Without a flaw, his pristine worth intact,—
While they, with all their claims and rights that cling, 615
Shall forthwith crumble off him every side,
Scorched into dust, a plaything for the winds.
As when, in our Campagna,[5] there is fired
The nest-like work that overruns a hut;
And, as the thatch burns here, there, everywhere,   620
Even to the ivy and wild vine, that bound
And blessed the home where men were happy once,
There rises gradual, black amid the blaze,
Some grim and unscathed nucleus of the nest,—
Some old malicious tower, some obscene tomb   625
They thought a temple in their ignorance,
And clung about and thought to lean upon—
There laughs it o'er their ravage,—where are they?
So did his cruelty burn life about,
And lay the ruin bare in dreadfulness,   630
Try the persistency of torment so
Upon the wife, that, at extremity,
Some crisis brought about by fire and flame,
The patient frenzy-stung must needs break loose,
Fly anyhow, find refuge anywhere,   635
Even in the arms of who should front her first,

5. The ruin-dotted plain surrounding Rome.

No monster but a man—while nature shrieked
"Or thus escape, or die!" The spasm arrived,
Not the escape by way of sin,—O God,
Who shall pluck sheep Thou holdest, from Thy hand?[6]   640
Therefore she lay resigned to die,—so far
The simple cruelty was foiled. Why then,
Craft to the rescue, let craft supplement
Cruelty and show hell a masterpiece!
Hence this consummate lie, this love-intrigue,   645
Unmanly simulation of a sin,
With place and time and circumstance to suit—
These letters false beyond all forgery—
Not just handwriting and mere authorship,
But false to body and soul they figure forth—   650
As though the man had cut out shape and shape
From fancies of that other Aretine,[7]
To paste below—incorporate the filth
With cherub faces on a missal-page!

Whereby the man so far attains his end   655
That strange temptation is permitted,—see!
Pompilia wife, and Caponsacchi priest,
Are brought together as nor priest nor wife
Should stand, and there is passion in the place,
Power in the air for evil as for good,   660
Promptings from heaven and hell, as if the stars
Fought in their courses for a fate to be.
Thus stand the wife and priest, a spectacle,
I doubt not, to unseen assemblage there.
No lamp will mark that window for a shrine,   665
No tablet signalize the terrace, teach
New generations which succeed the old
The pavement of the street is holy ground;
No bard describe in verse how Christ prevailed
And Satan fell like lightning![8] Why repine?   670
What does the world, told truth, but lie the more?

A second time the plot is foiled; nor, now,
By corresponding sin for countercheck,
No wile and trick that baffle trick and wile,—
The play o' the parents! Here the blot is blanched   675
By God's gift of a purity of soul
That will not take pollution, ermine-like
Armed from dishonour by its own soft snow.
Such was this gift of God who showed for once
How He would have the world go white: it seems   680
As a new attribute were born of each
Champion of truth, the priest and wife I praise,—

---

6. John 10:28.
7. Pietro Aretino (1492–1556), author of   satires and obscene sonnets.
8. Luke 10:18.

As a new safeguard sprang up in defence
Of their new noble nature: so a thorn
Comes to the aid of and completes the rose— 685
Courage to-wit, no woman's gift nor priest's,
I' the crisis; might leaps vindicating right.
See how the strong aggressor, bad and bold,
With every vantage, preconcerts[9] surprise,
Leaps of a sudden at his victim's throat 690
In a byeway,—how fares he when face to face
With Caponsacchi? Who fights, who fears now?
There quails Count Guido armed to the chattering teeth,
Cowers at the steadfast eye and quiet word
O' the Canon of the Pieve![1] There skulks crime 695
Behind law called in to back cowardice:
While out of the poor trampled worm the wife,
Springs up a serpent![2]

But anon of these.
Him I judge now,—of him proceed to note,
Failing the first, a second chance befriends 700
Guido, gives pause ere punishment arrive.
The law he called, comes, hears, adjudicates,
Nor does amiss i' the main,—secludes the wife
From the husband, respites the oppressed one, grants
Probation to the oppressor, could he know 705
The mercy of a minute's fiery purge!
The furnace-coals alike of public scorn,
Private remorse, heaped glowing on his head,
What if,—the force and guile, the ore's alloy,
Eliminate, his baser soul refined— 710
The lost be saved even yet, so as by fire?[3]
Let him, rebuked, go softly all his days[4]
And, when no graver musings claim their due,
Meditate on a man's immense mistake
Who, fashioned to use feet and walk, deigns crawl— 715
Takes the unmanly means—ay, though to ends
Man scarce should make for, would but reach thro' wrong,—
May sin, but nowise needs shame manhood so:
Since fowlers hawk, shoot, nay and snare the game,
And yet eschew vile practice, nor find sport 720
In torch-light treachery or the luring owl.

But how hunts Guido? Why, the fraudful trap—
Late spurned to ruin by the indignant feet
Of fellows in the chase who loved fair play—
Here he picks up its fragments to the least, 725
Lades him and hies to the old lurking-place

---

9. Plans.
1. Caponsacchi's church at Arezzo.
2. Pompilia drew a sword and brandished it when Guido caught the pair at
Castelnuovo. Cf. Caponsacchi's account,
VI.1518–23.
3. 1 Corinthians 3:15.
4. Isaiah 38:15.

Where haply he may patch again, refit
The mischief, file its blunted teeth anew,
Make sure, next time, first snap shall break the bone.
Craft, greed and violence complot revenge: 730
Craft, for its quota, schemes to bring about
And seize occasion and be safe withal:
Greed craves its act may work both far and near,
Crush the tree, branch and trunk and root beside,
Whichever twig or leaf arrests a streak   735
Of possible sunshine else would coin itself,
And drop down one more gold piece in the path:
Violence stipulates "Advantage proved
And safety sure, be pain the overplus!
Murder with jagged knife![5] Cut but tear too!   740
Foiled oft, starved long, glut malice for amends!"
And what, craft's scheme? scheme sorrowful and strange
As though the elements, whom mercy checked,
Had mustered hate for one eruption more,
One final deluge to surprise the Ark   745
Cradled and sleeping on its mountain-top:
Their outbreak-signal—what but the dove's coo,
Back with olive in her bill for news
Sorrow was over?[6] 'T is an infant's birth,
Guido's first born, his son and heir, that gives   750
The occasion:[7] other men cut free their souls
From care in such a case, fly up in thanks
To God, reach, recognize His love for once:
Guido cries "Soul, at last the mire is thine!
Lie there in likeness of a money-bag   755
My babe's birth so pins down past moving now,
That I dare cut adrift the lives I late
Scrupled to touch lest thou escape with them!
These parents and their child my wife,—touch one,
Lose all! Their rights determined on[8] a head   760
I could but hate, not harm, since from each hair
Dangled a hope for me: now—chance and change!
No right was in their child but passes plain
To that child's child and through such child to me.
I am a father now,—come what, come will,   765
I represent my child; he comes between—
Cuts sudden off the sunshine of this life
From those three: why, the gold is in his curls!
Not with old Pietro's, Violante's head,
Not his grey horror, her more hideous black—   770

5. Guido's dagger had "little hook-teeth on the edge" (II.147).
6. Genesis 8:6–11.
7. The pope accepts the argument of Pompilia's lawyer Bottini that Guido had a strong motive to withhold revenge until Pompilia was delivered of a baby: if Guido had remained childless, the estate (to which Pietro had only the "usufruct," or temporary use) would revert to the kinsmen of the Comparini.
8. Settled upon.

Go these, devoted to the knife!"
                    'T is done:
Wherefore should mind misgive, heart hesitate?
He calls to counsel, fashions certain four
Colourless natures counted clean till now,
—Rustic simplicity, uncorrupted youth,   775
Ignorant virtue! Here's the gold o' the prime[9]
When Saturn ruled, shall shock our leaden day—
The clown abash the courtier! Mark it, bards!
The courtier tries his hand on clownship here,
Speaks a word, names a crime, appoints a price,—   780
Just breathes on what, suffused with all himself,
Is red-hot henceforth past distinction now
I' the common glow of hell. And thus they break
And blaze on us at Rome, Christ's birthnight-eve![1]
Oh angels that sang erst "On the earth, peace!   785
To man, good will!"—such peace finds earth to-day!
After the seventeen hundred years, so man
Wills good to man, so Guido makes complete
His murder! what is it I said?—cuts loose
Three lives that hitherto he suffered cling,   790
Simply because each served to nail secure,
By a corner of the money-bag, his soul,—
Therefore, lives sacred till the babe's first breath
O'erweights them in the balance,—off they fly!

So is the murder managed, sin conceived   795
To the full: and why not crowned with triumph too?
Why must the sin, conceived thus, bring forth death?
I note how, within hair's-breadth of escape,
Impunity and the thing supposed success,
Guido is found when the check comes, the change,   800
The monitory touch o' the tether—felt
By few, not marked by many, named by none
At the moment, only recognized aright
I' the fulness of the days, for God's, lest sin
Exceed the service, leap the line: such check—   805
A secret which this life finds hard to keep,
And, often guessed, is never quite revealed—
Needs must trip Guido on a stumbling-block
Too vulgar, too absurdly plain i' the path!
Study this single oversight of care,   810
This hebetude[2] that marred sagacity,
Forgetfulness of all the man best knew,—
How any stranger having need to fly,

9. The mythical Golden Age, when Saturn (Cronus) ruled the world. This age of rural simplicity and happiness was followed by the Silver, Bronze, Heroic, and Iron Ages, i.e., by almost unrelieved decline.

1. Gaetano was born December 18; Guido arrived in Rome December 24, but waited until January 2 to commit the crime. (See V.1561–1652 for Guido's version.)
2. Stupidity.

Needs but to ask and have the means of flight.
Why, the first urchin tells you, to leave Rome,   815
Get horses, you must show the warrant, just
The banal scrap, clerk's scribble, a fair word buys,
Or foul one, if a ducat[3] sweeten word,—
And straight authority will back demand,
Give you the pick o' the post-house![4]—how should he,   820
Then, resident at Rome for thirty years,
Guido, instruct a stranger! And himself
Forgets just this poor paper scrap, wherewith
Armed, every door he knocks at opens wide
To save him: horsed and manned, with such advance   825
O' the hunt behind, why, 't were the easy task
Of hours told on the fingers of one hand,
To reach the Tuscan frontier, laugh at-home,
Light-hearted with his fellows of the place,—
Prepared by that strange shameful judgment, that   830
Satire upon a sentence just pronounced
By the Rota[5] and confirmed by the Granduke,—
Ready in a circle to receive their peer,
Appreciate his good story how, when Rome,
The Pope-King and the populace of priests   835
Made common cause with their confederate
The other priestling who seduced his wife,
He, all unaided, wiped out the affront
With decent bloodshed and could face his friends,
Frolic it in the world's eye. Ay, such tale   840
Missed such applause, and by such oversight!
So, tired and footsore, those blood-flustered five
Went reeling on the road through dark and cold,
The few permissible miles, to sink at length,
Wallow and sleep in the first wayside straw,   845
As the other herd quenched, i' the wash o' the wave,
—Each swine, the devil inside him: so slept they,
And so were caught and caged—all through one trip,
One touch of fool in Guido the astute!
He curses the omission, I surmise,   850
More than the murder. Why, thou fool and blind,
It is the mercy-stroke that stops thy fate,
Hamstrings and holds thee to thy hurt,—but how?
On the edge o' the precipice! One minute more,
Thou hadst gone farther and fared worse, my son,   855
Fathoms down on the flint and fire beneath!
Thy comrades each and all were of one mind,

---

3. Gold coin.
4. I.e., the fastest horses, which Guido could not use for escape to Tuscany because of his failure to obtain a pass through the city gates.
5. The Criminal Rota of Florence, the court of last appeal, which had con-firmed the sentence of the Commissary of Arezzo in the case of Pompilia's flight. Pompilia's "trial" at Arezzo, resulting in her being sentenced to life imprisonment, was nugatory since she was then under Roman jurisdiction.

Thy murder done, to straightway murder thee
In turn, because of promised pay withheld.
So, to the last, greed found itself at odds   860
With craft in thee, and, proving conqueror,
Had sent thee, the same night that crowned thy hope,
Thither where, this same day, I see thee not,
Nor, through God's mercy, need, to-morrow, see.

Such I find Guido, midmost blotch of black   865
Discernible in this group of clustered crimes
Huddling together in the cave they call
Their palace outraged day thus penetrates.
Around him ranged, now close and now remote,
Prominent or obscure to meet the needs   870
O' the mage and master, I detect each shape
Subsidiary i' the scene nor loathed the less,
All alike coloured, all descried akin
By one and the same pitchy furnace stirred
At the centre: see, they lick the master's hand,—   875
This fox-faced horrible priest, this brother-brute
The Abate,—why, mere wolfishness looks well,
Guido stands honest in the red o' the flame,
Beside this yellow that would pass for white,
Twice Guido, all craft but no violence,   880
This copier of the mien and gait and garb
Of Peter and Paul, that he may go disguised,
Rob halt and lame, sick folk i' the temple-porch![6]
Armed with religion, fortified by law,
A man of peace, who trims the midnight lamp   885
And turns the classic page—and all for craft,
All to work harm with, yet incur no scratch!
While Guido brings the struggle to a close,
Paul steps back the due distance, clear o' the trap
He builds and baits.[7] Guido I catch and judge;   890
Paul is past reach in this world and my time:
That is a case reserved. Pass to the next,
The boy of the brood, the young Girolamo[8]
Priest, Canon, and what more? nor wolf nor fox,
But hybrid, neither craft nor violence   895
Wholly, part violence part craft: such cross
Tempts speculation—will both blend one day,
And prove hell's better product? Or subside
And let the simple quality emerge,
Go on with Satan's service the old way?   900
Meanwhile, what promise,—what performance too!
For there's a new distinctive touch, I see,
Lust—lacking in the two—hell's own blue tint
That gives a character and marks the man

6. Acts 3:1–11.
7. See note to V.1400.
8. Pompilia had charged Girolamo with making "dishonorable advances" to her.

More than a match for yellow and red. Once more,   905
A case reserved: why should I doubt? Then comes
The gaunt grey nightmare in the furthest smoke,
The hag that gave these three abortions birth,
Unmotherly mother and unwomanly
Woman, that near turns motherhood to shame,   910
Womanliness to loathing: no one word,
No gesture to curb cruelty a whit
More than the she-pard thwarts her playsome whelps
Trying their milk-teeth on the soft o' the throat
O' the first fawn, flung, with those beseeching eyes,   915
Flat in the covert! How should she but couch,
Lick the dry lips, unsheath the blunted claw,
Catch 'twixt her placid eyewinks at what chance
Old bloody half-forgotten dream may flit,
Born when herself was novice to the taste,   920
The while she lets youth take its pleasure. Last,
These God-abandoned wretched lumps of life,
These four companions,—country-folk this time,
Not tainted by the unwholesome civic breath,
Much less the course o' the Court! Mere striplings too,   925
Fit to do human nature justice still!
Surely when impudence in Guido's shape
Shall propose crime and proffer money's-worth
To these stout tall rough bright-eyed black-haired boys,
The blood shall bound in answer to each cheek   930
Before the indignant outcry break from lip!
Are these i' the mood to murder, hardly loosed
From healthy autumn-finish of ploughed glebe,[9]
Grapes in the barrel, work at happy end,
And winter near with rest and Christmas play?   935
How greet they Guido with his final task—
(As if he but proposed "One vineyard more
To dig, ere frost come, then relax indeed!")
"Anywhere, anyhow and anywhy,
Murder me some three people, old and young,   940
Ye never heard the names of,—and be paid
So much!" And the whole four accede at once.
Demur? Do cattle bidden march or halt?
Is it some lingering habit, old fond faith
I' the lord o' the land, instructs them,—birthright badge   945
Of feudal tenure claims its slaves again?
Not so at all, thou noble human heart!
All is done purely for the pay,—which, earned,
And not forthcoming at the instant, makes
Religion heresy, and the lord o' the land   950
Fit subject for a murder in his turn.
The patron with cut throat and rifled purse,

9. Field.

Deposited i' the roadside-ditch, his due,
Nought hinders each good fellow trudging home,
The heavier by a piece or two in poke, 955
And so with new zest to the common life,
Mattock and spade, plough-tail and waggon-shaft,
Till some such other piece of luck betide,
Who knows? Since this is a mere start in life,
And none of them exceeds the twentieth year. 960
Nay, more i' the background yet? Unnoticed forms
Claim to be classed, subordinately vile?
Complacent lookers-on that laugh,—perchance
Shake head as their friend's horse-play grows too rough
With the mere child he manages amiss— 965
But would not interfere and make bad worse
For twice the fractious tears and prayers: thou know'st
Civility better, Marzi-Medici,[1]
Governor for thy kinsman the Granduke!
Fit representative of law, man's lamp 970
I' the magistrate's grasp full-flare, no rushlight-end
Sputtering 'twixt thumb and finger of the priest!
Whose answer to the couple's cry for help
Is a threat,—whose remedy of Pompilia's wrong,
A shrug o' the shoulder, and facetious word 975
Or wink, traditional with Tuscan wits,
To Guido in the doorway. Laud to law!
The wife is pushed back to the husband, he
Who knows how these home-squabblings persecute
People who have the public good to mind, 980
And work best with a silence in the court!

Ah, but I save my word at least for thee,
Archbishop,[2] who art under, i' the Church,
As I am under God,—thou, chosen by both
To do the shepherd's office, feed the sheep— 985
How of this lamb that panted at thy foot
while the wolf pressed on her within crook's[3] reach?
Wast thou the hireling that did turn and flee?[4]
With thee at least anon the little word!

Such denizens o' the cave now cluster round 990
And heat the furnace sevenfold: time indeed
A bolt from heaven should cleave roof and clear place,
Transfix and show the world, suspiring[5] flame,
The main offender, scar and brand the rest
Hurrying, each miscreant to his hole: then flood 995
And purify the scene with outside day—

1. Governor of Arezzo, no kin to the Medici, as Innocent supposes.
2. Bishop of Arezzo.
3. The crook or crozier symbolizes a bishop's office as spiritual shepherd.
4. John 10:12–13.
5. Breathing.

Which yet, in the absolutest drench of dark,
Ne'er wants a witness, some stray beauty-beam
To the despair of hell.

              First of the first,
Such I pronounce Pompilia, then as now   1000
Perfect in whiteness: stoop thou down, my child,
Give one good moment to the poor old Pope
Heart-sick at having all his world to blame—
Let me look at thee in the flesh as erst,
Let me enjoy the old clean linen garb,   1005
Not the new splendid vesture! Armed and crowned,
Would Michael, yonder,[6] be, nor crowned nor armed,
The less pre-eminent angel? Everywhere
I see in the world the intellect of man,
That sword, the energy his subtle spear,   1010
The knowledge which defends him like a shield—
Everywhere; but they make not up, I think,
The marvel of a soul like thine, earth's flower
She holds up to the softened gaze of God!
It was not given Pompilia to know much,   1015
Speak much, to write a book, to move mankind,
Be memorized by who records my time.
Yet if in purity and patience, if
In faith held fast despite the plucking fiend,
Safe like the signet stone with the new name   1020
That saints are known by,—if in right returned
For wrong, most pardon for worst injury,
If there be any virtue, any praise,[7]—
Then will this woman-child have proved—who knows?—
Just the one prize vouchsafed unworthy me,   1025
Seven years a gardener of the untoward ground,
I till,—this earth, my sweat and blood manure
All the long day that barrenly grows dusk:
At least one blossom makes me proud at eve
Born 'mid the briers of my enclosure! Still   1030
(Oh, here as elsewhere, nothingness of man!)
Those be the plants, imbedded yonder South
To mellow in the morning, those made fat
By the master's eye, that yield such timid leaf,
Uncertain bud, as product of his pains!   1035
While—see how this mere chance-sown cleft-nursed seed
That sprang up by the wayside 'neath the foot
Of the enemy, this breaks all into blaze,
Spreads itself, one wide glory of desire
To incorporate the whole great sun it loves   1040
From the inch-height whence it looks and longs! My flower,
My rose, I gather for the breast of God,

---

6. St. Michael's statue atop the Mauso-   7. Philippians 4:8.
leum of Hadrian.

This I praise most in thee, where all I praise,
That having been obedient to the end
According to the light allotted, law   1045
Prescribed thy life, still tried, still standing test,—
Dutiful to the foolish parents first,
Submissive next to the bad husband,—nay,
Tolerant of those meaner miserable
That did his hests, eked out the dole of pain,—   1050
Thou, patient thus, couldst rise from law to law,
The old to the new, promoted at one cry
O' the trump of God to the new service, not
To longer bear, but henceforth fight, be found
Sublime in new impatience with the foe!   1055
Endure man and obey God: plant firm foot
On neck of man, tread man into the hell
Meet for him, and obey God all the more!
Oh child that didst despise thy life so much
When it seemed only thine to keep or lose,   1060
How the fine ear felt fall the first low word
"Value life, and preserve life for My sake!"
Thou didst . . . how shall I say? . . . receive so long
The standing ordinance of God on earth,
What wonder if the novel claim had clashed   1065
With old requirement, seemed to supersede
Too much the customary law? But, brave,
Thou at first prompting of what I call God,
And fools call Nature, didst hear, comprehend,
Accept the obligation laid on thee,   1070
Mother elect, to save the unborn child,
As brute and bird do, reptile and the fly,
Ay and, I nothing doubt, even tree, shrub, plant
And flower o' the field, all in a common pact
To worthily defend the trust of trusts,   1075
Life from the Ever Living:—didst resist—
Anticipate the office that is mine—
And with his own sword stay the upraised arm,
The endeavour of the wicked, and defend
Him[8] who,—again in my default,—was there   1080
For visible providence: one less true than thou
To touch, i' the past, less practised in the right,
Approved less far in all docility
To all instruction,—how had such an one
Made scruple "Is this motion a decree?"   1085
It was authentic to the experienced ear
O' the good and faithful servant. Go past me
And get thy praise,—and be not far to seek
Presently when I follow if I may!

And surely not so very much apart   1090

8. Caponsacchi.

Need I place thee, my warrior-priest,—in whom
What if I gain the other rose, the gold,[9]
We grave to imitate God's miracle,
Greet monarchs with, good rose in its degree?
Irregular noble 'scapegrace—son the same!   1095
Faulty—and peradventure ours the fault
Who still misteach, mislead, throw hook and line,
Thinking to land leviathan[1] forsooth,
Tame the scaled neck, play with him as a bird,
And bind him for our maidens! Better bear   1100
The King of Pride go wantoning awhile,
Unplagued by cord in nose and thorn in jaw,
Through deep to deep, followed by all that shine,
Churning the blackness hoary: He who made
The comely terror, He shall make the sword   1105
To match that piece of netherstone his heart,
Ay, nor miss praise thereby; who else shut fire
I' the stone, to leap from mouth at sword's first stroke,
In lamps of love and faith, the chivalry
That dares the right and disregards alike   1110
The yea and nay o' the world? Self-sacrifice,—
What if an idol took it? Ask the Church
Why she was wont to turn each Venus here,—
Poor Rome perversely lingered round, despite
Instruction, for the sake of purblind love,—   1115
Into Madonna's shape,[2] and waste no whit
Of aught so rare on earth as gratitude!
All this sweet savour was not ours but thine,
Nard[3] of the rock, a natural wealth we name
Incense, and treasure up as food for saints,   1120
When flung to us—whose function was to give
Not find the costly perfume. Do I smile?
Nay, Caponsacchi, much I find amiss,
Blameworthy, punishable in this freak
Of thine, this youth prolonged, though age was ripe,   1125
This masquerade in sober day, with change
Of motley too,—now hypocrite's disguise,
Now fool's costume:[4] which lie was least like truth,
Which the ungainlier, more discordant garb
With that symmetric soul inside my son,   1130
The churchman's or the worldling's,—let him judge,
Our adversary who enjoys the task!
I rather chronicle the healthy rage,—

9. The pope's gift of a golden rose, annually given a king or notable person to whom the Holy See was obliged.
1. Sea monster. Lines 1096–1107 loosely paraphrase several verses from Job 41. Cf. V.1497–98.
2. "After a period of merciless destruction, some classical monuments were spared by the Popes; temples were converted into churches, and statues of pagan gods were occasionally made to do duty as Christian images" (Alexander Pope, note to *The Dunciad*, III.101).
3. Or spikenard, aromatic herb.
4. I.e., the garb of a layman, worn to help Pompilia escape from Arezzo.

When the first moan broke from the martyr-maid
At that uncaging of the beasts,—made bare   1135
My athlete on the instant, gave such good
Great undisguised leap over post and pale
Right into the mid-cirque, free fighting-place.
There may have been rash stripping—every rag
Went to the winds,—infringement manifold   1140
Of law's prescribed pudicity,[5] I fear,
In this impulsive and prompt self-display!
Ever such tax comes of the foolish youth;
Men mulct[6] the wiser manhood, and suspect
No veritable star swims out of cloud.   1145
Bear thou such imputation, undergo
The penalty I nowise dare relax,—
Conventional chastisement and rebuke.
But for the outcome, the brave starry birth
Conciliating earth with all that cloud,   1150
Thank heaven as I do! Ay, such championship
Of God at first blush, such prompt cheery thud
Of glove on ground that answers ringingly
The challenge of the false knight,—watch we long
And wait we vainly for its gallant like   1155
From those appointed to the service, sworn
His body-guard with pay and privilege—
White-cinct,[7] because in white walks sanctity,
Red-socked, how else proclaim fine scorn of flesh,
Unchariness of blood[8] when blood faith begs!   1160
Where are the men-at-arms with cross on coat?
Aloof, bewraying their attire: whilst thou
In mask and motley, pledged to dance not fight,[9]
Sprang'st forth the hero! In thought, word and deed,
How throughout all thy warfare thou wast pure,   1165
I find it easy to believe: and if
At any fateful moment of the strange
Adventure, the strong passion of that strait,
Fear and surprise, may have revealed too much,—
As when a thundrous midnight, with black air   1170
That burns, rain-drops that blister, breaks a spell,
Draws out the excessive virtue of some sheathed
Shut unsuspected flower that hoards and hides
Immensity of sweetness,—so, perchance,
Might the surprise and fear release too much   1175
The perfect beauty of the body and soul
Thou savedst in thy passion for God's sake,
He who is Pity. Was the trial sore?
Temptation sharp? Thank God a second time!

5. Modesty prescribed by law.
6. Punish, as by a fine.
7. With a belt of white. The pope describes a cardinal's garb.
8. I.e., willingness to shed blood.
9. Caponsacchi's superior had urged him to pay court to the ladies of Arezzo. (See VI.264–388.)

Why comes temptation but for man to meet   1180
And master and make crouch beneath his foot,
And so be pedestaled in triumph? Pray
"Lead us into no such temptations, Lord!"
Yea, but, O Thou whose servants are the bold,
Lead such temptations by the head and hair,   1185
Reluctant dragons,[1] up to who dares fight,
That so he may do battle and have praise!
Do I not see the praise?—that while thy mates
Bound to deserve i' the matter, prove at need
Unprofitable through the very pains   1190
We gave to train them well and start them fair,—
Are found too stiff, with standing ranked and ranged,
For onset in good, earnest, too obtuse
Of ear, through iteration of command,
For catching quick the sense of the real cry,—   1195
Thou, whose sword-hand was used to strike the lute,
Whose sentry-station graced some wanton's gate,
Thou didst push forward and show mettle, shame
The laggards, and retrieve the day. Well done!
Be glad thou hast let light into the world   1200
Through that irregular breach o' the boundary,—see
The same upon thy path and march assured,
Learning anew the use of soldiership,
Self-abnegation, freedom from all fear,
Loyalty to the life's end! Ruminate,   1205
Deserve the initiatory spasm,[2]—once more
Work, be unhappy but bear life, my son!

And troop you, somewhere 'twixt the best and worst,
Where crowd the indifferent product, all too poor
Makeshift, starved samples of humanity!   1210
Father and mother, huddle there and hide!
A gracious eye may find you! Foul and fair,
Sadly mixed natures: self-indulgent,—yet
Self-sacrificing too: how the love soars,
How the craft, avarice, vanity and spite   1215
Sink again! So they keep the middle course,
Slide into silly crime at unaware,
Slip back upon the stupid virtue, stay
Nowhere enough for being classed, I hope
And fear. Accept the swift and rueful death,   1220
Taught, somewhat sternlier than is wont, what waits
The ambiguous creature,—how the one black tuft
Steadies the aim of the arrow just as well
As the wide faultless white on the bird's breast!
Nay, you were punished in the very part   1225

---

1. Echo of Horace's phrase *reluctantes*
dracones in *Odes*, IV.iv.11. For Horace,
however, *reluctantes* meant "struggling,

resisting," not "battle-shy."
2. I.e., "rebirth" into a life of selfless
service.

That looked most pure of speck,—'t was honest love
Betrayed you,—did love seem most worthy pains,
Challenge such purging, since ordained survive
When all the rest of you was done with? Go!
Never again elude the choice of tints! 1230
White shall not neutralize the black, nor good
Compensate bad in man, absolve him so:
Life's business being just the terrible choice.

So do I see, pronounce on all and some
Grouped for my judgment now,—profess no doubt 1235
While I pronounce: dark, difficult enough
The human sphere, yet eyes grow sharp by use,
I find the truth, dispart the shine from shade,
As a mere man may, with no special touch
O' the lynx-gift[3] in each ordinary orb: 1240
Nay, if the popular notion class me right,
One of well-nigh decayed intelligence,—
What of that? Through hard labour and good will,
And habitude that gives a blind man sight
At the practised finger-ends of him, I do 1245
Discern, and dare decree in consequence,
Whatever prove the peril of mistake.
Whence, then, this quite new quick cold thrill,—cloudlike,
This keen dread creeping from a quarter scarce
Suspected in the skies I nightly scan? 1250
What slacks the tense nerve, saps the wound-up spring
Of the act that should and shall be, sends the mount
And mass o' the whole man's-strength,—conglobed so late—
Shudderingly into dust, a moment's work?
While I stand firm, go fearless, in this world, 1255
For this life recognize and arbitrate,
Touch and let stay, or else remove a thing,
Judge "This is right, this object out of place,"
Candle in hand that helps me and to spare,—
What if a voice deride me, "Perk and pry![4] 1260
Brighten each nook with thine intelligence!
Play the good householder, ply man and maid
With tasks prolonged into the midnight, test
Their work and nowise stint of the due wage
Each worthy worker: but with gyves[5] and whip 1265
Pay thou misprision of a single point
Plain to thy happy self who lift'st the light,
Lament'st the darkling,—bold to all beneath!
What if thyself adventure, now the place
Is purged so well? Leave pavement and mount roof, 1270
Look round thee for the light of the upper sky,

---

3. Piercing eyesight possessed by the fabulous lynx, half dog and half panther.
4. Perk: carry oneself smartly; pry: inquire into (*OED*).
5. Shackles.

The fire which lit thy fire which finds default
In Guido Franceschini to his cost!
What if, above in the domain of light,
Thou miss the accustomed signs, remark eclipse?   1275
Shalt thou still gaze on ground nor lift a lid,—
Steady in thy superb prerogative,
Thy inch of inkling,—nor once face the doubt
I' the sphere above thee, darkness to be felt?"

Yet my poor spark had for its source, the sun;[6]   1280
Thither I sent the great looks which compel
Light from its fount: all that I do and am
Comes from the truth, or seen or else surmised,
Remembered or divined, as mere man may:
I know just so, nor otherwise. As I know,   1285
I speak,—what should I know, then, and how speak
Were there a wild mistake of eye or brain
As to recorded governance above?
If my own breath, only, blew coal alight
I styled celestial and the morning-star?   1290
I, who in this world act resolvedly,
Dispose of men, their bodies and their souls,
As they acknowledge or gainsay the light
I show them,—shall I too lack courage?—leave
I, too, the post of me, like those I blame?   1295
Refuse, with kindred inconsistency,
To grapple danger whereby souls grow strong?
I am near the end; but still not at the end;
All to the very end is trial in life:
At this stage is the trial of my soul   1300
Danger to face, or danger to refuse?
Shall I dare try the doubt now, or not dare?

O Thou,—as represented here to me
In such conception as my soul allows,—
Under Thy measureless, my atom width!—   1305
Man's mind, what is but a convex glass
Wherein are gathered all the scattered points
Picked out of the immensity of sky,
To re-unite there, be our heaven for earth,
Our known unknown, our God revealed to man?   1310
Existent somewhere, somehow, as a whole;
Here, as a whole proportioned to our sense,—
There, (which is nowhere, speech must babble thus!)
In the absolute immensity, the whole
Appreciable solely by Thyself,—   1315
Here, by the little mind of man, reduced
To littleness that suits his faculty,

6. Here Browning gives his own interpretation of Christianity, emphasizing the Incarnation.

In the degree appreciable too;
Between Thee and ourselves—nay even, again,
Below us, to the extreme of the minute, 1320
Appreciable by how many and what diverse
Modes of the life Thou madest be! (why live
Except for love,—how love unless they know?)
Each of them, only filling to the edge,
Insect or angel, his just length and breadth, 1325
Due facet of reflection,—full, no less,
Angel or insect, as Thou framedst things.
I it is who have been appointed here
To represent Thee, in my turn, on earth,
Just as, if new philosophy[7] know aught, 1330
This one earth, out of all the multitude
Of peopled worlds, as stars are now supposed,—
Was chosen, and no sun-star of the swarm,
For stage and scene of Thy transcendent act[8]
Beside which even the creation fades 1335
Into a puny exercise of power.
Choice of the world, choice of the thing I am,
Both emanate alike from Thy dread play
Of operation outside this our sphere
Where things are classed and counted small or great,— 1340
Incomprehensibly the choice is Thine!
I therefore bow my head and take Thy place.
There is, beside the works, a tale of Thee
In the world's mouth, which I find credible:
I love it with my heart: unsatisfied, 1345
I try it with my reason, nor discept
From any point I probe and pronounce sound.
Mind is not matter nor from matter, but
Above,—leave matter then, proceed with mind!
Man's be the mind recognized at the height,— 1350
Leave the inferior minds and look at man!
Is he the strong, intelligent and good
Up to his own conceivable height? Nowise.
Enough o' the low,—soar the conceivable height,
Find cause to match the effect in evidence, 1355
The work i' the world, not man's but God's; leave man!
Conjecture of the worker by the work:
Is there strength there?—enough: intelligence?
Ample: but goodness in a like degree?
Not to the human eye in the present state, 1360
An isoscele[9] deficient in the base.
What lacks, then, of perfection fit for God
But just the instance which this tale supplies

7. I.e., science, especially the new as-
tronomy of Copernicus.
8. The Incarnation, ultimate proof of
God's love.

9. Here, triangle with two equal sides,
representing strength and intelligence;
the base is love.

Of love without a limit? So is strength,
So is intelligence; let love be so,   1365
Unlimited in its self-sacrifice,
Then is the tale true and God shows complete
Beyond the tale, I reach into the dark,
Feel what I cannot see, and still faith stands:
I can believe this dread machinery   1370
Of sin and sorrow, would confound me else,
Devised,—all pain, at most expenditure
Of pain by Who devised pain,—to evolve,
By new machinery in counterpart,
The moral qualities of man—how else?—   1375
To make him love in turn and be beloved,
Creative and self-sacrificing too,
And thus eventually God-like, (ay,
"I have said ye are Gods,"[1]—shall it be said for nought?)
Enable man to wring, from out all pain,   1380
All pleasure for a common heritage
To all eternity: this may be surmised,
The other is revealed,—whether a fact,
Absolute, abstract, independent truth,
Historic, not reduced to suit man's mind,—   1385
Or only truth reverberate, changed, made pass
A spectrum into mind, the narrow eye,—
The same and not the same, else unconceived—
Though quite conceivable to the next grade
Above it in intelligence,—as truth   1390
Easy to man were blindness to the beast
By parity of procedure,—the same truth
In a new form, but changed in either case:
What matter so intelligence be filled?
To a child, the sea is angry, for it roars: 1395
Frost bites, else why the tooth-like fret[2] on face?
Man makes acoustics deal with the sea's wrath,
Explains the choppy[3] cheek by chymic law,—
To man and child remains the same effect
On drum of ear and root of nose, change cause   1400
Never so thoroughly: so my heart be struck,
What care I,—by God's gloved hand or the bare?[4]
Nor do I much perplex me with aught hard,
Dubious in the transmitting of the tale,—
No, nor with certain riddles set to solve.   1405
This life is training and a passage; pass,—
Still, we march over some flat obstacle
We made give way before us; solid truth
In front of it, what motion for the world?[5]

---

1. Psalms 82:6; John 10:34.
2. Chapped spot.
3. Chapped. Chymic: related to the digestive process.
4. I.e., by myths or by facts.

5. I.e., absolute ("solid") truth, if presented to man at once, would be an obstacle to his moral growth, since there would be no need for him to search onward.

The moral sense grows but by exercise.   1410
'T is even as man grew probatively
Initiated in Godship, set to make
A fairer moral world than this he finds,
Guess now what shall be known hereafter. Deal
Thus with the present problem: as we see,   1415
A faultless creature is destroyed, and sin
Has had its way i' the world where God should rule.
Ay, but for this irrelevant circumstance
Of inquisition after blood, we see
Pompilia lost and Guido saved: how long?   1420
For his whole life: how much is that whole life?
We are not babes, but know the minute's worth,
And feel that life is large and the world small,
So, wait till life have passed from out the world.
Neither does this astonish at the end,   1425
That whereas I can so receive and trust,
Other men, made with hearts and souls the same,
Reject and disbelieve,—subordinate
The future to the present,—sin, nor fear.
This I refer still to the foremost fact,   1430
Life is probation and the earth no goal
But starting-point of man: compel him strive,
Which means, in man, as good as reach the goal,—
Why institute that race, his life, at all?
But this does overwhelm me with surprise,   1435
Touch me to terror,—not that faith, the pearl,
Should be let lie by fishers wanting food,—
Nor, seen and handled by a certain few
Critical and contemptuous, straight consigned
To shore and shingle for the pebble it proves,—   1440
But that, when haply found and known and named
By the residue made rich for evermore,
These,—that these favoured ones, should in a trice
Turn, and with double zest go dredge for whelks,[6]
Mud-worms that make the savoury soup! Enough   1445
O' the disbelievers, see the faithful few!
How do the Christians here deport them, keep
Their robes of white unspotted by the world?
What is this Aretine Archbishop, this
Man under me as I am under God,   1450
This champion of the faith, I armed and decked,
Pushed forward, put upon a pinnacle,
To show the enemy his victor,—see!
What's the best fighting when the couple close?
Pompilia cries, "Protect me from the wolf!"   1455
He—"No, thy Guido is rough, heady, strong,
Dangerous to disquiet: let him bide!
He needs some bone to mumble, help amuse

6. Marine snails.

The darkness of his den with: so, the fawn
Which limps up bleeding to my foot and lies,   1460
—Come to me, daughter!—thus I throw him back!"
Have we misjudged here, over-armed our knight,
Given gold and silk where plain hard steel serves best,
Enfeebled whom we sought to fortify,
Made an archbishop and undone a saint?   1465
Well, then, descend these heights, this pride of life,
Sit in the ashes with a barefoot monk
Who long ago stamped out the worldly sparks,
By fasting, watching, stone cell and wire scourge,
—No such indulgence as unknits the strength—   1470
These breed the tight nerve and tough cuticle,[7]
And the world's praise or blame runs rillet-wise
Off the broad back and brawny breast, we know!
He meets the first cold sprinkle of the world,
And shudders to the marrow. "Save this child?   1475
Oh, my superiors, oh, the Archbishop's self!
Who was it dared lay hand upon the ark
His betters saw fall nor put finger forth?[8]
Great ones could help yet help not: why should small?
I break my promise: let her break her heart!"   1480
These are the Christians not the worldlings, not
The sceptics, who thus battle for the faith!
If foolish virgins disobey and sleep,[9]
What wonder? But, this time, the wise that watch,
Sell lamps and buy lutes, exchange oil for wine,   1485
The mystic Spouse betrays the Bridegroom here.[1]
To our last resource, then! Since all flesh is weak,
Bind weaknesses together, we get strength:
The individual weighed, found wanting, try
Some institution, honest artifice   1490
Whereby the units grow compact and firm!
Each props the other, and so stand is made
By our embodied cowards that grow brave.
The Monastery called of Convertites,[2]
Meant to help women because these helped Christ,—   1495
A thing existent only while it acts,
Does as designed, else a nonentity,—
For what is an idea unrealized?—
Pompilia is consigned to these for help.

7. Skin.
8. It was the hapless Uzzah who sacrilegiously touched the ark of God when it tottered. God killed him for his error (2 Samuel 6:6–7).
9. Their error, rather, was failure to get oil for their lamps before sleeping. They were thus unready for the arrival of the Bridegroom (Matthew 25:1–13).
1. The church (Spouse) betrays Christ (Bridegroom). The symbolism is that of St. Paul (Ephesians 5:23–24).
2. The convent of Santa Maria Maddalena della Convertite, founded to save immoral women. After Pompilia's death, the Convertites, who had a legal right to claim the property of loose women, attempted to defame her in order to acquire her estate. But the court, declaring her innocent of adultery, rejected the convent's suit.

They do help: they are prompt to testify   1500
To her pure life and saintly dying days.
She dies, and lo, who seemed so poor, proves rich.
What does the body[3] that lives through helpfulness
To women for Christ's sake? The kiss turns bite,
The dove's note changes to the crow's cry: judge!   1505
"Seeing that this our Convent claims of right
What goods belong to those we succour, be
The same proved women of dishonest life,—
And seeing that this Trial made appear
Pompilia was in such predicament,—   1510
The Convent hereupon pretends to said
Succession of Pompilia, issues writ,
And takes possession by the Fisc's[4] advice."
Such is their attestation to the cause
Of Christ, who had one saint at least, they hoped: 1515
But, is a title-deed to filch, a corpse
To slander, and an infant-heir to cheat?
Christ must give up his gains then! They unsay
All the fine speeches,—who was saint is whore.
Why, scripture yields no parallel for this!   1520
The soldiers only threw dice for Christ's coat;[5]
We want another legend of the Twelve
Disputing if it was Christ's coat at all,
Claiming as prize the woof of price[6]—for why?
The Master was a thief, purloined the same,   1525
Or paid for it out of the common bag!
Can it be this is end and outcome, all
I take with me to show as stewardship's fruit,
The best yield of the latest time, this year
The seventeen-hundredth since God died for man?   1530
Is such effect proportionate to cause?
And still the terror keeps on the increase
When I perceive . . . how can I blink the fact?
That the fault, the obduracy to good,
Lies not with the impracticable stuff   1535
Whence man is made, his very nature's fault,
As if it were of ice the moon may gild
Not melt, or stone 't was meant the sun should warm
Not make bear flowers,—nor ice nor stone to blame:
But it can melt, that ice, can bloom, that stone,   1540
Impassible to rule of day and night!
This terrifies me, thus compelled perceive,
Whatever love and faith we looked should spring
At advent of the authoritative star,

3. The nunnery.
4. The Fisc is Bottini, prosecutor at Guido's trial. His associate Gambi made application to the court on behalf of the
Convertites. Bottini's cynical "defense"
of Pompilia (Book IX) amounts to an
attack upon her innocence.
5. Matthew 27:35.
6. Costly fabric.

Which yet lie sluggish, curdled at the source,— 1545
These have leapt forth profusely in old time,
These still respond with promptitude to-day,
At challenge of—what unacknowledged powers
O' the air, what uncommissioned meteors, warmth
By law, and light by rule should supersede? 1550
For see this priest, this Caponsacchi, stung
At the first summons,—"Help for honour's sake,
Play the man, pity the oppressed!"—no pause,
How does he lay about him in the midst,
Strike any foe, right wrong at any risk, 1555
All blindness, bravery and obedience!—blind?
Ay, as a man would be inside the sun,
Delirious with the plenitude of light
Should interfuse him to the finger-ends—
Let him rush straight, and how shall he go wrong? 1560
Where are the Christians in their panoply?
The loins we girt about with truth, the breasts
Righteousness plated round, the shield of faith,
The helmet of salvation, and that sword
O' the Spirit, even the word of God,[7]—where these? 1565
Slunk into corners! Oh, I hear at once
Hubbub of protestation! "What, we monks,
We friars, of such an order, such a rule,
Have not we fought, bled, left our martyr-mark
At every point along the boundary-line 1570
'Twixt true and false, religion and the world,
Where this or the other dogma of our Church
Called for defence?" And I, despite myself,
How can I but speak loud what truth speaks low,
"Or better than the best, or nothing serves! 1575
What boots deed, I can cap and cover straight
With such another doughtiness to match,
Done at an instinct of the natural man?"
Immolate body, sacrifice soul too,—
Do not these publicans the same?[8] Outstrip! 1580
Or else stop race you boast runs neck and neck,
You with the wings, they with the feet,—for shame!
O, I remark your diligence and zeal![9]
Five years long, now, rounds faith into my ears,
"Help thou, or Christendom is done to death!" 1585
Five years since, in the Province of To-kien,[1]
Which is in China as some people know,
Maigrot, my Vicar Apostolic there,

---

7. Ephesians 6:14–17.
8. Matthew 5:46–47. In the Gospels, the publican or tax-collector is a symbol of corruption.
9. That the zeal of the church is often misplaced is illustrated by the following true narrative of a semantic controversy in China. The resolution of the quarrel was left to Innocent's successor, Clement XI.
1. Actually Fukien.

Having a great qualm, issues a decree.
Alack, the converts use as God's name, not   1590
Tien-chu but plain *Tien* or else mere *Shang-ti*,
As Jesuits please to fancy politic,
While, say Dominicans, it calls down fire,—
For *Tien* means heaven, and *Shang-ti*, supreme prince,
While *Tien-chu* means the lord of heaven: all cry,   1595
"There is no business urgent for despatch
As that thou send a legate, specially
Cardinal Tournon, straight to Pekin, there
To settle and compose the difference!"
So have I seen a potentate all fume   1600
For some infringement of his realm's just right,
Some menace to a mud-built straw-thatched farm
O' the frontier; while inside the mainland lie,
Quite undisputed-for in solitude,
Whole cities plague may waste or famine sap: 1605
What if the sun crumble, the sands encroach,
While he looks on sublimely at his ease?
How does their ruin touch the empire's bound?

And is this little all that was to be?
Where is the gloriously-decisive change,   1610
Metamorphosis the immeasurable
Of human clay to divine gold, we looked
Should, in some poor sort, justify its price?
Had an adept of the mere Rosy Cross[2]
Spent his life to consummate the Great Work,   1615
Would not we start to see the stuff it touched
Yield not a grain more than the vulgar got
By the old smelting-process years ago?
If this were sad to see in just the sage
Who should profess so much, perform no more,   1620
What is it when suspected in that Power
Who undertook to make and made the world,
Devised and did effect man, body and soul,
Ordained salvation for them both, and yet . . .
Well, is the thing we see, salvation?
                                        I   1625
Put no such dreadful question to myself,
Within whose circle of experience burns
The central truth, Power, Wisdom, Goodness,—God:
I must outlive a thing ere know it dead:
When I outlive the faith there is a sun,   1630
When I lie, ashes to the very soul,—
Someone, not I, must wail above the heap,
"He[3] died in dark whence never morn arose."

---

2. A Rosicrucian, adherent of seven-
teenth- and eighteenth-century religious
movement devoted to esoteric wisdom.
Their "Great Work" was the alchemical
transmutation of base metal into gold.
3. Jesus (see Matthew 27:45).

While I see day succeed the deepest night—
How can I speak but as I know?—my speech   1635
Must be, throughout the darkness, "It will end:
The light that did burn, will burn!" Clouds obscure—
But for which obscuration all were bright?
Too hastily concluded! Sun-suffused,
A cloud may soothe the eye made blind by blaze,—   1640
Better the very clarity of heaven:
The soft streaks are the beautiful and dear.
What but the weakness in a faith supplies
The incentive to humanity, no strength
Absolute, irresistible, comports?[4]   1645
How can man love but what he yearns to help?
And that which men think weakness within strength,
But angels know for strength and stronger yet—
What were it else but the first things made new,
But repetitition of the miracle,   1650
The divine instance of self-sacrifice
That never ends and aye begins for man?
So, never I miss footing in the maze,
No,—I have light nor fear the dark at all.

But are mankind not real, who pace outside   1655
My petty circle, world that's measured me?
And when they stumble even as I stand,
Have I a right to stop ear when they cry,
As they were phantoms who took clouds for crags,
Tripped and fell, where man's march might safely move?   1660
Beside, the cry is other than a ghost's,
When out of the old time there pleads some bard,
Philosopher, or both,[5] and—whispers not,
But words it boldly. "The inward work and worth
Of any mind, what other mind may judge   1665
Save God who only knows the thing He made,
The veritable service He exacts?
It is the outward product men appraise.
Behold, an engine hoists a tower aloft:
'I looked that it should move the mountain too!'   1670
Or else 'Had just a turret toppled down,
Success enough!'—may say the Machinist[6]
Who knowns what less or more result might be:
But we, who see that done we cannot do,
'A feat beyond man's force,' we men must say.   1675
Regard me and that shake I gave the world!
I was born, not so long before Christ's birth
As Christ's birth haply did precede thy day,—
But many a watch before the star of dawn:

---

4. I.e., an incentive which absolute strength does not bring with it (Cook).
5. Euripides, Greek dramatist (ca. 484– 407 B.C.) who is the imagined speaker in lines 1664–1784.
6. Zeus.

Therefore I lived,—it is thy creed affirms,   1680
Pope Innocent, who art to answer me!—
Under conditions, nowise to escape,
Whereby salvation was impossible.
Each impulse to achieve the good and fair,
Each aspiration to the pure and true,   1685
Being without a warrant or an aim,
Was just as sterile a felicity
As if the insect, born to spend his life
Soaring his circles, stopped them to describe
(Painfully motionless in the mid-air)   1690
Some word of weighty counsel for man's sake,
Some 'Know thyself' or 'Take the golden mean!'
—Forwent his happy dance and the glad ray,
Dided half an hour the sooner and was dust.
I, born to perish like the brutes, or worse,   1695
Why not live brutishly, obey brutes' law?
But I, of body as of soul complete,
A gymnast at the games, philosopher
I' the schools, who painted, and made music,—all
Glories that met upon the tragic stage   1700
When the Third Poet's tread surprised the Two,[7]—
Whose lot fell in a land where life was great
And sense went free and beauty lay profuse,
I, untouched by one adverse circumstance,
Adopted virtue as my rule of life,   1705
Waived all reward, loved but for loving's sake,
And, what my heart taught me, I taught the world,
And have been teaching now two thousand years.
Witness my work,—plays that should please, forsooth!
'They might please, they may displease, they shall teach,   1710
For truth's sake,' so I said, and did, and do.
Five hundred years ere Paul spoke, Felix heard,[8]—
How much of temperance and righteousness,
Judgment to come, did I find reason for,
Corroborate with my strong style[9] that spared   1715
No sin, nor swerved the more from branding brow
Because the sinner was called Zeus and God?
How nearly did I guess at that Paul knew?
How closely come, in what I represent
As duty, to his doctrine yet a blank?   1720
And as that limner not untruly limns
Who draws an object round or square, which square
Or round seems to the unassisted eye,
Though Galileo's tube display the same
Oval or oblong,—so, who controverts   1725
I rendered rightly what proves wrongly wrought

7. When Euripides began to rival the older Aeschylus and Sophocles.
8. Acts 24:22–27.
9. Stylus or pen.

Beside Paul's picture? Mine was true for me.
I saw that there are, first and above all,
The hidden forces, blind necessities,
Named Nature, but the thing's self unconceived: 1730
Then follow,—how dependent upon these,
We know not, how imposed above ourselves,
We well know,—what I name the gods, a power
Various or one: for great and strong and good
Is there, and little, weak and bad there too,   1735
Wisdom and folly: say, these make no God,—
What is it else that rules outside man's self?
A fact then,—always, to the naked eye,—
And so, the one revealment possible
Of what were unimagined else by man.   1740
Therefore, what gods do, man may criticize,
Applaud, condemn,—how should he fear the truth?—
But likewise have in awe because of power,
Venerate for the main munificence,
And give the doubtful deed its due excuse   1745
From the acknowledged creature of a day
To the Eternal and Divine. Thus, bold
Yet self-mistrusting, should man bear himself,
Most assured on what now concerns him most—
The law of his own life, the path he prints,—   1750
Which law is virtue and not vice, I say,—
And least inquisitive where search least skills,
I' the nature we best give the clouds to keep.
What could I paint beyond a scheme like this
Out of the fragmentary truths where light   1755
Lay fitful in a tenebrific[1] time?
You have the sunrise now, joins truth to truth,
Shoots life and substance into death and void;
Themselves compose the whole we made before:
The forces and necessity grow God,—   1760
The beings so contrarious that seemed gods,
Prove just His operation manifold
And multiform, translated, as must be,
Into intelligible shape so far
As suits our sense and sets us free to feel.   1765
What if I let a child think, childhood-long,
That lightning, I would have him spare his eye,
Is a real arrow shot at naked orb?
The man knows more, but shuts his lids the same:
Lightning's cause comprehends nor man nor child.   1770
Why then, my scheme, your better knowledge broke,
Presently re-adjusts itself, the small
Proportioned largelier, parts and whole named new:
So much, no more two thousand years have done!

1. Dark.

Pope, dost thou dare pretend to punish me,   1775
For not descrying sunshine at midnight,
Me who crept all-fours, found my way so far—
While thou rewardest teachers of the truth,
Who miss the plain way in the blaze of noon,—
Though just a word from that strong style of mine,   1780
Grasped honestly in hand as guiding-staff,
Had pricked them a sure path across the bog,
That mire of cowardice and slush of lies
Wherein I find them wallow in wide day!"

How should I answer this Euripides?   1785
Paul,—'t is a legend,—answered Seneca,[2]
But that was in the day-spring; noon is now:
We have got too familiar with the light.
Shall I wish back once more that thrill of dawn?
When the whole truth-touched man burned up, one fire?   1790
—Assured the trial, fiery, fierce, but fleet,
Would, from his little heap of ashes, lend
Wings to that conflagration of the world
Which Christ awaits ere He makes all things new:
So should the frail become the perfect, rapt   1795
From glory of pain to glory of joy; and so,
Even in the end,—the act renouncing earth,
Lands, houses, husbands, wives and children here,—
Being that other act which finds all, lost,
Regained, in this time even, a hundredfold,   1800
And, in the next time, feels the finite love
Blent and embalmed with the eternal life.
So does the sun ghastlily seem to sink
In those north parts, lean all but out of life,
Desist a dread mere breathing-stop, then slow   1805
Re-assert day, begin the endless rise.
Was this too easy for our after-stage?
Was such a lighting-up of faith, in life,
Only allowed initiate, set man's step
In the true way by help of the great glow?   1810
A way wherein it is ordained he walk,
Bearing to see the light from heaven still more
And more encroached on by the light of earth,
Tentatives earth puts forth to rival heaven,
Earthly incitements that mankind serve God   1815
For man's sole sake, not God's and therefore man's.
Till at last, who distinguishes the sun
From a mere Druid[3] fire on a far mount?
More praise to him who with his subtle prism

Shall decompose both beams and name the true.   1820
In such sense, who is last proves first indeed;
For how could saints and martyrs fail see truth
Streak the night's blackness? Who is faithful now?
Who untwists heaven's white from the yellow flare
O' the world's gross torch, without night's foil that helped   1825
Produce the Christian act so possible
When in the way stood Nero's cross and stake,[4]—
So hard now when the world smiles "Right and wise!
Faith points the politic, the thrifty way,
Will make who plods it in the end returns   1830
Beyond mere fool's-sport and improvidence.
We fools dance thro' the cornfield of this life,
Pluck ears to left and right and swallow raw,
—Nay, tread, at pleasure, a sheaf underfoot,
To get the better at some poppy-flower,—   1835
Well aware we shall have so much less wheat
In the eventual harvest: you meantime
Waste not a spike,—the richlier will you reap!
What then? There will be always garnered meal
Sufficient for our comfortable loaf,   1840
While you enjoy the undiminished sack!"
Is it not this ignoble confidence,
Cowardly hardihood, that dulls and damps,
Makes the old heroism impossible?

Unless . . . what whispers me of times to come?   1845
What if it be the mission of that age[5]
My death will usher into life, to shake
This torpor of assurance from our creed,
Re-introduce the doubt discarded, bring
That formidable danger back, we drove   1850
Long ago to the distance and the dark?
No wild beast now prowls round the infant camp:
We have built wall and sleep in city safe:
But if some earthquake try the towers that laugh
To think they once saw lions rule outside,   1855
And man stand out again, pale, resolute,
Prepare to die,—which means, alive at last?
As we broke up that old faith of the world,
Have we, next age, to break up this the new—
Faith, in the thing, grown faith in the report—   1860
Whence need to bravely disbelieve report
Through increased faith i' the thing reports belie?
Must we deny,—do they, these Molinists,[6]
At peril of their body and their soul,—
Recognized truths, obedient to some truth   1865
Unrecognized yet, but perceptible?—

4. For immolation of Christian martyrs.   the "Age of Reason."
5. The eighteenth century, often called   6. See note to V.203.

Correct the portrait by the living face,
Man's God, by God's God in the mind of man?
Then, for the few that rise to the new height,
The many that must sink to the old depth,   1870
The multitude found fall away! A few,
E'en ere new law speak clear, may keep the old,
Preserve the Christian level, call good good
And evil evil, (even though razed and blank
The old titles,) helped by custom, habitude,   1875
And all else they mistake for finer sense
O' the fact that reason warrants,—as before,
They hope perhaps, fear not impossibly.
At least some one Pompilia left the world
Will say "I know the right place by foot's feel,   1880
I took it and tread firm there; wherefore change?"
But what a multitude will surely fall
Quite through the crumbling truth, late subjacent,
Sink to the next discoverable base,
Rest upon human nature, settle there   1885
On what is firm, the lust and pride of life!
A mass of men, whose very souls even now
Seem to need re-creating,—so they slink
Worm-like into the mud, light now lays bare,—
Whose future we dispose of with shut eyes   1890
And whisper—"They are grafted, barren twigs,
Into the living stock of Christ: may bear
One day, till when they lie death-like, not dead,"—
Those who with all the aid of Christ succumb,
How, without Christ, shall they, unaided, sink?   1895
Whither but to this gulf before my eyes?
Do not we end, the century and I?
The impatient antimasque treads close on kibe[7]
O' the very masque's self it will mock,—on me,
Last lingering personage, the impatient mime   1900
Pushes already,—will I block the way?
Will my slow trail of garments ne'er leave space
For pantaloon, sock, plume and castanet?
Here comes the first experimentalist
In the new order of things,—he plays a priest;   1905
Does he take inspiration from the Church,
Directly make her rule his law of life?
Not he: his own mere impulse guides the man—
Happily sometimes, since ourselves allow
He has danced, in gaiety of heart, i' the main   1910
The right step through the maze we bade him foot.
But if his heart had prompted him break loose
And mare the measure? Why, we must submit,

7. Antimasque: Interlude, often mock-   elaborately staged drama. Kibe: sore
ing, between the acts of a masque, an   heel.

And thank the chance that brought him safe so far.
Will he repeat the prodigy? Perhaps.   1915
Can he teach others how to quit themselves,
Show why this step was right while that were wrong?
How should he? "Ask your hearts as I asked mine,
And get discreetly through the morrice[8] too;
If your hearts misdirect you,—quit the stage,   1920
And make amends,—be there amends to make!"
Such is, for the Augustin[9] that was once,
This Canon Caponsacchi we see now.
"But my heart answers to another tune,"
Puts in the Abate, second in the suite,[1]   1925
"I have my taste too, and tread no such step!
You choose the glorious life, and may, for me!
I like the lowest of life's appetites,—
So you judge,—but the very truth of joy
To my own apprehension which decides.   1930
Call me knave and you get yourself called fool!
I live for greed, ambition, lust, revenge;
Attain these ends by force, guile: hypocrite,
To-day, perchance to-morrow recognized
The rational man, the type of common sense."   1935
There's Loyola[2] adapted to our time!
Under such guidance Guido plays his part,
He also influencing in the due turn
These last clods where I track intelligence
By any glimmer, these four at his beck   1940
Ready to murder any, and, at their own,
As ready to murder him,—such make the world!
And, first effect of the new cause of things,
There they lie also duly,—the old pair
Of the weak head and not so wicked heart,   1945
With the one Christian mother, wife and girl,
—Which three gifts seem to make an angel up,—
The world's first foot o' the dance is on their heads!
Still, I stand here, not off the stage though close
On the exit: and my last act, as my first,   1950
I owe the scene, and Him who armed me thus
With Paul's sword[3] as with Peter's key. I smite
With my whole strength once more, ere end my part,
Ending, so far as man may, this offence.
And when I raise my arm, who plucks my sleeve?   1955
Who stops me in the righteous function,—foe
Or friend? Oh, still as ever, friends are they

---

8. Or morris, English folk dance performed by costumed men.
9. St. Augustine (354–430), Bishop of
Hippo, who here symbolizes the church
as institution (cf. lines 1906–1907).
1. Procession.

2. St. Ignatius Loyola (1491–1556),
founder of the Jesuit order.
3. Symbol of Paul's defence of Christianity; not mentioned of Paul in Scripture, but attributed to him in art from
the eleventh century.

Who, in the interest of outraged truth
Deprecate such rough handling of a lie!
The facts being proved and incontestable, 1960
What is the last word I must listen to?
Perchance—"Spare yet a term this barren stock
We pray thee dig about and dung and dress
Till he repent and bring forth fruit even yet!"[4]
Perchance——"So poor and swift a punishment 1965
Shall throw him out of life with all that sin:
Let mercy rather pile up pain on pain
Till the flesh expiate what the soul pays else!"
Nowise! Remonstrants on each side commence
Instructing, there's a new tribunal now 1970
Higher than God's—the educated man's!
Nice sense of honour in the human breast
Supersedes here the old coarse oracle—
Confirming none the less a point or so
Wherein blind predecessors worked aright 1975
By rule of thumb: as when Christ said,—when, where?
Enough, I find it pleaded in a place,[5]—
"All other wrongs done, patiently I take:
But touch my honour and the case is changed!
I feel the due resentment,—*nemini* 1980
Honorem trado is my quick retort."
Right of Him, just as if pronounced to-day!
Still, should the old authority be mute
Or doubtful or in speaking clash with new,
The younger takes permission to decide. 1985
At last we have the instinct of the world
Ruling its household without tutelage:
And while the two laws, human and divine,
Having busied finger with this tangled case,
In pushes the brisk junior, cuts the knot, 1990
Pronounces for acquittal. How it trips
Silverly o'er the tongue! "Remit the death!
Forgive, . . . well, in the old way, if thou please,
Decency and the relics of routine
Respected,—let the Count go free as air! 1995
Since he may plead a priest's immunity,—
The minor orders help enough for that,
With Farinacci's[7] licence,—who decides
That the mere implication of such man,
So privileged, in any cause, before 2000
Whatever Court except the Spiritual,
Straight quashes law-procedure,—quash it, then!

4. Parable of the fig tree (Luke 8:8–9).
5. By Guido's attorney, Arcangeli (VIII.658).
6. The pope is wrong, for the (mis-quoted) words are not Christ's but

God's: *Gloriam meam alteri non dabo*, "My glory will I not give to another" (Isaiah 42:8, Vulgate).
7. Authority on canon law.

Remains a pretty loophole of escape
Moreover, that, beside the patent fact
O' the law's allowance, there's involved the weal   2005
O' the Popedom: a son's privilege at stake,
Thou wilt pretend the Church's interest,
Ignore all finer reasons to forgive!
But herein lies the crowning cogency—
(Let thy friends teach thee while thou tellest beads)   2010
That in this case the spirit of culture speaks,
Civilization is imperative.
To her shall we remand all delicate points
Henceforth, nor take irregular advice
O' thy sly, as heretofore: she used to hint   2015
Remonstrances, when law was out of sorts
Because a saucy tongue was put to rest,
An eye that roved was cured of arrogance:
But why be forced to mumble under breath
What soon shall be acknowledged as plain fact,   2020
Outspoken, say, in thy successor's time?
Methinks we see the golden age return!
Civilization and the Emperor
Succeed to Christianity and Pope.
One Emperor then, as one Pope now: meanwhile,   2025
Anticipate a little! We tell thee 'Take
Guido's life, sapped society shall crash,
Whereof of the main prop was, is, and shall be
—Supremacy of husband over wife!'
Does the man rule i' the house, and may his mate   2030
Because of any plea dispute the same?
Oh, pleas of all sorts shall abound, be sure,
One but allowed validity,—for, harsh
And savage, for, inept and silly-sooth,
For, this and that, will the ingenious sex   2035
Demonstrate the best master e'er graced slave:
And there's but one short way to end the coil,[8]—
Acknowledge right and reason steadily
I' the man and master: then the wife submits
To plain truth broadly stated. Does the time   2040
Advise we shift—a pillar? nay, a stake
Out of its place i' the social tenement?[9]
One touch may send a shudder through the heap
And bring it toppling on our children's heads!
Moreover, if our breed a qualm in thee,   2045
Give thine own better feeling play for once!
Thou, whose own life winks o'er the socket-edge,
Wouldst thou it went out in such ugly snuff
As dooming sons dead, e'en though justice prompt?
Why, on a certain feast, Barabbas' self   2050

8. Confusion.   9. Structure.

Was set free, not to cloud the general cheer:[1]
Neither shalt thou pollute thy Sabbath close![2]
Mercy is safe and graceful. How one hears
The howl begin, scarce the three little taps
O' the silver mallet[3] silent on thy brow,—   2055
'His last act was to sacrifice a Count
And thereby screen a scandal of the Church!
Guido condemned, the Canon justified
Of course,—delinquents of his cloth go free!'
And so the Luthers chuckle, Calvins scowl,   2060
So thy hand helps Molinos to the chair
Whence he may hold forth till doom's day on just
The *petit-maître*[4] priestlings,—in the choir
Sanctus et Benedictus, with a brush
Of soft guitar-strings that obey the thumb,   2065
Touched by the bedside, for accompaniment!
Does this give umbrage to a husband? Death
To the fool, and to the priest impunity!
But no impunity to any friend
So simply over-loyal as these four   2070
Who made religion of their patron's cause,
Believed in him and did his bidding straight,
Asked not one question but laid down the lives
This Pope took,—all four lives together make
Just his own length of days,—so, dead they lie,   2075
As these were times when loyalty's a drug,
And zeal in a subordinate too cheap
And common to be saved when we spend life!
Come, 't is too much good breath we waste in words:
The pardon, Holy Father! Spare grimace,   2080
Shrugs and reluctance! Are not we the world,
Art not thou Priam?[5] Let soft culture plead
Hecuba-like, '*non tali*' (Virgil serves)
'*Auxilio*' and the rest! Enough, it works!
The Pope relaxes, and the Prince is loth,   2085
The father's bowels yearn, the man's will bends,
Reply is apt. Our tears on tremble, hearts
Big with a benediction, wait the word
Shall circulate thro' the city in a trice,
Set every window flaring, give each man   2090
O' the mob his torch to wave for gratitude.
Pronounce then, for our breath and patience fail!"

I will, Sirs: but a voice other than yours

---

1. Acceding to the will of the people, Pilate released Barabbas and delivered Christ to be crucified (Matthew 27:15–26).
2. I.e., your final days.
3. Part of a ceremony performed at the death bed of a pope before formal announcement of his passing.
4. Foppish.
5. Aged king of Troy, who dressed for battle as Troy was falling, but was restrained by his wife Hecuba saying, "It is not aid like that, nor any armed defence, which is needed now" (*Aeneid*, II.521–522).

Quickens my spirit. *"Quis pro Domino?*
Who is upon the Lord's side?" asked the Count.[6]   2095
I, who write—
    "On receipt of this command,
Acquaint Count Guido and his fellows four
They die to-morrow: could it be to-night,
The better, but the work to do, takes time.
Set with all diligence a scaffold up,   2100
Not in the customary place, by Bridge
Saint Angelo, where die the common sort;
But since the man is noble, and his peers
By predilection haunt the People's Square,[7]
There let him be beheaded in the midst,   2105
And his companions hanged on either side:
So shall the quality see, fear and learn.
All which work takes time: till to-morrow, then,
Let there be prayer incessant for the five!"

For the main criminal I have no hope   2110
Except in such a suddenness of fate.
I stood at Naples once, a night so dark
I could have scarce conjectured there was earth
Anywhere, sky or sea or world at all:
But the night's black was burst through by a blaze—   2115
Thunder struck blow on blow, earth groaned and bore,
Through her whole length of mountain visible:
There lay the city thick and plain with spires,
And, like a ghost disshrouded, white the sea.
So may the truth be flashed out by one blow,   2120
And Guido see, one instant, and be saved.
Else I avert my face, nor follow him
Into that sad obscure sequestered state[8]
Where God unmakes but to remake the soul
He else made first in vain; which must not be.[9]   2125
Enough, for I may die this very night
And how should I dare die, this man let live?

Carry this forthwith to the Governor!

6. Guido has quoted Moses' words to justify his stepping "beyond the law" to commit the vengeful murders. (See note to V.1542.)
7. Piazza del Popolo, where the executions took place on February 22, 1698.
8. Purgatory.
9. For the pope it is unthinkable that any soul would be eternally damned; even Guido can be salvaged ultimately by an all-loving God.

The Later Achievement
(After 1870)

From *Fifine at the Fair* (1872)

Prologue

AMPHIBIAN[1]

I
The fancy I had to-day,
    Fancy which turned a fear!
I swam far out in the bay,
    Since waves laughed warm and clear.

II
I lay and looked at the sun,   5
    The noon-sun looked at me:
Between us two, no one
    Live creature, that I could see.

III
Yes! There came floating by
    Me, who lay floating too,   10
Such a strange butterfly![2]
    Creature as dear as new:

IV
Because the membraned wings
    So wonderful, so wide,
So sun-suffused, were things   15
    Like soul and nought beside.

V
A handbreadth over head!
    All of the sea my own,
It owned the sky instead;
    Both of us were alone.   20

VI
I never shall join its flight,

1. This lyric serves as prologue to the long casuistical monologue *Fifine at the Fair* (1872), a latter-day Don Juan's defense of infidelity. Here swimming, a new pleasure for the aging poet, provides the vehicle for speculation upon the function of poetry. As in the main poem, the setting is the resort town of Pornic in Brittany.
2. In antiquity the butterfly symbolized the soul. In Christian art the life cycle of the caterpillar, chrysalis, and butterfly stood for life, death, and resurrection. (See lines 33–34, 39–40.)

For, nought buoys flesh in air.
  If it touch the sea—good night!
    Death sure and swift waits there.

VII

Can the insect feel the better   25
  For watching the uncouth play
Of limbs that slip the fetter,
  Pretend as they were not clay?

VIII

Undoubtedly I rejoice
  That the air comports so well   30
With a creature which had the choice
  Of the land once. Who can tell?

IX

What if a certain soul[3]
  Which early slipped its sheath,[4]
And has for its home the whole   35
  Of heaven, thus look beneath,

X

Thus watch one who, in the world,
  Both lives and likes life's way,
Nor wishes the wings unfurled[5]
  That sleep in the worm,[6] they say?   40

XI

But sometimes when the weather
  Is blue, and warm waves tempt
To free oneself of tether,
  And try a life exempt

XII

From worldly noise and dust,   45
  In the sphere which overbrims
With passion and thought,—why, just
  Unable to fly, one swims!

XIII

By passion and thought upborne,
  One smiles to oneself—"They fare   50
Scarce better, they need not scorn
  Our sea, who live in the air!"

XIV

Emancipate[7] through passion
  And thought, with sea for sky,
We substitute, in a fashion,   55
  For heaven—poetry:

XV

Which sea,[8] to all intent,
  Gives flesh such noon-disport
As a finer element
  Affords the spirit-sort.   60

---

3. The poet's dead wife.   6. Corporeal existence.
4. Chrysalis; i.e., flesh.   7. Emancipated.
5. I.e., does not wish to die.   8. The medium of human expression.

XVI

Whatever they are, we seem:
　　Imagine the thing they know;
All deeds they do, we dream;
　　Can heaven be else but so?

XVII

And meantime, yonder streak　　　　　　65
　　Meets the horizon's verge;
That is the land, to seek
　　If we tire or dread the surge:

XVIII

Land the solid and safe—
　　To welcome again (confess!)　　　　　70
When, high and dry, we chafe
　　The body, and don the dress.

XIX

Does she look, pity, wonder
　　At one who mimics flight,
Swims—heaven above, sea under,　　　　75
　　Yet always earth in sight?

Epilogue

THE HOUSEHOLDER[1]

I

Savage I was sitting in my house, late, lone:
　　Dreary, weary with the long day's work:[2]
Head of me, heart of me, stupid as a stone:
　　Tongue-tied now, now blaspheming like a Turk;
When, in a moment, just a knock, call, cry,　　　　5
　　Half a pang and all a rapture, there again were we!—
"What, and is it really you again?" quoth I:
　　"I again, what else did you expect?" quoth She.

II

"Never mind, hie away from this old house—
　　Every crumbling brick embrowned[3] with sin and shame!　　10
Quick, in its corners ere certain shapes arouse!
　　Let them—every devil of the night—lay claim,
Make and mend, or rap and rend, for me! Good-bye!
　　God be their guard from disturbance at their glee,
Till, crash, comes down the carcass in a heap!" quoth I:　　15
　　"Nay, but there's a decency required!" quoth She.

III

"Ah, but if you know how time has dragged, days, nights!
　　All the neighbour-talk with man and maid—such men!

1. Unmistakably autobiographical, this lyric serves as epilogue to *Fifine at the Fair*. The scene may be Browning's house in London.
2. Echoes of the situation and style of Poe's "The Raven" are evident ("Once upon a midnight dreary, while I pondered, weak and weary, / . . . came a tapping . . .").
3. It is not difficult to detect here a pun on Browning's name.

All the fuss and trouble of street-sounds, window-sights:
   All the worry of flapping door and echoing roof; and then,   20
All the fancies . . . Who were they had leave, dared try
   Darker arts that almost struck despair in me?
If you knew but how I dwelt down here!" quoth I:
   "And was I so better off up there?" quoth She.

IV

"Help and get it over! *Re-united to his wife*   25
   (How draw up the paper lets the parish-people know?)
Lies M., or N., departed from this life,
   Day the this or that, month and year the so and so.
What i' the way of final flourish? Prose, verse? Try!
   Affliction sore long time he bore, or, what is it to be?   30
Till God did please to grant him ease. Do end!" quoth I:
   "I end with—Love is all and Death is nought!" quoth She.

From *Aristophanes' Apology* (1875)

[Thamuris Marching][1]

* * *

               "Once and only once, trod stage,
Sang and touched lyre in person, in his youth,
Our Sophokles,[2]—youth, beauty, dedicate
To Thamuris who named the tragedy.
The voice of him was weak; face, limbs and lyre,   5
These were worth saving: Thamuris stands yet
Perfect as painting helps in such a case.
At least you know the story, for 'best friend'[3]
Enriched his 'Rhesos' from the Blind Bard's store;
So haste and see the work, and lay to heart   10
What it was struck me when I eyed the piece!
Here stands a poet punished for rash strife
With Powers above his power, who see with sight
Beyond his vision, sing accordingly
A song, which he must needs dare emulate!   15
Poet, remain the man nor ape the Muse!

"But—lend me the psalterion![4] Nay, for once—

1. This song is excerpted from *Aristophanes' Apology* (lines 5167–5264), an elaborate defense of the Greek tragedian Euripides, whom Browning deeply admired. Here Aristophanes sings of the legendary Thracian poet Thamyris, who marches exultantly to challenge the Muses to a poetic contest at Dorion in Messenia. Angered at his presumption, they are to blind Thamyris and deprive him of his gift of song (see *Iliad*, II.594ff., and *Paradise Lost*, III.35). Browning enjoyed reading these lines aloud.
2. Sophocles, preeminent Greek tragedian.
3. Euripides. The *Rhesos* (line 9) is a tragedy doubtfully attributed to Euripides.
4. Psaltery, stringed instrument resembling the zither.

Once let my hand fall where the other's lay!
I see it, just as I were Sophokles,
That sunrise and combustion of the east!"   20

And then he sang—are these unlike the words?

Thamuris marching,—lyre and song of Thrace—
(Perpend[5] the first, the worst of woes that were
Allotted lyre and song, ye poet-race!)

Thamuris from Oichalia, feasted there   25
By kingly Eurutos of late, now bound
For Dorion at the uprise broad and bare

Of Mount Pangaios[6] (ore with earth enwound
Glittered beneath his footstep)—marching gay
And glad, Thessalia[7] through, came, robed and crowned,   30

From triumph on to triumph, mid a ray
Of early morn,—came, saw and knew the spot
Assigned him for his worst of woes, that day.

Balura[8]—happier while its name was not—
Met him, but nowise menaced; slipt aside,   35
Obsequious river to pursue its lot

Of solacing the valley—say, some wide
Thick busy human cluster, house and home,
Embanked for peace, or thrift that thanks the tide.

Thamuris, marching, laughed "Each flake of foam"   40
(As sparkingly the ripple raced him by)
"Mocks slower clouds adrift in the blue dome!"

For Autumn was the season; red the sky
Held morn's conclusive signet of the sun
To break the mists up, bid them blaze and die.   45

Morn had the mastery as, one by one,
All pomps produced themselves along the tract
From earth's far ending to near heaven begun.

Was there a ravaged tree? it laughed compact
With gold, a leaf-ball crisp, high-brandished now,   50
Tempting to onset frost which late attacked.

Was there a wizened shrub, a starveling bough,
A fleecy thistle filched from by the wind,
A weed, Pan's[9] trampling hoof would disallow?

5. Ponder.
6. Mountain in Thrace containing deposits of gold and silver. (See Aeschylus, *Persae*, 494.)
7. Thessaly, region of eastern Greece between the Pindus mountains and the Aegean.
8. The river Balyra ("cast away"), so named because Thamyris after being blinded threw his lyre into it.
9. Greek god of flocks and shepherds, represented as goatlike. He is supposed to have invented the musical pipe of seven reeds.

Each, with a glory and a rapture twined   55
About it, joined the rush of air and light
And force: the world was of one joyous mind.

Say not the birds flew! they forebore their right—
Swam, revelling onward in the roll of things.
Say not the beasts' mirth bounded! that was flight—   60

How could the creatures leap, no lift of wings?
Such earth's community of purpose, such
The ease of earth's fulfilled imaginings,—

So did the near and far appear to touch
I' the moment's transport,—that an interchange   65
Of function, far with near, seemed scarce too much;

And had the rooted plant aspired to range
With the snake's license, while the insect yearned
To glow fixed as the flower, it were not strange—

No more than if the fluttery tree-top turned   70
To actual music, sang itself aloft;
Or if the wind, impassioned chantress, earned

The right to soar embodied in some soft
Fine form all fit for cloud-companionship,
And, blissful, once touch beauty chased so oft.   75

Thamuris, marching, let no fancy slip
Born of the fiery transport; lyre and song
Were his, to smite with hand and launch from lip—

Peerless recorded, since the list grew long
Of poets (saith Homeros) free to stand   80
Pedestalled mid the Muses' temple-throng,

A statued service, laurelled, lyre in hand,
(Ay, for we see them)—Thamuris of Thrace
Predominating foremost of the band.

Therefore the morn-ray that enriched his face,   85
If it gave lambent chill, took flame again
From flush of pride; he saw, he knew the place.

What wind arrived with all the rhythms from plain,
Hill, dale, and that rough wildwood interspersed?
Compounding these to one consummate strain,   90

It reached him, music; but his own outburst
Of victory concluded the account,
And that grew song which was mere music erst.

"Be my Parnassos,[1] thou Pangaian mount!
And turn thee, river, nameless hitherto!   95

1. Parnassus, mountain near Delphi, sacred to Apollo and the Muses.

Famed shalt thou vie with famed Pieria's² fount!

"Here I await the end of this ado:
Which wins—Earth's poet or the Heavenly Muse."³ . . .

* * *

From *Pacchiarotto and How He Worked in Distemper: With Other Poems* (1876)

House¹

I

Shall I sonnet-sing you about myself?
　　Do I live in a house you would like to see?²
Is it scant of gear, has it store of pelf?³
　　"Unlock my heart with a sonnet-key?"⁴

II

Invite the world, as my betters⁵ have done?　　　　　　5
　　"Take notice: this building remains on view,
Its suites of reception every one,
　　Its private apartment and bedroom too;

III

"For a ticket, apply to the Publisher."
　　No: thanking the public, I must decline.　　　　　10
A peep through my window, if folk prefer;
　　But, please you, no foot over threshold of mine!

IV

I have mixed with a crowd and heard free talk

2. District on northern slope of Mt. Olympus sacred to the Muses.
3. The song ends abruptly here. (Aristophanes adds: " 'Tell the rest, / Who may!' ")
1. This is the best known poem in *Pacchiarotto* (1876), a volume largely devoted to castigating the poet's critics, chief among whom was Alfred Austin (1835–1913), who was to succeed Tennyson as poet laureate. "House" is a rather shrill defense of the author's right to privacy—a right which the reticent Browning went to extremes to protect, especially in the 1870s and 1880s, when he enjoyed lionization in London. During this period there developed two disparate Robert Brownings: the public self —sociable, talkative, and prosperous-looking—erected as a façade to mask the private self, revealed only to a select few. So intrigued was Henry James by this role-playing that he made Browning the model for his Clare Vawdrey, the enigmatic novelist of *The Private Life*

(1893): "The poet and the 'member of society' were, in a word, dissociated in him as they can rarely elsewhere have been."
2. Browning's focusing on a house exposed catastrophically to public view may be a pointed reply to D. G. Rossetti's sonnet sequence *The House of Life* (1870), which had a "confessional" tone he must have found deplorable (De Vane, pp. 400–401).
3. Riches.
4. Loose paraphrase of Wordsworth's "Scorn not the sonnet" (1827), lines 2–3; the same lines are quoted (inaccurately) in lines 38–39. The "key" is of course the sonnet form, which enjoyed a notable revival in the nineteenth century. Browning himself wrote very few sonnets.
5. Browning has in mind the poets extolled as masters of the sonnet in "Scorn not the sonnet": Shakespeare, Petrarch, Tasso, Camoëns, Dante, Spenser, and Milton.

In a foreign land where an earthquake chanced:
And a house stood gaping, nought to baulk   15
    Man's eye wherever he gazed or glanced.
                        V
The whole of the frontage shaven sheer,
    The inside gaped: exposed to day,
Right and wrong and common and queer,
    Bare, as the palm of your hand, it lay.   20
                        VI
The owner? Oh, he had been crushed. no doubt!
    "Odd tables and chairs for a man of wealth!
What a parcel of musty old books about!
    He smoked,—no wonder he lost his health!
                        VII
"I doubt if he bathed before he dressed.   25
    A brasier?—the pagan, he burned perfumes!
You see it is proved, what the neighbours guessed:
    His wife and himself had separate rooms."
                        VIII
Friends, the goodman of the house at least
    Kept house to himself till an earthquake came: 30
'T is the fall of its frontage permits you feast
    On the inside arrangement you praise or blame.
                        IX
Outside should suffice for evidence:
    And whoso desires to penetrate
Deeper, must dive by the spirit-sense—   35
    No optics like yours, at any rate!
                        X
"Hoity toity! A street to explore,
    Your house the exception! 'With this same key
Shakespeare unlocked his heart,' once more!"[6]
    Did Shakespeare? If so, the less Shakespeare he![7]   40
1874   1876

Fears and Scruples[1]

                        I
Here's my case. Of old I used to love him
    This same unseen friend, before I knew:
Dream there was none like him, none above him,—
    Wake to hope and trust my dream was true.
                        II
Loved I not his letters[2] full of beauty?   5

---

6. Lines 2–3 of "Scorn not the sonnet"; Browning added the word "same."
7. I.e., insofar as he laid bare his private feelings, Shakespeare was acting uncharacteristically. In his *Essay on Shelley*, Browning sees Shakespeare as a purely "objective" or dramatic poet; the sonnets are not mentioned.
1. This parable of religious doubt foreshadows the long poem "La Saisiaz" (1878).
2. The Scriptures.

Not his actions[3] famous far and wide?
Absent, he would know I vowed him duty;
   Present, he would find me at his side.

III

Pleasant fancy! for I had but letters,
   Only knew of actions by hearsay: 10
He himself was busied with my betters;
   What of that? My turn must come some day.

IV

"Some day" proving—no day! Here's the puzzle.
   Passed and passed my turn is. Why complain?
He's so busied! If I could but muzzle   15
   People's foolish mouths that give me pain!

V

"Letters?" (hear them!) "You a judge of writing?
   Ask the experts![4]—How they shake the head
O'er these characters, your friend's inditing—
   Call them forgery from A to Z!   20

VI

"Actions? Where's your certain proof" (they bother)
   "He, of all you find so great and good,
He, he only, claims this, that, the other
   Action—claimed by men, a multitude?"

VII

I can simply wish I might refute you,   25
   Wish my friend would,—by a word, a wink,—
Bid me stop that foolish mouth,—you brute you!
   He keeps absent,—why, I cannot think.

VIII

Never mind! Though foolishness may flout me,
   One thing's sure enough: 't is neither frost,   30
No, nor fire, shall freeze or burn from out me
   Thanks for truth—though falsehood, gained—though lost.

IX

All my days, I'll go the softlier,[5] sadlier,
   For that dream's[6] sake! How forget the thrill
Through and through me as I thought "The gladlier   35
   Lives my friend because I love him still!"

X

Ah, but there's a menace someone utters!
   "What and if your friend at home play tricks?
Peep at hide-and-seek behind the shutters?
   Mean your eyes should pierce through solid bricks?   40

XI

"What and if he, frowning, wake you, dreamy?

---

3. Miracles, now explained in purely human terms.
4. The "higher critics" of the Bible (Strauss, Renan, and others), who were questioning the authenticity of certain portions of Scripture.
5. Isaiah 38:15: "I shall go softly all my years in the bitterness of my soul."
6. His conception of God.

Lay on you the blame that bricks—conceal?
Say '*At least I saw who did not see me,*
   Does see now, and presently shall feel'?"

IIX

"Why, that makes your friend a monster!" say you: 45
   "Had his house no window? At first nod,
Would you not have hailed him?" Hush, I pray you!
   What if this friend happen to be—God?[7]

Numpholeptos[1]

Still you stand, still you listen, still you smile!
Still melts your moonbeam[2] through me, white awhile,
Softening, sweetening, till sweet and soft
Increase so round this heart of mine, that oft
I could believe your moonbeam-smile has past   5
The pallid limit, lies, transformed at last
To sunlight and salvation—warms the soul
It sweetens, softens! Would you pass that goal,
Gain love's birth at the limit's happier verge,
And, where an iridescence lurks, but urge   10
The hesitating pallor on to prime
Of dawn!—true blood-streaked, sun-warmth, action-time,
By heart-pulse ripened to a ruddy blow
Of gold above my clay—I scarce should know
From gold's self, thus suffused! For gold means love.   15
What means the sad slow silver smile above
My clay but pity, pardon?—at the best,
But acquiescence that I take my rest,
Contented to be clay, while in your heaven
The sun reserves love for the Spirit-Seven[3]   20
Companioning God's throne they lamp before,
—Leaves earth a mute waste only wandered o'er
By that pale soft sweet disempassioned moon
Which smiles me slow forgiveness! Such the boon
I beg? Nay, dear, submit to this—just this   25
Supreme endeavour! As my lips now kiss
Your feet, my arms convulse your shrouding robe,
My eyes, acquainted with the dust, dare probe

7. Browning believed that God accepts the love and forgives the ignorance of His faithful.
1. The poem has been interpreted autobiographically as Browning's expression of rebellion against the fifteen-year bondage to the memory of his dead wife (*Portrait*, pp. 259–61; DeVane, pp. 405–06). But Browning said, "I had no particular woman in my mind," and called the poem "an allegory . . . of an impossible ideal object of love" held by a man sadly aware that the "being is imaginary, not real, a nymph and no woman" (DeVane, p. 405). The title, adapted from Plutarch, means "caught or entranced by a nymph." In Greek mythology nymphs were beautiful female personifications of natural objects. Though they evoked passion, they could feel none. "Numpholeptos" resembles Tennyson's early monologue "Tithonus" (1833) in subject, tone, and imagery.
2. Cf. Elizabeth Barrett Browning as "my moon of poets" in "One Word More," line 188.
3. See Revelation 4:5: "seven lamps of fire burning before the throne, which are the seven Spirits of God."

Your eyes above for—what, if born, would blind
Mine with redundant bliss, as flash may find   30
The inert nerve, sting awake the palsied limb,
Bid with life's ecstasy sense overbrim
And suck back death in the resurging joy—
Love, the love whole and sole without alloy!

Vainly! The promise withers! I employ   35
Lips, arms, eyes, pray the prayer which finds the word,
Make the appeal which must be felt, not heard,
And none the more is changed your calm regard:
Rather, its sweet and soft grow harsh and hard—
Forbearance, then repulsion, then disdain.   40
Avert the rest! I rise, see!—make, again
Once more, the old departure for some track
Untried yet through a world which brings me back
Ever thus fruitlessly to find your feet,
To fix your eyes, to pray the soft and sweet   45
Which smile there—take from his new pilgrimage
Your outcast, once your inmate, and assuage
With love—not placid pardon now—his thirst
For a mere drop from out the ocean erst
He drank at! Well, the quest shall be renewed.   50
Fear nothing! Though I linger, unembued
With any drop, my lips thus close. I go!
So did I leave you, I have found you so,
And doubtlessly, if fated to return,
So shall my pleading persevere and earn   55
Pardon—not love—in that same smile, I learn,
And lose the meaning of, to learn once more,
Vainly!

      What fairy track do I explore?
What magic hall return to, like the gem
Centuply-angled[4] o'er a diadem?   60
You dwell there, hearted; from your midmost home
Rays forth—through that fantastic world I roam
Ever—from centre to circumference,
Shaft upon coloured shaft: this crimsons thence,
That purples out its precinct through the waste.   65
Surely I had your sanction when I faced,
Fared forth upon that untried yellow ray
Whence I retrack my steps? They end to-day
Where they began—before your feet, beneath
Your eyes, your smile: the blade is shut in sheath,   70
Fire quenched in flint; irradiation, late
Trimphant through the distance, finds its fate,
Merged in your blank pure soul, alike the source
And tomb of that prismatic glow:[5] divorce
Absolute, all-conclusive! Forth I fared,   75

4. Possessing a hundred facets.
5. Cf. "My Star," where the soul-mate throws off color like a prism.

Treading the lambent flamelet: little cared
If now its flickering took the topaz tint,
If now my dull-caked path gave sulphury hint
Of subterranean rage—no stay nor stint
To yellow, since you sanctioned that I bathe,   80
Burnish me, soul and body, swim and swathe
In yellow license. Here I reek suffused
With crocus, saffron, orange, as I used
With scarlet, purple, every dye o' the bow
Born of the storm-cloud. As before, you show   85
Scarce recognition, no approval, some
Mistrust, more wonder at a man become
Monstrous in garb, nay—flesh disguised as well,
Through his adventure. Whatsoe'er befell,
I followed, whereso'er it wound, that vein   90
You authorized should leave your whiteness, stain
Earth's sombre stretch beyond your midmost place
Of vantage,—trode that tinct whereof the trace
On garb and flesh repel you! Yes, I plead
Your own permission—your command, indeed,   95
That who would worthily retain the love
Must share the knowledge shrined those eyes above,
Go boldly on adventure, break through bounds
O' the quintessential whiteness that surrounds
Your feet, obtain experience of each tinge   100
That bickers[6] forth to broaden out, impinge
Plainer his foot its pathway all distinct
From every other. Ah, the wonder, linked
With fear, as exploration manifests
What agency it was first tipped the crests   105
Of unnamed wildflower, soon protruding grew
Portentous mid the sands, as when his hue
Betrays him and the burrowing snake gleams through;
Till, last . . . but why parade more shame and pain?
Are not the proofs upon me? Here again   110
I pass into your presence, I receive
Your smile of pity, pardon, and I leave . . .
No, not this last of times I leave you, mute,
Submitted to my penance, so my foot
May yet again adventure, tread, from source   115
To issue, one more ray of rays which course
Each other, at your bidding, from the sphere
Silver and sweet, their birthplace, down that drear
Dark of the world,—you promise shall return
Your pilgrim jewelled as with drops o' the urn   120
The rainbow paints from, and no smatch[7] at all
Of ghastliness at edge of some cloud-pall
Heaven cowers before, as earth awaits the fall
O' the bolt and flash of doom. Who trusts your word

6. Flickers.   7. Slight trace.

Tries the adventure: and returns—absurd   125
As frightful—in that sulphur-steeped disguise
Mocking the priestly cloth-of-gold, sole prize
The arch-heretic was wont to bear away
Until he reached the burning. No, I say:
No fresh adventure! No more seeking love   130
At end of toil, and finding, calm above
My passion, the old statuesque regard,
The sad petrific[8] smile!

               O you—less hard
And hateful than mistaken and obtuse
Unreason of a she-intelligence!   135
You very woman with the pert pretence
To match the male achievement![9] Like enough!
Ay, you were easy victors, did the rough
Straightway efface itself to smooth, the gruff
Grind down and grow a whisper,—did man's truth   140
Subdue, for sake of chivalry and ruth,
Its rapier-edge to suit the bulrush-spear
Womanly falsehood fights with! O that ear
All facts pricks rudely, that thrice-superfine
Feminity of sense, with right divine   145
To waive all process, take result stain-free
From out the very muck wherein . . .

                  Ah me!
The true slave's querulous outbreak! All the rest
Be resignation! Forth at your behest
I fare. Who knows but this—the crimson-quest—   150
May deepen to a sunrise, not decay
To that cold sad sweet smile?—which I obey.

From *Jocoseria* (1883)

Adam, Lilith, and Eve[1]

One day it thundered and lightened.
Two women, fairly frightened,
Sank to their knees, transformed, transfixed,
At the feet of the man who sat betwixt;

8. Able to petrify; ironic echo of "beatific."
9. It is difficult to believe Browning had "no particular woman" in mind here.
1. Irritated by a friend's misinterpretation of this poem, Browning gave the following reading: ". . . the story is simply that a man once knew a woman who, while she loved him, pretended that she did not—which pretence, like a man and a fool, he believed, so of course was not married to her—but to a woman who did *not* love him but another though she said she did love him—which, like a man and a fool—he believed: one day as they sat together, each, on a sudden impulse, told him the truth—which, like a man and a fool, he disbelieved. Surely there is nothing so difficult here . . ." (*Learned Lady,* p. 156).

And "Mercy!" cried each—"if I tell the truth   5
Of a passage in my youth!"

Said This[2]: "Do you mind the morning
I met your love with scorning?
As the worst of the venom left my lips,
I thought 'If, despite this lie, he strips   10
The mask from my soul with a kiss—I crawl
His slave,—soul, body and all!' "

Said That[3]: "We stood to be married;
The priest, or someone, tarried;
'If Paradise-door prove locked?' smiled you.   15
I thought, as I nodded, smiling too,
'Did one, that's away, arrive—nor late
Nor soon should unlock Hell's gate!' "

It ceased to lighten and thunder.
Up started both in wonder,   20
Looked round and saw that the sky was clear,
Then laughed "Confess you believed us, Dear!"
"I saw through the joke!" the man replied
They re-seated themselves beside.

Never the Time and the Place

Never the time and the place
     And the loved one all together![1]
This path—how soft to pace!
     This May—what magic weather!
Where is the loved one's face?   5
In a dream that loved one's face meets mine,
     But the house is narrow, the place is bleak
Where, outside, rain and wind combine
     With a furtive ear, if I strive to speak,
     With a hostile eye at my flushing cheek,   10
With a malice that marks each word, each sign!
O enemy sly and serpentine,
     Uncoil thee from the waking man!
          Do I hold the Past
          Thus firm and fast   15
     Yet doubt if the Future hold I can?
This path so soft to pace shall lead
Thro' the magic of May to herself indeed!
Or narrow if needs the house must be,
Outside are the storms and strangers: we—   20
Oh, close, safe, warm sleep I and she,
     —I and she!

2. Lilith, important figure in Jewish legend. In rabbinic literature Lilith is a
demon of the night and seducer of men.
She was regarded as Adam's first wife;
their union was marred by strife.

3. Eve.
1. The "loved one" is Elizabeth Barrett
Browning. Cf. "The Householder"
("Epilogue" to *Fifine at the Fair*).

From *Parleyings with Certain People of Importance in Their Day* (1887)

Reticent in the extreme about his private life (see "House"), Browning held biographers suspect. To handicap any effort at chronicling his own life he burned many of his private papers in 1885. Believing that his poetry alone should represent him to the world, he wrote no memoirs—though rumors persisted that he would do so. Speculation was ended by the publication in 1887 of *Parleyings with Certain People of Importance in Their Day*, aptly characterized as "notes for Browning's mental autobiography" (DeVane, p. 491). Dropping entirely his usual dramatic mask, Browning speaks his mind to seven figures of importance to his own intellectual development. The seven—Bernard de Mandeville, Daniel Bartoli, Christopher Smart, George Bubb Dodington, Francis Furini, Gerard de Lairesse, and Charles Avison—represent seven lifelong interests: philosophy, history, poetry, politics, painting, the classics, and music. After airing his settled opinions, Browning contrasts them with those of several outstanding contemporaries. Thus in "Bernard de Mandeville" the always optimistic Browning deplores the cosmic pessimism of Thomas Carlyle; in "Gerard de Lairesse" he criticizes the "Hellenism" of Matthew Arnold; and in "Christopher Smart" he attacks the poetry of "Aesthetes" such as A. C. Swinburne. The *Parleyings* are thoroughly and admirably treated in William C. DeVane's *Browning's Parleyings: The Autobiography of a Mind*, 2nd ed. (New York, 1964).

The English poet Christopher Smart (1722–71), whose irregular habits did not prevent his becoming a fellow of Pembroke College, Cambridge, went to London about 1752 to take up the life of a writer. His forgotten *Poems on Several Occasions* (1752) proved him at best a mediocre versifier. His unhappy life, complicated by drink and ill health, was after 1751 marked by periods of insanity. By 1756 he had developed a religious mania, which, according to his friend Samuel Johnson, took the form of "falling upon his knees, and saying his prayers in the street, or in any other unusual place. . . ." In 1763 he was confined in a madhouse, where he wrote the ecstatic "Song to David," by far his greatest poem, and today the only one by which he is remembered. Neglected in the eighteenth century as the product of a deranged mind, it was greatly appreciated by the romantics. In this "Parleying," Browning perpetuates the legend that Smart, lacking writing materials, indented the poem with a key on the wainscot of his madhouse room.

With Christopher Smart

I

It seems as if . . . or did the actual chance
Startle me and perplex? Let truth be said!
How might this happen? Dreaming, blindfold led
By visionary hand, did soul's advance

Precede my body's, gain inheritance   5
Of fact by fancy—so that when I read
At length with waking eyes your Song, instead
Of mere bewilderment, with me first glance
Was but full recognition that in trance
Or merely thought's adventure some old day   10
Of dim and done-with boyishness, or—well,
Why might it not have been, the miracle
Broke on me as I took my sober way
Through veritable regions of our earth
And made discovery, many a wondrous one?   15

II

Anyhow, fact or fancy, such its birth:
I was exploring some huge house, had gone
Through room and room complacently, no dearth
Anywhere of the signs of decent taste,
Adequate culture: wealth had run to waste   20
Nowise, nor penury was proved by stint:
All showed the Golden Mean without a hint
Of brave extravagance that breaks the rule.
The master of the mansion was no fool
Assuredly, no genius just as sure!   25
Safe mediocrity had scorned the lure
Of now too much and now too little cost,
And satisfied me sight was never lost
Of moderate design's accomplishment
In calm completeness. On and on I went,   30
With no more hope than fear of what came next,
Till lo, I push a door, sudden uplift
A hanging, enter, chance upon a shift
Indeed of scene! So—thus it is thou deck'st,
High heaven, our low earth's brick-and-mortar work?   35

III

It was the Chapel. That a star, from murk
Which hid, should flashingly emerge at last,
Were small surprise: but from broad day I passed
Into a presence that turned shine to shade.
There fronted me the Rafael Mother-Maid,[1]   40
Never to whom knelt votarist in shrine
By Nature's bounty helped, By Art's divine
More varied—beauty with magnificence—
Than this: from floor to roof one evidence
Of how far earth may rival heaven. No niche   45
Where glory was not prisoned to enrich
Man's gaze with gold and gems, no space but glowed
With colour, gleamed with carving—hues which owed
Their outburst to a brush the painter fed

---

1. Raphael Sanzio (1483–1520) painted a   clear which of these Browning has in
number of famous Madonnas. It is not   mind.

With rainbow-substance—rare shapes never wed   50
To actual flesh and blood, which, brain-born once,
Became the sculptor's dowry, Art's response
To earth's despair. And all seemed old yet new:
Youth,—in the marble's curve, the canvas' hue,
Apparent,—wanted not the crowning thrill   55
Of age the consecrator.[2] Hands long still
Had worked here—could it be, what lent them skill
Retained a power to supervise, protect,
Enforce new lessons with the old, connect
Our life with theirs? No merely modern touch   60
Told me that here the artist, doing much,
Elsewhere did more, perchance does better, lives—
So needs must learn.

IV
                 Well, these provocatives
Having fulfilled their office, forth I went
Big with anticipation—well-nigh fear—   65
Of what next room and next for startled eyes
Might have in store, surprise beyond surprise.
Next room and next and next—what followed here?
Why, nothing! not one object to arrest
My passage—everywhere too manifest   70
The previous decent null and void of best
And worst, mere ordinary right and fit,
Calm commonplace which neither missed, nor hit
Inch-high, inch-low, the placid mark proposed.

V
Armed with this instance, have I diagnosed   75
Your case, my Christopher? The man was sound
And sane at starting: all at once the ground
Gave way beneath his step, a certain smoke
Curled up and caught him, or perhaps down broke
A fireball wrapping flesh and spirit both   80
In conflagration.[3] Then—as heaven were loth
To linger—let earth understand too well
How heaven at need can operate—off fell
The flame-robe, and the untransfigured man
Resumed sobriety,—as he began,   85
So did he end nor alter pace, not he!

VI
Now, what I fain would know is—could it be
That he—whoe'er he was that furnished forth
The Chapel, making thus, from South to North,[4]

2. I.e., Raphael's painting, while reflecting the "new art" of the Italian Renaissance, did not lack a classical background. (The work of his Roman period
[1508–20] was strongly influenced by his
study of ancient sculpture.)
3. Cf. the transfiguration of Christ
(Mark 9:1–8).
4. From Italy to England.

Rafael touch Leighton,[5] Michelagnolo   90
Join Watts, was found but once combining so
The elder and the younger, taking stand
On Art's supreme,[6]—or that yourself who sang
A Song[7] where flute-breath silvers trumpet-clang,
And stations you for once on either hand   95
With Milton and with Keats,[8] empowered to claim
Affinity on just one point—(or blame
Or praise my judgment, thus it fronts you full)—
How came it you resume the void and null,
Subside to insignificance,—live, die   100
—Proved plainly two mere mortals who drew nigh
One moment—that,[9] to Art's best hierarchy,
This,[1] to the superhuman poet-pair?
What if, in one point only, then and there
The otherwise all-unapproachable   105
Allowed impingement? Does the sphere pretend
To span the cube's breadth, cover end to end
The plane with its embrace? No, surely! Still,
Contact is contact, sphere's touch no whit less
Than cube's superimposure. Such success   110
Befell Smart only out of throngs between
Milton and Keats that donned the singing-dress[2]—
Smart, solely of such songmen, pierced the screen
'Twixt thing and word, lit language straight from soul,—
Left no fine film-flake on the naked coal   115
Live from the censer—shapely or uncouth,
Fire-suffused through and through, one blaze of truth
Undeadened by a lie,—(you have my mind)—
For, think! this blaze outleapt with black behind
And blank before, when Hayley[3] and the rest . . .   120
But let the dead successors worst and best
Bury their dead: with life be my concern—
Yours with the fire-flame: what I fain would learn
Is just—(suppose me haply ignorant
Down to the common knowledge, doctors vaunt[4])   125

5. I.e., synthesizing old and new. The painters are: Sir Frederick Leighton (1830–96), English painter and sculptor, who had painted a portrait of Browning and had designed Elizabeth Barrett Browning's monument; Michelangelo (Michelagniolo Buonarroti, 1475–1564), greatest Florentine painter of the Renaissance; and George Frederic Watts (1817–1904), English painter and sculptor, who also had painted Browning's portrait.
6. Supreme height, summit.
7. "A Song to David."
8. John Milton (1608–74) and John Keats (1795–1821); the "flute-breath" is associated with the latter, the "trumpet-clang" with the former. Smart's poem synthesizes Miltonic grandeur and Keat-sian sensuousness, reconciles the baroque and "modern" styles.
9. The one "that furnished forth / The chapel" (lines 88–89).
1. Christopher Smart.
2. Eighteenth-century poets.
3. William Hayley (1745–1820), English poet and biographer. He "and the rest" represent mediocrity.
4. I.e., assume that I am ignorant, possessing only the common sense the philosophers make so much of. (Browning perhaps alludes to the "Scottish common-sense philosophers" of the late eighteenth century. Thomas Reid, Dugald Stewart, and others hoped to counter excessively metaphysical or skeptical points of view by appealing to common sense in philosophical disputes.)

Just this—why only once the fire-flame was:
No matter if the marvel came to pass
The way folk judged—if power too long suppressed
Broke loose and maddened, as the vulgar guessed,
Or simply brain-disorder (doctors said)   130
A turmoil of the particles disturbed
Brain's workaday performance in your head,
Spurred spirit to wild action health had curbed:
And so verse issued in a cataract
Whence prose, before and after, unperturbed   135
Was wont to wend its way. Concede the fact
That here a poet was who always could—
Never before did—never after would—
Achieve the feat: how were such fact explained?

VII

Was it that when, by rarest chance, there fell   140
Disguise from Nature, so that Truth remained
Naked, and whoso saw for once could tell
Us others of her majesty and might
In large, her lovelinesses infinite
In little,—straight you used the power wherewith   145
Sense, penetrating as through rind to pith
Each object, thoroughly revealed might view
And comprehend the old things thus made new,[5]
So that while eye saw, soul to tongue could trust
Thing which struck word out,[6] and once more adjust   150
Real vision to right language, till heaven's vault
Pompous with sunset, storm-stirred sea's assault
On the swilled[7] rock-ridge, earth's embosomed brood
Of tree and flower and weed, with all the life
That flies or swims or crawls, in peace or strife,   155
Above, below—each had its note and name
For Man to know by,—Man who, now—the same
As erst in Eden, needs that all he sees
Be named him[8] ere he note by what degrees
Of strength and beauty to its end Design   160
Ever thus operates—(your thought and mine,
No matter for the many dissident[9])—
So did you sing your Song, so truth found vent
In words for once with you?

VIII

                        Then—back was furled
The robe thus thrown aside, and straight the world   165
Darkened into the old oft-catalogued

---

5. Revelation 21:5: ". . . Behold, I make all things new."
6. Called the words forth.
7. Drenched.
8. For him. (Cf. Genesis 2:19–20; Adam's naming of creatures.) For Browning a main function of art is awakening men to the wonders of nature; cf. "Fra Lippo Lippi," lines 300–302.
9. I.e., we share the same philosophy, regardless of the many who disagree with us. (Probably Browning has poets like A. C. Swinburne in mind.)

Repository of things that sky, wave, land,
Or show or hide, clear late, accretion-clogged
Now, just as long ago, by tellings and
Re-tellings to satiety, which strike   170
Muffled upon the ear's drum. Very like
None was so startled as yourself when friends
Came, hailed your fast-returning wits: "Health mends
Importantly, for—to be plain with you—
This scribble on the wall was done—in lieu   175
Of pen and paper—with—ha, ha!—your key
Denting it on the wainscot! Do you see
How wise our caution was? Thus much we stopped
Of babble that had else grown print: and lopped
From your trim bay-tree this unsightly bough—   180
Smart's who translated Horace![1] Write us now" . . .
Why, what Smart did write—never afterward
One line to show that he, who paced the sward,[2]
Had reached the zenith from his madhouse cell.

IX

Was it because you judged (I know full well   185
You never had the fancy)—judged—as some—
That who makes poetry must reproduce
Thus ever and thus only, as they come,
Each strength, each beauty, everywhere diffuse
Throughout creation, so that eye and ear,   190
Seeing and hearing, straight shall recognize,
At touch of just a trait, the strength appear,—
Suggested by a line's lapse see arise
All evident the beauty,—fresh surprise
Startling at fresh achievement? "So, indeed,   195
Wallows the whale's bulk in the waste of brine,
Nor otherwise its feather-tufts make fine
Wild Virgin's Bower when stars faint off to seed!"[3]
(My prose—your poetry I dare not give,
Purpling too much my mere grey argument.)   200
—Was it because you judged—when fugitive
Was glory found, and wholly gone and spent
Such power of startling up deaf ear, blind eye,
At truth's appearance,—that you humbly bent
The head and, bidding vivid work good-bye,   205
Doffed lyric dress and trod the world once more
A drab-clothed decent proseman as before?
Strengths, beauties, by one word's flash thus laid bare

1. Roman poet Horace (Quintus Horatius Flaccus, 65–8 B.C.) was widely imitated and translated by the English "neo-classical" writers. Smart's having translated him would have been evidence of sanity as well as good taste. (Skeptical of poetic inspiration through Dionysiac frenzy, Horace concludes his *Ars Poetica* with a caricature of the mad poet who wanders about "spewing out verses.")
2. Grass, here symbolic of commonness or mediocrity.
3. The purple virgin's bower is a kind of wild clematis, a shrubby climber the fruits of which bear feathered seeds, often called "old man's beard." The plant's purple and gray are alluded to in line 200.

—That was effectual service: made aware
Of strengths and beauties, Man but hears the text,   210
Awaits your teaching.[4] Nature? What comes next?
Why all the strength and beauty?—to be shown
Thus in one word's flash, thenceforth let alone
By Man who needs must deal with aught that's known
Never so lately and so little? Friend,   215
First give us knowledge, then appoint its use!
Strength, beauty are the means: ignore their end?
As well you stopped at proving how profuse
Stones, sticks, nay stubble lie to left and right
Ready to help the builder,—careless quite   220
If he should take, or leave the same to strew
Earth idly,—as by word's flash bring in view
Strength, beauty, then bid who beholds the same
Go on beholding. Why gains unemployed?
Nature was made to be by Man enjoyed   225
First; followed duly by enjoyment's fruit,
Instruction—haply leaving joy behind:
And you, the instructor, would you slack pursuit
Of the main prize, as poet help mankind
Just to enjoy, there leave them? Play the fool,   230
Abjuring a superior privilege?
Please simply when your function is to rule—
By thought incite to deed?[5] From edge to edge
Of earth's round, strength and beauty everywhere
Pullulate[6]—and must you particularize   235
All, each and every apparition? Spare
Yourself and us the trouble! Ears and eyes
Want so much strength and beauty, and no less
Nor more, to learn life's lesson by. Oh, yes—
The other method's favoured in our day![7]   240
The end ere the beginning: as you may,
Master the heavens before you study earth,
Make you familiar with the meteor's birth
Ere you descend to scrutinize the rose!
I say, o'erstep no least one of the rows   245
That lead man from the bottom where he plants
Foot first of all, to life's last ladder-top:
Arrived there, vain enough will seem the vaunts
Of those who say—"We scale the skies, then drop

4. The metaphor is that of a preacher who had read the Bible lesson but has yet to deliver his sermon based on that "text."

5. In his moral emphasis Browning recalls Sir Philip Sidney's "Apology for Poetry" (1595): Poetry must both "teach and delight" and must "draw us to as high a perfection as our degenerate souls . . . can be capable of"; at its noblest the art can move men to "virtuous action." Browning's statement, "your function is to rule" (line 232),

paraphrases the last sentence of Shelley's "Defence of Poetry" (1821): "Poets are the unacknowledged legislators of the world."

6. Abound.

7. Under attack here is the English "Aesthetic Movement," led in poetry by A. C. Swinburne (1837–1909), whose "pagan" and sensual verse in *Atalanta* (1865) and *Poems and Ballads* (1866) made him the literary sensation of the time.

To earth—to find, how all things there are loth   250
To answer heavenly law: we understand
The meteor's course, and lo, the rose's growth—
How other than should be by law's command!"
Would not you tell such—"Friends, beware lest fume
Offuscate sense: learn earth first ere presume   255
To teach heaven legislation. Law must be
Active in earth or nowhere: earth you see,—
Or there or not at all, Will, Power and Love[8]
Admit discovery,—as below, above
Seek next law's confirmation! But reverse   260
The order, where's the wonder things grow worse
Than, by the law your fancy formulates,
They should be? Cease from anger at the fates
Which thwart themselves so madly. Live and learn,
Not first learn and then live, is our concern."   265

ca. 1885

From *Asolando: Fancies and Facts* (1889)

Prologue[1]

"The Poet's age is sad: for why?[2]
   In youth, the natural world could show
No common object but his eye
   At once involved with alien glow—[3]
His own soul's iris-bow.[4]   5

"And now a flower is just a flower:
   Man, bird, beast are but beast, bird, man—
Simply themselves, uncinct by dower
   Of dyes[5] which, when life's day began,
Round each in glory ran."   10

Friend, did you need an optic glass,
   Which were your choice? A lens to drape
In ruby, emerald, chrysopras,[6]

8. Browning often speaks of this triad of divine attributes; see for example "Saul," XVIII, and *The Ring and the Book*, X.1350ff.

1. *Asolando: Fancies and Facts*, Browning's last volume of poetry, was published on December 12, 1889, the day of his death in Venice; in his final hours he heard of its enthusiastic reception by the British public. In September 1889 Browning had returned to Asolo, the Italian town that is the setting for *Pippa Passes* (1841), to compose or revise poems for *Asolando*. As Roma King has stated, "In spite of the audaciousness of the love lyrics, there is a solemnity about the volume. Browning writes with a finality which suggests that he knew it would perhaps be his last work" (*The Focusing Artifice* [1968], p. 234).

The "Prologue" recalls the poet's first visit to Asolo in June 1838.

2. The first two stanzas are spoken by an unreflective friend of the poet's.

3. Cf. Wordsworth's "Ode: Intimations of Immortality," st. 1.

4. Iris was goddess of rainbows.

5. I.e., not enveloped by rich colors.

6. Apple-green silica which grows paler on exposure to light.

Each object—or reveal its shape
Clear outlined, past escape,   15

The naked very thing?—so clear
    That, when you had the chance to gaze,
You found its inmost self appear
    Through outer seeming—truth ablaze,
Not falsehood's fancy-haze?   20

How many a year, my Asolo,
    Since—one step just from sea to land—
I found you, loved yet feared you so—
    For natural objects seemed to stand
Palpably fire-clothed! No—   24

No mastery of mine o'er these!
    Terror with beauty, like the Bush[7]
Burning but unconsumed. Bend knees,
    Drop eyes to earthward! Language? Tush!
Silence 't is awe decrees.   30

And now? The lambent flame is—where?
    Lost from the naked world: earth, sky,
Hill, vale, tree, flower,—Italia's rare
    O'er-running beauty crowds the eye—
But flame? The Bush is bare.   35

Hill, vale, tree, flower—they stand distinct,
    Nature to know and name. What then?
A Voice spoke thence which straight unlinked
    Fancy from fact: see, all's in ken:[8]
Has once my eyelid winked?   40

No, for the purged ear apprehends
    Earth's import, not the eye late dazed:
The Voice said "Call my works thy friends!
    At Nature dost thou shrink amazed?
God is it who transcends."   45

ASOLO: Sept. 6, 1889.

Bad Dreams. I[1]

Last night I saw you in my sleep:[2]
    And how your charm of face was changed!

---

7. See Exodus 3, in which the Lord appears to Moses as a burning bush. Cf. lines 27ff.
8. View.
1. This sequence of poems shares with "James Lee's Wife" (1864) and George Meredith's *Modern Love* (1862) the theme of the estrangement of a modern couple. The obscurity, partly due to the dream symbolism, is perhaps traceable to the autobiographical element. A close friend, the young and wealthy American widow, Mrs. Clara Bloomfield-Moore, insisted that "no one can understand ['Bad Dreams'] so well as myself" (*Portrait*, p. 268). Browning apparently had a painful emotional experience as her guest at St. Moritz, Switzerland, in the fall of 1888, of which this may be the esoteric and ambiguous psychological record.
2. The speaker is probably the woman, though this is by no means clear.

I asked "Some love, some faith you keep?"
　You answered "Faith gone, love estranged."

Whereat I woke—a twofold bliss: 5
　Waking was one, but next there came
This other: "Though I felt, for this,[3]
　My heart break, I loved on the same."

Bad Dreams. II

You in the flesh and here—[4]
　Your very self! Now, wait!
One word! May I hope or fear?
　Must I speak in love or hate?
Stay while I ruminate!   5

The fact and each circumstance
　Dare you disown? Not you!
That vast dome, that huge dance,
　And the gloom which overgrew
A—possibly festive crew!   10

For why should men dance at all—
　Why women—a crowd of both—
Unless they are gay? Strange ball—
　Hands and feet plighting troth,
Yet partners enforced and loth!   15

Of who danced there, no shape
　Did I recognize: thwart, perverse,
Each grasped each, past escape
　In a whirl or weary or worse:
Man's sneer met woman's curse,   20

While he and she toiled as if
　Their guardian set galley-slaves
To supple chained limbs grown stiff:
　Unmanacled trulls and knaves—
The lash for who misbehaves!   25

And a gloom was, all the while,
　Deeper and deeper yet
O'ergrowing the rank and file
　Of that army of haters—set
To mimic love's fever-fret.   30

By the wall-side close I crept,
　Avoiding the livid maze.
And, safely so far, outstepped
　On a chamber—a chapel, says
My memory or betrays—   35

---

3. I.e., "because of this," the dream lover's denial of love.

4. The first dream, the man's, is an allegory of loveless marriage.

Closet-like, kept aloof
  From unseemly witnessing
What sport made floor and roof
  Of the Devil's palace ring

While his Damned amused their king.   40
Ay, for a low lamp burned,
  And a silence lay about
What I, in the midst, discerned
  Though dimly till, past doubt,
'T was a sort of throne stood out—   45

High seat with steps, at least:
  And the topmost step was filled
By—whom? What vestured priest?
  A stranger to me,—his guild,
His cult, unreconciled   50

To my knowledge how guild and cult
  Are clothed in this world of ours:
I pondered, but no result
  Came to—unless that Giaours[5]
So worship the Lower Powers.   55

When suddenly who entered?
  Who knelt—did you guess I saw?
Who—raising that face where centred
  Allegiance to love and law
So lately—off-casting awe,   60

Down-treading reserve, away
  Thrusting respect . . . but mine
Stands firm—firm still shall stay!
  Ask Satan! for I decline
To tell—what I saw, in fine!   65

Yet here in the flesh you come—
  Your same self, form and face,—
In the eyes, mirth still at home!
  On the lips, that commonplace
Perfection of honest grace!   70

Yet your errand is—needs must be—
  To palliate—well, explain,
Expurgate in some degree
  Your soul of its ugly stain.
Oh, you—the good in grain—   75

How was it your white took tinge?
  "A mere dream"—never object!
Sleep leaves a door on hinge
  Whence soul, ere our flesh suspect,
Is off and away: detect   80

5. Infidels.

Her vagaries when loose, who can!
    Be she pranksome, be she prude,
Disguise with the day began:
    With the night—ah, what ensued
From draughts of a drink hell-brewed?   85

Then She: "What a queer wild dream!
    And perhaps the best fun is—
Myself had its fellow—I seem
    Scarce awake from yet. 'T was this—
Shall I tell you? First, a kiss!   90

"For the fault was just your own,—
    'T is myself expect apology:
You warned me to let alone
    (Since our studies were mere philology)
That ticklish[6] (you said) Anthology.[7]   95

"So, I dreamed that I passed *exam*
    Till a question posed me sore:
'Who translated this epigram
    By—an author we best ignore?'[8]
And I answered 'Hannah More'!"[9]   100

Bad Dreams. III

This was my dream: I saw a Forest[1]
    Old as the earth, no track nor trace
Of unmade man. Thou, Soul, explorest—
    Though in a trembling rapture—space
Immeasurable! Shrubs, turned trees,   5
Trees that touch heaven, support its frieze
Studded with sun and moon and star:
While—oh, the enormous growths that bar
Mine eye from penetrating past
    Their tangled twine where lurks—nay, lives   10
Royally lone, some brute-type cast
    I' the rough, time cancels, man forgives.

On, Soul! I saw a lucid City[2]
    Of architectural device

6. Prurient, lewd.

7. Probably the Greek Anthology, a collection of epigrams, short elegiac poems composed between the seventh century B.C. and the tenth century A.D. Some are humorous or satirical. But Browning may have had in mind the Latin Anthology (sixth century A.D.), which includes the erotic poem *Pervigilium Veneris*, a song celebrating Venus Genetrix (mother of the Romans).

8. Possibly Martial (ca. A.D. 40–104), many of whose epigrams are spiced with obscenities. Her ludicrous answer (line 100) reflects the man's attempt to keep her sheltered intellectually.

9. Ethical and religious writer and reformer (1745–1833), a member of the Evangelical "Clapham Sect." Among her works is *Practical Piety* (1811).

1. The man's dream. The forest recalls the setting of the first dream in II. The symbolic opposition of Forest to City resembles the cultural antithesis defined by Friedrich Nietzsche in *The Birth of Tragedy* (1872): the "Dionysian" (passion, excess) vs. the "Apollonian" (restraint, harmony).

2. Cf. Tennyson's "The Palace of Art" (1832, 1842), an allegory of purely intellectual delights experienced by the Soul.

Every way perfect. Pause for pity,   15
   Lighting! nor leave a cicatrice
On those bright marbles, dome and spire,
Structures palatial,—streets which mire
Dares not defile, paved all too fine
For human footstep's smirch, not thine—   20
Proud solitary traverser.
   My Soul, of silent lengths of way—
With what ecstatic dread, aver,
   Lest life start sanctioned by thy stay!

Ah, but the last sight was the hideous!   25
   A City, yes,—a Forest, true,—
But each devouring each. Perfidious
   Snake-plants had strangled what I knew
Was a pavilion once: each oak
Held on his horns some spoil he broke   30
By surreptitiously beneath
Upthrusting: pavements, as with teeth,
Griped huge weed widening crack and split
   In squares and circles stone-work erst.
Oh, Nature—good! Oh, Art—no whit   35
   Less worthy! Both in one—accurst!

Bad Dreams. IV

It happened thus: my slab, though new,[3]
   Was getting weather-stained,—beside,
Herbage, balm, peppermint o'ergrew
   Letter and letter: till you tried
Somewhat, the Name was scarce descried.   5

That strong stern man my lover came:
   —Was he my lover? Call him, pray,
My life's cold critic bent on blame
   Of all poor I could do or say
To make me worth his love one day—   10

One far day when, by diligent
   And dutiful amending faults,
Foibles, all weaknesses which went
   To challenge and excuse assaults
Of culture wronged by taste that halts[4]—   15

Discrepancies should mar no plan
   Symmetric of the qualities
Claiming respect from—say—a man
   That's strong and stern. "Once more he pries
Into me with those critic eyes!"   20

No question! so—"Conclude, condemn
   Each failure my poor self avows!

---

3. The woman's dream.   4. Falters, wavers.

Leave to its fate all you contemn!
   There's Solomon's selected spouse:[5]
Earth needs must hold such maids—choose them!"   25

Why, he was weeping! Surely gone
   Sternness and strength: with eyes to ground
And voice a broken monotone—
   "Only be as you were! Abound
In foibles, faults,—laugh, robed and crowned   30

"As Folly's veriest queen,—care I
   One feather-fluff? Look pity, Love,
On prostrate me—your foot shall try
   This forehead's use—mount thence above,
And reach what Heaven you dignify!"   35

Now, what could bring such change about?
   The thought perplexed: till, following
His gaze upon the ground,—why, out
   Came all the secret! So, a thing
Thus simple has deposed my king!   40

For, spite of weeds that strove to spoil
   Plain reading on the lettered slab,
My name was clear enough—no soil
   Effaced the date when one chance stab
Of scorn . . . if only ghosts might blab!   45

"Imperante Augusto Natus Est—"[1]

What it was struck the terror into me?
This, Publius: closer! while we wait our turn
I'll tell you. Water's warm (they ring inside)
At the eighth hour, till when no use to bathe.

Here in the vestibule where now we sit,   5

5. See Song of Solomon 4:9: "Thou hast ravished my heart, my sister, my spouse. . . ."
1. Like "Karshish" and "Cleon," this monologue re-creates pagan antiquity on the verge of the Christian era. It is set during the thirteenth consulship of Augustus (ca. 2 B.C.) in Rome, where a senator and his friend Publius await their turn at the public bath. The senator's prophecy of Christ's coming (lines 158–59) is taken from *The Sibylline Oracles* (III.47–51, 55–60) hailing the advent of an "immortal" and "holy king" and from Virgil's *Fourth Ecologue* (Pollio), which celebrates a "boy's birth, in whom the iron race shall begin to cease, and the golden to arise over all the world." The title, meaning "He [Christ] was born in the reign of Augustus," is from St. Augustine's *The City of God*, XVIII. chap. 46.

For the portrait of Augustus the poet drew upon Suetonius' *De vita Caesarum* (*The Lives of the Caesars*). "Augustus" ("Exalted One") was the title awarded Gaius Julius Caesar Octavianus (63 B.C.–A.D. 14) in 27 B.C. in recognition that he has brought peace and saved the Roman republic through the defeat of Antony and Cleopatra at Actium (31 B.C.) and through the restoration of order at home. As "first citizen," Octavian was invested with comprehensive authority, wielding domestic power through a series of consulships. He revived the Roman state religion, was named *Pontifex Maximus* (head of the council of priests), and arranged to have his "genius" deified. As patron of the arts and literature he has had few equals; in his reign flourished Ovid, Horace, and Virgil.

One scarce stood yesterday, the throng was such
Of loyal gapers, folk all eye and ear
While Lucius Varius Rufus[2] in their midst
Read out that long-planned late-completed piece,
His Panegyric on the Emperor.   10
"Nobody like him" little Flaccus[3] laughed
"At leading forth an Epos[4] with due pomp!
Only, when godlike Caesar[5] swells the theme,
How should mere mortals hope to praise aright?
Tell me, thou offshoot of Etruscan kings!"   15
Whereat Mæcenas[6] smiling sighed assent.

I paid my quadrans,[7] left the Thermæ's roar
Of rapture as the poet asked "What place
Among the godships Jove, for Cæsar's sake,
Would bid its actual occupant vacate   20
In favour of the new divinity?"
And got the expected answer "Yield thine own!"—
Jove thus dethroned, I somehow wanted air,
And found myself a-pacing street and street,
Letting the sunset, rosy over Rome,   25
Clear my head dizzy with the hubbub—say
As if thought's dance therein had kicked up dust
By trampling on all else: the world lay prone,
As—poet-propped, in brave hexameters[8]—
Their subject triumphed up from man to God.   30
Caius Octavius Caesar the August—
Where was escape from his prepotency?
I judge I may have passed—how many piles
Of structure dropt like doles from his free hand
To Rome on every side? Why, right and left,   35
For temples you've the Thundering Jupiter,
Avenging Mars, Apollo Palatine:
How count Piazza, Forum—there's a third
All but completed. You've the Theatre
Named of Marcellus—all his work, such work!—   40
One thought still ending, dominating all—
With warrant Varius sang "Be Cæsar God!"
By what a hold arrests he Fortune's wheel,
Obtaining and retaining heaven and earth
Through Fortune, if you like, but favour—no!   45
For the great deeds flashed by me, fast and thick

2. Esteemed epic and tragic poet (64 B.C.–A.D. 9); none of Varius' work is extant except for two lines of a panegyric on Augustus, quoted by Horace in *Epistle 1*.
3. Horace, or Quintus Horatius Flaccus (65–8 B.C.), five years younger than Virgil; famous for his odes, epistles, and satires. Suetonius describes him as short and stout.
4. Heroic poem.
5. Augustus was widely regarded as divine. (See Virgil, *Aeneid*, VI.788–805.)
6. Died 8 B.C. Enlightened patron of a circle including Varius, Horace, and Virgil; also friend and counselor to Augustus.
7. Roman coin. *Thermae*: warm baths.
8. Classical six-measure line, primarily the meter of epic poetry.

As stars which storm the sky on autumn nights—
Those conquests! but peace crowned them,—so, of peace!
Count up his titles only—these, in few—
Ten years Triumvir, Consul thirteen times,   50
Emperor, nay—the glory topping all—
Hailed Father of his Country, last and best
Of titles, by himself accepted so:
And why not? See but feats achieved in Rome—
Not to say, Italy—he planted there   55
Some thirty colonies—but Rome itself
All new-built, "marble now, brick once," he boasts:
This Portico, that Circus. Would you sail?
He has drained Tiber for you: would you walk?
He straightened out the long Flaminian Way.[9]   60
Poor? Profit by his score of donatives!
Rich—that is, mirthful? Half-a-hundred games
Challenge your choice! There's Rome—for you and me
Only? The centre of the world besides!
For, look the wide world over, where ends Rome?   65
To sunrise? There's Euphrates—all between!
To sunset? Ocean and immensity:
North,—stare till Danube stops you: South, see Nile,
The Desert and the earth-upholding Mount.[1]
Well may the poet-people each with each   70
Vie in his praise, our company of swans,
Virgil and Horace, singers—in their way—
Nearly as good as Varius, though less famed:
Well may they cry, "No mortal, plainly God!"

Thus to myself myself said, while I walked: 75
Or would have said, could thought attain to speech,
Clean baffled by enormity of bliss
The while I strove to scale its heights and sound
Its depths—this masterdom o'er the world
Of one who was but born,—like you, like me,   80
Like all the world he owns,—of flesh and blood.
But he—how grasp, how gauge his own conceit
Of bliss to me near inconceivable?
Or—since such flight too much makes reel the brain—
Let's sink—and so take refuge, as it were,   85
From life's excessive altitude—to life's
Breathable wayside shelter at its base!
If looms thus large this Caesar to myself
—Of senatorial rank and somebody—
How must he strike the vulgar nameless crowd,   90

9. Northern road of ancient Italy, leading from the Flaminian gate of Rome to
Ariminium (Rimini).
1. Mount Atlas (actually a mountain
range in northwest Africa), where Atlas
was supposed to have stood holding the
earth on his shoulders. Lines 66–69 outline world geography as the Romans understood it in 2 B.C.

Innumerous swarm that's nobody at all?
Why,—for an instance,—much as yon gold shape
Crowned, sceptred, on the temple opposite—
Fulgurant[2] Jupiter—must daze the sense
Of—say, yon outcast begging from its step!   95
What, anti-Cæsar, monarch in the mud,
As he is pinnacled above thy pate?
Ay, beg away! thy lot contrasts full well
With his whose bounty yields thee this support—
Our Holy and Inviolable One,   100
Cæsar, whose bounty built the fane[3] above!
Dost read my thought? Thy garb, alack, displays
Sore usage truly in each rent and stain—
Faugh! Wash though in Suburra![4] 'Ware the dogs
Who may not so disdain a meal on thee!   105
What, stretchest forth a palm to catch my alms?
Aha, why yes: I must appear—who knows?—
I, in my toga, to thy rags and thee—
Quæstor—nay, Ædile, Censor[5]—Pol! perhaps
The very City-Prætor's[6] noble self!   110
As to me Caesar, so to thee am I?
Good: nor in vain shall prove thy quest, poor rogue!
Hither—hold palm out—take this quarter-as![7]

And who did take it? As he raised his head,
(My gesture was a trifle—well, abrupt),   115
Back fell the broad flap of the peasant's-hat,
The homespun cloak that muffled half his cheek
Dropped somewhat, and I had a glimpse—just one!
One was enough. Whose—whose might be the face?
That unkempt careless hair—brown, yellowish—   120
Those sparkling eyes beneath their eyebrows' ridge
(Each meets each, and the hawk-nose rules between)
—That was enough, no glimpse was needed more!
And terrifyingly into my mind
Came that quick-hushed report was whispered us,   125
"They do say, once a year in sordid garb
He plays the mendicant, sits all day long,
Asking and taking alms of who may pass,
And so averting, if submission help,
Fate's envy, the dread chance and change of things   130
When Fortune—for a word, a look, a nought—
Turns spiteful and—the petted lioness—
Strikes with her sudden paw, and prone falls each
Who patted late her neck superiorly,
Or trifled with those claw-tips velvet-sheathed."   135

2. Emitting flashes of lightning.
3. Temple.
4. Low street in Rome.
5. Three municipal offices in ascending
order of importance. *Pol!*: an oath by
Pollux, twin of Castor.
6. The *praetor urbanus* was the highest
magistrate in a Latin town.
7. Very small coin.

"He's God!" shouts Lucius Varius Rufus: "Man
And worms'-meat any moment!" mutters low
Some Power, admonishing the mortal-born.

Ay, do you mind? There's meaning in the fact
That whoso conquers, triumphs, enters Rome,   140
Climbing the Capitolian,[8] soaring thus
To glory's summit,—Publius, do you mark—
Ever the same attendant who, behind,
Above the Conqueror's head supports the crown
All-too-demonstrative for human wear,   145
—One hand's employment—all while reserves
Its fellow, backward flung, to point how, close
Appended from the car, beneath the foot
Of the up-borne exulting Conqueror,
Frown—half-descried—the instruments of shame,   150
The malefactor's due. Crown, now—Cross, when?

Who stands secure? Are even Gods so safe?
Jupiter that just now is dominant—
Are not there ancient dismal tales how once
A predecessor[9] reigned ere Saturn came,   155
And who can say if Jupiter be last?
Was it for nothing the grey Sibyl[1] wrote
"Cæsar Augustus regnant, shall be born
In blind Judæa"—one to master him,
Him and the universe? An old-wife's tale?   160

Bath-drudge! Here, slave! No cheating! Our turn next.
No loitering, or be sure you taste the lash!
Two strigils,[2] two oil-dippers, each a sponge!

Development[1]

My Father was a scholar and knew Greek.
When I was five years old, I asked him once
",What do you read about?"
                        "The siege of Troy."[2]

8. Capitol on the hill.
9. Uranus, father of the race of Titans or Elder Gods, among whom was Saturn (Cronus). According to Hesiod (*Theogony*, 133–87), Saturn castrated Uranus with a sickle, then ruled over the other Titans until his son Zeus (Jupiter) dethroned him. Saturn fled to Italy, inaugurating the Golden Age; he was the Roman agricultural deity.
1. The Erythraean sibyl, credited by St. Augustine with having "sung many things about Christ more plainly than the other sibyls" (*City of God*, XVIII. chap. 23). Augustus, it is said, consulted the oracles at Delphi to learn of his successor. When told a Judean child was his enemy and lord, he built an altar on the Capitoline Hill with the inscription *Ara Primogeniti Dei* ("Altar of God's First-Born").
2. Scrapers used at the baths.
1. Temperamentally unsuited to systematic instruction, Browning never earned a university degree. From boyhood his unorthodox education consisted mainly of reading for pleasure in his father's excellent library, where he developed a lifelong interest in the Greek classics. See the early "Artemis Prologizes" (1842) and the late poems containing translations from Euripides: *Balaustion's Adventure* (1871) and *Aristophanes' Apology* (1875).
2. The *Iliad*.

"What is a siege and what is Troy?"

                                        Whereat
He piled up chairs and tables for a town,   5
Set me a-top for Priam,[3] called our cat
—Helen, enticed away from home (he said)
By wicked Paris,[4] who couched somewhere close
Under the footstool, being cowardly,
But whom—since she was worth the pains, poor puss—   10
Towzer and Tray,—our dogs, the Atreidai,[5]—sought
By taking Troy to get possession of
—Always when great Achilles ceased to sulk,[6]
(My pony in the stable)—forth would prance
And put to flight Hector—our page-boy's self.   15
This taught me who was who and what was what:
So far I rightly understood the case
At five years old: a huge delight it proved
And still proves—thanks to that instructor sage
My Father, who knew better than turn straight   20
Learning's full flare on weak-eyed ignorance,
Or, worse yet, leave weak eyes to grow sand-blind,
Content with darkness and vacuity.

It happened, two or three years afterward,
That—I and playmates playing at Troy's Siege—   25
My Father came upon our make-believe.
"How would you like to read yourself the tale
Properly told, of which I gave you first
Merely such notion as a boy could bear?
Pope,[7] now, would give you the precise account   30
Of what, some day, by dint of scholarship,
You'll hear—who knows?—from Homer's very mouth.
Learn Greek by all means, read the 'Blind Old Man,
Sweetest of Singers'—*tuphlos* which means 'blind,'
Hedistos which means 'sweetest.' Time enough!   35
Try, anyhow, to master him some day;
Until when, take what serves for substitute,
Read Pope, by all means!"

                              So I ran through Pope,
Enjoyed the tale—what history so true?
Also attacked my Primer, duly drudged,   40
Grew fitter thus for what was promised next—
The very thing itself, the actual words,
When I could turn—say, Buttmann[8] to account.

3. King of Troy and father of Paris and Hector.
4. His carrying Helen off to Troy precipitated the Trojan War.
5. Sons of Atreus: Menelaus and Agamemnon.
6. Achilles sulked in his tent when Briseis, a beautiful captive, was taken from him by Agamemnon; he entered battle to avenge the death of his friend Patroclus, killing the Trojan leader Hector.
7. Alexander Pope (1688–1744), whose translation of the *Iliad* (1720) in heroic couplets was very popular.
8. Philipp Karl Buttman (1764–1829), author of a standard Greek grammar for schoolboys.

Time passed, I ripened somewhat: one fine day,
"Quite ready for the Iliad, nothing less?   45
There's Heine,[9] where the big books block the shelf:
Don't skip a word, thumb well the Lexicon!"

I thumbed well and skipped nowise till I learned
Who was who, what was what, from Homer's tongue,
And there an end of learning. Had you asked   50
The all-accomplished scholar, twelve years old,
"Who was it wrote the Iliad?"—what a laugh!
"Why, Homer, all the world knows: of his life
Doubtless some facts exist: it's everywhere:
We have not settled, though, his place of birth: 55
He begged, for certain, and was blind beside:
Seven cities claimed him—Scio, with best right,[1]
Thinks Byron. What he wrote? Those Hymns[2] we have.
Then there's the 'Battle of the Frogs and Mice,'[3]
That's all—unless they dig 'Margites'[4] up   60
(I'd like that) nothing more remains to know."

Thus did youth spend a comfortable time;
Until—"What's this the Germans say is fact
The Wolf[5] found out first? It's unpleasant work
Their chop and change, unsettling one's belief: 65
All the same, while we live, we learn, that's sure."
So, I bent brow o'er *Prolegomena.*
And, after Wolf, a dozen of his like
Proved there was never any Troy at all,
Neither Besiegers nor Besieged,—nay, worse,—   70
No actual Homer, no authentic text,
No warrant for the fiction I, as fact,
Had treasured in my heart and soul so long—
Ay, mark you! and as fact held still, still hold,
Spite of new knowledge, in my heart of hearts   75
And soul of souls, fact's essence freed and fixed
From accidental fancy's guardian sheath.
Assuredly thenceforward—thank my stars!—
However it got there, deprive who could—
Wring from the shrine my precious tenantry,   80

9. Christian Gottlob Heyne (1729–1812), editor of a standard text of the *Iliad*.
1. More than seven cities have claimed the honor. Modern scholars favor Smyrna or the island of Chios ("Scio").
2. The Homeric Hymns, collection of invocations and epic narratives of unknown authorship.
3. The *Batrachomyomachia*, burlesque epic attributed to Homer, but probably of much later date.
4. Lost satirical poem, authorship unknown but attributed to Homer by Aristotle and Zeno.
5. Friedrich August Wolf (1759–1824), a founder of modern classical philology and author of the famous *Prolegomena in Homerum* (1795), which theorized that the *Iliad* and *Odyssey* were not by one author but were the blending of several poems handed down by oral recitation and unified by subsequent treatment. The analogy of modern Homeric scholarship to the work of the biblical critics is clear: as Wolf was to Homer, so were Strauss and Renan to the Gospels. See "Christmas-Eve," XV (1850) and "A Death in the Desert" (1864) for the poet's reply to the so-called "Higher Criticism."

Helen, Ulysses, Hector and his Spouse,[6]
Achilles and his Friend?—though Wolf—ah, Wolf!
Why must he needs come doubting, spoil a dream?

But then "No dream's worth waking"[7]—Browning says:
And here's the reason why I tell thus much.   85
I, now mature man, you anticipate,
May blame my Father justifiably
For letting me dream out my nonage[8] thus,
And only by such slow and sure degrees
Permitting me to sift the grain from chaff,   90
Get truth and falsehood known and named as such.
Why did he ever let me dream at all,
Not bid me taste the story in its strength?
Suppose my childhood was scarce qualified
To rightly understand mythology,   95
Silence at least was in his power to keep:
I might have—somehow—correspondingly—
Well, who knows by what method, gained my gains,
Been taught, by forthrights not meanderings,
My aim should be to loathe, like Peleus' son,[9]   100
A lie as Hell's Gate, love my wedded wife,
Like Hector, and so on with all the rest.
Could not I have excogitated this
Without believing such men really were?
That is—he might have put into my hand   105
The "Ethics"?[1] In translation, if you please,
Exact, no pretty lying that improves,
To suit the modern taste: no more, no less—
The "Ethics": 't is a treatise I find hard
To read aright now that my hair is grey,   110
And I can manage the original.
At five years old—how ill had fared its leaves!
Now, growing double o'er the Stagirite,[2]
At least I soil no page with bread and milk,
Nor crumple, dogsear and deface—boys' way.   115

Epilogue[1]

At the midnight in the silence of the sleep-time,
    When you set your fancies free,

---

6. Andromache. Achilles' friend is Patroclus (line 82).
7. The controlling idea of *Asolando*, which repeatedly states the poet's preference for fact over fancy, reality over "dreaming's vapour-wreath" ("Dubiety," line 12).
8. Youth.
9. Achilles, whose resentment at Agamemnon's breach of faith is the theme of the *Iliad* (see Book I).
1. The *Nichomachean Ethics*, treatise on morals by Aristotle.

2. Aristotle (384–322 B.C.), born at Stagira, a Greek colonial town on the Aegean.
1. Of the poem Browning is reported to have said, "It almost looks like bragging to say this, and as if I ought to cancel it; but it's the simple truth; and as it's true, it shall stand." The "Epilogue" has traditionally concluded all editions of Browning's poetry. Cf. Tennyson's "Crossing the Bar."

Will they pass to where—by death, fools think, imprisoned—
Low he lies who once so loved you, whom you loved so,
   —Pity me?   5

Oh to love so, be so loved, yet so mistaken![2]
 What had I on earth to do
With the slothful, with the mawkish, the unmanly?
Like the aimless, helpless, hopeless, did I drivel
   —Being—who?   10

One who never turned his back but marched breast forward,
 Never doubted clouds would break,
Never dreamed, though right were worsted, wrong would triumph,
Held we fall to rise, are baffled to fight better,
   Sleep to wake.   15

No, at noonday in the bustle of man's work-time
 Greet the unseen with a cheer!
Bid him forward, breast and back as either should be,
"Strive and thrive!" cry "Speed,[3]—fight on, fare ever
   There as here!"   20

2. You (the person addressed in line 2)   3. Godspeed; a prosperous journey.
are mistaken in pitying me.

Prose

From "Introductory Essay" to the
Letters of Percy Bysshe Shelley (1852)

Browning published very little formal prose. His only signed critical work of importance is the "Introductory Essay" to the *Letters of Percy Bysshe Shelley* (1852), now called the *Essay on Shelley*. After touching briefly upon its ostensible subject, literary biography, the essay falls into two sections: in the first Browning advances the theory that successive literary periods are dominated by "objective" and "subjective" poetry in alternation; in the second he attempts to fix Shelley's unique place in this scheme of literary history and to vindicate the character of the poet, whom Browning then regarded as a maligned and neglected genius. After his momentous discovery of Shelley's poetry in 1826, Browning had undergone an intellectual conversion to Shelleyan principles, from which he was largely "unconverted" by 1833 (see notes to *Pauline*). Yet for two decades more Shelley was to remain a star of the first magnitude in Browning's firmament (see "Memorabilia" [1855]). When in 1851 he strove to formulate the reasons for his longstanding admiration of Shelley the poet, he as yet knew little (save fragmentary accounts) of Shelley the man. But disenchantment was not long in coming: as early as 1856 Browning was forcibly made aware of Shelley's desertion of his first wife, Harriet; thereafter his faith in Shelley's character remained badly shaken. Because the chasm between the poet and the man had widened unacceptably for Browning, he was to refuse in 1885 the presidency of the newly founded Shelley Society.

The *Essay on Shelley* was written in late 1851 at the request of Browning's friend and erstwhile publisher, Edward Moxon, who needed a preface to his newly acquired collection of twenty-five unpublished Shelley letters. The volume was printed in early 1852 but was suppressed forthwith, owing to the timely discovery that at least one of the letters was spurious. The essay was, however, reprinted in Browning's lifetime by both the Browning and the Shelley Societies. The extract here is from the opening paragraphs; the text is that of H. F. B. Brett-Smith (1921, 1923), a transcription of the 1852 Moxon volume in the Bodleian Library, Oxford.

An opportunity having presented itself for the acquisition of a series of unedited letters by Shelley, all more or less directly supplementary to and illustrative of the collection already published by Mr. Moxon,[1] that gentleman has decided on securing them. They will

1. *Essays, Letters from Abroad, Translations and Fragments,* ed. Mary W. Shelley, 2 vols. (1840, 1852). The Brownings owned a copy of the 1840 edition.

prove an acceptable addition to a body of correspondence, the value of which towards a right understanding of its author's purpose and work, may be said to exceed that of any similar contribution exhibiting the worldly relations of a poet whose genius has operated by a different law.

Doubtless we accept gladly the biography of an objective[2] poet, as the phrase now goes; one whose endeavour has been to reproduce things external (whether the phenomena of the scenic universe, or the manifested action of the human heart and brain) with an immediate reference, in every case, to the common eye and apprehension of his fellow men, assumed capable of receiving and profiting by this reproduction. It has been obtained through the poet's double faculty of seeing external objects more clearly, widely, and deeply, than is possible to the average mind, at the same time that he is so acquainted and in sympathy with its narrower comprehension as to be careful to supply it with no other materials than it can combine into an intelligible whole. The auditory of such a poet will include, not only the intelligences which, save for such assistance, would have missed the deeper meaning and enjoyment of the original objects, but also the spirits of a like endowment with his own, who, by means of his abstract, can forthwith pass to the reality it was made from, and either corroborate their impressions of things known already, or supply themselves with new from whatever shows in the inexhaustible variety of existence may have hitherto escaped their knowledge. Such a poet is properly the ποιητης, the fashioner;[3] and the thing fashioned, his poetry, will of necessity be substantive, projected from himself and distinct. We are ignorant what the inventor of "Othello" conceived of that fact as he beheld it in completeness, how he accounted for it, under what known law he registered its nature, or to what unknown law he traced its coincidence. We learn only what he intended we should learn by that particular exercise of his power,—the fact itself,—which, with its infinite significances, each of us receives for the first time as a creation, and is hereafter left to deal with, as, in proportion to his own intelligence, he best may. We are ignorant, and would fain be otherwise.

Doubtless, with respect to such a poet, we covet his biography. We desire to look back upon the process of gathering together in a lifetime, the materials of the work we behold entire; of elaborating, perhaps under difficulty and with hindrance, all that is familiar to our admiration in the apparent facility of success. And the inner impulse of this effort and operation, what induced it? Did a soul's

2. The distinction between "objective" and "subjective" writing was appropriated from German thought in the 1820s by Coleridge and other English romantic critics. Browning's use of the terms is typical.
3. Greek *poiētēs*, from *poiein*, "to make."

delight in its own extended sphere of vision set it, for the gratification of an insuppressible power, on labour, as other men are set on rest? Or did a sense of duty or of love lead it to communicate its own sensations to mankind? Did an irresistible sympathy with men compel it to bring down and suit its own provision of knowledge and beauty to their narrow scope? Did the personality of such an one stand like an open watch-tower in the midst of the territory it is erected to gaze on, and were the storms and calms, the stars and meteors, its watchman was wont to report of, the habitual variegation of his every-day life, as they glanced across its open roof or lay reflected on its four-square parapet? Or did some sunken and darkened chamber of imagery witness, in the artificial illumination of every storied compartment we are permitted to contemplate, how rare and precious were the outlooks through here and there an embrasure upon a world beyond, and how blankly would have pressed on the artificer the boundary of his daily life, except for the amorous diligence with which he had rendered permanent by art whatever came to diversify the gloom? Still, fraught with instruction and interest as such details undoubtedly are, we can, if needs be, dispense with them. The man passes, the work remains. The work speaks for itself, as we say: and the biography of the worker is no more necessary to an understanding or enjoyment of it, than is a model or anatomy of some tropical tree, to the right tasting of the fruit we are familiar with on the market-stall,—or a geologist's map and stratification, to the prompt recognition of the hill-top, our land-mark of every day.

We turn with stronger needs to the genius of an opposite tendency—the subjective poet of modern classification. He, gifted like the objective poet with the fuller perception of nature and man, is impelled to embody the thing he perceives, not so much with reference to the many below as to the One above him, the supreme Intelligence which apprehends all things in their absolute truth,— an ultimate view ever aspired to, if but partially attained, by the poet's own soul. Not what man sees, but what God sees—the *Ideas* of Plato,[4] seeds of creation lying burningly on the Divine Hand—it is toward these that he struggles. Not with the combination of humanity in action, but with the primal elements of humanity he has to do; and he digs where he stands,—preferring to seek them in his own soul as the nearest reflex of that absolute Mind, according to the intuitions of which he desires to perceive and speak. Such a poet does not deal habitually with the picturesque groupings and tempestuous tossings of the forest-trees, but with their roots and

4. The Platonic Idea is "a supposed eternally existing pattern or archetype of any class of things, of which the individual things in that class are imperfect copies, and from which they derive their existence" (*OED*).

fibres naked to the chalk and stone. He does not paint pictures and hang them on the walls, but rather carries them on the retina of his own eyes: we must look deep into his human eyes, to see those pictures on them. He is rather a seer, accordingly, than a fashioner, and what he produces will be less a work than an effluence. That effluence cannot be easily considered in abstraction from his personality,—being indeed the very radiance and aroma of his personality, projected from it but not separated. Therefore, in our approach to the poetry, we necessarily approach the personality of the poet; in apprehending it we apprehend him, and certainly we cannot love it without loving him. Both for love's and for understanding's sake we desire to know him, and as readers of his poetry must be readers of his biography also.

I shall observe, in passing, that it seems not so much from any essential distinction in the faculty of the two poets or in the nature of the objects contemplated by either, as in the more immediate adaptability of these objects to the distinct purpose of each, that the objective poet, in his appeal to the aggregate human mind, chooses to deal with the doings of men, (the result of which dealing, in its pure form, when even description, as suggesting a describer, is dispensed with, is what we call dramatic poetry), while the subjective poet, whose study has been himself, appealing through himself to the absolute Divine mind, prefers to dwell upon those external scenic appearances which strike out most abundantly and uninterruptedly his inner light and power, selects that silence of the earth and sea in which he can best hear the beating of his individual heart, and leaves the noisy, complex, yet imperfect exhibitions of nature in the manifold experience of man around him, which serve only to distract and suppress the working of his brain. These opposite tendencies of genius will be more readily descried in their artistic effect than in their moral spring and cause. Pushed to an extreme and manifested as a deformity, they will be seen plainest of all in the fault of either artist, when subsidiarily to the human interest of his work his occasional illustrations from scenic nature are introduced as in the earlier works of the originative painters[5]— men and women filling the foreground with consummate mastery, while mountain, grove and rivulet show like an anticipatory revenge on that succeeding race of landscape-painters[6] whose "figures" disturb the perfection of their earth and sky. It would be idle to inquire, of these two kinds of poetic faculty in operation, which is

5. Browning may have in mind such Italian Renaissance painters as Ghirlandaio, Botticelli, and Leonardo da Vinci, in whose work the natural setting is often a distant backdrop.
6. Perhaps the great English landscape painters John Constable (1776–1837) and J. M. W. Turner (1775–1851), who often placed their human figures in the middle distance or background and made them appear diminutive amid the grandeur of their surroundings.

the higher or even rarer endowment. If the subjective might seem to be the ultimate requirement of every age, the objective, in the strictest state, must still retain its original value. For it is with this world, as starting point and basis alike, that we shall always have to concern ourselves: the world is not to be learned and thrown aside, but reverted to and relearned.[7] The spiritual comprehension may be infinitely subtilised, but the raw material it operates upon, must remain. There may be no end of the poets who communicate to us what they see in an object with reference to their own individuality; what it was before they saw it, in reference to the aggregate human mind, will be as desirable to know as ever. Nor is there any reason why these two modes of poetic faculty may not issue hereafter from the same poet in successive perfect works, examples of which, according to what are now considered the exigences of art, we have hitherto possessed in distinct individuals only.[8] A mere running in of the one faculty upon the other, is, of course, the ordinary circumstance. Far more rarely it happens that either is found so decidedly prominent and superior, as to be pronounced comparatively pure: while of the perfect shield, with the gold and the silver side set up for all comers to challenge,[9] there has yet been no instance. Either faculty in its eminent state is doubtless conceded by Providence as a best gift to men, according to their especial want. There is a time when the general eye has, so to speak, absorbed its fill of the phenomena around it, whether spiritual or material, and desires rather to learn the exacter significance of what it possesses, than to receive any augmentation of what is possessed. Then is the opportunity for the poet of loftier vision, to lift his fellows, with their half-apprehensions, up to his own sphere, by intensifying the import of details and rounding the universal meaning. The influence of such an achievement will not soon die out. A tribe of successors (Homerides)[1] working more or less in the same spirit, dwell on his discoveries and reinforce his doctrine; till, at unawares, the world is found to be subsisting wholly on the shadow of a reality, on sentiments diluted from passions, on the tradition of a fact, the convention of a moral, the straw of last year's harvest. Then is the imperative call for the appearance of another sort of poet,[2] who shall at

---

7. This sentence fairly states the theme of "Fra Lippo Lippi"; see especially lines 282–315.

8. At this point it becomes clear that Browning's classification of poets is tripartite, the third class emerging from the fusion of the subjective and the objective elements.

9. According to a medieval allegory, two knights came from opposite directions upon a shield suspended from a tree. One side was gold, the other silver. The knights hotly disputed its metallic composition, their debate finally flaring into combat. Luckily a third knight rode up, settling the matter by informing the combatants that the shield was made of both metals.

1. The Homerides, or "clan of Homer," were a guild of professional poets and reciters living at ancient Chios in Asia Minor. They were dedicated to preserving the Homeric tradition.

2. The objective poet.

once replace this intellectual rumination of food swallowed long ago, by a supply of the fresh and living swathe; getting at new substance by breaking up the assumed wholes into parts of independent and unclassed value, careless of the unknown laws for recombining them (it will be the business of yet another poet[3] to suggest those hereafter), prodigal of objects for men's outer and not inner sight, shaping for their uses a new and different creation from the last, which it displaces by the right of life over death,—to endure until, in the inevitable process, its very sufficiency to itself shall require, at length, an exposition of its affinity to something higher, —when the positive yet conflicting facts shall again precipitate themselves under a harmonising law, and one more degree will be apparent for a poet to climb in that mighty ladder, of which, however cloud-involved and undefined may glimmer the topmost step, the world dares no longer doubt that its gradations ascend.[4]

Such being the two kinds of artists, it is naturally, as I have shown, with the biography of the subjective poet that we have the deeper concern. Apart from his recorded life altogether, we might fail to determine with satisfactory precision to what class his productions belong, and what amount of praise is assignable to the producer. Certainly, in the face of any conspicuous achievement of genius, philosophy, no less than sympathetic instinct, warrants our belief in a great moral purpose having mainly inspired even where it does not visibly look out of the same. Greatness in a work suggests an adequate instrumentality; and none of the lower incitements, however they may avail to initiate or even effect many considerable displays of power, simulating the nobler inspiration to which they are mistakenly referred, have been found able, under the ordinary conditions of humanity, to task themselves to the end of so exacting a performance as a poet's complete work. As soon will the galvanism[5] that provokes to violent action the muscles of a corpse, induce it to cross the chamber steadily: sooner. The love of displaying power for the display's sake, the love of riches, of distinction, of notoriety,—the desire of a triumph over rivals, and the vanity in the applause of friends,—each and all of such whetted appetites grow intenser by exercise and increasingly sagacious as to the best and readiest means of self-appeasement,—while for any of their ends, whether the money or the pointed finger of the crowd, or the flattery and hate to heart's content, there are cheaper prices to pay, they will all find soon enough, than the bestowment of a life upon

3. The subjective poet.
4. Browning's theory of literary history, while obviously cyclic, is also "progressivist" or transcendental, as the metaphor of the "mighty ladder" suggests. It is in keeping with that branch of Victorian evolutionary thought (Hegelian at base) which optimistically posited the continual upward progress of culture.
5. Physiological stimulation by application of electricity.

a labour, hard, slow, and not sure. Also, assuming the proper moral aim to have produced a work, there are many and various states of an aim: it may be more intense than clear-sighted, or too easily satisfied with a lower field of activity than a steadier aspiration would reach. All the bad poetry in the world (accounted poetry, that is, by its affinities) will be found to result from some one of the infinite degrees of discrepancy between the attributes of the poet's soul, occasioning a want of correspondency between his work and the verities of nature,—issuing in poetry, false under whatever form, which shows a thing not as it is to mankind generally, nor as it is to the particular describer, but as it is supposed to be for some unreal neutral mood, midway between both and of value to neither, and living its brief minute simply through the indolence of whoever accepts it or his incapacity to denounce a cheat. Although of such depths of failure there can be no question here, we must in every case betake ourselves to the review of a poet's life ere we determine some of the nicer questions concerning his poetry,—more especially if the performance we seek to estimate aright, has been obstructed and cut short of completion by circumstances,—a disastrous youth or a premature death. We may learn from the biography whether his spirit invariably saw and spoke from the last height to which it had attained. An absolute vision is not for this world, but we are permitted a continual approximation to it, every degree of which in the individual, provided it exceed the attainment of the masses, must procure him a clear advantage. Did the poet ever attain to a higher platform than where he rested and exhibited a result? Did he know more than he spoke of?

I concede however, in respect to the subject of our study as well as some few other illustrious examples, that the unmistakable quality of the verse would be evidence enough, under usual circumstances, not only of the kind and degree of the intellectual but of the moral constitution of Shelley: the whole personality of the poet shining forward from the poems, without much need of going further to seek it. The "Remains"—produced within a period of ten years,[6] and at a season of life when other men of at all comparable genius have hardly done more than prepare the eye for future sight and the tongue for speech—present us with the complete enginery of a poet, as signal in the excellence of its several adaptitudes as transcendent in the combination of effects,—examples, in fact, of the whole poet's function of beholding with an understanding keenness the universe, nature and man, in their actual state of perfection in imperfection,[7]—of the whole poet's virtue of being untempted

6. From 1813 (*Queen Mab*) to 1822 (*The Triumph of Life*, unfinished). Shelley died by drowning in 1822.

7. This paradox is developed in "Andrea del Sarto" (1855).

by the manifold partial developments of beauty and good on every side, into leaving them the ultimates he found them,—induced by the facility of the gratification of his own sense of those qualities, or by the pleasure of acquiescence in the short-comings of his predecessors in art, and the pain of disturbing their conventionalisms,—the whole poet's virtue, I repeat, of looking higher than any manifestation yet made of both beauty and good, in order to suggest from the utmost actual realisation of the one a corresponding capability in the other, and out of the calm, purity and energy of nature, to reconstitute and store up for the forthcoming stage of man's being, a gift in repayment of that former gift, in which man's own thought and passion had been lavished by the poet on the else-incompleted magnificence of the sunrise, the else-uninterpreted mystery of the lake,—so drawing out, lifting up, and assimilating this ideal of a future man, thus descried as possible, to the present reality of the poet's soul already arrived at the higher state of development, and still aspirant to elevate and extend itself in conformity with its still-improving perceptions of, no longer the eventual Human, but the actual Divine. In conjunction with which noble and rare powers, came the subordinate power of delivering these attained results to the world in an embodiment of verse more closely answering to and indicative of the process of the informing spirit, (failing as it occasionally does, in art, only to succeed in highest art),—with a diction more adequate to the task in its natural and acquired richness, its material colour and spiritual transparency,—the whole being moved by and suffused with a music at once of the soul and the sense, expressive both of an external might of sincere passion and an internal fitness and consonancy,—than can be attributed to any other writer whose record is among us. Such was the spheric poetical faculty of Shelley, as its own self-sufficing central light, radiating equally through immaturity and accomplishment, through many fragments and occasional completion, reveals it to a competent judgment.

* * *

1851

Criticism

Victorian Views

JOHN FORSTER

Evidences of a New Genius for Dramatic Poetry†

* * *

This is the simple and unaffected title of a small volume[1] which was published some half-dozen months ago, and which opens a deeper vein of thought, of feeling, and of passion, than any poet has attempted for years. Without the slightest hesitation we name Mr. Robert Browning at once with Shelley, Coleridge, Wordsworth. He has entitled himself to a place among the acknowledged poets of the age. This opinion will possibly startle many persons; but it is most sincere. It is no practice of ours to think nothing of an author because all the world have not pronounced in his favour, any more than we would care to offer him our sympathy and concern on the score of the world's indifference. A man of genius, we have already intimated, needs neither the one nor the other. He who is conscious of great powers can satisfy himself by their unwearied exercise alone. His day will come. He need never be afraid that truth and nature will wear out, or that Time will not eventually claim for its own all that is the handywork of Nature. Mr. Browning is a man of genius, he has in himself all the elements of a great poet, philosophical as well dramatic,—

> The youngest he
> That sits in shadow of Apollo's tree

—but he sits there, and with as much right to his place as the greatest of the men that are around him have to theirs. For the reception that his book has met with he was doubtless already well prepared,—as well for the wondering ignorance that has scouted it, as for the condescending patronage which has sought to bring it forward, as one brings forward a bashful child to make a doubtful display of its wit and learning. "We hope the best; put a good face on the matter; but are sadly afraid the thing cannot answer." We tell

† From his unsigned article in *The New Monthly Magazine and Literary Journal,* XLVI (March 1836), 289–308.
1. *Paracelsus* (1835), which Forster had already favorably reviewed in *The Exam-iner* for Sept. 6, 1835 (pp. 563–65). Forster and W. J. Fox, editor of *The Monthly Repository*, were the unknown Browning's earliest champions. [*Editor.*]

Mr. Browning, on the other hand, what we do not think *he* needs to be told, that the thing WILL answer. He has written a book that will live—he has scattered the seeds of much thought among his countrymen—he has communicated an impulse and increased activity to reason and inquiry, as well as a pure and high delight to every cultivated mind;—and this is the little and scantily-noticed volume of *Paracelsus!*

Before going farther, it may be as well to come to some understanding with the reader respecting the course of this article. In sitting down to write, we confess we had intended to limit ourselves to the matters strictly embraced in our title, and we took up Mr. Browning's volume with the intention of waiving many new and striking points of philosophical suggestion contained in it, for the purpose of considering more emphatically the evidences it abundantly presents of a new genius for dramatic poetry. We find, however, on examination, that we cannot restrict ourselves to so narrow a view of the poem. Its subject-matter and treatment are both so startlingly original, and both so likely to be altogether misunderstood; it embraces in its development so many of the highest questions, and glances with such a masterly perception at some of the deepest problems, of man's existence; that we feel, while to touch upon these various topics will not interfere with the object we first proposed, it is only in this way that a proper and just appreciation of the singular power and beauty, even of the dramatic portions of this poem, can be conveyed to the reader. We venture to promise him, in accompanying us through our criticism, that if, in its course, we do not break even a wholly new ground of philosophical inquiry into character, we shall at least suggest to him some valuable and very interesting trains of thought. It is the greatest glory of such labours as those of Mr. Browning, that they open up, on every side of us in the actual world, new sources of understanding and sympathy. * * *

* * * Passion is invariably displayed, and never merely analysed. Even at those moments when we seem most of all to be listening to its results alone, we are made most vividly sensible of the presence of the very agents by which the results have been determined. Mr. Browning has the power of a great dramatic poet; we never think of Mr. Browning while we read his poem; we are not identified with him, but with the persons into whom he has flung his genius. The objections to a dialogue of the French school do not apply. We get beyond conjecture and reasoning, beyond a general impression of the situation of the speakers, beyond general reflections on their passions, and hints as to their rise, continuance, and fall. We are upon the scene ourselves,—we hear, feel, and see,—we are face to face with the actors,—we are a party to the tears that are shed, to

the feelings and passions that are undergone, to the "flushed cheek and intensely sparkling eye." The same unrelaxing activity of thought and of emotion, by which the results of the poem are meant to be produced, is made to affect the reader in its progress; and he is as certain of the immediate presence of all that is going on, as in life he would be certain of any thing that made him laugh or weep. *In the agitation of the feelings, sight is given to the imagination.* This is an essential dramatic test, in which Mr. Browning is never found wanting.

* * *

THOMAS CARLYLE

[Letter to Browning]†

My dear Sir—Many months ago you were kind enough to send me your *Sordello*; and now this day I have been looking into your *Pippa Passes*, for which also I am your debtor. If I have made no answer hitherto, it was surely not for want of interest in you, for want of estimation of you: both Pieces have given rise to many reflexions in me, not without friendly hopes and anxieties in due measure. Alas, it is so seldom that any word one can speak is not worse than a word still unspoken;—seldom that one man, by his speaking or his silence, can, in great vital interests, help another at all!—

Unless I very greatly mistake, judging from these two works, you seem to possess a rare spiritual gift, poetical, pictorial, intellectual, by whatever name we may prefer calling it; to unfold which into articulate clearness is naturally the problem of all problems for you. This noble endowment, it seems to me farther, you are *not* at present on the best way for unfolding;—and if the world had loudly called itself content with these two Poems, my surmise is, the world could have rendered you no fataller disservice than that same! Believe me I speak with sincerity; and if I had not loved you well, I would not haver spoken at all.

A long battle, I could guess, lies before you, full of toil and pain, and all sorts of real *fighting*: a man attains to nothing here below without that. Is it not verily the highest prize you fight for? Fight on; that is to say, follow truly, with steadfast singleness of purpose, with valiant humbleness and openness of heart, what best light *you* can attain to; following truly so, better and ever better light will rise on you. The light we ourselves gain, by our very errors if not other-

† From his letter dated June 21, 1841; in *New Letters of Thomas Carlyle*, ed. Alexander Carlyle (London: John Lane, 1904), I. 233–34.

wise, is the only precious light. Victory, what I call victory, if well fought for, is sure to you.

If your own choice happened to point that way, I for one should hail it as a good omen that your next work were written in prose! Not that I deny you poetic faculty; far, very far from that. But unless poetic faculty mean a higher-power of common understanding, I know not what it means. One must first make a *true* intellectual representation of a thing, before any poetic interest that is true will supervene. All *cartoons* are geometrical withal; and cannot be made till we have fully learnt to make mere *diagrams* well. It is this that I mean by prose;—which hint of mine, most probably inapplicable at present, may perhaps at some future day come usefully to mind.

But enough of this: why have I written all this? Because I esteem yours no common case; and think such a man is not to be treated in the common way.

And so persist in God's name, as you best see and can; and understand always that my true prayer for you is, Good Speed in the name of God!

* * *

GEORGE ELIOT

[Review of *Men and Women* (1855)]†

We never read Heinsius—a great admission for a reviewer—but we learn from M. Arago that the formidably erudite writer pronounces Aristotle's works to be characterized by a *majestic obscurity which repels the ignorant*.[1] We borrow these words to indicate what is likely to be the first impression of a reader who, without any previous familiarity with Browning, glances through his two new volumes of poems. The less acute he is, the more easily will he arrive at the undeniable criticism, that these poems have a 'majestic obscurity,' which repels not only the ignorant but the idle. To read poems is often a substitute for thought: fine-sounding conventional phrases and the sing-song of verse demand no co-operation in the reader; they glide over his mind with the agreeable unmeaningness of 'the compliments of the season,' or a speaker's exordium on 'feelings too deep for expression.' But let him expect no such drowsy passivity in reading Browning. Here he will find no conventionality, no melodious commonplace, but freshness, originality, sometimes

† From her unsigned review in *The Westminster Review*, 65 (January 1856), 290–96. Footnotes are by editor.
1. Daniel Heinsius (or Heins, 1580–1655), classical scholar of the Dutch Renaissance; Étienne Vincent Arago (1802–92), French dramatist.

eccentricity of expression; no didactic laying-out of a subject, but dramatic indication, which requires the reader to trace by his own mental activity the underground stream of thought that jets out in elliptical and pithy verse. To read Browning he must exert himself, but he will exert himself to some purpose. If he finds the meaning difficult of access, it is always worth his effort—if he has to dive deep, 'he rises with his pearl.' Indeed, in Browning's best poems he makes us feel that what we took for obscurity in him was superficiality in ourselves. We are far from meaning that all his obscurity is like the obscurity of the stars, dependent simply on the feebleness of men's vision. On the contrary, our admiration for his genius only makes us feel the more acutely that its inspirations are too often straitened by the garb of whimsical mannerism with which he clothes them. This mannerism is even irritating sometimes, and should at least be kept under restraint in *printed* poems, where the writer is not merely indulging his own vein, but is avowedly appealing to the mind of his reader.

Turning from the ordinary literature of the day to such a writer as Browning, is like turning from Flotow's music,[2] made up of well-pieced shreds and patches, to the distinct individuality of Chopin's Studies or Schubert's Songs. Here, at least, is a man who has something of his own to tell us, and who can tell it impressively, if not with faultless art. There is nothing sickly or dreamy in him: he has a clear eye, a vigorous grasp, and courage to utter what he sees and handles. His robust energy is informed by a subtle, penetrating spirit, and this blending of opposite qualities gives his mind a rough piquancy that reminds one of a russet apple. His keen glance pierces into all the secrets of human character, but, being as thoroughly alive to the outward as to the inward, he reveals those secrets, not by a process of dissection, but by dramatic painting. We fancy his own description of a poet applies to himself:

> He stood and watched the cobbler at his trade,
> The man who slices lemons into drink,
> The coffee-roaster's brazier, and the boys
> That volunteer to help him turn its winch.
> He glanced o'er books on stalls with half an eye,
> And fly-leaf ballads on the vendor's string,
> And broad-edge bold-print posters by the wall.
> *He took such cognizance of men and things,*
> *If any beat a horse, you felt he saw;*
> *If any cursed a woman, he took note;*
> *Yet stared at nobody,—they stared at him,*
> *And found, less to their pleasure than surprise,*
> *He seemed to know them and expect as much.*[3]

2. Friedrich von Flotow (1812–83), German operatic composer.

3. "How It Strikes a Contemporary," lines 23–35; Eliot's emphasis.

Browning has no soothing strains, no chants, no lullabys; he rarely gives voice to our melancholy, still less to our gaiety; he sets our thoughts at work rather than our emotions. But though eminently a thinker, he is as far as possible from prosaic; his mode of presentation is always concrete, artistic, and, where it is most felicitous, dramatic. Take, for example, 'Fra Lippo Lippi,' a poem at once original and perfect in its kind. The artist-monk, Fra Lippo, is supposed to be detected by the night-watch roaming the streets of Florence, and while sharing the wine with which he makes amends to the Dogberrys[4] for the roughness of his tongue, he pours forth the story of his life and his art with the racy conversational vigour of a brawny genius under the influence of the Care-dispeller.[5]

* * *

Extracts cannot do justice to the fine dramatic touches by which Fra Lippo is made present to us, while he throws out this instinctive Art-criticism. And extracts from 'Bishop Blougram's Apology,' an equally remarkable poem of what we may call the dramatic-psychological kind, would be still more ineffective. 'Sylvester Blougram, styled *in partibus Episcopus*,' is talking

> Over the glass's edge when dinner's done,
> And body gets its sop and holds its noise
> And leaves soul free a little,[6]

with 'Gigadibs the literary man,' to whom he is bent on proving by the most exasperatingly ingenious sophistry, that the theory of life on which he grounds his choice of being a bishop, though a doubting one is wiser in the moderation of its ideal, with the certainty of attainment, than the Gigadibs theory, which aspires after the highest and attains nothing. The way in which Blougram's motives are dug up from below the roots, and laid bare to the very last fibre, not by a process of hostile exposure, not by invective or sarcasm, but by making himself exhibit them with a self-complacent sense of supreme acuteness, and even with a crushing force of worldly common sense, has the effect of masterly satire. But the poem is too strictly consecutive for any fragments of it to be a fair specimen. Belonging to the same order of subtle yet vigorous writing are the 'Epistle of Karshish, the Arab physician,' 'Cleon,' and 'How it Strikes a Contemporary.' 'In a Balcony,' is so fine, that we regret it is not a complete drama instead of being merely the suggestion of a drama. One passage especially tempts us to extract.

All women love great men

4. Dogberry is a constable in Shakespeare's *Much Ado about Nothing*.
5. Eliot's extract of lines 81–306 of "Fra Lippo Lippi" is omitted.
6. Lines 18–20.

If young or old—it is in all the tales—
Young beauties love old poets who can love—
Why should not he the poems in my soul,
The love, the passionate faith, the sacrifice,
The constancy? I throw them at his feet.
Who cares to see the fountain's very shape
And whether it be a Triton's or a Nymph's
That pours the foam, makes rainbows all around?
You could not praise indeed the empty conch;
But I'll pour floods of love and hide myself.[7]

These lines are less rugged than is usual with Browning's blank verse; but generally, the greatest deficiency we feel in his poetry is its want of music. The worst poems in his new volumes are, in our opinion, his lyrical efforts; for in these, where he engrosses us less by his thought, we are more sensible of his obscurity and his want of melody. His lyrics, instead of tripping along with easy grace, or rolling with a torrent-like grandeur, seem to be struggling painfully under a burthen too heavy for them; and many of them have the disagreeable puzzling effect of a charade, rather than the touching or animating influence of song. We have said that he is never prosaic; and it is remarkable that in his blank verse, though it is often colloquial, we are never shocked by the sense of a sudden lapse into prose. Wordsworth is, on the whole, a far more musical poet than Browning, yet we remember no line in Browning so prosaic as many of Wordsworth's, which in some of his finest poems have the effect of bricks built into a rock. But we must also say that though Browning never flounders helplessly on the plain, he rarely soars above a certain table-land—a footing between the level of prose and the topmost heights of poetry. He does not take possession of our souls and set them aglow, as the greatest poets— the greatest artists do. We admire his power, we are not subdued by it. Language with him does not seem spontaneously to link itself into song, as sounds link themselves into melody in the mind of the creative musician; he rather seems by his commanding powers to compel language into verse. He has *chosen* verse as his medium; but of our greatest poets we feel that they had no choice: Verse chose them. Still we are grateful that Browning chose this medium: we would rather have 'Fra Lippo Lippi' than an essay on Realism in Art; we would rather have 'The Statue and the Bust' than a three-volumed novel with the same moral; we would rather have 'Holy-Cross Day' than 'Strictures on the Society for the Emancipation of the Jews.'

* * *

7. Lines 509–19; Eliot's emphasis.

WILLIAM MORRIS

[Browning's Alleged Carelessness] †

* * *

Yet a few words, and I have done. For, as I wrote this, many times angry indignant words came to my lips, which stopped my writing till I could be quieter. For I suppose, reader, that you see whereabouts among the poets I place Robert Browning; high among the poets of all time, and I scarce know whether first, or second, in our own: and, it is a bitter thing to me to see the way in which he has been received by almost everybody; many having formed a certain theory of their own about him, from reading, I suppose, some of the least finished poems among the "Dramatic Lyrics," make all the facts bend to this theory, after the fashion of theory-mongers: they think him, or say they think him, a careless man, writing down anyhow anything that comes into his head. Oh truly! "The Statue and the Bust" shows this! or the soft solemn flow of that poem, "By the Fireside!" "Paracelsus!"—that, with its wonderful rhythm, its tender sadness, its noble thoughts, must have been very easy to write, surely!

Then they say, too, that Browning is so obscure as not to be understood by any one. Now, I know well enough what they mean by "obscure," and I know also that they use the word wrongly; meaning difficult to understand fully at first reading, or, say at second reading, even: yet, taken so, in what a cloud of obscurity would "Hamlet" be! Do they think this to be the case? they daren't *say* so at all events, though I suspect some of them of thinking so.

Now I don't say that Robert Browning is not sometimes really obscure. He would be a perfect poet (of some calibre or other) if he were not; but I assert, fearlessly, that this obscurity is seldom so prominent as to make his poems hard to understand on this ground: while, as to that which they call obscurity, it results from depth of thought, and greatness of subject, on the poet's part, and on his readers' part, from their shallower brains and more bounded knowledge; nay, often I fear from mere wanton ignorance and idleness.

So I believe that, though this obscurity, so called, would indeed be very objectionable, if, as some seem to think, poetry is merely a department of "light literature"; yet, if it is rather one of the very grandest of all God's gifts to men, we must not think it hard if we have sometimes to exercise thought over a great poem, nay, even

† From his unsigned review of *Men and*   *Magazine*, 1:3 (March 1856) 162–72.
Women in *Oxford and Cambridge*

sometimes the utmost straining of all our thoughts, an agony almost equal to that of the poet who created the poem.

However, this accusation against Browning of carelessness, and consequent roughness in rhythm, and obscurity in language and thought, has come to be pretty generally believed; and people, as a rule, do not read him; this evil spreading so, that many, almost unconsciously, are kept from reading him, who, if they did read, would sympathize with him thoroughly.

But it was always so; it was so with Tennyson when he first published his poems; it was so last year with *Maud*; it is so with Ruskin; they petted him indeed at first; his wonderful eloquence having some effect even upon the critics; but, as his circle grew larger, and larger, embracing more and more truth, they more and more fell off from him; his firm faith in right they call arrogance and conceit now; his eager fighting with falsehood and wrong they call unfairness. I wonder what they will say to his new volume.[1]

The story of the Præ-Raphaelites[2]—we all know that, only here, thank Heaven! the public has chosen to judge for itself somewhat, though to this day their noblest pictures are the least popular.

Yes, I wonder what the critics would have said to "Hamlet Prince of Denmark," if it had been first published by Messrs. Chapman and Hall in the year 1855.

JOHN RUSKIN

[Browning and the Italian Renaissance]†

* * *

How far in these modern days, emptied of splendour, it may be necessary for great men having certain sympathies for those earlier ages, to act in this differently from all their predecessors; and how far they may succeed in the resuscitation of the past by habitually dwelling in all their thoughts among vanished generations, are questions, of all practical and present ones concerning art, the most difficult to decide; for already in poetry several of our truest men have set themselves to this task, and have indeed put more vitality into the shadows of the dead than most others can give the presences of the living. Thus Longfellow, in the *Golden Legend*, has entered more closely into the temper of the Monk, for good and for evil,

1. *Modern Painters*, vols. III and IV (1856). [*Editor*.]
2. A group of contemporary painters and poets (among whom were D. G. Rossetti, A. C. Swinburne, and Morris himself), the Pre-Raphaelites praised Browning's

work well before it was widely accepted. [*Editor*.]
† From *Modern Painters*, IV (1856); in *The Works of John Ruskin*, ed. E. T. Cook and Alexander Wedderburn (London: Allen, 1903–12), VI, 446–49.

than ever yet theological writer or historian, though they may have given their life's labour to the analysis; and, again, Robert Browning is unerring in every sentence he writes of the Middle Ages; always vital, right, and profound; so that in the matter of art, with which we have been specially concerned, there is hardly a principle connected with the mediæval temper, that he has not struck upon in those seemingly careless and too rugged rhymes of his. There is a curious instance, by the way, in a short poem referring to this very subject of tomb and image sculpture; and illustrating just one of those phases of local human character which, though belonging to Shakespere's own age, he never noticed, because it was specially Italian and un-English; connected also closely with the influence of mountains on the heart, and therefore with our immediate inquiries. I mean the kind of admiration with which a southern artist regarded the *stone* he worked in; and the pride which populace or priest took in the possession of precious mountain substance, worked into the pavements of their cathedrals, and the shafts of their tombs.

Observe, Shakespere, in the midst of architecture and tombs of wood, or freestone, or brass, naturally thinks of *gold* as the best enriching and ennobling substance for them;—in the midst also of the fever of the Renaissance he writes, as every one else did, in praise of precisely the most vicious master of that school—Giulio Romano;[1] but the modern poet, living much in Italy, and quit of the Renaissance influence, is able fully to enter into the Italian feeling, and to see the evil of the Renaissance tendency, not because he is greater than Shakespere, but because he is in another element, and has *seen* other things.[2]

* * *

I know no other piece of modern English, prose or poetry, in which there is so much told, as in these lines, of the Renaissance spirit,—its worldliness, inconsistency, pride, hypocrisy, ignorance of itself, love of art, of luxury, and of good Latin. It is nearly all that I said of the central Renaissance in thirty pages of the *Stones of Venice* put into as many lines, Browning's being also the antecedent work. The worst of it is that this kind of concentrated writing needs so much *solution* before the reader can fairly get the good of it, that people's patience fails them, and they give the thing up as insoluble; though, truly, it ought to be to the current of common thought like Saladin's talisman, dipped in clear water, not soluble altogether, but making the element medicinal.

* * *

1. Italian painter (ca. 1499–1546), praised in *The Winter's Tale*, V.ii.97. [*Editor*.]

2. Ruskin quotes forty-four lines of "The Bishop Orders His Tomb at St. Praxed's Church" (1845). [*Editor*.]

WALTER BAGEHOT

[Browning's Grotesque Art]†

* * *

There is . . . a third kind of art which differs from these [the pure and the ornate][1] on the point in which they most resemble one another. Ornate and pure art have this in common, that they paint the types of literature in as good perfection as they can. Ornate art, indeed, uses undue disguises and unreal enchancements; it does not confine itself to the best types; on the contrary it is its office to make the best of imperfect types and lame approximations; but ornate art, as much as pure art, catches its subject in the best light it can, takes the most developed aspect of it which it can find, and throws upon it the most congruous colours it can use. But grotesque art does just the contrary. It takes the type, so to say, *in difficulties*. It gives a representation of it in its minimum development, amid the circumstances least favourable to it, just while it is struggling with obstacles, just where it is encumbered with incongruities. It deals, to use the language of science, not with normal types but with abnormal specimens; to use the language of old philosophy, not with what nature is striving to be, but with what by some lapse she has happened to become.

This art works by contrast. It enables you to see, it makes you see, the perfect type by painting the opposite deviation. It shows you what ought to be by what ought not to be, when complete it reminds you of the perfect image, by showing you the distorted and imperfect image. Of this art we possess in the present generation one prolific master. Mr. Browning is an artist working by incongruity. Possibly hardly one of his most considerable efforts can be found which is not great because of its odd mixture. He puts together things which no one else would have put together, and produces on our minds a result which no one else would have produced, or tried to produce. His admirers may not like all we may have to say of him. But in our way we too are among his admirers. No one ever read him without seeing not only his great ability but his great *mind*. He not only possesses superficial useable talents, but the strong something, the inner secret something which uses them and controls them; he is great, not in mere accomplishments, but in himself. He has applied a hard strong intellect to real life; he has

† From "Wordsworth, Tennyson, and Browning; or, Pure, Ornate, and Grotesque Art in English Poetry," *The National Review*, 19 (Nov. 1864), 27–67.

Footnotes are by editor.
1. Exemplified by Wordsworth and Tennyson, respectively.

applied the same intellect to the problems of his age. He has striven to know what *is*: he has endeavoured not to be cheated by counterfeits, to be infatuated with illusions. His heart is in what he says. He has battered his brain against his creed till he believes it. He has accomplishments too, the more effective because they are mixed. He is at once a student of mysticism, and a citizen of the world. He brings to the club sofa distinct visions of old creeds, intense images of strange thoughts: he takes to the bookish student tidings of wild Bohemia, and little traces of the *demi-monde*. He puts down what is good for the naughty and what is naughty for the good. Over women his easier writings exercise that imperious power which belongs to the writings of a great man of the world upon such matters. He knows women, and therefore they wish to know him. If we blame many of Browning's efforts, it is in the interest of art, and not from a wish to hurt or degrade him.

If we wanted to illustrate the nature of grotesque art by an exaggerated instance we should have selected a poem which the chance of late publication brings us in this new volume. Mr. Browning has undertaken to describe what may be called *mind in difficulties*—mind set to make out the universe under the worst and hardest circumstances. He takes "Caliban," not perhaps exactly Shakespeare's Caliban, but an analogous and worse creature; a strong thinking power, but a nasty creature—a gross animal, uncontrolled and unelevated by any feeling of religion or duty. The delineation of him will show that Mr. Browning does not wish to take undue advantage of his readers by a choice of nice subjects.[2]

* * *

It may seem perhaps to most readers that these lines are very difficult, and that they are unpleasant. And so they are. We quote them to illustrate, not the *success* of grotesque art, but the *nature* of grotesque art. It shows the end at which this species of art aims, and if it fails it is from over-boldness in the choice of a subject by the artist, or from the defects of its execution. A thinking faculty more in difficulties—a great type,—an inquisitive, searching intellect under more disagreeable conditions, with worse helps, more likely to find falsehood, less likely to find truth, can scarcely be imagined. Nor is the mere description of the thought at all bad: on the contrary, if we closely examine it, it is very clever. Hardly anyone could have amassed so many ideas at once nasty and suitable. But scarcely any readers—any casual readers—who are not of the sect of Mr. Browning's admirers will be able to examine it enough to appreciate it. From a defect, partly of subject, and partly

2. Quotes "Caliban Upon Setebos," lines 1–11, 24–56.

of style, many of Mr. Browning's works make a demand upon the reader's zeal and sense of duty to which the nature of most readers is unequal. They have on the turf the convenient expression "staying power": some horses can hold on and others cannot. But hardly any reader not of especial and peculiar nature can hold on through such composition. There is not enough of "staying power" in human nature. One of his greatest admirers once owned to us that he seldom or never began a new poem without looking on in advance, and foreseeing with caution what length of intellectual adventure he was about to commence. Whoever will work hard at such poems will find much mind in them: they are a sort of quarry of ideas, but whoever goes there will find these ideas in such a jagged, ugly, useless shape that he can hardly bear them.

We are not judging Mr. Browning simply from a hasty recent production. All poets are liable to misconceptions, and if such a piece as "Caliban upon Setebos" were an isolated error, a venial and particular exception, we should have given it no prominence. We have put it forward because it just elucidates both our subject and the characteristics of Mr. Browning. But many other of his best known pieces do so almost equally; what several of his devotees think his best piece is quite enough illustrative for anything we want. It appears that on Holy Cross day at Rome the Jews were obliged to listen to a Christian sermon in the hope of their conversion, though this is, according to Mr. Browning, what they really said when they came away:—[3]

* * *

It is very natural that a poet whose wishes incline, or whose genius conducts him to a grotesque art, should be attracted towards mediæval subjects. There is no age whose legends are so full of grotesque subjects, and no age where real life was so fit to suggest them. Then, more than at any other time, good principles have been under great hardships. The vestiges of ancient civilisation, the germs of modern civilisation, the little remains of what had been, the small beginnings of what is, were buried under a cumbrous mass of barbarism and cruelty. Good elements hidden in horrid accompaniments are the special theme of grotesque art, and these mediæval life and legends afford more copiously than could have been furnished before Christianity gave its new elements of good, or since modern civilisation has removed some few at least of the old elements of destruction. A *buried* life like the spiritual mediæval was Mr. Browning's natural element, and he was right to be attracted by it. His mistake has been, that he has not made it pleasant; that

3. Quotes "Holy-Cross Day," lines 1–18, 61–120.

he has forced his art to topics on which no one could charm, or on which he, at any rate, could not; that on these occasions and in these poems he has failed in fascinating men and women of sane taste.

We say "sane" because there is a most formidable and estimable *insane* taste. The will has great though indirect power over the taste, just as it has over the belief. There are some horrid beliefs from which human nature revolts, from which at first it shrinks, to which, at first, no effort can force it. But if we fix the mind upon them they have a power over us just because of their natural offensiveness. They are like the sight of human blood: experienced soldiers tell us that at first men are sickened by the smell and newness of blood almost to death and fainting, but that as soon as they harden their hearts and stiffen their minds, as soon as they *will* bear it, then comes an appetite for slaughter, a tendency to gloat on carnage, to love blood, at least for the moment, with a deep eager love. It is a principle that if we put down a healthy instinctive aversion, nature avenges herself by creating an unhealthy insane attraction. For this reason the most earnest truth-seeking men fall into the worst delusions; they will not let their mind alone; they force it towards some ugly thing, which a crotchet of argument, a conceit of intellect recommends, and nature punishes their disregard of her warning by subjection to the holy one, by belief in it. Just so the most industrious critics get the most admiration. They think it unjust to rest in their instinctive natural horror: they overcome it, and angry nature gives them over to ugly poems and marries them to detestable stanzas.

Mr. Browning possibly, and some of the worst of Mr. Browning's admirers certainly, will say that these grotesque objects exist in real life, and therefore they ought to be, at least may be, described in art. But though pleasure is not the end of poetry, pleasing is a condition of poetry. An exceptional monstrosity of horrid ugliness cannot be made pleasing, except it be made to suggest—to recall— the perfection, the beauty, from which it is a deviation. Perhaps in extreme cases no art is equal to this; but then such self-imposed problems should not be worked by the artist; these out-of-the-way and detestable subjects should be let alone by him. It is rather characteristic of Mr. Browning to neglect this rule. He is the most of a realist, and the least of an idealist of any poet we know.

* * *

Something more we had to say of Mr. Browning, but we must stop. It is singularly characteristic of this age that the poems which rise to the surface, should be examples of ornate art, and grotesque art, not of pure art. We live in the realm of the half educated. The number of readers grows daily, but the quality of readers does not improve rapidly. The middle class is scattered, headless; it is well-meaning but aimless; wishing to be wise, but ignorant how to be wise. The aristocracy of England never was a literary aristocracy, never even in the days of its full power—of its unquestioned predominance did it guide—did it even seriously try to guide—the taste of England. Without guidance young men, and tired men are thrown amongst a mass of books; they have to choose which they like; many of them would much like to improve their culture, to chasten their taste, if they knew how. But left to themselves they take, not pure art, but showy art; not that which permanently relieves the eye and makes it happy whenever it looks, and as long as it looks, but *glaring* art which catches and arrests the eye for a moment, but which in the end fatigues it. But before the wholesome remedy of nature—the fatigue arrives—the hasty reader has passed on to some new excitement, which in its turn stimulates for an instant, and then is passed by for ever. These conditions are not favourable to the due appreciation of pure art—of that art which must be known before it is admired—which must have fastened irrevocably on the brain before you appreciate it—which you must love ere it will seem worthy of your love. Women too, whose voice in literature counts as well as that of men—and in a light literature counts for more than that of men—women, such as we know them, such as they are likely to be, ever prefer a delicate unreality to a true or firm art. A dressy literature, an exaggerated literature seem to be fated to us. These are our curses, as other times had theirs.

* * *

ROBERT W. BUCHANAN

[The Ring and the Book]†

At last, the *opus magnum* of our generation lies before the world —the "ring is rounded"; and we are left in doubt which to admire most, the supremely precious gold of the material or the wondrous beauty of the workmanship. The fascination of the work is still so strong upon us, our eyes are still so spell-bound by the immortal features of Pompilia (which shine through the troubled mists of the story with almost insufferable beauty), that we feel it difficult to write calmly and without exaggeration; yet we must record at once

† From his unsigned review in *The Atheneum*, March 20, 1869, pp. 399–400.

our conviction, not merely that *The Ring and the Book* is beyond all parallel the supremest poetical achievement of our time, but that it is the most precious and profound spiritual treasure that England has produced since the days of Shakspeare. Its intellectual greatness is as nothing compared with its transcendent spiritual teaching. Day after day it grows into the soul of the reader, until all the outlines of thought are brightened and every mystery of the world becomes more and more softened into human emotion. Once and for ever must critics dismiss the old stale charge that Browning is a mere intellectual giant, difficult of comprehension, hard of assimilation. This great book *is* difficult of comprehension, *is* hard of assimilation; not because it is obscure—every fibre of the thought is clear as day; not because it is intellectual,—and it is intellectual in the highest sense,—but because the capacity to comprehend such a book must be spiritual; because, although a child's brain might grasp the general features of the picture, only a purified nature could absorb and feel its profoundest meanings. The man who tosses it aside because it is "difficult" is simply adopting a subterfuge to hide his moral littleness, not his mental incapacity. It would be unsafe to predict anything concerning a production so many-sided; but we quite believe that its true public lies outside the literary circle, that men of inferior capacity will grow by the aid of it, and that feeble women, once fairly initiated into the mystery, will cling to it as a succour passing all succour save that which is purely religious.

* * *

We should be grossly exaggerating if we were to aver that Mr. Browning is likely to take equal rank with the supreme genius of the world; only a gallery of pictures like the Shakspearean group could enable him to do that; and, moreover, his very position as an educated modern must necessarily limit his field of workmanship. What we wish to convey is, that Mr. Browning exhibits—to a great extent in all his writings, but particularly in this great work—a wealth of nature and a perfection of spiritual insight which we have been accustomed to find in the pages of Shakspeare, and in those pages only. His fantastic intellectual feats, his verbosity, his power of quaint versification, are quite other matters. The one great and patent fact is, that, with a faculty in our own time at least unparalleled, he manages to create beings of thoroughly human fibre; he is just without judgment, without preoccupation, to every being so created; and he succeeds, without a single didactic note, in stirring the soul of the spectator with the concentrated emotion and spiritual exaltation which heighten the soul's stature in the finest moments of life itself.

* * *

ALFRED AUSTIN

The Poetry of the Period: Mr. Browning†

* * *

* * * Whether Mr. Browning keeps a Commonplace Book, we have no means of knowing; but we have every means of knowing that he thinks in prose, for the prose thoughts are there before us, gratuitiously turned by some arbitrary whim, which we confess completely puzzles us, into metre. Mr. Browning is, as we have said, a profound thinker, and nearly all his thoughts have the quality of depth. Now, probably all thoughts to which this quality of depth can be ascribed, arrive at the portals of the brain in this prose— their natural vesture; whilst, on the contrary, lofty thoughts, their antitheses, usually enter it in the subtle garb of music. Here we have a clear difference in kind; prose thoughts, so to speak, from below—poetical thoughts, so to speak, from above. If we suppose a permeable plane dividing these two regions of thought, we can easily understand how there comes to be what we may call a sliding scale of poets, and a sliding scale of philosophical thinkers; some of the latter, to whom the faculty of philosophising cannot be denied, being rather shallow—some of the former, whose claims to poetical status cannot fairly be questioned, not being very soaring; and we can further understand how the natural denizens of one sphere may ever and anon cross the permeable plane, invade the other sphere, and seem to belong to it in the sense in which foreigners belong to a country they are constantly visiting. But for all that there ever remains a substantial difference between the two spheres and between their respective native inhabitants, between the country of poetry and the country of prose, between poetical power and instinct and philosophical power and proclivity. Accordingly, where a man talks the language of the sphere to which he properly belongs —in other words, when a philosophical thinker publishes his thoughts in prose, or a poetical thinker addresses us in verse—our task is comparatively simple. All we have got to do is to decide whether the former be profound or shallow, and whether the latter have a lofty or a lagging pinion. It is when a man affects to talk the language of the sphere to which he does not essentially belong, that he deceives some people, and puzzles us all. This is precisely what Mr. Browning has done. Hence most people scarcely know what to

† From "The Poetry of the Period," *Temple Bar*, 26 (June 1869), 316–33. This article by Austin (1835–1913; poet laureate 1896–1913) is famous for having provoked Browning to reply with the peppery volume *Pacchiarotto and How He Worked in Distemper: With Other Poems* (1876). Footnotes are by editor.

make of this poetico-philosophical hybrid, this claimant to the great inheritance of bardic fame, whose hands are the hands of Esau, but whose voice is the voice of Jacob. Several, whose eyes, like those of Isaac, are dim, and who therefore cannot see, admit the claim—hesitatingly, it is true, again like Isaac—of the hands,[1] and accept him as a poet. But it is the true resonant voice, not the made-up delusive hand, which is the test of the singer; and to those whose sight is not dim, Mr. Browning is not a poet at all—save in the sense that all cultivated men and women of sensitive feelings are poets—but a deep thinker, a profound philosopher, a keen analyser, and a biting wit. With this key to what to most persons is a riddle—for, despite the importunate attempts of certain critics who, as we have already said, having placed Mr. Tennyson on a poetical pedestal considerably too high for him, are now beginning to waver in their extravagant creed, and are disposed to put him on one a trifle lower, placing Mr. Browning there instead, the general public has not yet become quite reconciled to the operation—we think we shall be able to rid them of their perplexities. * * *

* * *

But how about "Andrea del Sarto," "Fra Lippo Lippi," "A Death in the Desert," "Caliban on Setebos," and "Bishop Blougram's Apology?" What have we to say about these? This much. That, with the exception of "Caliban on Setebos"—which, on account of its rendering certain prevailing modes of thought on theological questions, has been very much over-estimated—they are productions betraying the possession of peculiar imagination, of mordant wit of almost the highest kind, of a delicious sense of humour, and, in "Andrea del Sarto," of deep tenderness. But neither tenderness, nor humour, nor wit, nor even imagination, nor indeed all these together, will constitute a man a poet. Laplace, Bacon, Copernicus, Newton, Mr. Darwin, all have immense imagination; and we might, of course, extend the list indefinitely. We think we have allowed it to be seen that we regard Mr. Browning's intellectual powers as very considerable indeed. "Bishop Blougram's Apology" is an astonishing production, which we invariably read almost throughout with unflagging zest. But it is not poetry. There is not a line of poetry in it from first to last, and we confess we prefer it to all Mr. Browning's compositions. Suppose he had never written anything else, would it have occurred to anybody that he was a poet, or even aspiring to be a poet? In order still further to illustrate our meaning, suppose Mr. Tennyson had never written

1. To obtain the blessing due his elder brother Esau, Jacob deceived his blind father Isaac by disguising his smooth hands with goatskins (Genesis 27:1–29).

anything but "The Northern Farmer"—a piece we chuckle over with
inexpressible delight—again, would it have occurred to anybody
that Mr. Tennyson was a poet, or was pretending to be such? Of
course not; no more than it would have occurred to his contemporaries to have regarded Cowper as a poet if he had never written
anything but "John Gilpin," whose pre-eminent success positively
annoyed its author? So with "Bishop Blougram's Apology," and all
of Mr. Browning's compositions, or passages in his compositions,
which are *ejusdem generis*[2] with it. They are witty, wise, shrewd,
deep, true, wonderful—anything or everything but poetry. It is the
greatest, though apparently the commonest, mistake in the world to
suppose that the quality of verse, provided the thoughts it expresses
are excellent thoughts, involves for those thoughts and their expression the quality of poetry. This has been Mr. Browning's *ignis
fatuus*[3] through life; and the absurd chase it has led him he in turn
has led those who have not found out what it is he has all along
been following. In a word, Mr. Browning's so-called Muse is a *lusus
naturæ*,[4] a sport, to use gardeners' language; but certain sapient
critics have been exulting over it, as though it were a new and finer
specimen of the old true poetic stock. Moreover, Mr. Browning's
undoubted faculty of depth has bewitched and bewrayed them.
Despite their protestations of being perfectly content with Mr. Tennyson as the great poet who justifies the period, they are not content with him. They have all along more or less consciously felt
what we insisted on in our article last month—his want of loftiness.
Now, in Mr. Browning they have found something that unquestionably is not in Mr. Tennyson, and they have begun to fancy that
that something may possibly supply Mr. Tennyson's shortcomings.
That comes of not having thought the matter out with regard to
either of these authors. They know Mr. Tennyson wants something
or other: they know Mr. Browning has something or other. But
from lack of patient reflection and investigation they fail to perceive
for themselves that what Mr. Tennyson wants is height, and what
Mr. Browning has is depth. This once clearly perceived, it is
obvious that the latter characteristic cannot mend the imperfection
of the former characteristic. You might just as well try to make a
mountain higher by excavating round it, or make swallows fly more
soaringly by yourself descending a coal-pit. We have already very
explicitly given our estimate of Mr. Tennyson as a poet; and though
it is such as thousands of men who have fancied themselves beloved
of the Muses would have given anything to have honestly formed of
them, it is far removed from that in which his more ardent admirers

2. Of the same kind.
3. Literally, "foolish fire"; a delusive or
impractical aim.
4. A freak of nature.

at times affect to indulge. One thing, however, is certain. They need be in no fear lest Mr. Tennyson should be displaced by any critic in his sound senses to make way for Mr. Browning. When men desire to behold the flight of an eagle, and cannot get it, they do not usually regard the tramp of an elephant as a substitute.

We therefore beg of the general public to return to the bent of its own original judgment, and, unbewildered by those who would fain be its guides, to treat Mr. Browning's "Poetical Works" as it treated "Paracelsus," &c., on its first appearance—as though they were non-existent. We know it has now much to contend against. When the academy and the drawing-room, when pedantry and folly, combine to set a fashion, it requires more self-confidence than the meek public commonly possesses to laugh the silly innovation down. To Mr. Tennyson's credit be it spoken, he has never gone looking for fame. The ground we tread on is delicate; and we will, therefore, only add that we should have been better pleased if the author, who is now so ridiculously obtruded as his rival, had imitated him in that particular. Small London literary coteries, and large fashionable London salons, cannot crown a man with the bays of Apollo. They may stick their trumpery tinsel wreaths upon him, but these will last no longer than the locks they encircle. They may confer notoriety, but fame is not in their gift. All they can bestow is as transitory as themselves. Let the sane general public, therefore, we say, take heart, and bluntly forswear Mr. Browning and all his works. It is bad enough that there should be people, pretending to authority among us, who call a man a great poet when, though unquestionably a poet, he has no marks of greatness about him. But that is a venial error, and a trifling misfortune, compared to what would be the misery of living in an age which gibbetted itself beforehand for the pity of posterity, by deliberately calling a man a poet who—however remarkable his mental attributes and powers—is not specifically a poet at all. We hope we shall be spared this humiliation. At any rate, we must protest against being supposed willingly to participate in it.

P.S.—It will be observed that we have abstained from all mention of "The Ring and the Book." Our readers must not, however, suppose that the foregoing paper was written before that work appeared. Not at all. But "The Ring and the Book" throws no new light on the subject; and what we have said of Mr. Browning's aim, method, and manner, whilst examining his other compositions, holds equally good of his latest, wonderful but unpoetical, production. We have refrained from scrutinising it, only because conscientious criticism of art, like art itself, is long, and Magazine articles are short.

ALGERNON CHARLES SWINBURNE

[Browning's Obscurity]†

* * *

The charge of obscurity is perhaps of all charges the likeliest to impair the fame or to imperial the success of a rising or an established poet. It is as often misapplied by hasty or ignorant criticism as any other on the roll of accusations; and was never misapplied more persistently and perversely than to an eminent writer of our own time. The difficulty found by many in certain of Mr. Browning's works arises from a quality the very reverse of that which produces obscurity properly so called. Obscurity is the natural product of turbid forces and confused ideas; of a feeble and clouded or of a vigorous but unfixed and chaotic intellect. Such a poet as Lord Brooke, for example—and I take George Chapman and Fulke Greville[1] to be of all English poets the two most genuinely obscure in style upon whose works I have ever adventured to embark in search of treasure hidden beneath the dark gulfs and crossing currents of their rocky and weedy waters, at some risk of my understanding being swept away by the groundswell—such a poet, overcharged with overflowing thoughts, is not sufficiently possessed by any one leading idea, or attracted towards any one central point, to see with decision the proper end and use with resolution the proper instruments of his design. Now if there is any great quality more perceptible than another in Mr. Browning's intellect it is his decisive and incisive faculty of thought, his sureness and intensity of perception, his rapid and trenchant resolution of aim. To charge him with obscurity is about as accurate as to call Lynceus[2] purblind or complain of the sluggish action of the telegraphic wire. He is something too much the reverse of obscure; he is too brilliant and subtle for the ready reader of a ready writer to follow with any certainty the track of an intelligence which moves with such incessant rapidity, or even to realize with what spider-like swiftness and sagacity his building spirit leaps and lightens to and fro and backward and forward as it lives along the animated line of its labour, springs from thread to thread and darts from centre to circumference of the glittering and quivering web of living thought woven from the inex-

† From Algernon Charles Swinburne, *George Chapman: A Critical Essay* (London: Chatto and Windus, 1875), pp. 15–24. Footnotes are by editor.
1. George Chapman (ca. 1559–1634), English dramatist, best known for his translations of Homer; Sir Fulke Greville, Lord Brooke (1554–1628), English poet.
2. One of the Argonauts, whose sight was so keen that he could see through the earth.

haustible stores of his perception and kindled from the inexhaustible fire of his imagination. He never thinks but at full speed; and
the rate of his thought is to that of another man's as the speed of a
railway to that of a waggon or the speed of a telegraph to that of a
railway. It is hopeless to enjoy the charm or to apprehend the gist of
his writings except with a mind thoroughly alert, an attention awake
at all points, a spirit open and ready to be kindled by the contact of
the writer's. To do justice to any book which deserves any other sort
of justice than that of the fire or the wastepaper basket, it is necessary to read it in the fit frame of mind; and the proper mood in
which to study for the first time a book of Mr. Browning's is the
freshest, clearest, most active mood of the mind in its brightest and
keenest hours of work. Read at such a time, and not "with half-shut
eyes falling asleep in a half-dream,"[3] it will be found (in Chapman's phrase) "pervial" enough to any but a sluggish or a sand-
blind eye; but at no time and in no mood will a really obscure
writer be found other than obscure. The difference between the two
is the difference between smoke and lightning; and it is far more
difficult to pitch the tone of your thought in harmony with that of
a foggy thinker, than with that of one whose thought is electric in
its motion. To the latter we have but to come with an open and
pliant spirit, untired and undisturbed by the work or the idleness of
the day, and we cannot but receive a vivid and active pleasure in
following the swift and fine radiations, the subtle play and keen vi-
bration of its sleepless fires; and the more steadily we trace their
course the more surely do we see that these forked flashes of fancy
and changing lights of thought move unerringly around one centre,
and strike straight in the end to one point. Only random thinking
and random writing produce obscurity; and these are the radical
faults of Chapman's style of poetry. We find no obscurity in the
lightning, whether it play about the heights of metaphysical speculation or the depths of character and motive; the mind derives as
much of vigorous enjoyment from the study by such light of the
one as of the other. The action of so bright and swift a spirit gives
insight as it were to the eyes and wings to the feet of our own; the
reader's apprehension takes fire from the writer's, and he catches
from a subtler and more active mind the infection of spiritual interest; so that any candid and clear-headed student finds himself able
to follow for the time in fancy the lead of such a thinker with equal
satisfaction on any course of thought or argument; when he sets
himself to refute Renan through the dying lips of St. John or to try
conclusions with Strauss in his own person, and when he flashes at
once the whole force of his illumination full upon the inmost

3. Adapted from Tennyson's "The Lotos-Eaters," lines 100–101.

thought and mind of the most infamous criminal, a Guido Franceschini or a Louis Bonaparte,[4] compelling the black and obscene
abyss of such a spirit to yield up at last the secret of its profoundest
sophistries, and let forth the serpent of a soul that lies coiled under
the most intricate and supple reasonings of self-justified and self-
conscious crime. And thanks to this very quality of vivid spiritual
illumination, we are able to see by the light of the author's mind
without being compelled to see with his eyes, or with the eyes of
the living mask which he assumes for his momentary impersonation
of saint or sophist, philosopher or malefactor; without accepting one
conclusion, conceding one point, or condoning one crime. It is evident that to produce any such effect requires above all things
brightness and decision as well as subtlety and pliancy of genius;
and this is the supreme gift and distinctive faculty of Mr. Browning's mind. If indeed there be ever any likelihood of error in his
exquisite analysis, he will doubtless be found to err rather through
excess of light than through any touch of darkness; we may doubt,
not without a sense that the fittest mood of criticism might be that
of a self-distrustful confidence in the deeper intuition of his finer
and more perfect knowledge, whether the perception of good or evil
would actually be so acute in the mind of the supposed reasoner;
whether for instance a veritable household assassin, a veritable
saviour of society or other incarnation of moral pestilence, would in
effect see so clearly and so far, with whatever perversion or distortion of view, into the recesses of the pit of hell wherein he lives and
moves and has his being; recognising with quick and delicate apprehension what points of vantage he must strive to gain, what outposts
of self-defence he may hope to guard, in the explanation and vindication of the motive forces of his nature and the latent mainspring of
his deeds. This fineness of intellect and dramatic sympathy which is
ever on the watch to anticipate and answer the unspoken imputations and prepossessions of his hearer, the very movements of his
mind, the very action of his instincts, is perhaps a quality hardly
compatible with a nature which we might rather suppose, judging
from public evidence and historic indication, to be sluggish and
short-sighted, "a sly slow thing with circumspective eye"[5] that can
see but a little way immediately around it, but neither before it nor
behind, above it nor beneath; and whose introspection, if ever that
eye were turned inward, would probably be turbid, vacillating,
cloudy and uncertain as the action of a spirit incapable of self-
knowledge but not incapable of self-distrust, timid and impenitent,
abased and unabashed, remorseless but not resolute, shameless but

4. Swinburne refers to "A Death in the
Desert," "Christmas-Eve" (XVI), *The
Ring and the Book,* and "Prince Hohen-
stiel-Schwangau, Saviour of Society."
5. Adapted from Pope's *Essay on Man,*
IV.226.

not fearless. If such be in reality the public traitor and murderer of a nation, we may fairly infer that his humbler but not viler counterpart in private life will be unlikely to exhibit a finer quality of mind or a clearer faculty of reason. But this is a question of realism which in no wise affects the spiritual value and interest of such work as Mr. Browning's. What is important for our present purpose is to observe that this work of exposition by soliloquy and apology by analysis can only be accomplished or undertaken by the genius of a great special pleader, able to fling himself with all his heart and all his brain, with all the force of his intellect and all the strength of his imagination, into the assumed part of his client; to concentrate on the cause in hand his whole power of illustration and illumination, and bring to bear upon one point at once all the rays of his thought in one focus. Apart from his gift of moral imagination, Mr. Browning has in the supreme degree the qualities of a great debater or an eminent leading counsel; his finest reasoning has in its expression and development something of the ardour of personal energy and active interest which inflames the argument of a public speaker; we feel, without the reverse regret of Pope, how many a firstrate barrister or parliamentary tactician has been lost in this poet.[6] The enjoyment that his best and most characteristic work affords us is doubtless far other than the delight we derive from the purest and highest forms of lyric or dramatic art; there is a radical difference between the analyst and the dramatist, the pleader and the prophet. It would be clearly impossible for the subtle tongue which can undertake at once the apology and the anatomy of such motives as may be assumed to impel or to support a "Prince Hohenstiel-Schwangau" on his ways of thought and action, ever to be touched with the fire which turns to a sword or to a scourge the tongue of a poet[7] to whom it is given to utter as from Patmos or from Sinai the word that fills all the heaven of song with the lightnings and thunders of chastisement. But in place of lyric rapture or dramatic action we may profitably enjoy the unique and incomparable genius of analysis which gives to these special pleadings such marvellous life and interest as no other workman in that kind was ever or will ever again be able to give; we may pursue with the same sense of strenuous delight in a new exercise of intellect and interest the slender and luminous threads of speculation wound up into a clue with so fine a skill and such happy sleight of hand in *Fifine at the Fair* or the sixth book of *Sordello*, where the subtle secret of spiritual weakness in a soul of too various powers and too restless refinement

6. Allusion to *Dunciad,* IV.170: "How many Martials were in PULTENEY lost!" Martial was a Roman poet; William Pulteney, Earl of Bath (1684–1764), an English politician and pamphleteer.
7. Victor Hugo, whose *Les Châtiments* (1853), like "Prince Hohenstiel-Schwangau," satirizes Napoleon III.

is laid bare with such cunning strength of touch, condemned and consoled with such far-sighted compassion and regret.

* * *

GERARD MANLEY HOPKINS

[Strictures on Browning]†

* * *

* * * Browning has, I think, many frigidities. Any untruth to nature, to human nature, is frigid. Now he has got a great deal of what came in with Kingsley and the Broad Church school,[1] a way of talking (and making his people talk) with the air and spirit of a man bouncing up from table with his mouth full of bread and cheese and saying that he meant to stand no blasted nonsense. There is a whole volume of Kingsley's essays which is all a kind of munch and a not standing of any blasted nonsense from cover to cover. Do you know what I mean? The *Flight of the Duchess*, with the repetition of "My friend," is in this vein. Now this is *one* mood or vein of human nature, but they would have it all and look at all human nature through it. And Tennyson in his later works has been "carried away with their dissimulation."[2] The effect of this style is a frigid bluster. A true humanity of spirit, neither mawkish on the one hand nor blustering on the other, is the most precious of all qualities in style, and this I prize in your poems, as I do in Bridges'.[3] After all it is the breadth of his human nature that we admire in Shakespeare.

I read some, not much, of the *Ring and the Book*, but as the tale was not edifying and one of our people, who had been reviewing it, said that further on it was coarser, I did not see, without a particular object, sufficient reason for going on with it. So far as I read I was greatly struck with the skill in which he displayed the facts from different points of view: this is masterly, and to do it through three volumes more shews a great body of genius. I remember a good case of "the impotent collection of particulars" of which you speak in the description of the market place at Florence where he

† From a letter to R. W. Dixon (Oct. 12, 1881) in *The Correspondence of Gerard Manley Hopkins and Richard Watson Dixon,* ed. C. C. Abbott (London: Oxford University Press, 1935), pp. 74–75. Footnotes are by editor.
1. Charles Kingsley (1819–75), novelist, clergyman, and leader of the "Broad Church" or liberal wing of the established church. He was an apostle of a "healthful and manly" religious outlook, dubbed "Muscular Christianity."
2. Galatians 2:13.
3. Robert Bridges (1844–1930), poet laureate 1913–30.

found the book of the trial: it is a pointless photograph of still life, such as I remember in Balzac, minute upholstery description; only that in Balzac, who besides is writing prose, all tells and is given with a reserve and simplicity of style which Browning has not got. Indeed I hold with the oldfashioned criticism[4] that Browning is not really a poet, that he has all the gifts but the one needful and the pearls without the string; rather one should say raw nuggets and rough diamonds. I suppose him to resemble Ben Jonson, only that Ben Jonson has more real poetry.

* * *

OSCAR WILDE

[Browning as "Writer of Fiction"]

* * *

The members of the Browning Society,[1] like the theologians of the Broad Church Party, or the authors of Mr. Walter Scott's Great Writers' Series, seem to me to spend their time in trying to explain their divinity away. Where one had hoped that Browning was a mystic, they have sought to show that he was simply inarticulate. Where one had fancied that he had something to conceal, they have proved that he had but little to reveal. But I speak merely of his incoherent work. Taken as a whole, the man was great. He did not belong to the Olympians, and had all the incompleteness of the Titan. He did not survey, and it was but rarely that he could sing. His work is marred by struggle, violence, and effort, and he passed not from emotion to form, but from thought to chaos. Still, he was great. He has been called a thinker, and was certainly a man who was always thinking, and always thinking aloud; but it was not thought that fascinated him, but rather the processes by which thought moves. It was the machine he loved, not what the machine makes. The method by which the fool arrives at his folly was so dear to him as the ultimate wisdom of the wise. So much, indeed, did the subtle mechanism of mind fascinate him that he despised language, or looked upon it as an incomplete instrument of expression. Rhyme, that exquisite echo which in the Muse's hollow hill creates and answers its own voice; rhyme, which

4. Represented at its most negative by Alfred Austin's "The Poetry of the Period: Mr. Browning" (1869), an excerpt from which appears in this volume.
† From "The True Function and Value of Criticism," *Nineteenth Century*, 28 (July 1890), 123–47. Footnotes are by editor.

1. The London Browning Society, organized in 1881 by Frederick J. Furnivall and Miss Emily Hickey. Though much ridiculed during its eleven-year history, it helped establish Browning's reputation as a profound thinker.

in the hands of a real artist becomes not merely a material element of metrical beauty, but a spiritual element of thought and passion also, waking a new mood, it may be, or stirring a fresh train of ideas, or opening by mere sweetness and suggestion of sound some golden door at which the Imagination itself had knocked in vain; rhyme, which can turn man's utterance to the speech of gods; rhyme, the one chord we have added to the Greek lyre, became in Robert Browning's hands a grotesque, misshapen thing, which made him at times masquerade in poetry as a low comedian, and ride Pegasus too often with his tongue in his cheek. There are moments when he wounds us by monstrous music. Nay, if he can only get his music by breaking the strings of his lute, he breaks them, and they snap in discord, and no Athenian tettix,[2] making melody from tremulous wings, lights on the ivory horn to make the movement perfect or the interval less harsh. Yet, he was great: and though he turned language into ignoble clay, he made from it men and women that live. He is the most Shakespearian creature since Shakespeare. If Shakespeare could sing with myriad lips, Browning could stammer through a thousand mouths. Even now, as I am speaking, and speaking not against him but for him, there glides through the room the pageant of his persons. There, creeps Fra Lippo Lippi with his cheeks still burning from some girl's hot kiss. There, stands dread Saul with the lordly male-sapphires gleaming in his turban. Mildred Tresham[3] is there, and the Spanish monk, yellow with hatred, and Blougram, and the Rabbi Ben Ezra, and the Bishop of St. Praxed's. The spawn of Setebos gibbers in the corner, and Sebald, hearing Pippa pass by, looks on Ottima's haggard face, and loathes her and his own sin and himself. Pale as the white satin of his doublet, the melancholy king watches with dreamy treacherous eyes too loyal Strafford[4] pass to his doom, and Andrea shudders as he hears the cousin's whistle in the garden, and bids his perfect wife go down. Yes, Browning was great. And as what will he be remembered? As a poet? Ah, not as a poet! He will be remembered as a writer of fiction, as the most supreme writer of fiction, it may be, that we have ever had. His sense of dramatic situation was unrivalled, and, if he could not answer his own problems, he could at least put problems forth. Considered from the point of view of a creator of character he ranks next to him who made Hamlet. Had he been articulate he might have sat beside him. The only man living who can touch the hem of his garment is George Meredith. Meredith is a prose-Browning, and so is Browning. He used poetry as a medium for writing in prose.

* * *

2. Or tetrix, genus of grouse locusts.
3. Young heroine of Browning's tragedy *A Blot in the 'Scutcheon* (1843).

4. Hero of Browning's drama *Strafford* (1837).

HENRY JAMES

Browning in Westminster Abbey†

The lovers of a great poet are the people in the world who are most to be forgiven a little wanton fancy about him, for they have before them, in his genius and work, an irresistible example of the application of the imaginative method to a thousand subjects. Certainly, therefore, there are many confirmed admirers of Robert Browning to whom it will not have failed to occur that the consignment of his ashes to the great temple of fame of the English race was exactly one of those occasions in which his own analytic spirit would have rejoiced and his irrepressible faculty for looking at human events in all sorts of slanting coloured lights have found a signal opportunity. If he had been taken with it as a subject, if it had moved him to the confused yet comprehensive utterance of which he was the great professor, we can immediately guess at some of the sparks he would have scraped from it, guess how splendidly, in the case, the pictorial sense would have intertwined itself with the metaphysical. For such an occasion would have lacked, for the author of "The Ring and the Book," none of the complexity and convertibility that were dear to him. Passion and ingenuity, irony and solemnity, the impressive and the unexpected, would each have forced their way through; in a word the author would have been sure to take the special, circumstantial view (the inveterate mark of all his speculation) even of so foregone a conclusion as that England should pay her greatest honour to one of her greatest poets. As they stood in the Abbey, at any rate, on Tuesday last, those of his admirers and mourners who were disposed to profit by his warrant for enquiring curiously may well have let their fancy range, with its muffled step, in the direction which *his* fancy would probably not have shrunk from following, even perhaps to the dim corners where humour and the whimsical lurk. Only, we hasten to add, it would have taken Robert Browning himself to render the multifold impression.

One part of it on such occasion is of course irresistible—the sense that these honours are the greatest that a generous nation has to confer and that the emotion that accompanies them is one of the high moments of a nation's life. The attitude of the public, of the multitude, at such hours, is a great expansion, a great openness to ideas of aspiration and achievement; the pride of possession and of

† First published in *The Speaker*, 1 (Jan. 4, 1891), 11–12; reprinted in *English Hours* (Boston: Houghton Mifflin, 1905), pp. 51–59. Reprinted by permission of the James Estate and the publisher.

bestowal, especially in the case of a career so complete as Mr.
Browning's, is so present as to make regret a minor matter. We possess a great man most when we begin to look at him through the
glass plate of death; and it is a simple truth, though containing an
apparent contradiction, that the Abbey never takes us so benign-
antly as when we have a valued voice to commit to silence there.
For the silence is articulate after all, and in worthy instances the
preservation great. It is the other side of the question that would
pull most the strings of irresponsible reflection—all those conceivable postulates and hypotheses of the poetic and satiric mind to
which we owe the picture of how the bishop ordered his tomb in
St. Praxed's. Macaulay's "temple of silence and reconciliation"—
and none the less perhaps because he himself is now a presence there
—strikes us, as we stand in it, not only as local but as social, a sort
of corporate company; so thick, under its high arches, its dim tran-
septs and chapels, is the population of its historic names and
figures. They are a company in possession, with a high standard of
distinction, of immortality, as it were; for there is something
serenely inexpugnable even in the position of the interlopers. As
they look out, in the rich dusk, from the cold eyes of statues and
the careful identity of tablets, they seem, with their converging
faces, to scrutinise decorously the claims of each new recumbent
glory, to ask each other how he is to be judged as an accession. How
difficult to banish the idea that Robert Browning would have
enjoyed prefiguring and playing with the mystifications, the reserva-
tions, even perhaps the slight buzz of scandal, in the Poets' Corner,
to which his own obsequies might give rise! Would not his great
relish, in so characteristic an interview with his crucible, have been
his perception of the bewildering modernness, to much of the
society, of the new candidate for a niche? That is the interest and
the fascination, from what may be termed the inside point of view,
of Mr. Browning's having received, in this direction of becoming a
classic, the only official assistance that is ever conferred upon English writers.

It is as classics on one ground and another—some members of it
perhaps on that of not being anything else—that the numerous
assembly in the Abbey holds together, and it is as a tremendous and
incomparable modern that the author of "Men and Women" takes
his place in it. He introduces to his predecessors a kind of contemporary individualism which surely for many a year they had not been
reminded of with any such force. The tradition of the poetic character as something high, detached, and simple, which may be
assumed to have prevailed among them for a good while, is one that
Browning has broken at every turn; so that we can imagine his new
associates to stand about him, till they have got used to him, with

rather a sense of failing measures. A good many oddities and a good many great writers have been entombed in the Abbey; but none of the odd ones have been so great and none of the great ones so odd. There are plenty of poets whose right to the title may be contested, but there is no poetic head of equal power—crowned and recrowned by almost importunate hands—from which so many people would withhold the distinctive wreath. All this will give the marble phantoms at the base of the great pillars, and the definite personalities of the honorary slabs something to puzzle out until, by the quick operation of time, the mere fact of his lying there among the classified and protected makes even Robert Browning lose a portion of the bristling surface of his actuality.

For the rest, judging from the outside and with his contemporaries, we of the public can only feel that his very modernness—by which we mean the all-touching, all-trying spirit of his work, permeated with accumulations and playing with knowledge—achieves a kind of conquest, or at least of extension, of the rigid pale. We cannot enter here upon any account either of that or of any other element of his genius, though surely no literary figure of our day seems to sit more unconsciously for the painter. The very imperfections of this original are fascinating, for they never present themselves as weaknesses; they are boldnesses and overgrowths, rich roughnesses and humours, and the patient critic need not despair of digging to the primary soil from which so many disparities and contradictions spring. He may finally even put his finger on some explanation of the great mystery, the imperfect conquest of the poetic form by a genius in which the poetic passion had such volume and range. He may successfully say how it was that a poet without a lyre—for that is practically Browning's deficiency: he had the scroll, but not often the sounding strings—was nevertheless, in his best hours, wonderfully rich in the magic of his art, a magnificent master of poetic emotion. He will justify on behalf of a multitude of devotees the great position assigned to a writer of verse of which the nature or the fortune has been (in proportion to its value and quantity) to be treated rarely as quotable. He will do all this and a great deal more besides; but we need not wait for it to feel that something of our latest sympathies, our latest and most restless selves, passed the other day into the high part—the show-part, to speak vulgarly—of our literature. To speak of Mr. Browning only as he was in the last twenty years of his life, how quick such an imagination as his would have been to recognise all the latent or mystical suitabilities that, in the last resort, might link to the great Valhalla by the Thames a figure that had become so conspicuously a figure of London! He had grown to be intimately and inveterately of the London world; he was so familiar and recurrent, so responsive to all its solicitations, that, given the endless incarnations he stands for to-day, he would have been missed from the congregation of worthies whose memorials are the special pride of the Londoner. Just as his great sign to those who knew him was that he was a force of health, of temperament, of tone, so what he takes into the Abbey is an immense expression of life—of life rendered with large liberty and free experiment, with an unprejudiced intellectual eagerness to put himself in other people's place, to participate in complications and consequences; a restlessness of psychological research that might well alarm any pale company for their formal orthodoxies.

But the illustrious whom he rejoins may be reassured, as they will not fail to discover: in so far as they are representative it will clear itself up that, in spite of a surface unsuggestive of marble and a reckless individualism of form, he is quite as representative as any of them. For the great value of Browning is that at bottom, in all the deep spiritual and human essentials, he is unmistakably in the great tradition—is, with all his Italianisms and cosmopolitanisms, all his victimisation by societies organised to talk about him, a magnificent example of the best and least dilettantish English spirit. That constitutes indeed the main chance for his eventual critic, who will have to solve the refreshing problem of how, if subtleties be not what the English spirit most delights in, the author of, for instance, "Any Wife to Any Husband" made them his perpetual pasture, and yet remained typically of his race. He was indeed a wonderful mixture of the universal and the alembicated. But he played with the curious and the special, they never submerged him, and it was a sign of his robustness that he could play to the end. His voice sounds loudest, and also clearest, for the things that, as a race, we like best—the fascination of faith, the acceptance of life, the respect for its mysteries, the endurance of its charges, the vitality of the will, the validity of character, the beauty of action, the seriousness, above all, of the great human passion. If Browning had spoken for us in no other way, he ought to have been made sure of, tamed and chained as a classic, on account of the extraordinary beauty of his treatment of the special relation between man and woman. It is a complete and splendid picture of the matter, which somehow places it at the same time in the region of conduct and responsibility. But when we talk of Robert Browning's speaking "for us," we go to the end of our privilege, we say all. With a sense of security, perhaps even a certain complacency, we leave our sophisticated modern conscience, and perhaps even our heterogeneous modern vocabulary, in his charge among the illustrious. There will possibly be moments in which these things will seem to us to have widened the allowance, made the high abode more comfortable, for some of those who are yet to enter it.

Modern Essays in Criticism

Revaluations

GEORGE SANTAYANA

The Poetry of Barbarism†

* * *

If we would do justice to Browning's work as a human document, and at the same time perceive its relation to the rational ideals of the imagination and to that poetry which passes into religion, we must keep, as in the case of Whitman,[1] two things in mind. One is the genuineness of the achievement, the sterling quality of the vision and inspiration; these are their own justification when we approach them from below and regard them as manifesting a more direct or impassioned grasp of experience than is given to mildly blatant, convention-ridden minds. The other thing to remember is the short distance to which this comprehension is carried, its failure to approach any finality, or to achieve a recognition even of the traditional ideals of poetry and religion.

In the case of Walt Whitman such a failure will be generally felt; it is obvious that both his music and his philosophy are those of a barbarian, nay, almost of a savage. Accordingly there is need of dwelling rather on the veracity and simple dignity of his thought and art, on their expression of an order of ideas latent in all better experience. But in the case of Browning it is the success that is obvious to most people. Apart from a certain superficial grotesqueness to which we are soon accustomed, he easily arouses and engages the reader by the pithiness of his phrase, the volume of his passion, the vigour of his moral judgment, the liveliness of his historical fancy. It is obvious that we are in the presence of a great writer, of a great imaginative force, of a master in the expression of emotion. What is perhaps not so obvious, but no less true, is that

† From *Interpretations of Poetry and Religion* (New York: Scribner, 1900), pp. 188–216. Footnotes are by editor. 1. The subject of Santayana's unfavorable criticism in the preceding section. Whitman and Browning are presented as illustrations of the thesis that modern poets "have no total vision, no grasp of the whole reality. . . ."

we are in the presence of a barbaric genius, of a truncated imagination, of a thought and an art inchoate and ill-digested, of a vol-
canic eruption that tosses itself quite blindly and ineffectually into
the sky.

The points of comparison by which this becomes clear are perhaps not in every one's mind, although they are merely the elements of traditional culture, æsthetic and moral. Yet even without
reference to ultimate ideals, one may notice in Browning many
superficial signs of that deepest of all failures, the failure in rationality and the indifference to perfection. Such a sign is the turgid style,
weighty without nobility, pointed without naturalness or precision.
Another sign is the "realism" of the personages, who, quite like
men and women in actual life, are always displaying traits of character and never attaining character as a whole. Other hints might be
found in the structure of the poems, where the dramatic substance
does not achieve a dramatic form; in the metaphysical discussion,
with its confused prolixity and absence of result; in the moral ideal,
where all energies figure without their ultimate purposes; in the religion, which breaks off the expression of this life in the middle, and
finds in that suspense an argument for immortality. In all this, and
much more that might be recalled, a person coming to Browning
with the habits of a cultivated mind might see evidence of some
profound incapacity in the poet; but more careful reflection is necessary to understand the nature of this incapacity, its cause, and the
peculiar accent which its presence gives to those ideas and impulses
which Browning stimulates in us.

There is the more reason for developing this criticism (which
might seem needlessly hostile and which time and posterity will
doubtless make in their own quiet and decisive fashion) in that
Browning did not keep within the sphere of drama and analysis,
where he was strong, but allowed his own temperament and opinions to vitiate his representation of life, so that he sometimes
turned the expression of a violent passion into the last word of what
he thought a religion. He had a didactic vein, a habit of judging the
spectacle he evoked and of loading the passions he depicted with
his visible sympathy or scorn.

Now a chief support of Browning's popularity is that he is, for
many, an initiator into the deeper mysteries of passion, a means of
escaping from the moral poverty of their own lives and of feeling
the rhythm and compulsion of the general striving. He figures,
therefore, distinctly as a prophet, as a bearer of glad tidings, and it
is easy for those who hail him as such to imagine that, knowing the
labour of life so well, he must know something also of its fruits, and
that in giving us the feeling of existence, he is also giving us its
meaning. There is serious danger that a mind gathering from his

pages the raw materials of truth, the unthreshed harvest of reality, may take him for a philosopher, for a rationalizer of what he describes. Awakening may be mistaken for enlightenment, and the galvanizing of torpid sensations and impulses for wisdom.

Against such fatuity reason should raise her voice. The vital and historic forces that produce illusions of this sort in large groups of men are indeed beyond the control of criticism. The ideas of passion are more vivid than those of memory, until they become memories in turn. They must be allowed to fight out their desperate battle against the laws of Nature and reason. But it is worth while in the meantime, for the sake of the truth and of a just philosophy, to meet the varying though perpetual charlatanism of the world with a steady protest. As soon as Browning is proposed to us as a leader, as soon as we are asked to be not the occasional patrons of his art, but the pupils of his philosophy, we have a right to express the radical dissatisfaction which we must feel, if we are rational, with his whole attitude and temper of mind.

The great dramatists have seldom dealt with perfectly virtuous characters. The great poets have seldom represented mythologies that would bear scientific criticism. But by an instinct which constituted their greatness they have cast these mixed materials furnished by life into forms congenial to the specific principles of their art, and by this transformation they have made acceptable in the æsthetic sphere things that in the sphere of reality were evil or imperfect: in a word, their works have been beautiful as works of art. Or, if their genius exceeded that of the technical poet and rose to prophetic intuition, they have known how to create ideal characters, not possessed, perhaps, of every virtue accidentally needed in this world, but possessed of what is ideally better, of internal greatness and perfection. They have also known how to select and reconstruct their mythology so as to make it a true interpretation of moral life. When we read the maxims of Iago, Falstaff, or Hamlet, we are delighted if the thought strikes us as true, but we are not less delighted if it strikes us as false. These characters are not presented to us in order to enlarge our capacities of passion nor in order to justify themselves as processes of redemption; they are there, clothed in poetry and imbedded in plot, to entertain us with their imaginable feelings and their interesting errors. The poet, without being especially a philosopher, stands by virtue of his superlative genius on the plane of universal reason, far above the passionate experience which he overlooks and on which he reflects; and he raises us for the moment to his own level, to send us back again, if not better endowed for practical life, at least not unacquainted with speculation.

With Browning the case is essentially different. When his heroes are blinded by passion and warped by circumstance, as they almost always are, he does not describe the fact from the vantage-ground of the intellect and invite us to look at it from that point of view. On the contrary, his art is all self-expression or satire. For the most part his hero, like Whitman's, is himself; not appearing, as in the case of the American bard, *in puris naturalibus*, but masked in all sorts of historical and romantic finery. Sometimes, however, the personage, like Guido in *The Ring and the Book* or the "frustrate ghosts" of other poems, is merely a Marsyas, shown flayed and quivering to the greater glory of the poet's ideal Apollo. The impulsive utterances and the crudities of most of the speakers are passionately adopted by the poet as his own. He thus perverts what might have been a triumph of imagination into a failure of reason.

This circumstance has much to do with the fact that Browning, in spite of his extraordinary gift for expressing emotion, has hardly produced works purely and unconditionally delightful. They not only portray passion, which is interesting, but they betray it, which is odious. His art was still in the service of the will. He had not attained, in studying the beauty of things, that detachment of the phenomenon, that love of the form for its own sake, which is the secret of contemplative satisfaction. Therefore, the lamentable accidents of his personality and opinions, in themselves no worse than those of other mortals, passed into his art. He did not seek to elude them: he had no free speculative faculty to dominate them by. Or, to put the same thing differently, he was too much in earnest in his fictions, he threw himself too unreservedly into his creations. His imagination, like the imagination we have in dreams, was merely a vent for personal preoccupations. His art was inspired by purposes less simple and universal than the ends of imagination itself. His play of mind consequently could not be free or pure. The creative impulse could not reach its goal or manifest in any notable degree its own organic ideal.

* * *

Aristotle observes that we do not think the business of life worthy of the gods, to whom we can only attribute contemplation; if Browning had had the idea of perfecting and rationalizing this life rather than of continuing it indefinitely, he would have followed Aristotle and the Church in this matter. But he had no idea of anything eternal; and so he gave, as he would probably have said, a filling to the empty Christian immortality by making every man busy in it about many things. And to the irrational man, to the boy, it is no unpleasant idea to have an infinite number of days to live through, an infinite number of dinners to eat, with an infinity of fresh fights and new love-affairs, and no end of last rides together.

But it is a mere euphemism to call this perpetual vagrancy a development of the soul. A development means the unfolding of a definite nature, the gradual manifestation of a known idea. A series of phases, like the successive leaps of a water-fall, is no development. And Browning has no idea of an intelligible good which the phases of life might approach and with reference to which they might constitute a progress. His notion is simply that the game of life, the exhilaration of action, is inexhaustible. You may set up your tenpins again after you have bowled them over, and you may keep up the sport for ever. The point is to bring them down as often as possible with a master-stroke and a big bang. That will tend to invigorate in you that self-confidence which in this system passes for faith. But it is unmeaning to call such an exercise heaven, or to talk of being "with God" in such a life, in any sense in which we are not with God already and under all circumstances. Our destiny would rather be, as Browning himself expresses it in a phrase which Attila or Alaric might have composed, "bound dizzily to the wheel of change to slake the thirst of God."[2]

Such an optimism and such a doctrine of immortality can give no justification to experience which it does not already have in its detached parts. Indeed, those dogmas are not the basis of Browning's attitude, not conditions of his satisfaction in living, but rather overflowings of that satisfaction. The present life is presumably a fair average of the whole series of "adventures brave and new" which fall to each man's share; were it not found delightful in itself, there would be no motive for imagining and asserting that it is reproduced *ad infinitum*. So too if we did not think that the evil in experience is actually utilized and visibly swallowed up in its good effects, we should hardly venture to think that God could have regarded as a good something which has evil for its condition and which is for that reason profoundly sad and equivocal. But Browning's philosophy of life and habit of imagination do not require the support of any metaphysical theory. His temperament is perfectly self-sufficient and primary; what doctrines he has are suggested by it and are too loose to give it more than a hesitant expression; they are quite powerless to give it any justification which it might lack on its face.

It is the temperament, then, that speaks; we may brush aside as unsubstantial, and even as distorting, the web of arguments and theories which it has spun out of itself. And what does the temperament say? That life is an adventure, not a discipline; that the exercise of energy is the absolute good, irrespective of motives or of consequences. These are the maxims of a frank barbarism; nothing

2. Paraphrases "Rabbi Ben Ezra," lines 184–86. Attila and Alaric were barbarian rulers.

could express better the lust of life, the dogged unwillingness to learn from experience, the contempt for rationality, the carelessness about perfection, the admiration for mere force, in which barbarism always betrays itself. The vague religion which seeks to justify this attitude is really only another outburst of the same irrational impulse.

In Browning this religion takes the name of Christianity, and identifies itself with one or two Christian ideas arbitrarily selected; but at heart it has far more affinity to the worship of Thor or of Odin than to the religion of the Cross. The zest of life becomes a cosmic emotion; we lump the whole together and cry, "Hurrah for the Universe!" A faith which is thus a pure matter of lustiness and inebriation rises and falls, attracts or repels, with the ebb and flow of the mood from which it springs. It is invincible because unseizable; it is as safe from refutation as it is rebellious to embodiment. But it cannot enlighten or correct the passions on which it feeds. Like a servile priest, it flatters them in the name of Heaven. It cloaks irrationality in sanctimony; and its admiration for every bluff folly, being thus justified by a theory, becomes a positive fanaticism, eager to defend any wayward impulse.

Such barbarism of temper and thought could hardly, in a man of Browning's independence and spontaneity, be without its counterpart in his art. When a man's personal religion is passive, as Shakespeare's seems to have been, and is adopted without question or particular interest from the society around him, we may not observe any analogy between it and the free creations of that man's mind. Not so when the religion is created afresh by the private imagination; it is then merely one among many personal works of art, and will naturally bear a family likeness to the others. The same individual temperament, with its limitations and its bias, will appear in the art which has appeared in the religion. And such is the case with Browning. His limitations as a poet are the counterpart of his limitations as a moralist and theologian; only in the poet they are not so regrettable. Philosophy and religion are nothing if not ultimate; it is their business to deal with general principles and final aims. Now it is in the conception of things fundamental and ultimate that Browning is weak; he is strong in the conception of things immediate. The pulse of the emotion, the bobbing up of the thought, the streaming of the reverie—these he can note down with picturesque force or imagine with admirable fecundity.

Yet the limits of such excellence are narrow, for no man can safely go far without the guidance of reason. His long poems have no structure—for that name cannot be given to the singular mechanical division of *The Ring and the Book*. Even his short poems have no completeness, no limpidity. They are little torsos made broken so as to stimulate the reader to the restoration of their missing legs and arms. What is admirable in them is pregnancy of phrase, vividness of passion and sentiment, heaped-up scraps of observation, occasional flashes of light, occasional beauties of versification,—all like

> the quick sharp scratch
> And blue spurt of a lighted match.[3]

There is never anything largely composed in the spirit of pure beauty, nothing devotedly finished, nothing simple and truly just. The poet's mind cannot reach equilibrium; at best he oscillates between opposed extravagances; his final word is still a *boutade*,[4] still an explosion. He has no sustained nobility of style. He affects with the reader a confidential and vulgar manner, so as to be more sincere and to feel more at home. Even in the poems where the effort at impersonality is most successful, the dramatic disguise is usually thrown off in a preface, epilogue or parenthesis. The author likes to remind us of himself by some confidential wink or genial poke in the ribs, by some little interlarded sneer. We get in these tricks of manner a taste of that essential vulgarity, that indifference to purity and distinction, which is latent but pervasive in all the products of this mind. The same disdain of perfection which appears in his ethics appears here in his verse, and impairs its beauty by allowing it to remain too often obscure, affected, and grotesque.

Such a correspondence is natural: for the same powers of conception and expression are needed in fiction, which, if turned to reflection, would produce a good philosophy. Reason is necessary to the perception of high beauty. Discipline is indispensable to art. Work from which these qualities are absent must be barbaric; it can have no ideal form and must appeal to us only through the sensuousness and profusion of its materials. We are invited by it to lapse into a miscellaneous appreciativeness, into a subservience to every detached impression. And yet, if we would only reflect even on these disordered beauties, we should see that the principle by which they delight us is a principle by which an ideal, an image of perfection, is inevitably evoked. We can have no pleasure or pain, nor any preference whatsoever, without implicitly setting up a standard of excellence, an ideal of what would satisfy us there. To make these implicit ideals explicit, to catch their hint, to work out their theme, and express clearly to ourselves and to the world what they are demanding in the place of the actual—that is the labour of reason and the task of genius. The two cannot be divided. Clarification of ideas and disentanglement of values are as essential to æs-

3. From "Meeting at Night," lines 9–10.   4. Sally.

thetic activity as to intelligence. A failure of reason is a failure of art and taste.

* * *

G. K. CHESTERTON

[Reply to Santayana]†

* * *

Browning's optimism is of that ultimate and unshakeable order that is founded upon the absolute sight, and sound, and smell, and handling of things. If a man had gone up to Browning and asked him with all the solemnity of the eccentric, "Do you think life is worth living?" it is interesting to conjecture what his answer might have been. If he had been for the moment under the influence of the orthodox rationalistic deism of the theologian he would have said, "Existence is justified by its manifest design, its manifest adaptation of means to ends," or, in other words, "Existence is justified by its completeness." If, on the other hand, he had been influenced by his own serious intellectual theories he would have said, "Existence is justified by its air of growth and doubtfulness," or, in other words, "Existence is justified by its incompleteness." But if he had not been influenced in his answer either by the accepted opinions, or by his own opinions, but had simply answered the question "Is life worth living?" with the real, vital answer that awaited it in his own soul, he would have said as likely as not, "Crimson toadstools in Hampshire." Some plain, glowing picture of this sort left on his mind would be his real verdict on what the universe had meant to him. To his traditions hope was traced to order, to his speculations hope was traced to disorder. But to Browning himself hope was traced to something like red toadstools. His mysticism was not of that idle and wordy type which believes that a flower is symbolical of life; it was rather of that deep and eternal type which believes that life, a mere abstraction, is symbolical of a flower. With him the great concrete experiences which God made always come first; his own deductions and speculations about them always second. And in this point we find the real peculiar inspiration of his very original poems.

One of the very few critics who seem to have got near to the actual secret of Browning's optimism is Mr. Santayana in his most interesting book *Interpretations of Poetry and Religion*. He, in con-

† From G. K. Chesterton, *Robert Browning* (London: Macmillan, 1903), pp. 182–87. George Santayana's essay is reprinted above.

tradistinction to the vast mass of Browning's admirers, had discovered what was the real root virtue of Browning's poetry; and the curious thing is, that having discovered that root virtue, he thinks it is a vice. He describes the poetry of Browning most truly as the poetry of barbarism, by which he means the poetry which utters the primeval and indivisible emotions. "For the barbarian is the man who regards his passions as their own excuse for being, who does not domesticate them either by understanding their cause, or by conceiving their ideal goal." Whether this be or be not a good definition of the barbarian, it is an excellent and perfect definition of the poet. It might, perhaps, be suggested that barbarians, as a matter of fact, are generally highly traditional and respectable persons who would not put a feather wrong in their head-gear, and who generally have very few feelings and think very little about those they have. It is when we have grown to a greater and more civilised stature that we begin to realise and put to ourselves intellectually the great feelings that sleep in the depths of us. Thus it is that the literature of our day has steadily advanced towards a passionate simplicity, and we become more primeval as the world grows older, until Whitman writes huge and chaotic psalms to express the sensations of a schoolboy out fishing, and Maeterlinck embodies in symbolic dramas the feelings of a child in the dark.

Thus, Mr. Santayana is, perhaps, the most valuable of all the Browning critics. He has gone out of his way to endeavour to realise what it is that repels him in Browning, and he has discovered the fault which none of Browning's opponents have discovered. And in this he has discovered the merit which none of Browning's admirers have discovered. Whether the quality be a good or a bad quality, Mr. Santayana is perfectly right. The whole of Browning's poetry does rest upon primitive feeling; and the only comment to be added is that so does the whole of every one else's poetry. Poetry deals entirely with those great eternal and mainly forgotten wishes which are the ultimate despots of existence. Poetry presents things as they are to our emotions, not as they are to any theory, however plausible, or any argument, however conclusive. If love is in truth a glorious vision, poetry will say that it is a glorious vision, and no philosophers will persuade poetry to say that it is the exaggeration of the instinct of sex. If bereavement is a bitter and continually aching thing, poetry will say that it is so, and no philosophers will persuade poetry to say that it is an evolutionary stage of great biological value. And here comes in the whole value and object of poetry, that it is perpetually challenging all systems with the test of a terrible sincerity. The practical value of poetry is that it is realistic upon a point upon which nothing else can be realistic, the point of the actual desires of man. Ethics is the science of actions, but poetry is the science of motives. Some actions are ugly, and therefore some parts of ethics are ugly. But all motives are beautiful, or present themselves for the moment as beautiful, and therefore all poetry is beautiful. If poetry deals with the basest matter, with the shedding of blood for gold, it ought to suggest the gold as well as the blood. Only poetry can realise motives because motives are all pictures of happiness. And the supreme and most practical value of poetry is this, that in poetry, as in music, a note is struck which expresses beyond the power of rational statement a condition of mind, and all actions arise from a condition of mind. Prose can only use a large and clumsy notation; it can only say that a man is miserable, or that a man is happy; it is forced to ignore that there are a million diverse kinds of misery and a million diverse kinds of happiness. Poetry alone, with the first throb of its metre, can tell us whether the depression is the kind of depression that drives a man to suicide, or the kind of depression that drives him to the Tivoli. Poetry can tell us whether the happiness is the happiness that sends a man to a restaurant, or the much richer and fuller happiness that sends him to church.

Now the supreme value of Browning as an optimist lies in this that we have been examining, that beyond all his conclusions, and deeper than all his arguments, he was passionately interested in and in love with existence. If the heavens had fallen, and all the waters of the earth run with blood, he would still have been interested in existence, if possible a little more so. He is a great poet of human joy for precisely the reason of which Mr. Santayana complains: that his happiness is primal, and beyond the reach of philosophy. He is something far more convincing, far more comforting, far more religiously significant than an optimist: he is a happy man.

This happiness he finds, as every man must find happiness, in his own way. He does not find the great part of his joy in those matters in which most poets find felicity. He finds much of it in those matters in which most poets find ugliness and vulgarity. He is to a considerable extent the poet of towns. "Do you care for nature much?" a friend of his asked him. "Yes, a great deal," he said, "but for human beings a great deal more." Nature, with its splendid and soothing sanity, has the power of convincing most poets of the essential worthiness of things. There are few poets who, if they escaped from the rowdiest waggonette of trippers, could not be quieted again and exalted by dropping into a small wayside field. The speciality of Browning is rather that he would have been quieted and exalted by the waggonette.

To Browning, probably the beginning and end of all optimism was to be found in the faces in the street. To him they were all the masks of a deity, the heads of a hundred-headed Indian god of nature. Each one of them looked towards some quarter of the heavens, not looked upon by any other eyes. Each of them wore some expression, some blend of eternal joy and eternal sorrow, not to be found in any other countenance. The sense of the absolute sanctity of human difference was the deepest of all his senses. He was hungrily interested in all human things, but it would have been quite impossible to have said of him that he loved humanity. He did not love humanity but men. His sense of difference between one man and another would have made the thought of melting them into a lump called humanity simply loathsome and prosaic. It would have been to him like playing four hundred beautiful airs at once. The mixture would not combine all, it would lose all. Browning believed that to every man that ever lived upon this earth had been given a definite and peculiar confidence of God. Each one of us was engaged on secret service; each one of us had a peculiar message; each one of us was the founder of a religion. Of that religion our thoughts, our faces, our bodies, our hats, our boots, our tastes, our virtues, and even our vices, were more or less fragmentary and inadequate expressions.

* * *

WILLIAM O. RAYMOND

The Infinite Moment†

Though it is now sixty-five years since the death of Robert Browning, the time is yet unripe for a definitive estimate of his place amongst English men of letters. During his lifetime he experienced, perhaps to a greater extent than any of his contemporaries, the vicissitudes of a poet's lot. A long period of depreciation, in which his poetry was a byword for difficulty and obscurity, was followed by a sudden access of fame. From the time of the publication of *The Ring and the Book* in 1868–69 until his death in 1889, his niche beside Tennyson as one of the two master poets of the Victorian era was secure. Criticism was succeeded by panegyric, reaching its acme in the adulation of the Browning Society and its mushroom offshoots in England and America.

In the sixty-five years that have passed since Browning's death, his poetic reputation has varied as widely as in his lifetime. The pendulum of critical opinion has again swung violently from one extreme to the other. In particular, Browning has suffered, along

† From *The Infinite Moment and Other Essays in Robert Browning*, 2nd ed. (To-ronto: University of Toronto Press, 1965), pp. 3–18.

with Tennyson, from the general reaction inimical to Victorianism and all its works which has characterized the opening decades of the twentieth century. There are signs that the nadir has been reached, and that a juster and truer appreciation of the Victorian epoch is at hand. But we are still in the wake of that inevitable shift of literary evaluation which marks the transition from one generation to the next. The baiting of Victorianism continues to be a favourite sport of modern writers; and prevailing currents of present-day historical and aesthetic criticism run counter to some of the cherished ideals and standards in life and art of our Victorian forerunners. Part of this censure is wholesome, part is regrettable, but the winnowing of our Victorian inheritance by the fan of time is as yet incomplete.

A tentative estimate, within brief compass, of Browning's place in English letters must strive for centrality of view. In reckoning with a poet of such far-ranging interests, it is important to insist that he be appraised first of all as an artist. However beguiling the bypaths of his work in literature may be, it is essential to keep steadily in sight the beaten highway, lit by the flash of his genius, where his powers are exhibited at full stretch.

Yet such an emphasis should not be inconsistent with a recognition of the composite nature of Browning's contribution to English poetry. In certain ways he is both an intellectual and a moralist, and the philosophical, ethical, and theological aspects of his writings are fruitful subjects of inquiry. Much has been said concerning the confinement of these elements of his work within a set Victorian mould. But in dealing with a mind of a rare order and a poet of genius, stress should be laid upon those gleams of intuition which break through the conventional Victorian framework with keen insight into the heart of life and the problem of man's destiny. Such a reverie as that of Pope Innocent XII, in *The Ring and the Book*, is no mere collection of theological platitudes. It is a definitive summing-up of Browning's philosophy of life, and a high watermark of metaphysical thought in nineteenth-century poetry, enriched by acute religious perception.

Nevertheless, it is inevitable that a study of the didactic interests of Browning often leads to the periphery rather than to the centre of his poetry. Within their sphere, prodigious mental energy or moral fervour tends to obscure the poet. There is in him a conflict between imagination and intellect, only resolved in the poems of happiest vein, written between 1840 and 1870, beginning with *Pippa Passes* and ending with *The Ring and the Book*. For the understanding of his view of life, the deep-seated opposition between faith and reason pivotal to his thought, his ethical outlook, his conception of the relation between God and man and of man's place in the universe, a consideration of the earlier and later poems lying outside his golden period of imaginative vision is indispensable. Nor can the depths of Browning's analysis of character be plumbed without a knowledge of those stages of his work which abound in subtle probing of impulse and motive, the incidents in the development of the soul underlying outward action.

In order to comprehend these varying interests, a student must toil through the labyrinth of *Sordello*, "a bewildering potpourri of poetry, psychology, love, romance, humanitarianism, philosophy, fiction, and history."[1] He must wrestle with poems which in the aggregate, at any rate, tax his patience and mental faculties even more than that "Giant Despair" of English letters. Some of the later writings of Browning, while they contain lines and passages of sheer poetic beauty, are jungles of involved argument. The mind reels amid the elusive, ever shifting sophistries of *Fifine at the Fair* and *Aristophanes' Apology*, or is repelled by the sordidness of *Red Cotton Night Cap Country*. Though the poet tells us that a delectable ortolan is sandwiched between the plain bread of *Ferishtah's Fancies*, the appetite of the average reader is hardly reconciled to the crust he must crunch before reaching the toothsome bird.

Even the wit and dexterity of Browning's numerous studies in casuistry scarcely atone for their redundancy. We are dizzied by their juggling and wearied by their tortuousness. *Mr. Sludge, "the Medium," Bishop Blougram's Apology*, and *Prince Hohenstiel-Schwangau* are overweighted with ratiocination. The hairsplitting arguments of the lawyers in *The Ring and the Book* make gnarly and tiresome reading, and their crabbed forensic quibbles are only slightly enlivened by quaint Latin puns illustrating the humour of pedants. Whatever tribute is due to Browning's ingenuity in constructing these cumbersome leviathans of verse, the most ardent devotee of the poet, when caught in their toils, must compare his state of mind to that of Milton's spirits in torment, who "found no end in wandering mazes lost."

Happily for Browning's enduring fame as an artist, he has written a large body of fine poetry in which he was able to exorcize his intellectual devil. He cast it from him, even as the hero of one of his poems, in rollicking mockery of arid scholasticism, tossed the bulky tome of Sibrandus Schafnaburgensis into the crevice of a garden tree. "Plague take all your pedants, say I!" It is a pleasure to turn from the "grey argument" of tracts of his verse to the magic of such poetry as is garnered in *Dramatic Romances* and *Men and Women*. Here imagination has not been supplanted by dialectic; and passion and intuition are enlisted in the depicting of character and situation with swift and brilliant portraiture. The sweep and vivacity of Browning's humanism are a perpetual source of delight.

1. William Clyde DeVane, *A Browning Handbook* (New York, 1935), p. 79.

As a humanist he is of the lineage of Chaucer and Shakespeare, a poet of whose work it may be said, "here is God's plenty." Above all other Victorian writers, he has that spaciousness of mind we are wont to link with the Elizabethans. Spiritually a disciple of the Renaissance, he is akin to that great age in his zest of life, *élan* of temperament, overflowing curiosity regarding the ways and works of man. His creative genius has many facets and in richness and versatility is unsurpassed in nineteenth-century English literature. How far flung is his poetic net and what treasure trove he brings to land! Strange fish sometimes, but all

> Live whelks, each lip's beard dripping fresh,
> As if they still the water's lisp heard
> Through foam the rock-weeds thresh.

I intend to centre my estimate of Browning on his artistic quality. This, in itself, has various aspects, and many of them must be left untouched. His dramatic gift, its capacity and limitation, is a fascinating theme, but it has been exhaustively written on from various points of view. The style and diction of his verse have been the subject of a number of technical treatises. I have in mind, rather, to dwell on what may be called the elemental spirit of Browning's art. This choice is in part due to a wish to take issue with what I conceive to be the general drift of Browning criticism at present. If I interpret this rightly, its quarrel is with the whole tone and temper of the poet's work, not with this or that specific weakness.

An initial definition is, therefore, necessary. What is the basic element which inhabits and glints through the body of Browning's verse as its pervasive and animating soul? Can we in reading his numerous poems, so diverse in theme and setting, "loose their subtle spirit" in cruce, like the Arab sage of *In a Gondola*?

Writing to Elizabeth Barrett in 1845,[2] Browning spoke of his poetry as momentary escapes of a bright and alive inner power and (in a figure of speech) compared it to flashes of light he had seen at sea leaping out at intervals from a narrow chink in a Mediterranean pharos.[3] The vehemence and impulsiveness of Browning's verse have been universally recognized. Both the form and the content of his poetry are vividly impressionistic. His favourite medium is the dramatic monologue, which in his best work is the distillation of a crucial moment of human experience. Light is focused at one point in a white heat of concentration and intensity. In the revelation of the significance of the precipitous moment, vivacity and turbulence are outstanding attributes of his poetic diction and spirit.

Yet the general recognition of the flair or impetuosity of Brown-

2. *The Letters of Robert Browning and Elizabeth Barrett Browning, 1845–1846* (London, 1899), I, 17.

3. Lighthouse or beacon. The letter referred to is that of February 11, 1845 (Kintner, I. 16). [*Editor.*]

ing's poetry has by no means been accompanied by unanimity of opinion concerning its merit. Differing judgments of this essential quality have led to a battle of controversy, dividing the poet's admirers and detractors into hostile camps. Before singling it out for praise, it is, therefore, well to glance at some of the criticism it has provoked. "Cockney Sublime, Cockney Energy," was Fitz-Gerald's jaundiced comment.[4] In our own day, Mr. Santayana, in an essay "The Poetry of Barbarism," has scored the work of Browning as that of "a thought and an art inchoate and ill-digested, of a vocanic eruption that tosses itself quite blindly and ineffectually into the sky."[5] Santayana likens Browning to Whitman, and in this comparison has been followed by T. S. Eliot.

The germ of that approach to Browning's writings which emphasizes their so-called barbaric, Gothic, ultra-romantic elements, may be found back in 1864, in Bagehot's "Wordsworth, Tennyson, and Browning, or Pure, Ornate, and Grotesque Art in English Poetry."[6] It is a conception that was taken up and enlarged upon by Chesterton in his arresting but untrustworthy biography of the poet. Of late it has been made a formidable weapon of attack in the hands of a school of aesthetic thought which extols classical standards and is deeply distrustful of romanticism. F. L. Lucas has given recent expression to this neo-classicist credo in *The Decline and Fall of the Romantic Ideal*. Our appraisal of it will depend on whether we regard romanticism as abnormal and pathological, or as rooted in an experience of life as normative and intrinsic as that on which the classic tradition is based. It is important to recognize that criticism of Browning as voiced by Irving Babbitt, Santayana, F. L. Lucas, and T. S. Eliot is an offshoot of a general neo-classicist position.

Viewed as a whole, the modern indictment of the energy of Browning's poetry seems a weighty one. At present, the moral, intellectual, and aesthetic aspects of his outlook on life are all suspect. To Santayana, the poet's vagrancy of impulse is indicative of the barbarity of his genius, the essence of which lies in the fact that to him "life is an adventure, not a discipline; that the exercise of energy is the absolute good, irrespective of motives or of consequences."[7] To Babbitt, Browning's unrestrained emotion is an example of those centrifugal and neurotic tendencies that, from the standpoint of neo-classicism, are regarded as evidence of a decadent romanticism. Passion and sensation, we are told, run riot in his poetry, and there is an utter lack of classical decorum, balance, and repose. To Mr. Lucas, there is a trace of a bouncing vulgarity in

---

4. A. M. Terhune, *The Life of Edward FitzGerald* (New Haven, 1947), p. 254.
5. From *Interpretations of Poetry and Religion* (New York, 1900), p. 189. [See excerpt from Santayana in this edition. —*Editor*.]
6. See excerpt from Bagehot in this edition. [*Editor*.]
7. *Interpretations*, p. 206.

Browning's energetic verse, which smacks too much of the hearty hail-fellow-well-met manner of a Philistine. Metaphorically speaking, the unfastidious poet slaps his readers on the back. His "stamping and shouting," the jarring dissonances of his verse, "his hastily scribbled poems as fuzzy and prickly and tangled as a furze-bush"[8] are at once excesses of his temperament and an undisciplined romanticism. Such comments are reminiscent of an earlier criticism that all of Browning's poetry is summed up in the line, "*Bang-whang-whang* goes the drum, *tootle-te-tootle* the fife."[9]

Although, in justice to Mr. Lucas, it should be noted that he does recognize the vitality of Browning's dramatic portrayal of human life, the general tenor of his criticism seems to me indicative of a mental twist which inhibits him from depicting the great men of letters of the Victorian age with disinterested objectivity. It is the fate of every generation to have its idols shattered by the hammer blows of the succeeding generation. Since the publication of Lytton Strachey's life of Queen Victoria, there have been many acute and witty *exposés* of the foibles, conventions, and conservatisms of the Victorian era. Yet what so many twentieth-century critics lack is a perception of the dignity, poise, and stability of that era, an ethos contributing to the endowment of its principal personages with nobility of character. To ignore these basic elements in Victorianism in delineating its great men is to view the age through a subtly distorted mirror in which every figure is out of focus.

Every man, it has been said, has the defect of his quality, and it might be added, every poet in his art has the defect of his quality. Browning's energy and vitality at times din the ear and become strident and overpowering. Though "barbarism" is not supposed to be a mid-Victorian vice, there is something unbridled in his rush of passion and the militant romanticism of his verse. He can write metallic poems and rhyming exercises. When he is lost in the Cretan labyrinth of his longer poems, his style is as crabbed and involved as his subject-matter.

But the error and insufficiency of the criticism I have been reviewing seems to be that it fastens exclusively on the negative rather than on the positive aspect of the poet's elemental attribute. For it is precisely the dash or verve of his poetry which constitutes its perennial originality and attractiveness. It is a strain running like an *elixir vitae* through his verse in its golden era, giving it headiness and flavour. We are reminded of the violent rush of a mountain torrent frothing and seething amongst rocks and fretting its chan-

8. F. L. Lucas, *Ten Victorian Poets* (Cambridge, 1948), pp. 36; 23.
9. Cf. Browning's letter to Isabella Blagden, cited in *Letters of Robert Browning*, collected by Thomas J. Wise and ed. by Thurman L. Hood (New Haven, 1933), p. 82. See also F. R. G. Duckworth, *Browning: Background and Conflict* (London, 1931), p. 121.

nel, but compensating for its lack of smooth rhythmical flow by the spin and dance, the spray and sparkle of its waters. "Passion's too fierce to be in fetters bound." From the critical censure of Browning's energy and impulsiveness we turn away, as our eye falls, perchance, with renewed delight on the opening lines of *Pippa Passes*:

> Day!
> Faster and more fast,
> O'er night's brim, day boils at last:
> Boils, pure gold, o'er the cloud-cup's brim
> Where spurting and suppressed it lay. . . .

The relation between the form and the content of the poetry of Browning is often a tension rather than a harmony. All poetry, he once wrote to Ruskin, is the problem of "putting the infinite within the finite."[1] It would carry us too far afield to show how the antithesis of infinite and finite is perpetually in his thought. But it is clear that the crux of the struggle in his life as an artist was the difficulty of bodying forth the content of his imagination and intellect in adequate poetic forms. In *Sordello*, which in many ways is a confessional document, there is a vivid account of the hero's attempt to forge a new language, in an Italian dialect, capable of expressing the novelty of his thoughts and perceptions. The analogy between this and Browning's wrestling with language is unmistakable. Like Sordello, he was striving to make his diction a suitable vehicle for the new type of analytic poetry he was writing. The arduousness of the process is realistically described:

> He left imagining, to try the stuff
> That held the imaged thing, and, let it writhe
> Never so fiercely, scarce allowed a tithe
> To reach the light—his Language.   (II. 570–73)

Sordello, from the point of view of style, is a gigantic experiment in artistic technique. It is apprentice work of a faulty kind, yet through its convolutions the poet was feeling his way towards his true manner.

And when, after the murkiness of *Sordello*, the art of Browning begins to clear nobly in *Pippa Passes*, discovers its true bent in *Dramatic Lyrics* and *Dramatic Romances*, and reaches its meridian in *Men and Women*, the triumph of his style is all the more impressive because it has been hardly won. In the dramatic monologue of medium length, he found the poetic instrument he had vainly sought in *Sordello*. His metres and diction instinctively adapt themselves to impressionistic vignettes of picturesque situations and crucial moments in the lives of men and women, often enriched by

1. *The Works of John Ruskin*, ed. by   XXXVI (London, 1909), xxxiv.
E. T. Cook and Alexander Wedderburn,

pregnant historical or artistic backgrounds. Tension of style remains, but it is a close-packed, sensitive tension that is responsive to the subtle and varied play of highly charged thought and emotion. The tempo of Browning's diction in his great dramatic monologues is rapid to the point of abruptness. The metres have the beat of a driving energy. The music of his verse is uneven rather than smooth flowing, involving frequent suspensions and resolutions.

Le style c' est l'homme;[2] and the racy, colloquial style of Browning in the best of his dramatic monologues is a revelation of his intrinsic quality. He has used a greater variety of metres than any other modern poet, but his verse is never rigidly set in a conventional mould. In reading Tennyson's lines,

> All in the blue unclouded weather
> Thick-jewell'd shone the saddle-leather,

we realize that the imagery is enclosed in a sedate metrical framework. But when Browning writes,

> To mine, it serves for the old June weather
> Blue above lane and wall,

there is a natural felicity in the utterance which shakes itself free from formal trappings.

Within its own province, there is a finality in the organic structure, the Sophia and Technê of Greek art; where communication is so wedded to inspiration, form to content, that, as Browning has pointed out in *Old Pictures in Florence*, it achieves perfection in the sphere of the finite. But romantic art, as an emanation of the spirit of man in one of the two basic moments of his experience, has a genius of its own. It may lack the radiance of classic art, that clarity and harmony representative of "the depth and not the tumult of the soul." Yet there is a place on the altars of literature for the Dionysiac fire of romantic art: Dionysiac fire at times, but, when it burns as a purer flame, the light of the Holy Grail. Poetry must in certain moods reveal the tension of the spirit straining at the leash of form, and infinite passion shattering the web of finite expression:

> Thoughts hardly to be packed
> Into a narrow act,
> Fancies that broke through language and escaped.

Therefore, despite the frown of the classicist, a lover of Browning's poetry may take pleasure in its romantic beauty and in the free rein given to passion and sensation. He may enjoy its impressionistic glooms and glances, its live and nervous diction responsive to the

---

2. "The style is the man" (Buffon). [*Editor.*]

"moment one and infinite" of electrically charged emotion. He may feel the justification of a content that overweighs the form, and a tension that is like the pent-up energy of a storm-cloud:

> There are flashes struck from midnights,
> There are fire-flames noondays kindle. . . .

A few examples of the flair and verve of Browning's verse may be cited at random from the poems composed between 1840 and 1870.

The sensuousness of Browning's imagery is vivid and often opulent, but never cloying or languorous. He has too much energy ever to indulge in the sleepy sensuousness of Spenser. Frequently his imagery is associated with a wealth and exotic splendour of colour. In *Popularity*, his eye revels in the Tyrian blue or purple dye extracted from a secretion in the shell of the murex, and he combines this colour with the lustre of gold in two dazzling pictures. The dye, he tells us, is

> Enough to furnish Solomon
> Such hangings for his cedar-house,
> That, when gold-robed he took the throne
> In that abyss of blue, the Spouse
> Might swear his presence shone

> Most like the centre-spike of gold
> Which burns deep in the blue-bell's womb,
> What time, with ardours manifold,
> The bee goes singing to her groom,
> Drunken and overbold.

Images of light, sound, and motion are conjoined in the triumphant close of *Rabbi Ben Ezra*, where the philosophic argument of the Jewish sage takes imaginative wings:

> Look not thou down but up!
> To uses of a cup,
> The festal board, lamp's flash and trumpet's peal,
> The new wine's foaming flow,
> The Master's lips a-glow!
> Thou, heaven's consummate cup, what need'st thou
>   with earth's wheel?   (ll. 175–80)

Abt Vogler is a fine example of a sustained piece of imagery, representing a crescendo of feeling evoked by music. In other poems, imagery flares forth at the peak of an emotional mood like a beacon of passion. How the lines kindle in *The Statue and the Bust* when the cowardly and procrastinating lovers are contrasted with the militant saints of God!

> Only they see not God, I know,
> Nor all that chivalry of his,
> The soldier-saints who, row on row,
> Burn upward each to his point of bliss. . . .   (ll. 220–23)

Browning's descriptions of nature are as impressionistic as his vistas of human life, and reveal to an equal degree his elemental property. There is occasional tranquillity in his landscapes, but as a rule this is the brief hush that follows or precedes a moment of highly wrought emotional tension. As the lovers in *By the Fire-side* wait for the flash of revelation that is to fuse their lives in one, the brooding quietness of evening o'erhangs woodland and mountain.

> Oh moment, one and infinite!
> The water slips o'er stock and stone;
> The West is tender, hardly bright:
> How grey at once is the evening grown—
> One star, its chrysolite!   (ll. 181–85)

But Browning's typical delineation of nature is in keeping with the high tide of dramatic passion that surges through his poetry. In *Pippa Passes*, the lightning seems to search for the guilty lovers, Sebald and Ottima, like the bared sword of divine justice.

> Buried in the woods we lay, you recollect;
> Swift ran the searching tempest overhead;
> And ever and anon some bright white shaft
> Burned thro' the pine-tree roof, here burned and there,
> As if God's messenger thro' the close wood screen
> Plunged and replunged his weapon at a venture,
> Feeling for guilty thee and me: then broke
> The thunder like a whole sea overhead. . . .   (I. 190–97)

In *The Ring and the Book*, the Pope's one hope for the salvation of Guido is visualized through a similar piece of fiery landscape painting.

> I stood at Naples once, a night so dark
> I could have scarce conjectured there was earth
> Anywhere, sky or sea or world at all:
> But the night's black was burst through by a blaze—
> Thunder struck blow on blow, earth groaned and bore,
> Through her whole length of mountain visible:
> There lay the city thick and plain with spires,
> And, like a ghost disshrouded, white the sea.
> So may the truth be flashed out by one blow,
> And Guido see, one instant, and be saved.   (X. 219–28)

Browning's delight in brilliant and intense colour blends with his love of Italian scenery. In *De Gustibus*, he prefers a Mediterranean vista, "the great opaque blue breadth of sea without a break," to the pastoral lanes and coppices of England. He takes particular pleasure in the semi-tropical bounty of nature in June in these lines of *Pippa Passes*:

> Well for those who live through June!
> Great noontides, thunder-storms, all glaring pomps

> That triumph at the heels of June the god
> Leading his revel through our leafy world.   (III. 153–56)

The freshness and animation of the poet's landscapes are as typical as their emotional thrust. He pictures Florence as seen in spring "through the live translucent bath of air," when "river and bridge and street and square" are as clear "as the sights in a magic crystal ball." The common phenomenon of the breaking of ice in a pond gives birth, in *The Flight of the Duchess*, to the following exquisite description:

> Well, early in autumn, at first winter-warning,
> When the stag had to break with his foot, of a morning,
> A drinking-hole out of the fresh tender ice
> That covered the pond till the sun, in a trice,
> Loosening it, let out a ripple of gold,
> And another and another, and faster and faster,
> Till, dimpling to blindness, the wide water rolled. . . .
>
> (ll. 216–22)

Il fait vivre ses phrases.[3] It is, as I have striven to show, the incomparable gusto of Browning's poetry that is its essential quality. And this gusto is not the outpouring in art of the hearty exuberance of a Philistine, or the pietistic enthusiasm of an irresponsible optimist. It is rather—if one may apply to it words used by Arthur Symons in connection with the humour of the *The Pied Piper of Hamelin* and *Confessions*—"the jolly laughter of an unaffected nature, the effervescence of a sparkling and overflowing brain."[4] It has its roots in a sound physical constitution, a fine fibre of intellect, and a glow of life which, to cite Elizabeth Barrett's tribute, "shows a heart within blood-tinctured, of a veined humanity."[5]

Undoubtedly, Browning's superb physical health is an element of this gusto. In *Saul*, David sings of "our manhood's prime vigour," the play of muscle and sinew, "the leaping from rock up to rock," and "the plunge in a pool's living water." Idealist though the poet is, there is a genial and aromatic flavour of mother earth in his writings, and he draws sustenance from her which races through his veins like the sap of trees in spring. "Oh, good gigantic smile o' the brown old earth!" he exclaims in *James Lee's Wife*. This touch with earth is reflected in his unique chronicling of insect life, that form of animal existence which is in most intimate conjunction with the soil. The prodigal and spawning energy of nature, riotous with life, is whimsically portrayed in *Sibrandus Schafnaburgensis*. The worm, slug, eft, water-beetle, and newt, invading the covers of a ponderous volume, are symbolic of sheer animal frolic, mocking

3. "He makes his phrases live." [Editor.]
4. *An Introduction to the Study of* *Browning* (London, 1916), p. 27.
5. *Lady Geraldine's Courtship*, stanza 41.

dry-as-dust pedantry and the dead bones of a musty scholasticism:

> All that life and fun and romping,
> All that frisking and twisting and coupling,
> While slowly our poor friend's leaves were swamping
> And clasps were cracking and covers suppling!

Allied with this love of energy in the physical world is Browning's keen perception of the grotesque. For the grotesque is a bold and permptory shattering of conventional moulds. As Chesterton has said: "The element of the grotesque in art, like the element of the grotesque in nature, means, in the main, energy, the energy which takes its own forms and goes its own way."[6]

But the *élan* of the poet's art has more subtle and spiritual springs in his intellectual and emotional gifts. These gifts have their extravagances. The suppleness of Browning's mind and his temperamental impetuosity often lead him to strain at the curb of form. Yet the turns and twists of his verse, his metrical liberties, his unexpected and at times somersaulting rhymes, are usually the bubbling-up of irrepressible high spirits, chafing at the yoke of aught that is tame or conventional. It should be noted that he only gives rein to an "outrageous gallop of rhymes" in poems having a certain raciness of bohemianism of content, such as *The Flight of the Duchess, Old Pictures in Florence*, or *Pacchiarotto*. When set in their proper perspective and viewed in relation to the whole body of his poetry, these outward flourishes of style, even when pushed to the verge of idiosyncrasy, are not to be condemned sweepingly as barbaric wilfulness. They are often the frothings of a superabundant vitality, a tang of life like that of Fra Lippo Lippi, shattering the moulds of artistic decorum in a spirit of Puckish impishness.

> A laugh, a cry, the business of the world . . .
> And my whole soul revolves, the cup runs over,
> The world and life's too big to pass for a dream,
> And I do these wild things in sheer despite,
> And play the fooleries you catch me at,
> In pure rage!   (ll. 247–54)

Though we must look to the future for an impartial evaluation of Victorian literature, it is evident that Browning, with the possible exception of Carlyle, had a more robust and sinewy mind than any of his contemporaries. He is a great humanist; and however deeply and broadly he quarries in the mine of the thoughts and emotions of men and women, the vein never runs thin, though it may lead at times through tortuous tunnels. The horizons of an intellect of such power and fertility are vast; and linked with this amplitude is the

6. G. K. Chesterton, *Robert Browning* (New York, 1903), p. 149.

gift of communicating the joy and tingle of his contact with life. In this respect he allies himself with Chaucer, Fielding, and Scott. Like theirs his interest in humanity is unflagging, and while he does not maintain their objectivity of representation, he probes deeper than any of his forerunners into the inner springs of character.

As we travel imaginatively with Browning in many climes and ages, a panorama full of light and colour is unrolled. On a spacious canvas, through an astonishing variety of circumstance, he mirrors the subtle and ceaseless play of impulse and motive flaming up in moments of highly wrought passion into the crux of action,

> When a soul declares itself—to wit,
> By its fruit, the thing it does![7]

In speaking of the poems of Browning that culminate with *The Ring and the Book,* Mr. Osbert Burdett has said: "If it be still urged that the poetry of Browning loses for want of repose, the reply is that, in these poems, we do not miss it but are carried by the poet while we read into his own world of vigorous healthy imagination, a world so rich, vivid, and finely fashioned that it is one of the most original and dramatic possessions of our literature."[8]

While individual judgments are always relative, it is a test of quality when we can return in later years with unabated pleasure to the work of a poet loved in youth, and "obey the voice at eve, obeyed at prime." Browning measures up to this test, because the volume of his poetry is "the precious life-blood of a master spirit." Into its pages, through the alchemy of genius, the elixir of a generous personality has been distilled. In a large human sense, the best of Browning's work does not date—always a touchstone of worth.

In the most famous passage of *The Advancement of Learning,* Bacon says of poetry: "And, therefore it was ever thought to have some participation of divineness, because it doth raise and erect the mind, by submitting the shows of things to the desires of the mind." The classicist may complain that Browning bullies "the shows of things" into submission. Despite his recognition of "the value and significance of flesh," he does at times wrest the body of art, its sensuous elements, in order to

> Make new hopes shine through the flesh they fray,
> New fears aggrandize the rags and tatters:
> To bring the invisible full into play!
> Let the visible go to the dogs—what matters?[9]

Yet it is the informing presence of a discursive, fully charged mind that is an unfailing source of enjoyment to the sympathetic reader

---

7. "By the Fire-Side," lines 244–45.
8. *The Brownings* (London, 1928), p. 338.
9. "Old Pictures in Florence," lines 149–52.

of his poetry. Like Donne, whom in many ways Browning strikingly resembles, he might have spoken of "the sinewy thread my brain lets fall." In this fibre of thought, interwoven with ardour of temperament, lies the genesis of his verve and originality—that flash of life which I have singled out as the essential quality of his poetry.

J. HILLIS MILLER

[Browning's Language]†

* * *

The first principle of Browning's poetry is his attempt to make the words of the poem participate in the reality they describe, for he seeks to capture the "stuff/O' the very stuff, life of life, and self of self."[1] He wants his words to be thick and substantial, and to carry the solid stuff of reality. He wants, as he said in a striking phrase, "word pregnant with thing."[2] To read a poem by Browning should be a powerful sensuous experience, a tasting and feeling, not a thinking. The poem should go down like thick strong raw wine, "strained, turbid still, from the viscous blood/Of the snaky bough."[3] It must make the same kind of assault on the reader that the poet has made on reality to seize its pith.

How does Browning manage to make his words pregnant with things?

Sometimes he achieves his goal by the plastic re-creation of the appearances of a scene, after the manner of Goethe or Keats, as in the deliberately classical frieze in the "Parleying with Gerard de Lairesse," where Browning is trying to show that he can, if he wants, be as lucid and sculptural as the Greek or Roman poets.[4] More often he is not satisfied with such a distant vision of a scene. He wants the reader to feel what he describes as if it were part of his own body, and to achieve this he must appeal to the more intimate senses of taste, smell, and touch, and to the kinesthetic sense whereby we make sympathetic muscular movements in response to the motion of things. All the ways in which Browning conveys his sense of being at the center of unformed matter are also used, with appropriate modifications, to express his experiences when he places himself at the interior of particular forms. The pervasive qualities of

† From J. Hillis Miller, *The Disappearance of God: Five Nineteenth-Century Writers* (Cambridge, Mass.: The Belknap Press of Harvard University Press, 1963), pp. 118–24.
1. "Mr. Sludge, 'The Medium,'" lines 1009–10. [*Editor*.]
2. Preface to *Agamemnon*. [*Editor*.]
3. "Epilogue" to *Pacchiarotto*, lines 11–12.
4. "Parleying with Gerard de Lairesse," st. VIII–XII.

Browning's poetry are roughness and thickness. There are two opposite, yet related, causes for this texture. It expresses the shapeless
bubbling chaos. It also expresses the substantial solidity of realized
forms.

Browning wants to make the movement, sound, and texture of
his verse an imitation of the vital matter of its subject, whether that
subject is animate or inanimate, molten lava, flower, bird, beast,
fish, or man. He thinks of matter, in whatever form, as something
dense, heavy, rough, and strong-flavored, and there is for him a
basic similarity between all forms of life—they are all strong solid
substance inhabited by a vital energy. There are everywhere two
things: the thick weight of matter, and within it an imprisoned
vitality which seethes irresistibly out. The particular forms, however
finely developed, are still rooted in the primal mud, and the means
of expressing one are not unrelated to the means of expressing the
other. It is by imitation of the roughness of a thing that one has
most chance to get inside it. Things are not made of smooth
appearances, but of the dense inner core which is best approached
through heavy language.

Grotesque metaphors, ugly words heavy with consonants, stutter-
ing alliteration, strong active verbs, breathless rhythms, onomatopoeia, images of rank smells, rough textures, and of things fleshy,
viscous, sticky, nubbly, slimy, shaggy, sharp, crawling, thorny, or
prickly—all these work together in Browning's verse to create an
effect of unparalleled thickness, harshness, and roughness. These
elements are so constantly combined that it is difficult to demonstrate one of them in isolation, but their simultaneous effect gives
Browning's verse its special flavor, and could be said to be the most
important thing about it. They are the chief means by which he
expresses his sense of what reality is like. No other poetry can be at
once so ugly, so "rough, rude, robustious,"[5] and so full of a joyous
vitality.

Sometimes Browning achieves his effect by a direct appeal to the
kinesthetic sense. The words invite us to imitate with our bodies
what they describe, or to react to the poem as if it were a physical
stimulus:

> As he uttered a kind of cough-preludious
>   That woke my sympathetic spasm . . .[6]

>   . . . the pig-of-lead-like pressure
>   Of the preaching man's immense stupidity . . .[7]

> Aaron's asleep—shove hip to haunch,
>   Or somebody deal him a dig in the paunch![8]

5. "Parleying with Charles Avison," line 414.
6. "Christmas-Eve," lines 818–19.
7. "Christmas-Eve," lines 143–44.
8. "Holy Cross Day," lines 25–26.

Sometimes the chief means is onomatopoeia—language at the
level of interjection, exclamation, the sound of the word echoing
the reality, often an affirmation of the body's organic life:

> Fee, faw, fum! bubble and squeak![9]

> . . . the thump-thump and shriek-shriek
> Of the train . . .[1]

> He blindly guzzles and guttles . . .[2]

> . . . their blood gurgles and grumbles afresh . . .[3]

Sometimes it is the use of words clotted with consonants, for
bunched consonants seem to have power to express not only
unformed chaos, but also the sharp texture of particular things:

> . . . slimy rubbish, odds and ends and orts . . .[4]

> And one sharp tree—'t is a cypress—stands,
> By the many hundred years red-rusted,
> Rough iron-spiked, ripe fruit-o'ercrusted . . .[5]

Sometimes, as in the last quotation, it is the use of verbs of violent action, whether in their primary form or in the form of participles which have become part of the substance of what they modify:

> Yataghan, kandjar, things that rend and rip,
> Gash rough, slash smooth, help hate so many ways . . .[6]

> If there pushed any ragged thistle-stalk
> Above its mates, the head was chopped; the bents
> Were jealous else. What made those holes and rents
> In the dock's harsh swarth leaves, bruised as to baulk
> All hope of greenness? 't is a brute must walk
> Pashing their life out, with a brute's intents.[7]

Sometimes the chief device giving strength and substance to the
line is alliteration, often of explosive consonants:

> Here's John the Smith's rough-hammered head. Great eye,
> Gross jaw and griped lips do what granite can
> To give you the crown-grasper. What a man![8]

> First face a-splutter at me got such splotch
> Of prompt slab mud as, filling mouth to maw, . . .
> Immortally immerded . . .[9]

> No, the balled fist broke brow like thunderbolt,
> Battered till brain flew![1]

> The barrel of blasphemy broached once, who bungs?[2]

9. "Holy-Cross Day," line 1.
1. "Christmas-Eve," lines 250–51.
2. "Ponte dell'Angelo, Florence," line 72.
3. "Ponte dell'Angelo, Florence," line 148.
4. "Parleying with George Bubb
Dodington," line 52.
5. "De Gustibus ———," lines 23–25.
6. "A Forgiveness," lines 250–51.

7. " 'Childe Roland to the Dark Tower
Came,' " lines 67–72.
8. "Protus," lines 55–57.
9. *Aristophanes' Apology*, lines 1661–62,
1670.
1. *Aristophanes' Apology*, lines 1725–26.
2. "An Epilogue" to *Parleyings* ["Fust
and His Friends"], line 465.

Sometimes the chief effect is produced by the quick heavy, often syncopated, rhythm, the heartbeat of the verse helping the reader to participate in the substance of the thing or person and the pace of its life. The rhythm of Browning's poems is internal, vegetative. It is not the mind speaking, but the depths of corporeal vitality, the organic pulsation of life. Browning manages, better than any other poet, to convey the bump, bump, bump of blood coursing through the veins, the breathless rush of excited bodily life, the vital pulse of the visceral level of existence, the sense of rapid motion. No other poetry is more robust in tempo:

> I sprang to the stirrup, and Joris, and he;
> I galloped, Dirck galloped, we galloped all three . . .[3]

> Boh, here's Barnabas! Job, that's you?
> Up stumps Solomon—bustling too?[4]

> Fife, trump, drum, sound! and singers then,
> Marching, say "Pym, the man of men!"
> Up, heads, your proudest—out, throats, your loudest—
> "Somerset's Pym!"[5]

> Noon strikes,—here sweeps the procession! our Lady borne
> smiling and smart
> With a pink gauze gown all spangles, and seven swords
> stuck in heart!
> *Bang-whang-whang* goes the drum, *tootle-te-tootle* the fife;
> No keeping one's haunches still: it's the greatest pleasure in life.[6]

Sometimes the effect is produced by a cascade of grotesque metaphors. In Browning's world anything can be a metaphor for anything else, and often he gets an effect of uncouth vitality by piling up a heap of idiosyncratic things, each living violently its imprisoned life:

> Higgledy piggledy, packed we lie,
> Rats in a hamper, swine in a stye,
> Wasps in a bottle, frogs in a sieve,
> Worms in a carcase, fleas in a sleeve.[7]

Sometimes, however, it is a more subtle use of metaphor. Browning tends to qualify his description of external events with metaphors taken from the human body. This humanizing of dead objects is so pervasive in Browning's verse that it is easy not to notice it. His anthropomorphizing of the landscape is not achieved by a strenuous act of the imagination which transfers bodily processes to mountains or rivers. Everything in the world is already

3. " 'How They Brought the Good News from Ghent to Aix,' " lines 1–2.
4. "Holy-Cross Day," lines 7–8.
5. Parleying with Charles Avison," lines 422–25.
6. "Up at a Villa—Down in the City," lines 51–54.
7. "Holy-Cross Day," lines 13–16.

humanized for Browning, as soon as he sees it, and can be experienced as intimately as if it were his own body. The best proof of this is the casual and habitual way in which body-words are applied to the external world:

> Oh, those mountains, their infinite movement!
>   Still moving with you;
> For, ever some new head and breast of them
>   Thrust into view
> To observe the intruder; you see it
>   If quickly you turn
> And, before they escape you, surprise them.[8]

"Childe Roland to the Dark Tower Came" is a masterpiece of this kind of empathy. The effect of this weird poem comes not so much from the grotesque ugliness and scurfy "penury" of the landscape, as from the fact that the reader is continually coaxed by the language to experience this ghastly scene as if it were his own body which had got into this sad state:

> Now blotches rankling, coloured gay and grim,
>   Now patches where some leanness of the soil's
>   Broke into moss or substances like boils;
> Then came some palsied oak, a cleft in him
> Like a distorted mouth that splits its rim
>   Gaping at death, and dies while it recoils.[9]

Kinesthesia, onomatopoeia, "consonanted"[1] words, verbs of violent action, alliteration, visceral rhythm, grotesque metaphors, pathetic fallacy—by whatever means, Browning's aim is to get to the inmost center of the other life, and working out from it, to express that life as it is lived, not as it appears from the outside to a detached spectator. This power of what Hazlitt called "gusto" is surely one of Browning's chief qualities as a poet. His ability to convey the "thingness" of things, in his own special apprehension of it, belongs not at all to the realm of ideas, and yet is at once the most obvious thing about his verse, and, it may be, the most profound. Certain of his very best poems are not at all complicated thematically, but they succeed magnificently in expressing Browning's strong feeling for the density, roughness, and vitality of matter. Such a poem is "Sibrandus Schafnaburgensis," with its extraordinary description of the adventures of a book he has pitched into the rain-filled crevice of a hollow plum-tree, and later fished up:

> Here you have it, dry in the sun,
>   With all the binding all of a blister,

8. "An Englishman in Italy," lines 181–87.

9. " 'Childe Roland,' " lines 151–56.

1. Preface to *Agamemnon*.

And great blue spots where the ink has run,
 And reddish streaks that wink and glister
O'er the page so beautifully yellow . . .
How did he like it when the live creatures
 Tickled and toused and browsed him all over,
And worm, slug, eft, with serious features,
 Came in, each one, for his right of trover?
—When the water-beetle with great blind deaf face
 Made of her eggs the stately deposit . . .?[2]

Only Browning could have written such a poem, and only he could have written "The Englishman in Italy," with its admirable representation of an Italian landscape on a stormy autumn afternoon. Perhaps the best lines of all in this splendid poem are those describing the "sea-fruit." All the linguistic devices I have examined separately here work in concert, and, as in "Sibrandus Schafnaburgensis," word is indeed "pregnant with thing":

 —Our fisher [will] arrive,
And pitch down his basket before us,
 All trembling alive
With pink and gray jellies, your sea-fruit;
 You touch the strange lumps,
And mouths gape there, eyes open, all manner
 Of horns and of humps,
Which only the fisher looks grave at,
 While round him like imps
Cling screaming the children as naked
 And brown as his shrimps . . .[3]

* * *

The Dramatic Monologue

ROBERT LANGBAUM

The Dramatic Monologue:

Sympathy versus Judgment†

Writers on the dramatic monologue never fail to remark how little has been written on the subject—and I shall be no exception. The reason for the neglect is, I think, that no one has quite known

2. Lines 89–93, 97–102.
3. Lines 54–64.
† From Robert Langbaum, *The Poetry of Experience: The Dramatic Monologue* *in Modern Literary Tradition* (New York: Random House, 1957; London: Chatto & Windus, 1957; New York: W. W. Norton, 1963), pp. 75–88, 96–108.

what to do with the dramatic monologue except to classify it, to distinguish kinds of dramatic monologues and to distinguish the dramatic monologue from both the lyrical and the dramatic or narrative genres. Such classifications are all too easily made and have a way of killing off further interest in the subject. For they too often mean little beyond themselves, they close doors where they ought to open them.

The usual procedure in discussing the dramatic monologue is to find precedents for the form in the poetry of all periods, and then to establish, on the model of a handful of poems by Browning and Tennyson, objective criteria by which the form is henceforth to be recognized and judged. The procedure combines, I think, opposite mistakes; it is at once too restrictive and not restrictive enough, and in either case tells us too little. For once we decide to treat the dramatic monologue as a traditional genre, then every lyric in which the speaker seems to be someone other than the poet, almost all love-songs and laments in fact (*Lycidas*, *The Song of Songs*, *Polyphemus' Complaint* by Theocritus, the Anglo-Saxon *Banished Wife's Complaint*) become dramatic monologues; as do all imaginary epistles and orations and all kinds of excerpts from plays and narratives—e.g. all long speeches and soliloquies, those portions of epics in which the hero recounts the events that occurred before the opening of the poem, Chaucer's prologues to the *Canterbury Tales* and the tales themselves since they are told by fictitious persons: almost all first person narratives, in fact, become dramatic monologues. While such a classification is *true* enough, what does it accomplish except to identify a certain mechanical resemblance?—since the poems retain more affinity to the lyric, the drama, the narrative than to each other.

But if we are, on the other hand, too restrictive, we do little more than describe the handful of Browning and Tennyson poems we are using as models. We come out with the idea that dramatic monologues are more or less like Browning's *My Last Duchess*, and that most dramatic monologues being rather less like it are not nearly so good. We are told, for example, that the dramatic monologue must have not only a speaker other than the poet but also a listener, an occasion, and some interplay between speaker and listener. But since a classification of this sort does not even cover all the dramatic monologues of Browning and Tennyson, let alone those of other poets, it inevitably leads to quarrels about which poems are to be admitted into the canon; and worse, it leads to sub-classifications, to a distinction between what one writer calls "formal" dramatic monologues, which have only three of the necessary criteria, and "typical" dramatic monologues, which have all four. As for poems with only the dramatized speaker and perhaps the occasion—poems like

Tennyson's *St Simeon Stylites* and Browning's *Childe Roland* and *Caliban*, which are among the best and most famous of all dramatic monologues—this writer, in order to salvage her classification, calls them "approximations."[1]

The trouble with so narrow a criterion is that it suggests a decline of the dramatic monologue since Browning's time. It blinds us to the developing life of the form, to the importance of dramatic monologues in the work of such twentieth-century poets as Yeats, Eliot, Pound, Frost, Masters, Robinson and both Lowells, Amy and Robert (the form is particularly favoured by American poets). Robert Lowell's latest volume (*The Mills of the Kavanaughs*, 1951) consists entirely of dramatic monologues; while Pound, who in many places acknowledges his debt to Browning, has said of the dramatic monologues of Browning's *Men and Women* that "the form of these poems is the most vital form of that period,"[2] and has called a volume of his own *Personae*. Although Eliot has little to say in favour of Browning, the dramatic monologue has been the main form in his work until he assumed what appears to be a personal voice in the series of religious meditations beginning with *Ash Wednesday*. The dramatic monologue is proportionately as important in Eliot's work as in Browning's, Eliot having contributed more to the development of the form than any poet since Browning.[3] Certainly *Prufrock, Portrait of a Lady, Gerontion, Journey of the Magi, A Song for Simeon* and *Marina* do as much credit to the dramatic monologue as anything of Browning's; while in *The Waste Land* Eliot has opened new possibilities for the form by constructing a kind of *collage of* dramatic monologues as perceived by Tiresias, whose dramatic monologue the poem is.[4]

To understand the continuing life of the dramatic monologue, we must abandon the exclusive concern with objective criteria by which

1. Ina Beth Sessions, in her book, *A Study of the Dramatic Monologue in American and Continental Literature* (San Antonio, Texas: Alamo Printing Co., 1933). An extract with revisions appears as "The Dramatic Monologue," *PMLA*, June 1947. For other examples of this approach, see the only other book-length study: S. S. Curry, *Browning and the Dramatic Monologue* (Boston: Expression Co., 1908); and papers by Claud Howard, "The Dramatic Monologue: Its Origin and Development," *Studies in Philology*, IV (Chapel Hill, N.C.: University of North Carolina Press, 1910), and R. H. Fletcher, "Browning's Dramatic Monologs [*sic*]," *Modern Language Notes*, April 1908.

2. Reviewing Eliot's *Prufrock and Other Observations* in 1917. Reprinted as "T. S. Eliot," *Literary Essays*, edited with an introduction by T. S. Eliot (Norfolk, Conn.: New Directions; London: Faber and Faber, 1954), p. 419.

3. "For the eventual writer of the literary history of the twentieth century, Eliot's development of the dramatic soliloquy, a form that has been called 'the most flexible and characteristic genre of English verse,' cannot be divorced from the impetus furnished by *Men and Women* to *Personae*." (Matthiessen, *Achievement of Eliot*, p. 73, London: Oxford Univ. Press, 1935.)

4. "Tiresias, although a mere spectator and not indeed a 'character,' is yet the most important personage in the poem, uniting all the rest. Just as the one-eyed merchant, seller of currants, melts into the Phoenician Sailor, and the latter is not wholly distinct from Ferdinand Prince of Naples, so all the women are one woman, and the two sexes meet in Tiresias. What Tiresias *sees*, in fact, is the substance of the poem." (Eliot's *Notes* on *The Waste Land*, III.218.)

poems are either combined when they lack any effect in common, or else are separated when they have a common effect but lack the necessary mechanical resemblance. It is when we look inside the dramatic monologue, when we consider its effect, its *way* of meaning, that we see its connection with the poetry that precedes and follows Browning. We see, on the one hand, that the dramatic monologue is unprecedented in its effect, that its effect distinguishes it, in spite of mechanical resemblance, from the monologues of traditional poetry; and on the other hand, we welcome as particularly illuminating just those "approximations" that distress the classifiers. We welcome them because, having without the mechanical resemblance the same effect as the so-called "typical" dramatic monologues, they show us what the form is essentially doing.

One writer on the dramatic monologue has managed to suggest what it is essentially doing; and he has done this at just the point where he abandons objective criteria to make an intuitive leap inside the form. In a Warton Lecture of 1925 which remains the best study of the dramatic monologue, M. W. MacCallum sees sympathy as its way of meaning:

> But in every instance . . . the object [of the dramatic monologue] is to give facts from within. A certain dramatic understanding of the person speaking, which implies a certain dramatic sympathy with him, is not only the essential condition, but the final cause of the whole species.[5]

Unfortunately, MacCallum does not pursue the implications of this insight. If he had, he would not be so disposed to isolate the dramatic monologue within the Victorian period, and he would not confine his consideration to its quality as a monologue. Although the fact that a poem is a monologue helps to determine our sympathy for the speaker, since we must adopt his viewpoint as our entry into the poem, the monologue quality remains nevertheless a means, and not the only means, to the end—the end being to establish the reader's sympathetic relation to the poem, to give him "facts from within."

The distinction may seem niggling unless we see that, by subordinating the dramatic monologue's quality as a monologue to the larger question of the reader's relation to it, we are able to under-

5 ."The Dramatic Monologue in the Victorian Period," *Proceedings of the British Academy 1924–1925*, p. 276. See also an earlier paper which moves in the same direction, though not nearly so far: G. H. Palmer. "The Monologue of Browning," *Harvard Theological Review*, April 1918; and the three pages Bliss Perry devotes to the subject in *A Study of Poetry* (Boston: Houghton Mifflin, 1920), pp. 267–70. Stopford Brooke makes the pioneering remarks on the dramatic monologue in Chap. XIII of *Tennyson: His Art and Relation to Modern Life* (London: Isbister, 1895). But Brooke in his *Tennyson* and William Lyon Phelps in Chap. V of *Robert Browning, How to Know Him* (Indianapolis: Bobbs-Merrill, 1915), are more concerned with the content of individual dramatic monologues than with generic characteristics.

stand the wider connections of the form. For to give facts from within, to derive meaning that is from the poetic material itself rather than from an external standard of judgment, is the specifically romantic contribution to literature; while sympathy or projectiveness, what the Germans call *Einfühlung*, is the specifically romantic way of knowing. Once we consider the dramatic monologue as a poetry of sympathy, we are in a position to see the connection not only between the dramatic monologues of the nineteenth and twentieth centuries but between the dramatic monologue and all that is unprecedented in poetry since the latter eighteenth century. We can see in the differences between the dramatic monologue on the one hand, and the dramatic lyric and lyrical drama of the romanticists on the other, the articulation of a form potential in romantic poetry from the start.

The standard account of the dramatic monologue is that Browning and Tennyson conceived it as a reaction against the romantic confessional style. This is probably true. Both poets had been stung by unfriendly criticism of certain early poems in which they had too much revealed themselves; and both poets published, in 1842, volumes which were a new departure in their careers and which contained dramatic monologues. The personal sting was probably responsible for Tennyson's decade of silence before 1842; it was almost certainly responsible for the disclaimer attached by Browning to his 1842 *Dramatic Lyrics*: "so many utterances of so many imaginary persons, not mine." Yet the reserve of the two poets cannot explain the coincidence that, working independently, they both arrived at the same form and produced at first try dramatic monologues so perfect (Browning's *My Last Duchess* and Tennyson's *Ulysses* and *St Simeon Stylites*) that they were never themselves to surpass them. We must look for precedents; we must suspect that they inherited a form which required only one more step in its development to achieve the objectivity they desired.

Browning's poetry before 1842 suggests by the manner of its failure the kind of precedent that lay behind the dramatic monologue, and the kind of problem that remained for the dramatic monologue to solve. His first published work, *Pauline* (1833), is the poem in which he too much revealed himself. It is transparently autobiographical (although the fictitious identity of the lady addressed provides a disguise of a sort), tracing the poet's intellectual development up to the age of twenty, the time of writing. It was of *Pauline* that John Stuart Mill said: "The writer seems to me possessed with a more intense and morbid self-consciousness than I ever knew in any sane human being"—a criticism Browning took so to heart that he would not allow *Pauline* to be published again until 1867; and then with an apologetic preface which repeats the disclaimer of

1842: "The thing was my earliest attempt at 'poetry always dramatic in principle. and so many utterances of so many imaginary persons, not mine.'" In spite of which disclaimer, he is reported to have said in his old age that "his early poems were so transparent in their meaning as to draw down upon him the ridicule of the critics, and that, boy as he was, this ridicule and censure stung him into quite another style of writing."[6]

We can follow his attempts at "another style" in *Paracelsus* (1835), a dramatic poem, and *Sordello* (1833-40), an historical narrative. There is, however, little enough drama in *Paracelsus*, and the narrative line is at best intermittent in *Sordello*; in both poems the style that takes over is the introspective, transparently autobiographical history of a soul in the manner of *Pauline*—the soul being in all three recognizable as the same passionately idealistic and endlessly ambitious, endlessly self-absorbed disciple of Shelley. In the preface to the first edition of *Paracelsus*, Browning says that he has reversed the usual method of drama:

> Instead of having recourse to an external machinery of incidents to create and evolve the crisis I desire to produce, I have ventured to display somewhat minutely the mood itself in its rise and progress, and have suffered the agency by which it is influenced and determined to be generally discernible in its effects alone, and subordinate throughout, if not altogether excluded.

And reflecting in 1863 on the failure of *Sordello*, he says in the preface dedicating the new edition of the poem to his friend, the French critic Milsand: "My stress lay on the incidents in the development of a soul: little else is worth study. I, at least, always thought so—you, with many known and unknown to me, think so—others may one day think so."

Did Browning forget that the romantic poets had thought so, that even Arnold, who disagreed, could hardly help but write poetry as though he too thought so, and that the enormous popularity of the "spasmodic"[7] poets gave evidence that by mid-century almost everyone thought so? The question is perhaps answered by Milsand, who, in reviewing *Men and Woman* for the *Revue Contemporaine* of September 1856, describes Browning's dramatic monologues in terms applicable to the whole of what I have been calling the

6. Quoted in W. C. DeVane, *A Browning Handbook* (New York: Appleton-Century-Crofts, 1955), pp. 46–47; (London: John Murray, 1937), p. 44. Just as the failure of *Pauline* is considered responsible for Browning's reluctance to speak in his own voice, so Tennyson seems to have been similarly wounded by the failure of his 1832 volume, especially by Lockhart's personally insulting review of it in the *Quarterly*. Harold Ni-colson gives an amusing account of this review, considering it as "undoubtedly one of the main causes of the silent and morose decade which was to follow." (*Tennyson*, London: Constable, 1949, pp. 112–17.)
7. Term applied to English poets of the 1840s and 1850s (Sydney Dobell, P. J. Bailey, Alexander Smith, and others) whose verse was often uneven in style and exaggerated in emphasis. [*Editor.*]

poetry of experience. "What Mr Browning has attempted," says
Milsand, "is the fusion of two kinds of poetry into one." And after
citing Browning's remarks in the *Essay on Shelley* on the distinction between subjective and objective poetry:

> This alone indicates that he sympathizes equally with both kinds
> of inspiration, and I am inclined to think that from the begin-
> ning, and partly without his knowing it, his constant effort has
> been to reconcile and combine them, in order to find a way of
> being, not in turn but simultaneously, lyric and dramatic, subjec-
> tive and pictorial . . . [His poetry] would have us conceive the
> inner significance of things by making us see their exteriors.[8]

Compare these remarks of Milsand and Browning with Wordsworth's: "the feeling therein developed gives importance to the
action and situation, and not the action and situation to the feeling," and with Pound's description of his own poetry:

> To me the short so-called dramatic lyric—at any rate the sort
> of thing I do—is the poetic part of a drama the rest of which (to
> me the prose part) is left to the reader's imagination or implied
> or set in a short note. I catch the character I happen to be inter-
> ested in at the moment he interests me, usually a moment of
> song, self-analysis, or sudden understanding or revelation. And
> the rest of the play would bore me and presumably the reader.[9]

Add to the comparison Pound's idea that drama is less poetic than
other kinds of poetry because "the maximum charge of verbal
meaning cannot be used on the stage,"[1] and Virginia Woolf's aim
"to saturate" in her novels "every atom":

> I mean to eliminate all waste, deadness, superfluity: to give the
> moment whole; whatever it includes. . . . Waste, deadness, come
> from the inclusion of things that don't belong to the moment;
> this appalling narrative business of the realist: getting on from
> lunch to dinner: it is false, unreal, merely conventional. Why
> admit anything to literature that is not poetry—by which I mean
> saturated?[2]

And we see Browning's innovations as part of a general change of
sensibility—a demand that all literature yield much the same effect,
an effect of lyrical intensity.

When we have said all the objective things about Browning's *My
Last Duchess*, we will not have arrived at the meaning until we
point out what can only be substantiated by an appeal to effect—
that moral judgment does not figure importantly in our response to

8. Pp. 545–46.
9. To William Carlos Williams, 21 October 1908, *Letters 1907–1941*, ed. D. D.
Paige (New York: Harcourt, Brace,
1950), pp. 3–4; (London: Faber and
Faber, 1951), p. 36.

1. *ABC of Reading* (New Haven: Yale
University Press, 1934), p. 33; London:
Routledge, 1934), p. 31.
2. *A Writer's Diary*, ed. Leonard Woolf
(London: The Hogarth Press, 1953), p.
139.

the duke, that we even identify ourselves with him. But how is such an effect produced in a poem about a cruel Italian duke of the Renaissance who out of unreasonable jealousy has had his last duchess put to death, and is now about to contract a second marriage for the sake of dowry? Certainly, no summary or paraphrase would indicate that condemnation is not our principal response. The difference must be laid to form, to that extra quantity which makes the difference in artistic discourse between content and meaning.

The objective fact that the poem is made up entirely of the duke's utterance has of course much to do with the final meaning, and it is important to say that the poem is in form a monologue. But much more remains to be said about the way in which the content is laid out, before we can come near accounting for the whole meaning. It is important that the duke tells the story of his kind and generous last duchess to, of all people, the envoy from his prospective duchess. It is important that he tells his story while showing off to the envoy the artistic merits of a portrait of the last duchess. It is above all important that the duke carries off his outrageous indiscretion, proceeding triumphantly in the end downstairs to conclude arrangements for the dowry. All this is important not only as content but also as form, because it establishes a relation between the duke on the one hand, and the portrait and the envoy on the other, which determines the reader's relation to the duke and therefore to the poem—which determines, in other words, the poem's meaning.

The utter outrageousness of the duke's behaviour makes condemnation the least interesting response, certainly not the response that can account for the poem's success. What interests us more than the duke's wickedness is his immense attractiveness. His conviction of matchless superiority, his intelligence and bland amorality, his poise, his taste for art, his manners—high-handed aristocratic manners that break the ordinary rules and assert the duke's superiority when he is being most solicitous of the envoy, waiving their difference of rank ("Nay, we'll go/Together down, sir"); these qualities overwhelm the envoy, causing him apparently to suspend judgment of the duke, for he raises no demur. The reader is no less overwhelmed. We suspend moral judgment because we prefer to participate in the duke's power and freedom, in his hard core of character fiercely loyal to itself. Moral judgment is in fact important as the thing to be suspended, as a measure of the price we pay for the privilege of appreciating to the full this extraordinary man.

It is because the duke determines the arrangement and relative subordination of the parts that the poem means what it does. The duchess's goodness shines through the duke's utterance; he makes no attempt to conceal it, so preoccupied is he with his own standard of judgment and so oblivious of the world's. Thus the duchess's case is subordinated to the duke's, the novelty and complexity of which engages our attention. We are busy trying to understand the man who can combine the connoisseur's pride in the lady's beauty with a pride that caused him to murder the lady rather than tell her in what way she displeased him, for in that

> would be some stooping; and I choose
> Never to stoop.

The duke's paradoxical nature is fully revealed when, having boasted how at his command the duchess's life was extinguished, he turns back to the portrait to admire of all things its life-likeness:

> There she stands
> As if alive.

This occurs ten lines from the end, and we might suppose we have by now taken the duke's measure. But the next ten lines produce a series of shocks that outstrip each time our understanding of the duke, and keep us panting after revelation with no opportunity to consolidate our impression of him for moral judgment. For it is at this point that we learn to whom he has been talking; and he goes on to talk about dowry, even allowing himself to murmur the hypocritical assurance that the new bride's self and not the dowry is of course his object. It seems to me that one side of the duke's nature is here stretched as far as it will go; the dazzling figure threatens to decline into paltriness admitting moral judgment, when Browning retrieves it with two brilliant strokes. First, there is the lordly waiving of rank's privilege as the duke and the envoy are about to proceed downstairs, and then there is the perfect all-revealing gesture of the last two and a half lines when the duke stops to show off yet another object in his collection:

> Notice Neptune, though,
> Taming a sea-horse, thought a rarity,
> Which Claus of Innsbruck cast in bronze for me!

The lines bring all the parts of the poem into final combination, with just the relative values that constitute the poem's meaning. The nobleman does not hurry on his way to business, the connoisseur cannot resist showing off yet another precious object, the possessive egotist counts up his possessions even as he moves toward the acquirement of a new possession, a well-dowered bride; and most important, the last duchess is seen in final perspective. She takes her place as one of a line of objects in an art collection; her sad story becomes the *cicerone's* anecdote lending piquancy to the portrait. The duke has taken from her what he wants, her beauty, and thrown the life away; and we watch with awe as he proceeds to take what he wants from the envoy and by implication from the new duchess. He carries all before him by sheer force of will so unde-flected by ordinary compunctions as even, I think, to call into ques-tion—the question rushes into place behind the startling illumina-tion of the last lines, and lingers as the poem's haunting afternote—the duke sanity.

The duke reveals all this about himself, grows to his full stature, because we allow him to have his way with us; we subordinate all other considerations to the business of understanding him. If we allowed indignation, or pity for the duchess, to take over when the duke moves from his account of the murder to admire the life-like-ness of the portrait, the poem could hold no further surprises for us; it could not even go on to reinforce our judgment as to the duke's wickedness, since the duke does not grow in wickedness after the account of the murder. He grows in strength of character, and in the arrogance and poise which enable him to continue command of the situation after his confession of murder has threatened to turn it against him. To take the full measure of the duke's distinction we must be less concerned to condemn than to appreciate the trium-phant transition by which he ignores clean out of existence any judgment of his story that the envoy might have presumed to invent. We must be concerned to appreciate the exquisite timing of the duke's delay over Neptune, to appreciate its fidelity to the duke's own inner rhythm as he tries once more the envoy's already sorely tried patience, and as he teases the reader too by delaying for a lordly whim the poem's conclusion. This willingness of the reader to understand the duke, even to sympathize with him as a necessary condition of reading the poem, is the key to the poem's form. It alone is responsible for a meaning not inherent in the content itself but determined peculiarly by the treatment.

I have chosen *My Last Duchess* to illustrate the working of sym-pathy, just because the duke's egregious villainy makes especially apparent the split between moral judgment and our actual feeling for him. The poem carries to the limit an effect peculiarly the genius of the dramatic monologue—I mean the effect created by the tension between sympathy and moral judgment. Although we seldom meet again such an unmitigated villian as the duke, it is safe to say that most successful dramatic monologues deal with speakers who are in some way reprehensible.

Browning delighted in making a case for the apparently immoral position; and the dramatic monologue, since it requires sympathy for the speaker as a condition of reading the poem, is an excellent vehicle for the "impossible" case. Mr. Sludge and Bishop Blougram in matters of the spirit, Prince Hohenstiel-Schwangau in politics, and in love Don Juan of *Fifine*, are all Machiavellians who defend themselves by an amoral casuistry. The combination of villian and aesthete creates an especially strong tension, and Browning exploits the combination not only in *My Last Duchess* but again in *The Bishop Orders His Tomb*, where the dying Renaissance bishop reveals his venality and shocking perversion of Christianity together with his undeniable taste for magnificence:

> Some lump, ah God, of *lapis lazuli*,
> Big as a Jew's head cut off at the nape,
> Blue as a vein o'er the Madonna's breast . . .

and again in *The Laboratory* where the Rococo court lady is much concerned with the colour of the poison she buys and would like

> To carry pure death in an earring, a casket,
> A signet, a fan-mount, a filigree basket!

To the extent that these poems are successful, we admire the speaker for his power of intellect (as in *Blougram*) or for his aesthetic passion and sheer passion for living (as in *The Bishop Orders His Tomb*). *Hohenstiel-Schwangau* and *Fifine* are not successful because no outline of character emerges from the intricacy of the argument, there is no one to sympathize with and we are therefore not convinced even though the arguments are every bit as good as in the successful poems. Arguments cannot make the case in the dramatic monologue but only passion, power, strength of will and intellect, just those existential virtues which are independent of logical and moral correctness and are therefore best made out through sympathy and when clearly separated from, even opposed to, the other virtues. Browning's contemporaries accused him of "perversity" because they found it necessary to sympathize with his reprehensible characters.

But Browning's perversity is intellectual and moral in the sense that most of his characters have taken up their extraordinary positions through a perfectly normal act of will. Tennyson, on the other hand, although less interested in novel moral positions, goes much farther than Browning in dealing in his successful dramatic monologues with an emotional perversity that verges on the pathological. Morally, Tennyson's *St Simeon Stylites* is a conventional liberal Protestant attack upon asceticism. But the poem is unusual because the saint's passion for a heavenly crown is shown as essentially demonic; his hallucinations, self-loathing and insatiable lust for self-punishment suggest a psyche as diseased (we should nowadays call it sado-masochistic) as the ulcerous flesh he boasts of. St Simeon conceives himself in both body and soul as one disgusting sore:

> Altho' I be the basest of mankind,
> From scalp to sole one slough and crust of sin,

and there is in his advice to his disciples a certain obscene zest:

Mortify
Your flesh, like me, with scourges and with thorns;
Smite, shrink not, spare not.

Browning would have complicated the case against asceticism, he might have emphasized the moral ambiguity presented by the saintly ambition which does not differ in quality from the ambition for money or empire; or if he did simplify, it would be to present the case against ascetic ritualism satirically as in *The Spanish Cloister*. Tennyson, however, is more interested in the psychological ambiguity, pursuing the saint's passion to its obscurely sexual recesses.

Treating a similar example of religious buccaneering, Browning has written in *Johannes Agricola in Meditation* a dramatic monologue of sheer lyric exultation. Johannes is, like St Simeon, on a rampage for salvation and confident of attaining it. But compare with St Simeon's the beauty of Johannes' conception of his own spiritual position:

> There's heaven above, and night by night
>   I look right through its gorgeous roof;
> No suns and moons though e'er so bright
>   Avail to stop me; splendour-proof
>   I keep the broods of stars aloof:
> For I intend to get to God,
>   For 'tis to God I speed so fast,
> For in God's breast, my own abode,
>   Those shoals of dazzling glory passed,
>   I lay my spirit down at last.

Although Browning clearly intends us to disapprove of Johannes' Antinomianism, he complicates the issue by showing the lofty passion that can proceed from the immoral doctrine. Nevertheless, the passion is rationally accounted for by the doctrine; Johannes is a fanatic, one who has gone to a philosophical extreme. A moral and and philosophical term like *fanatic* will not suffice, however, to characterize St Simeon; we need also a term out of abnormal psychology. It is interesting to note in this connection that *Johannes Agricola* originally appeared together with *Porphyria's Lover* under the common heading of *Madhouse Cells*, but the poems were later separated and the heading abandoned. Without the heading, there is nothing in *Johannes Agricola* to make us suppose that the speaker is mad, that he is anything more than fanatically devoted to his Antinomian principles. That is because Browning does not, like Tennyson in *St Simeon*, pursue the passion downward to those subrational debths where lurk unsuspected motives.

In *Porphyria's Lover*, the speaker is undoubtedly mad. He strangles Porphyria with her own hair, as a culminating expression of his love and in order to preserve unchanged the perfect moment of her surrender to him. But even here, Browning is relying upon an extraordinary complication of what still remains a rationally understandable motive. The motive and action are no more unreasonable than in A *Forgiveness*, where we do not consider the speaker of his wife mad. She is unfaithful because of her great love for him, and he eventually forgives her by awarding her hate instead of contempt; she allows the life blood to flow out of her to help his hate pass away in vengeance. The motives in both poems are likely to demonstrate for us rather more ingenuity than madness; and it is generally true that extraordinary motives in Browning come not from disordered subconscious urges but, as in Henry James, from the highest moral and intellectual refinement.

* * *

* * * Since the past is understood in the same way that we understand the speaker of the dramatic monologue, the dramatic monologue is an excellent instrument for projecting an historical point of view. For the modern sense of the past involves, on the other hand, a sympathy for the past, a willingness to understand it in its own terms as different from the present; and on the other hand it involves a critical awareness of our own modernity. In the same way, we understand the speaker of the dramatic monologue by sympathizing with him, and yet by remaining aware of the moral judgment we have suspended for the sake of understanding. The combination of sympathy and judgment makes the dramatic monologue suitable for expressing all kinds of extraordinary points of view, whether moral, emotional or historical—since sympathy frees us for the widest possible range of experience, while the critical reservation keeps us aware of how far we are departing. The extraordinary point of view is characteristic of all the best dramatic monologues, the pursuit of experience in all its remotest extensions being the genius of the form.

We are dealing, in other words, with empiricism in literature. The pursuit of all experience corresponds to the scientific pursuit of all knowledge; while the sympathy that is a condition of the dramatic monologue corresponds to the scientific attitude of mind, the willingness to understand everything for its own sake and without consideration of practical or moral value. We might even say that the dramatic monologue takes toward its material the literary equivalent of the scientific attitude—the equivalent being, where men and women are the subject of investigation, the historicizing and psychologizing of judgment.

Certainly the Italian Renaissance setting of *My Last Duchess* helps us to suspend moral judgment of the duke, since we partly at least take an historical view; we accept the combination of villainy with taste and manners as a phenomenon of the Renaissance and of the old aristocratic order generally. The extraordinary combination pleases us the way it would the historian, since it impresses upon us the difference of the past from the present. We cannot, however, entirely historicize our moral judgment in this poem, because the duke's crime is too egregious to support historical generalization. More important, therefore, for the suspension of moral judgment is our psychologizing attitude—our willingness to take up the duke's view of events purely for the sake of understanding him, the more outrageous his view the more illuminating for us the psychological revelation.

In *The Bishop Orders His Tomb*, however, our judgment is mainly historicized, because the bishop's sins are not extraordinary but the universally human venalities couched, significantly for the historian, in the predilections of the Italian Renaissance. Thus, the bishop gives vent to materialism and snobbery by planning a bigger and better tomb than his clerical rival's. This poem can be read as a portrait of the age, our moral judgment of the bishop depending upon our moral judgment of the age. Ruskin praised the poem for its historical validity: "It is nearly all that I said of the Central Renaissance in thirty pages of *The Stones of Venice* put into as many lines"; but being no friend of the Renaissance, this is the spirit of the age he conceived Browning to have caught: "its worldliness, inconsistency, pride, hypocrisy, ignorance of itself, love of art, of luxury, and of good Latin."[3] Browning, who admired the Renaissance, would have admitted all this but he would have insisted, too, upon the enterprise and robust aliveness of the age. What matters, however, is that Browning has presented an historical image the validity of which we can all agree upon, even if our moral judgments differ as they do about the past itself.

In the same way, our understanding of the duke in *My Last Duchess* has a primary validity which is not disturbed by our differing moral judgments after we have finished reading the poem—it being characteristically the style of the dramatic monologue to present its material empirically, as a fact existing before and apart from moral judgment which remains always secondary and problematical. Even where the speaker is specifically concerned with a moral question, he arrives at his answer empirically, as a necessary outcome of conditions within the poem and not through appeal to an outside moral code. Since these conditions are always psychological and sometimes historical as well—since the answer is determined, in other words, by the speaker's nature and the time he inhabits—the

3. *Modern Painters* (London: Routledge; New York: Dutton, 1907), iv, 370. [See   excerpt from Ruskin in this edition.— *Editor.*]

moral meaning is of limited application but enjoys within the limit-
ing conditions of the poem a validity which no subsequent differences in judgment can disturb.

Take as an example Browning's dramatic monologues in defence
of Christianity. Although the poet has undoubtedly an axe to grind,
he maintains a distinction between the undeniable fact of the
speaker's response to the conditions of the poem and the general
Christian formulation which the reader may or may not draw for
himself. The speaker starts with a blank slate as regards Christianity, and is brought by the conditions of the poem to a perception of
need for the kind of answer provided by Christianity. Nevertheless,
the perception is not expressed in the vocabulary of Christian
dogma and the speaker does not himself arrive at a Christian formulation.

The speakers of the two epistolary monologues, *Karshish* and
Cleon, are first-century pagans brought by the historical moment
and their own psychological requirements to perceive the need for a
God of Love (*Karshish*) and a promise of personal immorality
(*Cleon*). But they arrive at the perception through secular concepts, and are prevented by these same concepts from embracing
the Christian answer that lies before them. Karshish is an Arab physician travelling in Judea who reports the case of the risen Lazarus
as a medical curiosity, regarding Jesus as some master physician with
the cure for a disease that simulates death. He is ashamed, writing
to his medical teacher, of the story's mystical suggestions and purposely mixes it up with, and even tries to subordinate it to, reports
of cures and medicinal herbs. Yet it is clear throughout that the
story haunts him, and he has already apologized for taking up so
much space with it when he interrupts himself in a magnificent
final outburst that reveals the story's impact upon his deepest feelings:

> The very God! Think, Abib; dost thou think?
> So, the All-Great, were the All-Loving too—.

Nevertheless, he returns in the last line to the scientific judgment,
calling Lazarus a madman and using to characterize the story the
same words he has used to characterize other medical curiosities: "it
is strange."

Cleon is a Greek of the last period; master of poetry, painting,
sculpture, music, philosophy, he sums up within himself the whole
Greek cultural accomplishment. Yet writing to a Greek Tyrant who
possesses all that Greek material culture can afford, he encourages
the Tyrant's despair by describing his own. The fruits of culture—
self-consciousness and the increased capacity for joy—are curses, he
says, since they only heighten our awareness that we must die with-

out ever having tasted the joy our refinement has taught us to conceive. He demonstrates conclusively, in the manner of the Greek
dialectic, that life without hope of immortality is unbearable. "It is
so horrible," he says,

> I dare at times imagine to my need
> Some future state revealed to us by Zeus,
> Unlimited in capability
> For joy, as this is in desire for joy,
> —To seek which, the joy-hunger forces us.

He despairs because Zeus has not revealed this. Nevertheless, he dis-
misses in a hasty postscript the pretensions of "one called Paulus,"
"a mere barbarian Jew," to have "access to a secret shut from us."

The need for Christianity stands as empiric fact in these poems,
just because it appears in spite of intellectual and cultural objections. In *Saul* there are no objections, but the need is still empiric
in that it appears before the Christian formulation of it. The young
David sings to Saul of God's love, of His sacrifice for man, and His
gift of eternal life, because he needs to sing of the highest conceivable joy, his songs about lesser joys having failed to dispel Saul's
depression. David "induces" God's love for Saul from his own,
God's willingness to suffer for Saul from his own willingness, and
God's gift of eternal life from his own desire to offer Saul the most
precious gift possible.

> "O Saul,
> it shall be
> A Face like my face that receives thee; a Man
> like to me,
> Thou shalt love and be loved by, for ever:
> a Hand like this hand
> Shall throw open the gates of new life to thee!
> See the Christ stand!"

The speaker of *A Death in the Desert* is a Christian—St John,
the beloved disciple and author of the Fourth Gospel, conceived as
speaking his last words before dying at a very old age. He has out-
lived the generation that witnessed the miracles of Christ and the
apostles, and has lived to see a generation that questions the promise of Christ's coming and even His existence. As the last living
eye-witness, John has been able to reassure this generation; but
dying, he leaves a kind of Fifth Gospel for the skeptical generations
to follow, generations that will question the existence of John himself. It is an empiricist gospel. "I say, to test man, the proofs shift,"
says John. But this is well, since belief in God would have no moral
effect were it as inevitable as belief in the facts of nature. Myth,
man's apprehension of truth, changes; but Truth remains for each

generation to rediscover for itself. The later generations will have sufficiently profited from the moral effect of Christianity, so as not to require proof by miracle or direct revelation. They will be able to "induce" God's love from their own and from their need to conceive a love higher than theirs. Thus, Browning invests with dogmatic authority his own anti-dogmatic line of Christian apologetics.

In *Bishop Blougram's Apology*, the case is complicated by the inappropriateness of the speaker and his argument to the Christian principles being defended. Blougram, we are told in an epilogue, "said true things, but called them by wrong names." A Roman Catholic bishop, he has achieved by way of the Church the good things of this world and he points to his success as a sign that he has made the right choice. For his relatively unsuccessful opponent, the agnostic literary man, Gigadibs, the bishop is guilty of hypocrisy, a vice Gigadibs cannot be accused of since he has made no commitments. Since the bishop admits to religious doubt (Gigadibs lives "a life of doubt diversified by faith," the bishop "one of faith diversified by doubt"), Gigadibs can even take pride in a superior respect for religion, he for one not having compromised with belief. Thus, we have the paradox of the compromising worldly Christian against the uncompromising unworldly infidel—a conception demonstrating again Browning's idea that the proofs do not much matter, that there are many proofs better and worse for the same Truth. For if Blougram is right with the wrong reasons, Gigadibs with admirable reasons or at least sentiments is quite wrong.

The point of the poem is that Blougram makes his case, even if on inappropriate grounds. He knows his argument is not the best ("he believed," according to the epilogue, "say, half he spoke"), for the grounds are his opponent's; it is Blougram's achievement that he makes Gigadibs see what the agnostic's proper grounds are. He is doing what Browning does in all the dramatic monologues on religion—making the empiricist argument, starting without any assumptions as to faith and transcendental values. Granting that belief and unbelief are equally problematical, Blougram proceeds to show that even in terms of this world only belief bears fruit while unbelief does not. This is indicated by Blougram's material success, but also by the fact that his moral behaviour, however imperfect, is at least in the direction of his professed principles; whereas Gigadibs' equally moral behaviour is inconsistent with his principles. Who, then, is the hypocrite? "I live my life here," says Blougram; "yours you dare not live."

But the fact remains—and this is the dramatic ambiguity matching the intellectual—that the bishop is no better than his argument, though he can conceive a better argument and a better kind of person. He cannot convert Gigadibs because his argument, for all its suggestion of a Truth higher than itself, must be understood dramatically as rationalizing a selfish worldly existence. What Gigadibs apparently does learn is that he is no better than the bishop, that he has been the same kind of person after the same kind of rewards only not succeeding so well, and that he has been as intellectually and morally dishonest with his sentimental liberalism as the bishop with his casuistry. All this is suggested indirectly by the last few lines of the epilogue, where we are told that Gigadibs has gone off as a settler to Australia. Rid of false intellectual baggage (the bishop's as well as his own), he will presumably start again from the beginning, "inducing" the Truth for himself. "I hope," says Browning,

> By this time he has tested his first plough,
> And studied his last chapter of St John.

St John, note, who makes the empiricist argument in *A Death in the Desert*, and whose Gospel Browning admired because of its philosophical rather than thaumaturgic treatment of Christianity.

Although *Blougram* and *A Death in the Desert* are too discursive to communicate their religious perceptions in the manner of *Karshish*, *Cleon* and *Saul*, as the speaker's immediate experience, they make their case empirically because in non-Christian terms. They might be considered as setting forth the rhetorical method of the more dramatic poems, a method for being taken seriously as intelligent and modern when broaching religion to the skeptical post-Enlightenment mind. The reader is assumed to be Gigadibs (it is because the bishop is so intelligent that Gigadibs finds it difficult to understand how he can believe), and the poet makes for his benefit a kind of "minimum argument," taking off from his grounds and obtruding no dogmatic assertions.

Eliot addresses his religious poetry to the same kind of reader, communicating his religious perceptions in terms that fall short of Christian dogma. This is especially interesting in Eliot since his concern has been with dogmatic religion, whereas Browning was always anti-dogmatic. Of course, the method is in both poets not merely a deliberate rhetorical device but the necessary outcome of their own religious uncertainties, and a sign that they share like Blougram the post-Enlightenment mind. This is again especially apparent in Eliot, who has dramatized in his poetry his movement from skepticism to orthodoxy, whereas Browning's poetry shows no significant religious *development*. Nevertheless, there is something of the obtuseness of Karshish and Cleon in those speakers of Eliot's dramatic monologues whose religious perceptions fall short of the Christian truth—and with the same effect as in Browning, that the reader can give assent to the speaker's experience without having to agree on doctrine.

In *Journey of the Magi*, one of the Magi describes with great clarity and detail the hardships of the journey to Bethlehem, but cannot say for certain what he saw there or what it meant. The Magi returned to their Kingdoms, like Karshish and Cleon "no longer at ease here, in the old dispensation," but still without light. The old Jew Simeon, in *A Song for Simeon*, is somewhat in the position of Browning's David in *Saul*; he sees clearly the glory of Christianity, but is too old to embrace it— not for him "the ultimate vision," the new dispensation is ahead of his time. In *Marina*, the speaker apparently finds the ultimate vision in the face of his newly recovered daughter and in the woodthrush song through the fog, but the vision is still not intelligible, not translated into Christian terms.

In the earlier skeptical poems, the fog is even thicker and no song of revelation comes through it. But Eliot uses idolatrous or "minimum" analogues to the Christian myth to indicate the groping for meaning, his own groping and that of the characters within the poem. The characters in *Gerontion* and *The Waste Land* practise idolatries, aesthetic and occultist. *Gerontion* ends with an occultist vision of the modern, cosmopolitan, unbelieving dead whirled around the universe on a meaningless wind:

> De Bailhache, Fresca, Mrs Cammel, whirled
> Beyond the circuit of the shuddering Bear
> In fractured atoms.

Yet seen in the subsequent lines as a natural phenomenon, the wind has a certain meaning in that it unites the parts of nature, north and south, into a single living whole:

> Gull against the wind, in the windy straits
> Of Belle Isle, or running on the Horn,
> White feathers in the snow, the Gulf claims,

and there is, I think, the suggestion that the wind may be a cleansing wind, one which may bring the rain the aged speaker has been waiting for. The same wind that carries off the dead may bring renewal to the depleted living; that is as much meaning and as much hope as the speaker can achieve.

It is as much meaning as our pagan ancestors achieved in the primitive vegetation myths of death and renewal, and Eliot uses the analogy of these myths to give at least that much meaning to the jumbled fragments of *The Waste Land*. Just as the vegetation gods were slain so they might rise renewed and restore the fertility of the land; so the longing for death, which pervades the modern waste land, is a longing for renewal and, if the reader wants to carry the analogy a step farther, a longing for redemption through the blood of Christ, the slain God.

The analogy with the vegetation myths is maintained even in the

Four Quartets, which are written from a solidly orthodox position. The religious perceptions of these poems are couched less in Christian terms than in terms of that mystical fusion of anthropology and psychology, of myth and the unconscious, that Jung effected.[4] One wonders if the *Four Quartets* are not, for all their orthodoxy, more satisfying to the skeptical than to the orthodox, since the latter might well prefer an articulation of religious truth no less explicit than their own convictions. Post-Enlightenment minds, on the other hand, are particularly fascinated by the mystique of myth and the unconscious as a way back, I think, to a kind of religious speculation which commits them to nothing while preserving intact their status as intelligent, scientific and modern. Myth and the unconscious are contemporary equivalents of Browning's pragmatism in making the "minimum" argument for Christianity..

Although not the only way to talk religion empirically, the dramatic monologue offers certain advantages to the poet who is not committed to a religious position, or who is addressing readers not committed and not wanting to be. The use of the speaker enables him to dramatize a position the possibilities of which he may want to explore as Browning explores the "impossible" case. The speaker also enables him to dramatize an emotional apprehension in advance of or in conflict with his intellectual convictions—a disequilibrium perhaps inevitable to that mind which I have been calling post-Enlightenment or romantic because, having been intellectually through the Enlightenment, it tries to re-establish some spiritual possibility. Browning's St. John, in *A Death in the Desert,* defends religious myth as the expression of just this disequilibrium, of the emotional apprehension that exceeds formulated knowledge:

> "man knows partly but conceives beside,
> Creeps ever on from fancies to the fact,
> And in this striving, this converting air
> Into a solid he may grasp and use,
> Finds progress, man's distinctive mark alone,
> Not God's, and not the beasts'."

Even Eliot who professes to be against this "dissociation" of emotional apprehension from its formulated articulation (which for him is dogma), even in Eliot's poetry emotion is always a step ahead of reason—as for example the dim adumbrations of Christianity provided by the vegetation mythology of *The Waste Land,* or the disturbance of the Magi that exceeds their understanding, or that ultimate vision in *Marina* the articulation of which is obscured by the fog.

4. For a discussion of Eliot's use of Jungian ideas and symbols, see Elizabeth Drew, *T. S. Eliot: The Design of His* *Poetry* (New York: Scribner's, 1949; London: Eyre and Spottiswoode, 1950).

Not only can the speaker of the dramatic monologue dramatize a position to which the poet is not ready to commit himself intellectually, but the sympathy which we give the speaker for the sake of the poem and apart from judgment makes it possible for the reader to participate in a position, to see what it feels like to believe that way, without having finally to agree. There is, in other words, the same split between sympathy and judgment that we saw at work in our relation to the duke of *My Last Duchess*. The split is naturally most apparent in those dramatic monologues where the speaker is in some way reprehensible, where sympathy is in conflict with judgment, but it is also at work where sympathy is congruent with judgment although a step ahead of it. The split must in fact be at work to some degree, if the poem is to generate the effect which makes it a dramatic monologue.

Browning's *Rabbi Ben Ezra* is a dramatic monologue by virtue of its title only; otherwise it is a direct statement of a philosophical idea, because there is no characterization or setting. Because the statement is not conditioned by a speaker and a situation, there is no way of apprehending it other than intellectually; there is no split between its validity as somebody's apprehension and its objective validity as an idea. But in *Abt Vogler*, where the statement is also approved of, it is conditioned by the speaker's ecstasy as he extemporizes on the organ. His sublime vision of his music as annihilating the distinction between heaven and earth has validity as part of the ecstatic experience of extemporizing, but becomes a matter of philosophical conjecture as the ecstasy subsides and the music modulates back into the "C Major of this life." The disequilibrium between the empiric vision that lasts as long as the ecstasy and the music, and its philosophical implication, makes sympathy operative; and the tension between what is known through sympathy and what is only hypothesized through judgment generates the effect characteristic of the dramatic monologue.

Since sympathy is the primary law of the dramatic monologue, how does judgment get established at all? How does the poet make clear what we are to think of the speaker and his statement? Sometimes it is not clear. The Catholic reader might well consider Tennyson's St Simeon admirable and holy. Readers still try to decide whether Browning is for or against Bishop Blougram. Browning was surprised at accusations of anti-Catholicism that followed the publication of the poem, but he was even more surprised when Cardinal Wisemen (the model for Bloughram) wrote in reviewing the poem for a Catholic journal: *"we should never feel surprise at his* [Browning's] *conversion."*[5] We now know, at least from external

5. E. R. Houghton has established that   [*Editor.*]
Wiseman was not the reviewer after all.

evidence if not from more careful reading, that Browning's final judgment is against Don Juan of *Fifine* and Prince Hohenstiel-Schwangau (representing Napoleon III). But the reviewers considered that he was defending the incontinent Don Juan and accused him of perversity; while of *Hohenstiel-Schwangau*, one reviewer said that it was a "eulogism on the Second Empire," and another called it "a scandalous attack on the old constant friend of England."[6]

But these are exceptional cases, occurring mainly in Browning and the result partly of Browning's sometimes excessive ingenuity, partly of a judgment more complex than the reader is expecting, partly of careless reading. Certainly Don Juan's desertion of his wife and return to the gipsy girl in the end—even though he says it is for five minutes and "to clear the matter up"—ought for the careful reader to show up his argument as rationalizing a weak character, although the argument contains in itself much that is valid. In the same way, the final reference to Gigadibs as starting from the beginning with a plough and the Gospel of St John ought to indicate that he is getting closer to the truth than Blougram. I have tried to indicate that more is involved in our judgment of the bishop than the simple alternatives of *for* and *against*. As the bishop himself says of the modern interest in character, which interest is precisely the material of the dramatic monologue:

> Our interest's on the dangerous edge of things.
> The honest thief, the tender murderer,
> The superstitious atheist, demirep
> That loves and saves her soul in new French books—
> We watch while these in equilibrium keep
> The giddy line midway: one step aside,
> They're classed and done with. I, then, keep the line
> Before your sages,—just the men to shrink
> From the gross weights, coarse scales and labels broad
> You offer their refinement. Fool or knave?
> Why needs a bishop be a fool or knave
> When there's a thousand diamond weights between?

There is judgment all right among modern empiricists, but it follows understanding and remains tentative and subordinate to it. In trying to take into account as many facts as possible and to be as supple and complex as the facts themselves, judgment cuts across the conventional categories, often dealing in paradoxes—the honest thief, the tender murderer. Above all, it brings no ready-made yardstick; but allows the case to establish itself in all its particularity, and to be judged according to criteria generated by its particularity.

In other words, judgment is largely psychologized and histori-

6. Quoted in DeVane, *Browning Handbook* (New York: Appleton-Century-Crofts), pp. 243, 369, 363; (London: John Murray), pp. 216, 327, 321.

cized. We adopt a man's point of view and the point of view of his age in order to judge him—which makes the judgment relative, limited in applicability to the particular conditions of the case. This is the kind of judgment we get in the dramatic monologue, which is for this reason an appropriate form for an empiricist and relativist age, an age which has come to consider value as an evolving thing dependent upon the changing individual and social requirements of the historical process. For such an age judgment can never be final, it has changed and will change again; it must be perpetually checked against fact, which comes before judgment and remains always more certain.

Interpretations of Poems

W. DAVID SHAW

Browning's Duke as Theatrical Producer†

The Duke of "My Last Duchess" (1842) occupies the same position in Browning's canon as Hamlet does in Shakespeare's. His power as a dramatic character resides in his endless suggestiveness, in the play of enigmatic forces that continue to seduce and inspire his subtlest critics. With the Bishop of St. Praxed's and Count Guido Franceschini, he is Browning's most convincing portrayal of the aesthetic stage.[1] His complexity arises from the accuracy with which Browning reproduces the baffling contradictions of the aesthetic man who, in attempting to shock and entertain the envoy, is also trying to make his existence durable to himself.

Some of the best commentators on the poem believe that the Duke delivers his speech as a warning which he wants the envoy to convey to his future wife. Professors E. K. Brown and J. O. Bailey summarize this view when they state that the Duke "expects from his bride single-hearted, worshipful loyalty, and will tolerate no less. He tells the story of his last duchess as a subtle means of making this point."[2] But other critics have objected that the Duke is more interested in obtaining a dowry than a submissive wife, and if the envoy were to report this speech to the Count's daughter, it is

† From W. D. Shaw, *The Dialectical Temper: The Rhetorical Art of Robert Browning* (Ithaca, N.Y.: Cornell University Press, 1968), pp. 92–104.
1. The term is that of Søren Kierkegaard, whose dialectical structuring of experience includes three phases: the aesthetic, the ethical, and the religious. [*Editor.*]
2. *Victorian Poetry*, ed. E. K. Brown and J. O. Bailey (New York, 1962), p. 774.

unlikely that the dowry would be forthcoming. It is possible, of course, that the duaghter would have no choice in the matter, since Italian women of the sixteenth century were still treated as chattels on the marriage market. But if the daughter has no choice, there is even less reason to suppose that the Duke is delivering his speech as a warning. For him to do so under such circumstances would be to grant the possibility of an unruly chattel and to suggest that the marital rights of a duke are only nominal. On the other hand, the Duke is too adroit and sophisticated to indulge in plain effrontery. It would not be in character for the Duke crudely and openly to challenge the envoy to report the Duke's story if he dared.

Thomas Assad argues that the Duke stoops to reveal a domestic frustration because the revelation enables him to demonstrate his knowledge of art. But the role of art is not as important in "My Last Duchess" as it is in "Fra Lippo Lippi" or "Andrea del Sarto." One cannot help feeling that Mr. Assad has mistaken a subordinate theme for the primary one. After all, could a mere taste for appreciating art make the Duke do what "he claims he never chooses to do, and that is to stoop?"[3] Neither B. R. Jerman's thesis that the Duke is witless[4] nor Robert Langbaum's hypothesis of the Duke's insanity[5] can explain convincingly why the Duke should volunteer all the shocking information that he does. As in a portrait of Pontormo, there is a presumption of superiority in the Duke's manner that will accept no question from the outside would nor admit any satisfaction of our curiosity. Indeed, the usual roles of speaker and reader are reversed: the reader, like the envoy, feels that he, and not the Duke, is being inspected. The critic's inquiring gaze at the Duke is at first rejected; nor does it perceive any simple explanation of his motives.

I believe that the clue to this mystery lies in an area which other critics have indicated, but which no one seems to have explored at length. Commentators have sensed that the Duke is staging a "show" for the envoy by drawing and closing curtains and speaking rhetorically. George Monteiro, in particular, has stressed the dramatic basis of the Duke's speech: "Virtually a libretto, the Duke's monologue sustains a central metaphor of drama and performance." He begins his play with a curtain, and "sees himself in a dramatic light."[6] But because most critics have paid too little attention to the Duke's language and gestures, they have not generally recognized the full extent to which he is involved in a drama of social

3. "Browning's 'My Last Duchess,' " *Tulane Studies in English*, 10 (1960), 117–28.
4. "Browning's Witless Duke," *PMLA*, 72 (1957), 488–93.

5. *The Poetry of Experience* (London, 1957), p. 85.
6. "Browning's 'My Last Duchess,' " *Victorian Poetry*, 1 (1963), 235.

pretension—of ceremonious posturing, play acting, and verbal artifice. The ceremony is part of the stagecraft. He was like the producer of a play till life, in the form of his Duchess' admirers, moved
into his theatre and set up its counterplay. Isolated by the greedy
idolatries of his producer's art, the Duke's theatrical self has fiercely
willed the extinction of every other self. Now, in the perfect theatre
of the dramatic monologue, with the envoy as his captive audience,
the Duke must restage the uneven drama of his domestic life in the
form most flattering to his producer's ego. He is at last ready to give
the faultless performance which, as we gradually infer, he has never
had the absolute mastery to stage in real life.

The opening lines have a sweep of godlike omnipotence. The
Duke's lordly gesture "calls" into being, as though by a fiat of
divine creation, an acknowledged "wonder":

> I call
> That piece a wonder, now: Frà Pandolf's hands
> Worked busily a day, and there she stands   [ll. 2–4].

The paratactic syntax sounds impressively oracular. Like Belinda's
echo of Genesis in "The Rape of the Lock" ("Let Spades be
trumps! she said, and trumps they were"), the very grammar invites
a biblical parody. The Duke has dazzled his auditor with a magnificent opening, and fully conscious of the effect he has made, he can
now afford to descend from this plateau of ceremony, with its operatic pointing at the picture, to a drawing-room atmosphere of mere
formality. In extending his civilities to the envoy, this autocratic
spellbinder, while choosing "Never to stoop" himself, becomes a
subtle social parody of the Christian God of Browning's St. John,
who "stoops . . . to rise . . . Such ever was love's way" ("A Death in
the Desert," I.134). The Duke pretends to "stoop," not out of love
(for his melodramatic pretensions exclude the imagination of love),
but only out of a selfish desire to dramatize his own importance.

The speaker is producing a play in which the envoy must act his
proper role. Thus the profession of feeling in "Will't please you sit"
is offset by the Duke's self-important quotation of himself ("I
said") and by the studied artifice of his "by design." Feeling is further displaced by the classificatory instinct evident in the phrase
"Strangers like you" and by the placid rationality of the causal
"for," as though the envoy were simply another statistic, his
response a calculated theatrical effect, something which the Duke
has already predicted with scientific accuracy. Instead of speaking of
the Duchess' "deep passion," he uses hendiadys ("The depth and
passion of its earnest glance") to give an increased formality and an
emphasis in keeping with the Latinate elegance of "that pictured
countenance." An austere note enters with the aggressive insolence of
the first parenthesis: "(since none puts by / The curtain I have

drawn for you, but I)." Its audacity is a theatrical triumph which further accentuates the displacement of tone in the slightingly acrid "Strangers like you," and which reaches a minor climax in the insolent threat—"if they durst"—he casually tosses off. His lofty rhetoric corresponds in the social realm to the sublime in the aesthetic: each is tinged with as much terror as dignity. The use of first-person pronouns ("As they would ask me," "But to myself they turned"), the studied indifference of the parenthesis, which is really a stage direction, and, above all, the frightening brevity of the arresting "if they durst," which owes half its power to its appearance as a careless afterthought, all enable the Duke to glory in an authority which the Duchess' spontaneity never allowed him to possess while she was alive. The very disparity of meaning between the rhyming words "breast" and "West," which the heroic couplet brings into one web of sense, confirms our suspicion that the Duke lacked this kind of mastery in his married life. The rhymes, which are irrational satellites revolving around the rhetoric, imply that, like "the dropping of the daylight," the Duchess' "breast" had indeed become for him a sinking sun. In order to dramatize his complete possession of the Duchess' "smile," the Duke in his little play takes keen delight in turning that smile on and off, merely by pulling a rope, with all the absorption of a child with a toy. But from what he proceeds to say we gather that the Duchess would never have allowed the curtain to be drawn over her in real life.

What is most repulsive in the Duke's manner is the callous precision of an insane rationalist. The Duke casts his critique of the instinctive and humane into the brainlessly analytic mode of a social geometer:

> "Just this
> Or that in you disgusts me; here you miss,
> Or there exceed the mark" [ll. 37–39].

The speaker has the hypersensitive nerves of an infallible producer and rejects as vulgar any rational discussion with his star performer. His moral calculus transforms the rationality of the Duchess into the impudence of a saucy schoolgirl, "plainly" setting "Her wits to [his]," as though chopping logic with her master.

By way of a transitional "Oh sir," as though to anticipate and forestall the mingled outrage and amazement of his auditor, the Duke passes to a fleeting reminder, in the two words "she smiled," of the Duchess' instinctive humanity:

> Oh sir, she smiled, no doubt,
> Whene'er I passed her; but who passed without
> Much the same smile? [ll. 43–45].

The jealous producer finds intolerable the spontaneous warmth of an actress who dares move beyond the role in which he has cast her by extending to others "Much the same smile." The third and final use of "smile" communicates in a lightning stroke the full extent of the Duke's despotism: "This grew; I gave commands;/Then all *smiles* stopped together" (italics mine). The account of the march to power of this conqueror, whose use of asyndeton resembles Caesar's "I came, I saw, I conquered," shifts at once from the height of cruelty to a producer's sensitive appreciation of the Duchess' portrait, valued by the Duke now, in his theatrical performance before the envoy, as his most striking stage property. The impresario remains polished and unperturbed; his dissociation of brutality from the usual signs defines a peculiarly intense animus and contempt for everyone around him.

The Duke's assurance that he is more interested in obtaining a wife than a dowry is a transparent deception. Hedged round with double negatives and alliterating Latinisms, the indirection of the grammar reflects the indirection of the Duke's motives, which are precisely the opposite of what he avows. His condescension, as he steps back to allow the deferential envoy to accompany him, as a social equal, out of the room, is devoid of feeling: it is a subtle theatrical trick, a way of affirming the pride it seems to modify. Only the arrogant aristocrat who chooses "Never to stoop" can afford to stoop at all without loss of dignity. Hence the weird feel of the social play acting; everything moves by mysterious theatrical convention. The envoy and the Duchess are puppets controlled by unseen machinery, and even the Duke, in extending civilities to a menial he despises, seems to be speaking through a ventriloquist. By rhyming "rarity" and "me," the last couplet reminds us that the Duke is a unique specimen and can properly be connected only with a "rarity." The very task of relating several of the terms placed together makes the reader aware of new combinations. The "fair daughter's self" will never be as "fair" as the more concretely described statue or as any of the other works of art that her dowry will allow the Duke to buy. By concentrating meaning into the pure forms of marital property and financial obligation, abstractions like "fair daughter's self" and "known munificence" admit sharp contrasts to the speaker's lively appreciation of his art.

The final picture of the Duke, pointing with a grand gesture to his statue of Neptune boldly "Taming a sea-horse," brings to mind the contrasting picture of the Duchess, riding round the terrace on her mule. The mule and the sea horse are superficially appropriate to the Duchess and the Duke, respectively. But if the Duke identifies himself with the lusty Neptune mastering the unruly beast, it is the Duchess herself who must figure as the sea horse; submissive only in death, as the sea horse is in art, she has always been indomitable in real life.

The final images carry a great weight of meaning, once we make relevant associations with the earlier "fool" and "mule." The images are sufficiently generalized to effect a reversal unobtrusively, but suggestive enough to accommodate Browning's own indictment of the speaker. When the Duke refers to his statue of Neptune's taming a sea horse, a lurking suspicion that the Duke is indulging in wish fulfillment leaps suddenly to attention to assert its primacy. For, as we have seen, the Duke reveals just enough about the Duchess to indicate that she would not allow the curtain to be drawn over her while alive. His wife's picture is the Duke's "hang-up," in both a literal and Freudian sense.[7] By reducing his frustrations to the theatrics of social play acting, the Duke's speech is a means of re-enacting, and thus of artfully discharging, the real humiliation which he suffered in his last marriage, and which has been revived on the present occasion by the distasteful act of having to "stoop" to negotiate another marriage—to a mere Count's daughter—and with a social inferior at that. Browning has not chosen his auditor casually. The envoy on his marriage mission is precisely the person to revive the Duke's memories of his last marriage. As an emissary of a count, he is important enough to give the Duke a sense of power in manipulating his responses, yet at the same time he is insignificant enough to remove any of the Duke's fears that his puppet might take on independent life. The envoy's mission revives traumatic memories from the Duke's past. But they are memories which, once revived, the Duke can amplify and correct before a submissive auditor who enables him to transform the past into what it ought to have been.

The Duke's theatrical indirection is really evidence of his psychological complexity, suggesting Freud's profoundly dramatic notion of compulsive or obsessive behavior that attains expression by theatrical subterfuges designed to evade traumatic psychological experiences, often sexual in their origin. The Duke's behavior conforms precisely to Freud's classic analysis of the obsessional neurosis.[8] It transforms and corrects the domestic situation giving rise to his obsession. The ceremonious rhetoric, matchlessly contrived to secure, from the first lordly gesture to the final impudent levity, a breath-taking progression of dramatic shocks, keeps suggesting that the Duke is play acting, and that however reprehensible he may really be, he is not Satanic in the grand Miltonic way he would like the envoy and the reader to believe he is. As Robert Langbaum finely says, the last ten lines "produce a series of shocks that outstrip each time our understanding of the duke, and keep us panting after revelation."[9] It is almost as though the Duke is afraid to be

7. I am indebted for this observation to Professor Dean Blehert.
8. Sigmund Freud, *A General Introduction to Psychoanalysis,* tr. Joan Riviere (New York, 1960), pp. 268–83.
9. *The Poetry of Experience,* p. 84.

dull and must keep up a rapid succession of dazzling paradoxes and ever more violent shocks, which a less inwardly disturbed or compulsive rhetorician would be content to let lapse. One keeps sensing that the Duke is trying to evade the threat of personal catastrophe by building a fence and by constantly busying himself with doing something. According to Freud, "The actions performed in an obsessional condition are supported by a kind of energy which probably has no counterpart in normal mental life."[1] The Duke makes a tyranny, not only within his own domestic life, but also within the theatrical domain of art. The Duke resembles Browning himself in relation to the reader, and calculates every phrase and gesture that will force his own will or aesthetic intention on the envoy.

Like most victims of obsessional neurosis, the Duke occupies himself with such matters as the envoy's sitting and rising, which do not really interest him. Freud observes that such people "perform actions which . . . afford [them] no pleasure"—like the Duke's telling of his wife's attentions to Fra Pandolf, for example, which must be painful to recall but which he is compelled to talk about. The behavior of the neurotic may, according to Freud, be "absolutely silly," as the Duke's revelations would seem to be in view of his negotiations for another wife. Though such apparent "silliness" has led critics like B. R. Jerman to call the speaker "witless," the Duke seems more the obsessional neurotic as Freud describes him. He is "originally always a person of a very energetic disposition, often highly opinionated, and as a rule intellectually gifted above the average."[2] Laurence Perrine's excellent analysis of the Duke's shrewdness, a valuable antidote to theories of his witlessness, emphasizes this aspect of his character.[3] The Duke is overconscientious and more than usually correct in extending his courtesies to the envoy. In keeping with Freud's diagnosis, the Duke's genius in controlling the responses of the envoy and his skillful use of rhetoric are evidence of superior intellect. But he devotes these powers to such ostensibly "silly" ends that, as Freud observes of the neurotic, "it is a sufficiently arduous task to find one's bearings in this maze of contradictory character-traits and morbid manifestations. . . . Only one thing is open to him . . . instead of one silly idea he can adopt another of a slightly milder character."[4] This is precisely what the Duke does at the end of the poem, when he identifies himself with the lusty Neptune and sees the woman as the mule. He "can displace his sense of compulsion, but he cannot dispel it." He must repeat and correct the traumatic domestic situation that has given rise to his ceremonial compulsion.

The Duke forgets the nominal purpose of his interview and sub-

1. *A General Introduction to Psychoanalysis*, pp. 270–71.
2. *Ibid.*, p. 271.
3. "Browning's Shrewd Duke," *PMLA*, 74 (1959), 157–59.
4. *A General Introduction to Psychoanalysis*, p. 277.

stitutes a fantasy of sexual seduction for the immediate rhetorical "seduction" of the envoy. His monologue is a grotesque form of social courtship, involving as it does communication between hierarchically related orders. Verbal "courtship" of an inferior embodies the hierarchical principle of which the Duke is so conscious, and it is a surrogate for the rhetoric of sexual courtship, much of whose "mystery" likewise proceeds from inequalities in social status. "The Bishop Orders His Tomb" offers a similar parody of courtship when the old ecclesiastic turns his death bed into a satyr's bed and acts out in fantasy a kind of sexual seduction of his late mistress but fails in his "courtship" of the heirs. But whereas the Bishop's failure is largely a result of the disparity between the two kinds of "courtship," the Duke's substitution of a verbal and dramatic mode of "seduction" provides him with a vicarious thrill. His private satisfaction is to that extent a "mystery" and admittedly more important to the Duke than the purchase of a dowry, as he himself avows, though without ever understanding in what sense his repudiation of the financial motivation is valid. His rhetoric is a parody of disinterested persuasion, designed less to sway an auditor than to gratify that psychotic need of dominion and ownership which compels him to treat the envoy, like his "last Duchess," as another stage property.

The Duke's spellbinding performance before his auditor enables him to glory in what Kenneth Burke has called "an aesthetic of crime which is infused, however perversely, with the 'mystery' of aristocracy."[5] He represents "aristocratic vice," criminality that has the appeal of dramatic style. This is because Browning has cast the Duke as the outrageous producer of a social play which must bring into harmony with the prejudices of the speaker's own taste every spontaneous action of the Duchess. The Duke's theatrical sense, finely adjusted and revealing no more than a shadow of concern with the nominal purpose of his interview, results in the removal of the speaker from the reader and in the willed isolation of his person. He is the compulsive producer who must re-enact on a stage flattering to his thwarted ego the drama of his past domestic life, and who, with all the craft of the spellbinder's art, deliberately sets out to control the responses of the envoy. The Duke's treatment of his auditor is strikingly rhetorical; he gives evidence of what Burke would call a "pantomimic" morality always on the alert for slight advantages. Even his self-abasement before his visitor is a form of self-exaltation, "the first 'stratagem' of pride."

Thus, to see Browning's Duke as a theatrical producer is not to suspend our moral judgment of him. The intellectual sympathy that allows Browning to understand a point of view so different from his own allows him to uncover its internal contradictions. Beneath the

5. *A Rhetoric of Motives*, p. 145.

surface brilliance lies the doom of Auden's "intellectuals without love." The poem's last phrase, "for me," re-establishes the whole proprietary nature of the Duke and rules out any possibility of a final redemption before he disappears forever by descending the staircase into what is at once a literary immortality and in insolently courted hell of personal damnation. The speaker is as surely imprisoned by his senses as any inhabitant of Dante's Inferno. Only an interpretation of this kind can account for the complex moral and aesthetic response which Browning's Duke arouses. The present reading enriches existing ideas about the poem by linking a disciplined attention to rhetoric with the hypothesis that the Duke is staging a "show" which enables him to transform his domestic past into what he believes it should have been. The Duchess, of course, may be the victim and the envoy the stooge, but only the Duke, in his bland amorality, is duped. The craft of the producer, whose theatrical self fiercely wills the extinction of every other self, becomes a metaphor for the damnation of all self-deceived and egocentric men.

HAROLD BLOOM

Browning's "Childe Roland": All Things Deformed and Broken†

"What in the midst lay but the Tower itself?" The quester, "after a life spent training for the sight," sees nothing but everything he has estranged from himself. Browning's poem, to me his finest, is a crucial test for any reader, but peculiarly so for a reader rendered aware of Romantic tradition, and the anxieties fostered by its influence. What happens in the poem, difficult to determine, perhaps impossible to know with final assurance, depends upon the reader's judgment of Roland, the poem's speaker. How far can he be trusted in recounting his own catastrophe?

On New Year's Day, 1852, in Paris, Browning strenuously resolved to write a poem a day, a resolution kept for a fortnight, producing successively in its first three days *Women and Roses*, "*Childe Roland to the Dark Tower Came*," and *Love Among The Ruins*.[1] *Women and Roses*, as William Clyde DeVane commented, is wholly uncharacteristic of its poet, and is far likelier to

† From Harold Bloom, *The Ringers in the Tower: Studies in Romantic Tradition* (Chicago and London: The University of Chicago Press, 1971), pp. 157–67. Footnotes below are by editor.

1. The order given by Browning's biographers is "Love Among the Ruins" (Jan. 1), "Women and Roses" (Jan. 2), and "Childe Roland" (Jan. 3); see *BRP*, p. 293.

make current readers think of Yeats than of Browning. Its curious structure alternates tercets and nine-line stanzas, the tercets introducing the roses of a dream-vision, and the longer stanzas presenting the poet's almost frantic responses to the vision's sexual appeal. Past, present, and future women dance to one cadence, each circling their rose on the poet's rose tree, and each evading his attempts "to possess and be possessed." Even the prophetic vision, a kind of Yeatsian *antithetical* influx, refuses the maker's shapings:

> What is far conquers what is near.
> Roses will bloom nor want beholders,
> Spring from the dust where our flesh moulders,
> What shall arrive with the cycle's change?
> A novel grace and a beauty strange.
> I will make an Eve, be the artist that began her,
> Shaped her to his mind!—Alas! in like manner
> They circle the rose on my rose tree.

Browning's experience of what Blake called the Female Will had been confined largely to his mother and his wife, neither of whom he had shaped to his mind; rather he had yielded to both. If *Women and Roses* indeed was "the record of a vivid dream" DeVane), then the dream was of reality, and not a wish-fulfillment. A greater, though nightmare, vision of reality came the next day.

> My first thought was, he lied in every word,
>   That hoary cripple, with malicious eye
>   Askance to watch the working of his lie
> On mine, and mouth scarce able to afford
> Suppression of the glee, that pursed and scored
>   Its edge, at one more victim gained thereby.
>
> What else should he be set for, with his staff?
>   What, save to waylay with his lies, ensnare
>   All travellers who might find him posted there,
> And ask the road? I guessed what skull-like laugh
> Would break, what crutch 'gin write my epitaph
>   For pastime in the dusty thoroughfare,
>
> If at his counsel I should turn aside
>   Into that ominous tract which, all agree,
>   Hides the Dark Tower.

The cripple's motives, the actual look of him, even whether his mouth worked with suppressed glee or with terror, or compassion, or whatever, we will never know, for we have only Childe Roland's monologue, and it takes less than the first fifteen lines he speaks for us to suspect all his impressions. Whether, if we rode by his side, we too would see all things deformed and broken, would depend

upon the degree to which we shared in his desperation, his hopeless-
ness not only of his quest but of himself and of all questings and
questers. Why not throw up the irksome charge at once? If Roland
tempts us to this question, asked of Paracelsus by Festus in the second of Browning's Shelleyan quest-romances, we can be assuaged by
the great charlatan's reply:

> A task, a task!
> But wherefore hide the whole
> Extent of degradation once engaged
> In the confessing vein? Despite of all
> My fine talk of obedience and repugnance,
> Docility and what not, 'tis yet to learn
> If when the task shall really be performed,
> My inclination free to choose once more,
> I shall do aught but slightly modify
> The nature of the hated task I quit.
> In plain words, I am spoiled . . .
> . . . God! how I essayed
> To live like that mad poet, for a while,
> To love alone; and how I felt too warped
> And twisted and deformed! What should I do,
> Even though released from drudgery, but return
> Faint, as you see, and halting, blind and sore,
> To my old life and die as I began?
> I cannot feed on beauty for the sake
> Of beauty only, nor can drink in balm
> From lovely objects for their loveliness;
> My nature cannot lose her first imprint;
> I still must hoard and heap and class all truths
> With one ulterior purpose: I must know!
>
> . . . .
> . . . alas,
> I have addressed a frock of heavy mail
> Yet may not join the troop of sacred knights;
> And now the forest-creatures fly from me,
> The grass-banks cool, the sunbeams warm no more,
> Best follow, dreaming that ere night arrive,
> I shall o'ertake the company and ride
> Glittering as they!

This company, in *"Childe Roland to the Dark Tower Came,"* has
become "The Band" of failures, who glitter only in the Yeatsian
Condition of Fire that Roland enters also in his dying:

> There they stood, ranged along the hillsides, met
> To view the last of me, a living frame
> For one more picture! in a sheet of flame
> I saw them and I knew them all.

The company of Browning scholars, notably DeVane, F. A.

Pottle, W. O. Raymond, and Betty Miller, have charted for us the complexities of Browning's Shelleyan heritage, and his equivocal denial of that heritage. Mrs. Miller in particular reads *Childe Roland* in the context of the denial, as a poem of retribution appropriate to Browning's own sin in murdering his earlier, Shelleyan self as a sacrifice to his Oedipal anxieties, to his love for his Evangelical mother. The poem, like Coleridge's three poems of natural magic, *Christabel, The Ancient Mariner, Kubla Khan*, becomes a ballad of the imagination's revenge against the poet's unpoetic nature, against his failure to rise out of the morass of family romance into the higher romance of the autonomous spirit questing for evidences of its own creative election. Mrs. Miller's view seems to me the indispensable entry into Browning's darkest and most powerful romance, and once within we will find the fullest phenomenology of a consciousness of creative failure available to us in our language, fuller even than in Coleridge, whose censorious and magnificent intellect fought back too effectively against romance, in the holy name of the Logos. Browning embraced that name also, but in *Childe Roland* happily the embrace is evaded, and a terrible opening to vision is made instead.

If we go a day past *Childe Roland's* composition, to 3 January 1852, we find the indefatigable Browning writing *Love Among The Ruins*, where fallen Babylon exposes only a ruined tower:

> Now,—the single little turret that remains
>   On the plains,
> By the caper overrooted, by the gourd
>   Overscored,
> While the patching houseleek's head of blossom winks
>   Through the chinks—
> Marks the basement whence a tower in ancient time
>   Sprang sublime,
> And a burning ring. . . .

It is "the Tower itself," but a day later, still "the round squat turret, blind as the fool's heart," but seen now in the mundane, nightmare fallen away into ruin, and Browning, blind to the night's lessons, falls back on: "Love is best." Doubtless it is, when the quester is free to find it, or be found by it. Shelley, who knew more about love than Browning, or most men (before or since), had the capacity of a stronger visionary, to confront the image of nightmare in the mundane:

> —so, o'er the lagune
> We glided; and from that funeral bark
> I leaned, and saw the city, and could mark
> How from their many isles, in evening's gleam,
> Its temples and its palaces did seem

Like fabrics of enchantment piled to Heaven.
I was about to speak, when—"We are even
Now at the point I meant," said Maddalo,
And bade the gondolieri cease to row.
"Look, Julian, on the west, and listen well
If you hear not a deep and heavy bell."
I looked, and saw between us and the sun
A building on an island; such a one
As age to age might add, for uses vile,
A windowless, deformed and dreary pile;
And on the top an open tower, where hung
A bell, which in the radiance swayed and swung
We could just hear its hoarse and iron tongue:
The broad sun sunk behind it, and it tolled
In strong and black relief.—
. . . .
"And such," he cried, "is our mortality,
And this must be the emblem and the sign
Of what should be eternal and divine!—
And like that black and dreary bell, the soul,
Hung in a heaven-illumined tower, must toll
Our thoughts and our desires to meet below
Round the rent heart and pray—as madmen do
For what? they know not—till the night of death
As sunset that strange vision, severeth
Our memory from itself, and us from all
We sought and yet were baffled."[2]

Though it is not traditional to find in this passage one of the
"sources" of *Childe Roland*, it seems to me the truest precursor to
Browning's poem, on evidence both internal and external. It lay
deep in his mind as he wrote his poem, and emerged in the emblem
of the commonplace yet unique tower where the quester is met by
his career's ambiguous truth, and triumphantly accepts destruction
by that truth. Externals can be postponed until Roland's truth
meets us in the poem, but the internal evidence of Romantic tradition finds us even as we enter Roland's realm of appearances, and
are accosted by his "hoary cripple," an amalgam of Spenser's Archi-
mago, Spenser's Despair, Shakespeare's Gloucester from *Lear*, and
perhaps Ahasuerus, the Wandering Jew of Shelley's *Queen Mab*
and *Hellas*. Gloucester as seen by Cornwall, I should amend, for the
verbal origins of *Childe Roland* are in the snatch of verse sung by
Edgar before his father suffers Cornwall's version of the Dark
Tower:

"Child Rowland to the dark tower came.
His word was still 'Fie, foh, and fum,
I smell the blood of a British man.' "

2. *Julian and Maddalo* (1818), lines 87–106, 120–30.

But the Browning version of the ogre is a *daimon* of self-betrayal, and the reader needs to trace influence in the manner of Borges, rather than of Lowes,[3] if source-study is to help in reading this poem. Kafka and Yeats, Gnostic[4] visionaries, are closer to the poem than Spenser and Shakespeare, or even Shelley, who in a true sense is the poem's pervasive subject, the betrayed ideal whose spirit haunts Roland, whose love chastizes Roland's way of knowing until it becomes a knowing that deforms and breaks all things it lights upon, and finds "all dark and comfortless," the blinded Gloucester's answer to Cornwall's vile taunt: "Where is thy luster now?"

To recognize Childe Roland as a Gnostic quester is to begin reading his poem as if it were a Borges parable of self-entrapment, another labyrinth made by men that men must decipher. A Gnostic quester is necessarily a kind of Quietist, for whom every landscape is infernal, and every shrine a squalor. In Shelleyan quest the objects of desire tend to touch the vanishing point of the visual and auditory, but the field of quest remains attractive, though not benign. Childe Roland moves in the Gnostic nightmare, where all natural context even looks and sounds malevolent, and the only goal of desire is to fail.

The greatest power of Browning's romance inheres not in its landscape (in which we are too ready to believe) but in the extraordinary, negative intensity of Childe Roland's consciousness, which brings to defeat an energy of perception so exuberant as to mock defeat's limits. This energy is very close to the remorseless drive of Shelley's Poet in *Alastor*, or of Shelley himself in *Epipsychidion*. The landscape of *"Childe Roland to the Dark Tower Came,"* like that of *Alastor*, is charged by the quester's own furious, self-frustrated energy, and cannot at last contain that energy. When Childe Roland burns through the context he has invented, in his closing epiphany, he sees and hears all things he has made and marred, or rather made by breaking, himself and his vision, everything finally except the landscape of estrangement he has been seeing all through the poem. "Burningly it came on me all at once," he says, and "it" is place imagined into full meaning, an uncovering so complete as to be triumph whatever else comes to him. The Roland who sets the slughorn to his lips does not accept a Gnostic conclusion, but ranges himself with those who have sounded the trumpet of a prophecy to unawakened earth. A poem that commenced in the

3. I.e., the eclectic approach of the modern Argentinian writer and critic Jorge Luis Borges (who has traced his leading metaphors through wide-ranging research into recondite literature) rather than the more restrictive method of John Livingston Lowes in *The Road to Xanadu* (1927); Lowes demonstrated that images from Coleridge's reading were stored in his unconscious mind until fused imaginatively in the creative act.
4. Adherent of ancient cult which held matter to be evil; emancipation is reached through *gnosis*, immediate knowledge of spiritual truth.

spirit of *The Castle* or *Meditations in a Time of Civil War*[5] concludes itself deliberately in the Orphic spirit of the *Ode to the
West Wind's* last stanza.

Browning dates his *Introductory Essay* on Shelley[6] as "Paris,
December 4th, 1851," a month before the composition of *Childe
Roland*. The *Essay* on Shelley is, with one exception, Browning's
only prose work of consequence, the exception being the *Essay on
Tasso and Chatterton* done a decade before *Childe Roland*. In
Julian and Maddalo the "windowless, deformed and dreary pile"
with its "open tower" and "hoarse and iron tongue" of a tolling
bell is the madhouse of Tasso's confinement, and one can surmise
that "the round squat turret, blind as the fool's heart" has some
intimate relation to the madness of poets. Chatterton, coupled with
Tasso by Browning as a victimized mad poet, enters *Childe Roland*
at the close with the slug-horn, a nonexistent instrument that appears
only in his works, by a corruption of "slogan." As a cry-to-battle by
a crazed, self-defeated poet, its appropriateness is overwhelming at
Childe Roland's end. The *Essay on Tasso and Chatterton* is essentially a defense of Chatterton's assumption of the mask of Rowley,
anticipating Browning's extraordinary essay on Shelley, with its
implicit defense of Browning's assumption of the many masks of his
mature poetry. Contrasting Shakespeare as the objective poet to
Shelley as the subjective (and thus helping Yeats to his antinomies
of *primary* and *antithetical* in *A Vision*), Browning asks an unan-
swerable question about the unknowable objective artist:

> Did the personality of such an one stand like an open watch-
> tower in the midst of the territory it is erected to gaze on, and
> were the storms and calms, the stars and meteors, its watchman
> was wont to report of, the habitual variegation of his everyday
> life, as they glanced across its open door or lay reflected on its
> four-square parapet?

No such question need be asked concerning the subjective poet,
who is a seer, not a fashioner, and so produces "less a work than an
effluence." The open tower of Shelley radiates "its own self-sacrificing central light," making possible what Browning calls "his noblest
and predominating characteristic":

> This I call his simultaneous perception of Power and Love in
> the absolute, and of Beauty and Good in the concrete, while he
> throws, from his poet's station between both, swifter, subtler, and
> more numerous films for the connection of each with each, than
> have been thrown by any modern artificer of whom I have
> knowledge . . .

5. I.e., exhibiting the abject yearning for order and grace that mark Kafka's novel *The Castle* (1926) and Yeats' poem "Meditations in Time of Civil War" (1923). Orphic: prophetic.
6. See above, pp. 445–52.

Browning was thirty-nine when he wrote his Shelley essay, and then its sequel in *Childe Roland*. At thirty-nine the imagination has learned that no spring can flower past meridian, and in one sense we can regard *Childe Roland* as a classical poem of the fortieth year. Shelley had died in his thirtieth year, but his imagination might have declined the lesson in any case, for no imagination was ever so impatient of our staler realities, and Browning, who was a superb reader of Shelley, would have known this. Reading Shakespeare for his Shelley essay, Browning came upon Edgar's assumption of a mask, and his ballad-lines of the Dark Tower, and yoked together in his creative mind highly disparate towers. The *Essay on Shelley* twice names *Julian and Maddalo* as a major example of the poet's art, once citing it among "successful instances of objectivity" together with "the unrivalled Cenci." Browning is critically acute, for the landscape of *Julian and Maddalo* is not only marvelously rendered, but is one of the rare instances in nineteenth-century poetry of a landscape *not* estranged from the self, and so not seen merely as a portion of the self expelled:

> I rode one evening with Count Maddalo
> Upon the bank of land which breaks the flow
> Of Adria towards Venice: a bare strand
> Of hillocks, heaped from ever-shifting sand,
> Matted with thistles and amphibious weeds,
> Such as from earth's embrace the salt ooze breeds,
> Is this; an uninhabited sea-side,
> Which the lone fisher, when his nets are dried,
> Abandons; and no other object breaks
> The waste, but one dwarf tree and some few stakes
> Broken and unrepaired, and the tide makes
> A narrow space of level sand thereon,
> Where 'twas our wont to ride when day went down,
> This ride was my delight. I love all waste
> And solitary places; where we taste
> The pleasure of believing what we see
> Is boundless, as we wish our souls to be.[7]

This rider experiencing the Sublime is the polar contrary to Childe Roland, and to the mad poet dwelling in the "windowless, deformed and dreary pile;/And on the top an open tower," who in some sense is Roland's *daimon* or true self. In the debate between Shelley (as Julian) and Lord Byron (as Count Maddalo) it is Shelley who insists on the quester's will as being central and capable, and Byron who maintains a darker wisdom, to which Shelley, unlike Roland (or Browning), quietly declines surrender:

7. *Julian and Maddalo*, lines 1–17.

> "—it is our will
> That thus enchains us to permitted ill—
> We might be otherwise—we might be all
> We dream of happy, high majestical.
> Where is the love, beauty, and truth we seek
> But in our mind? and if we were not weak
> Should we be less in deed than in desire?"
> "Ay, if we were not weak—and we aspire
> How vainly to be strong!" said Maddalo:
> "You talk Utopia." "It remains to know,"
> I then rejoined, "and those who try may find
> How strong the chains are which our spirit bind;
> Brittle perchance as straw . . . we are assured
> Much may be conquered, much may be endured,
> Of what degrades and crushes us. We know
> That we have power over ourselves to do
> And suffer—what, we know not till we try;
> But something nobler than to live and die—"

The passage might well be epigraph to *Childe Roland*. Shelley, the sun-treading spirit of imaginative reproach or true Apollo of *Pauline*, the "mad poet" who sought love as opposed to Paracelsus's quest for knowledge, the spirit still not exorcised in *Sordello*, gives to *Childe Roland* and its nightmare landscape a sense of a hidden god, a presence felt by the void of its total absence. Roland rides across a world without imagination, seeing everywhere "such starved ignoble nature," his own, as he follows" my darkening path" to its conclusion.

DeVane found much of the "source" material for Roland's landscape in Gerard de Lairesse's *The Art of Painting in All its Branches*, a book Browning remembered as having read "more often and with greater delight, when I was a child, than any other." Lairesse, celebrated by Browning in the late *Parleyings*, gathered together the horrible in painting, as he saw it, in his Chapter 17, *Of Things Deformed and Broken, Falsely called Painter-like*, and DeVane demonstrated how many details Browning took from the one chapter, probably unknowingly. Childe Roland, like Browning, is painter as well as poet, and dies as a living picture, framed by "all the lost adventurers my peers," who like him found all things deformed and broken.

All this is the living circumference of *"Childe Roland to the Dark Tower Came"*; we move to the central meaning when we ponder the sorrow of this quester, this *aware* solipsist whose self-recognition has ceased to be an avenue to freedom. When Roland ceased to imagine (before his poem opens) he made it inevitable that he should be *found by* his phantasmagoria. By marching into that land of his own terrible force of failed will, he compels himself to know the degradation of what it is to be illuminated while himself giving no light. For this is the anxiety of influence, in that variety of poetic melancholy that issues from the terrible strength of post-Enlightenment literary tradition. Where *Childe Roland* excels, and makes its greatness as a poem, is in its unique and appalling swerve, its twist or Lucretian *clinamen* away from its precursors, from the whole line of internalized romance, and from Shelley in particular. This swerve is the vision of the end, where *all* the poets of the Romantic tradition are seen as having failed, to the degree where they stand together, ranged in the living flame, the fire the Promethean quester could not steal but had to burn through.

Yet Childe Roland dies in the courage of knowing—he too sees, and he knows, and so dies with a full intelligence as what Keats called an atom of perception; at the close, he ceases to be a figure of romance, for he knows too much.

Thomas Greene, in a superb insight, speaks of "the mystery and melancholy of romance, which always accepts less than total knowledge," since total knowledge successfully resists enchantment. Romance in *Childe Roland* passes into what George Ridenour has called "the typical mode," which though allegoric is yet allegorically self-contained, as though Browning's poem were that odd conceit, an allegory of allegorizing. Ridenour, in the most illuminating critical remarks yet made about the poem, relates the knight's trial by landscape (his reduced *geste*) to Browning's obsessive investigations into the nature of purposeful human act, and finds the poem to be finally a celebration. All men are questers, and capable of rising into the Burkean Sublime, however purposeless or compulsive their acts as they blunder toward goals both commonplace and unique, like the Dark Tower. Whether this is entirely celebration, since Roland fails his trial by landscape, may be doubted, but the triumphant surge of the end gives Ridenour considerable sanction, making his reading of the poem closer to what must be presumed as Browning's also than my own or Mrs. Miller's is.

If we follow Mrs. Miller by returning to the passage from *Paracelsus* quoted earlier in this essay, we can say that Roland is being punished, by himself, for having quested after knowledge rather than love, the punishment being to see all things as deformed and broken. One of Wordsworth's central insights is that to see without love, to see by knowing, is to deform and break, and Roland would thus exemplify a terrible Romantic truth. But this is to read as reductively as Roland sees, and to miss the awful greatness of Roland's landscape. Browning took Roland from Edgar's song, but giving the name to a quester means to invoke also, in some way, the rich romance associations of the name. In the *Chanson de Roland* the knight's loyalty to his lord, Charlemagne, is exemplary, and the final blast of his trumpet is a supreme self-sacrifice. In Ariosto though, Orlando is insane and disloyal through love's madness, with the love being silly, wretched, and unrequited at that. In contrast to Browning's Roland, we can say of Tasso, Chatterton, and Shelley, his precursors in the band of questers, what Yeats said of certain Irish poets and rebels who had confounded his expectations, that excess of love may have bewildered them until they died. But if the romance quest is, as Angus Fletcher suggests in his powerful study of allegory, an obsessive pattern of desire that becomes a compulsive act, then Browning's Roland too is journeying to rebeget himself, despite his conscious desire only to make an end, any end. Though he finds, and is annihilated in finding, an extraordinary if only partly communicable knowledge, the meaning of his quest was still in his search for love. Love of whom? Of his precursors, the band of brothers who, one by one, "failed" triumphantly at the Dark Tower. A poet's love for another poet is no more disinterested than any other variation upon family romance, but a final knowledge that it was indeed love may be the revelation that makes for a kind of triumph, though not a salvation, at a dark end.

F. E. L. PRIESTLEY

Blougram's Apologetics†

Most interpretations of "Bishop Blougram's Apology" have started with the assumption that the poem represents one of Browning's attempts to present the best that a generally contemptible character can say for himself, "an attempt to make a case for a sophistical and indulgent priest at his possible worst."[1] Such interpretations give to the word *apology* its popular meaning of a confession of error with a plea for lenience in judgment. As Miss Naish pointed out long ago, Browning's reported comments to Duffy are hard to reconcile with this view of the poem; if Browning drew a portrait of Wiseman as "a vulgar, fashionable priest, justifying his own cowardice,"[2] yet declared that the portrait was not a satire,

† From *University of Toronto Quarterly*, 15 (1946), 139–47.

1. W. C. DeVane, *A Browning Handbook* (New York, 1935), p. 215. Cf. E. Dowden, *Robert Browning* (London, 1904), pp. 197ff.: "a nineteenth century sceptic's exposition of his Christian faith." Cf. also J. Fotheringham, *Studies of the Mind and Art of Robert Browning* (London, 1898), pp. 363ff. Recognition in various degrees of what I take to be Browning's real intention is to be found in E. M. Naish, *Browning and Dogma* (London, 1908), pp. 63–91; J. A. Hutton, *Guidance from Robert Browning in Matters of Faith* (Edinburgh and London, 1903), pp. 24–42; and C. R. Tracy, "Bishop Blougram" (*Modern Language Review*, 34 [1939]), 422–25: "Browning's real purpose was to comment on the problem of faith in a sceptical world."

2. G. K. Chesterton, *Robert Browning* (New York, 1903), p. 201.

and had "nothing hostile about it,"[3] then Browning was either a hypocrite more brazen than Gigadibs thought Blougram, or incredibly naive.

As a matter of fact, the critics in general, even Miss Naish, have paid too little attention to the significance of the title, and far too little attention to Gigadibs. The whole monologue is an *apology* in the sense of a piece of apologetics; its whole course is dictated by Gigadibs. In no other monologue of Browning's is the *muta persona* so important; in no other monologue is Browning so careful to keep us aware of the presence of the auditor. Every word of the Bishop's is uttered with a full understanding of the character of his guest, and of what his guest is thinking.

Consider for a moment who Gigadibs is, and why he is in the Bishop's presence. Gigadibs is a thirty year old journalist, ambitious for "success" (if his name means anything, success in terms of a gig and "dibs"). His contributions to *Blackwood's* have so far attracted no attention; his scholarly work, as yet unprinted, consists of "two points in Hamlet's soul Unseized by the Germans yet"; his one success is an imitation of Dickens, a piece of sensational journalism with a second-hand literary flavour. His mind is that of the ordinary third-rate journalist; the Bishop calls him "You . . . the rough and ready man who write apace,/Read somewhat seldom, think perhaps even less"; he is on the alert for the sensational, the dramatic antithesis, "the honest thief, the tender murderer./The superstitious atheist"; he needs simple labels, neat summary phrases, "man of sense and learning too,/The able to think yet act, the this, the that," to embody these dramatic journalistic contrasts. Phrases, indeed, serve him instead of thought; he has never pursued thoughts far enough to reach solid ground; his opinions are "loose cards,/Flung daily down, and not the same way twice."

In his own estimation, however, Gigadibs is no ordinary figure. He is an artist-soul, with the artist's nobility of aim and stern integrity; "clever to a fault"; proud of his scepticism. since to him unbelief is a sign of honest thinking; proud of his vague aspirations, of his insistence on being himself, "imperial, plain and true," proud of his rigid certainty that "truth is truth."

He has come to interview the Bishop with a purpose perfectly evident to Blougram from the start. To Gigadibs, it is a self-evident proposition that intelligence and religious faith are incompatible. Consequently, Blougram must be either an imbecile or a hypocrite, a fool or a knave. And he is obviously no fool. Gigadibs is confident that, if granted an interview, he, the shrewd journalist, the trained ferret, can surely penetrate the pretence, and expose the impostor; through his skilful questioning, Blougram can be led to make "The

3. *Ibid.*, p. 188.

Eccentric Confidence," to admit, at least by implication, that "he's quite above their humbug in his heart."

His very presence is an insult to the Bishop. The problem facing Blougram is quite clear; Gigadibs is a recognizable type, and represents a familiar point of view. To insist that a man may be intelligent and yet accept the articles of Christian faith would merely confirm Gigadibs in his belief that the Bishop is a hypocrite. Moreover, Blougram, nettled by the reporter's smug self-conceit, his secure conviction of the rightness of his own point of view, his patronizing assumption of superior integrity, is in no mood for defence. Gigadibs has arrived, has spoken his home truths, has challenged Blougram to say what he can for his way of life, assuming always that his own way of life is the only one compatible with truth, honesty, and a lofty morality. Blougram is far from ready to admit that his own is the vulnerable position. He is not defending, but attacking. He has no great hope of changing Gigadibs' prejudices; he can perhaps make him realize that even the Gigadibsian philosophy, beautiful as it is in its simplicity, is not uniquely coherent and reasonable. Being a skilled apologist, he recognizes the necessity for attacking on his opponent's ground; since Gigadibs would scornfully reject all the Bishop's premises, the arguments must proceed from premises acceptable to the sceptic. Throughout, Blougram uses the apologetic method, stating Gigadibs' objections fairly and strongly, then replying to them. The stages in the argument are quite clear in the Bishop's mind as he drives Gigadibs systematically from one position to another, at every point anticipating the movements of his hearer's thoughts.

The Bishop is so much master of the situation, so much superior to his opponent, that he permits himself flourishes, or scores a point with insulting ease. The whole performance is shot through with irony, and Blougram enjoys it. He enjoys particularly giving Gigadibs the impression that he is about to hear what he has come to hear. ("These hot long ceremonies of our church Cost us a little— oh, they pay the price, You take me—amply pay it!" Is this a bit of the "truth that peeps Over the glasses' edge?" Or does "price" hold two possible meanings?) Gigadibs' naive conviction that a few glasses of wine will lead an intelligent prelate into indiscreet utterance, and the sight of the eager face across the table, waiting for the wine to work and the eccentric confidence to flow, offer Blougram tempting opportunities. He opens and closes the interview on the same theme: he begins by explaining, to Gigadibs' embarrassment, the sort of confidence Gigadibs expects, and ends by a challenge to Gigadibs to publish what he has learned. The full irony of the challenge is apparent only to those who stop to consider exactly what Gigadibs has learned in the course of the conversation. That will appear if we follow the conversation step by step.

As it opens, Blougram is examining Gigadibs' charges against him, his grounds for despising him. These are: first, that the Bishop's official position implies the possession of a religious faith which in Gigadibs' opinion is impossible to an intelligent man; and secondly, that the Bishop is less ascetic and other-worldly than a bishop, in Gigadibs' opinion, ought to be. If these charges were being made by a pious ascetic, they would be coherent; but they are proceeding from a sceptic and secularist, from one who denies the validity of the religious ideal and the utility of the ascetic ideal. Blougram at once proceeds to the attack. When Gigadibs condemns Blougram's way of life, what is his criterion? What is the ideal way of life by which he is measuring Blougram's? Gigadibs has not thought the matter out; he is sure only that he would like to be something distinguished (Blougram offers an anti-climactic trio of possibilities) and that the chief quality to be sought is integrity, which of course the Bishop lacks. Even as Pope, Blougram could not, thinks Gigadibs, realize the majestic ideal of being himself, "imperial, plain and true."

At this point, a less skilful apologist would have at once challenged Gigadibs' assumption of the unworthiness of the Bishop's way of life. But Blougram is patient and shrewd. The only approach to Gigadibs is through premises he will accept. By way of preliminary groundwork, then, the Bishop establishes the basic premise that a plan of life must relate to life as it is, not to an "abstract intellectual plan of life," but to the life "a man, who is man and nothing more, may lead." This is a premise which Gigadibs must accept. As a sceptic, he cannot admit other-worldly criteria; any admission that man is more than man, the natural being, makes his whole case against Blougram collapse. Measured by his own this-worldly criterion, then, is Gigadibs' plan of life superior to the Bishop's? If mundane values are the only ones we can accept, whose life is the better fitted to realize those values? This question, framed playfully in the "cabin" analogy, confronts Gigadibs at the outset with the basic problem of values, and tends to force him into a recognition of the inconsistency of his own axiology. If no other values than the simply material must guide our plan of life, then why is not the life of a bishop a choice one, since it brings the good things of this world (apart from any other good things)? Why will not Gigadibs be a bishop too?

Gigadibs' answer comes rapidly: he can't believe in any revelation called divine; that is, believe "fixedly And absolutely and exclusively." As Blougram indicates at this point, a great deal depends on what "believe" means, but discussion of that can come later. He is ready to admit ("To you, and over the wine") that there are doctrinal difficulties he cannot solve, dogmas he cannot "believe" in Gigdibs' sense of the word. But before considering the nature of faith, the Bishop proposes to start from Gigadibs' premise of the necessity of total unbelief ("I mean to meet you on your own premise") and examine its consequences.

Since they are both agreed that the primary concern of man is to find the fittest, most coherent way of life, Blougram raises the question, how can we make unbelief bear fruit to us? Gigadibs has challenged the utility of belief; now he must show the utility of unbelief. But first, again by way of applying Gigadibs' own logic to his argument, since he will not accept anything but complete and perfect belief, can he accept anything but complete and perfect unbelief? and how can he be certain of complete unbelief? This argument, combined perhaps with the warmth and evident sincerity of Blougram's assertion of the possibility of a divine purpose, leads Gigadibs to abandon his position of positive unbelief for the agnostic "chess-board."

Blougram is now ready for the next stage in the argument. "We'll proceed a step." The problem of belief or unbelief is not a simple matter of choice between equally tenable propositions of a theoretic nature. "Belief or unbelief Bears upon life, determines its whole course." Every act implies a faith; every effort a man makes implies faith in the value of what he strives for. The only consistent course for the thorough unbeliever is to keep his bed, to "abstain from healthy acts that prove you man." Even on the basis of material values, if Gigadibs wishes to exclude all others, the Bishop can show success in gaining the world's estimation, and its good things. If the sensitive artistic idealism of Gigadibs is repelled by the blunt way in which Blougram proclaims the goodness of worldly power and comforts, he must remember that consistent materialism admits only material values, naturalism only natural values, and draw his own conclusions. At this point he is ready to concede that "it's best believing if we may." He is next asked to concede, still on his own premises of unbelief, that "if once we choose belief, . . . We can't be too decisive in our faith. . . To suit the world which gives us the good things." Success in life (that is, in material terms of riches, honour, pleasure, work, repose) does not come to the indifferent; whatever a man chooses to pursue, we do not call him a fool "so long as he's consistent with his choice." The choice once made is irrevocable. Blougram's own choice, viewed (in accordance with the agreed premise of unbelief) from the merely material point of view, has given his life a singleness and continuity of purpose, and has brought the material returns. Gigadibs would object here that the Bishop's taste is gross; that were he made of "better elements" he would not call this sort of life successful. Again Blougram draws his attention to the logical inconsistency. Gigadibs is denying the validity of the ascetic ideal, and condemning the Bishop for not following it; he is proclaiming that the Bishop cannot be genuinely religious, yet blaming him for not being so. "Grant I'm a beast," says Blougram, "why, beasts must lead beasts' lives." Gigadibs is trying to have it both ways. Again the "cabin" is brought out to remind him that the discussion is concerned with living life as it is, not as it might be.

But the Bishop is by no means willing to grant that he is a beast; the patronizing assumption of moral superiority by Gigadibs is not patently justified. Gigadibs feels himself nobler simply because he is thoroughly convinced that Blougram is fool or hypocrite, and that he "pines among his million imbeciles" uneasily conscious of the piercing eyes of the Gigadibsian experts. As Verdi looked towards the true judge of music, Rossini. so must Blougram look towards the true judge of values, Gigadibs. But is a journalist the most expert judge of values, of ideals, of men? Is the journalistic habit of mind a critical habit? or does it rather seek the sensational, "see more in a truth than the truth's simple self," find interest only "on the dangerous edge of things," and strive to distinguish only by "gross weights, coarse scales and labels broad?" Why may not the simple truth be that Blougram actually believes what he professes to believe?

But even granted that Blougram's life is not one which Gigadibs can approve, what is his ideal? The direct question disconcerts Gigadibs; it is one thing to be complacently aware of lofty, if vague, aspirations; to define them is another matter involving more rigorous thinking. The Bishop waits in vain, then offers suggestions. Suppose that Gigadibs aspires to be a Napoleon, a man of action, and granted that he has the requisite qualities ("A large concession, clever as you are," says Blougram), then, remembering that we are still accepting the Gigadibsian premise of unbelief ("We can't believe, you know—We're still at that admission, recollect!"), what guiding principle will justify the life? What possible admirable worldly end can explain such a career? "What's the vague good o' the world, for which you dare With comfort to yourself blow millions up?" If this life is all, Napoleon wins a "dozen noisy years" and "ugly thoughts," while if "doubt may be wrong—there's judgment, life to come!" On either basis, Napoleon's life offers no admirable pattern. If not the man of action, then perhaps the great artist offers an ideal. Should we try to be Shakespeares? What aims in life did Shakespeare pursue? On the material level, he sought the kind of comfort which has come much more abundantly to Blougram: "We want the same things, Shakespeare and myself, And what I want, I have." *If this life's all*, then Blougram beats Shakespeare. With this *reductio ad absurdum* the attack on Gigadibs' first premise, the assumption of unbelief, is closed. Gigadibs is forced to recognize something beyond this life and its purely temporal and material values.

The discussion can now be moved on to an important new stage. "Believe—and our whole argument breaks up." Gigadibs has been forced by argument from his own premises to abandon them and accept the one basic premise of Blougram's position. He has been brought to acknowledge the use of faith, and as Blougram says, "We're back on Christian ground." What remains now is to proceed from that premise to Blougram's conclusion. The procedure is clearly to examine the nature of faith. Both are now agreed that "enthusiasm's the best thing," that "fire and life Are all, dead matter's nothing," and that faith has power to "penetrate our life with such a glow As fire lends wood and iron"; but fire in itself may be good or ill, enthusiasm may be well or ill directed. Moreover, how can we command it? "Paint a fire, it will not therefore burn." Gigadibs, having granted the value of enthusiasm, is inclined to restrict his approval to enthusiasm like Luther's, enthusiasm "on the denying side." But "ice makes no conflagration." Moreover, there is a limit to denying; after Luther comes Strauss, and once the denying has taught the world that it owes not a farthing (or a duty) to the Church or to St. Paul, what has been gained except the comfort (perhaps temporary) of him who denies? He may feel a Gigadibsian satisfaction at being himself, "imperial, plain and true," but the consequences of following the inner light of doubt may not be all good.

"But," objects Gigadibs, still convinced of the Bishop's secret scepticism, "imperfect faith is no more available to do faith's work than unbelief like mine. Whole faith, or none!" This is the objection Blougram has been waiting for, and, indeed, leading up to. It is time to attack Gigadibs' definition of faith, as he had promised to do earlier. ("Well, I do not believe—If you'll accept no faith that is not fixed, Absolute and exclusive, as you say. You're wrong—I mean to prove it in due time.") Faith is to be distinguished from empirical knowledge; "it is the idea, the feeling and the love, God means mankind should strive for and show forth Whatever be the process to that end." Faith is not solely an act of the intellect; it is a free act of will: "If you desire faith—then you've faith enough: What else seeks God—nay, what else seek ourselves?" "What matter though I doubt at every pore, Head-doubts, heart-doubts . . . If finally I have a life to show?" Gigadibs is demanding, not faith, but factual knowledge verifiable by the senses; like Thomas, he cannot believe until he has seen with his eyes and felt with his hands. Belief, he thinks, must have been easy centuries ago; he might believe in Genesis if he could meet the traveller who has seen the ark. But, Blougram points out, intellectual assent does not constitute a living belief. The important question is not "what could you accept?" but "how should you feel, in such an age, How act?"

Faith is something to live by; when it means an inner struggle with doubt, then "A man's worth something." At worst, a struggle to maintain the most difficult beliefs is at all events better than "acquitting God with grace."

If Gigadibs thinks that there have been times, or that there are places, in which belief as he defines it has ever prevailed, he is wrong. No intellectual acceptance of religious doctrines has ever been qualitatively the same as the acceptance of empirically observed experience. No "ragamuffin-saint Believes God watches him continually, As he believes in fire that it will burn, Or rain that it will drench him." The two sorts of knowledge, even as knowledge, are not alike, and can never be equally immediate. It is not part of the divine scheme that they should be so. "Some think, Creation's meant to show him forth: I say it's meant to hide him all it can. . . . Under a vertical sun, the exposed brain . . . less certainly would wither up at once/Than a mind, confronted with the truth of him."

It follows that the criteria to be applied to empirical knowledge are not applicable to the substance of faith. The demand to "decrassify" faith, to "experimentalize on sacred things," since it eventually means the rejection of all that cannot be empirically verified, must end in "Fichte's clever cut at God himself."

Gigadibs is still inclined to object to "leaving growths of lies unpruned," so Blougram again introduces the "cabin" analogy, to remind his hearer again that the Gigadibsian logic cannot be free to argue from diverse premises: the Bishop cannot be condemned for rejecting an empirical view of faith and in the same breath be condemned for accepting an empirical view of life. The "cabin" and the following "traveller" analogy, besides offering a logical objection, also put forward the characteristic Browning argument of the goodness and significance of this life. Whether this denial of asceticism is an important part of the Bishop's own belief does not, at this point, matter; it serves here to drive Gigadibs into asserting once and for all whether he recognizes absolute values. Presented with this clear-cut issue, Gigadibs meets it by maintaining the value of truth, and the necessity of acting up to it.

Now the attack can be pressed home: Gigadibs, who has accused the Bishop of failure to fit his life to his professed ideals, has now announced the transcendental rule by which *his* life is governed. Does he consistently live by the dictates of reason (as he would define reason) in search of truth (as he would define truth)? If he applies to natural religion the test he has used to demolish the revealed, what is left that checks his will? His behaviour is obviously not unrestrainedly amoral; upon what empirically rational grounds does he base his system of morality? Why is he chaste, for example?

After all, he rejects the religious ideal of chastity, and as for a natural law, what authority can it preserve against the analysis of the anthropologist? Natural morality can show no more validity than supernatural. Is Gigadibs chaste, then, from an instinctive feeling that self-restraint is good, and indulgence evil? If so, then his whole pretence of following "reason" breaks down with the introduction of an element which belongs not to his scheme of things, but to the Bishop's. Does he restrain himself from mere timid conformity to convention, because "your fellow-flock Open great eyes at you and even butt?" Conformity to convention can be justified on a utilitarian basis of weighing pleasures against pains, but what then becomes of the lofty pursuit of truth?

With this final challenge, Blougram has finished his argument. It is time to dismiss Gigadibs, and again the Bishop recalls why he has come. He is again aware of the ironic fact that the very worldly position which Gigadibs affects to despise him for valuing is all that makes him important in the journalist's eyes. The real lover of power, rank, luxury, and high worldly place in this same ambitious Gigadibs who is feeling so patronizingly superior. Once more the Bishop is moved to retaliate. Since it is power and social position that Gigadibs admires, it is only fitting to return his condescension with interest by reminding him of his own insignificance. The final insult is to offer the episcopal influence in the publishing world; the implications are that Gigadibs needs (or wants) the money, and that his writing is not good enough to be accepted on its own merits. The irony of the invitation to publish "The Outward-Bound" is effective and complicated. It carries a reminder of the journalist's insignificance, and it also draws attention to Gigadibs' original purpose of "exposing" the Bishop. He is now free to publish to the eager world the startling revelations that the Bishop, though not necessarily granting the good things of this world pre-eminence, does not despise them and actually enjoys good food, works of art, and a position of eminence; and that he, like most theologians, distinguishes between faith and knowledge, recognizing the activity of the will in belief. It would take more than the Dickens touch to give these revelations the sensational quality Gigadibs had anticipated. And so Gigadibs departs, still detesting Blougram perhaps, still eager to defame him, but at least not despising him as an opponent. There is a deliberate ambiguity, of course, in the Bishop's use of the word "despising."

Blougram, we are told, "believed, say, half he spoke." The rest was shaped "for argumentatory purposes." It should by now be evident enough which half Blougram believed. Quite clearly, the arguments from Gigadibsian premises are not, and are not intended to be, his own beliefs. The "arbitrary accidental thoughts That crossed his mind, amusing because new," are obviously the analogies of the "cabin" and the "traveller"; these are ingenious, are brought in more than once, and represent stages in the argument necessary for the attack on Gigadibs' assumptions. Blougram's own beliefs are indicated by the deeper tone, the heightened poetry of the expression in certain passages; they all deal with the affirmation of faith and the power of faith (ll. 182–97; 560–3; 621–5; 647–61; 693–7; 845–51). His deeper religious thoughts and feelings he did not utter, partly because they are not readily expressed, partly because their expression would have meant nothing to Gigadibs. His purpose was not to make a fruitless exposition of his own point of view for the scoffer's benefit, but to show the scoffer upon what crumbling ground his scoffing rested. After Gigadibs has seen the shallowness of his own thinking, then he can start the process of trying to reach firmer ground ("So, let him sit with me this many a year!").

But Blougram has been more successful than he had expected. Gigadibs, seized with a "sudden healthy vehemence," renounces his ambitions of power and place, of literary eminence, and sails for Australia. He has presumably found an ideal, and is proposing to follow it. Moreover, he is, apparently, intent on the study of the Gospels. He has in fact turned away from precisely those things in Blougram's career which he formerly valued, and is seeking that which he formerly despised; he who doubted above all the possibility of the life of faith is now pursuing it. The victory, unexpected to be sure in its scope, is Blougram's.

ROMA A. KING, JR.

Eve and the Virgin: "Andrea del Sarto"†

Browning characteristically begins "Andrea del Sarto" in the middle of an action, and concentrates the painter's situation into a single climactic experience. Yet before the drama is finished this pin-pointed moment has been related to the whole of Andrea's drab life. We have both the intense moment of revelation and the slow movement in time of past events which make the painter's final insight possible.

The poem is a psychological study in which the time element is an important part of structure. Andrea's initial surrender to his wife's demand that he paint for money is totally damning to the artist; its completeness and finality divert interest from what may

† From Roma A. King, Jr., *The Bow and the Lyre: The Art of Robert Browning* (Ann Arbor: The University of Michigan Press, 1957), pp. 11–31.

happen to why it has happened, from suspense in action to character analysis. The action moves from present to past, from past to
present, and, finally, to an imaginary future in the New Jerusalem.
Andrea's restless dissatisfaction with any time signals his personal
disturbances, his unwillingness to accept himself in any role, real or
imaginary, and provides a significant clue to the poem's meaning.

There can be no question about the sordidness of the present, for
Browning presents its most repelling aspects. Andrea, uncomfortable
over his capitulation to his wife, seeks renewed self-esteem in the
past which he tries to make palatable by recalling what he once was,
or what he imagines he was. A less honest nature might have found
comfort in such an escape, but Andrea, much too sensitive to be
easily deluded, is driven first to face and then to rationalize his
obvious failure. Ironically, he achieves not peace, but an increasing
self-awareness that makes the past as uncomfortable as the present.
In his primitive Garden he finds both the Tree of Knowledge and
an Eve. He comes to see that his failure is at least twofold—both as
artist and as lover—and that somehow these two are inseparably
related. His initial surrender of his art to Lucrezia is paralleled by a
final surrender of Lucrezia to her lover. From the reality of both
past and present, he is driven finally to seek refuge in an imaginary
heaven where, with Leonardo, Rafael, and Agnolo, he achieves illusory fulfillment.

This account of action inadequately describes the drama of the
poem, however, for it is given complexity and intensity both by
Andrea's conscious attempts to reject what he unconsciously knows
to be true, and by a series of dialectical movements within the
poem. Part of the intensity comes from the opposition of pairs, all
symbolic: summer and autumn, twilight and darkness, youth and
age, past and present, heaven and earth, hope and failure.

The first suggestion of meaning comes in the ambivalent subtitle,
"The Faultless Painter." The phrase, recognized as ironic, is too
often understood to mean that Browning said a thing ridiculous in
order to enforce a contradictory meaning. Accordingly, he did not
mean that Andrea was faultless, but that he was totally depraved. A
thoughtful reading discredits this one-dimensional interpretation.
Empson makes a statement about irony which applies here: "An
irony has no point unless it is true, in some degree, in both senses;
for it is imagined as a part of an argument; what is said is made
absurd, but it is what the opponent might say."[1] Precisely so in
"Andrea del Sarto." In a sense, Andrea is a faultless painter; at the
same time he is a mere craftsman. On another level, he is both husband and pander; Lucrezia is at once his Virgin and his Eve.

Andrea's roles are many and often contradictory. He becomes

1. William Empson, *Some Versions of Pastoral* (London: Chatto and Windus, 1935),
p. 56.

participant with the lover in a twofold drama, one in which lover and mistress provide contrasting comment upon husband and wife, and the other in which the two vie for Lucrezia's favor. Still again, Andrea is unwittingly cast in opposition to Agnolo and obliged to defend his faultless paintings against his rival's superior accomplishments. Torn between opposite but equally demanding claims and made constantly aware of failure, Andrea achieves not wholeness, but destructive self-realization.

His impulses run in counter directions. A remark of self-justification is followed by one of self-accusation; a spirit of bravado and assertiveness, by one of passive acceptance. His attitude toward Lucrezia fluctuates from contempt to deference; toward the lover, from resentment to grudging admiration; toward his public, from disdain to obsequiousness.

Andrea oscillates between assertiveness and passiveness, between projection and receptivity. His vision of what he should do as artist is remarkably clear and his desire for a normal relationship with Lucrezia is intense, but a spiritual and physical enervation prohibits him from being satisfactorily either the husband or artist. The conflict of the poem is between asserted artistic and masculine virility and a steadily increasing awareness of debility.

Andrea attempts to establish himself by recalling with justified pride the praise of his contemporaries; he is, indeed, a facile craftsman, and his attempt to improve Rafael is not mere bravado. He likes also to fancy himself as being masculine and irresistible. In the lines

> Your soft hand is a woman of itself,
> And mine the man's bared breast she curls inside

the words "bared breast" suggest masculine strength, and the "soft hand" feminine dependency and affection. The hand appropriately curls in his, a symbol of the personal union which he desires.

At the same time, he is aware of the superiority of Rafael's paintings, and he realizes too that his own sense of form and line can never compensate for an insight which he does not have. Simultaneously, he knows that the lover possesses Lucrezia in a way that he can never hope to rival. Suspecting that he is incapable of passion and devoid of masculine attractiveness, Andrea resembles a character out of the early Auden, Eliot's Prufrock, or James's Marcher, save that he, perhaps, is more aware of his deficiency. His despair is produced partly by the realization that Lucrezia can be, indeed has been, won. Even as he presses his ineffectual suit, outside waits a lover to whom she is willingly drawn. His failure and the lover's success tantalize him into speculation:

> Ah, but what does he,
> The Cousin! what does he to please you more?

If Andrea could answer this question he would at the same time answer a great many more. For his failure with Lucrezia is only a part of his total failure as son, friend, and artist. His strange, almost abnormal devotion to a woman who has so degraded him cannot have been other than devastating to his art. Yet, he realizes clearly that she is not wholly the cause of his failure:

> Beside, incentives come from the soul's self;
> The rest avail not. Why do I need you?
> What wife had Rafael, or has Agnolo?

What he calls lack of incentive from the soul's self is really passiveness, debility, receptivity. These qualities make necessary his attempts to escape from time and self and produce his ultimate weariness and despair.

Stopford Brooke and William Lyon Phelps have called attention to Andrea's uxoriousness, his "unconquerable passion," but have failed to note that what they speak of is largely illusory. Indeed, Andrea does seem to give up everything for Lucrezia—his family, his friends, his integrity, and finally his creative vision; yet with equal submissiveness he hands her over to the lover at the end of the poem: "Again the Cousin's whistle! Go, my Love." His attitude toward her wavers. His subservience is counterpointed by a bitterness, an antagonism that makes itself felt much too often to be ignored: "You don't understand/Nor care . . . ," "Had I been two, . . ." "Had you enjoined them on me, given me soul," "Had you, with these same, but brought a mind!" "And had you not grown restless. . . ."

Clearly, uxoriousness is only one manifestation of a more basic weakness. Attracted as he is by Lucrezia's body, he lacks, nevertheless, the virility of Fra Lippo Lippi and the passion of Sebald. What seems physical desire is partly enthusiasm for artistic form, and in the following it is the craftsman who speaks: "perfect ears . . . oh, so sweet," "perfect brow,/And perfect eyes, and more than perfect mouth,/And the low voice. . . ." Enamoured of his wife's beauty, Andrea runs his hands through her hair and remarks that it serves to frame her picture-perfect face:

> Let my hands frame your face in your hair's gold,
> You beautiful Lucrezia that are mine!

Actually, he is surprisingly passive and physically undemanding:

> . . . and it seems
> As if—forgive now—should you let me sit
> Here by the window with your hand in mine
> And look a half-hour forth on Fiesole,
> Both of one mind, as married people use,

> Quietly, quietly the evening through,
> I might get up to-morrow to my work
> Cheerful and fresh as ever.

The half-hour over, he states complacently:

> You loved me quite enough, it seems to-night.

That "enough" reflects a characteristic of Andrea's which is given additional emphasis by the poem's structure. Diction, sound repetition, rhythm, and sentence structure all unite to create an impression, emotionally and sensuously, of placidity and greyness, qualities by which Andrea describes his life and work.

The diction, lacking the colorfulness of Fra Lippo Lippi's, is abstract and conceptual rather than perceptive and sensory. There are an unusually large number of substantives and relatively few modifiers, an almost equal number of concrete and abstract nouns. Clear and sharp but not particularly sensuous, the concrete nouns are used primarily to establish character and setting. Many are descriptive or technical: *sun, tree, star, moon, bird, picture, chalk.* Others show a painter's interest in man's anatomy: *hand, head, face, breast, ears, arms, neck, shoulders.* Andrea habitually speaks professionally, detachedly of the human body. It is as model that he refers most often to Lucrezia.

The small number of modifiers suggests subordination of sensuous appeal. Only a few are sensory, and of these, two alone, *grey* and *golden,* appear more than once; even they lose most of their sensuousness since they are used as symbols, as I shall show later. On the whole, the diction in "Andrea del Sarto" contrasts sharply with that of the Ottima-Sebald scene in *Pippa Passes,* where Browning attempts to communicate physicality.

The greater number of modifiers is qualitative and quantitative: *glad, perfect, past, little, same, poor, great, good,* and *better.* Only a sprinkling of adjectives, *sober, pleasant, strange, festal, melancholy,* and *bright,* are romantically atmospheric. Browning begins "Andrea del Sarto" with a simple, straightforward, unemotional statement:

> But do not let us quarrel any more,
> No, my Lucrezia; bear with me for once:
> Sit down and all shall happen as you wish.

Andrea himself suffers from emotional sterility, reflected both by his "faultless" paintings (contrasted with the "soulful" works of his contemporaries) and by his relations with Lucrezia. His pleading, his promises, his bribes, elicit less response from her than the whistle of the lover. Andrea offers everything, the cousin nothing. Yet his "less" is "more," just as Rafael's is.

In "The Bishop Orders His Tomb" Browning partly characterizes the Bishop by frequent repetition of vowel sounds used for purely sensuous effects, but no such attempt is made in "Andrea del Sarto." Governed by the central meaning of the poem, he does avoid cacophony, the general placidity helping to present both in concept and in emotional texture Andrea's "grey world" and his "autumnal" and "twilight" life and work.

There is considerable alliteration, but it does not function primarily to convey sensuousness or to provide poetic decoration. Frequently, it emphasizes idea by calling attention to important thoughts, as in "mine the man's bared breast she curls inside." This line, containing a basic image, commands special attention because of the alliteration. Browning uses repetition (the *l*'s and the *f*'s in the following, for example) to link sentences and to gain conceptual unity and compactness:

> Love, we are in God's hand.
> How strange now, looks the life he makes us lead;
> So free we seem, so fettered fast we are!
> I feel he laid the fetter: let it lie!

My point is that Browning does not use alliteration in "Andrea del Sarto," as, for example, Swinburne does in "Dolores," to produce emotional and sensuous effects apart from meaning. Even when repetition calls attention to lines that appear sensuous the effect is actually ironic. For example, "Let my hands frame your face in your hair's gold" counterpoints sensuous with artistic attraction, passion with a painter's professional appraisal of a good subject.

Alliteration is used further as part of rhythm. Stressing lightly conceptually unimportant syllables, and calling attention to others by heavy stress and alliteration, Browning achieves simultaneously in some lines both the artistic effect of alliterative verse and an emphasis on idea. Thus, the rhythmic pattern of the poem becomes a part of the meaning much more profoundly than by merely echoing the sense. Though irregular, the poem is "unmusical" only if judged by Spenserian and Tennysonian standards. Closer to the Wyatt-Donne tradition, Browning uses a line basically conventional in that it has a predetermined number of syllables and stresses, but breaks with the musical tradition in the placement of syllables within the line, proposing to relate closely what is felt and said with the manner of saying it, to use rhythm both to create and to support meaning. The absence of a strong sensuous movement, such as that, for example, which creates so vividly the physicality of Shakespeare's "Venus and Adonis" and Marlowe's "Hero and Leander," emphasizes Andrea's passivity; its brokenness reflects at the same time his psychological chaos.

Andrea's weariness—physical, intellectual, emotional—is expressed both overtly and structurally.

> I often am much wearier than you think,
> This evening more than usual,

he says. And again:

> Too live the life grew, golden and not grey,
> And I'm the weak-eyed bat no sun should tempt
> Out of the grange whose four walls make his world.

Andrea's debility contrasts significantly with Lucrezia's assertiveness.

Such frequently used words as *silver, dream, quietly, evening, grey, greyness, twilight, autumn* create atmosphere and texture more because of their conceptual meaning than their emotional connotations. Their effect, therefore, is clear and sharp rather than vague and diffuse. Browning's diction, here and elsewhere, had a specificity not found in that of any other nineteenth-century poet before Meredith, Hardy, and Hopkins. It was this quality more than any other that recommended him to Ezra Pound in the twentieth century.

The smaller number of verbs slows down the action and heightens the sense of weariness. Browning uses a minimum of action words:

> I surely then could sometimes leave the ground,
> Put on the glory, Rafael's daily wear,
> In that humane great monarch's golden look,—
> One finger in his beard or twisted curl
> Over his mouth's good mark that made the smile,
> One arm about my shoulder, round my neck,
> The jingle of his gold chain in my ear,
> I painting proudly with his breath on me,
> All his court round him, seeing with his eyes,
> Such frank French eyes, and such a fire of souls
> Profuse, my hand kept plying by those hearts,—
> And, best of all, this, this, this face beyond,
> This in the background, waiting on my work,
> To crown the issue with a last reward!

In fourteen lines there are only three finite verbs. Others are implied, and participles function suggestively as verbs. By implication and substitution, however, Browning avoids disturbing the quiet autumnal atmosphere with active verbs. Some lines lack even participles:

> But all the play, the insight and the stretch—
> Out of me, out of me! And wherefore out?

The effect here should be contrasted with that of "Fra Lippo Lippi," where relatively a great many more verbs are used. Obviously, a difference in subject matter requires a difference in technique: Lippo, in contrast to Andrea, is virile and sensuous.

The structure of Andrea's sentences is on one level a projection of his inner emptiness, and on another a suggestion of his struggle against self-realization. They express an unwillingness to grapple realistically with his problem, a passive receptiveness of "fate" that contradicts his half-hearted attempts at assertiveness.

His imperatives, never strong, are characteristically more often entreaties than commands. He timidly requests that Lucrezia grant him partly what by rights he should command wholly. And though numerous, the interrogatory sentences are not at all like Lippo's startling demand:

> Come, what am I a beast for?

Andrea's is not a searching mind attempting to discover truth, but a timid one afraid of discovering too much. Lippo, more confident of himself, could with greater comfort face his problems. Andrea's exclamations lack force, the shock of immediate experience and spontaneous utterance having been absorbed by retrospection. The opening sentence reveals an emotional staleness produced by a situation so often repeated that it has lost all immediacy.

Andrea's speech, though not "literary," lacks the colloquial directness, the force, of Lippo's or Bishop Blougram's. Lucrezia is protagonist but not in the sense that Gigadibs and the Watchman are. Symbolic of the whole pattern of Andrea's life, she is in a sense a much richer auditor than either of the others. Her presence in the room, the turn of her head that brings face but not heart, the careless sweep of her skirt against wet paint, her indifference to Andrea's reputation among his contemporaries, her impatience to join her lover all combine to elicit from Andrea a complex response. In a sense, he speaks more to himself than directly to Lucrezia, and although we never forget that she is with him, we feel that she too is overhearing. Actually, the poem belongs somewhere between dramatic conversation and internal monologue. Andrea does not develop his thoughts logically, for he is not reasoning and coming to conclusions; rather he is reminiscing, justifying, excusing, and accepting. Consequently, units of expression often consist of conceptual or emotional rather than grammatical groups. Their unity is imaginative, hence not always immediately apparent.

These groups are frequently only fragments, many times containing a series of substantives and few or no verbs:

> That Francis, that first time,
> And that long festal year at Fontainebleau!

Their fragmentariness, the omission of co-ordinates and verbs, is significant. The absence of verbs I have already discussed as one indication of his passiveness. The omission of co-ordinate conjunctions between independent clauses serves to break the poem into a series of ungrammatically related reflections, and at the same time signals his incapacity for integrating counterimpulses and for forming relationships.

Lack of structural formality creates the impression of emotional and intellectual instability. In general, Andrea's sentences are of two types: either segmented, brief, independent clauses frequently not syntactically related to a larger unit; or complex sentences consisting of introductory independent clauses followed by one or more subordinate clauses. These complex sentences are frequently split into two or more segments by interpolations which may or may not be syntactically related:

> Well, I can fancy how he did it all,
> Pouring his soul, with kings and popes to see,
> Reaching, that heaven might so replenish him,
> Above and through his art—for it gives way;
> That arm is wrongly put—and there again—
> A fault to pardon in the drawing's lines,
> Its body, so to speak: its soul is right,
> He means right—that, a child may understand.

The complex sentences, the numerous subordinations, the interpolations, the exclamations, the lack of syntactical connections give the effect of thought in conflict, of intellectual uncertainty and emotional instability. Andrea's aim is self-justification, but since he has not ordered his thinking, he cannot proceed straightforwardly as Lippo does; rather he muses disjointedly and inconclusively on first one aspect and then another of his unpleasant experience. Andrea is afraid to pursue his speculations to a logical conclusion for he partly knows and rejects what he would find if he did.

His sentences reflect the tortured flow of thought that can neither stop nor come to a logical conclusion, a surplus of diffused intensity that decreases the finality of what he says. The *pasticcio* quality of his thinking is demonstrated by the fact that a reader is hardly aware of either the beginning or the end of many of his constructions.

Thus, the dialectical opposition between Andrea's physical and spiritual debility and his effort to avoid self-realization is communicated materially and structurally. These opposing forces are given both more precise definition and artistic unity particularly through symbol. Lucrezia herself is the dominant symbol. Briefly, Andrea's devotion to her "soulless" beauty signifies a personal and artistic deficiency; and her perfidy, fate's compensation to him for his weak-

ness. She is the materialization of his desires for human relationships and artistic achievement, reflecting his erroneous judgment,
his false standard of values.

She is the symbol of the emptiness which Andrea comes to
understand. He speaks of himself rightly as a "half-man." The
famous "Ah, but a man's reach should exceed his grasp" is ironical,
for Andrea is vaguely conscious of the discrepancy between his
higher vision (personal and artistic) and his spiritual and emotional
faculties to achieve; he is tormented by a stimulus greater than his
power to respond.

His eventual capitulation and destruction are suggested by a
group of frequently repeated words associated with values: *worth*,
pay, *gold*, *silver*, *gain*, *reward*. Each has a literal meaning, but as a
group and in context they are also symbolically significant. The two
basic adjectives are *golden* and *silver* (grey): in his "kingly days"
Andrea enjoyed the monarch's "golden look"; he worked with Francis' arm about him, the jingle of his gold chain in his ears; a "fire of
souls" kept his hand plying until "too live the life grew, golden and
not grey. . . ." He left the "golden look" of the monarch for the
gold of Lucrezia's hair, and his whole world changed:

> . . . the whole seems to fall into a shape
> As if I saw alike my work and self
> And all that I was born to be and do,
> A twilight-piece.

His attitude toward his work changed; seeing it degenerate into a
commodity, he came to speak of it in marketplace terms:

> I'll work then for your friend's friend, never fear,
> Treat his own subject after his own way,
> Fix his own time, accept too his own price,
> And shut the money into this small hand
> When next it takes mine.

He uses the same terminology when he attempts to describe the
relation between himself and his painting:

> I know both what I want and what might *gain*,
> And yet how *profitless* to know. . . .

The words *gain* and *profitless* suggest the hold which buying and
selling have upon him. His painting itself takes on the color of com-
mercialism:

> All is silver-grey
> Placid and perfect with my art.

Lucrezia is blamed because she failed to urge that he "never care for *gain*" (a pun that is ironic). Because of his perverted values, Andrea becomes paradoxical when he recognizes that Rafael, though lacking his technical skill, is the greater painter:

> Yet do much less, so much less, Someone says,
> (I know his name, no matter)—so much less!
> Well, less is more, Lucrezia.

Toward the conclusion of the poem, these market terms appear more frequently and in positions of greater emphasis. Heightening emotion and sharpening the irony, they become effective mediums for expressing meaning. The brick walls appear cemented with fierce bright gold; Andrea took money from Francis; he neglected to give money to his mother and father; he failed to make money for himself and Lucrezia. Most significantly they depict the degeneration of Andrea's standards of values, his genuine confusion, and ultimately his compromise with the tawdry and commonplace. They are all echoed in the lines:

> That Cousin here again? he waits outside,
> Must see you—you, and not with me? Those *loans?*
> More gaming *debts* to *pay?* you smiled for that?
> Well, let smiles *buy* me! have you more to *spend?*
> While hand and eye and something of a heart
> Are left me, work's my *ware*, and what's it *worth?*
> I'll *pay* my fancy.

Here everything is reduced to a mart where the lover makes debts which Andrea must pay, where Lucrezia barters her love, and where Andrea pays for her smiles with second-rate paintings. The climaxing line, "I'll pay my fancy," suggests the ironic state of Andrea's eixstence: the delight which he finds in his relationship with Lucrezia is capricious, not real, and even for that he pays dearly.

The words *golden* and *grey* have still another meaning. *Grey* best suggests Andrea's passive, colorless personality, and used in contrast to *golden* points up the difference between the life that he now lives and that he once lived; they also suggest, on another level, the breach between his actual existence and his imagined one. There was a time when life itself was golden, but that time is gone: "A common greyness silvers everything. . . ." Dusk falls outside as Andrea talks; dusk has long since settled over his life. Summer has given way to autumn in the natural world; within Andrea's inner world "autumn grows, autumn in everything." The merging of the outer world with the inner illustrates the success with which Browning handles symbol. Andrea's work, as well as his life, has been affected. "All that I was born to be and do" is "a twilight-piece." "My youth, my hope, my art, being all toned down. . . ." This is the figure which he uses to contrast his work with that of his more successful contemporaries. His is the hand of a patient, skilful, but uninspired craftsman, while in the works of his contemporaries "There burns a truer light of God. . . ."

Andrea regrets his lack of light, but at the same time, paradoxically, fears to venture into full day. In one powerful figure he expresses his inner paralysis and brings together the golden-grey with the wall figure. He says, referring to his earlier life with Francis:

> Too live the life grew, golden and not grey,
> And I'm the weak-eyed bat no sun should tempt
> Out of the grange whose four walls make his world.

The emphasis is on the "weak-eyed bat"—the natural lover of darkness. Andrea prefers the calm security and the comforting shades of four walls to the penetrating light of the world. Lucrezia is a symbol of darkness which he welcomes rather than fears, and he follows his own self-destroying impulses when he chooses her in preference to the world of Rafael and Agnolo. Now he lives within his four walls and takes comfort in the dusk of the late afternoon, his only light a false reflection created by a guilty conscience:

> . . . oft at nights
> When I look up from painting, eyes tired out,
> The walls become illumined, brick from brick
> Distinct, instead of mortar, fierce bright gold,
> That gold of his I did cement them with!

His personal limitations are imposed upon his paintings. He realizes that an artist should break through the boundaries of here and now to participate in the limitlessness of eternity. Spiritually and artistically imprisoned, however, he is unable to transcend the market place. His failure sets him apart from his more illustrious contemporaries:

> Their works drop groundward, but themselves, I know,
> Reach many a time a heaven that's shut to me,
> Enter and take their place there sure enough,
> Though they come back and cannot tell the world.
> My works are nearer heaven, but I sit here.

Indeed, it is understandable that in a moment of despair he should say, "I feel he laid the fetter: let it lie!"

Paradoxically, also, he realizes that Lucrezia is a part of his failure and sometimes blames her for the whole of it; yet he holds tenaciously to the small security which she brings. The fact that he legally possesses her beautiful body is comforting compensation for his personal ineffectualness. She is there as a bulwark against complete self-realization.

The epithet "serpentining beauty" is rich in connotations. It calls to mind the Garden of Eden story with its suggestions of feminine deception, loss of innocence, the curse of God, and spiritual death. In a sense, Lucrezia is his Eve; at the same time she is also his Virgin, the prototype of his technically faultless painting. Another expression of his ambivalent attitude toward her appears in the following:

> And the low voice my soul hears, as a bird
> The fowler's pipe, and follows to the snare.

The fowler is a destructive figure; the snare, a kind of trap serving to restrict and imprison. Browning uses the word *snare* and not *trap* because the snare quietly entangles; while a trap, more violent, suggests action inappropriate to the tone of the poem. Here, as in the serpent figure, the emphasis is on deception, and yet it must be noted again that Andrea's is a willing deception. He is the weak-eyed bat who "came home" to Lucrezia. If she were a deceiver, if he were snared, she was also his deliverer; he found a home, a resting place in the snare.

Browning uses these figures to achieve tragic irony. Andrea both desires and fears light, both resents and welcomes the snare; he prefers the grey autumnal shades, yet nostalgically recalls his golden days. His desire to break his prison walls and reach the heaven of others is expressed in the ironic figure coming at the conclusion of the poem:

> What would one have?
> In heaven, perhaps, new chances, one more chance—
> Four great walls in the New Jerusalem,
> Meted on each side by the angel's reed.

Andrea is tragically incapable of either conceiving or enjoying complete freedom.

Actually, in the "bared breast" figure, quoted earlier as an expression of Andrea's desire for a normal marital relationship, the word *bared* is a pun. Literally, it suggests qualities of masculine strength which Andrea desires, at the same time points up the bareness of his soul. There is nothing there for Lucrezia. In fact, ultimately it is Andrea who seeks Lucrezia's breast, not she his. This reversal of roles should be noted. It is Lucrezia who calls, not Andrea; she who is the assertive, Andrea the receptive member of the pair. Andrea's behavior contrasts with that of the lover; his passive submission to Lucrezia's call, with the command of the lover's whistle. Equally ironic and effective as the subtitle is the line: "You beautiful Lucrezia that are mine." For she was never his. It was Andrea's misfortune to know this.

E. D. H. JOHNSON

Robert Browning's Pluralistic Universe:
A Reading of *The Ring and the Book*†

* * *

I

Speaking to the Harvard Young Men's Christian Association in 1895 on the subject "Is Life Worth Living?", William James declared: "Yet, on more intimate acquaintance, the visible surfaces of heaven and earth refuse to be brought by us into any intelligible unity at all. Every phenomenon that we would praise there exists cheek by jowl with some contrary phenomenon that cancels all its religious effect upon the mind. Beauty and hideousness, love and cruelty, life and death keep house together in indissoluble partnership. . . ." The imperviousness of the perceptual world to man's age-old aspiration to discover in it evidence of some unified plan or meaning lay at the root of the philosophic system which James called radical empiricism. As he wrote in the Preface to his collection of popular addresses, *The Will to Believe*: "There is no possible point of view from which the world can appear an absolutely single fact. Real possibilities, real indeterminations, real beginnings, real ends, real evil, real crises, catastrophes, and escapes, a real God, and a real moral life, just as common-sense conceives these things, may remain in empiricism as conceptions which that philosophy gives up the attempt either to 'overcome' or to reinterpret in monistic form."

The variousness of human nature and the incommensurateness of any individual's experiences with those of his fellows oblige us, James maintains, to adopt a pluralistic habit of mind: that is, to view life as an indeterminate and contingent process. The day-to-day events of existence reveal to rational inquiry no intelligible order or purpose; the things that happen to us are "partly joined and partly disjoined," composite of good and evil, essentially ambiguous. To replace the ideal demand for absolutes with a common-sense acceptance of the actual in all its multiplicity and heterogeneity is the mark of the Jamesian pluralist. "The obvious outcome of our total experience," said James in his Gifford lectures on *The Varieties of Religious Experience*, "is that the world can be handled according to many systems of ideas, and is so handled by different

† From *University of Toronto Quarterly*, 31 (1961), 20–41. Reprinted by permission of the author and the publisher, University of Toronto Press.

men, and will each time give some characteristic kind of profit, for which he cares, to the handler, while at the same time some other kind of profit has to be omitted or postponed."

That Robert Browning fully subscribed to such a view of the world must be evident to any reader of his early volumes of poetry, whether *Pippa Passes, Dramatic Romances and Lyrics, Men and Women,* or *Dramatic Personae.* The total impression created by this work is of a pluralistic universe made up of people of all sorts and conditions, living in all ages and climes, each uniquely inclined to a course of action by character and circumstance. These actions portend no final resolutions; at best they are approximations more or less satisfactory according to the number of truths which they embody. For Cleon, Karshish, and the Saint John of "A Death in the Desert" the problems posed by the Christian revelation are wholly distinct, and each tries to come to terms with its enigma in his own way. The conditions which make for artistic success or failure are variously assessed by Fra Lippo Lippi, Andrea del Sarto, and the Pictor Ignotus.

Correspondingly, in the dramatic monologue Browning developed a medium extraordinarily responsive to his sense of the indeterminacy of the human condition. However artful and persuasive the pleading of any speaker in his own behalf, the reader is kept constantly mindful that this body of testimony is susceptible of interpretations at variance with its avowed tenor. Through the poet's handling the most trivial incident takes on implications suggestive of the many facets of truth. In "My Last Duchess," for example, the Duke, although bent on presenting his previous marriage in the light most flattering to himself, inadvertently prejudices his case by instilling in the reader's mind three alternate positions from which to judge it: that of the dead wife whose behaviour, as reported, stirs our sympathy; that of the Count's emissary whose implied distaste for the Duke we share; and finally, that more objective evaluation of the speaker's character symbolically configured in the piece of sculpture to which he draws attention at the end of the poem.

It is *The Ring and the Book,* however, which both in conception and form most comprehensively exhibits Browning's pluralism. Here the poet's method of allowing nine different individuals to present their separate reconstructions of a single series of happenings has the effect of investing with tragic grandeur events which on their surface would seem to constitute, in Henry James's phrase, "a mere vulgar criminal anecdote." Browning insisted that his poem was built on facts throughout; and each of those who bears witness to these facts is sure that he is rendering them veraciously. This holds even for Guido, of whom Pompilia says "hate was thus the truth of him," a sentiment echoed in the Pope's saddened admission: "Out

of some core of truth the excrescence comes. . . ." And however partial the truth emerging from most of the monologues, however
much it comes to us perverted by malice or the errors of self-delu-
sion, we yet find that the limited awareness of each successive
speaker has contributed to the total awareness which Browning is
building up in our minds. The cumulative effect of so many conflicting versions is to evoke that kind of complex response to existence for which William James was to become the philosophic advocate. "For pluralism," as James stated in his lectures on A *Pluralistic Universe*, "all that we are required to admit as the constitution
of reality is . . . that nothing real is absolutely simple, that every
smallest bit of experience is a *multum in parvo* plurally related, that
each relation is one aspect, character, or function, way of its being
taken, or way of its taking something else. . . ."

That Browning had deliberately adopted a pluralistic approach to
each material is demonstrable from certain analogies which he
invokes at the outset of the poem. As the months in their rotation
strike forth "Each facet-flash of the revolving year," so will the
twelve books of the poem project a series of kaleidoscopic views:
"The variance now, the eventual unity,/Which makes the miracle."
Confronted by first one, then another aspect of the story, the reader
will be baffled in his inclination to settle for easy answers, to cast
his "sentence absolute for shine or shade." The ring metaphor, furthermore, operates in two ways to call attention to the poem's pluralistic implications. In the first place, it symbolizes the plasticity
of factual reality. And secondly, through likening the separate monologues to the segments of a circle within the circumference of which
the elusive truth resides, its aspect altering with every change in
perspective, the poet expresses his sense of the multiform nature of
all truth.

Browning's pluralism provides the structural key to *The Ring and
the Book*. Postponing for later discussion the first and last books
which the poet reserved for his own comments, the remaining monologues present in chronological sequence the testimony of nine witnesses. This body of evidence falls, as Browning himself noted, into
three categories: Books II–IV being devoted to the gossip current in
Rome in the days immediately following the crime; Books V–VII
and Book XI giving the statements of the three principal actors;
and Books VIII—X containing the summations of the representa-
tives of the law. Each speaker, isolated from the others, addresses an
audience not immediately implicated in the action (the Pope alone
soliloquizes). The monologues thus offer a serial pattern of discrete
narratives which, nevertheless, constantly intersect, supplementing,
qualifying, or contradicting each other as the case may be. There
results an impression of unity in apparent disunity remarkably con-

formable to William James's description of the nature of reality, as contained in the following passage from *A Pluralistic Universe*: "If the each-form be the eternal form of reality no less than it is the form of temporal appearance, we still have a coherent world, and not an incarnate incoherence, as is charged by so many absolutists. Our 'multiverse' still makes a 'universe'; for every part, tho it may not be in actual or immediate connexion, is nevertheless in some possible or mediated connexion, with every other part however remote, through the fact that each part hangs together with its very next neighbors in inextricable interfusion."

The three monologues which contain samplings of the hearsay in Roman society at once establish the author's pluralistic approach to his "murder story." "Half-Rome's feel after the vanished truth" yields to the Other Half-Rome's "opposite feel / For truth," to which then succeeds Tertium Quid's "reasoned statement of the case." The three speakers rest their verdicts on ascertainable facts; yet what disparate meanings each deduces from these facts! As a jealous husband, Half-Rome cannot but side with Guido; the Other Half-Rome, a sentimental bachelor, is no less strongly drawn to Pompilia's defence; while Tertium Quid, he of the "critical mind," displays the born sceptic's inability to make a choice. Meanwhile the sequential ordering of these monologues makes for a steady accumulation of fresh details ("So do the facts abound and super-abound," says Tertium Quid); and correspondingly, the speakers show themselves increasingly scrupulous in sifting the bits of evidence, so that Tertium Quid's suspension of judgment in the fourth book is a real measure of the ambiguities which the affair has taken on.

It was Henry James who, in his brilliant paper on "The Novel in *The Ring and the Book*," first pointed out the additional purpose which these opening monologues serve in evoking as the poem's setting "those wonderful, dreadful, beautiful particulars of the Italy of the eve of the eighteenth century. . . ." The atmosphere created by Browning "stirs up, to my vision," said Henry, "a perfect cloud of gold-dust. . . ." This figure may well have lingered in the novelists's memory out of an extraordinary passage from his brother's *A Pluralistic Universe*, where Wiliam comments, as follows, on the teeming and random mediocrity which in this world environs every form of excellence:

Since when, in this mixed world, was any good thing given us in purest outline and isolation? One of the chief characteristics of life is life's redundancy. The sole condition of our having anything, no matter what, is that we should have so much of it. . . . Everything is smothered in the litter that is fated to accompany it. Without too much you cannot have enough, of anything. Lots of inferior books, lots of bad statues, lots of dull speeches, of tenth-rate men and women, as a condition of the few precious specimens in either kind being realized! The gold-dust comes to birth with the quartz-sand all around it. . . .

If the second, third, and fourth books of the poem are primarily narrative in interest, the dramatic aspects of the case are played up in the three following monologues which give a hearing to the trio of leading characters, while in Books VIII–X the emphasis shifts once more, now towards the philosophic, as the foregoing evidence undergoes judicial examination. In this way, a single set of circumstances is not only appraised from different points of view, but with varying degrees of intensity referable to the demands of each speaker's role, whether it calls for the casual curiosity of the spectator, the life-and-death involvement of the protagonist, or the theoretic detachment of the arbiter. Within the three groupings of monologues there exist, furthermore, certain structural parallels which confirm the pluralistic implications of the subject-matter. Books II, V, and VIII, given to Half-Rome, Guido, and the latter's attorney for the defence, develop complementary arguments in Guido's support; whereas the case for Pompilia is pleaded by the Other Half-Rome, Caponsacchi, and the prosecutor in Books III, VI, and IX. The duplicating interplay between thesis and antithesis thus established is then resolved in the syntheses recurrently proposed in the culminating monologue of each triad. Tertium Quid's weighing of pros and cons steers a sober middle course between the irrational prejudices which sway the partisans of Guido and Pompilia. By the same token, Pompilia's intuitive grasp of essentials rectifies the self-delusions to which her husband and her champion are subject. And lastly, the Pope's monologue, combining Tertium Quid's objectivity with Pompilia's insight, disengages the truth so sorely travestied in the lawyer's speeches.

The monologues of Tertium Quid, Pompilia, and the Pope have this additional quality in common, that the speakers are equally cognizant and tolerant of the aberrant motives which have split Rome into opposing camps. In other words, these three, who otherwise have so little in common, share the attribute of open-mindedness which, according to William James, characterizes the pluralist in his confrontation of reality. For Tertium Quid, as has already been observed, the indeterminacy of the issues involved hopelessly complicates the apportioning of innocence and guilt. Pompilia, dying, would forgive all those who have wronged her. "Wherefore should I blame you much?" she humbly asks:

> So we are made, such difference in minds,
> Such difference too in eyes that see the minds!

It is the Pope, however, who, as Browning's mouthpiece, most clearly takes up a pluralistic position in his grappling with the ultimate bearings of the case. Significant in this connection are Innocent's preliminary deliberations on the subject of papal infallibility, occasioned by his study of the perplexed history of Pope Formosus. Chastened by the errors of his predecessors in office, he turns to review the facts appealed to him with full awareness of their ambiguity:

> Truth, nowhere, lies yet everywhere in these—
> Not absolutely in a portion, yet
> Evolvable from the whole . . .

At line 1252, roughly the midpoint of his monologue, the Pope is ready to condemn Guido; yet he is withheld from signing the death-warrant by a host of new doubts, all resulting from his recognition that human faculties can at best attain to partial glimpses of truth:

> Man's mind—what is it but a convex glass
> Wherein are gathered all the scattered points
> Picked out of the immensity of sky,
> To reunite there, be our heaven on earth,
> Our known unknown, our God revealed to man?
> Existent somewhere, somehow, as a whole;
> Here, as a whole proportioned to our sense,—
> There, (which is nowhere, speech must babble thus!)
> In the absolute immensity, the whole
> Appreciable solely by Thyself,—
> Here, by the little mind of man, reduced
> To littleness that suits his faculty,
> Appreciable too in the degree . . .

He hears ghostly voices, the advocates of views not endorsed by the Church. First speaks Euripides, who would defer the determination of justice to God ("who only knows the thing He made"), and who questions whether Christian ethics have promoted conduct nobler than that which prevailed in ancient Greece. The Quietist doctrines of the Molinists next come forward to trouble the old man's thoughts. In heretically denying "At peril of their body and their soul,—/Recognized truths," were they not, he asks himself

> obedient to some truth
> Unrecognized yet, but perceptible?

And lastly, "the spirit of culture," premonitory of the age of enlightenment dawning with the new century, solicits Innocent with its seductive worldly pleas: "Mercy is safe and graceful." The Pope at no point endeavours to oppose a reasoned rebuttal to any of these arguments which, as projections of his anti-dogmatism, are perhaps irrefutable on pluralistic grounds. Rather, he invokes the appeal to which Guido has given so cynical a twist in Book V, "*Quis pro Domino?*", and acting under the kind of instinctual compulsion which William James was to call the will to believe, he seals the murderer's doom with lightning pen-strokes.

There remain the eleventh and the narrative portions of the twelfth books, the structural and thematic functions of which have habitually stirred up controversy among admirers of *The Ring and the Book*. In his first monologue Guido uttered what he hoped would seem true to his inquisitors in the witness-chamber; allowed a second chance to justify his actions, he speaks his own "naked truth." When Julia Wedgwood, Browning's friend and sympathetic critic, protested against the unrelieved evil of Guido's character, as depicted in Book V, the poet replied that his portrait was faithful to the recorded facts: "But here,—given the subject, I cannot but still say, given the treatment too: the business has been, as I specify, to explain *fact*—and the fact is what you see and, worse, are to see. . . . here my pride was concerned to invent nothing: the minutest circumstance that denotes character is *true*: the black is so much— the white, no more." In sending Miss Wedgwood the concluding books of the poem, Browning added: "The worst is, I think myself dreadfully in the right, all the while, in everything: apart, of course, from my own incapacities of whatever kind, I think this *is* the world as it is, and will be—*here* at least." Hate is Guido's truth, as Pompilia had perceived; and he goes to his death unregenerate. For it is surely inconsistent with his nature to interpret that last despairing apostrophe to his wife as a token of grace. Nor does the aftermath in Book XII materially lighten the gloom cast by Guido's second monologue. Here again Browning's method is pluralistic: the details which wind up the story are presented through a series of letters from individuals variously implicated. Their total effect is to give substance to the Pope's desponding observation: "What does the world, told truth, but lie the more?" Even Fra Celestino, whose sermon is reported verbatim by Bottini, derives no lasting consolation from the issue of the trial:

> Because Pompilia's truth prevails,
> Conclude you, all truth triumphs in the end?

But while those who would read an unmitigatedly hopeful message into Browning's poetry must be disconcerted by the conclusion of *The Ring and the Book*, the impression which it creates is quite consistent with a pluralistic interpretation. For the pluralist in William James's definition is prepared to accept the actuality of evil in the natural order of things as a given fact, inexplicable perhaps, but incontrovertible and inescapable. James's conception, delivered in the following passage from his important address, "The Dilemma of

Determinism," might, indeed, be taken as a gloss on the kind of world in which *The Ring and the Book* is set:

> The world is enigmatical enough in all conscience, whatever theory we may take up toward it. The indeterminism I defend, the free-will theory of popular sense based on the judgment of regret, represents that world as vulnerable, and liable to be injured by certain of its parts if they act wrong. And it represents their acting wrong as a matter of possibility or accident, neither inevitable nor yet to be infallibly warded off. In all this, it is a theory devoid either of transparency or of stability. It gives us a pluralistic, restless universe, in which no single point of view can ever take in the whole scene; and to a mind possessed of the love of unity at any cost, it will, no doubt, remain forever inacceptable.

II

So far the purpose of this discussion has been to suggest that in *The Ring and the Book* Browning projects a world-view which is remarkably conformable to that elaborated in William James's philosophy. It remains to show that the poet also shared the ethical suppositions which the philosopher associated with this world-view. Put simply, Browning anticipated James's contention in "Is Life Worth Living?" that man is at home in a pluralistic universe: "For such a half-wild, half-saved universe our nature is adapted."

The very manifoldness and indeterminacy of the phenomenal world exists, as James said in his address entitled "The Sentiment of Rationality," "to elicit from the man every form of triumphant endurance and conquering moral energy." In choosing amidst conflicting alternatives, the individual exercises, again in James's words, this time from *Varieties of Religious Experience*, "mankind's common instinct for reality, which in point of fact has always held the world to be essentially a theatre for heroism." To this end the plasticity of circumstance contributes. The given lends itself to remoulding; and we find, as James declared in *Pragmatism*, that "in our cognitive as well as our active life we are creative. We *add*, both to the subject and to the predicate part of reality. The world stands really malleable, waiting to receive its final touches at our hands. Like the kingdom of heaven, it suffers human violence willingly. Man *engenders* truths upon it." The primacy which James accorded to the creative impulse as a component of the pluralistic habit of mind may be inferred from the fact that he particularly stressed this aspect of his philosophy in an interview which he granted the *New York Times* in 1907:

> Mind *engenders* truth *upon* reality. . . . Our minds are not here simply to copy a reality that is already complete. They are here to

complete it, to add to its importance, by their own remodeling of it, to decant its contents over, so to speak, into a more significant shape. In point of fact, the *use* of most of our thinking is to help us to *change* the world.

The ethical postulates of pluralism are dramatically realized in the central conflicts of *The Ring and the Book*; thus, Caponsacchi and Pompilia on conventional grounds betray their prescribed duties, he as a priest, she as a wife. For the pluralist, as we have seen, however, the imperfections inherent in the status quo call for unconventional measures. The compulsion on which Caponsacchi acts,

> That dares the right and disregards alike
> The yea and nay o' the world,

is an heroic one, accompanied by a sense of religious conversion: "Into another state, under new rules/I knew myself was passing swift and sure. . . . In the chapter entitled "Saintliness" from *Varieties of Religious Experience* occurs the following passage which might have been inspired by the example of Caponsacchi:

> The man who lives in his religious centre of personal energy, and is actuated by spiritual enthusiasms, differs from his previous carnal self in perfectly definite ways. The new ardor which burns in his breast consumes in its glow the lower "noes" which formerly beset him, and keeps him immune against infection from the entire groveling portion of his nature. Magnanimities once impossible are now easy; paltry conventionalities and mean incentives once tyrannical hold no sway.

The resolve to assert their wills, however unorthodox the consequences, comes to Pompilia and Caponsacchi alike through the recognition of evil. For the pluralist, as we have also seen, evil is an existing fact, ingrained in the very texture of reality, not to be overlooked or temporized with or explained away. The Comparinis, with their "Sadly mixed natures: self-indulgent,—yet/Self-sacrificing too," constitute for the Pope an object lesson in the price individuals must pay for moral obliquity: "Life's business being," as he says, "just the terrible choice." In contrast, Pompilia and Caponsacchi stand fully exonerated in his eyes because they have fearlessly acted, in William James's words from *Varieties of Religious Experience*, on "the belief that there is an element of real wrongness in this world, which is neither to be ignored nor evaded, but which must be squarely met and overcome by an appeal to the soul's heroic resources, and neutralized and cleansed away by suffering."

A world without evil, as both Browning and James believed, would be a world without conflict, wherein there would be no opportunity for ethical discriminations. Over and over again, the Pope's monologue testifies to the speaker's conviction that human existence acquires its highest meaning under the stress of alternative possibilities, in choosing amongst which the individual's moral attributes are perpetually searched and tested: "All till the very end is trial in life," and "This life is training and a passage." James reaches an identical conclusion in "The Dilemma of Determinism":

> Not the absence of vice, but vice there, and virtue holding her by the throat, seems the ideal human state. And there seems no reason to suppose it not a permanent human state. . . . Our moral horizon moves with us as we move, and never do we draw nearer to the far-off line where the black waves and the azure meet. The final purpose of our creation seems most plausibly to be the greatest possible enrichment of our ethical consciousness, through the intensest play of contrasts and the widest diversity of characters.

And this argument is significantly amplified in *Varieties of Religious Experience*, where the author states that saints are the true world-changers by virtue of their genius for creativity affirming those transcendent values which point the way to higher states of being:

> The saints are authors, *auctores*, increasers of goodness. The potentialities of development in human souls are unfathomable. . . . The saints, with their extravagance of human tenderness are the great torch-bearers . . . , the tip of the wedge, the clearers of the darkness. Like the single drops which sparkle in the sun as they are flung far ahead of the advancing edge of a wave-crest or of a flood, they show the way and are forerunners. The world is not yet with them, so they often seem in the midst of the world's affairs to be preposterous. They are impregnators of the world, vivifiers and animators of potentialities of goodness which but for them would lie forever dormant. It is not possible to be quite as mean as we naturally are, when they have passed before us. One fire kindles another; and without that over-trust in human worth which they show, the rest of us would lie in spiritual stagnancy.

It is on precisely such grounds that the Pope derives from the conduct of Pompilia and Caponsacchi not only private spiritual consolation, but also faith in man's perfectibility:

> The moral sense grows but by exercise.
> 'T is even as man grew probatively
> Initiated in Godship, set to make
> A fairer moral world than this he finds . . .

In summary, then, it is apparent that Browning's poetry supports William James's pluralistic contentions that the individual engenders truths on the world, that he does so by rebelliously asserting his will in opposition to the evil which he perceives, and that through the resulting conflict he not only grows in moral stature but also acts as a redemptive agent in the cause of humanity. This is the point at which to investigate still another important link between Browning's thought and the psychological premises on which James's pluralism rests. Recent research has called attention to the significant ways in which his early exposure to evangelical Christianity influenced the poet's intellectual development. And the sources cited in *Varieties of Religious Experience* are evidence enough that the same Protestant tradition is instrumental to an understanding of the Jamesian philosophy. But even allowing for this common background, one cannot but be struck by the similarities which the two writers present in their treatment of the psychology of the religious experience.

James's pluralism does not end with the manifoldness of perceptual reality; it is extended to include the hypothesis (which can be matched in many of Browning's poems, "Rephan" for example) that this world is only one among many, that, in other words, we inhabit a pluralistic universe. "The whole drift of my education," James confessed in *Varieties of Religious Experience*, "goes to persuade me that the world of our present consciousness is only one out of many worlds of consciousness that exist, and that those other worlds must contain experiences which have a meaning for our life also; and that although in the main their experiences and those of this world keep discrete, yet the two become continuous at certain points, and higher energies filter in." To the eloquent elaboration of this belief James devoted himself in the concluding lectures of both *A Pluralistic Universe* and *Varieties of Religious Experience*; but he had introduced it in pragmatic terms as early as his address, "Is Life Worth Living?", in a passage which is worth quoting at length for the light it throws on Browning's own preoccupation with surmises of a like nature:

> Suppose, however thickly evils crowd upon you, that your unconquerable subjectivity proves to be their match, and that you find a more wonderful joy than any passive pleasure can bring in trusting ever in the larger whole. . . .

> Now, in this description of faiths that verify themselves I have assumed that our faith in an invisible order is what inspires those efforts and that patience which make this visible order good for moral men. Our faith in the seen world's goodness (goodness now meaning fitness for successful moral and religious life) has verified itself by leaning on our faith in the unseen world. But will our faith in the unseen world similarly verify itself? Who knows?

> Once more it is a case of *maybe*; and once more *maybes* are the

essence of the situation. I confess that I do not see why the very existence of an invisible world may not in part depend on the personal response which any one of us may make to the religious appeal. God himself, in short, may draw vital strength and increase of very being from our fidelity. For my own part, I do not know what the sweat and blood and tragedy of this life mean, if they mean anything short of this. If this life be not a real fight, in which something is eternally gained for the universe by success, it is not better than a game of private theatricals from which one may withdraw at will. But it *feels* like a real fight,—as if there were something really wild in the universe which we, with all our idealities and faithfulnesses, are needed to redeem; and first of all to redeem our own hearts from atheisms and fears. For such a half-wild, half-saved universe our nature is adapted. The deepest thing in our nature is this *Binnenleben* (as a German doctor lately has called it), this dumb region of the heart in which we dwell alone with our willingnesses and unwillingnesses, our faiths and fears. As through the cracks and crannies of caverns those waters exude from the earth's bosom which then form the fountain-heads of springs, so in these crepuscular depths of personality the sources of all our outer deeds and decisions take their rise. Here is our deepest organ of communication with the nature of things; and compared with these concrete movements of our soul all abstract statements and scientific arguments —the veto, for example, which the strict positivist pronounces upon our faith—sound to us like mere chatterings of the teeth. For here possibilities, not finished facts, are the realities with which we have actively to deal . . .

From the foregoing passage emerge at least three ideas which are relevant to the present discussion. The first of these is self-evident, and need only be noted in passing. The higher realms of being postulated by James lie beyond cognition, and are solely apprehensible through influxes of intuitive knowledge coming from the subliminal consciousness. James's conviction that ultimate truths exceed man's rational faculties has its counterpart in Browning's exaltation of the wisdom of the heart over the wisdom of the head, a tendency which the poet shared with many of his contemporaries—Carlyle and Dickens to name only the most famous.

In the second place and as an outgrowth of his insistence on the plastic nature of reality, James suggests that the will to believe may be the best means of actualizing the thing believed in. Inherent in this theory is the concept of a finite creative power whose purposes in this world can only be accomplished through the co-operation of its inhabitants. In his address, "Reflex Action and Theism," James had remarked: "God's being is sacred from ours. To co-operate with his creation by the best and rightest response seems all he wants of us. In such co-operation with his purposes, not in any chimerical speculative conquest of him, not in any theoretic drinking of him up, must lie the real meaning of our destiny." And the same notion recurs in the Postscript to *Varieties of Religious Experience*.

Here, at first glance, the philosopher would seem to take radical issue with Browning's faith in the all-knowing, all-powerful deity of Biblical revelation. Yet, as James was at pains to emphasize in "The Dilemma of Determinism," the hypothesis which impugned God's sovereignty was not an essential article in the pluralistic creed:

> . . . it is entirely immaterial, in this scheme, whether the creator leave the absolute chance-possibilities to be decided by himself, each when its proper moment arrives, or whether, on the contrary, he alienate this power from himself, and leave the decision out and out to finite creatures such as we men are. The great point is that the possibilities are really *here*. Whether it be we who solve them, or he working through us, at those soul-trying moments when fate's scales seem to quiver, and good snatches the victory from evil or shrinks nerveless from the fight, is of small account, so long as we admit that the issue is decided nowhere else than *here* and *now*.

With the general drift of this passage Browning could have had no quarrel; and it is doubtful whether James, on the other hand, would have found any significant basis for distinguishing between his own belief and Browning's concept of a transcendent God whose will remains inscrutable until brought to pass by the agency of his creatures. Certainly, Browning would have given full assent to James's assertion in "The Sentiment of Rationality" that "Truths cannot become true till our faith had made them so," with its corollary: "There are then cases where faith creates its own verification."

Finally, man's creative potentiality, his capacity for embodying new truths in thought and action, constitutes for James the really hopeful element in the human situation. This meliorism, however, is not to be dissociated from its setting in the pluralistic habit of mind. For, as James declared in *A Pluralistic Universe*:

> What really *exists* is not things made but things in the making. Once made, they are dead, and an infinite number of alternative conceptual decompositions can be used in defining them. But put yourself *in the making* by a stroke of intuitive sympathy with the thing and, the whole range of possible decompositions coming at once into your possession, you are no longer troubled with the question which of them is absolutely true. Reality *falls* in passing into conceptual analysis; it *mounts* in living its own undivided life—it buds and burgeons, changes and creates. Once adopt the movement of this life in any given instance and you know what Bergson calls the *devenir réel* by which the thing evolves and grows.

Here, as it may well seem, is the proper perspective wherein to evaluate Browning's own optimism which can realistically confront a world so riddled with imperfection as that portrayed in *The Ring and the Book* and yet discern in such an environment the conditions for moral growth.

William James habitually appealed the tenets of his pluralism to the touchstone of individual experience. In explanation of this pragmatic procedure he offered the following statement in the concluding lecture of *Varieties of Religious Experience*:

> You see now why I have been so individualistic throughout these lectures, and why I have seemed so bent on rehabilitating the element of feeling in religion and subordinating its intellectual part. Individuality is founded in feeling; and the recesses of feeling, the darker, blinder strata of character, are the only places in the world in which we catch real fact in the making, and directly perceive how events happen, and how work is actually done. Compared with this world of living individualized feelings, the world of generalized objects which the intellect contemplates is without solidity or life.

Browning's intellectual temper was equally individualistic and empirical; and the kind of religious faith sanctioned by James's philosophy could hardly be better illustrated than through the poet's rendering in *The Ring and the Book* of the experiences which motivate Pompilia, Caponsacchi, and the Pope.

Pompilia belongs in the company of Browning's saintly innocents, along with Pippa, the Duke's last duchess, Brother Lawrence of the "Soliloquy of the Spanish Cloister," and so many others. She exhibits in its purest form what E. M. Forster has called "the holiness of the heart's imagination." For guidance in the crucial moments of her life she relies exclusively on the promptings of intuition; yet her actions, thus dictated, are the transcendent force for good in the world of the poem. It is a measure of Browning's artistry that Pompilia's impressionability compels the reader to imagine for her a role to which in her humility she would never have dreamed of aspiring. Thus, when she describes the morning on which she was first visited by the mystic intimation of approaching motherhood, she does so in language that can only evoke the scene of the Annunciation:

> When, what, first thing at daybreak, pierced the sleep
> With a summons to me? Up I sprang alive,
> Light in me, light without me, everywhere
> Change! A broad yellow sun-beam was let fall
> From heaven to earth,—a sudden drawbridge lay,
> Along which marched a myriad merry motes,
> Mocking the flies that crossed them and recrossed

In rival dance, companions new-born too.
On the house-eaves, a dripping shag of weed
Shook diamonds on each dull grey lattice-square,
As first one, then another bird leapt by,
And light was off, and lo was back again,
Always with one voice,—where are two such joys?—

To be sure, Gaetano's birth at Christmastide does wring from the dying girl the wondering admission, "This time I felt like Mary"; and at one point Caponsacchi likens her to "Our Lady of all the Sorrows." But it is otherwise left to the reader to shape the tragic context for her sufferings out of such intuitions as those which led her to worship when a child

the poor Virgin that I used to know
At our street-corner in a lonely niche,—
The babe, that sat upon her knees, broke off—;

or to deny Guido's paternity of her son:

No father that he ever knew at all,
Nor ever had—no, never had, I say!;

or, finally, to go to her death with an unconscious recollection of the Assumption: "And I rise."

Their involvement in Pompilia's fate completes Caponsacchi and the Pope, the one as a man of action, the other as a religious philosopher. "She has done the good to me," says the priest. And he recalls the circumstances under which there had miraculously awakened in him the sense of mission which was to change him from a foppish worldling into Pompilia's Saint George, the Pope's "warrior-priest":

Pompilia spoke, and I at once received,
Accepted my own fact, my miracle
Self-authorised and self-explained . . .

The revelation of truth, originating outside the rational mind with its logical inhibitions, had come like "the cleaving of a cloud, a cry, a crash":

'Thought?' nay, Sirs, what shall follow was not thought:
I have thought sometimes, and thought long and hard.
I have stood before, gone round a serious thing,
Tasked my whole mind to touch and clasp it close,
As I stretch forth my arm to touch this bar.
God and man, and what duty I owe both,—
I dare to say I have confronted these
In thought; but no such faculty helped here.
I put forth no thought,—powerless, all that night
I paced the city: it was the first Spring.

> By the invasion I lay passive to,
> In rushed new things, the old were rapt away . . .

Yet, Caponsacchi is not fully "saved" by his initial meeting with Pompilia. Less incorruptible than she, he is not equal to achieving at a single leap the required pinnacle of heroism. At first he delays, aware as never before of the duties of his priestly function, but restrained from action by submission to those religious disciplines which have only now become fully meaningful to him. Caponsacchi's conversion is not completed until a second encounter brings him a deeper and truer intuition of Pompilia's need. After that he is to think of himself as God's militant deputy, dedicated solely to furthering the divine plan whereby

> one purpose and one will
> Evolve themselves i' the world, change wrong to right . . .

Pompilia's role with regard to the Pope, downhearted before the evil which surrounds him on every side, is that of a restorer rather than a revealer of faith. Her saintliness conveys to the old man, as to Fra Celestino, a sense of personal reward:

> Yet if in purity and patience, if
> In faith held fast despite the plucking fiend,
> Safe like the signet-stone with the new name
> That saints are known by,—if in right returned
> For wrong, most pardon for worst injury,
> If there be any virtue, any praise,—
> Then will this woman-child have proved—who knows?—
> Just the one prize vouchsafed unworthy me,
> Ten years a gardener of the untoward ground,
> I till,—this earth, my sweat and blood manure
> All the long day that barrenly grows dusk;
> At least one blossom makes me proud at eve
> Born 'mid the briers of my enclosure!

This individual response, however, is absorbed in Innocent's concern for his official responsibilities, as he debates "what gain or loss to God" has come of his pontificate. In passing judgment, he is called on to speak as Christ's vicar; and his reading of the evidence irresistibly impels him to the conclusion that, by actively resisting Guido's menace to her unborn child and to Caponsacchi, Pompilia did "anticipate the office that is mine." To the extent, furthermore, that he recognizes in Pompilia's rebellion a radical outgrowth of the meekly submissive spirit in which she had accepted her earlier trials, the Pope is confirmed in his faith that higher truths are dynamically evolved from lower under the stress of conflict:

> Thou, patient thus, couldst rise from law to law,
> The old to the new, promoted at one cry

> O' the trump of God to the new service, not
> To longer bear, but henceforth fight, be found
> Sublime in new impatience with the foe!
> Endure man and obey God: plant firm foot
> On neck of man, tread man into hell
> Meet for him, and obey God all the more!

The conduct which the world has deemed unwifely on Pompilia's part, unpriestly on Caponsacchi's, and unchristian for both, the Pope thus understands as the manifestation of spiritual rebirth:

> . . . it seems
> As a new attribute were born of each
> Champion of truth, the priest and wife I praise,—
> As a new safeguard sprang up in defence
> Of their new noble nature . . .

That the advancement of truth should entail on heroic individuals great suffering and apparent waste is in the pluralistic view only to be expected. "Life is probation and this earth no goal/But starting-point of man": this for the Pope is "the foremost fact." On any other hypothesis the spectacle of evil would be insupportable:

> I can believe this dread machinery
> Of sin and sorrow, would confound me else,
> Devised,—all pain, at most expenditure
> Of pain by Who devised pain,—to evolve,
> By new machinery in counterpart,
> The moral qualities of man . . .

In Innocent's eyes, then, Pompilia and Caponsacchi are redeemed by their moral *creativity*. Whereas the other characters in *The Ring and the Book* have through their actions helped to compound the indeterminacy of this pluralistic world, they alone have ventured "the terrible choice" which is "life's business." And just as the Pope subjects to judicial scrutiny the deeds of the beings committed to his care, so, he thinks, will his own deeds be judged when shortly he faces God and hears:

> 'Since by its fruit a tree is judged,
> 'Show me thy fruit, the latest act of thine!
> 'For in the last is summed the first and all,—
> 'What thy life last put heart and soul into,
> 'There shall I taste thy product.'

Thus it is that, acting on a conviction no less intuitive than those which prompted Pompilia and Caponsacchi to vindicate the truth, each according to his own best lights, Innocent makes his choice: "And how should I dare die, this man let live?"

The truth which the Pope declared for the Rome of his day,

Browning undertook through his poem to proclaim for all time. Enough has been said to suggest how closely *The Ring and the Book* corresponds, both in form and conception, to the central assumptions of William James's pluralistic philosophy. Equally amenable to discussion in the context of pluralism is the poet's own statement of his aesthetic relationship to his material, as set forth in the first and last books. Browning records that he was directed as if by predestination to the Old Yellow Book, wherein lay the "pure crude fact" of the Roman murder-case. Buried within the indiscriminate welter of detail which made up the volume, as he sensed from the outset, "lay absolutely truth,—/Fanciless fact." Browning's equation of truth with fact, however, is somewhat misleading, since the facts ostensibly mirrored in the original documents had in actuality been refracted in passing through the minds of the various witnesses to suit their special purposes. Even the final verdict, however just, had been delivered under circumstances so ambiguous as to consign the truth to oblivion. Nor could the resurrection of this truth be accomplished by the simple skills of the literary detective. What was called for was a process of re-creation. The artist's approach to his subject must be that of the Jamesian pluralist for whom the given facts of existence are not intractable, but malleable, awaiting the act of human violence which will engender truth on them. "I fused my live soul with that inert stuff," writes the poet; "The life in me abolished the death of things." This does not mean that the artist in the process of creation has any disposition to relax his grasp on the actual. On the contrary, his effort is by intuitive means to identify himself ever more intimately with factual reality:

> Yet by a special gift, an art of arts,
> More insight and more outsight and much more
> Will to use both of these than boast my mates,
> I can detach from me, commission forth
> Half of my soul . . .

In Browning's view, then, the imagination is instrumental to the elucidation of truth. "Fancy with fact is just one fact the more," writes the poet; and rhetorically he asks

> Are means to the end, themselves in part the end?
> Is fiction which makes fact alive, fact too?

Browning's many poems about painters, musicians, and poets attest to the author's exalted concept of the creative faculty. His most notable spokesman, perhaps, is Fra Lippo Lippi, that passionate lover of life in all its pluralistic variety. To the captain of the watch, who has taken him in custody, the artist explains how the vicissitudes of existence have made the "soul and sense of him grow sharp alike." And his gain as a painter has been the capacity so to represent appearances as to enable men to see through his eyes the beauty and the ugliness which they were incapable of perceiving for themselves:

> For, don't you mark? we're made so that we love
> First when we see them painted, things we have passed
> Perhaps a hundred times nor cared to see;
> And so they are better, painted—better to us,
> Which is the same thing. Art was given for that;
> God uses us to help each other so,
> Lending our minds out.

Lippi, however, thinks of himself as the interpreter of existing, rather than the discoverer of new truths; and Browning is careful in the opening monologue of *The Ring and the Book* not to claim more of his own poetry. God alone is truly creative. Individual man tries to duplicate the divine process, not with the intention of usurping God's prerogative, but because in imitating it, however distantly, he produces works which embody as much of the ideal as lies within human scope:

> I find first
> Writ down for very A.B.C. of fact,
> 'In the beginning God made heaven and earth;'
> From which, no matter with what lisp, I spell
> And speak you out a consequence—that man,
> Man,—as befits the made, the inferior thing,—
> Purposed, since made, to grow, not make in turn,
> Yet forced to try and make, else fail to grow,—
> Formed to rise, reach at, if not grasp and gain
> The good beyond him,—which attempt is growth,—
> Repeats God's process in man's due degree,
> Attaining man's proportionate result,—
> Creates, no, but resuscitates, perhaps.
> Inalienable, the arch-prerogative
> Which turns thought, act—conceives, expresses too!
> No less, man, bounded, yearning to be free,
> May so project his surplusage of soul
> In search of body, so add self to self
> By owning what lay ownerless before,—
> So find, so fill full, so appropriate forms—
> That, although nothing which had never life
> Shall get life from him, be, not having been,
> Yet something dead may get to live again,
> Something with too much life or not enough,
> Which, either way imperfect, ended once:
> An end whereat man's impulse intervenes,
> Makes new beginning, starts the dead alive,
> Completes the incomplete and saves the thing.

Yet, in asserting that through his poem he had educed the ultimate and enduring truth of Pompilia's story, does not Browning
imply for the artistic imagination a higher function on pluralistic
premises than he was willing explicitly to avow? The world of *The
Ring and the Book* can only be described as indeterminate, "half-
wild, half-saved," as James would say. It is a world in which God
relies on human assistance for the fulfilment of his intent, a world
wherein heroic deeds and inspired words initiate the serial stages in
the progressive revelation of truth. It is, in short, a pluralistic world,
according to the Jamesian definition. And if this world seems, nevertheless, to exhibit moral order and purpose, that impression is ultimately dependent on nothing less than the poet's ability to impose
his own will to believe through the resources of an art which does
not simply enunciate, but which actually becomes the vital form of
that belief:

> But Art,—wherein man nowise speaks to men,
> Only to mankind,—Art may tell a truth
> Obliquely, do the thing shall breed the thought,
> Nor wrong the thought, missing the mediate word.
> So may you paint your picture, twice show truth,
> Beyond mere imagery on the wall,—
> So, note by note, bring music from your mind,
> Deeper than ever e'en Beethoven dived,—
> So write a book shall mean, beyond the facts,
> Suffice the eye and save the soul beside.

Selected Bibliography

In this listing, recent scholarship and criticism have been emphasized as most relevant to the needs of contemporary readers. Excluded are (1) works already represented in the Criticism section of this volume; and (2) works not in English.

I. COLLECTED EDITIONS

Authoritative modern collected editions have been based mainly on the "Fourth and complete edition" of *The Poetical Works of Robert Browning* (17 vols. London: Smith, Elder, 1888–94), all supervised by Browning except for the final volume. The best editions aiming at completeness are:

The Works of Robert Browning ["Centenary Edition"]. Ed. F. G. Kenyon. 10 vols. London: Smith, Elder, 1912. Reprint (10 vols.), New York: Barnes & Noble, 1966.

The Complete Works of Robert Browning ["Florentine Edition"]. Ed. Charlotte Porter and Helen A. Clarke. 12 vols. New York: Crowell, 1910. Excellent notes on works not commonly anthologized.

[The "Centenary" and "Florentine" editions are supplemented by *New Poems by Robert Browning and Elizabeth Barrett Browning*. Ed. F. G. Kenyon. London: Smith, Elder, 1914; New York: Macmillan, 1915].

The Complete Poetical Works of Robert Browning, New Edition with Additional Poems First Published in 1914 ["Macmillan Edition"]. Ed. Augustine Birrell. New York: Macmillan, 1915. Best one-volume edition.

The Complete Poetic and Dramatic Works of Robert Browning ["Cambridge Edition"]. Ed. Horace E. Scudder. Boston and New York: Houghton Mifflin, 1895. Includes Browning's *Essay on Shelley*.

II. BIBLIOGRAPHY, CONCORDANCE, HANDBOOKS

The standard bibliography is L. N. Broughton, C. S. Northrup, and R. B. Pearsall, *Robert Browning: A Bibliography, 1830–1950* (Ithaca, N.Y., 1953. Reprint, New York, 1970). Pearsall's updating is found in his "Robert Browning," *New Cambridge Bibliography of English Literature*, Vol. 3 (1969), listing principal publications down to 1966. A thorough compilation by Boyd Litzinger in *The Browning Critics* (Lexington, Ky., 1965) covers 1951-May 1965. Annual bibliographies are found in "MLA International Bibliography" (in *PMLA*) and *Victorian Studies* (from 1958). A very useful "Guide to the Year's Work in Victorian Poetry and Prose," with authoritative surveys on Browning, appears annually in *Victorian Poetry*. Quarterly checklists appear in *Studies in Browning and His Circle* and its predecessor, *The Browning Newsletter* (from June 1968).

Two selective guides through Browning scholarship are Park Honan's chapter in *The Victorian Poets: A Guide to Research*, ed. Frederic E. Faverty, 2nd ed. (Cambridge, Mass., 1968) and P. J. Keating, "Robert Browning: A Reader's Guide" in *Robert Browning* (Writers and Their Background Series), ed. Isobel Armstrong (London, 1974).

The definitive concordance is L. N. Broughton and B. F. Stelter, *A Concordance to the Poems of Robert Browning*, 2 vols. (New York, 1924–25).

William Clyde DeVane's *A Browning Handbook*, 2nd ed. (New York, 1955), remains the single most useful commentary on Browning. Others still valuable are:

Orr, Mrs. Sutherland. *A Handbook to the Works of Robert Browning*. 6th ed. London. 1892. Reprint, New York, 1969. Authorized by the poet.

Symons, Arthur. *An Introduction to the Study of Browning*. London, 1886.

III. BIOGRAPHY

The standard biography is William Irvine and Park Honan, *The Book, the*

Selected Bibliography · 597

Ring, and the Poet (New York, 1974), superseding W. H. Griffin and H. C. Minchin, The Life of Robert Browning, 3rd ed. (London, 1938). As its title suggests, Maisie Ward's copious Robert Browning and His World (2 vols.; New York, 1967–69) sets the poet in his literary and social milieu. Other important studies:

Altick, Richard D. "The Private Life of Robert Browning." Yale Review, 41 (1951–52), 247–62. Examines the poet's psyche. For reply to Altick, see K. L. Knickerbocker, "A Tentative Apology for Browning," Tennessee Studies in Literature, 1 (1956), 75–82. (Both in Browning Critics.)
Cohen, J. M. Robert Browning. London, 1952. Biocritical study.
DeVane, William C. Browning's Parleyings: The Autobiography of a Mind. 2nd ed. New York, 1964.
DeVane, William C. "The Virgin and the Dragon." Yale Review, 37 (1947–48), 33–46. Browning's predilection for Perseus-Andromeda myth. (In Drew collection.)
Duckworth, F. R. G. Browning: Background and Conflict. New York, 1932.
Gosse, Edmund. Robert Browning: Personalia. London, 1890.
Holmes, Stewart W. "Browning's Sordello and Jung: Browning's Sordello in the Light of Jung's Theory of Types." PMLA, 56 (1941), 758–96.
Holmes, Stewart W. "Browning: Semantic Stutterer." PMLA, 60 (1945), 231–55.
James, Henry. "The Private Life." 1893. Browning fictionalized as Clare Vawdrey, novelist with two personalities.
Miller, Betty. Robert Browning: A Portrait. London, 1952. Controversial psychological interpretation.
Orr, Mrs. Sutherland. Life and Letters of Robert Browning. Revised by Frederic G. Kenyon. Boston, 1908. Reprint, Westport, Conn., 1973. Quasi-official life.
Raymond, W. O. "Browning's Dark Mood: A Study of Fifine at the Fair." Studies in Philology, 31 (1934), 578–99. (In his Infinite Moment [Toronto, 1950, 1965].) Poem reflects Browning's feeling that he had betrayed his dead wife by proposing to Lady Ashburton

IV. LETTERS

There is presently no collected edition of Robert Browning's letters; they are distributed among several volumes (minor collections omitted):

Browning to His American Friends: Letters between the Brownings, The Storys and James Russell Lowell 1841–1890. Ed. Gertrude Reese Hudson. New York, 1965.
Dearest Isa: Robert Browning's Letters to Isabella Blagden. Ed. Edward C. McAleer. Austin, Tex., 1951. Period: 1850–72.
Learned Lady: Letters from Robert Browning to Mrs. Thomas FitzGerald 1876–1889. Ed. Edward C. McAleer. Cambridge, Mass., 1966.
The Letters of Robert Browning and Elizabeth Barrett Barrett 1845–1846. Ed. Elvan Kintner. 2 vols. Cambridge, Mass., 1969. The love letters.
Letters of Robert Browning Collected by Thomas J. Wise. Ed. Thurman L. Hood. New Haven, 1933. Supplemented by New Letters of Robert Browning, ed. W. C. DeVane and K. L. Knickerbocker (New Haven, 1950; London, 1951). The important general collections.
Orr, Mrs. Sutherland. Life and Letters of Robert Browning.
Robert Browning and Alfred Domett. Ed. Frederic G. Kenyon. London, 1906.
Robert Browning and Julia Wedgwood: A Broken Friendship as Revealed by Their Letters. Ed. Richard Curle. New York, 1937. Period: 1863–70; letters shed light on The Ring and the Book.
Whiting, Lilian. The Brownings: Their Life and Art. Boston, 1911. Late letters to Mrs. Bronson.

V. ESSAY COLLECTIONS

There are several accessible essay collections, with minimal overlap. Selected titles from these are distributed in the following sections, using the cue-titles noted here:

Armstrong, Isobel, ed. The Major Victorian Poets: Reconsiderations. London, 1969; Lincoln, Nebr., 1969. Four essays on Browning. (MVP)
Armstrong, Isobel, ed. Writers and Their Background: Robert Browning. London, 1974. (RB)
Drew, Philip, ed. Robert Browning: A Collection of Critical Essays. London and Boston, 1966. (Drew)

Litzinger, Boyd, and K. L. Knickerbocker, eds. *The Browning Critics*. Lexington, Ky., 1965. (*Browning Critics*)
Litzinger, Boyd, and Donald Smalley. *Browning: The Critical Heritage*. New York, 1970. Nineteenth-century reviews and criticism, excluding continental.
Tracy, Clarence, ed. *Browning's Mind and Art*. Edinburgh and London, 1968. (Tracy)
Watson, J. R., ed. *Browning: "Men and Women" and Other Poems*. London, 1974. (Watson)

VI. GENERAL CRITICISM

Armstrong, Isobel. "Browning and the 'Grotesque' Style." (In *MVP*.)
Armstrong, Isobel. "Browning and Victorian Poetry of Sexual Love." (In *RB*.)
Badger, Kingsbury. "'See the Christ Stand!': Browning's Religion." *Boston Univ. Studies in English*, 1 (1955–56), 53–73. (In Drew.)
Ball, Patricia M. "Browning's Godot." *Victorian Poetry*, 3 (1965), 245–53. (In Watson.)
Beach, Joseph Warren. "Browning." *The Concept of Nature in Nineteenth-Century English Poetry*. New York, 1936. Reprint, New York, 1966.
Beckson, Karl, and John M. Munro. "Symons, Browning, and the Development of the Modern Aesthetic." *Studies in English Literature*, 10 (1970), 687–99.
Brooke, Stopford A. *The Poetry of Robert Browning*. London, 1902.
Burrows, Leonard. *Browning the Poet: An Introductory Study*. Nedlands, W. Australia, 1969.
Bush, Douglas. "Browning and Meredith." *Mythology and the Romantic Tradition in English Poetry*. Cambridge, Mass., 1937. Reprint, New York. 1963.
Cadbury, William. "Lyric and Anti-Lyric Forms: A Method for Judging Browning." *Univ. of Toronto Quarterly*, 34 (1964–65), 49–67. (In Tracy.)
Charlton, H. B. "Browning as Dramatist." *Bulletin of the John Rylands Library*, 23 (1939), 33–67.
Charlton, H. B. "The Making of the Dramatic Lyric." *Bulletin of the John Rylands Library*, 35 (1953), 349–84.
Collins, Thomas J. *Browning's Moral-Aesthetic Theory 1833–1855*. Lincoln, Nebr., 1967.
Cook, Eleanor. *Browning's Lyrics: An Exploration*. Toronto, 1974.
Cramer, Maurice B. "What Browning's Literary Reputation Owed to the Pre-Raphaelites, 1847–1856." *ELH*, 8 (1941), 305–21.
Drew, Philip. *The Poetry of Browning: A Critical Introduction*. London, 1970.
Drinkwater, John. "Browning's Diction" and "Browning's Influence." *Victorian Poetry*. London [1923]; New York, 1924.
Duncan, J. E. "The Intellectual Kinship of John Donne and Robert Browning." *Studies in Philology*, 50 (1953), 81–100.
Elliott, G. R. "Shakespeare's Significance for Browning." *Anglia*, 32 (1909), 90–162.
Elton, Oliver. "The Brownings." *A Survey of English Literature 1830–1880*. London, 1920. I, 364–97.
Fairchild, H. N. "Browning the Simple-Hearted Casuist." *Univ. of Toronto Quarterly*, 18 (1948–49), 234–40. (In *Browning Critics*.)
Fairchild, H. N. *Religious Trends in English Poetry. Vol. IV: 1830–1880, Christianity and Romanticism in the Victorian Era*. New York, 1957.
Greer, Louise. *Browning and America*. Chapel Hill, N.C., 1952.
Gridley, Roy E. *Browning* [Routledge Author Guides]. London and Boston, 1972.
Groom, Bernard. "Tennyson, Browning, and Arnold." *The Diction of Poetry from Spenser to Bridges*. Toronto, 1955.
Hair, Donald S. *Browning's Experiments with Genre*. Toronto, 1972.
Harrold, William E. *The Variance and the Unity: A Study of the Complementary Poems of Robert Browning*. Athens, Ohio, 1973.
Hartle, R. W. "Gide's Interpretation of Browning." *University of Texas Studies in English*, 28 (1949), 244–56.
Hatcher, H. H. *The Versification of Robert Browning*. Columbus, Ohio, 1928. Reprint, Brooklyn, N.Y., 1968.
Honan, Park. *Browning's Characters: A Study in Poetic Technique*. New Haven, 1961. Reprint, Hamden, Conn., 1969. An important study.
Honan, Park. "The Iron String in the Victorian Lyre: Browning's Lyric Versification." (In Tracy.)
Hood, Thurman L. *Browning's Ancient Classical Sources*. Cambridge, Mass., 1922.

Jones, Henry. *Browning as a Philosophical and Religious Teacher.* New York, 1891. Influential early study.

King, Roma A., Jr. *The Focusing Artifice: The Poetry of Robert Browning.* Athens, Ohio, 1968.

Langbaum, Robert. "Browning and the Question of Myth." *PMLA,* 81 (1966), 575–84.

Lloyd, Trevor. "Browning and Politics." (In *RB.*)

Lounsbury, Thomas R. *The Early Literary Career of Robert Browning.* New York, 1911.

Lubbock, Percy. "Robert Browning." *Quarterly Review,* 217 (1912), 437–57.

Lucas, F. L. *Ten Victorian Poets.* 2nd ed. Cambridge, 1940. Largely negative view.

McCormick, J. P. "Robert Browning and the Experimental Drama." *PMLA,* 68 (1953), 982–91.

McNally, James. "Browning's Political Thought." *Queen's Quarterly,* 77 (1970), 568–90.

Peckham, Morse. "Personality and the Mask of Knowledge." *Victorian Revolutionaries.* New York, 1970.

Peterson, William S. *Interrogating the Oracle: A History of the London Browning Society.* Athens, Ohio, 1969.

Phelps, William Lyon. *Robert Browning.* 2nd ed. Indianapolis, 1932.

Preyer, Robert. "Two Styles in the Verse of Robert Browning." *ELH,* 32 (1965), 62–84.

Priestley, F. E. L. "Some Aspects of Browning's Irony." (In Tracy.)

Raymond, W. O. " 'The Jewelled Bow': A Study in Browning's Imagery and Humanism." (In his *Infinite Moment* and in Drew.)

Ridenour, George M. "Browning's Music Poems: Fancy and Fact." *PMLA,* 78 (1963), 369–77. (In Tracy.)

Ridenour, George M. Introduction to *Robert Browning: Selected Poetry.* New York and Toronto, 1966. Usefully classifies the monologues into four major "types."

Roppen, Georg. *Evolution and Poetic Belief: A Study in Some Victorian and Modern Writers.* Oslo, 1956. Places Browning with Tennyson in "the Platonic tradition."

Routh, H. V. *Towards the Twentieth Century.* Cambridge, 1937. Sees Browning as failure "in the highest sense."

Ryan, William M. "The Classifications of Browning's 'Difficult' Vocabulary." *Studies in Philology,* 60 (1963), 542–48.

Sharrock, Roger. "Browning and History." (In *RB.*)

Shaw, W. David. *The Dialectical Temper: The Rhetorical Art of Robert Browning.* Ithaca, N.Y., 1968.

Smith, C. Willard. *Browning's Star-Imagery: The Study of a Detail in Poetic Design.* Princeton, 1941. Scope far broader than title suggests.

Somervell, D. C. "The Reputation of Robert Browning." *Essays and Studies by Members of the English Association,* 15 (1929), 122–38.

Stange, G. Robert. "Browning and Modern Poetry." (In Tracy.)

Stevenson, Lionel. "Robert Browning." *Darwin Among the Poets.* Chicago, 1932. Reprint, New York. 1963.

Stevenson, Lionel. "The Pertinacious Victorian Poets." *Univ. of Toronto Quarterly,* 21 (1951–52), 232–45.

Stevenson, Lionel. "Tennyson, Browning, and a Romantic Fallacy." *Univ. of Toronto Quarterly,* 13 (1943–44), 175–95.

Tracy, C. R. "Browning's Heresies." *Studies in Philology,* 33 (1936), 610–25.

Whitla, William. *The Central Truth: The Incarnation in Robert Browning's Poetry.* Toronto, 1963.

Woolford, John. "Sources and Resources in Browning's Early Reading." (In *RB.*)

VII. THE DRAMATIC MONOLOGUE

Culler, A. Dwight. "Monodrama and the Dramatic Monologue." *PMLA,* 90 (1975), 366–85.

Curry, S. S. *Browning and the Dramatic Monologue: Nature and Interpretation of an Overlooked Form of Literature.* Boston, 1908. Reprint, New York, 1969.

Fuson, B. W. *Browning and His English Predecessors in the Dramatic Monolog* [sic]. State University of Iowa Humanistic Studies, 8. Iowa City, 1948.

Garratt, Robert F. "Browning's Dramatic Monologue: The Strategy of the Double Mask." *Victorian Poetry,* 11 (1973), 115–25.

Grandsen, K. W. "The Uses of Personae." (In Tracy.)

Honan, Park. "The Solitary Voice." Chap. 4 of his *Browning's Characters*.
MacCallum, M. W. "The Dramatic Monologue in the Victorian Period." *Proceedings of the British Academy, 1924–1925*, pp. 265–82.
Mason, Michael. "Browning and the Dramatic Monologue." (In *RB*.)
Sessions, Ina Beth. "The Dramatic Monologue." *PMLA*, 62 (1947), 503–16.

VIII. STUDIES OF SINGLE WORKS

1833–1852

Assad, Thomas J. "Browning's 'My Last Duchess.'" *Tulane Studies in English*, 10 (1960), 117–28.
Drew, Philip. "Browning's *Essay on Shelley*." *Victorian Poetry*, 1 (1963), 1–6. Challenged in Thomas J. Collins, "Browning's *Essay on Shelley:* In Context." *Victorian Poetry*, 2 (1964), 119–24.
Eggenschwiler, David. "Psychological Complexity in 'Porphyria's Lover.'" *Victorian Poetry*, 8 (1970), 39–48.
Glen, Margaret E. "The Meaning and Structure of *Pippa Passes*." *University of Toronto Quarterly*, 24 (1954–55), 410–26.
Greenberg, Robert A. "Ruskin, Pugin, and the Contemporary Context of 'The Bishop Orders His Tomb.'" *PMLA*, 84 (1969), 1588–94.
Guskin, Phyllis J. "Ambiguities in the Structure and Meaning of Browning's *Christmas-Eve*." *Victorian Poetry*, 4 (1966), 21–28.
Hancher, Michael. "The Dramatic Structure in Browning's 'Pauline.'" *Yearbook of English Studies*, 1 (1971), 149–59.
Hilton, Earl. "Browning's *Sordello* as a Study of the Will." *PMLA*, 69 (1954), 1127–34.
Holloway, Sister M. M. "A Further Reading of 'Count Gismond.'" *Studies in Philology*, 60 (1963), 549–53.
Jerman, B. R. "Browning's Witless Duke." *PMLA*, 72 (1957), 488–93. On "My Last Duchess"; challenged in Laurence Perrine, "Browning's Shrewd Duke," *PMLA*, 74 (1959), 157–59. (Both in *Browning Critics*.)
King, Roma. "Ecclesiastical Vision in Stone: 'The Bishop Orders His Tomb.'" (In his *The Bow and the Lyre*; also in Watson.)
Korg, Jacob. "A Reading of *Pippa Passes*." *Victorian Poetry*, 6 (1968), 5–19.
Mason, Michael. "The Importance of *Sordello*." (In *MVP*.)
Miyoshi, Masao. "Mill and 'Pauline': The Myth and Some Facts." *Victorian Studies*, 9 (1965), 154–63. Mill's critique of *Pauline* did not alter the course of Browning's career.
Monteiro, George. "The Apostasy and Death of St. Praxed's Bishop." *Victorian Poetry*, 8 (1970), 209–18.
Pottle, Frederick A. *Shelley and Browning: A Myth and Some Facts*. Chicago, 1923. Reprint, New York, 1965.
Preyer, Robert. "Robert Browning: A Reading of the Early Narratives." *ELH*, 26 (1959), 531–48. Chiefly on *Pauline*. (In *Browning Critics* and Drew.)
Priestley, F. E. L. "The Ironic Pattern of Browning's *Paracelsus*." *University of Toronto Quarterly*, 34 (1964–65), 68–81.
Smalley, Donald. "Special-Pleading in the Laboratory." *Browning's Essay on Chatterton*. Cambridge, Mass., 1948.
Starkman, M. K. "The Manichee in the Cloister: A Reading of Browning's 'Soliloquy of the Spanish Cloister.'" *Modern Language Notes*, 75 (1960), 399–405.
Stempel, Daniel. "Browning's *Sordello*: The Art of the Makers-See." *PMLA*, 80 (1965), 554–61.
Tilton, J. W., and R. D. Tuttle. "A New Reading of 'Count Gismond.'" *Studies in Philology*, 59 (1962), 83–95.
Yetman, Michael G. "Exorcising Shelley out of Browning: *Sordello* and the Problem of Poetic Identity." *Victorian Poetry*, 13 (1975), 79–98.

1855–1864

Aiken, Susan Hardy. "On Clothes and Heroes: Carlyle and 'How It Strikes a Contemporary.'" *Victorian Poetry*, 13 (1975), 99–109.
Altick, R. D. "'Andrea del Sarto': The Kingdom of Hell Is Within." (In Tracy and Watson.)
Altick, R. D. "Browning's 'Transcendentalism.'" *Journal of English and Germanic Philology*, 58 (1959), 24–28.
Altick, R. D. "'A Grammarian's Funeral': Browning's Praise of Folly?" *Studies in English Literature*, 3 (1963), 449–60. (In Drew.)
Altick, R. D. "Lovers' Finiteness: Browning's 'Two in the Campagna.'" *Papers on Language and Literature*, 3 (1967), 75–80.

Altick, R. D. "The Symbolism of Browning's 'Master Hugues of Saxe-Gotha.' " *Victorian Poetry*, 3 (1965), 1–7.

Armstrong, Isobel. "Browning's *Mr. Sludge, 'The Medium.'* " *Victorian Poetry*, 2 (1964), 1–9. (In Drew.)

Bieman, Elizabeth. "An Eros *Manqué*: Browning's 'Andrea del Sarto.' " *Studies in English Literature*, 10 (1970), 651–68. Discusses poem in light of Plato's *Symposium*.

Golder, Harold. "Browning's *Childe Roland*." *PMLA*, 39 (1924), 963–78. Browning's unconscious borrowing from children's tales and romances.

Guerin, W. L. "Irony and Tension in Browning's 'Karshish.' " *Victorian Poetry*, 1 (1963), 132–39.

Hellstrom, Ward. "Time and Type in Browning's *Saul*." *ELH*, 33 (1966), 370–89.

Howard, John. "Caliban's Mind." *Victorian Poetry*, 1 (1963), 249–57. (In Drew.)

Irvine, William. "Four Monologues in Browning's *Men and Women*." *Victorian Poetry*, 2 (1964), 155–64. On "Fra Lippo Lippi," "Bishop Blougram's Apology," "Karshish," and "Cleon."

Kelly, Robert L. "Dactyls and Curlews: Satire in 'A Grammarian's Funeral.' " *Victorian Poetry*, 5 (1967), 105–12.

King, R. A. "Browning: 'Mage' and 'Maker'—A Study in Poetic Purpose and Method." *Victorian Newsletter*, No. 20 (Fall 1961), 21–25. On "Cleon." (In Drew.)

King, R. A. "Karshish Encounters Himself: An Interpretation of Browning's 'Epistle.' " *Concerning Poetry*, 1 (1968), 23–33.

King, R. A. "Sportive Ladies and Patron Saint: 'Fra Lippo Lippi.' " (In his *The Bow and the Lyre*.)

McAleer, Edward C. "Browning's 'Cleon' and Auguste Comte." *Comparative Literature*, 8 (1956), 142–45.

Raymond, W. O. "The Statue and the Bust." (In his *Infinite Moment* and in Tracy.)

Sandstrom, Glenn. " 'James Lee's Wife'—and Browning's." *Victorian Poetry*, 4 (1966), 259–70.

Shaffer, Elinor. "Browning's St. John: The Casuistry of the Higher Criticism." *Victorian Studies*, 16 (1972), 205–21. On "A Death in the Desert."

Shaw, W. David. "The Analogical Argument of Browning's 'Saul.' " *Victorian Poetry*, 2 (1964), 277–82.

Svaglic, Martin J. "Browning's Grammarian: Apparent Failure or Real?" *Victorian Poetry*, 5 (1967), 93–104.

Timko, Michael. "Browning upon Butler; or, Natural Theology in the English Isle." *Criticism*, 7 (1965), 141–50.

Tracy, C. R. "Bishop Blougram." *Modern Language Review*, 34 (1939), 422–25.

Tracy, C. R. "Caliban Upon Setebos." *Studies in Philology*, 35 (1938), 487–99.

Willoughby, John. "Browning's *'Childe Roland to the Dark Tower Came.'* " *Victorian Poetry*, 1 (1963), 291–99.

The Ring and the Book

W. C. DeVane's *Handbook* provides vital facts and summaries. For detailed, line by line annotation, see A. K. Cook's *A Commentary upon Browning's "The Ring and the Book"* (London and New York, 1920. Reprint, Hamden, Conn., 1966). Browning's source, the Old Yellow Book, is translated by Charles W. Hodell (Washington, 1908) and by J. M. Gest (Boston, 1925; Philadelphia, 1927). Hodell's essay "The Making of a Great Poem," accompanying his translation, perceptively discusses the poem in the light of its source. (This essay is unfortunately not included in the Everyman's Library reprint of Hodell's book [1911].)

Altick, R. D., and James F. Loucks, II. *Browning's Roman Murder Story: A Reading of "The Ring and the Book."* London and Chicago, 1968.

Armstrong, Isobel. *"The Ring and the Book*: The Uses of Prolixity." (In *MVP*.)

Chesterton, G. K. *"The Ring and the Book." Robert Browning*. London, 1903.

Corrigan, Beatrice. *Curious Annals: New Documents Relating to Browning's Roman Murder Story*. Toronto, 1956. Fullest account of Guido's family, the Franceschini.

Gridley, R. E. "Browning's Caponsacchi: 'How the Priest Caponsacchi said his say.' " *Victorian Poetry*, 6 (Autumn-Winter 1968), 281–95. The whole of this double issue is devoted to *The Ring and the Book*.

Gridley, R. E. "Browning's Pompilia." *Journal of English and Germanic Philology*, 67 (1968), 64–83.

Gridley, R. E. "Browning's Two Guidos." *Univ. of Toronto Quarterly*, 37 (1967–68), 51–68.
James, Henry. "The Novel in *The Ring and the Book*." *Quarterly Review*, 217 (1912), 68–87. (In his *Notes on Novelists*, 1914).
Langbaum, Robert. *"The Ring and the Book:* A Relativist Poem." *The Poetry of Experience.* New York, 1957; 1963.
Phipps, C. T. "Adaptation from the Past, Creation for the Present: A Study of Browning's 'The Pope.' " *Studies in Philology*, 65 (1968), 702–22.
Phipps, C. T. "Browning's Canon Giuseppe Caponsacchi: Warrior-Priest, Dantean Lover, Critic of Society." *ELH*, 36 (1969), 696–718.
Shaw, J. E. "The 'Donna Angelicata' in *The Ring and the Book*." *PMLA*, 41 (1926), 55–81. On Pompilia.
Sullivan, Mary Rose. *Browning's Voices in "The Ring and the Book": A Study of Method and Meaning.* Toronto, 1969.
Yetman, Michael G. " 'Count Guido Franceschini': The Villain as Artist in *The Ring and the Book*." *PMLA*, 87 (1972), 1093–1102.

1871–1889

DeVane, W. C. *Browning's Parleyings: The Autobiography of a Mind.* 2nd ed. New York, 1964.
Drew, Philip. "Another View of *Fifine at the Fair*." *Essays in Criticism*, 17 (1967), 244–55.
Priestley, F. E. L. "A Reading of *La Saisiaz*." *Univ. of Toronto Quarterly*, 25 (1955–56), 47–59.
Ryals, Clyde de L. *"Balaustion's Adventure:* Browning's Greek Parable." *PMLA*, 88 (1973), 1040–48.
Ryals, Clyde de L. *"Prince Hohenstiel-Schwangau*: Browning's 'Ghostly Dialogue.' " *Nineteenth-Century Literary Perspectives: Essays in Honor of Lionel Stevenson.* Ed. Clyde de L. Ryals, et al. Durham, N.C., 1974.
Watkins, C. C. "The 'Abstruser Themes' of Browning's *Fifine at the Fair*." *PMLA*, 74 (1959), 426–37.

Index of Titles

"Abt Vogler," 243
"Adam, Lilith, and Eve," 421
"Amphibian," see "Prologue" to *Fifine at the Fair*
"Andrea del Sarto," 184
"Any Wife to Any Husband," 123
"Apparent Failure," 261
Aristophanes' Apology: ["Thamuris Marching"], 412
"Bad Dreams, I–IV," 431
"Bishop Blougram's Apology," 158
"Bishop Orders His Tomb at Praxed's Church, The," 87
"By the Fire-Side," 116
"Caliban upon Setebos," 252
"Caponsacchi, Giuseppe," see *The Ring and the Book*
" 'Childe Roland to the Dark Tower Came,' " 134
"Christopher Smart," see *Parleyings*
"Cleon," 207
"Confessions," 259
"Count Gismond," 59
"Count Guido Franceschini," see *The Ring and the Book*
"Cristina," 70
"Development," 440
"Dîs aliter Visum," 239
"Epilogue" to *Asolando*, 443
"Epilogue" to *Dramatis Personæ*, 263
"Epilogue" to *Fifine at the Fair*, 411
"Epistle . . . of Karshish, An," 127
"Evelyn Hope," 100
"Fears and Scruples," 416
"Fra Lippo Lippi," 105
"Giuseppe Caponsacchi," see *The Ring and the Book*
"Grammarian's Funeral, A," 219
"Guardian-Angel, The," 205
"Guido Franceschini, Count," see *The Ring and the Book*
" 'Here's to Nelson's Memory,' " see "Home-Thoughts, from Abroad: II"
"Holy-Cross Day," 201
"Home-Thoughts, from Abroad," 86
"Home-Thoughts, from Abroad: II," 86
"Home-Thoughts, from the Sea," 87
"House," 415
"Householder, The," see "Epilogue" to *Fifine at the Fair*
"How It Strikes a Contemporary," 149
" 'How They Brought the Good News from Ghent to Aix,' " 82
" 'Imperante Augusto Natus Est—,' " 436
"In a Gondola," 64
"Introductory Essay" to the *Letters of Percy Bysshe Shelley*, 445
"James Lee's Wife," 229

"Johannes Agricola in Meditation," 72
"Karshish, Epistle of," see "Epistle . . . of Karshish"
"Laboratory, The," 91
"Last Ride Together, The," 151
"Light Woman, A," 140
"Love among the Ruins," 94
"Lovers' Quarrel, A," 96
"Master Hugues of Saxe-Gotha," 154
"Meeting at Night; Parting at Morning," 92
"Memorabilia," 183
"My Last Duchess," 58
"My Star," 134
"Nationality in Drinks," 93
"Never the Time and the Place," 422
"Numpholeptos," 418
"One Word More," 224
Paracelsus (lyrics), 4
Parleyings with Certain People of Importance in Their Day: "With Christopher Smart," 423
"Parting at Morning," see "Meeting at Night; Parting at Morning"
Pauline (lyrics), 1
"Pictor Ignotus," 84
"Pied Piper of Hamelin, The," 75
Pippa Passes, 18
"Pope, The," see *The Ring and the Book*
"Popularity," 215
"Porphyria's Lover," 74
"Prologue" to *Asolando*, 430
"Prologue" to *Fifine at the Fair*, 409
"Prospice," 260
"Rabbi Ben Ezra," 246
"Respectability," 140
Ring and the Book, The, Headnote to, 266; Book V: "Count Guido Franceschini," 270; Book VI: "Giuseppe Caponsacchi," 316; Book X: "The Pope," 361
"Saul," 191
"Shelley, Essay on," see "Introductory Essay"
"Soliloquy of the Spanish Cloister," 62
Sordello, 12
"Statue and the Bust, The," 142
["Thamuris Marching"], see *Aristophanes' Apology*
"Toccata of Galuppi's, A," 114
" 'Transcendentalism,' " 222
"Two in the Campagna," 217
"Up at a Villa—Down in the City," 101
"With Christopher Smart," see *Parleyings*
"Woman's Last Word, A," 104
"Women and Roses," 200

NORTON CRITICAL EDITIONS

AUSTEN *Emma* edited by Stephen M. Parrish

AUSTEN *Pride and Prejudice* edited by Donald J. Gray

Beowulf (the Donaldson translation) edited by Joseph M. Tuso

Blake's Poetry and Designs selected and edited by Mary Lynn Johnson and John E. Grant

BOCCACCIO *The Decameron* selected, translated, and edited by Mark Musa and Peter E. Bondanella

BRONTË, CHARLOTTE *Jane Eyre* edited by Richard J. Dunn

BRONTË, EMILY *Wuthering Heights* edited by William M. Sale, Jr. *Second Edition*

Robert Browning's Poetry selected and edited by James F. Loucks

Byron's Poetry selected and edited by Frank D. McConnell

CARROLL *Alice in Wonderland* selected and edited by Donald J. Gray

CERVANTES *Don Quixote* (the Ormsby translation, substantially revised) edited by Joseph R. Jones and Kenneth Douglas

Anton Chekhov's Plays translated and edited by Eugene K. Bristow

Anton Chekhov's Short Stories selected and edited by Ralph E. Matlaw

CHOPIN *The Awakening* edited by Margaret Culley

CLEMENS *Adventures of Huckleberry Finn* edited by Sculley Bradley, Richmond Croom Beatty, E. Hudson Long, and Thomas Cooley *Second Edition*

CLEMENS *A Connecticut Yankee in King Arthur's Court* edited by Allison R. Ensor

CLEMENS *Pudd'nhead Wilson* and *Those Extraordinary Twins* edited by Sidney E. Berger

CONRAD *Heart of Darkness* edited by Robert Kimbrough *Second Edition*

CONRAD *Lord Jim* edited by Thomas Moser

CONRAD *The Nigger of the "Narcissus"* edited by Robert Kimbrough

CRANE *Maggie: A Girl of the Streets* edited by Thomas A. Gullason

CRANE *The Red Badge of Courage* edited by Sculley Bradley, Richmond Croom Beatty, E. Hudson Long, and Donald Pizer *Second Edition*

Darwin edited by Philip Appleman *Second Edition*

DEFOE *Moll Flanders* edited by Edward Kelly

DEFOE *Robinson Crusoe* edited by Michael Shinagel

DICKENS *Bleak House* edited by George Ford and Sylvère Monod

DICKENS *Hard Times* edited by George Ford and Sylvère Monod

John Donne's Poetry selected and edited by A. L. Clements

DOSTOEVSKY *Crime and Punishment* (the Coulson translation) edited by George Gibian *Second Edition*

DOSTOEVSKY *The Brothers Karamazov* (the Garnett translation revised by Ralph E. Matlaw) edited by Ralph E. Matlaw

DREISER *Sister Carrie* edited by Donald Pizer

ELIOT *Middlemarch* edited by Bert G. Hornback

FIELDING *Tom Jones* edited by Sheridan Baker

FLAUBERT *Madame Bovary* edited with a substantially new translation by Paul de Man

GOETHE *Faust* translated by Walter Arndt and edited by Cyrus Hamlin

HARDY *Jude the Obscure* edited by Norman Page

HARDY *The Mayor of Casterbridge* edited by James K. Robinson

HARDY *The Return of the Native* edited by James Gindin

HARDY *Tess of the d'Urbervilles* edited by Scott Elledge *Second Edition*

HAWTHORNE *The Blithedale Romance* edited by Seymour Gross and Rosalie Murphy

HAWTHORNE *The House of the Seven Gables* edited by Seymour Gross

HAWTHORNE *The Scarlet Letter* edited by Sculley Bradley, Richmond Croom Beatty, E. Hudson Long, and Seymour Gross *Second Edition*

George Herbert and the Seventeenth-Century Religious Poets selected and edited by Mario A. Di Cesare

HOMER *The Odyssey* translated and edited by Albert Cook
HOWELLS *The Rise of Silas Lapham* edited by Don L. Cook
IBSEN *The Wild Duck* translated and edited by Dounia B. Christiani
JAMES *The Ambassadors* edited by S. P. Rosenbaum
JAMES *The American* edited by James A. Tuttleton
JAMES *The Portrait of a Lady* edited by Robert D. Bamberg
JAMES *The Turn of the Screw* edited by Robert Kimbrough
JAMES *The Wings of the Dove* edited by J. Donald Crowley and
    Richard A. Hocks
Ben Jonson and the Cavalier Poets selected and edited by Hugh Maclean
Ben Jonson's Plays and Masques selected and edited by Robert M. Adams
MACHIAVELLI *The Prince* translated and edited by Robert M. Adams
MALTHUS *An Essay on the Principle of Population* edited by Philip Appleman
MELVILLE *The Confidence-Man* edited by Hershel Parker
MELVILLE *Moby-Dick* edited by Harrison Hayford and Hershel Parker
MEREDITH *The Egoist* edited by Robert M. Adams
MILL *On Liberty* edited by David Spitz
MILTON *Paradise Lost* edited by Scott Elledge
MORE *Utopia* translated and edited by Robert M. Adams
NEWMAN *Apologia Pro Vita Sua* edited by David J. DeLaura
NORRIS *McTeague* edited by Donald Pizer
Adrienne Rich's Poetry selected and edited by Barbara Charlesworth Gelpi and
    Albert Gelpi
The Writings of St. Paul edited by Wayne A. Meeks
SHAKESPEARE *Hamlet* edited by Cyrus Hoy
SHAKESPEARE *Henry IV, Part I* edited by James J. Sanderson *Second Edition*
Bernard Shaw's Plays selected and edited by Warren Sylvester Smith
Shelley's Poetry and Prose edited by Donald H. Reiman and Sharon B. Powers
SOPHOCLES *Oedipus Tyrannus* translated and edited by Luci Berkowitz and
    Theodore F. Brunner
SMOLLET *The Expedition of Humphry Clinker* edited by James Thorson
SPENSER *Edmund Spenser's Poetry* selected and edited by Hugh Maclean
    Second Edition
STENDHAL *Red and Black* translated and edited by Robert M. Adams
STERNE *Tristram Shandy* edited by Howard Anderson
SWIFT *Gulliver's Travels* edited by Robert A. Greenberg *Revised Edition*
The Writings of Jonathan Swift edited by Robert A. Greenberg and
    William B. Piper
TENNYSON *In Memoriam* edited by Robert Ross
Tennyson's Poetry selected and edited by Robert W. Hill, Jr.
THOREAU *Walden and Civil Disobedience* edited by Owen Thomas
TOLSTOY *Anna Karenina* (the Maude translation) edited by George Gibian
TOLSTOY *War and Peace* (the Maude translation) edited by George Gibian
TURGENEV *Fathers and Sons* edited with a substantially new translation by
    Ralph E. Matlaw
VOLTAIRE *Candide* translated and edited by Robert M. Adams
WATSON *The Double Helix* edited by Gunther S. Stent
WHITMAN *Leaves of Grass* edited by Sculley Bradley and Harold W. Blodgett
WOLLSTONECRAFT *A Vindication of the Rights of Woman* edited by
    Carol H. Poston
WORDSWORTH *The Prelude: 1799, 1805, 1850* edited by Jonathan Wordsworth,
    M. H. Abrams, and Stephen Gill
Middle English Lyrics selected and edited by Maxwell S. Luria and
    Richard L. Hoffman
Modern Drama edited by Anthony Caputi
Restoration and Eighteenth-Century Comedy edited by Scott McMillin